Kickstart Artificial Intelligence Fundamentals

Master Machine Learning, Neural Networks, and Deep Learning from Basics to Build Modern AI Solutions with Python and TensorFlow-Keras

Dr. S.Mahesh Anand

www.orangeava.com

Copyright © 2025, Orange Education Pvt Ltd, AVA®

All rights reserved. No part of this book may be reproduced, stored in a retrieval system, or transmitted in any form or by any means, without the prior written permission of the publisher, except in the case of brief quotations embedded in critical articles or reviews.

Every effort has been made in the preparation of this book to ensure the accuracy of the information presented. However, the information contained in this book is sold without warranty, either express or implied. Neither the author nor **Orange Education Pvt Ltd** or its dealers and distributors, will be held liable for any damages caused or alleged to have been caused directly or indirectly by this book.

Orange Education Pvt Ltd has endeavored to provide trademark information about all of the companies and products mentioned in this book by the appropriate use of capital. However, **Orange Education Pvt Ltd** cannot guarantee the accuracy of this information. The use of general descriptive names, registered names, trademarks, service marks, etc. in this publication does not imply, even in the absence of a specific statement, that such names are exempt from the relevant protective laws and regulations and therefore free for general use.

First Published: March 2025
Published By: Orange Education Pvt Ltd, AVA®
Address: 9, Daryaganj, Delhi, 110002, India

275 New North Road Islington Suite 1314 London,
N1 7AA, United Kingdom

ISBN (PBK): 978-93-48107-13-8
ISBN (E-BOOK): 978-93-48107-22-0

Scan the QR code to explore our entire catalogue

www.orangeava.com

Dedicated To

My Beloved Family,

And

Every Student and Professional Who Has Been a Part of My Teaching Journey.

About the Author

Dr. S.Mahesh Anand is a distinguished educator, corporate trainer, keynote speaker, and consultant specializing in data science, machine learning, and artificial intelligence. With over two decades of experience, Dr. Anand has been instrumental in shaping the learning journey of more than 50,000 students and professionals across India.

Dr. Anand served as a full-time faculty member at VIT University (Vellore) for a decade, where he honed his academic and research skills. In 2012, he founded his consulting and training firm, Scientific Computing Solutions (SCS-India).

His professional footprint includes delivering transformative corporate training sessions for leading organizations such as Great Learning, Chegg, TNQTech, CGI, Mad Street Den, and numerous startups. Additionally, he has conducted over 800 master training sessions for faculty members at higher education institutions across India.

Among his accolades, Dr. Anand is the recipient of the AT&T Labs Award from IEEE Headquarters and the M.V. Chauhan Award from the IEEE India Council for his pioneering work on the ANN-Fuzzy hybrid AI model for cancer prediction. In 2022, he was also honored with the Best Data Science and AI Educator Award by AI Global Media, UK.

As the founder of "Learn AI with Anand," a flagship program of SCS-India, he continues to inspire learners through his online cohort courses, technical books, published works, and innovative teaching methodologies. Dr. Anand's love for reading, exploring new destinations, and writing fuels his passion for learning, discovering fresh perspectives, and sharing knowledge through his work.

About the Technical Reviewer

Sudin Baraokar holds a Bachelor's degree in Computer Engineering from the University of Mumbai. He is an innovator in emerging and deep technologies, with extensive experience as CIO, CTO, and IT Advisor at major organizations such as SBI, Barclays, IBM, and GE. Currently, he is an IT Advisor to global organizations and academia, as well as the founder of a deep tech startup.

Sudin has expertise in over 70 technologies and platforms, including AI, cybersecurity, quantum computing, data science, IoT, blockchain, cloud computing, low code/no code development, digital transformation, and enterprise architecture. He established the Bankchain Alliance, a consortium of over 30 banks focused on emerging tech solutions.

At SBI, Sudin transformed the core banking systems to handle 24,000 transactions per second and 1.5 billion transactions per day, serving over 500 million customers and 700 million accounts. He also developed the SBI YONO smart mobile banking application, which has over 50 million users.

Currently, Sudin is developing AI-based digital transformation platforms for supply chain management (SCM), trade tech, fintech, regtech, and risk tech. He has trained over 1 million professionals, entrepreneurs, faculty, and students in deep tech and emerging technologies. With more than 1,000 technology and digital transformation events delivered, he has also mentored over 500 startups.

Sudin is a global keynote speaker on topics such as emerging tech, deep tech, innovations, and collaboration. In his free time, he enjoys golfing, singing, volunteering for charity, and researching future tech, economics, sports, and history.

Acknowledgements

Hailing from a middle-class family, my parents instilled in me the belief that education is the greatest asset one can possess, far surpassing material wealth. I am deeply grateful for their unconditional love, unwavering support, and the values they have passed on to me. I also extend my heartfelt gratitude to my younger brothers and sisters, who have always stood by me with their encouragement and support.

A warm thanks to my maternal uncle and grandfather, who played a pivotal role in nurturing my love for writing in English. They introduced me to the habit of writing postal letters during my school days, long before the advent of mobile phones, planting the seeds of my passion for storytelling and communication.

To my supportive wife and my lovely daughters, thank you for standing by me throughout this journey. Their patience, understanding, and willingness to sacrifice family time while I worked during early mornings and late nights have been invaluable. They have been my silent strength, and their love and support have fueled my perseverance.

I extend my heartfelt gratitude to my professor, Dr. Harikumar Rajaguru, whose inspiring guidance during my undergraduate years ignited my passion for ANN and soft computing, laying the foundation for my journey in this field.

To my students, who are my greatest source of inspiration. Their curiosity, enthusiasm, and hunger for knowledge have motivated me to write this book.

Finally, I extend my gratitude to my publishers, Orange Education Pvt Ltd, particularly Ms. Sreeja Nair and Ms. Priyanka Arora. The team's creative freedom, steadfast patience, and unwavering support have made this year-long writing journey a truly fulfilling experience. Thank you for believing in this project and for helping bring it to life.

Preface

Artificial Intelligence (AI) has revolutionized the way we interact with technology, shaping innovations across industries and redefining what machines are capable of achieving. From its theoretical roots to practical applications, AI continues to be a field that sparks curiosity and drives innovation. *Kickstart Artificial Intelligence Fundamentals* is crafted to provide a structured and comprehensive introduction to this fascinating domain.

This book is designed for students, professionals, and enthusiasts who are keen to delve into the world of AI, starting from foundational concepts to the implementation of cutting-edge technologies. The book begins with the basics of Machine Learning models and their evolution into Artificial Neural Networks. It then ventures into advanced architectures such as Convolutional Neural Networks and Recurrent Neural Networks, equipping readers with the theoretical knowledge and practical insights needed to navigate the AI landscape. Each chapter is enriched with Python-based examples using TensorFlow and Keras frameworks, enabling hands-on learning and fostering a deeper understanding of the subject.

This book not only serves as an educational resource but also inspires its readers to embark on their own journeys of discovery in the ever-evolving world of AI. May it provide the readers with the confidence and foundational knowledge to explore the limitless possibilities of Artificial Intelligence.

Happy learning, and welcome to the future of technology!

This book is thoughtfully divided into 17 chapters, each designed to progressively build your understanding of Artificial Intelligence (AI) and its foundational concepts.

Chapter 1. Introduction and Evolution of AI Technologies: This chapter provides a historical overview of Artificial Intelligence (AI), tracing its evolution from symbolic reasoning and rule-based systems to modern-day neural networks. Key milestones, significant breakthroughs, and the growth of AI as a field are discussed to set the stage for exploring its transformative potential.

Chapter 2. Modern Approach to AI: This chapter delves into the shift from traditional AI approaches to data-driven machine learning models. It introduces the role of data, algorithms, and computational power in enabling modern AI, emphasizing their convergence in creating advanced intelligent systems.

Chapter 3. Introduction to Machine Learning: This chapter presents Machine Learning (ML) as the backbone of modern AI. This chapter introduces the core concepts of ML, including supervised, unsupervised, and reinforcement learning, alongside practical steps such as data preparation, feature engineering, and model evaluation.

Chapter 4. Regression Versus Classification Model: This chapter contrasts regression and classification tasks, exploring their significance in predicting continuous values and categorizing data points. Examples and hands-on Python implementations provide a practical understanding of these fundamental ML paradigms.

Chapter 5. Naive Bayes as a Linear Classifier: This chapter explores the Naive Bayes algorithm, with an emphasis on its assumptions, applications, and effectiveness as a linear classifier. Real-world use cases, such as spam detection and sentiment analysis, illustrate its utility.

Chapter 6. Tree-Based Machine Learning Models: This chapter examines tree-based ML models, including Decision Trees, Random Forest, and Gradient Boosting. These models are highlighted for their interpretability and effectiveness in handling complex, non-linear data.

Chapter 7. Distance-Based Machine Learning Models: This chapter focuses on algorithms such as K-Nearest Neighbors (KNN) and distance metrics and their application in classification and regression tasks. It emphasizes the simplicity and adaptability of distance-based learning.

Chapter 8. Support Vector Machines: This chapter introduces Support Vector Machines, detailing their mathematical foundations, kernel functions, and effectiveness in classification tasks. Examples demonstrate SVM's ability to handle high-dimensional data and complex decision boundaries.

Chapter 9. Introduction to Artificial Neural Networks: This chapter transitions from classical ML to Neural Networks, explaining their structure, activation functions, and layers. The foundational concepts of Artificial Neural Networks (ANNs) set the stage for deep learning models.

Chapter 10. Training Neural Networks: This chapter shifts to the mechanics of training neural networks, including gradient descent, backpropagation, and optimization techniques. Practical Python implementations illustrate the training process.

Chapter 11. Introduction to Convolutional Neural Networks: This chapter introduces Convolutional Neural Networks (CNNs) as a powerful tool for image-related tasks. The chapter covers convolutional layers, pooling, and activation functions, building the foundation for deeper exploration.

Chapter 12. Classification Using CNN: This chapter expands on the basics of CNNs. It delves into image classification, demonstrating step-by-step model implementation using TensorFlow-Keras. Practical insights and results are presented for hands-on learning.

Chapter 13. Pre-trained CNN Architectures: This chapter explores popular pre-trained CNN models such as VGG, ResNet, and YOLO, showcasing their applications in object detection, semantic segmentation, and transfer learning. Readers are encouraged to experiment with these models for various tasks.

Chapter 14. Introduction to Recurrent Neural Networks: This chapter introduces RNNs for handling sequential data such as time series and text. This chapter explains their architecture, working principles, and challenges, paving the way for more advanced models such as LSTMs.

Chapter 15. Introduction to Long Short-Term Memory (LSTM): The chapter focuses on LSTM networks, designed to overcome the long-term dependency problem in RNNs. It explains their architecture and advantages, providing insights into how they manage temporal dependencies effectively.

Chapter 16. Application of LSTM in NLP and TS Forecasting: This chapter applies LSTMs and GRUs to real-world tasks such as time-series forecasting, sentiment analysis, language translation, and chatbot development. It emphasizes hands-on implementations with Python.

Chapter 17. Emerging Trends and Ethical Considerations in AI: This chapter navigates advanced applications in AI, including multimodal models and generative AI. It also addresses ethical considerations such as bias, privacy, and societal impacts, urging readers to approach AI responsibly and innovatively.

Downloading the code bundles and colored images

Please follow the links or scan the QR codes to download the **Code Bundles and Images** of the book:

https://github.com/ava-orange-education/Kickstart-Artificial-Intelligence-Fundamentals

The code bundles and images of the book are also hosted on
https://rebrand.ly/f26206

In case there's an update to the code, it will be updated on the existing GitHub repository.

Errata

We take immense pride in our work at **Orange Education Pvt Ltd**, and follow best practices to ensure the accuracy of our content to provide an indulging reading experience to our subscribers. Our readers are our mirrors, and we use their inputs to reflect and improve upon human errors, if any, that may have occurred during the publishing processes involved. To let us maintain the quality and help us reach out to any readers who might be having difficulties due to any unforeseen errors, please write to us at :

errata@orangeava.com

Your support, suggestions, and feedback are highly appreciated.

DID YOU KNOW

Did you know that Orange Education Pvt Ltd offers eBook versions of every book published, with PDF and ePub files available? You can upgrade to the eBook version at **www.orangeava.com** and as a print book customer, you are entitled to a discount on the eBook copy. Get in touch with us at: **info@orangeava.com** for more details.

At **www.orangeava.com**, you can also read a collection of free technical articles, sign up for a range of free newsletters, and receive exclusive discounts and offers on Print Books and eBooks.

PIRACY

If you come across any illegal copies of our works in any form on the internet, we would be grateful if you would provide us with the location address or website name. Please contact us at **info@orangeava.com** with a link to the material.

ARE YOU INTERESTED IN AUTHORING WITH US?

If there is a topic that you have expertise in, and you are interested in either writing or contributing to a book, please write to us at **business@orangeava.com**. We are on a journey to help developers and tech professionals to gain insights on the present technological advancements and innovations happening across the globe and build a community that believes Knowledge is best acquired by sharing and learning with others. Please reach out to us to learn what our audience demands and how you can be part of this educational reform. We also welcome ideas from tech experts and help them build learning and development content for their domains.

REVIEWS

Please leave a review. Once you have read and used this book, why not leave a review on the site that you purchased it from? Potential readers can then see and use your unbiased opinion to make purchase decisions. We at Orange Education would love to know what you think about our products, and our authors can learn from your feedback. Thank you!

For more information about Orange Education, please visit **www.orangeava.com**.

Table of Contents

1. Introduction and Evolution of AI Technologies 1
    Introduction 1
    Structure 1
    Brief Introduction and Evolution of AI 2
    Historical Developments in AI 2
    Milestones in AI Development 3
    Rule-Based System and Symbolic Reasoning in AI 5
        Historical Background of Rule-Based System 6
        Components of Rule-Based System 7
        Symbolic Reasoning in AI 9
        Logic and Inference Engines 11
    Expert Systems: A Practical Application of
    Symbolic Reasoning 12
        Knowledge Representation in Rule-Based Systems 14
    Examples and Case Studies of Rule-Based Systems 16
        Example in Health Care and Medical Diagnosis 16
        *Case Study-1: Enhancing Pediatric Respiratory
        Diagnostics with Rule-Based Systems* 16
        Example in Banking and Finance 17
        *Case Study-2: Streamlining Credit Risk Assessment
        with Rule-Based Systems* 17
        Example in Manufacturing and Production Industry 18
        *Case Study-3: Optimizing Manufacturing Efficiency
        with Rule-Based Systems* 18
    Limitations and Challenges of Rule-Based Systems 19
        Pediatric Case Study 19
        Banking Loan Defaulter Case Study 20
        Manufacturing and Production Case Study 20
    Future Directions and Trends in Rule-Based AI Research 21

  Conclusion 21
  Multiple Choice Questions 22
  Answers 24
  Keywords 25
  References 25

2. Modern Approach to AI 26
  Introduction 26
  Structure 26
  The Evolution from Rule-Based to Data-Driven AI 27
  Fundamentals of Data-Driven AI 27
  Understanding Big Data Variables in the Business Context 28
  A Brief Overview of Machine Learning and its Types 30
    Conventional Programming: The Traditional Route 30
    Machine Learning: A Data-Driven Approach 31
    Types of Machine Learning 32
  Introduction to Machine Learning Life Cycle 36
  Applications of Modern Data-Driven AI across Data Structures 38
    Tabular Data: The Backbone of Conventional AI Applications 38
    Image-Based Datasets 39
    Text-Based Applications 39
    Time Series Dataset Applications 40
  Challenges in Data-Driven AI 41
  Conclusion 42
  Multiple Choice Questions 43
  Answers 46
  Keywords 46

3. Introduction to Machine Learning 48
  Introduction 48
  Structure 48
  Machine Learning Concepts and Definitions 49
  Landscapes of Machine Learning Models 49
  Key Components: Features, Label and Models 50

    Features 51
    Labels 51
    Algorithms 52
    Model Training 52
    Model Validation 53
    Model Evaluation 53
Data Preparation for Machine Learning Models 55
    Data Preparation Using Python 56
    Handling Missing Values 58
    Feature Scaling 60
    Outlier Treatment 62
Exploratory Data Analysis 64
Introduction to Unsupervised Learning 73
    K-Means Clustering 74
    Hierarchical Clustering 77
Introduction to Supervised Learning 81
    Regression Models 81
    Classification Models 82
Introduction to ML Model Evaluation Method and Metrics 83
Conclusion 84
Practice Exercises 85
Answers 86
Multiple Choice Questions 87
Answers 90
Keywords 91
References 91

4. Regression Versus Classification Model **92**
Introduction 92
Structure 93
Linear Regression 93
    Mathematical Definitions 93
    Interpreting the Coefficients 94

- Gradient Descent Learning 95
  - Mathematics of Gradient Calculation 96
  - Demonstration of Gradient Descent Learning with Contrived Data 97
- Implementation of Multiple Linear Regression in Python 99
  - Introducing the Use Case and Dataset 99
  - Implementation in Python 100
  - Exploratory Data Analysis (EDA) on Real Estate Data 101
  - Bivariate Analysis 103
  - Implementing MLR Model in Python 105
  - Performance Evaluation by K-Fold Cross Validation 108
    - Final Inference 109
- Logistic Regression as a Classifier Model 109
  - Illustrative Example with Contrived Data 111
- Implementation of Logistic Regression Model in Python 113
  - Interpretation of Model Coefficients 117
- Limitations of Linear Models and Assumptions 118
- Model Evaluation Techniques and Different Performance Metrics 120
- Conclusion 124
- Practice Exercises 124
- Answers 125
- Multiple Choice Questions 126
- Answers 130
- Keywords 131
- References 131

5. Naive Bayes as a Linear Classifier 132
- Introduction 132
- Structure 132
- Overview of Naïve Bayes Algorithm 133
  - Mathematical Definitions 133
  - Extending Bayes Formula into Naïve Bayes Classifier 134

Types of Naïve Bayes Classifiers 136
    Gaussian Naïve Bayes 137
    Multinomial Naïve Bayes 137
    Bernoulli Naïve Bayes 137
Applications of Naïve Bayes in Classification Task 138
Python Implementation and Use Case 140
    A Use Case with GaussianNB Scikit Learn Library 143
    Exploratory Data Analysis with Heart Disease Dataset 144
    Model Building and Evaluation 153
    Model Performance Summary 156
Challenges and Constraints in the Naïve Bayes Model 156
Conclusion 157
Practice Exercises... 158
Answers 159
Multiple Choice Questions 159
Answers 161
Keywords 161
References 162

6. Tree-Based Machine Learning Models 163
Introduction 163
Structure 164
Overview of Decision Tree Model 164
    Mathematical Foundation 166
    Decision Tree as a Classifier: An Illustrative
    Example with Contrived Dataset 166
    Root Node Split 167
    Split of the Right Node at Depth-1 169
    Split of the Left Node at Depth-1 170
Python Implementation of Decision Tree Classifier 171
    Decision Tree as a Regressor: An Illustrative
    Example with Contrived Dataset 174
    Split of the Left Node at Depth-1 176

  Split of the Right Node at Depth-1.. 177
 Python Implementation of Decision Tree Regressor 178
 Limitations and Drawbacks in Decision Tree Models 180
 Random Forest Model as Ensemble Learning 181
  Bagged Decision Trees and Bootstrap Sampling 182
 Python Implementation of Random Forest Models.. 183
  Random Forest as a Classifier..184
  Inference..185
  Random Forest as a Regressor 185
  Inference..186
 Ensemble Learning: Bagging and Boosting..187
  Bootstrap Aggregation or Bagging 187
  Boosting Techniques 188
  Adaptive Boosting (AdaBoost) Learning 189
  GradientBoost Learning... 190
  XGBoost Learning..194
   Key Features of XGBoost..194
  Stacked Ensemble Models...195
  Voting Ensemble Models 196
 Conclusion..197
 Practice Exercises.. 198
 Answers 199
 Multiple Choice Questions 200
 Answers 202
 Keywords 202
 References 203

7. Distance-Based Machine Learning Models 204
 Introduction 204
 Structure 204
 Introduction to K-Nearest Neighbor (KNN) Model..205
 Mathematical Foundation with Hand-Worked
 Calculation with Contrived Dataset.. 206

- *Exploring Different Distance Metrics in KNN* 208
  - *Euclidean Distance* 208
  - *Manhattan Distance* 208
  - *Minkowski Distance* 208
  - *Cosine Similarity* 209
  - *Hamming Distance* 209
  - *Impact on Model Performance* 209
- KNN as a Classifier: An Illustrative Example with Contrived Dataset 210
- KNN as a Regressor: An Illustrative Example with Contrived Dataset 213
- Python Implementation of KNN Classifier 217
  - *Inference* 219
- Python Implementation of KNN Regressor 220
  - *Inference* 224
- Limitations in Distance-Based ML Models 225
- Conclusion 226
- Practice Exercises 227
- Answers 228
- Multiple Choice Questions 228
- Answers 230
- Keywords 231
- References 231

8. Support Vector Machines 232
- Introduction 232
- Structure 232
- Understanding the Principles of Support Vector Machines 233
- Mathematical Foundation of Kernel Functions and Their Role in SVMs 235
  - *Types of Kernel Functions* 235
  - *Kernel Trick* 236
  - *SVM Hand-Worked Calculation with Contrived Dataset* 238

  Properties of Kernel Functions 241
 Python Implementation and Use Case with
 SVM as a Regressor 241
  Inference 244
 Python Implementation and Use Case with SVM
 as a Classifier 244
  Inference 248
 Pros and Cons of Support Vector Machines...............................248
 Conclusion..250
 Practice Exercises..250
 Answers 252
 Multiple Choice Questions..252
 Answers 254
 Keywords 255
 References 255

9. Introduction to Artificial Neural Networks.............................. 256
 Introduction...256
 Structure..257
 Fundamentals of Artificial Neural Networks 257
 Structure and Architecture of Artificial Neural Networks......258
 Activation Functions and Their Significance 261
 Layers in Neural Networks..264
  Input Layer 264
  Pre-Processing and Normalization...............................265
  Importance of the Input Layer.......................................265
  Hidden Layers..266
  Number of Hidden Layers and Neurons.....................266
  Role in Learning...266
  Challenges and Considerations.....................................267
  Output Layers 268
  Interactions Between Layers..268
 Conclusion..269

Practice Exercises	269
Answers	270
Multiple Choice Questions	270
Answers	272
Keywords	272
References	273

10. Training Neural Networks **274**

Introduction	274
Structure	274
Gradient Descent and Backpropagation Algorithm	275
ANN as a Classifier	276
ANN as a Regressor	281
Fine-Tuning Model Parameters	283
Coding Neural Networks in Python	285
Solving X-OR Problem Using ANN	286
ANN as a Classifier Use Case	289
ANN as a Regressor Use Case	292
Challenges in Traditional Neural Networks	294
Evolution of Technology Stack and Structured Data	296
Conclusion	297
Practice Exercise	297
Answers	298
Multiple Choice Questions	298
Answers	300
Keywords	300
References	301

11. Introduction to Convolutional Neural Networks **302**

Introduction	302
Structure	303
Evolution of Neural Networks for Unstructured Data	303
Introduction of Convolutional Neural Networks (CNNs)	305
Convolution Operations in CNN	306

xxi

    Understanding Strides in Convolution Operation 309
        Impact of Small Versus Large Strides 309
    Max Pooling Layer in CNN 310
    Flatten Layer 311
    Importance of Flattening 311
    Fully Connected FeedForward Layer 312
    Steps in Fully Connected Layers 312
    Importance of Fully Connected Layers 312
  Role of Filters in CNN 313
  Role of ReLU Activation Function in CNNs 314
  Conclusion 316
  Practice Exercises 316
  Answers 317
  Multiple Choice Questions 317
  Answers 319
  Keywords 320
  References 320

12. Classification Using CNN **321**
  Introduction 321
  Structure 322
  Dataset Preparation for Image Classification Tasks 322
  Training and Fine-Tuning the Model for Optimal
  Performance Using Conv2D Layers 323
    Implementing a CNN for MNIST Classification 324
  Evaluation Metrics for Image Classification 326
  Dataset Preparation for Time-Series Classification 327
  Training and Fine-Tuning the Model 331
  Conclusion 333
  Practice Exercises 334
  Answers 335
  Multiple Choice Questions 335
  Answers 337

Keywords 337

References 338

13. Pre-Trained CNN Architectures 339

Introduction 339

Structure 339

Introduction to Popular Pre-Trained CNN Architectures 340

    AlexNet 340

    VGGNet 341

    GoogleNet/Inception 341

    ResNet 342

    DenseNet 342

    MobileNet 343

    EfficientNet 343

Transfer Learning and its Significance in Deep Learning 344

    Types of Transfer Learning 344

    Benefits of Transfer Learning 345

Implementing Transfer Learning with Pre-Trained
CNN Models 345

    Introduction to the Problem Statement 346

Pre-Trained CNN Model as a Feature Extractor 352

    Exploring Different Configurations of
    Pre-Trained CNNs 353

    Pre-Trained Models as Direct Inference 353

    Full Model Training Configuration with
    Pre-Trained CNNs 354

    Customizing Only the Dense Layer
    (Fully Connected Layer) 354

    Transforming Images into Feature Vectors Using
    Pre-Trained CNNs 355

Case Studies Showcasing the Effectiveness of Pre-Trained
Architectures in Various Domains 356

    MedNet: Pre-Trained Model for Medical Imaging Tasks 356

    SatlasPretrain: Satellite Imagery Analysis 357

        A Mobile-Based DL Model for Cassava Disease Diagnosis 357
        Fashion and Apparel Classification Using CNNs 357
        Industrial Automation and Machine Vision 358
        Defense Sector: Automatic Target Recognition 358
    Conclusion 359
    Practice Exercises 360
    Answers 360
    Multiple Choice Questions 361
    Answers 363
    Keywords 363
    References 364

14. Introduction to Recurrent Neural Networks 365
    Introduction 365
    Structure 366
    Basics of Sequential Data and Time-Series Analysis 366
        Time-Series Analysis 367
        Challenges in Analyzing Sequential Data 370
    Understanding the Need for Recurrent Connections
    in Neural Networks 371
        Challenges of FeedForward Models for Sequential Data 372
        Next Word Prediction Challenge 372
        Sequence Classification Challenge 372
        Recurrent Connections in Neural Networks 373
    Architecture and Working Principle of a Basic RNN 374
        Training the RNN Architecture 376
        Backpropagation Through Time 376
            Output Gradients 377
            Hidden State Gradients 377
            Parameter Gradients 377
    Limitations of RNN 378
    Conclusion 380
    Practice Exercises 380

Answers	381
Multiple Choice Questions	381
Answers	383
Keywords	384
References	384

15. Introduction to Long Short-Term Memory (LSTM) 385

Introduction	385
Structure	385
Overcoming the Long-Term Dependency Problem in RNN	386
Advantages of LSTMs over Traditional RNNs	388
Architecture and Working Principles of LSTM	390
The Core Gates of LSTM	392
Forward Pass	392
Forget Gate	392
Update Gate	393
Candidate Cell State	393
Cell State Update	393
Output Gate and Final Hidden State	394
Training the LSTM Model	395
Applications and Use-Case of LSTM Models	396
Simplified Representation of LSTM as Gated Recurrent Unit (GRU)	397
Update Gate: Merging Forget and Input Gates	397
Pros and Cons of GRU Compared to LSTM	399
Pros of GRU Compared to LSTM	399
Cons of GRU Compared to LSTM	399
Applications and Use-Case of GRU Models	400
Conclusion	401
Practice Exercises	401
Answers	402
Multiple Choice Questions	403
Answers	404

Keywords	405
References	405

16. Application of LSTM in NLP and TS Forecasting 406

Introduction	406
Structure	407
TS Forecasting Using LSTM and its Implementation	407
Different Design Strategies of LSTM Architecture	413
LSTM as Encoder	414
LSTM as Encoder-Decoder	415
LSTM as Decoder	416
Language Modelling and Sentiment Analysis	418
Language Modelling using LSTM	418
Sentiment Analysis using LSTM	422
Language Translation and Chatbot Modeling	426
Conclusion	434
Practice Exercises	434
Answers	435
Multiple Choice Questions	436
Answers	437
Keywords	438
References	438

17. Emerging Trends and Ethical Considerations in AI 439

Introduction	439
Structure	439
Advanced Applications of CNN in Object Detection and Face Recognition	440
Advanced Applications of LSTM in the Form of Transformer Models	444
Scope of GenAI in Modern Day ChatGPT	449
Ethical Challenges and Societal Responsibilities in AI	451
Balancing Risks and Benefits in the AI Landscape	452
Economic, Cultural, and Social Impacts of AI	454

Conclusion 455
Multiple Choice Questions 455
Answers 457
Keywords 458
References 458

Index **459**

CHAPTER 1
Introduction and Evolution of AI Technologies

Introduction

This chapter embarks on a comprehensive journey into the realm of Artificial Intelligence (AI), unraveling its historical evolution, foundational technologies, and the pivotal role of rule-based systems. As we navigate through the intricacies of AI development, this chapter aims to provide a thorough understanding of how these technologies have shaped the landscape of modern computing and decision-making processes. By delving into the origins and advancements of rule-based systems, we illuminate the cornerstone upon which much of early AI research was built, showcasing the critical steps that have led us to today's sophisticated AI applications. This exploration is not just about chronicling milestones; it is about appreciating the complex interplay between theory, practice, and innovation in the AI field.

Structure

In this chapter we are going to cover the following main topics:
- Brief Introduction and Evolution of AI
- Historical Developments in AI
- Milestones in AI Development
- Rule-Based System and Symbolic Reasoning in AI
- Expert Systems: A Practical Application of Symbolic Reasoning
- Examples and Case Studies of Rule-Based Systems
- Limitations and Challenges of Rule-Based System
- Future Directions and Trends in Rule-Based AI Research

Brief Introduction and Evolution of AI

The term Artificial Intelligence (AI) was first coined by John McCarthy, an American computer scientist, in 1956 during the Dartmouth Summer Research Project on Artificial Intelligence. McCarthy and a group of researchers gathered at Dartmouth College to investigate the feasibility of developing machines capable of emulating human intelligence. The gathering at Dartmouth College is widely recognized as the inception of AI as an academic discipline. From that point forward, AI has undergone substantial development, propelled by advancements in computing capabilities, algorithmic innovations, and the abundance of data.

Artificial Intelligence (AI) stands as a pivotal branch within the domain of computer science, dedicated to crafting systems that emulate human intelligence to tackle tasks traditionally requiring human cognition. AI systems encompass a diverse range of approaches, from basic rule-based algorithms that follow predefined instructions to sophisticated neural networks modeled upon the human brain, equipped with the ability to perform intricate reasoning and decision-making processes.

Ultimately, AI endeavors to furnish machines with the capacity to replicate human-like intelligence, enabling them to undertake a multitude of tasks with efficacy and adaptability. These tasks span a wide spectrum, including but not limited to comprehending and generating natural language discerning intricate patterns within vast datasets, solving complex problems, learning from past experiences, and autonomously making decisions informed by acquired knowledge.

Furthermore, AI extends its reach to include tasks such as computer vision, enabling machines to perceive and interpret visual information; speech recognition, facilitating seamless interaction between humans and machines through spoken language; robotics, empowering machines with the ability to interact with the physical world; and predictive analytics, forecasting future outcomes based on historical data trends. In essence, AI serves as the bedrock for a myriad of applications across various industries, revolutionizing the way we work, communicate, and interact with technology.

Historical Developments in AI

Following the Dartmouth Conference, researchers began developing early AI programs that focused on symbolic reasoning and problem-solving. Notable examples include the Logic Theorist (1956), developed by Allen Newell and Herbert A. Simon, which could prove mathematical theorems, and the General Problem Solver (1959), which demonstrated problem-solving capabilities.

During the 1960s and 1970s, a significant discourse emerged within the AI community, cantering around Symbolic AI and Connectionism. Symbolic AI supporters advocated for rule-based systems and symbolic reasoning, emphasizing the explicit representation of knowledge and logical inference. Conversely, Connectionism proponents championed neural networks and distributed representations, which aimed to simulate the interconnected structure of the human brain and learn from patterns in data.

While Symbolic AI enjoyed widespread popularity during this era due to its intuitive approach to problem-solving, Connectionism laid the groundwork for future advancements in neural networks and deep learning. Despite facing skepticism at the time, Connectionism introduced innovative concepts such as parallel processing and distributed representation, which proved instrumental in the development of modern AI technologies. Over time, the principles of Connectionism evolved into the deep learning techniques that underpin many of today's AI applications, including computer vision and image recognition, natural language processing, and autonomous decision-making systems.

The field experienced periods of stagnation known as "AI Winters" in the 1970s and 1980s due to overpromising and underdelivering on the capabilities of AI systems. Despite initial optimism, the practical limitations of existing technologies prevailed during that time leading to a perception of AI as overhyped and underperforming. However, the landscape began to shift with the emergence of expert systems and advancements in computing power during the 1980s and 1990s. Expert systems, which relied on rule-based reasoning to solve specific problems, showcased practical applications of AI in areas such as medicine, finance, and engineering.

Additionally, the availability of more powerful computers enabled researchers to explore complex algorithms and models, reigniting interest and investment in AI research and development. This resurgence marked a turning point for the field, paving the way for subsequent breakthroughs and innovations in AI technology.

During the late 20th and early 21st centuries, machine learning underwent a transformative phase, marked by notable progress in key domains such as pattern recognition, reinforcement learning, and probabilistic reasoning. These advancements played a pivotal role in catapulting the field of artificial intelligence to unprecedented levels of sophistication and applicability. As algorithms reached new levels of sophistication, fuelled by breakthroughs in computational techniques, and the exponential growth of datasets, AI research and its real-world implementations witnessed a remarkable surge.

This convergence of algorithmic innovation, data abundance, and computational prowess became the cornerstone of AI's evolution, laying the foundation for a multitude of ground-breaking applications and shaping the trajectory of technological progress in the modern era.

Milestones in AI Development

Throughout its history, AI has achieved numerous milestones that have shaped its evolution and impact on society. Let us delve into some of the key milestones that have defined the history of AI, from its humble beginnings to the emergence of modern-day language models.

- **1956**: Dartmouth Conference - Coined the term "artificial intelligence" and marked the formal birth of the field.
- **1958**: McCulloch-Pitts Model - Introduced the first mathematical model of a neural network.
- **1959**: Perceptron - Frank Rosenblatt created the perceptron artificial neural model.
- **1966**: ELIZA - Joseph Weizenbaum developed the first chatbot, demonstrating natural language processing.
- **1969**: DENDRAL - The first expert system, designed for chemical analysis, was developed.
- **1973**: Lighthill Report - Highlighted the limitations of AI research, leading to an "AI Winter" period.
- **1980**: MYCIN - A rule-based expert system for diagnosing bacterial infections was developed.
- **1986**: Backpropagation - The backpropagation algorithm for training neural networks was popularized.
- **1988**: Neural Network Boom - Geoff Hinton and others proposed the "wake-sleep algorithm," sparking renewed interest in neural networks.
- **1997**: Deep Blue - IBM's chess-playing computer defeated world champion Garry Kasparov.
- **2005**: DARPA Grand Challenge - Autonomous vehicles completed a 131-mile course in the Mojave Desert.
- **2011**: Watson - IBM's AI system won the quiz show Jeopardy! Showcasing advancements in natural language processing.
- **2012**: AlexNet - A convolutional neural network achieved record-breaking performance in the ImageNet competition.
- **2015:** Driverless Cars on Public Roads - Google's self-driving car project, later branded as Waymo, became the first to operate fully autonomous vehicles on public roads without a steering wheel or driver. This marked a significant leap in AI and machine learning integration for real-world navigation and safety.
- **2016**: AlphaGo - DeepMind's AI defeated world champion Lee Sedol in the game of Go.
- **2018**: GPT (Generative Pre-trained Transformer) - OpenAI introduced the first large-scale language model.
- **2020s:** Autonomous Systems - AI-driven advancements led to the development

of autonomous tractors and autonomous vehicles, revolutionizing agriculture and transportation by integrating machine learning and real-time decision-making for fully autonomous operations.

- **2020**: GPT-3 - OpenAI released a 175 billion parameter model, capable of impressive natural language understanding and generation.
- **2022**: ChatGPT - OpenAI introduced ChatGPT, a conversational AI model based on the GPT-3 architecture.
- **2024**: Devin AI – Cognition AI developed the world's first fully autonomous AI software engineer.

These milestones reflect the progression of AI from its early conceptualization to the development of sophisticated AI models including large language models such as GPT-3 and ChatGPT. Alongside, advancements in symbolic and logical reasoning and expert systems have played a crucial role in shaping the field of AI.

Rule-Based System and Symbolic Reasoning in AI

Rule-based systems, a fundamental aspect of Artificial Intelligence (AI), are computational frameworks engineered to replicate human decision-making logic. These systems operate on a set of predefined rules or conditions, enabling them to analyze input data, make deductions, and generate responses or outputs accordingly. Unlike traditional programming paradigms, rule-based systems emphasize the encoding of knowledge and expertise in the form of rules, fostering a more intuitive and adaptable approach to problem-solving.

At the core of rule-based systems lies the concept of declarative knowledge representation, where domain-specific knowledge is expressed in the form of rules as shown in *Figure* 1.1, often following an "if-then" structure. These rules encapsulate logical relationships and dependencies between different variables or entities within a given domain, allowing the system to infer conclusions and make decisions autonomously. By leveraging this rule-based reasoning mechanism, AI systems can effectively handle complex decision-making tasks across diverse domains, ranging from expert systems in healthcare and finance to intelligent tutoring systems in education.

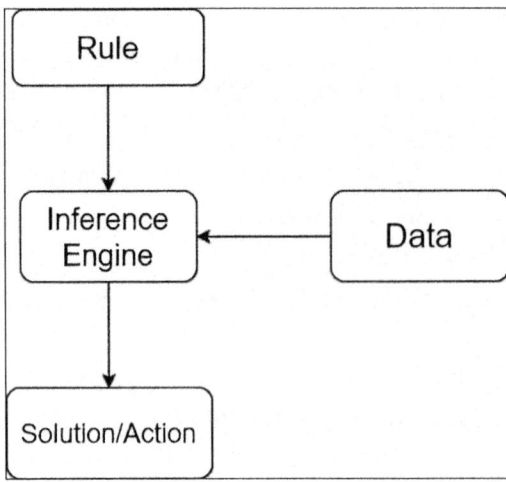

Figure 1.1: *Rule-Based System*

In recent years, advancements in rule-based systems have been fueled by innovations in knowledge engineering, machine learning, and natural language processing. These developments have enabled the creation of more sophisticated rule-based models capable of handling larger datasets, extracting insights from unstructured data, and interacting with users in natural language. As rule-based AI continues to evolve, it holds immense potential to drive transformative changes across various industries, empowering organizations to streamline operations, enhance decision-making processes, and deliver tailored solutions to complex problems.

Historical Background of Rule-Based System

The origins of rule-based systems can be traced back to the early days of artificial intelligence research in the 1950s and 1960s when pioneers such as John McCarthy and Marvin Minsky envisioned computational systems capable of emulating human reasoning. Initial efforts focused on developing symbolic AI approaches, which relied on explicit rules and logical reasoning to solve problems. One of the earliest rule-based systems, known as the Logic Theorist, was created by Allen Newell and Herbert Simon in 1956 to prove mathematical theorems using symbolic manipulation.

Throughout the following decades, rule-based systems gained prominence in various domains, including expert systems, natural language processing, and automated reasoning. The development of expert systems in the 1970s and 1980s marked a significant milestone in the evolution of rule-based AI, with systems such as MYCIN and DENDRAL demonstrating the practical applications of rule-based reasoning in complex problem domains such as medical diagnosis and chemical analysis. These early successes fuelled further research and innovation in rule-based systems, leading to the emergence of tools and methodologies for knowledge representation, inference, and rule-based programming.

In the modern era, rule-based systems continue to play a vital role in AI and cognitive computing, albeit alongside other paradigms such as machine learning and deep learning. With advancements in computational power, knowledge engineering techniques, and natural language processing, rule-based systems have evolved into sophisticated AI tools capable of handling large-scale knowledge bases, reasoning under uncertainty, and interacting with users in natural language. Today, rule-based systems are widely deployed in diverse applications, from intelligent virtual assistants and recommendation engines to fraud detection systems and autonomous vehicles, underscoring their enduring relevance in the field of artificial intelligence.

Components of Rule-Based System

Rule-based systems typically consist of several key components that work together to enable automated reasoning and decision-making. At the core of these systems are a set of rules or logical expressions that encode domain-specific knowledge and expertise. These rules are formulated using a formal language or notation, such as production rules or first-order logic, and are structured to capture the relationships and dependencies between different entities in the problem domain.

The representation of rules determines how they are stored, organized, and manipulated within the system. Common representations include if-then statements, production rules, decision tables, and semantic networks. The choice of rule representation impacts the system's efficiency, flexibility, and expressiveness in capturing domain knowledge and reasoning about complex situations. Effective rule representation facilitates the encoding of logical relationships, conditions, and actions, enabling the system to perform accurate inference and decision-making.

Moreover, rule representation techniques may incorporate features such as modularity, hierarchy, and abstraction to enhance the system's scalability, maintainability, and reusability of rules across different domains and applications. By employing suitable rule representation methods, rule-based systems can effectively model and automate decision-making processes, thereby enhancing their utility and applicability in various domains.

In addition to rules, rule-based systems often include a knowledge base, which serves as a repository for storing and organizing the domain knowledge. The knowledge base may contain facts, assertions, and other relevant information about the problem domain, which are used by the inference engine to derive new conclusions and make decisions. To facilitate efficient retrieval and manipulation of knowledge, the knowledge base is typically organized in a structured format, such as a semantic network, frame-based system, or relational database.

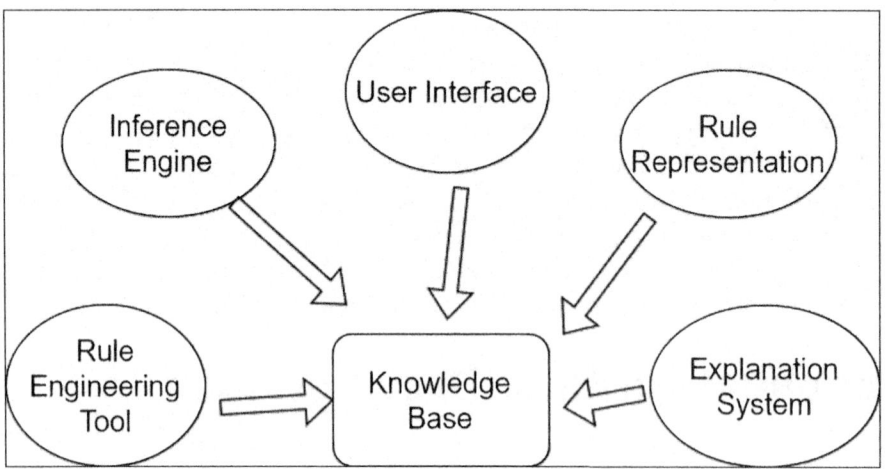

Figure 1.2: Components of Rule-Based System

Another essential component of rule-based systems is the inference engine as shown in *Figure 1.2*, which is responsible for interpreting and applying the rules to deduce new information and perform reasoning tasks. The inference engine employs various reasoning mechanisms, such as forward chaining, backward chaining, or truth maintenance, to evaluate the rules and derive logical consequences. By systematically applying the rules to the available knowledge, the inference engine can generate solutions, make predictions, and provide explanations in response to user queries or input. Overall, these components work in concert to enable rule-based systems to emulate human-like reasoning and problem-solving capabilities in diverse application domains.

In addition to rules, knowledge bases, and inference engines, user interfaces play a crucial role as a component of rule-based systems. The user interface serves as the bridge between the system and the human user, facilitating interaction, communication, and collaboration. Through the user interface, users can input queries, provide feedback, and interact with the system to access its capabilities and functionalities. A well-designed user interface enhances the usability, accessibility, and user experience of the rule-based system, enabling users to easily understand, navigate, and manipulate the system's functionalities. Moreover, user interfaces may incorporate features such as graphical displays, natural language processing, and visualization tools to enhance user interaction and comprehension. By integrating an intuitive and user-friendly interface, rule-based systems can empower users to effectively harness the system's capabilities and leverage its domain knowledge for decision-making and problem-solving tasks.

The final component within rule-based systems is the explanation system. This component is responsible for providing transparency and interpretability by explaining the reasoning behind the system's decisions and actions. Explanation systems help users understand how the system arrived at a particular conclusion or recommendation by tracing the application of rules and the inference process. They facilitate human-computer interaction by presenting the rationale and justification behind the system's behavior in a comprehensible manner.

Explanation systems may employ various techniques such as rule tracing, justification generation, and interactive interfaces to elucidate the underlying logic and rules involved in decision-making. By incorporating robust explanation mechanisms, rule-based systems enhance user trust, acceptance, and collaboration, fostering effective human-machine partnerships in problem-solving tasks.

Additionally, explanation systems enable users to validate the system's outputs, correct any errors or biases, and refine the rules based on domain expertise and feedback, thereby improving the system's accuracy and reliability over time.

Symbolic Reasoning in AI

Symbolic reasoning in AI refers to the process of manipulating symbols and rules to perform logical deductions, infer relationships, and solve problems in a structured manner. It is based on the principles of formal logic, where propositions and rules are represented symbolically, and reasoning is carried out through the application of deductive or inductive inference rules. Symbolic reasoning systems encode domain knowledge using symbolic representations such as predicates, variables, constants, and logical operators, allowing them to capture the semantics and structure of the problem domain. These systems employ symbolic manipulation techniques, such as theorem proving, resolution, and inference engines, to derive new knowledge from existing facts and rules.

One of the key characteristics of symbolic reasoning is its emphasis on explicit representation and manipulation of knowledge in a declarative form. This enables AI systems to express complex relationships and domain-specific constraints using formal languages such as first-order logic or propositional calculus. Symbolic reasoning systems employ logical inference mechanisms to derive conclusions from the available knowledge base by applying inference rules such as modus ponens, resolution, and backward chaining. These systems can perform tasks such as automated theorem proving, knowledge representation and reasoning, planning, and natural language understanding, making them well-suited for domains that require logical reasoning and rule-based decision-making.

Symbolic reasoning has been instrumental in various AI applications, including expert systems, knowledge-based systems, and natural language processing. Expert systems use symbolic reasoning to encode expert knowledge in the form of rules and facts, enabling them to emulate human expertise and provide advisory or diagnostic capabilities in specific domains. Knowledge-based systems leverage symbolic reasoning to represent and manipulate large knowledge bases, supporting tasks such as knowledge retrieval, inference, and explanation.

In natural language processing, symbolic reasoning techniques are employed for semantic analysis, syntactic parsing, and discourse understanding, enabling AI systems to comprehend and generate human language effectively. Overall, symbolic reasoning plays a crucial role in AI by enabling systems to perform complex reasoning tasks and exhibit intelligent behavior in various domains.

To delve deeper into the principles and techniques underlying symbolic reasoning, exploring its key components, challenges, and implications for AI research and application. The following points are summarized based on six key factors:

- **Knowledge Representation Formalisms**: Symbolic reasoning systems often utilize formalisms such as frames, semantic networks, and ontologies to represent knowledge in a structured and hierarchical manner. These formalisms enable the organization and manipulation of complex knowledge structures, facilitating effective reasoning and inference.
    - **Inference Mechanisms**: Symbolic reasoning involves various inference mechanisms, including forward chaining, backward chaining, and abduction. Forward chaining starts with known facts and derives new conclusions based on predefined rules, while backward chaining starts with a goal and works backward to find supporting evidence. Abduction involves generating plausible explanations for observed phenomena based on available evidence and background knowledge.
    - **Uncertainty Handling**: Symbolic reasoning systems often struggle with handling uncertainty and ambiguity inherent in real-world data and knowledge. Techniques such as fuzzy logic, probabilistic reasoning, and Bayesian networks have been introduced to address these challenges and enhance the robustness and flexibility of symbolic reasoning systems.
    - **Integration with Other AI Approaches**: Symbolic reasoning is often combined with other AI approaches, such as statistical learning and connectionist models, to create hybrid AI systems that leverage the strengths of each approach. For example, symbolic reasoning can provide high-level, structured reasoning capabilities, while statistical learning can handle large-scale data processing and pattern recognition tasks.
    - **Scalability and Efficiency**: One challenge faced by symbolic reasoning systems is scalability, especially when dealing with large knowledge bases or complex inference tasks. Research in optimization techniques, parallel and distributed computing, and knowledge compilation methods aims to improve the scalability and efficiency of symbolic reasoning systems, enabling them to handle increasingly complex problems.
    - **Ethical and Social Implications**: Symbolic reasoning raises ethical and social concerns related to the use of AI systems in decision-making contexts. Issues such as bias, fairness, transparency, and accountability

must be addressed to ensure that symbolic reasoning systems make decisions that align with ethical principles and societal values.

As we conclude our understanding of symbolic reasoning in artificial intelligence, it becomes evident that this approach offers a powerful framework for knowledge representation, reasoning, and problem-solving. By leveraging formal logic and symbolic manipulation, AI systems can effectively model and reason about complex domains, enabling them to make intelligent decisions and derive insights from data. Despite its strengths, symbolic reasoning also faces challenges, such as scalability and handling uncertainty, which continue to drive research and innovation in the field.

Moving forward, the integration of symbolic reasoning with other AI techniques promises to unlock new avenues for tackling real-world problems and advancing the frontiers of artificial intelligence.

Logic and Inference Engines

Logic plays a fundamental role in Artificial Intelligence (AI) as it provides a formal framework for representing knowledge and reasoning about it. In AI systems, logic-based representations facilitate the expression of facts, rules, and relationships in a structured manner, allowing the system to derive new information through logical inference. One of the key components of logic-based AI systems is the inference engine, which serves as the reasoning mechanism responsible for drawing conclusions from the given knowledge base. Inference engines employ various reasoning techniques, such as deduction, abduction, and induction, to process the available information and generate logical conclusions.

Deductive reasoning as shown in *Figure* 1.3, also known as top-down reasoning, involves deriving specific conclusions from general principles or rules. In deductive inference, the inference engine applies logical rules and deductions to reach a definitive conclusion based on the available premises. This form of reasoning is commonly used in rule-based systems and expert systems, where the knowledge base consists of a set of rules and facts, and the goal is to infer new facts or make decisions based on existing knowledge.

Figure 1.3: *Deductive Reasoning*

Abductive reasoning, on the other hand, operates in the opposite direction of deduction, starting from observations or evidence as shown in *Figure* 1.4, and working towards the best possible explanation or hypothesis. Abductive inference involves generating explanations that are consistent with the observed data, even if they may not be certain. This form of reasoning is particularly useful in diagnostic systems and problem-solving tasks, where the goal is to identify the most likely cause or solution given the observed symptoms or evidence.

Inductive reasoning, also known as bottom-up reasoning, involves deriving general principles or rules from specific observations or instances. Unlike deductive reasoning, which proceeds from the general to the specific, inductive inference starts with specific examples and generalizes patterns or trends to form more abstract rules or principles. Inductive reasoning is commonly used in machine learning algorithms, where patterns in data are identified and used to make predictions or classifications based on new instances.

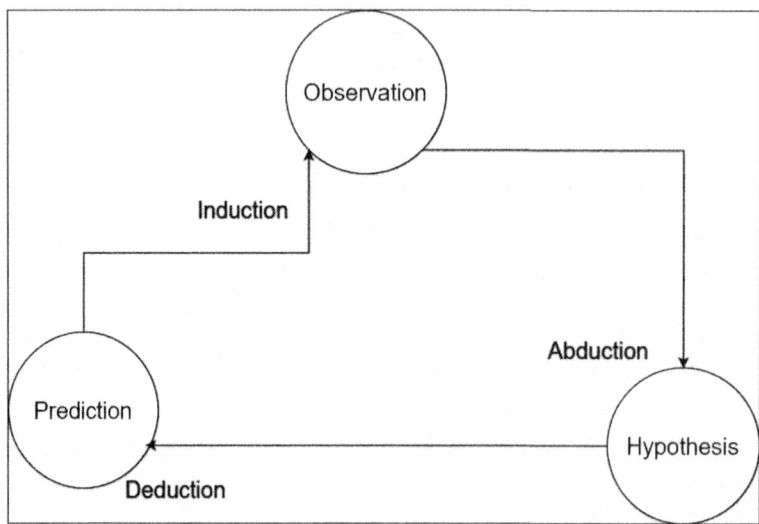

Figure 1.4: Different Reasoning Process

In summary, logic and inference engines are essential components of AI systems, enabling them to represent knowledge, perform reasoning, and make decisions. By employing various forms of logical inference, including deduction, abduction, and induction, AI systems can effectively process information and derive meaningful conclusions, thereby exhibiting intelligent behavior in a wide range of applications.

Expert Systems: A Practical Application of Symbolic Reasoning

Expert systems represent a practical application of symbolic reasoning in artificial intelligence, designed to emulate the problem-solving abilities of human experts in specific domains. These systems are built upon a foundation of knowledge engineering, which involves eliciting, organizing, and representing the expertise of human specialists in a structured form that can be processed by computers. The knowledge base of an expert system typically comprises a collection of rules, facts, and heuristics, derived from domain experts through interviews, documentation review, and other knowledge acquisition methods.

One of the key components of an expert system is the inference engine, which serves as the reasoning mechanism responsible for drawing conclusions and making decisions based on the available knowledge. The inference engine employs symbolic reasoning techniques, such as deduction, abduction, and pattern matching, to process the input data and generate output in the form of recommendations, diagnoses, or solutions. By leveraging the domain-specific knowledge encoded in its knowledge base, an expert system can provide intelligent assistance to users in problem-solving tasks within its domain of expertise.

Expert systems find applications in a wide range of fields, including medicine, finance, engineering, and customer support, where they serve as decision-support tools for professionals and domain experts. In medicine, for example, expert systems are used for diagnostic purposes, helping clinicians to identify diseases and recommend treatment options based on patient symptoms and medical history. In finance, expert systems assist financial analysts in evaluating investment opportunities, assessing risks, and making investment decisions in complex market conditions.

The development of an expert system is a multi-stage process that begins with knowledge acquisition, where domain experts and knowledge engineers collaborate closely to capture and formalize the expertise required for the system. In this phase, domain experts provide insights into the rules, heuristics, and decision-making criteria they use when solving problems within their domain. Knowledge engineers work alongside these experts to translate this tacit knowledge into a structured format that can be understood and processed by the computer. This involves identifying relevant concepts, relationships, and constraints, and representing those using formal languages such as production rules, semantic networks, or frames.

Once the knowledge acquisition phase is complete, the next step is knowledge representation, where the acquired knowledge is organized and encoded into a knowledge base. This knowledge base serves as the backbone of the expert system, containing all the rules, facts, and heuristics necessary for problem-solving. Knowledge representation involves structuring the knowledge in a way that facilitates efficient retrieval and reasoning by the inference engine. Various formal representation languages are used for this purpose, each suited to different types of knowledge and problem domains. By carefully designing the knowledge base and selecting appropriate representation languages, developers ensure that the expert system can effectively interpret and apply the domain expertise encoded within it, leading to accurate and reliable decision-making capabilities.

Once the knowledge representation is established, the next step is to design and implement the inference engine as shown in *Figure 1.5*, which interprets the input data, applies the rules and heuristics stored in the knowledge base, and generates the appropriate output. The inference engine may use various reasoning mechanisms, such as forward chaining, backward chaining, or fuzzy logic, depending on the nature of the problem and the requirements of the application. Succeeding the implementation of the expert system, it undergoes testing and validation to ensure that it behaves correctly and produces accurate results in real-world scenarios.

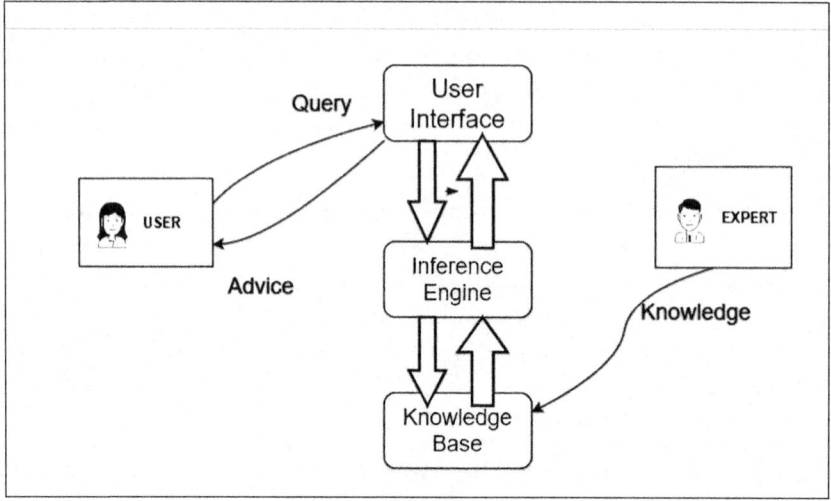

Figure 1.5: Expert System

Knowledge Representation in Rule-Based Systems

Knowledge representation is a fundamental aspect of rule-based systems, playing a crucial role in encoding and organizing the information required for decision-making and problem-solving. In these systems, knowledge is typically represented in a structured format that facilitates efficient storage, retrieval, and manipulation by the computer. Basically, there are four types of knowledge representation as shown in *Figure 1.6*.

One common approach to knowledge representation is the use of production rules, which consist of a set of conditional statements that describe relationships between different elements of knowledge. Each rule typically takes the form of an "if-then" statement, specifying a condition that must be met for a certain action or conclusion to be taken. These rules are stored in a knowledge base and can be invoked by an inference engine to derive new knowledge or make decisions based on the available information.

Imagine a rule-based system designed to assist doctors in diagnosing illnesses based on patient symptoms. One production rule in the system could be: "If the patient has a fever and cough, then consider the possibility of respiratory infection." Here, the

Introduction and Evolution of AI Technologies 15

condition "fever and cough" serves as the input, and the action "consider respiratory infection" represents the system's response based on that input. The system can contain numerous such rules, each capturing a specific symptom combination and corresponding diagnosis recommendation.

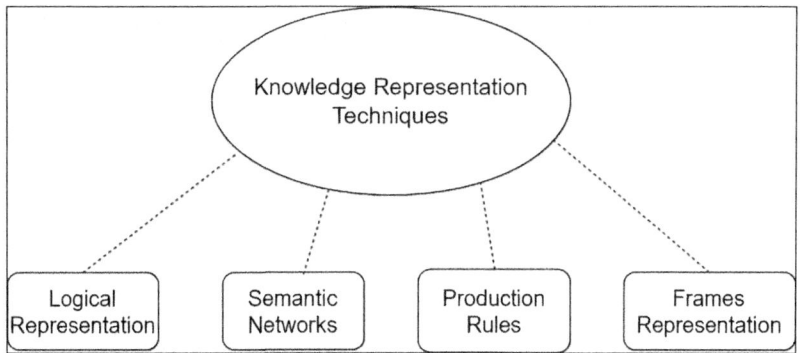

Figure 1.6: *Knowledge Representation Types*

Another widely used technique for knowledge representation in rule-based systems is semantic networks as shown in *Figure* 1.7, which represent knowledge in the form of interconnected nodes and edges. Nodes correspond to entities or concepts, while edges represent relationships or links between these entities. By organizing knowledge in this hierarchical and interconnected manner, semantic networks enable the representation of complex relationships and dependencies between different pieces of information. This facilitates efficient reasoning and inference, as the system can traverse the network to retrieve relevant information and draw conclusions based on the connections between nodes.

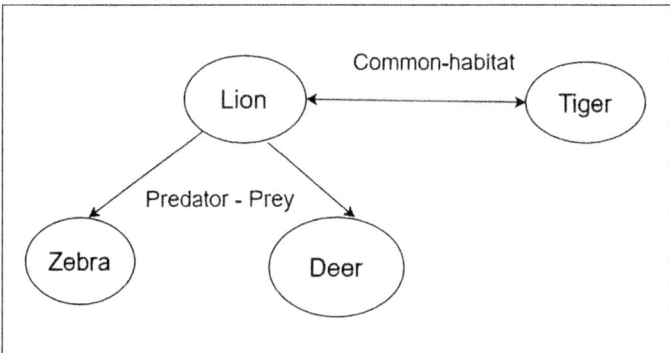

Figure 1.7: *Example of a Semantic Network*

Frames are another important tool for knowledge representation in rule-based systems, providing a structured way to represent objects, concepts, and their attributes. A frame consists of a set of slots, each of which represents a particular aspect or property of the object or concept being modeled. These slots can contain values or references to other frames, allowing for the representation of complex structures and relationships. Frames provide a flexible and intuitive way to organize knowledge, making it easier for developers to encode domain-specific information and capture the intricacies of real-world phenomena.

Consider a rule-based system designed to recommend personalized movie selections based on user preferences. Frames, a knowledge representation technique, can organize information about movies and users into structured entities. Each movie frame might include slots for attributes such as genre, director, and release year, along with associated values. Similarly, each user frame might contain slots for demographic information, viewing history, and preferred genres. By linking these frames together, the system can match user preferences with movie attributes to generate tailored recommendations that align with individual tastes and interests.

In addition to these formal representation languages, rule-based systems may also utilize more specialized knowledge representation techniques tailored to specific problem domains. For example, expert systems in medical diagnosis may employ ontologies to represent complex taxonomies of diseases, symptoms, and treatments, while those in natural language processing may use grammars and lexicons to represent linguistic rules and structures. Regardless of the specific approach used, effective knowledge representation is essential for the successful operation of rule-based systems, enabling them to interpret and reason with the available information to achieve their intended objectives.

Examples and Case Studies of Rule-Based Systems

We are going to walk through a few case studies in different domains, starting with:

Example in Health Care and Medical Diagnosis

Imagine a rule-based diagnostic system tailored for pediatric respiratory health, assisting pediatricians in identifying common childhood respiratory illnesses. The system operates by analyzing symptoms reported by parents or guardians during pediatric appointments. For instance, if a child presents with persistent coughing, wheezing, and difficulty breathing, the system may suggest a diagnosis of asthma or bronchiolitis based on established symptom-disease correlations in pediatric respiratory medicine.

Case Study-1: Enhancing Pediatric Respiratory Diagnostics with Rule-Based Systems

A pediatric clinic integrates a rule-based diagnostic system into its practice to aid pediatricians in diagnosing respiratory illnesses in children. Parents or guardians input their child's symptoms into the system during appointments, providing details such as cough frequency, presence of fever, and any accompanying symptoms. The system then applies a set of rules derived from pediatric respiratory guidelines and expert knowledge to generate potential diagnoses. Pediatricians review the system's suggestions alongside clinical observations to formulate an accurate diagnosis and treatment plan.

The rule-based diagnostic system enhances the efficiency of pediatric respiratory care, enabling pediatricians to promptly identify and address respiratory issues in children. By leveraging established symptom-disease correlations specific to pediatric patients, the system assists in early detection and intervention, ultimately leading to improved health outcomes for young patients. Additionally, the system continuously learns from diagnostic outcomes and pediatrician feedback, refining its rule set to enhance diagnostic accuracy and relevance in pediatric respiratory medicine over time.

Example in Banking and Finance

Consider a rule-based system implemented by a bank to assess the creditworthiness of loan applicants and identify potential loan defaulters. The system operates by analyzing various factors such as credit score, income level, employment status, and debt-to-income ratio. For instance, if an applicant has a low credit score, unstable employment history, and a high debt-to-income ratio, the system may flag them as a high-risk borrower based on predefined rules and thresholds established by the bank's risk management team.

Case Study-2: Streamlining Credit Risk Assessment with Rule-Based Systems

A leading bank employs a rule-based system to streamline the evaluation of loan applications and mitigate credit risk. Applicants provide financial information such as credit scores, income levels, employment history, and debt obligations through the bank's online portal. The rule-based system applies a structured set of predefined rules derived from established credit risk management guidelines to assess each applicant's creditworthiness.

For instance, the system may flag applicants with credit scores lower than a certain threshold or identify those with a history of late payments as high-risk borrowers. It also evaluates other criteria, such as debt-to-income ratios, to generate a risk profile for each applicant. Applicants flagged as high risk are automatically routed for additional manual review or required to provide supporting documentation. On the other hand, low-risk applicants benefit from a faster and more streamlined loan approval process.

The rule-based system ensures consistency and objectivity in credit risk evaluation by applying the same set of decision rules across all applications. This not only reduces the subjectivity of human judgment but also speeds up the initial screening process, enabling loan officers to focus on higher-value tasks such as reviewing complex cases or tailoring financial solutions for clients.

By leveraging this systematic approach, the bank enhances its ability to identify potential loan defaulters, reduces financial losses, and ensures compliance with credit regulations. While limited in its ability to learn from new patterns or data, the rule-based system remains a reliable tool for improving efficiency and minimizing risks in the lending process.

Example in Manufacturing and Production Industry

A manufacturing company implements a rule-based system to optimize production processes and minimize downtime on the factory floor. The system is designed to monitor various factors such as machine performance, equipment maintenance schedules, and production quotas. For instance, if a machine exceeds predefined temperature thresholds or shows signs of abnormal vibration patterns, the system triggers an alert to notify maintenance personnel for immediate inspection and repair. Additionally, the system automatically adjusts production schedules and allocates resources to prevent bottlenecks and ensure smooth operations.

Case Study-3: Optimizing Manufacturing Efficiency with Rule-Based Systems

A 'Z' Manufacturing, a leading player in the automotive industry, utilizes a rule-based system to enhance efficiency and productivity in its manufacturing plants. The rule-based system integrates with the company's production line and equipment sensors to monitor real-time data on machine performance and operational status. For example, sensors installed on assembly line robots detect anomalies in movement patterns or deviations from predefined production standards.

When deviations or potential issues are detected, the rule-based system triggers automated responses based on predefined rules and decision criteria. Maintenance alerts are sent to relevant personnel, specifying the nature of the issue and recommended actions for resolution. Simultaneously, the system adjusts production schedules and reassigns tasks to other machines or workstations to minimize disruptions and maintain optimal throughput.

By leveraging the rule-based system, 'Z' Manufacturing streamlines its production operations, reduces downtime, and ensures consistent product quality. The system's proactive approach to monitoring and maintenance enables the company to address potential issues preceding they escalate into costly delays or defects. Ultimately, the rule-based system contributes to 'Z' Manufacturing's competitiveness by maximizing efficiency, minimizing waste, and meeting customer demand effectively in the dynamic manufacturing environment.

Limitations and Challenges of Rule-Based Systems

While rule-based systems offer several advantages in terms of transparency, interpretability, and ease of implementation, they also face certain limitations and challenges that warrant consideration. One major limitation is the static nature of rule-based systems, which rely on predefined rules and decision criteria. These systems may struggle to adapt to changing environments or handle scenarios that fall outside the scope of their predefined rules. As a result, rule-based systems may lack flexibility and scalability, limiting their effectiveness in dynamic and complex problem domains.

Another challenge associated with rule-based systems is the potential for rule explosion, where the number of rules grows exponentially as the system attempts to capture all possible scenarios and exceptions. Rule explosion not only complicates system maintenance and management but also increases the risk of conflicts or inconsistencies between rules. Moreover, rule-based systems may suffer from brittleness, where minor changes or updates to rules can have unintended consequences or disrupt system functionality. This brittleness can undermine user trust and confidence in the system's reliability and robustness.

Furthermore, rule-based systems may struggle to handle uncertainty and ambiguity inherent in real-world problems. While rules provide clear instructions for decision-making, they may not adequately account for probabilistic reasoning or fuzzy logic, leading to suboptimal outcomes or erroneous conclusions in uncertain situations. Additionally, rule-based systems may face challenges in handling incomplete or noisy data, as they rely heavily on explicit rules and may struggle to generalize from limited or imperfect information.

Let us analyze these limitations and challenges for the case studies we have discussed in the previous section.

Pediatric Case Study

Let us take a brief look at the pediatric case study:

- **Rule Explosion:** The pediatric diagnosis system may face challenges due to the vast number of medical conditions and symptoms, leading to an extensive set of rules and potential conflicts.

- **Handling Uncertainty**: Medical diagnoses often involve uncertainty and ambiguity, which rule-based systems may struggle to address without incorporating probabilistic reasoning or fuzzy logic.
- **Adaptability**: As medical knowledge evolves and new diseases emerge, the static nature of rule-based systems may hinder their ability to adapt and incorporate new diagnostic criteria or treatment guidelines.

Banking Loan Defaulter Case Study

Let us take a brief look at the bank loan defaulter case study:

- **Rule Brittleness:** Minor changes in lending policies or economic conditions could lead to significant updates in loan approval rules, increasing the risk of unintended consequences or inconsistencies.
- **Handling Incomplete Data**: Loan applications may contain incomplete or inaccurate information, challenging the rule-based system's ability to make accurate decisions based on limited data.
- **Scalability**: As the number of loan applications increases, rule-based systems may struggle to efficiently process and evaluate each application within a reasonable timeframe, potentially leading to delays or inefficiencies.

Manufacturing and Production Case Study

Let us take a brief look at the manufacturing and production case study:

- **Rule Maintenance:** Manufacturing processes often involve complex interactions and dependencies, requiring frequent updates to production rules to reflect changes in equipment, materials, or operating conditions.
- **Handling Noisy Data**: Sensor readings and production data may contain errors or inconsistencies, posing challenges for rule-based systems in accurately detecting and responding to anomalies or quality issues.
- **Adaptability to Changing Demand**: Rule-based systems may face difficulties in dynamically adjusting production schedules or resource allocations in response to fluctuating market demand or supply chain disruptions.

Despite these limitations, rule-based systems continue to play a valuable role in various domains, particularly where transparency, interpretability, and domain expertise are paramount. However, addressing these challenges requires careful consideration of system design, rule management strategies, and integration with complementary techniques such as machine learning and probabilistic reasoning. By leveraging the strengths of rule-based systems while mitigating their limitations, practitioners can harness the full potential of these systems to address complex problems and support decision-making in diverse domains.

Future Directions and Trends in Rule-Based AI Research

As rule-based AI systems continue to evolve, researchers are exploring several avenues for future development and innovation. One promising direction is the integration of rule-based systems with other AI techniques, such as machine learning and deep learning. By combining rule-based reasoning with the ability to learn from data, researchers aim to create more flexible and adaptive AI systems capable of handling complex and dynamic environments.

Another area of interest is the development of hybrid AI architectures that leverage the strengths of both rule-based and probabilistic reasoning approaches. These hybrid systems aim to address the limitations of rule-based systems in handling uncertainty and incomplete information while preserving their ability to represent and reason about explicit knowledge and domain expertise.

Furthermore, there is growing interest in the application of rule-based AI to emerging domains such as explainable AI and AI ethics. Rule-based systems offer transparent and interpretable decision-making processes, making them valuable tools for ensuring accountability and fairness in AI applications. Research in this area aims to develop rule-based frameworks for addressing ethical considerations and biases in AI algorithms.

Additionally, advancements in natural language processing and human-computer interaction are driving research into rule-based AI systems that can understand and generate natural language instructions. These systems have applications in areas such as virtual assistants, chatbots, and intelligent tutoring systems, where intuitive interaction with users is essential for effective communication and collaboration.

Overall, the future of rule-based AI research holds promise for addressing complex real-world challenges across various domains. By leveraging interdisciplinary approaches and integrating diverse AI techniques, researchers aim to develop more robust, adaptive, and human-centered AI systems that can positively impact society and address the evolving needs of the digital age.

Conclusion

This chapter explored the foundational aspects of rule-based systems in AI. It began by providing an introduction to rule-based systems, highlighting their significance in AI research and applications. The historical background of rule-based systems is explored, tracing their evolution from early symbolic reasoning approaches to modern expert systems. The components of rule-based systems, including rule representation and explanation mechanisms, are examined in detail, shedding light on their inner workings.

Furthermore, the chapter delved into symbolic reasoning in AI, emphasizing its role in problem-solving and decision-making processes. Logic and inference engines are discussed as fundamental components of rule-based systems, enabling logical deduction and reasoning. Expert systems are presented as practical applications of symbolic reasoning, showcasing their use in various domains such as medicine, finance, and manufacturing.

The chapter also addresses knowledge representation in rule-based systems, exploring different formalisms and techniques for encoding domain knowledge. Through examples and case studies, readers gain insights into real-world applications of rule-based systems across different industries. Additionally, the chapter identifies the limitations and challenges faced by rule-based systems, paving the way for future research directions aimed at addressing these issues and advancing the field of rule-based AI.

In summary, this chapter provided a comprehensive overview of rule-based systems in AI, covering their historical background, components, applications, and future prospects. By understanding the principles and capabilities of rule-based systems, readers are equipped with valuable insights into this important area of AI research and development.

In the next chapter, we will delve into the fascinating world of data-driven AI and provide a comprehensive introduction to machine learning. Building upon the foundational knowledge established in this chapter, we will explore cutting-edge techniques and methodologies that harness the power of data to drive intelligent decision-making and problem-solving.

Multiple Choice Questions

1. Which of the following best defines Artificial Intelligence (AI)?

    a. A branch of physics that studies quantum computing

    b. A technology that enables machines to perform tasks requiring human intelligence

    c. A subset of robotics focused on physical automation

    d. A technique to enhance data storage capacity

2. The term "Artificial Intelligence" was first coined in which year?

    a. 1943

    b. 1956

    c. 1969

    d. 1985

3. What differentiates AI from traditional computer programs?

   a. AI systems can learn and improve from data

   b. AI systems rely solely on predefined instructions

   c. AI does not require human input for training

   d. AI programs do not use statistical models

4. Which AI program defeated world chess champion Garry Kasparov in 1997?

   a. AlphaGo

   b. DeepMind

   c. Deep Blue

   d. Watson

5. Which of the following is a key component of symbolic reasoning in AI?

   a. Neural networks

   b. Logical rules and knowledge representation

   c. Randomized decision-making

   d. Genetic algorithms

6. What type of reasoning is used in a rule-based AI system to derive conclusions?

   a. Inductive reasoning

   b. Deductive reasoning

   c. Probabilistic reasoning

   d. Heuristic reasoning

7. In a rule-based system, what happens if no rules match the given input?

   a. The system generates a default random output

   b. The system requests additional input or provides no conclusion

   c. The system automatically creates a new rule

   d. The system switches to a neural network approach

8. What are the two primary components of an expert system?

   a. Data warehouse and neural network

   b. Knowledge base and inference engine

c. Feature extraction module and optimizer
   d. Input layer and backpropagation module
9. Which of the following is a well-known early expert system?
   a. Deep Blue
   b. BERT
   c. MYCIN
   d. AlexNet
10. What was the primary purpose of the MYCIN expert system?
    a. Diagnosing bacterial infections and recommending antibiotic treatments
    b. Automating financial risk analysis
    c. Predicting weather patterns
    d. Assisting in satellite image classification
11. One of the biggest limitations of rule-based systems is their inability to:
    a. Process structured data
    b. Store and retrieve large amounts of data
    c. Perform mathematical computations
    d. Adapt to new situations without human intervention
12. Why do rule-based systems struggle with large and complex datasets?
    a. They require predefined rules for every possible scenario
    b. They can only handle numeric data
    c. They rely on deep learning models
    d. They are optimized for real-time decision-making

Answers

1. b
2. b
3. a
4. c

5. b

6. b

7. b

8. b

9. c

10. a

11. d

12. a

Keywords

- Artificial Intelligence (AI)
- Machine Learning (ML)
- Rule-Based Systems
- Expert Systems
- Symbolic Reasoning
- Knowledge Representation
- Turing Test
- Heuristics
- Inference Engine
- Forward Chaining and Backward Chaining
- Knowledge Base
- Automated Decision-Making

References

1. "A Logic-Based Framework for Reactive Systems," by Robert Kowalski, Lecture Notes in Computer Science, Proceedings of the 6th International Conference on Rules on the Web: Research and Applications, Aug 2012.

2. https://www.shortliffe.net/Buchanan-Shortliffe-1984/Chapter-01.pdf

CHAPTER 2
Modern Approach to AI

Introduction

This chapter delves into the transformative shift from traditional rule-based systems to the data-driven paradigms that currently dominate the field of artificial intelligence. This chapter aims to dissect the core mechanisms and innovative methodologies that underpin modern AI, from the foundational aspects of data-driven AI and the exploration of big data to the comprehensive overview of machine learning types and their life cycles. It navigates through the vibrant landscape of AI applications, addressing the challenges inherent in these advanced technologies. By providing a succinct yet profound exploration of how AI has evolved to leverage data in unprecedented ways, this chapter sets the stage for understanding the dynamic interplay between data, algorithms, and machine learning models, marking a significant leap in the journey of AI development.

Structure

In this chapter, we are going to cover the following main topics:

- The Evolution from Rule-Based to Data-Driven AI
- Fundamentals of Data-Driven AI
- Understanding Big Data and Variables in the Business Context
- A Brief Overview of Machine Learning (ML) and its Types
- Introduction to Machine Learning Life Cycle
- Applications of Modern Data-Driven AI across Data Structures
- Challenges in Data-Driven AI

The Evolution from Rule-Based to Data-Driven AI

The journey from rule-based to data-driven Artificial Intelligence (AI) marks a pivotal shift in the way we approach problem-solving and innovation within the technology landscape. Initially, AI was anchored in rule-based systems, which relied on clearly defined rules and logical sequences to make decisions as we discussed in the previous chapter. These systems were akin to well-organized libraries, where each book (or rule) had a specific place and purpose, but the library's capacity for knowledge was limited to what was already on its shelves.

As technology advanced, the limitations of rule-based AI became evident. These systems struggled with complexity and adaptability, unable to learn beyond their initial programming. Imagine a librarian tasked with sorting an influx of new books without knowing where to place them because the categories were too rigid or simply not inclusive enough. This metaphor captures the dilemma faced by rule-based systems when confronted with new, undefined, or complex scenarios.

Enter the era of data-driven AI, a paradigm shift powered by the digital age's most valuable resource: data. Unlike their rule-based predecessors, data-driven AI systems thrive on vast amounts of information, learning from patterns and making predictions. This is akin to transitioning from a static library to a dynamic, ever-expanding database that continuously learns and updates itself with every new piece of information it encounters.

The backbone of this new era is Machine Learning (ML), a subset of AI that automates analytical model building. Through algorithms that learn from data, machine learning allows computers to find hidden insights without being explicitly programmed where to look. This method of learning from data to improve over time is similar to a student who, instead of memorizing facts, learns to understand concepts and apply them to new problems.

This evolution from rule-based to data-driven AI represents a leap towards more flexible, intelligent, and autonomous systems capable of tackling complex and nuanced tasks. By leveraging the exponential growth of data and computational power, AI now promises solutions that are not only reactive but also predictive and adaptive to changing conditions. This marks a significant milestone in our journey towards creating machines that can learn, reason, and interact with the world in ways previously imagined only in the realm of science fiction.

Fundamentals of Data-Driven AI

In the exploration of data-driven AI, understanding the types of data encountered in business and real-world problems is foundational. Data, the cornerstone of modern AI systems, comes in various forms and complexities. At its core, data can be categorized into structured and unstructured types, each with its unique characteristics and challenges. Structured data is akin to a well-organized file cabinet, where everything is meticulously labeled and stored in predefined formats, such as tables or spreadsheets. This type of data is highly organized and easily searchable, making it ideal for traditional database systems. Examples include sales records, customer information, and financial transactions.

Conversely, unstructured data is similar to a vast, bustling city where information is scattered in different forms and locations. It encompasses a wide range of formats, including text, images, videos, voice recordings, and sensor data. This type of data does not fit neatly into traditional tables or databases. For instance, social media posts, video footage, and satellite images all fall under this category, offering rich insights but also presenting significant challenges in terms of processing and analysis.

In the realm of time series data, sensor readings collected over time provide another layer of complexity. This data type is crucial for monitoring and predicting trends in various sectors, such as finance, healthcare, and environmental studies. Time series data is inherently structured but requires specialized analysis techniques to uncover patterns, anomalies, and future predictions.

Given the vast landscape of data types, this book initially focuses on structured data in the context of the first few chapters. The reason for this focus is twofold. First, structured data provides a more accessible entry point for understanding the principles of data-driven AI. It allows us to explore fundamental concepts and techniques without the added complexity of processing and interpreting unstructured data. Second, structured data forms the basis for many business and operational decisions, making it immediately applicable to a wide range of readers.

As we progress and delve into the later chapters dealing with Artificial Neural Networks (ANN), the focus will shift towards unstructured data. ANNs are particularly well-suited for handling the complexity and variability of unstructured data, thanks to their ability to learn from vast amounts of examples. This transition marks a significant step in our journey through data-driven AI, moving from the structured and somewhat predictable world into the dynamic and richly informative domain of unstructured data. This shift not only expands the scope of problems AI can address but also showcases the flexibility and power of modern AI technologies.

Understanding Big Data Variables in the Business Context

In the vast expanse of the modern information age, structured big data stands as a beacon for organizations aiming to harness the power of data-driven AI. The sheer volume and complexity of data available today require a nuanced understanding and strategic approach, particularly when dealing with structured data forms such as big tables. These tables, organized into rows and columns, are the scaffolding upon which data-driven decisions are built.

Rows in these tables are akin to individual stories, each representing a record, observation, sample, or instance. Imagine each row as a unique narrative in a vast anthology, where every story contributes to the overall understanding of the theme. These narratives might detail customer transactions, patient records, or sensor readings, each one a snapshot of an event or state at a specific point in time.

Columns, on the other hand, are the themes that run through these stories, known as variables, features, or attributes. They provide structure and context, defining the characteristics that describe each row's narrative. For instance, in a customer database, columns could include attributes such as age, purchase history, and preferences, each column offering insights into different facets of the customer's interaction with the business.

Understanding the relationship between these rows and columns is crucial. Some columns might be dependent on others, indicating a relationship or influence between variables. For instance, a column representing salary per month as shown in *Figure 2.1* could be dependent on the column detailing the job role or years of experience. Recognizing these dependencies is the first step toward unraveling the complex web of interactions within your data. This understanding allows for the identification of patterns, trends, and anomalies, which are essential for predictive modeling and decision-making processes.

Moreover, aligning this structured data with the business context is paramount. The data must not only be relevant but also meticulously aligned with the business problem at hand. This alignment ensures that the insights gleaned from data analysis are actionable and directly applicable to solving real-world business challenges. It necessitates a deep dive into the nature of each column, discerning not just the type of data it represents but also its significance in the broader context of the business objectives. By doing so, organizations can ensure that their data-driven AI initiatives are not just technically sound but also strategically focused, paving the way for transformative outcomes in the competitive landscapes they navigate.

In sum, the journey towards mastering data-driven AI begins with a profound understanding of structured big data. Recognizing the narratives within rows and the themes represented by columns and how they correlate to business challenges is a foundational step. This approach not only demystifies the complexity of big data but also equips businesses with the knowledge to leverage AI effectively, ensuring that their ventures into the realm of data-driven decision-making are both informed and impactful.

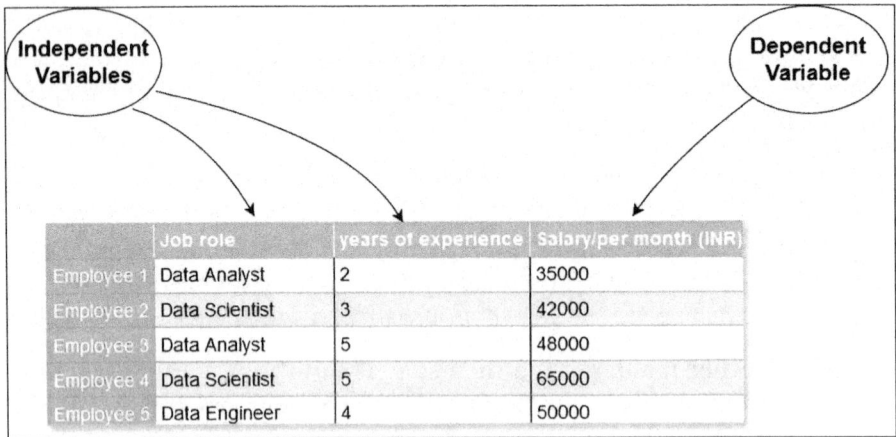

Figure 2.1: *Tabular Data Representation*

A Brief Overview of Machine Learning and its Types

Machine Learning (ML), a cornerstone of the modern data-driven AI landscape, represents a shift from explicit programming to data-centric learning. It is a method through which computers gain the ability to learn and adapt without being explicitly programmed for every task. This transformative technology has become integral to developing systems that can improve over time with exposure to more data.

At the heart of machine learning is the concept of enabling computers to learn from and make decisions based on data. Imagine teaching a child to differentiate between fruits and vegetables. Instead of memorizing every possible item, the child learns to recognize patterns and characteristics that define each category. Similarly, machine learning algorithms learn from data patterns, enabling them to make predictions or decisions when exposed to new data.

Conventional Programming: The Traditional Route

In conventional programming depicted in *Figure* 2.2, the process begins with the programmer who uses their knowledge and understanding of a problem to write explicit instructions or rules that the computer must follow to achieve a desired outcome. These rules are codified in a programming language and the computer executes them step by step. The data is then fed into these pre-defined rules to produce the output. Think of it as a recipe where the steps are carefully crafted and laid out by a chef, and the computer is the cook who follows each step to create the dish.

The rule-based system we discussed in the previous chapter is a clear reflection of conventional programming's philosophy where the programmer is the maestro, dictating each action the computer must take through a series of 'if-then' statements. This approach requires a comprehensive understanding of the problem space, anticipating every possible scenario to encode appropriate responses. It is a world where decisions are meticulously mapped out, leaving little room for deviation or learning from past interactions.

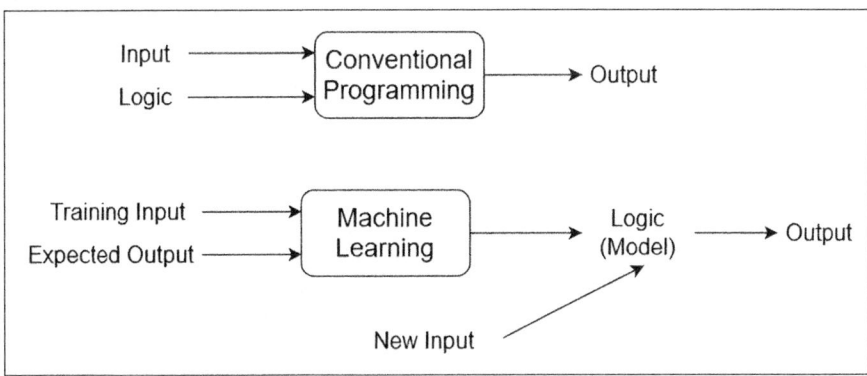

Figure 2.2: *Conventional Programming versus Machine Learning*

This approach works exceptionally well for problems that are well-understood and can be expressed in logical steps – for instance, calculating the monthly interest for a bank account or sorting a list of names alphabetically. The logic is clear, the steps are deterministic, and the outcomes are predictable. The programmer has full control over the process, and the computer acts as an efficient, but non-autonomous executor of the provided instructions.

Machine Learning: A Data-Driven Approach

Machine Learning, however, flips the script. Instead of being programmed with explicit instructions, the computer is given a large amount of data and the desired outcome, and it 'learns' the rules by finding patterns in the data. This is akin to a child learning to identify fruits not by memorizing a rule for each fruit but by looking at many different examples and developing an intuitive sense of what characterizes each one.

In this paradigm, a model (or algorithm) is trained using a dataset that includes both the inputs and the correct outputs. Over time, the model finds statistical structure in the data which allows it to make predictions or decisions without being explicitly programmed to perform the task. For instance, instead of writing code to detect spam emails, a machine learning model is fed millions of emails that are labeled as 'spam' or 'not spam,' and it learns to classify new emails based on its training.

This method is powerful for tasks that are too complex for traditional programming, where writing explicit rules is impractical or impossible. This includes recognizing speech, translating languages, or driving a car autonomously. The beauty of machine learning lies in its ability to adapt and improve as it is exposed to more data, often surpassing human performance in specific tasks.

The shift from conventional programming to machine learning is one of the most significant in the history of technology. Machine learning enables systems to not just follow instructions, but to develop their own instructions based on the data they process. This leads to a form of computational problem-solving that is dynamic, adaptable, and often more aligned with the complexities of real-world problems.

As we move through the chapters of this book, readers will gain a deeper understanding of how machine learning models are constructed, trained, and deployed. They will learn about the different types of machine learning approaches and how they can be applied to a diverse array of tasks, from simple to complex. This journey from the traditional to the modern approach to problem-solving is not just a technical evolution but a conceptual revolution, redefining what is possible in the world of computing.

Types of Machine Learning

Machine learning can be broadly classified into three types: supervised learning, unsupervised learning, and reinforcement learning. Each type represents a different learning strategy and is suited for various kinds of problems.

- **Supervised Learning**: This type involves learning a function that maps an input to an output based on example input-output pairs. It is similar to a student learning with the help of a tutor who provides practice problems along with the answers. In the context of ML, the algorithm makes predictions or judgments based on a dataset that includes both the inputs and the desired outputs. The key players in this process are the variables, which are divided into two groups: dependent and independent as shown as 'p' features in *Figure 2.3*. The dependent variable, also known as the target variable, is what the model aims to predict or classify, similar to a student's goal to find the correct answer in a test. The independent variables, on the other hand, are the inputs or features that provide the algorithm with information; they are the clues or textbook pages the student uses to deduce the answer. Supervised learning is akin to a teacher-student dynamic, where the 'teacher' is the training dataset with known answers.

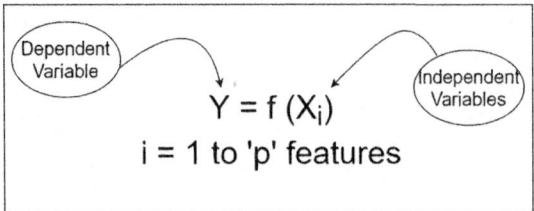

Figure 2.3: *Representation of Supervised Learning*

When the dependent variable is a continuous numeric quantity, such as rainfall in centimeters, blood sugar levels in mg/dL, or sales figures in INR, the task falls under the umbrella of regression prediction models. In a regression problem, the algorithm learns to predict a quantitative response. For instance, a real estate model might predict the price of a house (the dependent variable) based on features such as its size, location, and age (the independent variables).

Conversely, if the dependent variable is categorical, such as the stage of disease (early, middle, advanced), whether a transaction is fraudulent, or weather conditions (rainfall or clear sky), we enter the domain of classification prediction models.

In classification, the algorithm is trained to assign each input into one of the predefined categories. An email filtering system, for instance, might classify incoming messages as 'spam' or 'not spam' based on characteristics such as the sender's address, the email's content, and the time it was sent.

Regardless of the type of prediction—regression or classification—the hallmark of supervised learning is its use of historical data where the outcome is already known. It is similar to having a completed quiz to study from; the model uses this 'answer key' to understand the relationship between the inputs (independent variables) and the output (dependent variable). As it processes more data, it 'learns' the patterns and nuances, enabling it to make accurate predictions when faced with new, unseen data.

Supervised learning, therefore, is a robust approach for tackling problems where the relationship between the input data and the desired output is understood and can be taught to the model. From forecasting stock market trends to diagnosing medical conditions, supervised learning models stand at the forefront of AI applications, transforming historical data into predictive power.

- **Unsupervised Learning**: In unsupervised learning, the algorithm learns patterns from untagged data. The system tries to learn without instruction, similar to a student attempting to find patterns in their notes without knowing the questions that will be on the exam. This type is used for exploratory data analysis, clustering, and dimensionality reduction. It is useful in customer segmentation, anomaly detection, and organizing large data sets into coherent groups.

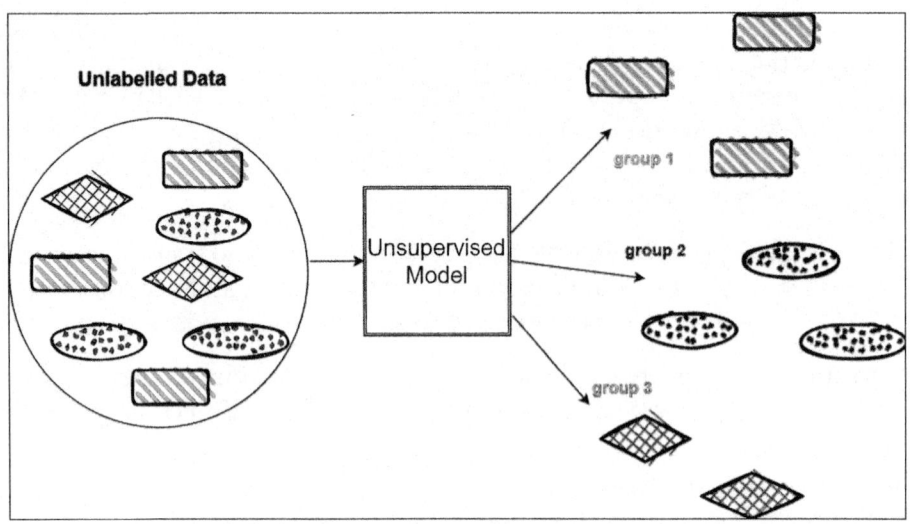

Figure 2.4: *Representation of Unsupervised Learning*

Here, the algorithm acts similar to an explorer, sifting through uncharted territory to find structure and patterns on its own. The model discerns the inherent groupings in the data, organizing them into clusters, similar to sorting a mixed collection of gems into separate classes based on their characteristics as depicted in *Figure* 2.4.

Unsupervised Learning (USL) algorithms thrive on the challenge of discovering hidden structures in data. They are not provided with the right answers at the outset; instead, they examine the data and identify patterns that segment it into clusters. Consider a vast array of stars in the night sky; unsupervised learning is akin to grouping these stars into constellations without a predefined guide. The algorithm might group data points based on similarities in features, which could correspond to anything from customer preferences to genetic markers, depending on the dataset at hand.

In the business world, unsupervised learning has practical and potent applications. Think of an online bookstore that wants to enhance its customers' shopping experience; it employs unsupervised learning to suggest books. The algorithm analyzes purchase histories, browsing behaviors, and book ratings across its entire user base. By identifying clusters of similar activities and preferences, the system can then recommend new books to a customer that others with similar tastes have enjoyed. This process does not require a 'correct answer'; the algorithm independently finds relationships within the data to provide recommendations. Similarly, in the field of bioinformatics, unsupervised learning can analyze gene expression data, grouping genes with similar expression patterns that may indicate a shared function or regulation.

The real magic of unsupervised learning lies in its capacity to reveal the unexpected. It provides businesses with the insights necessary to innovate, such as identifying a new target demographic or uncovering an unnoticed market trend. The process is less about predicting and more about understanding and providing a clearer picture of the data landscape that can lead to informed and data-driven decisions.

Unsupervised learning models are invaluable when the right questions to ask are not clear or when the richness of the data has not been fully explored. In an age where data is abundant yet its secrets are densely packed, unsupervised learning offers a lens through which hidden treasures within the data can be found and leveraged for strategic advantages.

- **Reinforcement Learning**: Reinforcement Learning (RL) stands out in the landscape of machine learning as the process akin to training an animal, as vividly depicted in *Figure 2.5*. This type of learning is centered on the concept of reward and punishment actions that lead to positive outcomes are reinforced, while those that result in negative outcomes are discouraged. Picture a scenario where a dog is learning to jump over a hurdle; every successful jump is met with a treat, while missed attempts receive no reward. Over time, the dog learns to associate the jump with the positive outcome of getting a treat.

Figure 2.5: An Illustrative Example of Reinforcement Learning Behavior of a Dog

Translating this concept into the digital world, reinforcement learning involves training algorithms to make a sequence of decisions. The algorithm executes actions within an environment to achieve a certain objective, refining its approach continuously to maximize a cumulative reward. It is similar to a video game, where the player (in this case, the algorithm) navigates through challenges, learning from past actions to improve future performance and achieve a higher score.

In the business realm, reinforcement learning has practical applications in areas requiring a series of decision-making steps. One such example is dynamic pricing models. Online retailers use RL to adjust prices in real time, learning from the interplay of market demand, supply constraints, and consumer behavior to maximize profits. Another example is inventory management, where RL algorithms determine optimal restocking strategies to reduce holding costs and prevent stockouts, adapting to changing patterns in consumer purchases and supply chain variables.

Reinforcement learning is particularly powerful in scenarios where the environment is complex and the consequences of decisions unfold over time. This allows businesses to model and optimize processes that are too intricate for traditional analytical approaches. For instance, in logistics and distribution, RL can optimize routing and delivery schedules in real time, considering traffic conditions, delivery windows, and fuel efficiency. As such, RL is not just a theoretical construct but a practical tool for businesses to navigate the complexities of the modern economy, driving efficiency and innovation through learned experience.

Acknowledging the vastness of the field of Artificial Intelligence (AI), this book has been meticulously curated to provide a robust and extensive understanding of the fundamentals, with a focused approach towards Machine Learning (ML) prediction models. The chapters are tailored to offer a deep dive into supervised learning, covering both regression and classification models, while paving the way towards more complex structures such as Artificial Neural Networks (ANN), Deep Learning, and Convolutional Neural Networks (CNN) for predictive applications. We will also touch upon the expansive domain of Unsupervised Learning, offering a glimpse into its potential and how it complements the predictive prowess of supervised learning.

The decision to concentrate the material of this book on the aforementioned areas is both intentional and strategic, recognizing that the field of Reinforcement Learning (RL) is burgeoning into a highly specialized and broad domain that deserves its own dedicated examination. RL stands out in the machine learning spectrum as a method where an agent learns through a system of rewards and consequences a process that echoes the principles of behaviorist psychology. This fascinating and complex subject, rich with nuance and potential, calls for an in-depth treatment that extends beyond the bounds of our current scope.

This book therefore channels its focus into laying down a solid foundation in the established areas of machine learning and AI, aiming to provide clarity and depth on well-vetted applications preceding one ventures into the nuanced world of RL. RL's intricacies, from setting up reward structures to developing algorithms that can navigate these dynamic environments, demand comprehensive attention and analysis, meriting a separate, focused discourse to do it justice. We encourage readers with a keen interest in RL to seek out resources that specifically navigate this advanced terrain, as they continue to build upon the knowledge base established here.

Introduction to Machine Learning Life Cycle

At its core, the machine learning lifecycle is a cyclical process designed to transform

Modern Approach to AI   37

data into actionable insights, driving informed business decisions. This lifecycle is an intricate dance of multiple stages as shown in *Figure 2.6*, each with its unique rhythm and tempo, and understanding this choreography is vital for anyone stepping into the world of machine learning.

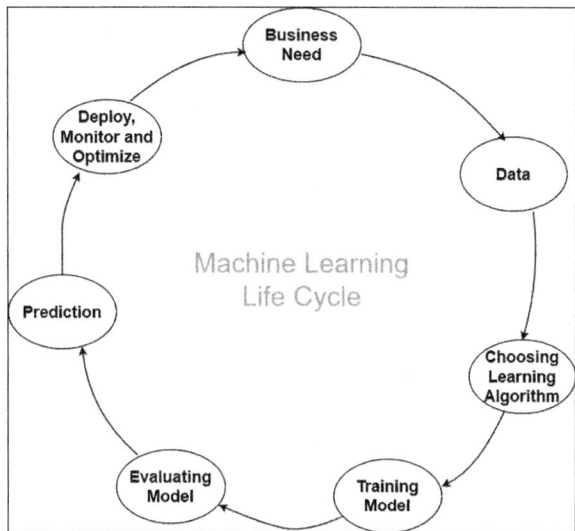

Figure 2.6: *End-to-End Machine Learning Workflow*

The first step is crystallizing the business need, which serves as the compass for the entire machine learning project. Identifying the problem to be solved or the question to be answered is foundational. It involves consulting with domain experts, analyzing business objectives, and determining how machine learning can add value. One must ask, "What business outcome do we seek to influence?" This could range from predicting customer churn to optimizing supply chain logistics.

Data is the lifeblood of machine learning, and sourcing the right data is crucial. It involves collecting, cleaning, and preprocessing data to ensure quality and relevance. The data may come in various forms and sizes, and it is important to treat it as a treasure trove of potential insights, waiting to be unlocked.

Choosing the right algorithm comes next. This decision hinges on the nature of the business problem and the type of data at hand. If the goal is to predict a continuous value, such as sales for the next quarter, regression models would be the tools of choice. Conversely, if the objective is to categorize data into distinct groups, such as identifying if an email is spam or not, classification algorithms would be employed.

Training the model is similar to teaching a child to ride a bike, requiring patience and iteration. The model learns from the training data, adjusting its parameters to minimize error. Each round of training is a chance to improve and inch closer to a model that can make accurate predictions or useful classifications. Evaluating the model's performance on a separate validation set helps ensure that it can generalize to new, unseen data, rather than just memorizing the training set. This stage tests the model's true understanding, similar to a pop quiz following a study session.

Fine-tuning the model is often necessary to improve its performance. This could involve adjusting the model's parameters, selecting different features, or even revisiting the choice of algorithm. The goal is to refine the model into a more precise instrument, tailored to the business need. Once the model demonstrates robust performance, it is time for deployment. This stage puts the model into action, integrating it with existing business systems to start providing insights, making predictions, or automating decisions in the real world.

But the journey does not end at deployment. Monitoring the model to ensure it continues to perform well over time, and optimizing it in response to new data or changing circumstances, is key to maintaining its relevance and effectiveness.

In summary, the machine learning lifecycle is a dynamic and iterative journey. It begins with a clear understanding of the business need and navigates through data preparation, algorithm selection, training, evaluation, and fine-tuning, culminating in the deployment of a model that can bring about tangible business impact. Each step is a critical part of the whole, ensuring that the final model is not only technically sound but also aligned with the strategic objectives it was meant to serve. As we delve into the following chapters, each of these stages will be explored in detail, providing readers with the knowledge and tools to navigate the lifecycle with confidence.

Applications of Modern Data-Driven AI across Data Structures

Data-driven AI's versatility is best showcased by its wide array of applications across various types of data structures. Each data structure offers unique opportunities for AI to flex its analytical prowess, from interpreting tabular datasets to deciphering complex images and text.

Tabular Data: The Backbone of Conventional AI Applications

Tabular data sets, with their structured grid of rows and columns, serve as the bedrock for numerous AI applications. Some of the applications but not limited to this list are as follows:

- **Regression Applications**
    - **Real Estate Pricing**: Utilizing a multitude of features such as location, square footage, and number of bedrooms to predict the market value of properties.

- o **Stock Price Forecasting**: Analyzing historical stock market data to predict future price movements based on trends and patterns.
- **Classification Applications**
  - o **Credit Scoring**: Assessing the risk profile of loan applicants by classifying them into 'creditworthy' or 'high risk' categories based on their financial history.
  - o **Disease Diagnosis**: Helping physicians diagnose diseases by classifying patient data as indicative of certain medical conditions or not, based on symptoms and test results.

Image-Based Datasets

Image-based datasets play a crucial role in modern AI applications, enabling models to analyze, classify, and generate visual content. Some of the applications but not limited to this list are as follows:

- **Image Classification**
  - o **Facial Recognition for Security**: Identifying individuals in security footage by matching their facial features to a database of known faces.
  - o **Agricultural Disease Detection**: Helping farmers detect plant diseases early by classifying images of crop leaves.
- **Object Detection and Semantic Segmentation**
  - o **Autonomous Vehicles**: Enabling self-driving cars to understand their environment by detecting and segmenting different objects such as pedestrians, other vehicles, and road signs.
  - o **Medical Imaging Analysis**: Assisting radiologists by detecting and outlining tumors or fractures in medical scans.

Text-Based Applications

Text-based datasets are fundamental in enabling AI models to process, understand, and generate human language. Some of the applications but not limited to this list are as follows:

- **Sentiment Analysis**
  - o **Market Research**: Analyzing customer reviews and feedback on social media to gauge public sentiment about products and services.
  - o **Political Campaign Analysis**: Monitoring public opinion on policy initiatives or political figures by analyzing sentiment in news articles and blog posts.

- **Advanced ANN-Based Architectures**
  - **Chatbot for Customer Service**: Engaging users in natural conversations to resolve queries or provide recommendations using advanced neural network models.
  - **Summarization Tools**: Automatically generating concise summaries of long documents, making it easier to digest large volumes of information quickly.
- **Large Language Models (LLMs)**
  - **ChatGPT**: One of the recent (2023) sensation; Open AI's ChatGPT and other equivalent LLMs have revolutionizing the AI market globally as a Generative AI(GenAI) applications. These models interact with users in a conversational manner, providing responses that can range from answering queries to generating human-like text based on prompts.
  - **Personalized Learning Assistants**: Tailoring educational content to individual users by generating explanations, quizzes, and summaries based on their learning progress and challenges.

Time Series Dataset Applications

Time series datasets consist of sequential data points recorded over time, enabling AI models to analyze trends, detect anomalies, and make future predictions. Some of the applications but not limited to this list are as follows:

- **Speech Recognition**
  - **Voice-Activated Assistants**: Translating spoken commands into action, enabling users to interact with technology through natural language.
  - **Language Translation Services**: Converting spoken language in one dialect to text in another, facilitating communication across language barriers.
- **Predictive Maintenance**
  - **Industrial Equipment Monitoring**: Predicting machinery failures preceding they occur by analyzing patterns in sensor data, thus reducing downtime and maintenance costs.
  - **Weather Forecasting**: Predicting weather conditions by analyzing sequential meteorological data, thereby aiding in disaster management and agricultural planning.

Through these examples, it is evident that modern ML and AI applications are not only diverse but also deeply integrated into various aspects of modern life. The upcoming chapters will delve into each of these domains, unpacking the complexities and exploring the technical underpinnings that make these innovative applications possible. As readers progress, they will gain not just an understanding of AI's practical applications but also the inspiration to conceptualize and develop their own solutions to the challenges within their fields of interest or expertise.

Challenges in Data-Driven AI

As we enter a new phase marked by the ascendancy of data-driven AI, a myriad of challenges emerge, ranging from technical complexities to ethical dilemmas.

- **Deployment Framework Diversity**

    One of the pressing challenges in the realm of AI is the abundance of deployment frameworks. With technology rapidly advancing, these frameworks are also in a state of flux, lacking standardization. This presents a difficulty for developers and businesses alike, as choosing the appropriate framework for deploying AI models becomes a complex task. Each framework has its nuances, requiring developers to stay constantly updated and flexible, adapting to the evolving tools and practices.

- **Vulnerability to Misuse and Cyber Threats**

    As AI becomes increasingly generative and autonomous, the potential for misuse and the risk of viral attacks grows. GenAI applications, capable of creating content or making decisions without human intervention, may become a tool for harm if not adequately protected. This raises the stakes for cyber security, necessitating robust security protocols to prevent malicious use of AI technologies that could lead to widespread misinformation or automated cyber-attacks.

- **Ethical and Responsible AI Considerations**

    The ethical landscape of AI is complex and multifaceted. From concerns about bias and fairness in algorithms to the broader impact on employment and societal structures, ethical considerations must be front and centre in the development and deployment of AI systems. Ensuring that AI operates in a manner that is just and equitable requires continuous scrutiny and the establishment of ethical guidelines that govern its use. Responsible AI practices prioritize inclusivity, making AI systems accessible and beneficial to diverse populations while mitigating disparities. Additionally, ethical AI requires explainability, enabling stakeholders to understand how decisions are made, and fostering trust in AI systems. Organizations and researchers must also address potential risks, such as automation-induced unemployment or misuse of AI technologies, by proactively implementing safeguards and adhering to guidelines for sustainable and human-centric AI development. Through these measures, ethical AI can contribute positively to society while respecting the rights and dignity of all stakeholders.

- **Dominance in Cloud Infrastructure**

    The cloud infrastructure that powers much of today's AI is dominated by a handful of tech giants. This concentration of power raises concerns about the democratization of AI. With only a few players controlling the AI infrastructure, there is a risk that innovation could be stifled, and access to these powerful tools could be limited to those who can afford it or who align with the providers' terms and services.

- **Data Privacy and Governance**

    In a world where AI systems are fuelled by data, privacy becomes a paramount concern. Ensuring the confidentiality and integrity of personal and sensitive data is a challenge that is yet to be fully resolved. Furthermore, data governance regulating who has access to what data and for what purpose remains a complex issue, intertwined with legal and regulatory aspects that vary across jurisdictions.

- **Bias and Representation in Data**

    The adage 'garbage in, garbage out' holds particularly true in AI. Bias in data can lead to biased AI systems, perpetuating and amplifying existing prejudices. Ensuring that datasets are representative and free of bias is a significant challenge that requires concerted efforts in data collection, pre-processing, and model evaluation.

In summary, while data-driven AI holds tremendous promise, it also presents a series of challenges that must be addressed to unlock its full potential. Tackling these issues demands a collaborative approach, involving stakeholders from across the spectrum, including technologists, policymakers, ethicists, and end-users. As we advance into the next chapters, these challenges will be dissected further, and potential pathways to address them will be discussed, ensuring that as we advance AI, we do so responsibly and inclusively.

Conclusion

In this chapter, we embarked on an enlightening journey, charting the course from the structured domain of rule-based AI to the dynamic and evolving realm of data-driven AI. We laid out the groundwork by elucidating the pivotal transition to modern AI practices, delving into the essentials of data-driven approaches. We have dissected the fundamentals, touched upon the burgeoning wealth of big data, and differentiated between the distinct natures of variables within this data. A panoramic view of the types of machine learning provided us with a primer on the subject, setting the stage for the intricate life cycle of a machine learning model. We delved into the rich tapestry of AI applications, showcasing how diverse data structures breathe life into myriad real-world AI solutions, from tabular data predictions to advanced ANN-driven text analysis. Finally, we confronted the multifaceted challenges that lie in the path of AI's advancement, pondering technical, ethical, and infrastructural quandaries.

The upcoming Chapter promises to be a continuation of this exciting expedition into the nucleus of machine learning. Here, readers will be invited to roll up their sleeves and dive into the practical aspects of AI development, from data preparation to feature selection. The chapter will unravel the intricacies of algorithm selection and shine a spotlight on Exploratory Data Analysis, the beating heart of understanding data preceding it is shaped and modeled. Stay tuned for a deep dive into the analytical processes that transform raw data into insightful, actionable knowledge, paving the way for robust AI models that not only predict but also inspire innovation. The next chapter is a testament to the promise of AI and an invitation to readers to deepen their understanding of this transformative field.

Multiple Choice Questions

1. What is the primary limitation of rule-based AI systems?

    a. They require minimal computational power

    b. They can automatically learn from data without explicit programming

    c. They struggle to adapt to new, unseen data

    d. They outperform data-driven AI in complex decision-making

2. How do data-driven AI systems differ from rule-based AI systems?

    a. They follow predefined rules set by experts

    b. They rely on structured programming logic

    c. They learn patterns from data without explicit rule definitions

    d. They only function with small datasets

3. Which of the following was a key factor in the shift from rule-based AI to data-driven AI?

    a. Growth in labeled datasets and computational power

    b. Increase in manual programming efficiency

    c. Reduction in the need for AI research

    d. Decrease in business reliance on AI

4. In which decade did data-driven AI models gain prominence over rule-based systems?

    a. 1970s

    b. 1980s

    c. 1990s

    d. 2000s

5. Why are rule-based AI systems still used in some industries?

    a. They are better at handling unstructured data

    b. They require large-scale labeled data for training

    c. They provide high interpretability and deterministic outputs

    d. They are the only AI approach that supports deep learning

6. What is a key characteristic of data-driven AI?

    a. It requires explicit rules for decision-making

    b. It relies on predefined logical structures

    c. It learns patterns and generalizes from data

    d. It only works with structured data

7. In data-driven AI, what is the role of training data?

    a. It is used to manually code decision rules

    b. It provides examples from which the AI model learns

    c. It serves as a backup for rule-based decision-making

    d. It is not necessary for AI models to function

8. Which type of AI model is most associated with data-driven approaches?

    a. Symbolic AI

    b. Knowledge-based AI

    c. Expert Systems

    d. Machine Learning and Deep Learning models

9. What are the five key characteristics of Big Data?

    a. Speed, Size, Scope, Security, and Sensitivity

    b. Volume, Velocity, Variety, Veracity, and Value

c. Scalability, Variance, Validation, Volume, and Vision

d. Visualization, Variability, Virtualization, Velocity, and Value

10. How is business data categorized based on its format and level of organization?

   a. Raw data and Processed data

   b. Primary data and Secondary data

   c. Structured, Semi-structured, and Unstructured

   d. Tabular, Hierarchical, and Sequential

11. Why is feature engineering important in AI models?

   a. It enables AI models to extract meaningful patterns

   b. It reduces data storage costs significantly

   c. It eliminates the need for labeled training data

   d. It speeds up the training process without requiring preprocessing

12. What are common issues found in raw business data prior to preprocessing?

   a. Excessive use of numerical variables

   b. Incomplete machine learning models

   c. Missing values and inconsistent formats

   d. High computational complexity in algorithms

13. Which of the following represents the three primary types of machine learning?

   a. Linear, Nonlinear, and Hybrid Learning

   b. Supervised, Unsupervised, and Reinforcement Learning

   c. Deep Learning, Shallow Learning, and Evolutionary Learning

   d. Training Learning, Validation Learning, and Testing Learning

14. What type of data does supervised learning require?

   a. Unstructured datasets with no clear relationships

   b. Time-series data only

   c. Datasets with only categorical variables

   d. Labeled datasets

15. Which machine learning technique is commonly used in unsupervised learning?

    a. Clustering

    b. Classification

    c. Regression

    d. Reinforcement Learning

Answers

1. c
2. c
3. a
4. d
5. c
6. c
7. b
8. d
9. b
10. c
11. a
12. c
13. b
14. d
15. a

Keywords

- Rule-Based AI
- Data-Driven AI
- Big Data
- Machine Learning Types

- Supervised Learning
- Unsupervised Learning
- AI Applications
- Machine Learning Life Cycle
- Business Intelligence
- Data Variables
- Feature Engineering
- Predictive Analytics
- Data Preprocessing
- Model Training
- Data Science

CHAPTER 3
Introduction to Machine Learning

Introduction

This chapter meticulously unpacks the essential concepts and definitions that underpin Machine Learning (ML), navigates through the diverse landscapes of ML models, and elucidates the key components vital for constructing effective machine learning systems. Through practical use cases demonstrated in Python, readers will engage with the critical processes of data pre-processing, cleaning, and exploratory data analysis, gaining hands-on experience that bridges theory with practice. The chapter further demystifies the distinctions between unsupervised and supervised learning, guiding readers through the intricacies of regression and classification models, and concludes with a thorough examination of model evaluation methods and metrics. Designed to empower readers with both the knowledge and tools necessary for delving into machine learning, this chapter lays the groundwork for understanding and leveraging the transformative potential of ML in solving complex problems and uncovering insights from data.

Structure

In this chapter, we're going to cover the following main topics:

- Machine Learning Concepts and Definitions
- Landscapes of Machine Learning (ML) Models
- Key components: Features, Label and Models
- Data Preparation for Machine Learning Models
- Exploratory Data Analysis
- Introduction to Unsupervised Learning
- Introduction to Supervised Learning
- Introduction to ML Model Evaluation Method and Metrics

Machine Learning Concepts and Definitions

Having already navigated a brief overview of Machine Learning (ML) in the previous chapter, we embark on a deeper journey into the nuances and detailed mechanisms that drive this pivotal technology. While we touched upon the transformative shift from traditional programming to a data-driven learning paradigm, this chapter is dedicated to unraveling the complex layers and mechanisms foundational to ML, shedding light on the intricate interplay among data, algorithms, and models.

The core of machine learning lies in its remarkable capacity to absorb and interpret data, mirroring the learning patterns of humans yet surpassing our limitations in both scale and velocity. This ability enables machines to identify complex patterns and make informed decisions, a feat achieved through the power of algorithms. These algorithms act as the blueprint for learning, comprising a series of rules and statistical models that direct the machine's process of analyzing data and recognizing patterns. This structured approach to learning allows machines to uncover insights from data that are vast and intricate, far beyond the human capability of processing and analysis. Through this sophisticated mechanism, machines can continually adapt and refine their understanding, leading to more accurate and nuanced predictions and decisions over time.

Andrew Ng, a prominent figure in modern AI and machine learning education, simplifies the concept by stating, "Machine learning is the science of getting computers to act without being explicitly programmed." This definition underscores the goal of ML to create systems that can independently adapt and make decisions.

Yann LeCun, another pioneer in deep learning, emphasizes the predictive aspect of machine learning, describing it as "a way to program computers to use example data or past experience." This perspective focuses on the use of historical data to forecast future outcomes, patterns, or behaviors.

These definitions, while diverse, all underscore the fundamental essence of machine learning: the ability of machines to autonomously learn from data, improve over time, and make decisions or predictions, marking a significant departure from traditional programming paradigms.

Landscapes of Machine Learning Models

Let us revisit the types of machine learning models from a fresh perspective, focusing on their practical applications and the underlying decision-making processes that differentiate them. This approach allows us to build upon the foundational knowledge introduced in *Chapter 2, Modern Approach to AI*, enriching our understanding with a focus on how these models are applied in real-world scenarios and the nuances of their operational mechanisms.

Supervised learning, a fundamental concept in artificial intelligence and machine learning, has been defined by various pioneers and experts in the field. Christopher M. Bishop: In his book, "Pattern Recognition and Machine Learning," Bishop describes supervised learning as involving the automatic discovery of the relationship between input variables and some output variable, with the aim of making predictions of the output for future input data. The definition points to the predictive nature of supervised learning and its reliance on historical data for model training.

On the other hand, unsupervised learning, a critical branch of machine learning, focuses on drawing inferences from datasets without labeled responses. The notable pioneers in the field of AI, Ian Good fellow, Yoshua Bengio, and Aaron Courville (2016), in their seminal work, "Deep Learning," the authors describe unsupervised learning as "the problem of trying to learn about the structure of the input distribution without any explicit feedback on what is correct or incorrect." This definition highlights the exploratory nature of unsupervised learning, where the goal is to uncover hidden patterns or structures in the data without pre-defined labels.

Reinforcement learning, a distinctive branch of machine learning, is characterized by an agent's ability to learn optimal behaviors through interactions with its environment by receiving feedback in the form of rewards or penalties. This dynamic field, inspired by behavioral psychology, simulates the process of learning from consequences, making it particularly suited for applications requiring sequential decision-making, such as autonomous driving, game playing, and robotics.

As mentioned in the previous chapter, the exploration of reinforcement learning, with its unique challenges and profound implications for artificial intelligence, extends beyond the scope of this book. Readers with a keen interest in delving deeper into the intricacies of reinforcement learning are encouraged to seek specialized resources that can offer a comprehensive understanding of this advanced learning landscape.

Key Components: Features, Label and Models

At the heart of every machine learning endeavor lies data, serving as the cornerstone upon which these intelligent systems are built and refined. The essence of machine learning's capacity to predict, classify, and make informed decisions is deeply rooted in its interaction with data, split into inputs, known as features, and outputs, referred to as labels or targets. Features provide the model with observable variables from which to learn, ranging from simple numerical values to complex structures such as images and text. Labels, on the other hand, offer the guiding light in supervised learning models, marking the correct outcome that the algorithm aims to predict based on the features. This symbiotic relationship between features and labels forms the blueprint from which models derive their learning capabilities.

The significance of data quality and volume cannot be overstated in the context of machine learning. High-quality and accurate data, relevant and devoid of biases ensures that the model has a strong foundation from which to learn, enhancing its ability to generalize from training data to real-world applications. Conversely, poor-quality data can mislead models, embedding errors and biases that compromise their functionality. Similarly, the quantity of data plays a pivotal role; ample data enables models to capture the diversity and complexity of the real world, whereas insufficient data may lead to underfitting, where the model fails to capture the underlying trends. Thus, the caliber and size of the dataset directly influence a model's performance, underscoring the critical importance of data as the foundational bedrock of machine learning.

Features

Features play a pivotal role as the individual measurable attributes or characteristics that serve as inputs for models. These features can range from simple numeric values to more complex data types such as strings or images, depending on the problem at hand. The art of selecting the right set of features is crucial, as it directly impacts the model's ability to learn and make accurate predictions. Features must be relevant, informative, and discriminative, capturing the essence of the underlying data in a form that the model can process and learn from.

The process of feature engineering, then, becomes an essential craft in the creation of effective machine learning models. It involves selecting, modifying, and sometimes creating new features from the raw data to enhance model performance. This process can include techniques such as normalization, where features are scaled to a uniform range, and transformation, where data is converted into a more suitable format for modeling (for example, turning categorical data into numerical values). Feature engineering can also involve more creative approaches, such as deriving new features from existing ones to expose hidden relationships or patterns to the model. The goal is to construct a feature set that not only accurately represents the data but also simplifies the model's learning process, ultimately leading to more accurate and robust predictions. Through careful feature engineering, data scientists can significantly influence the outcome of the machine learning pipeline, reinforcing the adage that the quality of input determines the quality of output.

Labels

Labels serve as the cornerstone, guiding the algorithm through the learning process by providing explicit examples of the correct outcomes associated with given inputs. These annotated data points, or labels, are what distinguish supervised learning from other types of machine learning methodologies. Essentially, labels are the answers to the questions posed by the input features, creating a clear pathway for the model to understand and predict outcomes. For instance, in a spam detection model, emails are the input features, and their labels indicate whether each email is "spam" or "not spam." This direct association allows the model to learn the characteristics that define each category based on the input data it is fed.

The role of labels in supervised learning cannot be overstated; they are the critical element that enables the model to learn the mapping between inputs and desired outputs. Through the training process, the model iteratively adjusts its parameters to minimize the difference between its predictions and the actual labels typically we define this as a cost function in the subsequent chapter, refining its ability to predict accurately. This constant feedback loop, where the model's predictions are compared against known labels, ensures that the learning is directed and purposeful. Over time, the model's capacity to generalize and make predictions on unseen data improves, rooted in the foundational knowledge it has acquired from the labeled training set. Thus, labels not only inform the model about the specific outcomes to learn but also shape its understanding of the underlying patterns that dictate those outcomes.

Algorithms

The selection of an algorithm is a critical decision that can significantly influence a model's learning efficiency and its performance on given tasks. This choice is often dictated by the nature of the problem, the type of data at hand, and the desired outcome. For instance, while linear regression might be suited for predicting continuous outcomes based on a linear relationship between features, convolutional neural networks are more adept at handling complex image recognition tasks. Each algorithm comes with its strengths and limitations, and understanding these nuances is key to harnessing their potential effectively. Moreover, the choice of algorithm impacts not just the accuracy of predictions but also factors such as training time and computational resource requirements. Thus, the role of algorithms in machine learning is both foundational and transformative, driving the evolution of models from simple pattern recognizers to complex decision-makers capable of tackling an array of sophisticated tasks.

Model Training

The training process is a fundamental phase in the lifecycle of a machine learning model, where the abstract becomes tangible, and data transforms into decision-making capability. During this stage, a model is exposed to a dataset, learning to make predictions or decisions based on the patterns it uncovers. This is where the theoretical designs and chosen algorithms are put to the test, and applied to real-world data.

The essence of model training lies in its ability to adapt and evolve. Initially, a model might perform poorly, its predictions far from the mark. However, with each iteration, the model adjusts, tuning its internal parameters based on the feedback received from the training process. This feedback loop, powered by techniques such as gradient descent, allows the model to navigate toward optimal performance, reducing error rates and enhancing its predictive or decision-making accuracy. The training phase is not just about feeding data into an algorithm; it is a carefully calibrated process of learning and adaptation that unfolds over time. As the model iterates through the data, it not only learns to predict more accurately but also becomes more attuned to the nuances and complexities of the data it is working with.

Model Validation

Validation and testing represent pivotal stages in the development of a machine learning model, serving as the benchmarks for assessing its performance against previously unseen data. These phases are essential for evaluating how well the model generalizes beyond the specific examples on which it was trained, thereby ensuring its applicability and reliability in real-world scenarios. Validation involves using a separate portion of the dataset (not used during the training phase) to provide an unbiased evaluation of a model's performance. This process helps in fine-tuning the model's parameters and in selecting the best version of the model that strikes a balance between learning from the training data and generalizing to new data.

Testing, on the other hand, is the final assessment stage, where the model is evaluated against another reserved subset of the data called a test set. This step is crucial for gauging the model's actual performance and its ability to make accurate predictions or decisions when faced with new, unseen data. It is akin to a final exam succeeding a period of learning and revision, providing a clear measure of how well the model has learned to generalize from its training.

The importance of validation and testing cannot be overstated; they safeguard against overfitting, a scenario where the model performs exceptionally well on the training data but poorly on any new data. This ensures that the model is robust, versatile, and reliable, capable of functioning effectively in diverse conditions and scenarios. Moreover, these stages provide critical insights into the model's strengths and weaknesses, offering guidance for further improvements and refinements. By rigorously validating and testing a model, data scientists can confidently deploy machine learning solutions that are not only powerful in their predictive capabilities but also steadfast and dependable in their application across various domains.

Model Evaluation

Evaluating the performance of a machine learning model is a nuanced process that relies on various metrics to measure its effectiveness accurately. These metrics are the yardsticks by which a model's ability to make correct predictions or decisions is judged, providing insight into its strengths and areas for improvement. For classification tasks, where the goal is to predict which category or class an observation belongs to, common metrics include accuracy, precision, recall, and the F1 score.

In contrast, regression tasks, aimed at predicting continuous values, rely on metrics such as Mean Squared Error (MSE), Root Mean Squared Error (RMSE), and Mean Absolute Error (MAE). MSE measures the average squared difference between the observed actual outcomes and the outcomes predicted by the model, emphasizing the penalty for large errors. RMSE, the square root of MSE, is particularly interpretable as it remains in the same units as the output variable and illustrates the model's error in terms of the predicted quantity. MAE, on the other hand, provides a linear score that averages the absolute differences between predicted and actual values, offering a more straightforward interpretation of the model's prediction error.

We shall deep dive into the detailed formula and definition of these metrics in the subsequent sections. These evaluation metrics serve not only to quantify a model's performance but also to guide the model development process, informing decisions about model selection, tuning, and improvement strategies. By meticulously applying and analyzing these metrics, we can refine the models to achieve higher levels of accuracy and reliability, ensuring that the deployed models meet the rigorous demands of real-world applications. Understanding and selecting the appropriate evaluation metric is thus a crucial step in the machine learning pipeline, pivotal to developing models that are both effective and aligned with the specific objectives of a given task.

MLOps Platforms and Tools: MLOps focuses on the seamless integration of validated machine learning models with deployment, monitoring, and maintenance processes. It provides the infrastructure and tools required to scale ML solutions effectively and ensure their reliability in real-world applications.

A few of the popular MLOps platforms include:

- **AWS SageMaker**: An end-to-end platform for building, training, and deploying machine learning models at scale. It integrates seamlessly with other AWS services, making it a popular choice for cloud-based ML solutions.
- **Microsoft Azure ML Studio**: Offers drag-and-drop interfaces, automated machine learning pipelines, and robust tools for managing production-grade ML workflows.
- **Google Vertex AI**: Google's comprehensive platform combines AutoML capabilities with custom model deployment, enabling organizations to manage the entire ML lifecycle efficiently.
- **Databricks MLflow**: An open-source platform that supports experiment tracking, model registry, and deployment. It simplifies the orchestration of ML pipelines across various environments.

A few essential tools in MLOps include:

- **Kubeflow**: A Kubernetes-native platform designed to build and manage scalable ML workflows. It allows for containerized model deployment and orchestration.
- **Airflow**: A workflow orchestration tool that automates and schedules ML pipelines, ensuring efficient execution of complex tasks.
- **Docker**: Facilitates containerization, ensuring ML models and dependencies are packaged together for consistent deployment across environments.

By leveraging MLOps platforms and tools, organizations can streamline their ML workflows, reduce manual intervention, and ensure robust model deployment. This approach enhances reproducibility, scalability, and monitoring, enabling machine learning solutions to adapt and perform optimally in dynamic environments.

Data Preparation for Machine Learning Models

Data preparation is an indispensable step in the machine learning pipeline, often determining the success or failure of the models built. This process involves transforming raw data into a clean, organized format that is suitable for use in machine learning algorithms. The importance of meticulous data preparation cannot be overstressed, as it directly impacts the model's ability to learn effectively and produce accurate predictions. Without proper preparation, even the most sophisticated algorithms can falter, misled by inconsistencies, missing values, and irrelevant information that can obscure the underlying patterns they are designed to discover.

At the heart of data preparation is the quest to enhance data quality and relevance, ensuring that the dataset reflects the problem at hand while being free from distortions that could skew the results. Activities such as handling missing values, correcting errors, and standardizing data formats are critical components of this process. Moreover, feature selection and transformation play a pivotal role in shaping the dataset into a form that not only represents real-world phenomena accurately but also aligns with the computational requirements of machine learning models.

Beyond cleaning and organizing data, data preparation also involves enriching the dataset to improve model performance. Techniques such as feature engineering, where new features are created from existing ones, and data augmentation, which artificially increases the size and diversity of the dataset, are employed to provide models with a deeper, more nuanced understanding of the problem space. These steps are crucial for avoiding overfitting, where a model performs well on training data but poorly on unseen data, and underfitting, where the model fails to capture the underlying trends altogether.

Ultimately, data preparation sets the stage for the learning process, creating a foundation upon which models can build their predictions. It is a meticulous and often iterative process that bridges the gap between raw data and actionable insights, ensuring that the data fed into machine learning algorithms is as informative and representative as possible.

Data Preparation Using Python

As we embark on the journey of understanding the data preparation process, we will utilize a contrived, small dataset to guide us through each step, complemented by Python code demonstrations. This approach allows us to explore the intricacies of data preparation in a detailed and manageable manner, making it easier to grasp the fundamental concepts and techniques involved. While the dataset we will use is intentionally simplified, it is important to note that the principles and processes we will discuss are fully scalable and applicable to larger, real-world datasets.

The decision to use a smaller dataset is driven by the need for clarity and conciseness in our demonstrations. In a book format, it is impractical to print thousands of records or delve into the complexity of big data. Instead, by focusing on an illustrative dataset, we can ensure that the core ideas and methods of data preparation are communicated effectively, without overwhelming readers with excessive details or data volume. Rest assured, the skills and knowledge you will acquire from these examples can be applied to much larger datasets, equipping you with the tools necessary to tackle real-world data preparation challenges. Whether working with small-scale projects or navigating the vast seas of big data, the principles of data preparation remain the same, serving as the foundation for any successful machine learning endeavor.

For readers embarking on their journey with Python and data analysis, choosing the right Integrated Development Environment (IDE) can significantly enhance the learning experience.

- **Jupyter Notebook**: Jupyter Notebooks offer an interactive computing environment where you can combine code execution, rich text, mathematics, plots, and rich media. Installing Anaconda, a popular Python distribution for data science, provides you with Jupyter and other useful libraries pre-installed.
- **PyCharm**: PyCharm is another powerful IDE that provides a comprehensive set of tools for Python developers. It features smart code navigation, error checking, and a debugging tool, making it a favorite among professionals. PyCharm offers a Community Edition that is free and open-source.
- **Spyder**: Spyder is an open-source IDE specifically designed for scientists, engineers, and data analysts. It features a unique combination of advanced editing, analysis, debugging, and profiling functionality with a comprehensive numerical computing environment. Spyder is also included with Anaconda.

- **Google Colab**: Google Colab is a free cloud service based on Jupyter Notebooks that supports Python. It requires no setup, offers free access to computing resources, including GPUs, and facilitates easy sharing of projects. Colab is particularly popular for machine learning and data analysis projects.
- **Online Editors**: For those who prefer not to install software or are unable to do so, online Python editors are a convenient option. These platforms allow you to write and run Python code directly in your web browser, without any setup. A few popular online Python editors include Repl.it and CodePen for Python.

Each of these environments has its unique strengths, and the choice largely depends on your personal preferences, project requirements, and whether you prioritize having a local development environment or prefer the flexibility of cloud-based platforms. For beginners, starting with Jupyter Notebooks (via Anaconda) or Google Colab can lower the entry barrier, providing an easy-to-use interface for learning Python and data analysis concepts.

Remember, while the tools and IDEs facilitate the development process, the core of learning involves understanding the principles of programming and data analysis. Feel free to experiment with different environments to find what best suits your learning style and project needs.

Preceding we deep dive into the Python exercise to perform different data preparation tasks, let us quickly explore a few prominent libraries which are very useful in our data science projects.

- **Pandas** is a powerful Python library for data manipulation and analysis. It provides fast, flexible data structures, such as Data Frames and Series, making it easy to manipulate structured data. Pandas is particularly suited for handling tabular data (such as our dataset), time series, and arbitrary matrix data with row and column labels.
- **NumPy** is a fundamental package for scientific computing in Python. It offers a powerful N-dimensional array object, sophisticated functions, tools for integrating C/C++ and Fortran code, and useful linear algebra, Fourier transform, and random number capabilities.
- **Matplotlib** is a plotting library for the Python programming language and its numerical mathematics extension, NumPy. It provides an object-oriented API for embedding plots into applications using general-purpose GUI toolkits such as Tkinter, wxPython, Qt, or GTK.
- **Seaborn** is a Python visualization library based on matplotlib. It provides a high-level interface for drawing attractive and informative statistical graphics. Seaborn is particularly good at making complex visualization tasks simpler and more approachable.

Let us consider a contrived dataset for an illustrative example, we are going to read customer data available in the form of a CSV file with the help of the pandas library as follows; we need to load the pandas library and read the file by specifying its path.

```
import pandas as pd

# Load dataset
df = pd.read_csv('path_to_your_file/data1_Ch_3.csv')

# Display the first 5 rows of the dataset
print(df.head())
```

The output of the first five records of the contrived dataset is shown in *Figure* 3.1.

	CustomerID	Age	Income	AccountCreated	Preference	EmailVerified
0	1	56.0	92955.0	2022-01-02	Product A	False
1	2	NaN	94925.0	2022-01-09	NaN	False
2	3	46.0	97969.0	2022-01-16	Service C	False
3	4	NaN	35311.0	2022-01-23	NaN	False
4	5	NaN	83707.0	2022-01-30	Product A	False

Figure 3.1: *Output of the First 5 Records of the Contrived Dataset*

This table shown in *Figure* 3.1 demonstrates how the data is structured, with some missing values (NaN) in the Age and Preference columns, showcasing a typical scenario we might encounter in real-world datasets. Next, we could explore how to address these missing values or proceed with other data preparation steps.

Handling Missing Values

The following are the techniques to deal with missing data points:

- **Removing Rows**: This method involves removing rows that contain missing values. It is straightforward but can result in a significant reduction of data, potentially losing valuable information.
- **Imputation**: Imputation replaces missing values with substitute values, which could be the mean, median, or mode of the column for numerical data, or the most frequent category for categorical data. Advanced imputation methods consider correlations between features.

We shall perform an imputation method to replace the missing value. Given our dataset contains both numerical (for example, Age, Income) and categorical (for example, Preference) data, we will use the median for numerical data and the most frequent value for categorical data.

Introduction to Machine Learning

```
from sklearn.impute import SimpleImputer

# Numerical data imputation
num_imputer = SimpleImputer(strategy='median')
df[['Age', 'Income']] = num_imputer.fit_transform(df[['Age', 'Income']])

# Categorical data imputation
cat_imputer = SimpleImputer(strategy='most_frequent')
df['Preference'] = cat_imputer.fit_transform(df[['Preference']])

# Display the first 5 rows after imputation
print(df.head())
```

Scikit-learn (Sklearn) is a free software machine learning library for the Python programming language. It features various classification, regression, and clustering algorithms designed to interoperate with the Python numerical and scientific libraries NumPy and SciPy. Within scikit-learn, the `SimpleImputer` class provides basic strategies for imputing missing values, which are common issues in real-world data sets. Missing values can be replaced by the mean, the median, and the most frequent value.

fill_value: When the strategy is "constant," **fill_value** is used to replace all occurrences of missing values. By default, **fill_value** is 0 when imputing numerical data and "`missing_value`" for strings or object data types.

Subsequent to treating the missing values in our dataset, here are the first five rows shown in *Figure* 3.2.

	CustomerID	Age	Income	AccountCreated	Preference	EmailVerified
0	1	56.0	92955.0	2022-01-02	Product A	False
1	2	51.0	94925.0	2022-01-09	Product A	False
2	3	46.0	97969.0	2022-01-16	Service C	False
3	4	51.0	35311.0	2022-01-23	Product A	False
4	5	51.0	93940.0	2022-01-30	Product A	False

***Figure* 3.2:** *Output of the First 5 Records Succeeding Missing Value Treatment*

Subsequent to treating missing values in our customer dataset, it is worthwhile to conduct a thorough review for any other potential issues or inconsistencies that might require further data preparation steps. Common areas to examine include, checking for and removing any duplicate entries, identifying and assessing outliers in numerical columns, and categorical variables (such as Preference in our dataset) should be converted into a numerical format through encoding methods such as one-hot encoding or label encoding.

There are no duplicate rows in our dataset. Based on a standard definition of outliers (values more than 3 standard deviations from the mean), there are no outliers in the 'Age' and 'Income' columns of our dataset.

```
from sklearn.preprocessing import LabelEncoder

# Initializing the label encoder
label_encoder = LabelEncoder()

# Applying label encoding to the 'Preference' column
df['Preference'] = label_encoder.fit_transform(df['Preference'])

# Saving the dataset with label-encoded 'Preference' column to a new CSV file
encoded_csv_file_path = "path_to_your_file /customer_data_encoded.csv"
df.to_csv(encoded_csv_file_path, index=False)
```

The output of the first five records subsequent to treating the preference column is shown in *Figure 3.3*.

CustomerID	Age	Income	AccountCreated	Preference	EmailVerified
1	56.0	92955.0	02-01-2022	0	False
2	40.0	94925.0	09-01-2022	0	False
3	46.0	97969.0	16-01-2022	2	False
4	40.0	35311.0	23-01-2022	0	False
5	40.0	83707.0	30-01-2022	0	False

Figure 3.3: Output of the First 5 Records Subsequent to Treating the Preference Column

Feature Scaling

Another important step in the data preparation task is feature scaling and normalization. These methods are crucial pre-processing steps in many machine learning workflows, ensuring that the numerical values of different features contribute equally to the model training process. A dataset often has different units of measurement and varying scales. This disparity can cause issues with machine learning algorithms that are sensitive to the magnitude of input features, mostly distance-based algorithms, gradient-descent-based algorithms, and regularization techniques that we will be discussing in forthcoming chapters. Feature Scaling involves transforming the values of numerical features to a common scale without distorting differences in the ranges of values. Techniques include Min-Max scaling, where values are scaled to a fixed range usually 0 to 1, and Standardization, where data is scaled to have a mean of 0 and a standard deviation of 1.

To understand the process with the help of Python code, let us consider a different

Introduction to Machine Learning

contrived dataset that includes features (columns) such as age in years and salary in INR which have different ranges and units of measurement. Scaling them to a similar range would help ensure that no single feature disproportionately influences the model's performance due to its scale. The choice between Min-Max scaling and Standardization would depend on the specifics of the model and the data distribution, but both approaches are commonly used in practice. Let us read the data and display the first 5 records of the dataset as shown in *Figure 3.4*.

```
import pandas as pd
# Load dataset
df = pd.read_csv('path_to_your_file/data2_Ch_3.csv')
# Display the first 5 rows of the dataset
print(df.head())
```

The output of the first five records of the contrived dataset is shown in *Figure 3.4*.

	Age	Salary	Credit_Score	Years_of_Experience	Number_of_Dependents
0	23	50000	650	2	0
1	45	55000	700	15	2
2	56	70000	750	25	3
3	30	65000	620	10	1
4	22	40000	680	1	0

Figure 3.4: *Output of the First 5 Records of the Contrived Dataset*

```
from sklearn.preprocessing import StandardScaler
import pandas as pd
# Initialize the StandardScaler
scaler = StandardScaler()
# Perform Min-Max scaling on all columns
scaled_features = scaler.fit_transform(df)
# Convert the scaled features back into a DataFrame
df_scaled = pd.DataFrame(scaled_features, columns=df.columns)
# Display the first 5 records of the scaled DataFrame
print(df_scaled.head())
```

The output of the first five records subsequent to scaling is shown in *Figure 3.5*.

	Age	Salary	Credit_Score	Years_of_Experience	Number_of_Dependents
0	-1.290052	-0.750981	-0.991454	-1.165857	-1.264391
1	0.577128	-0.392232	0.279641	0.458015	0.140488
2	1.510719	0.684015	1.550736	1.707148	0.842927
3	-0.695949	0.325266	-1.754111	-0.166551	-0.561951
4	-1.374924	-1.468479	-0.228797	-1.290771	-1.264391

Figure 3.5: *Output of the First 5 Records Subsequent to Scaling*

This transformation has adjusted all feature values to have a mean of 0 and a standard deviation of 1, making the data suitable for algorithms that assume the data is centered on zero and variance is the same for all features. We can observe positive high values such as 0.68 in salary indicates the highest salary and -1.47 indicates the lowest salary, very low from the mean value zero. Also, we can notice, that 1.55 is the highest credit score and the lowest is -1.75. In the same manner, we can investigate the rest of the columns even without the units.

Outlier Treatment

Outliers are data points that differ significantly from other observations in a dataset. They can arise due to variability in measurement, experimental errors, or genuinely extreme values. Outliers can influence the results of the data analysis and statistical modeling in significant ways, leading to potential misinterpretations. Linear models are sensitive to outliers because outliers can significantly influence the line of best fit. Outlier treatment is often mandatory to ensure the robustness of the model. Models such as decision trees or ensemble methods (random forests, gradient boosting) and Neural network models can handle outliers better due to their non-linear nature. They can learn the pattern of extreme values without being unduly influenced. Several methods exist for handling outliers, each suitable for different scenarios and assumptions about the data, including:

- **Trimming/Removing:** This involves removing outliers from the dataset. It is straightforward but can lead to loss of information.
- **Capping:** Outliers are capped at a certain percentile. For instance, values above the 95th percentile are set to the value at the 95th percentile.
- **Transformation:** Applying transformations (such as log, square root, and so on) can reduce the effect of outliers.
- **Imputation:** Replace outliers with estimates based on the rest of the data. This can be a mean, median, or a prediction from other data points.
- **Z-score Method:** Identifying outliers based on their Z-scores (the number of standard deviations away from the mean).
- **Interquartile Range (IQR) Method:** Outliers are defined as observations beyond the 1.5 * IQR above the third quartile or below the first quartile.

We shall understand the concept of outlier treatment with the help of a Python example. Consider a small dataset with features Age, Height (in cm), Weight (in kg), and Blood Pressure (Systolic/Diastolic) for a group of individuals. Let us load this dataset and display the summary of the dataset to understand the potential outliers.

```
import pandas as pd
# Load the original dataset with outliers
Df_original = pd.read_csv('path_to_your_file/data3_Ch3.csv')
```

Introduction to Machine Learning

```
# Display summary statistics before outlier treatment
summary_before = df_original.describe()
print(summary_before)
```

The summary statistics before the outlier treatment are shown in *Figure 3.6*.

	Age	Height_in_cm	Weight_in_kg	BP_Systolic	BP_Diastolic
count	27.000000	27.000000	27.000000	27.000000	27.000000
mean	40.481481	172.462760	74.395242	124.560979	79.839425
std	14.420526	27.618262	14.205768	21.258104	10.637850
min	18.000000	90.000000	48.399378	105.935947	30.000000
25%	27.500000	163.249773	64.890730	113.981792	78.644646
50%	45.000000	170.768949	73.394324	120.419801	81.286037
75%	52.000000	178.233651	85.699060	128.243255	84.443923
max	61.000000	278.000000	108.087441	220.000000	88.814687

***Figure 3.6**: Summary Statistics of Data*

We could notice outliers in the following columns.

- **Height_in_cm:** Values of 278 and 90 are unrealistic and likely represent data entry errors.
- **Blood_Pressure_Systolic:** A value of 220 might be considered an extreme outlier, potentially indicating a measurement error or a severe medical condition. A diastolic pressure of 30 is also unrealistic, likely a data entry error.

We shall perform the IQR method as mentioned here and replace the outlier with its median values as shown in the Python code. The whole piece of code is written in the form of a user-defined function for the reusability of the code.

```
def treat_outliers_with_median(df, column):
    Q1 = df[column].quantile(0.25)
    Q3 = df[column].quantile(0.75)
    IQR = Q3 - Q1
    median = df[column].median()
    lower_bound = Q1 - 1.5 * IQR
    upper_bound = Q3 + 1.5 * IQR
    # Replace outliers with the median
    df.loc[(df[column] < lower_bound) | (df[column] > upper_bound), column] = median
    return df
```

Let us treat the outliers in the 'Height_in_cm' and 'BP_Systolic' columns

```
df_treated = df_original.copy()
df_treated = treat_outliers_with_median(df_treated, 'Height_in_cm')
df_treated = treat_outliers_with_median(df_treated, 'BP_Systolic')
# Display summary statistics after outlier treatment
summary_after = df_treated.describe()
print(summary_after)
```

The summary statistics succeeding the outlier treatment are shown in *Figure* 3.7.

	Age	Height_in_cm	Weight_in_kg	BP_Systolic	BP_Diastolic
count	27.000000	27.000000	27.000000	27.000000	27.000000
mean	40.481481	171.482682	74.395242	120.872823	79.839425
std	14.420526	8.488828	14.205768	9.386688	10.637850
min	18.000000	157.771265	48.399378	105.935947	30.000000
25%	27.500000	164.659292	64.890730	113.981792	78.644646
50%	45.000000	170.768949	73.394324	120.419801	81.286037
75%	52.000000	177.702188	85.699060	127.551591	84.443923
max	61.000000	187.066050	108.087441	147.344222	88.814687

Figure 3.7: *Summary Statistics Succeeding Outlier Treatment*

In the same manner, other columns are treated if there is a potential outlier, here domain knowledge will be very helpful in understanding the reference values (mean/median).

Subsequent to completing the data preparation phase, the next critical step in the data analysis process is to perform Exploratory Data Analysis (EDA). The forthcoming section will delve into EDA, providing a platform to better comprehend the business process and derive actionable insights from the data.

Exploratory Data Analysis

EDA is an approach for summarizing the main characteristics of a dataset, often with visual methods. It is a crucial stage that allows analysts to uncover patterns, spot anomalies, test a hypothesis, or check assumptions with the help of summary statistics and graphical representations. Understanding the business context is equally important; it helps in making informed decisions about the significance of the patterns found during EDA.

Let us navigate the EDA process for the video game dataset. This dataset, often available on Kaggle or similar platforms, contains information about a comprehensive look at the sales (in millions) performance of video games across various regions, including North America, Europe, Japan, and other territories. It encompasses data on game titles, platforms (such as PlayStation, Xbox, Nintendo, and PC), genres (Action, Sports, Role-Playing, and more), and publisher information. Furthermore, it includes global sales figures, enabling an analysis of market trends, regional preferences, and the overall impact of different genres and platforms on the gaming industry. This dataset provides a fascinating glimpse into the dynamics of the video game market, highlighting the shifts in consumer preferences over time and the rise and fall of various gaming trends. It serves as an excellent resource for exploratory data analysis, offering insights into the factors that drive video game popularity and success across the globe.

Let us load this data and explore the variables.

```
import pandas as pd
data = pd.read_csv('path_to_your_file/data4_Ch3_vgsales.csv')
```

- **Rank:** Duplicate of row index
- **Name** : The game's name
- **Platform:** Platform of the game's release (that is PC, PS4, and more)
- **Year**: Year of the game's release
- **Genre**: Genre of the game
- **Publisher**: Publisher of the game
- **NA_Sales**: Sales in North America (in millions)
- **EU_Sales**: Sales in Europe (in millions)
- **JP_Sales**: Sales in Japan (in millions)
- **Other_Sales**: Sales in the rest of the world (in millions)
- **Global_Sales**: Total worldwide sales

The total number of records is 16,598 with 11 columns. We shall drop the following columns which do not add any value to the dataset, which includes Rank, Name, and Year. Rank is the duplicate of row index of the record, and has nothing to do with the original rank or popularity. Each game has a unique title, we have a Genre column that describes the nature of the game better, hence we drop the unique Name column. Also, the year the game was released does not add any value to the analysis. We shall proceed with dropping these columns and display the head of the data.

```
# Drop the 'Rank', 'Name', and 'Year' columns
data_dropped_columns = original_data.drop(columns=['Rank', 'Name', 'Year'])
# Display the first few rows of the modified dataframe
data_dropped_columns.head()
```

The head of the data showing the first five records subsequent to removing unwanted columns is shown in *Figure 3.8*.

Platform	Genre	Publisher	NA_Sales	EU_Sales	JP_Sales	Other_Sales	Global_Sales
Wii	Sports	Nintendo	41.49	29.02	3.77	8.46	82.74
NES	Platform	Nintendo	29.08	3.58	6.81	0.77	40.24
Wii	Racing	Nintendo	15.85	12.88	3.79	3.31	35.82
Wii	Sports	Nintendo	15.75	11.01	3.28	2.96	33.00
GB	Role-Playing	Nintendo	11.27	8.89	10.22	1.00	31.37

***Figure 3.8**: Head of the Data Showing First Five Records Subsequent to Removing Unwanted Columns*

Performing EDA on this video game sales dataset can provide valuable insights into market trends, platform preferences, genre popularity, and regional sales distributions. We shall begin the sales distribution analysis with respect to Genre. Box plots can effectively display the distribution of global sales across different genres, highlighting the median, quartiles, and potential outliers within each genre. This type of plot is great for comparing the central tendency and variability of sales among genres, as well as identifying genres with particularly high or low sales. Let us create a box plot using the seaborn package to visualize the distribution of global video game sales across different genres.

```
import seaborn as sns
# Creates a new figure for the box plot with specified size (width, height)
plt.figure(figsize=(14, 8))
sns.boxplot(x='Genre', y='Global_Sales', data=data_dropped)
plt.title('Genre vs. Global Sales Distribution')
plt.xlabel('Genre')
plt.ylabel('Global Sales (Millions)')
# Rotates the x-axis labels (genre names) by 45 degrees to prevent overlap and improve readability
plt.xticks(rotation=45)
# Sets the y-axis scale to logarithmic for a clearer view of data across orders of magnitude
plt.yscale('log')
# Enables the grid for better visibility, affecting both major and minor grid lines
plt.grid(True, which="both", ls="--")
plt.show()
```

The Genre versus Global Sales Distribution is illustrated in *Figure* 3.9.

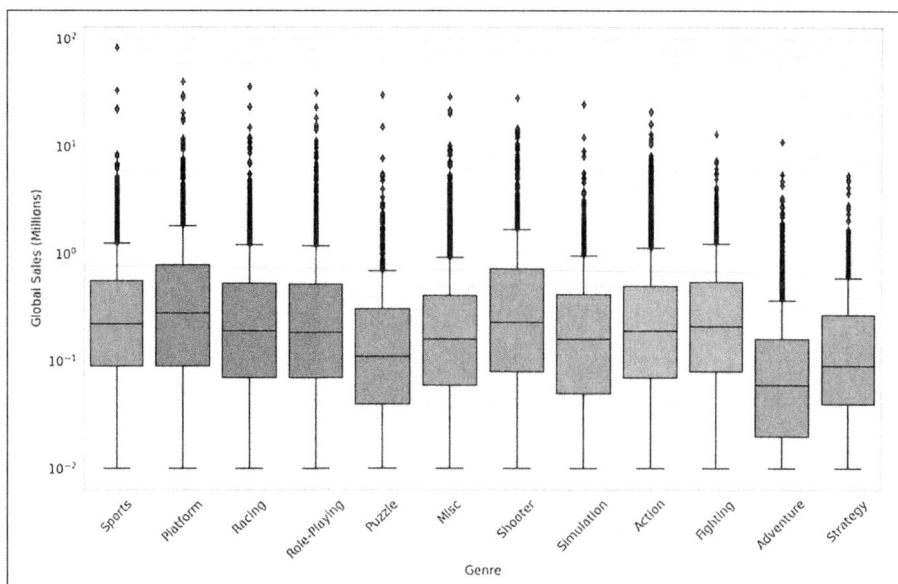

Figure **3.9**: *Genre versus Global Sales Distribution*

A few key observations from the preceding plot shown in *Figure* 3.9 indicate the following:

Median Sales: The line within each box represents the median sales of each genre, providing a sense of the central tendency of sales within genres.

Variability and Range: The length of the boxes and the whiskers show the variability and range of sales within each genre. A longer box or whisker indicates a wider distribution of sales figures.

Outliers: Points beyond the whiskers represent outliers, which are games that have achieved exceptionally high sales compared to other games in the same genre.

Some genres, such as **Action**, **Sports**, and **Shooter**, show a significant number of outliers indicating that a few titles in these genres have achieved exceptionally high global sales. This suggests that while the market is competitive, there are standout successes within each genre.

Next, to represent the market share of each genre as a percentage of total global sales, we can sum up the global sales for each genre, calculate the percentage of total sales for each, and then visualize this information using a pie chart. The pie chart will provide a clear visual representation of the market share held by each genre in the video game industry. Let us proceed with these steps:

```
# Summing up the global sales for each genre
genre_sales = data_dropped.groupby('Genre')['Global_Sales'].sum()
```

```
# Calculating the percentage of total sales for each genre
genre_sales_percentage = genre_sales / genre_sales.sum() * 100

# Plotting the market share of each genre as a pie chart
plt.figure(figsize=(10, 8))
#The use of sns.color_palette('pastel') gives the chart a pleasant
aesthetic with pastel colors.
genre_sales_percentage.plot.pie(autopct='%1.1f%%', startangle=140,
colors=sns.color_palette('pastel'))
plt.title('Market Share by Genre (Percentage of Global Sales)')
plt.ylabel('')   # Hide the y-label as it is unnecessary for a pie chart
plt.show()
```

The following pie chart depicts the market share by Genre:

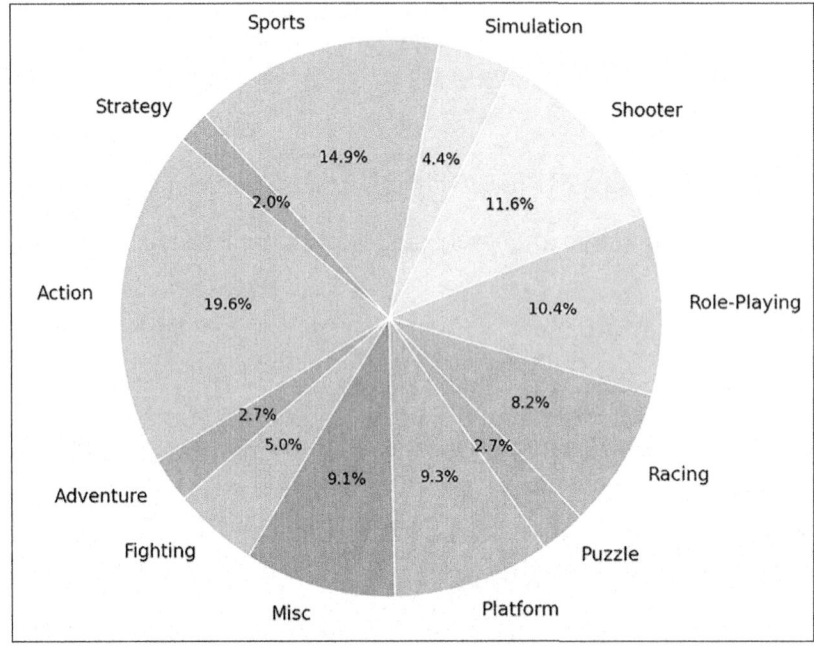

Figure 3.10: *Pie Chart Showing Market Share by Genre*

Each slice of the pie chart shown in *Figure* 3.10 corresponds to a different genre, with the size of each slice, indicating the proportion of global sales that genre contributes. This visual representation allows us to quickly grasp which genres dominate the market and how sales are distributed across different types of video games. For instance, genres with larger slices (Action, Sports, and Shooter) hold a top three larger share of the market, indicating their popularity and commercial success.

The dataset contains a total of 578 unique publishers. This indicates a diverse range of companies involved in publishing video games globally. We shall filter the top 12

Introduction to Machine Learning 69

publishers who are selling above 200 million total global sales and visualize their market share.

```
# Finding the top 12 publishers by their total global sales with more than 200 million

top_12_publishers = data_dropped.groupby('Publisher')['Global_Sales'].sum().sort_values(ascending=False).head(12)

# Calculating the market share percentage
top_publishers_market_share = top_12_publishers / top_12_publishers.sum() * 100

# Plotting the market share of the top publishers as a pie chart
plt.figure(figsize=(10, 8))
top_publishers_market_share.plot.pie(autopct='%1.1f%%', startangle=140, colors=sns.color_palette('pastel'))
plt.title('Market Share by Top Publishers (Above 200 Million Global Sales)')
plt.ylabel('')   # Hide the y-label as it is unnecessary for a pie chart
plt.show()
```

The following pie chart depicts market share by the top publishers:

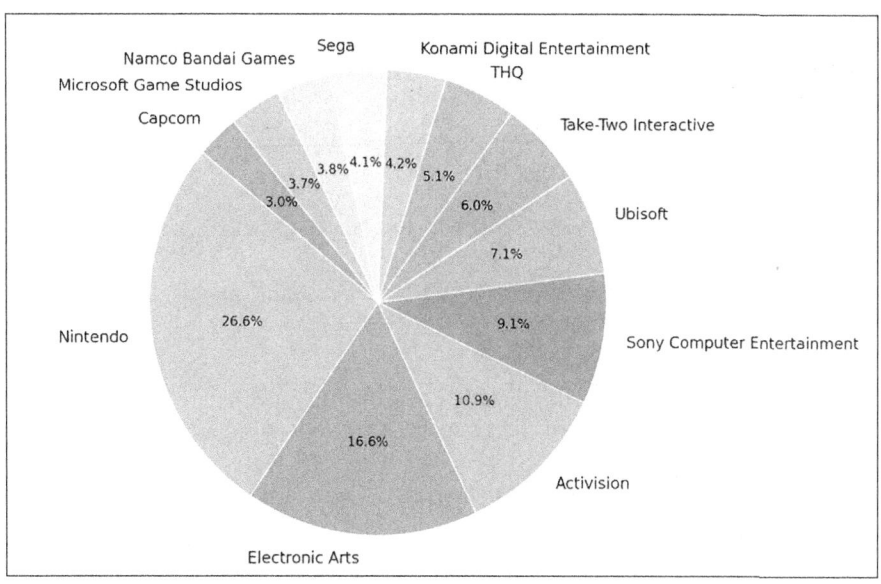

Figure 3.11: Pie Chart Showing Market Share by Top Publishers (above 200 Million)

Each slice in *Figure 3.11* represents the proportion of global sales contributed by these leading publishers, clearly illustrating their dominance and influence within the video game industry. Top publishers, highlighting Nintendo's leading position (26.6%) in the video game industry, followed by Electronic Arts (16.6%) and Activision (10.9%).

The dataset contains a total of 31 unique platforms. This indicates a wide variety of gaming consoles and systems for which games have been developed and sold globally.

The top ten platforms by total global sales are:

1. PlayStation 2 (PS2) - 1255.64 million
2. Xbox 360 (X360) - 979.96 million
3. PlayStation 3 (PS3) - 957.84 million
4. Wii - 926.71 million
5. Nintendo DS - 822.49 million
6. PlayStation (PS) - 730.66 million
7. Game Boy Advance (GBA) - 318.50 million
8. PlayStation Portable (PSP) - 296.28 million
9. PlayStation 4 (PS4) - 278.10 million
10. PC - 258.82 million

We shall visualize the preceding listing with an interesting bar chart.

```
# Finding the top 10 platforms by their total global sales
top_10_platforms = data_dropped.groupby('Platform')['Global_Sales'].sum().sort_values(ascending=False).head(10)
# Plotting the top 10 platforms by total global sales as a declining height bar chart
plt.figure(figsize=(12, 8))
sns.barplot(x=top_10_platforms.index, y=top_10_platforms.values, palette="viridis")
plt.title('Top 10 Platforms by Total Global Sales')
plt.xlabel('Platform')
plt.ylabel('Global Sales (Millions)')
plt.xticks(rotation=45)  # Rotating the x-axis labels for better readability
plt.show()
```

The following bar chart depicts top-10 platforms by Total Global Sales:

Introduction to Machine Learning   71

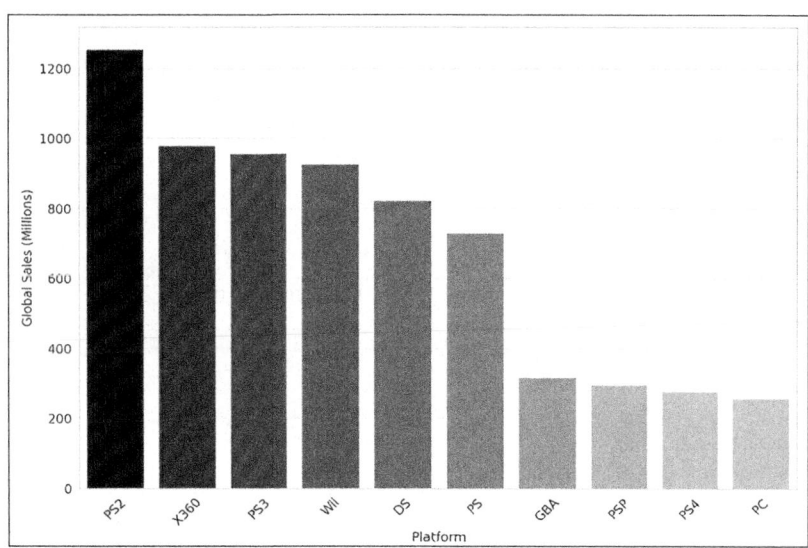

Figure 3.12: *Bar Chart Showing Top-10 Platforms by Total Global Sales*

The bar chart shown in *Figure* 3.12 visualizes the top 10 platforms by total global sales, presented in declining order of sales volume. Each bar represents a different platform, with the height of the bar indicating the total global sales in millions of units. The PlayStation 2 leads significantly, followed by the Xbox 360, PlayStation 3, and others, showcasing the competitive landscape of gaming platforms over the years. This representation makes it easy to compare the sales performance of these leading platforms visually.

To analyze regional platform preferences, we will compare the total sales in North America (NA), Europe (EU), Japan (JP), and other regions for the top platforms. We will aggregate the sales data for these regions and then create an overlaid bar plot. This visualization will allow us to observe any differences in platform popularity across these territories.

```
# Aggregating sales data for NA, EU, JP, and Other regions for the top
platforms
platform_sales_region = data_dropped.groupby('Platform').agg({'NA_
Sales': 'sum','EU_Sales': 'sum', 'JP_Sales': 'sum','Other_Sales':
'sum'})
# Identifying the top 10 platforms by global sales
top_10_platforms = data_dropped.groupby('Platform')['Global_Sales'].
sum().sort_values(ascending=False).head(10)
# Focusing on the regional sales for these top platforms
top_platforms_sales_region = platform_sales_region.loc[top_10_platforms.
index]
# Plotting the overlaid bar plot with contrasting colors ('#1f77b4',
'#ff7f0e', '#2ca02c', '#d62728')
```

```
top_platforms_sales_region.plot(kind='bar', figsize=(14, 10), width=0.8,
color=['#1f77b4', '#ff7f0e', '#2ca02c', '#d62728'])
plt.title('Regional Sales for Top 10 Platforms')
plt.xlabel('Platform')
plt.ylabel('Sales (Millions)')
plt.xticks(rotation=45)
plt.legend(title='Region')
plt.show()
```

The following overlaid bar chart depicts top-10 platforms by Regional Sales:

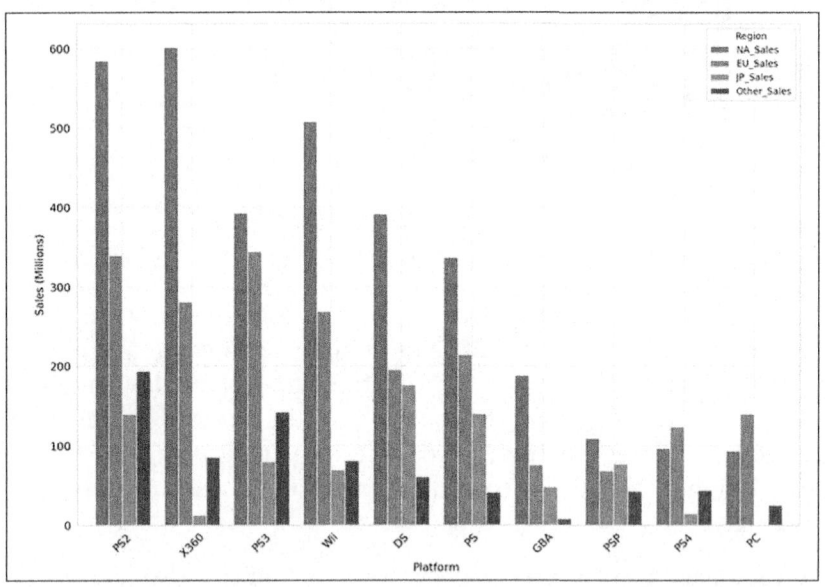

Figure 3.13: *Overlaid Bar Chart Showing Top-10 Platforms by Regional Sales*

The overlaid bar plot shown in *Figure* 3.13 illustrates the regional sales (North America, Europe, Japan, and other regions) for the top-10 platforms. This visualization enables us to observe differences in platform popularity across different territories. Key observations are listed in the chart as follows:

- **North America (NA) Sales:** Dominance in sales can be seen for certain platforms, reflecting a strong preference in this region. Platforms such as the X360 and PS2 show significant sales.

- **Europe (EU) Sales**: Similar to NA, certain platforms have a strong presence, with PS3 and PS2 showing substantial sales.

- **Japan (JP) Sales**: The preference in Japan can be quite distinct from NA and EU, with platforms such as the DS and PS showing higher sales proportions relative to other regions.

- **Other Regions Sales**: Reflects sales outside NA, EU, and JP, which can show a mix of preferences, often aligning more closely with global trends.

Given the depth and breadth of the video game sales data, there is significant scope for further detailed analysis and exploration. However, due to the constraints imposed by the length of this chapter, we must conclude our exploratory data analysis at this juncture. That said, it is highly recommended for readers to delve deeper into this dataset on their own. There are undoubtedly many more insights and patterns waiting to be uncovered, each potentially leading to a better understanding of the dynamics within the video game industry.

Introduction to Unsupervised Learning

Unsupervised Learning (USL) holds a unique and expansive role within the machine learning and AI model-building lifecycle. Unlike its supervised counterpart, USL does not rely on pre-labeled data to learn. Instead, it focuses on identifying patterns, structures, and relationships directly from the data itself. This intrinsic capability makes USL invaluable for discovering the underlying architecture of datasets, offering insights that might not be immediately apparent. Its broad scope extends from the initial stages of Exploratory Data Analysis (EDA) to enhance the performance of supervised learning models by uncovering hidden features in unlabeled data.

At the heart of USL's importance is its versatility and applicability across various domains and stages of the AI model-building process. During EDA, USL techniques such as clustering and dimensionality reduction can reveal natural groupings and associations within the data, guiding subsequent model development with enriched understanding. These insights are not just about simplifying complex data into more manageable forms; they also illuminate the intrinsic properties of the dataset, such as the distribution and relationships of features, which are critical for designing more effective machine learning models.

Moreover, USL's scope extends beyond just the analytical phase. It plays a pivotal role in refining and preparing data for supervised learning. By identifying patterns and features within unlabeled datasets, USL can help in creating pseudo-labels or in feature engineering, thereby augmenting the available training data for supervised models. This process can significantly improve model accuracy and robustness, especially in scenarios where labeled data is scarce or expensive to obtain. In essence, unsupervised learning is not merely a set of algorithms or an alternative approach to supervised learning; it is a foundational tool that permeates every stage of the AI model-building lifecycle. From initial data analysis to enhancing supervised model training, USL offers a lens through which data can be understood in its most authentic form.

Clustering algorithms are at the forefront of unsupervised learning, enabling the discovery of inherent groupings within data based on similarities among items. These algorithms leverage various distance metrics to evaluate and group data points, each bringing its own strengths and challenges to the task of clustering. Here, we explore some popular clustering algorithms, the distance metrics they utilize, and their respective advantages and disadvantages.

K-Means Clustering

K-means clustering is a fundamental algorithm in unsupervised learning that aims to partition a dataset into K distinct clusters. The "means" in its name refers to the averaging process involved in finding the center (centroid) of each cluster. Designed for simplicity and efficiency, K-means seeks to minimize the variance within each cluster, ensuring that data points are as close as possible to their respective centroids.

The process begins with the random selection of K points in the dataset as the initial centroids. The algorithm then iterates through two main steps: assignment and update. In the assignment step, each data point is assigned to the nearest centroid, with "nearest" typically defined by the Euclidean distance between the data point and the centroid. This step effectively partitions the dataset into clusters based on the current centroid positions. In the update step, the centroids are recalculated as the mean of all points assigned to their cluster, hence moving the centroid to the center of the points.

To understand the concept of clustering, let us consider a small contrived dataset showing a dataset that simulates environmental data collected from different locations. This data could be useful for clustering to identify areas with similar environmental characteristics, which could have applications in ecology, environmental management, or urban planning.

Here is the structure for our new dataset:

- **LocationID**: A unique identifier for each location where data is collected.
- **Temperature (°C)**: Average annual temperature in degrees Celsius.
- **Rainfall (mm)**: Average annual rainfall in millimeters.
- **pH Level**: Average soil pH level, indicating the acidity or alkalinity of the soil.

Let us read this dataset and display the head of the data as shown in *Figure 3.14*.

```
from sklearn.cluster import KMeans
from sklearn.preprocessing import StandardScaler
import matplotlib.pyplot as plt
import pandas as pd
import numpy as np

df = pd.read_csv('path_to_your_file/data5_Ch3.csv')
df.head()
```

The first five records of the environmental dataset are shown in *Figure* 3.14.

LocationID	Temperature (°C)	Rainfall (mm)	pH Level
6	3.07	744.96	5.34
22	20.19	98.12	7.73
13	13.61	1333.13	6.56
10	7.28	1489.96	6.26
12	13.18	1270.49	6.82

Figure 3.14: *First 5 Records of Environmental Dataset*

Choosing the optimal number of clusters from an elbow plot is a critical step in K-means clustering, a method that aims to partition 'n' observations into 'k' clusters in which each observation belongs to the cluster with the nearest mean.

The Elbow Method plot shows how the inertia (or within-cluster sum of squares) decreases as the number of clusters increases. The "elbow" point in the plot is typically considered an indicator of the optimal number of clusters because, beyond this point, the reduction in inertia slows down, indicating diminishing returns by increasing the cluster count.

```
# Scaling the features
scaler = StandardScaler()
scaled_features = scaler.fit_transform(df.drop('LocationID', axis=1))
# Elbow method to find the optimal number of clusters
inertia = []
k_values = range(1, 11)
for k in k_values:
    kmeans = KMeans(n_clusters=k, random_state=42)
    kmeans.fit(scaled_features)
    inertia.append(kmeans.inertia_)
# Plotting the elbow plot
plt.figure(figsize=(10, 6))
plt.plot(k_values, inertia, marker='o')
plt.title('Elbow Method For Optimal k')
plt.xlabel('Number of clusters')
plt.ylabel('Inertia')
plt.grid(True)
plt.show()
```

The first five records of the environmental dataset are shown in *Figure* 3.15.

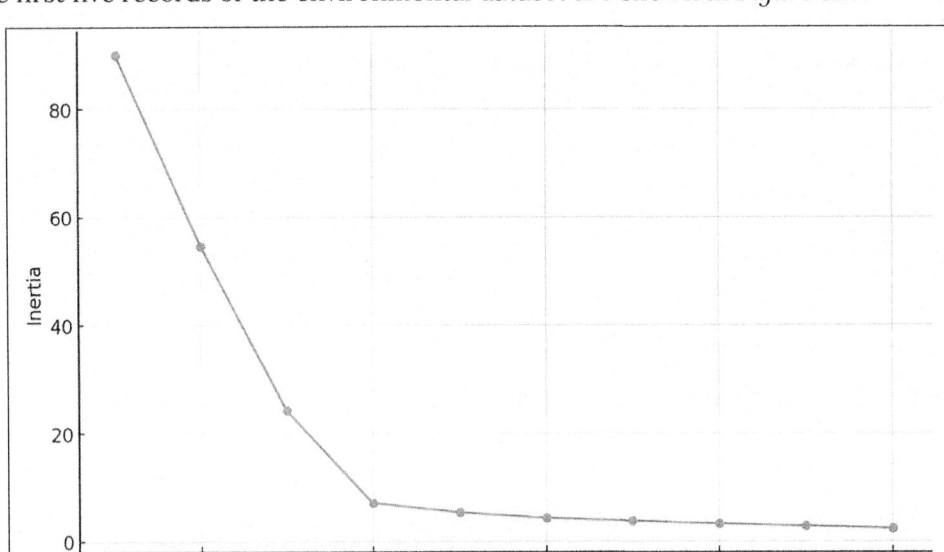

Figure 3.15: *First 5 Records of Environmental Dataset*

From the plot shown in *Figure* 3.15, it appears that the elbow point is around **3 or 4 clusters**. This suggests that 3 or 4 is a suitable number of clusters for our dataset. For a more detailed analysis, both values could be evaluated further, but for simplicity, we will proceed with **3 clusters** for our next steps, which include performing K-means clustering with this number of clusters and visualizing the results.

```
# Choose the number of clusters (for example, 3) based on the elbow plot
kmeans = KMeans(n_clusters=3, random_state=42)
clusters = kmeans.fit_predict(scaled_features)

# Adding cluster information to the DataFrame
df['Cluster'] = clusters

# Plotting the clusters
plt.figure(figsize=(10, 6))
colors = ['blue', 'green', 'red']
for i in range(3):
    plt.scatter(df[df['Cluster'] == i]['Temperature (°C)'],df[df
['Cluster'] == i]['Rainfall (mm)'], label=f'Cluster {i}', c=colors[i])
plt.title('Environmental Conditions Clustering')
plt.xlabel('Temperature (°C)')
plt.ylabel('Rainfall (mm)')
plt.legend()
plt.grid(True)
plt.show()
```

Introduction to Machine Learning

The K-means clustered result is shown in *Figure* 3.16.

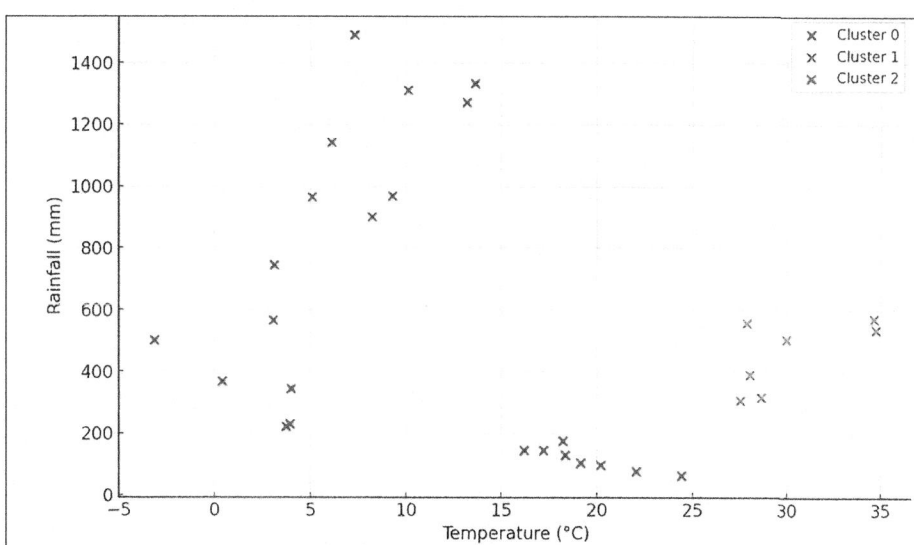

Figure 3.16: *K-means Clustered Result*

Figure 3.16 shows the distribution of locations across clusters. We can interpret the clusters as follows:

- **Cluster 0 (Blue)**: This is the largest cluster with 15 locations. It seems to represent areas with moderate temperatures and a wide range of rainfall, potentially indicative of temperate regions with varying levels of precipitation.

- **Cluster 1 (Green)**: Consisting of seven locations, this cluster might represent areas with higher temperatures and moderate to high rainfall, suggesting warm and wet climates, possibly tropical or subtropical regions.

- **Cluster 2 (Red)**: This cluster includes eight locations and appears to capture areas with lower rainfall and a range of temperatures, possibly indicating dryer climates or regions where precipitation is less common.

These clusters could serve various applications, such as ecological research, environmental monitoring, or regional planning, by helping to categorize locations based on their average temperature and rainfall characteristics.

Hierarchical Clustering

Hierarchical clustering stands out as a versatile and insightful method within the domain of unsupervised learning, offering a unique approach to understanding and visualizing the intrinsic groupings within a dataset. Unlike partitioning methods such as K-means, which require the number of clusters to be specified in advance, hierarchical clustering creates a dendrogram, or tree-like diagram as shown in *Figure*

3.17, that illustrates the arrangement and relationship of the clusters at every level of hierarchy. This method operates under two primary strategies: agglomerative, which is a bottom-up approach starting with each data point as a single cluster and merging them step by step; and divisive, a top-down approach that begins with all points in a single cluster and progressively divides them into smaller clusters.

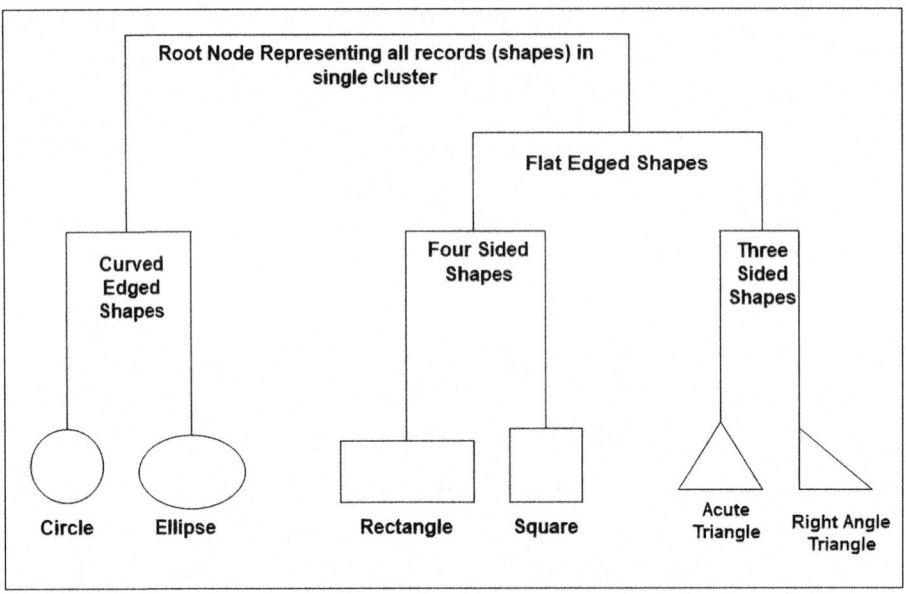

Figure 3.17: *Dendrogram Representation of Hierarchical Clustering*

However, hierarchical clustering's flexibility and depth come with computational challenges, particularly with large datasets. The complexity of the algorithm, especially in the agglomerative case, can lead to significant computational demands as the number of pairwise comparisons grows exponentially with the size of the dataset. Despite this, the method's ability to produce a nested series of partitions makes it invaluable for applications where the relationship between clusters is as important as the clusters themselves.

In practice, the choice between agglomerative and divisive approaches, as well as the selection of a distance metric (such as Euclidean, Manhattan, or cosine similarity), can significantly impact the results of hierarchical clustering. This requires careful consideration and experimentation to align with the specific goals and characteristics of the data being analyzed. Ultimately, hierarchical clustering serves as a powerful tool for data scientists seeking to uncover the layered complexities within their data, offering both the granularity and flexibility needed to navigate the multifaceted landscapes of unsupervised learning.

We shall perform agglomerative clustering to the same environmental dataset used for the earlier K-means clustering analysis.

Introduction to Machine Learning

```
from scipy.cluster.hierarchy import dendrogram, linkage
import matplotlib.pyplot as plt
import seaborn as sns
from sklearn.cluster import AgglomerativeClustering
# Using the scaled features for clustering
# Note: Excluding the LocationID since it is not part of the features to
cluster
X_cluster = scaled_features
# Perform Agglomerative Clustering with the 'ward' linkage method
# 'ward' minimizes the variance of clusters being merged.
agg_clustering = AgglomerativeClustering(n_clusters=3, affinity='
euclidean', linkage='ward')
clusters_agg = agg_clustering.fit_predict(scaled_features)
# Add the cluster labels to the original data
scaled_data_with_clusters['AggCluster'] = clusters_agg
# Plotting the dendrogram
linked = linkage(X_cluster, 'ward')
plt.figure(figsize=(10, 7))
dendrogram(linked,
           orientation='top',
           distance_sort='descending',
           show_leaf_counts=True)
plt.title('Dendrogram for Agglomerative Clustering')
plt.xlabel('Sample index')
plt.ylabel('Distance')
plt.show()
```

The Dendrogram for Agglomerative Clustering is shown in *Figure 3.18*.

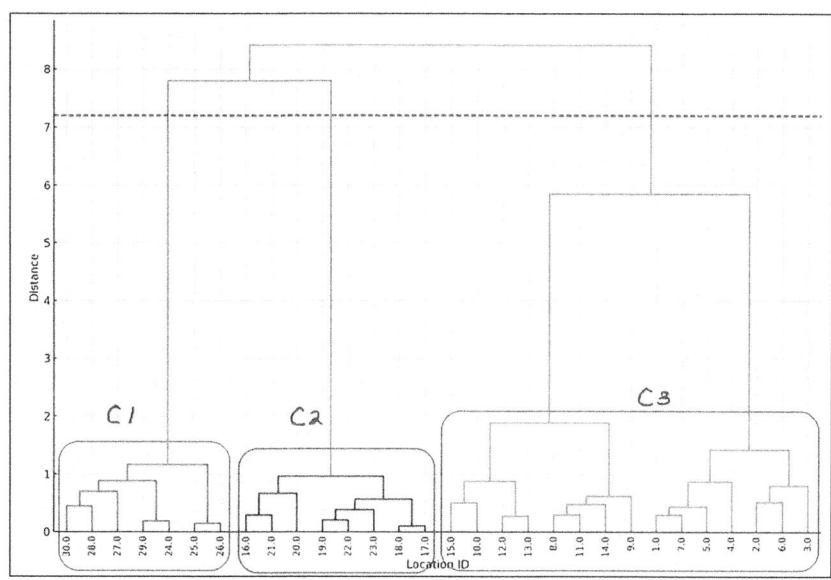

Figure 3.18: *Dendrogram for Agglomerative Clustering*

The beauty of hierarchical clustering lies in its ability to provide a detailed view of the data's structure, revealing not just the clusters but also how closely they are related to each other. The dendrogram output as shown in *Figure 3.18* is particularly informative, offering a visual representation of the clustering process and the hierarchical relationships between clusters. We could observe three clusters 'c1,' 'c2,' and 'c3' and their sub-clusters as well. This sub-cluster investigation is possible in hierarchical clustering, whereas K-means clustering is a flat approach. Also, we could notice the sub-clusters of 'c3' are a bit heterogeneous when compared to their counterparts 'c1' and 'c2.' This is also evident from the following scatter plot as shown in *Figure 3.19*, where 'c3' is a loosely packed cluster and marked as Label-0. This feature makes it an excellent tool for exploratory data analysis, where understanding the data's underlying structure is as crucial as the clustering itself.

```
# Scatter plot of Temperature vs. Rainfall colored by Agglomerative
Clusters
plt.figure(figsize=(10, 7))
sns.scatterplot(x='Temperature (°C)', y='Rainfall (mm)', hue='
AggCluster', data=scaled_data_with_clusters, palette='viridis',
alpha=0.6, s=100, edgecolor='k')
plt.title('Temperature vs. Rainfall - Clustered (Agglomerative
Clustering)')
plt.xlabel('Temperature (°C) - Scaled')
plt.ylabel('Rainfall (mm) - Scaled')
plt.legend(title='Cluster')
plt.show()
```

The scatter plot of records succeeding agglomerative clustering is shown in *Figure 3.19*.

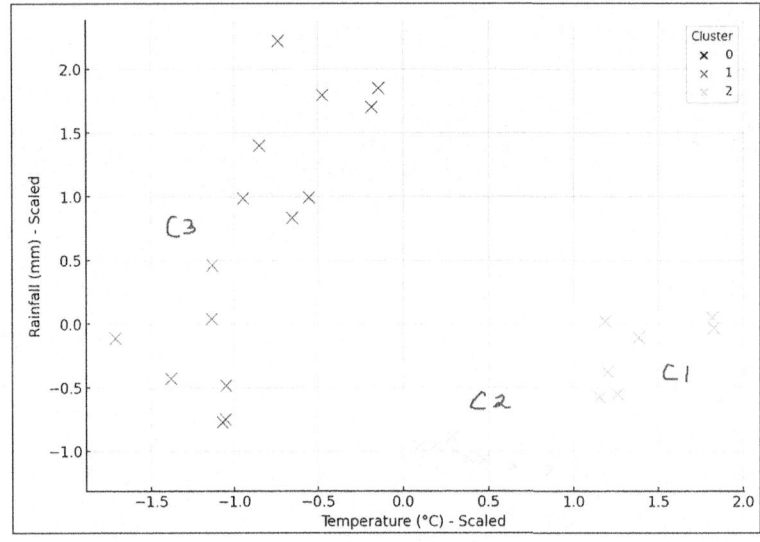

Figure 3.19: *Scatter Plot of Records Succeeding Agglomerative Clustering*

Beyond the well-trodden paths of K-means and hierarchical clustering, there exist less commonly explored yet equally fascinating clustering techniques such as Density-Based Spatial Clustering of Applications with Noise (DBSCAN) and spectral clustering. DBSCAN, for instance, excels in identifying clusters of arbitrary shapes by focusing on the density of data points, setting it apart from methods that assume spherical clusters. It is particularly adept at handling noise and outlier data, making it a robust choice for real-world datasets that defy neat categorization. Spectral clustering, on the other hand, takes a graph-based approach, using the eigenvectors of a similarity matrix to reduce dimensionality prior to applying traditional clustering techniques. This method shines in scenarios where the relationship between data points is best captured through their connectivity, offering an elegant solution to clustering non-convex shapes.

While these techniques might not boast the widespread popularity of K-means or hierarchical clustering, their unique strengths and capabilities make them invaluable tools in the data scientist's arsenal, especially for tasks where more conventional methods falter. Their relatively lower profile belies their potential to tackle complex clustering challenges with finesse, underscoring the rich diversity of strategies available in the pursuit of uncovering meaningful patterns in data.

Introduction to Supervised Learning

As discussed earlier, supervised learning involves training a model on a labeled dataset, where each training example is paired with an output label. The model's task is to learn the mapping from inputs to outputs, using this knowledge to predict the labels of new, unseen data. This process mirrors the way a student learns under the guidance of a teacher, with the labeled data providing clear examples of what the correct output should appear as for given inputs. Supervised learning's strength lies in its ability to apply these learned patterns to new data, making it incredibly powerful for a wide range of predictive tasks, from email filtering to medical diagnosis. Within the domain of supervised learning, two primary model types emerge: Regression and Classification models. Each serves a distinct purpose and operates under different paradigms of prediction.

Regression Models

Regression models stand as pivotal tools in the world of supervised learning, designed with the capability to predict continuous variables. These models find their strength in scenarios where the task at hand is to quantify an outcome – for example, estimating the selling price of homes based on their size, location, and other features, or predicting the daily temperature from historical weather data. The essence of regression lies in its ability to provide precise numerical values as predictions, making it indispensable for a wide array of applications where the objective is to forecast quantities that change fluidly and span a wide range.

At the core of regression analysis is the development of a mathematical model that captures the relationship between the dependent variable (the outcome we aim to predict) and one or more independent variables (the input features). This relationship is quantified in such a way that, given the values of input features, the model can accurately predict the outcome variable. Techniques range from simple linear regression, which assumes a straight-line relationship between inputs and outputs, to more complex forms such as polynomial and logistic regression, which can model non-linear relationships and are capable of handling a broader spectrum of real-world scenarios. The power of regression models lies not just in prediction but also in their ability to provide insights into which factors most significantly impact the outcome, offering valuable clues for decision-making processes.

The application of regression models transcends numerous fields and industries, from finance, where they predict stock prices, to healthcare, forecasting patient outcomes based on clinical data. Each use case benefits from the model's ability to dissect and utilize the intricate patterns hidden within the data, transforming raw information into precise estimates. As we delve deeper into the specific methodologies and technologies that enable these predictions in subsequent chapters, the foundational understanding of regression as a tool for quantitative prediction sets the stage for exploring its vast potential. By equipping readers with this knowledge, we pave the way for not only leveraging regression models in practical applications but also for appreciating the nuanced interplay between data and prediction in the broader context of machine learning.

Classification Models

Classification models represent a fundamental aspect of supervised learning, distinguished by their ability to categorize input data into discrete classes. Unlike regression models, which predict continuous outcomes, classification models deal with binary or multi-class outcomes, such as determining whether an email is spam or not, or diagnosing whether a medical scan indicates the presence of a malignant or benign tumor. This capability to discern and assign categorical labels to data makes classification models particularly valuable in scenarios requiring clear-cut decisions. The process involves analyzing the input features to predict which category or class the new data belongs to, facilitating critical decisions across various domains, from cyber security to healthcare.

At the heart of classification lies the intricacy of dividing data into distinct groups based on learned patterns from training data. This involves algorithms learning from pre-labeled examples, enabling them to apply these learned distinctions to new, unseen data. Techniques employed in classification range from simpler algorithms, such as logistic regression and decision trees, to more complex ones such as support vector machines and neural networks. Each of these algorithms brings its own strengths to the table, whether it be the interpretability of decision trees or the robustness of neural networks in handling complex patterns. The choice of algorithm often hinges on the specific nature of the data and the task at hand, highlighting the importance of understanding the underlying principles that guide these models.

The wide applicability of classification models is evident in their use across a spectrum of real-world applications. From filtering spam in our inboxes to enhancing customer segmentation in marketing strategies, and from fraud detection in financial transactions to aiding in critical medical diagnoses, the impact of classification models is profound. They not only automate the process of decision-making but also increase the accuracy and efficiency of these decisions, leveraging the vast amounts of data available today.

A more detailed exploration of both regression and classification models will be presented in subsequent chapters. There, we will delve into the intricacies of developing and fine-tuning these models, covering a range of techniques from linear regression to complex neural networks for regression tasks, and from logistic regression to neural network models for classification challenges. The upcoming chapters will provide a comprehensive guide to understanding, implementing, and leveraging these models for real-world applications, ensuring readers are well-equipped to tackle both quantitative and qualitative predictive tasks with confidence.

Introduction to ML Model Evaluation Method and Metrics

The evaluation of machine learning models is a crucial step in the model development process, providing insights into their performance and guiding the improvement of future models. Model evaluation methods and metrics are the tools that help data scientists understand the efficacy of their models in making accurate predictions or classifications. These metrics not only shed light on how well a model has learned from the training data but also predict its behavior on unseen data, ensuring that the model is both effective and reliable.

For regression models, evaluation metrics focus on quantifying the error between the predicted values and the actual values. Common metrics include Mean Absolute Error (MAE), Mean Squared Error (MSE), and Root Mean Squared Error (RMSE). MAE measures the average magnitude of errors in a set of predictions, without considering their direction. MSE, on the other hand, squares the errors prior to averaging them, penalizing larger errors more severely than smaller ones. RMSE takes the square root of MSE, scaling the error back to the original units of the output variable, making it easier to interpret. These metrics provide a clear sense of the model's accuracy in predicting quantitative outcomes.

In the realm of classification models, the evaluation focuses on how effectively the model can categorize data points. Accuracy is the simplest metric, measuring the proportion of correctly predicted instances out of all predictions made. However, in cases where the data is imbalanced, precision, recall, and the F1 score offer a more nuanced view. Precision assesses the model's ability to identify only the relevant objects, while recall evaluates how well the model can find all relevant cases within a dataset. The F1 score harmonizes precision and recall, providing a single metric that balances the two.

Beyond these basic metrics, advanced techniques such as Receiver Operating Characteristic (ROC) curves and Area Under the Curve (AUC) offer deeper insights into classification model performance, especially for binary classification problems. These methods consider the trade-offs between true positive rates and false positive rates, offering a comprehensive view of model performance across different threshold settings. Understanding and applying the appropriate evaluation metrics is vital for refining machine learning models, ensuring they meet the desired standards of accuracy and applicability. As the field of machine learning continues to evolve, so will the methods and metrics for model evaluation, adapting to new challenges and complexities in model development.

As we have introduced various model evaluation methods and metrics, it is important to note that the detailed exploration of these concepts, including their formulas and numerical examples, awaits in the forthcoming chapters. To enrich your understanding and application skills, we will delve into the intricacies of these metrics, supported by Python codes that bring these abstract concepts to life. This hands-on approach will not only demystify the underlying mathematics but also provide you with practical tools to assess and improve your machine learning models effectively. So, stay tuned for more interesting calculations and code-based demonstrations that promise to deepen your comprehension of machine learning model evaluation, making you well-equipped to tackle real-world data science challenges.

Conclusion

In this chapter, we navigated through the landscapes of machine learning models, examining the key components that underpin these technologies: features, labels, and the models themselves. Through practical use cases illustrated with Python programming, we peeled back the layers of data pre-processing and cleaning, as well as exploratory data analysis, demonstrating the critical role these processes play in preparing data for ML modeling. The chapter also introduced the realms of unsupervised learning with different clustering techniques with Python examples, offering insights into the techniques for uncovering hidden patterns within data,

Introduction to Machine Learning

and provided a brief introduction to supervised learning, highlighting the distinction between regression and classification models. Lastly, we touched upon the crucial aspect of ML model evaluation methods and metrics, preparing the ground for more detailed discussions in subsequent chapters.

In the next chapter, we will explore the fundamentals of Regression and Classification models, understanding their role in predictive analytics.

Practice Exercises

1. Calculate the mean, median, and mode of the following dataset representing the number of features in various machine learning models: [10, 12, 10, 15, 18, 10, 12, 20, 25, 10].

2. A dataset has a feature X with the following values: [2, 4, 4, 4, 5, 5, 7, 9]. Calculate the variance and standard deviation of this feature.

3. Given a dataset shown in *Figure* 3.20 with missing values, write a Python code snippet to handle these missing values by replacing them with the mean of the respective column.

Feature1	Feature2
1	NaN
2	2
NaN	3
4	4
5	5

Figure 3.20: Contrived Dataset with Missing Values

4. A dataset contains the ages of individuals in a group: [25, 30, 35, 40, 45, 50, 55, 60, 65, 70]. Calculate the range, interquartile range (IQR), and the standard deviation of the ages.

5. Perform a Z-score normalization on the following dataset: [50, 60, 70, 80, 90].

6. Given the following 2D data points: (1, 2), (2, 2), (3, 4), (5, 6), and (8, 8), perform the first iteration of the K-Means algorithm with K=2. Assume initial centroids are (1, 2) and (5, 6). Assign each point to the nearest centroid and calculate the new centroids.

7. Calculate the silhouette score for the following clustering of 5 data points into 2 clusters: Cluster 1: (1, 2), (2, 2), Cluster 2: (3, 4), (5, 6), (8, 8). The average intra-cluster distance for Cluster 1 is 1, and for Cluster 2 is 3. The average inter-cluster distance between points in Cluster 1 and Cluster 2 is 5.

8. A dataset is clustered using K-Means into three clusters with the following cluster centroids: C1 = (2, 3), C2 = (5, 7), C3 = (8, 9). Calculate the Euclidean distance between each centroid pair.

9. Perform a single iteration of agglomerative hierarchical clustering with the following points: (1, 1), (2, 1), (4, 3), (5, 4), (8, 8). Use the single-linkage method and describe the clusters succeeding the first merge.

10. Discuss various techniques for handling missing data during EDA. Provide examples of situations where each technique might be most appropriate.

Answers

1. Mean=14.2, Median=11 and Mode=10

2. Mean=5, Variance=4 and SD = 2

3. ```
   import pandas as pd
   import numpy as np
   # Sample dataset
   data = {'Feature1': [1, 2, np.nan, 4, 5], 'Feature2': [np.nan, 2, 3, 4, 5]}
   df = pd.DataFrame(data)
   # Replacing missing values with mean
   df.fillna(df.mean(), inplace=True)
   ```
   print(df)

4. Range = 45, Q1=35, Q3=55, IQR = Q3-Q1 = 20, SD=14.36

5. Mean=70, SD=14.14, Normalized values = [-1.41,-0.71, 0, 0.71, 1.41]

6. Initial Centroids: C1 = (1, 2), C2 = (5, 6)

   Distance calculations:

   Point (1, 2) to C1: 0, to C2: 5.66 (closer to C1)

   Point (2, 2) to C1: 1, to C2: 5 (closer to C1)

   Point (3, 4) to C1: 2.83, to C2: 3.61 (closer to C2)

   Point (5, 6) to C1: 5, to C2: 0 (closer to C2)

   Point (8, 8) to C1: 9.22, to C2: 4.47 (closer to C2)

   New Centroids: For C1: Mean of (1, 2) and (2, 2) = (1.5, 2)

   For C2: Mean of (3, 4), (5, 6), and (8, 8) = (5.33, 6)

7. For Cluster 1 points: (5-1)/5=0.8, For Cluster 2 points: 5-3/5=0.4, similarly for all data points and compute the average.
   ```

Average of scores = (0.8+0.8+0.4+0.4+0.45)/5=0.56

8. Distance between C1 and C2: 5, Distance between C1 and C3: 8.49, Distance between C2 and C3:3.61

9. Initial distances Between (1, 1) and (2, 1): 1, Between (4, 3) and (5, 4): 1.41, Smallest distance: 1

   Merge (1, 1) and (2, 1): New clusters: {(1, 1), (2, 1)}, {(4, 3)}, {(5, 4)}, {(8, 8)}

   Update distances considering the single-linkage method.

10. Removing rows with any missing values.

    Appropriate When: The dataset is large, and the proportion of missing data is small. For example, removing rows with missing values in a survey dataset with over 10,000 responses.

    Mean/Median/Mode Imputation: Replacing missing values with the mean, median, or mode of the column.

    Appropriate When: The data is missing at random and the proportion of missing values is low. For example, imputing missing test scores with the average score in a student performance dataset.

    K-Nearest Neighbors (KNN) Imputation: Replacing missing values based on the mean or median of the k-nearest neighbors.

    Appropriate When: The dataset is small to medium-sized, and there are patterns in the data that can be captured by the neighbors.

Multiple Choice Questions

1. What does 'supervised learning' refer to in machine learning?
   a. Models that are explicitly programmed to perform a task
   b. Models that learn from unlabeled data
   c. Models that learn from labeled data
   d. Models that operate without any data

2. In the context of machine learning, what are 'features'?
   a. The label we want to predict
   b. The algorithm used for modeling
   c. The individual measurable properties used as input
   d. The final model created subsequent to training

3. Which Python library is commonly used for data manipulation and analysis?

    a. TensorFlow

    b. PyTorch

    c. Pandas

    d. Keras

4. What is the main purpose of Exploratory Data Analysis (EDA)?

    a. To train the final model

    b. To test the model's performance

    c. To understand and summarize the main characteristics of the data

    d. To deploy the model into production

5. Which algorithm is an example of unsupervised learning?

    a. Linear Regression

    b. Decision Trees

    c. K-Means Clustering

    d. Logistic Regression

6. Which of the following is NOT a typical step in data preprocessing?

    a. Normalization

    b. Dimensionality reduction

    c. Hyperparameter tuning

    d. Handling missing values

7. What does 'unsupervised learning' refer to in machine learning?

    a. Models that learn without a specific task in mind

    b. Models that learn from unlabeled data to find patterns

    c. Models that require human supervision

    d. Models that are not based on data.

8. What does the Interquartile Range (IQR) measure in statistics?

    a. The range between the 1st quartile and the 3rd quartile in a dataset

    b. The total range of the dataset

c. The range between the minimum and maximum values

d. The variance of the dataset

9. In the context of data visualization, what does a scatter plot best illustrate?

   a. The distribution of a single variable

   b. The relationship between two numeric variables

   c. The comparison of quantitative data across categories

   d. The frequency of categorical data

10. Which type of visualization would be best to compare the number of sales across different regions?

    a. Scatter plot

    b. Boxplot

    c. Barplot

    d. Histogram

11. What statistical concept is used to define outliers in a boxplot?

    a. Standard deviation from the mean

    b. Distance from the median

    c. Number of occurrences below the 1st quartile

    d. Distance greater than 1.5 times the IQR from the quartiles

12. What is the primary purpose of using the Elbow Method in K-means clustering?

    a. To determine the optimal number of clusters

    b. To calculate the distance between clusters

    c. To choose the initial centroids

    d. To reduce the dimensionality of the dataset

13. Which of the following is a common distance metric used in hierarchical clustering?

    a. Manhattan distance

    b. Cosine similarity

    c. Euclidean distance

    d. All of the above

14. During the hierarchical clustering process, what does the term 'agglomerative' refer to?

    a. Dividing a large cluster into smaller clusters

    b. Combining small clusters into larger ones

    c. Assigning points randomly to different clusters

    d. Calculating distances between clusters using centroids

15. Why might you use a dendrogram in hierarchical clustering?

    a. To identify the optimal number of clusters by observing the longest vertical line not crossed by any horizontal lines

    b. To represent the number of iterations needed to converge

    c. To show the distribution of data points within each cluster

    d. To calculate the centroids of each cluster

Answers

1. c
2. c
3. c
4. c
5. c
6. c
7. b
8. a
9. b
10. c
11. d
12. a
13. d
14. b
15. a

Keywords

- Machine Learning
- Supervised Learning
- Unsupervised Learning
- Linear Models
- Non-Linear Models
- Features (Input Variables)
- Labels (Output Variables)
- Training Data
- Prediction
- Descriptive Statistics
- Data Visualization
- Correlation
- Python Libraries (for example, Matplotlib, Seaborn)
- Clustering
- K-Means
- Hierarchical Clustering
- Regression Analysis
- Classification
- Cross-Validation

References

1. https://www.kaggle.com/code/snanilim/video-games-sales-analysis-and-visualization

CHAPTER 4
Regression Versus Classification Model

Introduction

This chapter serves as a guide through the distinctive landscapes of these two fundamental approaches in ML modeling such as Regression and Classification models, illuminating the subtle yet crucial differences that set them apart. We start our journey with Linear Regression, venturing into the realm of predicting continuous numerical outcomes. Here, readers will gain insights into the mathematical underpinnings that enable the prediction of quantitative values, from housing prices to temperature forecasts. The narrative then shifts to Logistic Regression, steering us into the world of classification. This segment unveils how models categorize inputs into discrete classes, such as identifying whether an email is spam or not, showcasing the power of machine learning in decision-making scenarios.

Further enriching this exploration, we delve into the Gradient Descent Learning Approach, an optimization technique that lies at the heart of training both regression and classification models. By unpacking this fundamental process, the chapter aims to demystify how models iteratively adjust to minimize errors and enhance accuracy. Bridging theory with practice, we provide readers with hands-on Python implementations, empowering them to apply these concepts in tangible coding exercises. Lastly, the chapter concludes by examining performance evaluation metrics, equipping readers with the tools to assess and refine the effectiveness of their models. Through this comprehensive journey, this chapter aims to not only elucidate the technical intricacies of regression and classification models but also to highlight their practical applications, guiding readers towards mastering these essential machine learning techniques.

Structure

In this chapter, we're going to cover the following main topics:

- Linear Regression
- Gradient Descent Learning
- Implementation of Multiple Linear Regression in Python
- Logistic Regression as a Classifier Model
- Implementation of Logistic Regression Model in Python
- Limitations of Linear Models and Assumptions
- Model Evaluation Techniques and Different Performance Metrics

Linear Regression

Linear Regression stands as one of the most fundamental and widely used statistical methods in machine learning, aimed at predicting a continuous variable. **Francis Galton**, a British polymath often referred to as the father of Biostatistics, lays the groundwork for the concept of regression analysis, hinting at its potential to predict outcomes based on observable characteristics.

Another renowned statistician called **George E.P. Box**, who served as a Director of the Statistical Research Group, at Princeton University famously said, "*All models are wrong, but some are useful.*" This quote, while not exclusively about Linear Regression, speaks volumes about the nature of statistical modeling, including Linear Regression. It acknowledges that while no mathematical model perfectly captures the complexities of the real world, models such as Linear Regression can still provide valuable insights and predictions.

These perspectives from pioneers in the field highlight Linear Regression's fundamental role in statistical analysis and its enduring value in extracting meaningful information from data. Despite its simplicity, Linear Regression serves as a critical tool for understanding relationships between variables and making informed predictions, a testament to its foundational status in the landscape of machine learning and AI.

Mathematical Definitions

At its core, Linear Regression models the relationship between a dependent variable, Y, and one or more independent variables, X, assuming that the relationship can be described by a straight line. Mathematically, this relationship is often represented as follows:

$$Y = \beta_0 + \beta_1 X_1 + \varepsilon$$

Where β_0 is the intercept, β_1 is the slope of the line (indicating the weight of the independent variable), and ε is the error term, accounting for the variance not explained by the model.

Imagine you're curious about how different amounts of water, sunlight exposure, type of soil, and manure affect the growth of a particular plant species. In this scenario, the amount of sunlight (in hours/ per day), water (liters/per day), manure (grams/per day), and soil type (categorical variable) serve as the independent variables (X), and the plant's height (in centimeters) is the dependent variable (Y). By incorporating these variables into a Multiple Linear Regression model, we can create a more comprehensive model that predicts plant growth based on a combination of these factors. The model could take the form of,

$$\text{Plant Growth} = \beta_0 + \beta_1(\text{sunlight}) + \beta_2(\text{water}) + \beta_3(\text{soil Type}) + \beta_4(\text{manure}) + \varepsilon$$

The aforementioned expression indicates the Multiple Linear Regression model, on the other hand if the output variable depends on single independent variable, we shall call that model as a simple Linear Regression model. Here, β_0 represents the intercept, β_1, β_2, β_3, and β_4 are coefficients that represent the slope or weight of each predictor (independent variable) in the model, and ε is the error term as mentioned earlier in the definition.

The aforementioned example illustrates the complexity and interplay of various environmental factors on plant growth. By adjusting the amounts of water and manure, as well as selecting the appropriate soil type and optimizing sunlight exposure, one could theoretically predict and enhance the growth of the plant using the insights gained from the Multiple Linear Regression model. The coefficients indicate how much a unit increase in any predictor variable is expected to increase the plant's growth, holding all other variables constant.

Let us assign hypothetical values to the coefficients in our Multiple Linear Regression model for plant growth to illustrate how each predictor variable affects plant growth, holding other variables constant. Assume our model, succeeding analysis, provides the following equation,

$$\text{Plant Growth (cm)} = 2 + 0.5(\text{sunlight}) + 1.2(\text{water}) - 0.8(\text{soil type}) + 0.3(\text{manure})$$

Interpreting the Coefficients

The intercept ($\beta_0 = 2$) suggests that, in the absence of any of the predictors (sunlight, water, manure, and assuming sandy soil as it would be encoded as 0), the basic growth of the plant we might expect is 2 cm.

The coefficient for sunlight ($\beta_1 = 0.5$) indicates that for each additional hour of sunlight, holding all other variables constant, the plant's growth is expected to increase by 0.5 cm.

The coefficient for water (β_2=1.2) means that for every additional liter of water provided per day, the plant's growth is expected to increase by 1.2 cm, assuming sunlight, soil type, and manure quantities remain unchanged.

The coefficient for soil type (β_3=-0.8) shows a slightly more complex relationship. Moving from sandy to loamy soil (0 to 1) or loamy to clay soil (1 to 2) would decrease the expected plant growth by 0.8 cm, all else being equal. This could suggest that sandy soil (encoded as 0, thus not contributing to the decrease) is most conducive to growth in this hypothetical scenario, possibly due to better drainage or other factors not explicitly modeled.

Lastly, the coefficient for manure (β_4=0.3) suggests that for every additional gram of manure used per day, plant growth increases by 0.3 cm, holding other factors steady.

This example underscores the interpretive power of Multiple Linear Regression coefficients, offering insights into how varying each predictor within the context of a controlled experimental setting where other variables are kept constant can influence the outcome variable, and in this case, the growth of the plant. Also, this model not only aids in understanding the factors affecting plant growth but also in making informed decisions to optimize conditions for healthy plants.

Gradient Descent Learning

Gradient Descent Learning is a cornerstone optimization algorithm in machine learning, pivotal for refining model coefficients toward the closest target values. At its core, Gradient Descent iteratively adjusts the parameters of a model in order to minimize a given cost function, such as the Mean Squared Error in Linear Regression. This process begins with the selection of random initial values for the parameters, followed by successive adjustments made in the direction that most steeply reduces the cost function.

The fundamental nature of Gradient Descent is rooted in its capacity to traverse the intricate terrain of the cost function. It utilizes the gradient, a mathematical instrument indicating the direction of its course toward the lowest point, where the cost function reaches its minimal value.

The operation of Gradient Descent is characterized by two key concepts: the learning rate and the gradient itself. The learning rate determines the size of the steps taken towards the minimum of the cost function. A carefully chosen learning rate is crucial; too large a step can overshoot the minimum, while too small a step can result in a protracted journey toward the optimal parameters, significantly slowing down the learning process. The gradient, on the other hand, provides the direction for each step. By calculating the gradient of the cost function with respect to each parameter, Gradient Descent ensures that each adjustment is informed and purposeful, effectively navigating the parameter space.

Figure 4.1: *Picture Illustrating a Path Down a Hilly Terrain*

The illustration shown in *Figure* 4.1 captures a path down a hilly terrain, symbolizing the journey of finding the minimal value of the cost function in the complex landscape of machine learning.

Mathematics of Gradient Calculation

In this subsection, we delve into the mathematics underpinning the calculation of gradients, a pivotal step in the Gradient Descent Learning algorithm, using a simplified dataset to elucidate the process. This demonstration will focus on Full Batch Gradient Descent, a variation of the algorithm that utilizes the entire dataset to compute the gradient and update model parameters in each iteration.

Gradient calculation is the process by which we determine the direction and magnitude of the steps taken toward minimizing the cost function. For a regression model with parameters β_0 (intercept) and β_1 (slope), the gradient calculations with respect to these parameters are crucial for understanding how to update them. The partial derivative of the cost function with respect to β_0 tells us how the cost function changes with changes in the intercept, while the partial derivative with respect to β_1 does the same for the slope.

Regression Versus Classification Model

Mathematically, for a Mean Squared Error (MSE) cost function, the gradients are given by:

$$\frac{\partial \text{MSE}}{\partial \beta_0} = -\frac{1}{n}\sum_{i=1}^{n}(Y_i - (\beta_0 + \beta_1 x_i))$$

$$\frac{\partial \text{MSE}}{\partial \beta_1} = -\frac{1}{n}\sum_{i=1}^{n}(Y_i - (\beta_0 + \beta_1 x_i))x_i$$

Where n is the number of training records, Y_i is the actual value, and x_i is the input feature value for the ith record.

Demonstration of Gradient Descent Learning with Contrived Data

Let us consider a tiny dataset with just three records for ease of calculation:

X (Feature)	Y (Actual Output Values)
2	5
5	12
7	15

Table 4.1: *Contrived Tiny Dataset*

Table 4.1 outlines a tiny contrived dataset with values for X and Y. We will consider a simple linear regression model of the form $\hat{Y} = \beta_0 + \beta_1 * X$. Let us initialize random values for the coefficients β_0 and β_1, specifically 1 and 3, respectively.

Predicted Y using the assumed initial coefficients:

- For x=2, $\hat{Y}=1+3\times2=7$
- For x=5, $\hat{Y}=1+3\times5=16$
- For x=7, $\hat{Y}=1+3\times7=22$

The objective of gradient descent is to find the values of β_0 and β_1 that minimize the cost function, which we will define as the Sum Squared Error (SSE) with a scaling factor (1/2) for mathematical convenience.

$$\text{SSE} = \frac{1}{2}\sum_{i=1}^{n}(Y_i - \hat{Y}_i)^2$$

From the earlier section we know the error gradient of β_0 and β_1 are given as follows:

$$\frac{\partial_{\text{SSE}}}{\partial_{\beta_0}} = -(Y - \hat{Y})$$

$$\frac{\partial_{SSE}}{\partial_{\beta_1}} = -(Y - \hat{Y}) * X$$

Plugging in our values to get sum of the error gradients, since we have considered full batch gradient descent learning for this illustration, however for stochastic gradient descent we need to substitute the individual error gradient of each training record for the coefficient update.

$$\frac{\partial_{SSE}}{\partial_{\beta_0}} = -[(5-7) + (12-16) + (15-22)] = -[-2 -4 - 7] = 13$$

$$\frac{\partial_{SSE}}{\partial_{\beta_1}} = -[(5-7)*2 + (12-16)*5 + (15-22)*7] = -[-4 -20 - 49] = 73$$

Also, we shall calculate the total SSE before updating the coefficients with the calculated error gradients.

$$SSE = [(-2)^2 + (-4)^2 + (-7)^2] = [4+16+49] = [69] = 34.5$$

Now we are going to update the randomly initialized coefficients using gradient descent update rule, where α is the learning rate to control the size of the update step.

$$\beta_{0new} = \beta_{0old} - \alpha_*$$
$$\beta_{1new} = \beta_{1old} - \alpha_*$$

To update the coefficients using the calculated error gradients, we shall assume the learning rate (α) as 0.01 for this illustrative example.

$$\beta_{0new} = 1 - 0.01 \times 13 = 0.87$$

$$\beta_{1new} = 3 - 0.01 \times 73 = 2.27$$

Now, we shall predict Y with the updated coefficients:

- For $x=2$, $\hat{Y} = 0.87 + 2.27 \times 2 = 5.41$
- For $x=5$, $\hat{Y} = 0.87 + 2.27 \times 5 = 12.22$
- For $x=7$, $\hat{Y} = 0.87 + 2.27 \times 7 = 16.76$

We shall re-calculate the total SSE with the updated predictions,

$$SSE = [(5-5.41)^2 + (12-12.22)^2 + (15-16.76)^2] = [(-0.41)^2 + (-0.22)^2 + (-1.76)^2]$$

$$= [3.3141] = 1.65705$$

We could notice, that the predictions are much closer to the actual Y values than the initial predictions were. The overall SSE has also reduced significantly from the original calculation (which had a much larger SSE = 34.5 due to starting with random coefficients), showing that our model is improving and getting better at predicting the actual outcome. This indicates that the gradient descent optimization is working effectively to minimize the error between the predicted and actual values.

The process would be repeated with updated coefficients until the SSE no longer decreases significantly, indicating convergence to a minimum.

Implementation of Multiple Linear Regression in Python

In this section, we will immerse ourselves in the practical implementation of Multiple Linear Regression (MLR) using Python, an advanced leap from the handwork exercise of single-variable linear models to multiple predictors. Multiple linear regression allows us to unravel the influence of several independent variables on a single dependent variable, capturing the complex interplay that often exists in real-world data.

By employing libraries such as NumPy or pandas for data manipulation and statsmodels or scikit-learn for model building, we can construct a multiple linear regression model that considers various factors simultaneously, offering a multidimensional view of the relationships within our dataset. Readers will learn how to prepare their dataset for multiple regression, select appropriate variables, and interpret the output to make meaningful inferences about their data.

Introducing the Use Case and Dataset

To illustrate the application of Multiple Linear Regression (MLR) within a Python environment, let us consider the Real Estate Valuation dataset from the University of California Irvine's Machine Learning Repository. The dataset, originating from the Sindian District in New Taipei City, Taiwan, encompasses historical data on real estate transactions. It serves as a detailed resource, capturing various elements that impact property values such as the age of buildings, their proximity to major transportation links such as MRT stations, accessibility to convenience stores, and specific geographical coordinates.

Let us start by loading and examining the contents of the dataset to understand what variables it includes. The dataset contains 414 entries with the following variables:

- **No**: A unique identifier for each transaction.
- **X1 Transaction Date**: The transaction date, formatted as a floating point number representing the year and month (for example, 2013.250=2013 March, 2013.500=2013 June, and so on).
- **X2 House Age**: The age of the house at the time of transaction, in years.

- **X3 Distance to the Nearest MRT Station**: The distance to the nearest Mass Rapid Transit (MRT) station, in meters.
- **X4 Number of Convenience Stores**: The number of convenience stores within walking distance.
- **X5 Latitude**: Geographic coordinate specifying the north-south position.
- **X6 Longitude**: Geographic coordinate specifying the east-west position.
- **Y House Price of Unit Area**: The house price per unit area. (10000 New Taiwan Dollars/Ping, where Ping is a local unit, 1 Ping = 3.3 meter squared)

Implementation in Python

We are going to build an MLR model to predict the House Price expressed in terms of '10,000 New Taiwan Dollars per Ping.' This unit reflects the local pricing conventions and area measurements used in Taiwan. Let us load the dataset in Python and display the head of the data to understand its structure as shown in *Figure 4.2*.

```
import pandas as pd
# Load the dataset
file_path = 'path_to_your_data/data1_Ch4_Real estate.csv'
real_estate_data = pd.read_csv(file_path)
# Drop the 'No' column which has no significance here
real_estate_data.drop('No', axis=1, inplace=True)
# Display the first five rows of the dataset
real_estate_data.head()
```

The following figure illustrates the head of the data showing all predictor variables and dependent variables:

Transaction Date	House Age	Distance to Nearest MRT Station	Number of Convenience Stores	Latitude	Longitude	House Price per Unit Area
2012.917	32.0	84.87882	10	24.98298	121.54024	37.9
2012.917	19.5	306.5947	9	24.98034	121.53951	42.2
2013.583	13.3	561.9845	5	24.98746	121.54391	47.3
2013.500	13.3	561.9845	5	24.98746	121.54391	54.8
2012.833	5.0	390.5684	5	24.97937	121.54245	43.1

Figure 4.2: Head of the Data Showing all Predictor Variables and Dependent Variables

We shall explore the descriptive summary of the data to understand the variable better. The transaction dates cover a period from approximately mid-2012 to mid-2013. We shall ignore this variable since it does not explain the Price and more over there is no practical relevance.

The age of the houses varies widely, from newly built properties to those that are nearly 44 years old. On average, the houses are around 18 years old, indicating a mix of relatively newer and older homes in the data. The nearest MRT station can be as close as 23 meters and as far as approximately 6.5 kilometers from the houses. The number of nearby convenience stores varies from none up to 10 stores within a convenient distance. On average, there are about 4 convenience stores close to the properties, providing a good level of accessibility to daily necessities.

Latitude Range extends from about 24.93 to 25.01, indicating a relatively narrow geographical spread from north to south. The Longitude Range spans from approximately 121.47 to 121.57, also showing a compact area from east to west. The properties are clustered around a latitude of 24.97 and a longitude of 121.53, which may suggest a concentrated urban area.

The price per unit area varies significantly, from as low as about 7.6 to a high of 117.5, indicating a broad spectrum of property values. The average price per unit area is around 38, reflecting the general market conditions and property values in the area.

Exploratory Data Analysis (EDA) on Real Estate Data

For the dataset concerning real estate prices, EDA involves a thorough investigation of the dataset to understand its characteristics, uncover underlying patterns, identify anomalies, and test assumptions. This specific dataset includes variables such as house age, distance to the nearest MRT station, number of convenience stores, latitude, longitude, and house price per unit area. By exploring these variables, we aim to identify key factors that influence the price of real estate, thereby guiding the selection of appropriate variables for inclusion in a regression model.

In the context of building a multiple linear regression model, EDA helps in assessing the relationships between the predictor variables and the response variable, which is the house price per unit area in this case. One critical aspect of EDA in this context is to check the linearity assumptions that underpin linear regression models. Linear regression assumes that there is a linear relationship between the dependent variable and each of the independent variables. By visualizing these relationships through scatter plots and correlation matrices, we can determine if linear regression is a suitable model or if transformations and more complex modeling strategies are needed. These analyses help in fine-tuning the model to better predict real estate prices, thereby providing valuable insights for investors and policymakers in the real estate market.

We shall begin with the exploration of the dependent variable and its distribution of prices using a histogram plot.

```
import matplotlib.pyplot as plt
import seaborn as sns
# Plot the distribution of the house price of unit area
plt.figure(figsize=(10, 6))
sns.histplot(real_estate_data ['Y house price of unit area'], kde=True,
color='blue')
plt.xlabel('House Price of Unit Area')
plt.ylabel('Frequency')
plt.grid(True)
plt.show()
```

The following figure illustrates the distribution of house price of unit area:

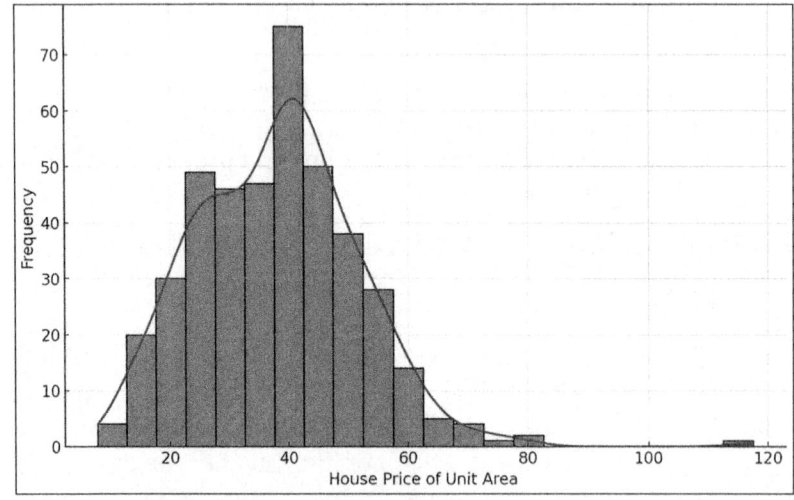

Figure 4.3: *Distribution of House Price of Unit Area*

The histogram shown in *Figure* 4.3 displays the distribution of the house price per unit area. The plot shows a near normal distribution with mild right-skewed distribution due to an outlier record with a 117.5 value, this value is about 4.75 IQRs above the first quartile. This further underscores the property's premium nature as it significantly exceeds the typical range of house prices observed in the dataset with very close proximity to an MRT station and the newer age of the property likely plays significant role in deeming this property as premium with high desirable geographical location. Since we are building a linear regression model and keeping this extreme value (outlier) in the dataset might affect model performance, hence we shall remove this record.

```
# Remove the outlier where the house price per unit area is 117.5
data_cleaned = real_estate_data [real_estate_data ['Y house price of
unit area']! = 117.5]
# Plot the histogram of the cleaned data
plt.figure(figsize=(10, 6))
sns.histplot(data_cleaned['Y house price of unit area'], kde=True,
color='blue')
```

```
plt.xlabel('House Price of Unit Area')
plt.ylabel('Frequency')
plt.grid(True)
plt.show()
```

The updated histogram is shown in *Figure* 4.4 illustrating the distribution of house price of unit area (without outlier):

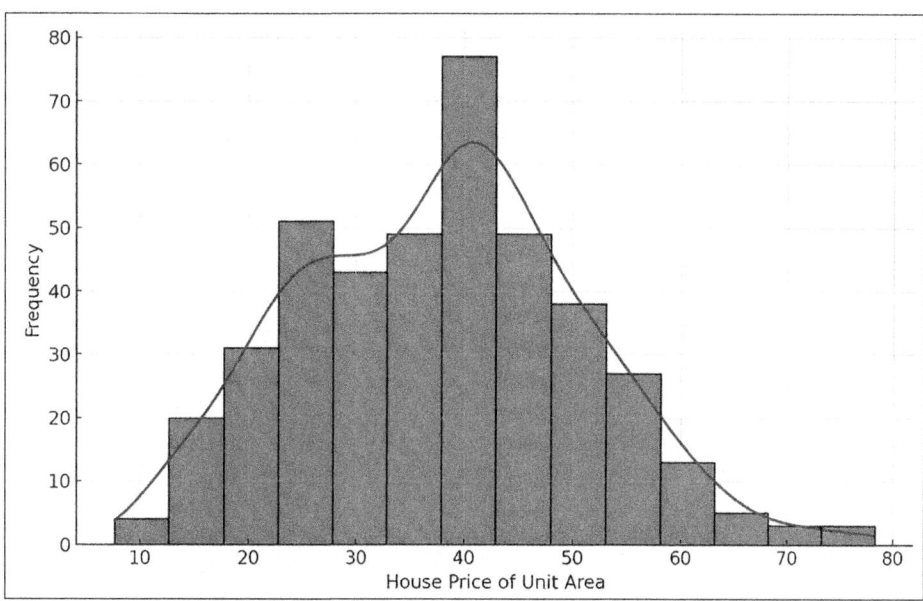

***Figure* 4.4**: *Distribution of House Price of Unit Area (Without Outlier)*

The distribution now might appear slightly different, potentially less skewed without the extreme value pulling the tail to the right. This adjusted view can offer a more representative understanding of the typical house prices in the dataset and is very well suitable for linear models.

Bivariate Analysis

Bivariate analysis involves the exploration and analysis of two variables to understand the relationships between them and how one variable may affect the other. We will exclude the transaction date from our pair plot analysis primarily because it has a very narrow range and may not provide significant practical insight into the relationships with house prices. This variable, representing the date of transaction, is likely to show limited variation over the dataset's span, which makes it less useful for understanding how house prices change over time in a short and specific timeframe. Instead, we will focus on other more informative features that are likely to have a direct impact on house prices, such as house age, distance to the nearest MRT station, number of convenience stores, and geographical coordinates.

```python
# Scatter plot of first three variables
label_font = {'size': 14, 'weight': 'bold'}
title_font = {'size': 16, 'weight': 'bold'}
data_subset = filtered_data.drop('X1 transaction date', axis=1)
independent_vars = ['X2 house age', 'X3 distance to the nearest MRT station','X4 number of convenience stores', 'X5 latitude', 'X6 longitude']
fig1, axes1 = plt.subplots(nrows=1, ncols=3, figsize=(27, 7))
for ax, var in zip(axes1, independent_vars[:3]):
    ax.scatter(data_subset[var], data_subset['Y house price of unit area'], alpha=0.6)
    ax.set_title(f'{var} vs House Price', fontdict=title_font)
    ax.set_xlabel(var, fontdict=label_font)
    ax.set_ylabel('House Price of Unit Area', fontdict=label_font)
    plt.tight_layout()
    plt.show()
# Scatter plot of geographical coordinates
fig2, axes2 = plt.subplots(nrows=1, ncols=2, figsize=(18, 7))  # Adjust size for two plots
for ax, var in zip(axes2, independent_vars[3:5]):
    ax.scatter(data_subset[var], data_subset['Y house price of unit area'], alpha=0.6)
    ax.set_title(f'{var} vs House Price', fontdict=title_font)
    ax.set_xlabel(var, fontdict=label_font)
    ax.set_ylabel('House Price of Unit Area', fontdict=label_font)
plt.tight_layout()
plt.show()
```

The following figure illustrates the Bivariate Scatter Plots:

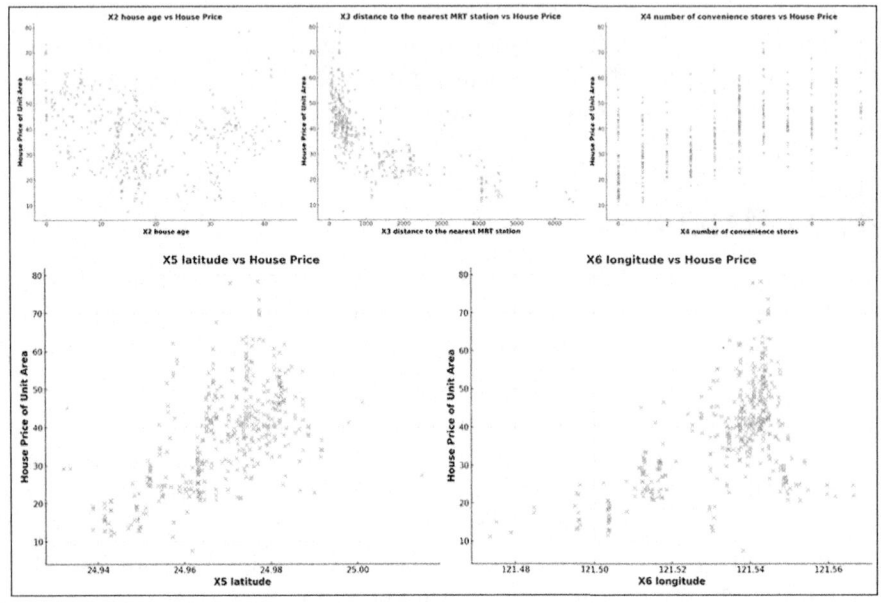

Figure 4.5: Bivariate Scatter Plots

The aforementioned scatter plots shown in Figure 4.5 reveal some interesting patterns and insights, we shall go through them one by one, starting with:

- We can see the house prices of the old houses (20-40) are less than newer ones (0-10 years).
- It is clear that the more distance to the nearest MRT station, the cheaper the house as it is less convenient.
- The more convenient stores are around a house, the more expensive the house.
- The more latitude and longitude, the more expensive the house. This likely reflects the property values being higher in more desirable or economically prosperous areas.

While a general linear trend appears to be present, certain data points stray notably from this linear path. This deviation could lead one to consider removing these outliers to tighten the trend's consistency. However, the exclusion of these data points risks discarding a significant portion of the data, potentially leading to a loss of valuable information.

Addressing these irregularities can be approached in two ways. One could opt for non-linear models, which may more accurately capture the nuanced patterns and trends within the data. Non-linear models can adapt to the complexities and bends in the data that a linear model might overlook. On the other hand, there is a compelling case for sticking with multiple linear regression models. Despite some data deviation, a linear model offers an element of explainability that is often favored in statistical analysis.

Particularly since we're currently focusing on linear regression, there is value in leveraging the interpretability of linear models. Even if 20-25% of the data appear not to align perfectly with a linear trend and straightly follow the linearity assumptions, the model's explanatory power can still yield insightful and meaningful results. This approach not only aligns with the educational focus of the chapter but also emphasizes the practical aspect of modeling, where perfect data alignment is the exception rather than the rule.

Implementing MLR Model in Python

Although we have explored the qualitative visual assessment of each predictor variable with respect to the house price, let us calculate the correlation score and display the heat map for better judgment of features to be included in the MLR model.

```
correlation_matrix = data_subset.corr()
plt.figure(figsize=(10, 8))
sns.heatmap(correlation_matrix, annot=True, fmt=".2f", cmap="coolwarm",
cbar=True)
plt.title("Correlation Heatmap")
plt.show()
```

The following figure illustrates the Correlation Heatmap:

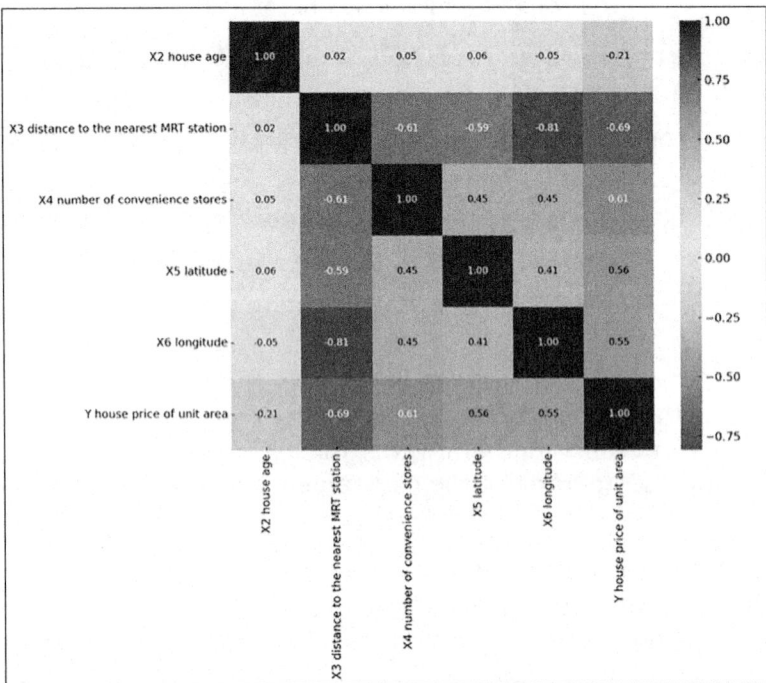

Figure 4.6: *Correlation Heatmap*

The heatmap of the correlation matrix in *Figure 4.6*, shows the relationships between the predictors and the house price. Positive values (warmer colors) indicate a positive correlation, where variables tend to increase together. Negative values (cooler colors) indicate a negative correlation, where one variable tends to increase as the other decreases.

From the heatmap, we could infer the following:

- **Distance to the Nearest MRT Station** has a strong negative correlation with house prices, suggesting that closer proximity to the MRT station is associated with higher house prices.
- **Number of Convenience Stores** shows a positive correlation with house prices, which aligns with the regression coefficient indicating that more nearby stores increase property values.
- **Latitude and Longitude** also show positive correlations with house prices, suggesting particular geographic areas are associated with higher property values.

Subsequent to understanding the features impacting dependent variable, let us scale the predictor variables using **StandardScaler** to standardize the predictor variables to have a mean of zero and a standard deviation of one. This is often beneficial for models such as linear regression. Subsequent to scaling the predictor variables, we shall fit a linear regression model.

```
from sklearn.preprocessing import StandardScaler
predictors = data_subset.drop('Y house price of unit area',axis=1)
target = data_subset['Y house price of unit area']
# Initialize the StandardScaler
scaler = StandardScaler()
# Scale the predictor variables
predictors_scaled = scaler.fit_transform(predictors)
MLR = LinearRegression()
MLR.fit(predictors_scaled, target)
# Retrieve the model coefficients
coefficients = pd.DataFrame(MLR.coef_, predictors.columns, columns=
['Coefficient'])
```

Let us interpret the coefficients from the linear regression model built with scaled predictors, explaining the impact of a one standard deviation increase in each predictor variable on the house price per unit area, measured in 10,000 New Taiwan Dollars/Ping.

House Age: A one standard deviation increase in the age of the house is associated with a decrease in the house price by approximately 2.965 units of 10,000 New Taiwan Dollars per Ping. This suggests that older houses tend to be valued lower, other factors being equal.

Distance to the Nearest MRT Station: A one standard deviation increase in the distance to the nearest MRT station is associated with a decrease in the house price by approximately 4.659 units of 10,000 New Taiwan Dollars per Ping. This highlights the importance of proximity to transport infrastructure in determining house prices.

Number of Convenience Stores: A one standard deviation increase in the number of convenience stores within walking distance is associated with an increase in the house price by approximately 3.869 units of 10,000 New Taiwan Dollars per Ping. This suggests that the availability of nearby amenities positively influences house values.

Latitude: A one standard deviation increase in latitude is associated with an increase in the house price by approximately 2.904 units of 10,000 New Taiwan Dollars per Ping. This indicates that properties located at higher latitudes within this dataset are generally priced higher, perhaps due to being in more desirable or affluent areas.

Longitude: A one standard deviation increase in longitude is associated with an increase in the house price by approximately 0.314 units of 10,000 New Taiwan Dollars per Ping. This smaller effect suggests that longitudinal location also impacts property values, though not as strongly as other factors.

The intercept value of the fitted MLR model is approximately 37.7877. This means that when all predictor variables X are at their mean values, the expected house price of unit area is about 37.7877. Since the unit of measurement for the target variable Y (house price of unit area) is expressed in 10,000 New Taiwan Dollars per Ping, this intercept value should be interpreted as 37.7877 * 10,000 New Taiwan Dollars per Ping. This translates to an expected house price of approximately 377,877 New Taiwan Dollars per Ping when all predictor variables are at their mean values.

These interpretations help understand how each predictor, normalized by its variability, influences house prices in the dataset.

Performance Evaluation by K-Fold Cross Validation

K-fold cross-validation is a statistical technique used to evaluate the performance of a predictive model more reliably. In this method, the dataset is randomly divided into 'k' equal-sized subsets or "*folds.*" For each iteration, one fold is reserved as the test set, and the remaining k-1 folds are used as the training set. The model is trained on the training set and validated on the test set, and this process is repeated k times, with each fold serving as the test set exactly once. The results from each fold can then be averaged to produce a single estimation. This technique is beneficial because it maximizes both the training and testing data so that the model is tested across all available data, ensuring the reliability and robustness of the performance evaluation.

K-fold cross-validation is particularly advantageous compared to a simple train-test split for several reasons:

- **Bias Reduction**: In a simple train-test split, the performance can significantly depend on how the data is split. In contrast, K-fold cross-validation averages the results over several subsets, which provides a more comprehensive evaluation and reduces the variance in performance metrics, leading to less biased estimates.
- **Efficient Use of Data**: Especially in scenarios where data is limited, using K-fold cross-validation ensures that every data point is used for both training and testing, which helps in learning more robust patterns without wasting data.
- **Generalizability**: By validating the model across multiple subsets, K-fold cross-validation checks for the model's ability to generalize to an independent dataset better than a single train-test split, which may be subject to specific idiosyncrasies of the split data.

Let us perform k-fold cross validation to the MLR model we have designed.

```
from sklearn.model_selection import cross_val_score
cv_scores = cross_val_score(MLR, predictors_scaled, Y, cv=3,
scoring='neg_root_mean_squared_error')
```

```
# Convert negative RMSE scores to positive
rmse_scores = -cv_scores
# Calculate the mean and standard deviation of the RMSE scores mean_rmse
= rmse_scores.mean()
std_dev_rmse = rmse_scores.std()
mean_rmse, std_dev_rmse
```

8.1829, 0.2765

The model's predictions deviate from the actual house prices by about 81,829 New Taiwan Dollars per Ping. This value provides a measure of the typical error magnitude you can expect from the model's predictions when estimating house prices. The standard deviation of the RMSE, which is 0.2765, tells us about the variability of the RMSE across the different folds of the cross-validation. Translated into the same units, this variability amounts to about 2,765 New Taiwan Dollars per Ping.

Final Inference

We can infer that the model predicts the property price with an average error of approximately 81,829 New Taiwan Dollars per Ping. This prediction error has a standard deviation of about ±2,765 New Taiwan Dollars, indicating the typical range of deviation around the average error.

Logistic Regression as a Classifier Model

Logistic regression stands as a fundamental analytical technique within the realm of machine learning, particularly distinguished for its role in classification tasks. Unlike linear regression, which is used to predict continuous outcomes, logistic regression is designed to predict categorical outcomes. This makes it an invaluable tool for scenarios where the result is categorical, such as determining whether an email is spam or not, or predicting whether a customer will purchase a product.

The essence of logistic regression lies in its ability to provide probabilities and classify data into categories. It achieves this through the logistic function, also known as the sigmoid function, which transforms any real-valued number into a value between 0 and 1, effectively mapping predictions to probabilities. This function is S-shaped, ensuring that predictions are bounded and interpretable as probabilities. Also, multinomial logistic regression generalizes logistic regression to multi-class problems without needing to decompose the problem, directly predicting probabilities of multiple classes as outputs through a single model. This flexibility allows logistic regression to be applied to a wide range of practical situations where the target variable includes three or more categories.

The logistic function, often symbolized as $\sigma(z)$, is defined by the formula:

$$\sigma(z) = \frac{1}{1+e^{-(\beta_0 + \beta_1 * X_1 + \beta_2 * X_2 + \cdots \beta_p * X_p)}}$$

Here, z represents the linear combination of the input features X weighted by the coefficients β, plus an intercept β_0.

The logistic function $\sigma(z)$ outputs values between 0 and 1, which are interpreted as probabilities. For binary classification, these probabilities indicate the likelihood of the data belonging to one of the two categories (usually classified as 1 if the probability is greater than 0.5, and 0 otherwise), however, we can evaluate the model with different thresholds other than default 0.5.

We are going to extend the mathematics of gradient descent discussed for Linear Regression to the Logistic Regression problem by additionally calculating the derivative of the logistic function, often called the logistic sigmoid function, which is crucial for understanding how changes in the input affect the output.

To ease the computation, let us consider $z = \beta_0 + \beta_1 * X_1 + \beta_2 * X_2 + \cdots \beta_p * X_p$ the logistic function can be represented in short as follows:

$$\sigma(z) = \frac{1}{1+e^{-(Z)}}$$

The derivative can be derived by differentiating the $\sigma(z)$ function with respect to z.

We can rewrite the function as $\sigma(z) = (1+e^{-(Z)})^{-1}$ and apply chain rule

$$\sigma'(Z) = -1 \cdot (1+e^{-(Z)})^{-2} \cdot (-e^{-Z}) = \frac{e^{-Z}}{(1+e^{-Z})^2}$$

$$\sigma'(Z) = \frac{1}{1+e^{-Z}} \cdot \left(1 - \frac{1}{1+e^{-Z}}\right) = \sigma(Z) \cdot (1 - \sigma(Z))$$

Let us express $\sigma(z)$ as $\hat{Y}$, and the error gradients of logistic regression model are summarized as follows,

$$\frac{\partial_{SSE}}{\partial_{\beta_0}} = -(Y - \hat{Y}) * \hat{Y} * (1 - \hat{Y})$$

$$\frac{\partial_{SSE}}{\partial_{\beta_1}} = -(Y - \hat{Y}) * \hat{Y} * (1 - \hat{Y}) * X$$

Illustrative Example with Contrived Data

Let us delve into the illustrative gradient descent learning mechanism in logistic regression using a contrived dataset for a better understanding of mathematics discussed in the preceding section. A small dataset shown in Table 4.2 with ages and corresponding labels reflects a binary classification problem where '0' might represent non-adults (teenagers) and '1' represents adults, based on their ages.

X (Age in Years)	Y (Output Class: Teen/Adult)
16	0
15	0
26	1
28	1

Table 4.2: Contrived Tiny Dataset

The logistic function to compute the prediction $\hat{Y}$ is: $\sigma(z) = \dfrac{1}{1+e^{-(z)}}$, where $z = \beta_0 + \beta_1 \cdot X$.

Let us proceed with the calculations for the logistic regression with the randomly initialized parameters $\beta_0 = -20$ and $\beta_1 = 0.8$.

For each record:

1. Record 1: $z = -20 + 0.8 \times 16 = -7.2$

   $\hat{Y}_1 = \dfrac{1}{1+e^{7.2}} \approx 0.00074$

2. Record 2: $z = -20 + 0.8 \times 15 = -8$

   $\hat{Y}_2 = \dfrac{1}{1+e^{8}} \approx 0.00033$

3. Record 3: $z = -20 + 0.8 \times 26 = 0.8$

   $\hat{Y}_3 = \dfrac{1}{1+e^{-(0.8)}} \approx 0.68997$

4. Record 4: $z = -20 + 0.8 \times 28 = 2.4$

   $\hat{Y}_4 = \dfrac{1}{1+e^{-(2.4)}} \approx 0.91682$

Let us calculate the error gradients based on the formula discussed in the preceding section.

$$\frac{\partial_{SSE}}{\partial_{\beta_0}} = -(Y - \hat{Y}) * \hat{Y} * (1 - \hat{Y})$$

$$\frac{\partial_{SSE}}{\partial_{\beta_1}} = -(Y - \hat{Y}) * \hat{Y} * (1 - \hat{Y}) * X$$

Gradients for Each Record:

Record 1 (Age = 16, Y = 0): Gradient contribution to β_0:(0−0.0007477)×0.0007477×(1−0.0007477)≈ −0.0005594

Gradient contribution to β_1: Same but×16= − 0.0089504

Record 2 (Age = 15, Y = 0):

Gradient contribution to β_0: (0−0.00033)× 0.00033×(1−0.00033)≈ −0.0001126

Gradient contribution to β_1: Same but×15= − 0.0016890

Record 3 (Age = 26, Y = 1):

Gradient contribution to β_0: (0−0.68997)× 0.68997×(1−0.68997)≈ 0.0667

Gradient contribution to β_1: Same but×26 ≈ 1.7342

Record 4 (Age = 28, Y = 1):

Gradient contribution to β_0: (0−0.91682)× 0.91682×(1−0.91682)≈ 0.0068

Gradient contribution to β_1: Same but×28 ≈ 0.1904

Summing Gradient Contributions for β_0 = 0.0628612

Summing Gradient Contributions for β_1 = 1.756

Updating Coefficients: Let us use a learning rate α=0.1 and apply the summed contributions:

- β_0 update: β0 = −20+0.1×0.0628612= **−19.9927182**
- β_1 update: β1= 0.8+0.1×1.756 = **0.9756**

Let us recalculate predictions for each record with updated coefficients:

1. Record 1: z =−19.99+0.97×16=−4.38

$$\hat{Y}_1 = \frac{1}{1+e^{4.38}} \approx 0.0124$$

2. Record 2: $z = -19.99 + 0.97 \times 15 = -5.36$

$$\hat{Y}_2 = \frac{1}{1+e^{5.36}} \approx 0.0047$$

3. Record 3: $z = -19.99 + 0.97 \times 26 = 5.37$

$$\hat{Y}_3 = \frac{1}{1+e^{-(5.37)}} \approx 0.9953$$

4. Record 4: $z = -19.99 + 0.97 \times 28 = 7.32$

$$\hat{Y}_4 = \frac{1}{1+e^{-(7.32)}} \approx 0.9993$$

The updated model parameters have significantly improved the predictive accuracy for the third and fourth records in our dataset, where the ages are 26 and 28, respectively. These ages represent individuals classified as adults (class 1). With the new coefficients, $\beta_0 = -19.9927182$ and $\beta_1 = 0.9756$, the predictions for these ages have resulted in probabilities of 0.9953 for age 26 and 0.9993 for age 28. These high probabilities closely align with the expected outcomes, demonstrating a strong model fit for these data points.

Implementation of Logistic Regression Model in Python

Lung Cancer Prediction public access dataset from https://www.kaggle.com/datasets is used for the implementation. This dataset sounds quite comprehensive and well-suited for logistic regression analysis, especially for predicting the likelihood of lung cancer based on a range of demographic, lifestyle, and health-related factors. The dataset includes various attributes related to the patients such as their gender, age, smoking habits, and several symptoms or conditions such as yellow fingers, anxiety, peer pressure, and more. The last column, **"LUNG_CANCER,"** indicates whether the patient was diagnosed with lung cancer ("YES" or "NO").

Let us load and display the data types of all columns to understand the variable nature.

```
# Load the dataset
file_path = 'file_path/Lung_Cancer_Dataset.csv'
lung_cancer_data = pd.read_csv(file_path)
lung_cancer_data.dtypes
```

- **GENDER**: object (string)
- **AGE**: int64 (integer)
- **SMOKING**: int64 (integer)

- **YELLOW_FINGERS**: int64 (integer)
- **ANXIETY**: int64 (integer)
- **PEER_PRESSURE**: int64 (integer)
- **CHRONIC DISEASE**: int64 (integer)
- **FATIGUE**: int64 (integer)
- **ALLERGY**: int64 (integer)
- **WHEEZING**: int64 (integer)
- **ALCOHOL CONSUMING**: int64 (integer)
- **COUGHING**: int64 (integer)
- **SHORTNESS OF BREATH**: int64 (integer)
- **SWALLOWING DIFFICULTY**: int64 (integer)
- **CHEST PAIN**: int64 (integer)
- **LUNG_CANCER**: object (string)

The following columns ['SMOKING', 'YELLOW_FINGERS', 'ANXIETY', 'PEER_PRESSURE', 'CHRONIC DISEASE', 'FATIGUE ','ALLERGY ', 'WHEEZING', 'ALCOHOL CONSUMING', 'COUGHING', 'SHORTNESS OF BREATH', 'SWALLOWING DIFFICULTY', 'CHEST PAIN'] are labeled as integer '1' and '2', which should be treated as categorical object data, so that model could make a reasonable understanding about these variables. Towards the first step, we are going to convert these columns into categorical object data types.

columns_to_convert = ['SMOKING', 'YELLOW_FINGERS', 'ANXIETY', 'PEER_PRESSURE', 'CHRONIC DISEASE', 'FATIGUE ', 'ALLERGY ', 'WHEEZING', 'ALCOHOL CONSUMING', 'COUGHING', 'SHORTNESS OF BREATH', 'SWALLOWING DIFFICULTY', 'CHEST PAIN']

```
# Convert 1 to 0 and 2 to 1 for the corrected list of columns
lung_cancer_data[columns_to_convert] = lung_cancer_data[columns_to_convert].replace({1: 0, 2: 1})
lung_cancer_data[columns_to_convert] = lung_cancer_data[columns_to_convert].astype('object')
```

Now the **GENDER** column needs to be encoded as follows, F as '0' and M as '1' and converted to object data type.

```
# Encode 'F' as 0 and 'M' as 1 in the Gender column
lung_cancer_data['GENDER'] = lung_cancer_data['GENDER'].replace({'F': 0, 'M': 1})

# Convert the 'GENDER' column back to object type
lung_cancer_data['GENDER'] = lung_cancer_data['GENDER'].astype('object')
```

Regression Versus Classification Model

Preceding we proceed with model building, we shall have a look at the dependent variable (**Lung_Cancer**) and we can observe the majority of the records are cancer cases (Yes-270) and non-cancer (No-39). The data should be the representation of the real-world population, nearly 88% of data is cancer records, and this does not sound realistic. Let us perform oversampling and under sampling techniques to bring the cancer categories with realistic proportions. Being a demonstrative exercise, we take liberty in doing this, however, while we handle such situations in real life, we can get more data from controls (non-cancer) cases.

```
# Separate the majority and minority classes
df_majority = lung_cancer_data[lung_cancer_data['LUNG_CANCER'] == 'YES']
df_minority = lung_cancer_data[lung_cancer_data['LUNG_CANCER'] == 'NO']
# Set target numbers for YES and NO cases
target_yes = 50
target_no = 150
# Random undersample the 'YES' cases to 50
df_yes_adjusted = df_majority.sample(target_yes, replace=False, random_state=42)
# Random oversample the 'NO' cases to 150
df_no_adjusted = df_minority.sample(target_no, replace=True, random_state=42)
# Combine the adjusted majority and minority classes
df_adjusted = pd.concat([df_yes_adjusted, df_no_adjusted])
adjusted_file_path = 'file_path/Adjusted_Lung_Cancer_Dataset.csv'
df_adjusted.to_csv(adjusted_file_path, index=False)
```

If the reader wants to load the adjusted dataset directly, you could skip all these steps, by loading the corrected and adjusted dataset. However, it is encouraged to practice such steps to gain more hands-on experience in data preparation. Let us proceed and build the model.

```
# Split the features (X) and target (Y) from the adjusted dataset
X = df_adjusted.drop('LUNG_CANCER', axis=1)
Y = df_adjusted['LUNG_CANCER']
# Initialize and train the logistic regression model on the entire adjusted dataset
from sklearn.linear_model import LogisticRegression
model = LogisticRegression()
model.fit(X_adjusted, y_adjusted)
# Predict on the entire adjusted dataset
y_adjusted_pred = complete_logistic_model.predict(X_adjusted)
# Compute the confusion matrix for the entire adjusted dataset
from sklearn import metrics
confusion_matrix_complete = confusion_matrix(y_adjusted, y_adjusted_pred)
```

The logistic regression model was trained and validated using the entire adjusted dataset. Here is the confusion matrix as shown in *Figure 4.7*. A confusion matrix is a powerful tool used in predictive analytics, particularly in classification problems, to visualize the performance of an algorithm. It is a table that allows you to compare the actual target values with those predicted by the model, providing insight into the correct and incorrect predictions made by the model across different categories. Each row of the matrix represents the instances in an actual class, while each column represents the instances in a predicted class.

	Predicted NO	Predicted YES
Actual NO	150	0
Actual YES	7	43

Figure 4.7: *Confusion Matrix Result of Logistic Regression*

True Negatives (TN): 150 - The model correctly predicted 'NO' lung cancer for all 150 cases.

False Positives (FP): 0 - There were no instances where the model incorrectly predicted 'YES' for a 'NO' case.

False Negatives (FN): 7 - The model incorrectly predicted 'NO' when the actual was 'YES.'

True Positives (TP): 43 - The model correctly predicted 'YES' lung cancer for 43 cases.

Let us calculate the overall accuracy of the model as follows:

```
overall_accuracy_metrics = metrics.accuracy_score(y_adjusted, y_adjusted_pred_default)
```

The overall accuracy of the model is 96.5%. This confirms the model's overall effectiveness in predicting Lung cancer reliably. Also, we could observe the sensitivity of predicting cancer cases is 43 out of 50 cases, which is 86%. However, K-fold cross validation will give a much reliable performance evaluation of the model. Let us perform 3-fold cross validation with respect to the recall score, which is the sensitivity of the model in predicting the cancer case, and is very crucial for medical diagnosis.

```
from sklearn.model_selection import cross_val_score
from sklearn.model_selection import KFold
from sklearn.metrics import make_scorer, recall_score
# Setup KFold cross-validation with shuffle enabled
sensitivity_scorer = make_scorer(recall_score, pos_label='YES')
kf = KFold(n_splits=3, shuffle=True, random_state=0)
kfold_sensitivity_scores = cross_val_score(model, X_adjusted,
y_adjusted, cv=kf, scoring=sensitivity_scorer)
```

The sensitivity (recall) scores for each fold are 0.882, 0.813, and 0.824, with the overall average of 84% being a quite decent score. Nonetheless, non-linear models will address this dataset with a significantly higher degree of sensitivity, a topic we will explore in more detail in upcoming chapters.

Interpretation of Model Coefficients

These coefficients provide insights into how each predictor variable influences the log odds of having lung cancer, with positive coefficients increasing the log odds of the event (lung cancer = YES) and negative coefficients decreasing it. The magnitude of these coefficients indicates the strength of the influence. Taking the exponent of the logistic regression coefficients converts them from log odds to odds ratios. This helps in understanding how the odds of the dependent event (in this case, lung cancer) change with a one-unit change in each predictor variable, holding all other variables constant.

Preceding we start interpreting the coefficients, let us quickly explore the definition of odds. Odds describe the ratio of the probability of an event occurring to the probability of it not occurring. In simpler terms, odds are a way of expressing the likelihood that a particular event will happen versus it not happening. For instance, if the probability of an event is 'p,' then the odds are . If an event has a probability of 0.75, the odds are = 3, often expressed as 3 to 1, which means the event is three times as likely to occur as not.

In logistic regression, the relationship between the predictor variables and the probability of the target variable (for example, having a disease, or choosing an option) being true is modeled using odds. The coefficients in a logistic regression model represent the change in the log of odds for a one-unit change in predictors. This is why we exponentiate these coefficients to interpret them as odds ratios, giving a multiplicative effect of predictors on the odds of the outcome.

The coefficients of the logistic regression model are expressed as odds ratios, along with the interpretation for each.

Intercept (Odds Ratio = 0.661): Represents the odds of having lung cancer when all predictor variables are at their baseline levels (typically 0 for categorical variables).

For features with categorical variables (such as CHRONIC DISEASE_1), the odds ratio represents how much the odds of having lung cancer multiply when the feature changes from the reference category (0) to the active category (1).

- **CHRONIC DISEASE_1**: An individual with a chronic disease is about 2.89 times more likely to have lung cancer compared to those without.
- **ALLERGY_1**: Having allergies increases the odds of having lung cancer by 2.52 times.
- **COUGHING_1**: Coughing increases the odds by about 2.24 times.

- **YELLOW FINGERS_1**: Yellow fingers increase the odds by about 2.24 times.
- **FATIGUE_1**: Fatigue increases the odds by about 2.23 times.
- **AGE**: Each additional year of age slightly increases the odds of having lung cancer (odds ratio = 1.03).
- **GENDER_0** (Female): Being female slightly decreases the odds compared to the reference category, which is male in this case (odds ratio = 0.98).
- **GENDER_1** (Male): Being male slightly decreases the odds compared to the reference category, which is female (odds ratio = 0.89).

Limitations of Linear Models and Assumptions

This section focuses on the limitations of linear models and the assumptions underlying both linear and logistic regression. This will help set a solid foundation for understanding when these models are appropriate and their potential pitfalls.

Linear models assume a linear relationship between the independent variables and the dependent variable. This can be overly simplistic as real-world data often exhibits non-linear patterns that linear models cannot capture.

- **Homoscedasticity**: Linear regression assumes that the variance of residual errors is constant across all levels of the independent variables. If the variance changes (heteroscedasticity), the model's reliability diminishes, especially for inference.
- **Influence of Outliers**: Linear Regression models are sensitive to outliers in the data. A few outliers can significantly influence the model's parameters and can lead to misleading interpretations or predictions.
- **Independence of Observations**: The model assumes that all observations are independent of each other. In real-world scenarios, especially in time series or spatial data, this assumption often does not hold.
- **Multicollinearity**: Multicollinearity, a phenomenon where independent variables in a regression model are highly correlated, poses a significant challenge as it can undermine the stability and interpretation of regression coefficients.

When multicollinearity is present, it becomes difficult to precisely estimate the contribution of each independent variable to the dependent variable, as the effects of correlated variables become confounded. This can lead to inflated standard errors, making the estimates unreliable and hindering the identification of significant predictors. Moreover, multicollinearity complicates the interpretation of coefficients, as it becomes unclear which variable is truly driving the outcome.

While multicollinearity can sometimes be mitigated through techniques such as variable selection or regularization, it remains a critical issue to address in regression analysis to ensure the validity and accuracy of the model. Similar to linear regression, logistic regression assumes little or no multicollinearity among the independent variables.

- **Normal Distribution of Errors**: The assumption that the residuals (errors) of a linear regression model should be normally distributed is pivotal for ensuring the validity and reliability of the model. This assumption facilitates robust statistical inference, as it ensures that estimates of regression coefficients are unbiased and have minimum variance.

Additionally, the normality of residuals validates one of the key assumptions of linear regression, enhancing the model's interpretability and prediction accuracy. Deviations from normality may compromise the efficiency of estimators, leading to biased parameter estimates and unreliable predictions.

While some deviation from normality may be acceptable, especially in large samples, assessing the normality of residuals remains a critical diagnostic check in linear regression analysis to maintain the model's integrity and trustworthiness.

- **Linearity of Independent Variables and Log Odds**: While the dependent variable need not be linearly related to the independent variables, logistic regression requires that the log odds of the dependent variable are linearly related to the independent variables.

Despite their limitations, linear and logistic regression models remain popular choices in data analysis and predictive modeling due to their simplicity, interpretability, and ease of implementation. These models provide straightforward insights into the relationship between independent and dependent variables, making those valuable tools for understanding and explaining the data.

However, it is essential to recognize that linear models rely on certain assumptions, such as linearity, independence of errors, homoscedasticity, and normality of residuals, which may not always hold true in real-world datasets. When faced with datasets that significantly violate these assumptions, it is prudent for researchers and practitioners to consider alternative modeling approaches, such as non-linear models. Non-linear models, such as decision trees, random forests, and neural networks, do not impose stringent assumptions on the data and have the flexibility to capture complex relationships and irregularities without the need for explicit specification.

Therefore, while linear and logistic regression models offer valuable insights, it is essential to be aware of their limitations and explore alternative approaches when necessary to ensure accurate and robust modeling results.

Model Evaluation Techniques and Different Performance Metrics

While we have explored practical use cases in Python where one or two metrics are often emphasized for their relevance, the evaluation of machine learning models extends beyond these select few. In this section, we delve into a variety of different performance metrics that provide comprehensive insights into the effectiveness and accuracy of regression and classification models. By examining each metric individually, we gain a deeper understanding of their significance and applicability in assessing model performance across diverse datasets and problem domains.

R-squared (R^2): R^2 represents the proportion of the variance in the dependent variable that is predictable from the independent variables.

$$R^2 = 1- \quad R^2 = 1 - \frac{SS_{res}}{SS_{tot}}$$

Where SS_{res} is the sum of squares of residuals and SS_{tot} is the total sum of squares.

Adjusted R^2: Adjusted R2R2 is a modified version of the coefficient of determination (R2R2) that adjusts for the number of predictors in the model. It penalizes the addition of unnecessary predictors, providing a more accurate assessment of the model's goodness of fit.

$$\text{Adjusted } R^2 = 1 - \frac{(1-R^2).(n-1)}{n-k-1}$$

Here *n* is the number of observations and *k* is the number of predictors in the model.

Adjusted R^2 ranges from 0 to 1, where a higher value indicates a better fit of the model to the data. It accounts for both the goodness of fit and the complexity of the model, making it a valuable metric for evaluating regression models.

Mean Squared Error (MSE): MSE measures the average squared difference between the predicted values and the actual values which are given by,

$$MSE = \frac{1}{n}\sum_{i=1}^{n}(Y_i - \hat{Y}_i)^2$$

where n is the number of samples, *Yi* is the actual value, and $\hat{Y}_i$ is the predicted value.

Mean Absolute Error (MAE): MAE calculates the average absolute difference between the predicted values and the actual values.

$$MAE = \frac{1}{n}\sum_{i=1}^{n}|Y_i - \hat{Y}_i|$$

Root Mean Squared Error (RMSE): RMSE is the square root of the MSE, providing an interpretable scale that matches the original units of the target variable.

$$\text{RMSE} = \sqrt{\text{MSE}}$$

RMSE stands out as one of the most preferred metrics due to its client-friendly nature. Clients often find RMSE intuitive and easy to understand, as it represents the average difference between actual and predicted values in the same units as the dependent variable. This makes it a straightforward measure of model performance that resonates well with stakeholders seeking clear insights into the accuracy of regression models.

Mean Absolute Percentage Error (MAPE): In addition to RMSE, another commonly used metric is MAPE, or Mean Absolute Percentage Error.

$$\text{MAPE} = \frac{100}{n} \sum_{i=1}^{n} \left| \frac{Y_i - \hat{Y}_i}{Y_i} \right|$$

Unlike RMSE, which expresses the average difference between actual and predicted values in the same units as the dependent variable, MAPE provides a percentage representation of the error. This makes MAPE particularly useful for interpreting the accuracy of predictions relative to the scale of the data. While RMSE offers insights into absolute errors, MAPE offers a relative perspective, allowing stakeholders to assess the model's performance in terms of percentage deviation from actual values.

Now, we delve into various performance metrics specifically designed for assessing the effectiveness of classification models. From measures such as accuracy and precision to more nuanced metrics such as ROC-AUC, each provides valuable insights into different aspects of a model's performance. Let us explore these metrics and understand how they contribute to evaluating the effectiveness of classification algorithms.

Accuracy: Overall accuracy is one of the fundamental metrics used to evaluate the performance of classification models. It measures the proportion of correctly classified instances among all instances in the dataset. In essence, it provides a general overview of how well the model performs across all classes or categories. While overall accuracy is a useful metric, especially when classes are balanced, it may not provide a complete picture of model performance in situations where class distributions are imbalanced. Nonetheless, it serves as a starting point for assessing the effectiveness of a classification model.

Confusion Matrix: The confusion matrix is a fundamental tool in evaluating the performance of classification models by tabulating the actual and predicted class labels. It provides a comprehensive summary of the model's predictions, breaking down the outcomes into four categories as shown in *Figure 4.8*: True Positives (TP), True Negatives (TN), False Positives (FP), and False Negatives (FN). These elements serve as the basis for computing various performance metrics, such as accuracy, sensitivity, specificity, precision, and recall. By visually representing the model's classification results, the confusion matrix offers valuable insights into its strengths and weaknesses, aiding in model refinement and optimization.

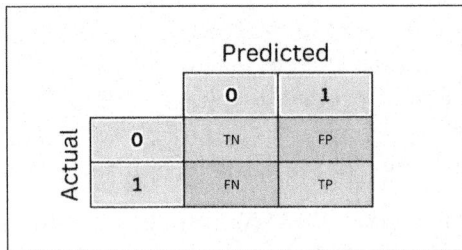

Figure 4.8: *Confusion Matrix*

Sensitivity: Sensitivity also known as Recall, measures the proportion of actual positive instances that were correctly predicted by the model. It quantifies the model's ability to identify positive instances.

$$\text{Sensitivity or Recall} = \frac{True\ Positives}{True\ Positives + False\ Negatives}$$

The importance of sensitivity lies in its ability to capture the model's effectiveness in correctly detecting positive instances, thereby minimizing the risk of false negatives. In medical diagnosis, for example, sensitivity indicates the proportion of individuals with a condition who are correctly identified by the model. A high sensitivity value implies that the model is adept at detecting positive instances, which is vital in situations where missing a positive case could have serious consequences.

Specificity: Specificity measures the proportion of correctly predicted negative instances out of all actual negative instances. It quantifies the model's ability to identify negative instances.

$$\text{Specificity} = \frac{True\ Negatives}{True\ Negatives + False\ Positives}$$

A high specificity value implies that the model is proficient at correctly excluding negative instances, which is essential for minimizing unnecessary interventions or treatments for individuals who do not have the condition.

Precision: Precision measures the proportion of correctly predicted positive instances out of all instances predicted as positive. It quantifies the accuracy of positive predictions.

$$\text{Precision} = \frac{True\ Positives}{True\ Positives + False\ Positives}$$

The importance of precision lies in its ability to evaluate the model's performance in making positive predictions and determining how many of those predictions are correct. In scenarios where correctly identifying positive instances is crucial, precision provides valuable insights into the model's effectiveness in minimizing false positives.

F1 Score: The F1 score is the harmonic mean of precision and recall. It provides a balanced measure of both precision and recall, making it useful when the class distribution is uneven.

$$\text{F1 score} = 2 * \frac{Precision * Recall}{Precision + Recall}$$

The F1 score is particularly valuable in scenarios where there is an imbalance between the number of positive and negative instances in the dataset. In such cases, accuracy alone may not provide a complete picture of the model's performance, as it can be skewed by the majority class. The F1 score, on the other hand, takes into account both false positives and false negatives, providing a more comprehensive assessment of the model's ability to correctly classify instances from both classes.

Receiver Operating Characteristic - Area Under Curve (ROC-AUC): ROC-AUC represents the area under the receiver operating characteristic curve, which plots the true positive rate (sensitivity) against the false positive rate (1 - specificity). It provides a single value that summarizes the model's performance across different thresholds. One of the key advantages of ROC AUC is its ability to provide a comprehensive summary of a model's performance across all possible classification thresholds. By plotting the True Positive Rate (TPR) against the False Positive Rate (FPR) at various threshold values, the ROC curve captures the trade-off between sensitivity and specificity.

The area under this curve, known as the ROC AUC score, quantifies the model's ability to distinguish between positive and negative instances. A higher ROC AUC score indicates better discrimination ability, with a score of 1 representing a perfect classifier and 0.5 representing a random classifier.

When assessing a model's effectiveness, it is crucial to consider the specific goals and requirements of the task at hand. Overall accuracy is a commonly used metric, providing a general indication of a model's correctness. However, in scenarios where class imbalance is present, metrics such as sensitivity, specificity, precision, and F1 score offer a more nuanced understanding of a model's ability to correctly classify positive and negative instances.

Additionally, ROC AUC provides a comprehensive summary of a model's performance across all possible classification thresholds, making it particularly useful for comparing models and assessing discrimination ability. Ultimately, the choice of metric depends on the specific objectives and constraints of the classification problem, and it is essential to carefully consider the trade-offs and implications of each metric when evaluating model performance. By leveraging a combination of these metrics, practitioners can gain a more holistic understanding of their classification models and make informed decisions to optimize model performance for real-world applications.

Conclusion

In this chapter, we embarked on an exploration of linear models, delving into both linear regression and logistic regression. We began by understanding the foundational principles behind these models, including the mathematics involved and the implementation in Python. Through practical examples and discussions, we gained insights into gradient descent learning, which lies at the heart of optimizing these models.

Moreover, we scrutinized the assumptions and limitations of linear models, highlighting their significance in real-world applications. To gauge the performance of our models, we examined various evaluation techniques and metrics tailored to regression and classification tasks.

As we move towards the next chapter, we find ourselves at the threshold of yet another intriguing topic, Naive Bayes Classifier. Building upon the foundation laid by linear models, Naive Bayes offers a unique perspective on classification tasks.

Practice Exercises

1. Given contrived data shown in *Figure* 4.9 following data points for hours studied (X) and exam scores (Y). Calculate the linear regression line Y=aX+b using the least squares method.

Hours Studied (X)	Exam Score (Y)
1	50
2	55
3	60
4	65
5	70

Figure 4.9: *Hours Studied (X) versus Exam Score (Y)*

2. For a logistic regression model with parameters 0 = -4 and 1 = 1, calculate the probability of a positive outcome (P(Y=1)) when X=5.

3. Calculate the sum of squared errors (SSE) for the linear regression model Y = 3 X + 2 using the following data points: (1,5), (2,8), (3,11), (4,14).

4. Given the data points shown in *Figure* 4.10 for advertising expenses (X) and sales revenue (Y), calculate the coefficient of determination (R2) for the linear regression model Y=2X+3000.

Regression Versus Classification Model

Advertising Expenses (X)	Sales Revenue (Y)
1000	5000
2000	7000
3000	9000
4000	11000
5000	13000

Figure 4.10: *Advertising Expense (X) versus Sales Revenue (Y)*

5. Calculate the Mean Absolute Error (MAE) for the linear regression model Y = 2 X + 1 using the following data points: (1, 3), (2, 5), (3, 7), (4, 9).

6. Given the predicted probabilities and actual outcomes for a binary classification problem, calculate the log-loss.

Predicted Probability	Actual Outcome
0.8	1
0.4	0
0.7	1
0.3	0
0.6	1

Figure 4.11: *Predicted Probability versus Actual Outcome*

7. Given the confusion matrix shown in Figure 4.12, calculate the sensitivity (recall) and specificity.

	Predicted Positive	Predicted Negative
Actual Positive	50	10
Actual Negative	5	35

Figure 4.12: *Confusion Matrix*

8. For the confusion matrix shown in Figure 4.12, calculate the precision and f1-score.

Answers

1. Calculate means: X = 3, Y = 60; Calculate the slope 1 = 5; Calculate the intercept 0= 45; Y = 5 X + 45

2. Probability = 0.731

3. X = 3, Ypred =5; X=2, Ypred =8; X=3, Ypred =11; X=4, Ypred =14, SSE=0

4. Y = 9000; Calculate Total Sum of Squares (TSS) and Sum of the Squared Errors (SSE); R2 =1
5. MAE =0
6. Log-loss = 0.504
7. Sensitivity: 0.833; Specificity: 0.875
8. Precision: 0.909; F1-score: 0.868

Multiple Choice Questions

1. Which of the following is a correct statement about the intercept term in Linear Regression?
    a. It represents the change in the dependent variable for a one-unit change in the independent variable.
    b. It represents the starting point of the regression line when all independent variables are zero.
    c. It is always zero in Linear Regression.
    d. It is the coefficient of determination.

2. In Linear Regression, what is the name given to the difference between the observed and predicted values?
    a. Variance
    b. Deviance
    c. Residuals
    d. Standard Error

3. What does the term "Multicollinearity" refer to in the context of Linear Regression?
    a. The relationship between multiple independent variables
    b. The correlation between the dependent and independent variables
    c. The presence of high correlation among independent variables
    d. The distribution of residuals

4. Which of the following metrics is commonly used to evaluate the performance of a Linear Regression model?
    a. Accuracy
    b. Precision

c. RMSE (Root Mean Squared Error)

   d. F1 Score

5. What is the formula for the coefficient of determination (R-squared) in Linear Regression?

   a. 1 - (SSR/SST)

   b. (SST - SSR) / SST

   c. SSR / SST

   d. 1 - (SSE/SST)

6. What does the term "Gradient Descent" refer to in the context of Linear Regression?

   a. A method to estimate the coefficients of the regression equation

   b. A method to minimize the cost function by adjusting the coefficients iteratively

   c. A method to calculate the correlation between independent variables

   d. A method to plot the regression line

7. What does the cost function represent in the context of Linear Regression?

   a. The sum of squared errors between observed and predicted values

   b. The correlation between independent and dependent variables

   c. The coefficient of determination

   d. The variance of the dependent variable

8. What is the primary difference between Linear Regression and Logistic Regression?

   a. Linear Regression predicts continuous outcomes, while Logistic Regression predicts categorical outcomes.

   b. Linear Regression uses gradient descent, while Logistic Regression uses decision trees.

   c. Linear Regression assumes linearity, while Logistic Regression assumes non-linearity.

   d. Linear Regression is a parametric model, while Logistic Regression is a non-parametric model.

9. Which of the following methods is commonly used to assess the goodness of fit of a Linear Regression model?

   a. Root Mean Squared Error (RMSE)

   b. R-squared (Coefficient of Determination)

   c. Mean Absolute Error (MAE)

   d. Mean Squared Error (MSE)

10. What is the primary purpose of feature scaling in Linear Regression?

    a. To remove outliers from the dataset

    b. To transform the target variable to have a normal distribution

    c. To standardize or normalize the scale of independent variables

    d. To increase the complexity of the model

11. In Logistic Regression, what type of function is used to model the relationship between the independent variables and the dependent variable?

    a. Linear function

    b. Quadratic function

    c. Sigmoid function

    d. Exponential function

12. Which of the following is a suitable evaluation metric for Logistic Regression models?

    a. Mean Squared Error (MSE)

    b. R-squared (R^2)

    c. Area Under the Receiver Operating Characteristic Curve (ROC-AUC)

    d. Mean Absolute Percentage Error (MAPE)

13. What is the range of values the sigmoid function outputs in Logistic Regression?

    a. [-1, 1]

    b. [0, 1]

    c. [1, ∞)

    d. (-∞, ∞)

14. What does the term "odds ratio" represent in Logistic Regression?

    a. The ratio of the odds of success to the odds of failure

    b. The ratio of the dependent variable to the independent variable

    c. The ratio of the coefficients of the model

    d. The ratio of the intercept to the slope

15. In Logistic Regression, what does the term "threshold" refer to?

    a. The value used to determine whether a prediction is classified as positive or negative

    b. The number of independent variables in the model

    c. The intercept of the regression line

    d. The slope of the regression line

16. Which performance metric penalizes false negatives more severely than false positives?

    a. Accuracy

    b. Precision

    c. Recall (Sensitivity)

    d. Specificity

17. Precision is defined as:

    a. The proportion of true positive predictions among all positive predictions

    b. The proportion of true negative predictions among all negative predictions

    c. The proportion of true positive predictions among all predictions

    d. The proportion of true negative predictions among all positive predictions

18. Which metric combines precision and recall into a single value?

    a. Accuracy

    b. F1 Score

    c. Specificity

    d. Area Under the Curve (AUC)

19. When interpreting the ROC AUC value, what does an AUC value of 0.5 signify?

    a. Perfect classification

    b. Random classification

    c. Poor classification

    d. Undefined classification

20. Which performance metric is suitable for imbalanced datasets?

    a. Accuracy

    b. Precision

    c. Recall

    d. F1 Score

Answers

1. b
2. c
3. c
4. c
5. d
6. b
7. a
8. a
9. b
10. c
11. c
12. c
13. b
14. a
15. a
16. c
17. a

18. b
19. b
20. d

Keywords

- Linear Regression
- Logistic Regression
- Gradient Descent
- Cost Function
- Intercept
- Slope
- Residuals
- Multicollinearity
- Linearity Assumptions
- Regression Metrics
- Mean Squared Error (MSE)
- Root Mean Squared Error
- Mean Absolute Error (MAE)
- Mean Absolute Percentage of Error (MAPE)
- Classification Metrics
- Sensitivity
- Specificity
- Precision
- F1 Score
- ROC AUC
- Confusion Matrix
- R Squared (R^2)
- Adjusted R^2

References

1. https://archive.ics.uci.edu/dataset/477/real+estate+valuation+data+set
2. https://www.kaggle.com/datasets

CHAPTER 5
Naive Bayes as a Linear Classifier

Introduction

This chapter embarks on an exploration of Naive Bayes as a Linear Classifier, a fundamental algorithm in the domain of machine learning. Naive Bayes, known for its simplicity and efficiency, offers a powerful tool for classification tasks across various domains. In this chapter, we delve into the intricacies of Naive Bayes, beginning with an in-depth overview of its algorithmic principles and underlying assumptions. Through this exploration, readers will gain a deep understanding of how Naive Bayes operates and its inherent strengths and limitations.

Furthermore, this chapter delves into the practical applications of Naive Bayes, elucidating its relevance in solving real-world classification problems. By examining use cases and scenarios where Naive Bayes has demonstrated its effectiveness, readers will glean insights into its versatility and applicability across different domains.

Additionally, the chapter provides hands-on experience with Naive Bayes through hand-worked calculations using contrived datasets, allowing readers to grasp the mathematical foundations of the algorithm. With a Python implementation and accompanying use case, readers will witness first-hand how Naive Bayes can be leveraged to address classification challenges, solidifying their understanding and proficiency in this essential machine learning technique.

Structure

In this chapter we are going to cover the following main topics:

- Overview of Naïve Bayes Algorithm
- Types of Naïve Bayes Classifiers
- Application of Naïve Bayes in Classification Tasks
- Python Implementation and Use Case
- Challenges and Constraints in the Naïve Bayes Model

Overview of Naïve Bayes Algorithm

The Naive Bayes algorithm finds its roots in the work of Reverend Thomas Bayes, an 18th-century mathematician. Bayes made significant contributions to the field of probability theory, particularly through his theorem, which provides a method for updating beliefs in the presence of new evidence. His theorem forms the foundation of Bayesian statistics, a powerful framework for reasoning under uncertainty.

In the context of machine learning, the Naive Bayes algorithm applies Bayes' theorem to classification problems. It is based on the assumption of conditional independence between features, hence the term "naïve." Despite its simplicity, Naive Bayes is widely used in various applications, including spam detection, sentiment analysis, and document categorization.

Mathematical Definitions

Bayes' theorem stands as a cornerstone in probability theory, offering a mechanism to adjust existing beliefs regarding the likelihood of an event in light of fresh evidence or data. This theorem serves as a pivotal tool for inference, enabling the refinement of predictions and assessments by incorporating new information into the probabilistic framework.

The formula for Bayes' theorem is as follows:

$$P(A|B) = \frac{P(B|A) * P(A)}{P(B)}$$

Here:

$P(A|B)$ is the probability of event 'A' occurring given that event 'B' has occurred.

$P(B|A)$ is the probability of event 'B' occurring given that event 'A' has occurred.

$P(A)$ and $P(B)$ are the probabilities of events 'A' and 'B' occurring independently of each other.

To understand the practical scope of the Bayes theorem, we shall consider a problem statement to predict whether an email is spam or not based on the presence of the word 'Lottery' in the email content. To better understand the relationship between the occurrences of this word and email categorization, the cross-tabulation is shown in *Table 5.1*. This table illustrates the distribution of emails based on their classification (spam or non-spam) and the presence or absence of the word 'Lottery.' We will leverage this information to apply Bayes' theorem and predict the likelihood of an email being spam given its content.

	Spam Email	Non-Spam Email
Contains 'Lottery'	50	5
Does not Contain 'Lottery'	10	435

Table 5.1: Cross-Tabulation

The Bayes' theorem formula for this problem statement can be written as:

$$P(Booking = 'Yes'|Red, Sports, Manual) = \frac{P(Red|Yes)*P(Sports|Yes)*P(Manual|Yes)*P(Yes)}{P(Red)*P(Sports)*P(Manual)}$$

We will use the provided information from the problem statement to calculate each of these probabilities and determine the likelihood of an email being spam given that it contains the word 'Lottery.'

P(Spam) is the overall probability of an email being spam = 60/500 = 12%

P(Email contains 'Lottery') is the probability that any given email contains the word 'Lottery' = 55/500 = 11%

P(Email contains 'Lottery' | Spam) is the probability that a spam email contains the word 'Lottery' = 50/60 = 83.33%

Let us incorporate these values into the formula as follows,

P(Spam | Email contains 'Lottery') = (0.8333*0.12)/0.11 = 90.90%

The probability of an email being spam given that it contains the word 'Lottery' is 90.90%.

In the case of spam email filtering, Bayes' theorem allows us to calculate the probability that an email is spam given certain features, such as the presence of specific words such as "Lottery." The strength of Bayes' theorem lies in its simplicity and effectiveness in practical applications, such as spam email filtering. This approach is particularly effective because it accounts for both the prior probability of an email being spam and the conditional probability of observing certain features given that the email is spam. As a result, spam filters can accurately classify emails as spam or non-spam by leveraging the probabilities calculated using Bayes' theorem. Moreover, Bayes' theorem is adaptable and can be updated with new evidence, allowing spam filters to continuously improve their performance over time as they encounter new types of spam emails.

Extending Bayes Formula into Naïve Bayes Classifier

In the context of classification tasks, we can extend Bayes' theorem to build a probabilistic classifier known as Naive Bayes. Naive Bayes makes the "naive" assumption that the features are conditionally independent given the class label. This assumption simplifies the calculation of the conditional probabilities and allows us to express the probability of a class given the features as,

$$P(C_k|x_1, x_2, \ldots x_n) = \frac{P(x_1|C_k) \cdot P(x_2|C_k) \cdot \ldots \cdot P(x_n|C_k) \cdot P(C_k)}{P(x_1) \cdot P(x_2) \cdot \ldots \cdot P(x_i)}$$

Here:

$P(C_k|x_1, x_2, \ldots x_n)$ is the probability of class C_k given the features $x_1, x_2, \ldots x_n$.

$P(C_k)$ is the prior probability of class C_k.

$P(x_i|C_k)$ is the conditional probability of feature x_i given the class C_k.

$P(x_i)$ is the probability of feature x_i.

We will illustrate this formula using contrived data shown in *Table 5.2*, incorporating a categorical variable. This approach simplifies our calculations, making it easier to grasp the underlying concepts and mechanics of the formula. This hands-on approach allows us to gain a deeper understanding of the formula's functionality and its application to real-world problems.

	Color	Variant	Transmission	Booking
1	Red	Sports	Manual	Yes
2	Red	Sports	Manual	No
3	Red	Sports	Manual	Yes
4	White	Sports	Manual	No
5	White	Sports	Automatic	Yes
6	White	Asta	Automatic	No
7	White	Asta	Automatic	Yes
8	White	Asta	Manual	No
9	Red	Asta	Automatic	No
10	Red	Sports	Manual	Yes
11	Red	Asta	Manual	Yes

Table 5.2: *Contrived Data*

A car showroom aims to optimize inventory management by predicting the likelihood of a customer booking a particular car variant based on historical booking patterns. Using the provided historical data, we are going to predict the probability of a booking being "Yes" for a car with the attributes Red color, Sports variant, and Manual transmission. This prediction will assist the showroom in maintaining appropriate stock levels of each car variant to meet customer demand effectively.

$$P(Booking = \text{'Yes'}|Red, Sports, Manual) = \frac{P(Red|Yes) \cdot P(Sports|Yes) \cdot P(Manual|Yes) \cdot P(Yes)}{P(Red) \cdot P(Sports) \cdot P(Manual)}$$

In our case, P(Red) = 6/11, P(Sports) = 6/11 and P(Manual) = 7/11 these values are going to be same for 'Yes' and 'No' class, since they are independent of class variable.

We shall compute the other probabilities from the table as follows:

$$P(Red|Yes) = \frac{4}{6}$$

$$P(Sports|Yes) = \frac{4}{6}$$

$$P(Manual|Yes) = \frac{4}{6}$$

$$P(Yes) = \frac{6}{11}$$

$$P(Booking = \text{'Yes'}|Red, Asta, Manual) = \frac{\frac{4}{6} \cdot \frac{4}{6} \cdot \frac{4}{6} \cdot \frac{6}{11}}{\frac{6}{11} \cdot \frac{6}{11} \cdot \frac{7}{11}} = 0.8533 = 85.33\%$$

The calculated probability of 85.33% suggests that there is a high likelihood of a booking being "Yes" for a car with the attributes Red color, Sports variant, and Manual transmission. This inference indicates that customers who prefer cars with these specific characteristics have a slightly higher tendency to book them. Therefore, the showroom may consider stocking an adequate number of Red, Sports variant with Manual transmission to cater to potential customers' preferences effectively.

This handwork calculation exemplified the simplicity and effectiveness of the Naive Bayes formula in the context of a classifier. By manually computing probabilities based on categorical variables, readers gained insight into how the algorithm predicts outcomes using conditional probabilities. However, when dealing with continuous variables, such as in real-world scenarios, manual calculations become impractical. Instead, dedicated libraries in Python, offer efficient methods to compute probabilities, allowing for seamless implementation and application of Naive Bayes classifiers to a wide range of real world datasets.

Types of Naïve Bayes Classifiers

In this section, we delve into the diverse landscape of Naive Bayes classifiers, exploring three prominent variants: Gaussian, Multinomial, and Bernoulli Naive Bayes. Each variant is tailored to handle specific types of data, offering unique approaches to classification tasks. By understanding the distinguishing characteristics and underlying assumptions of each variant, we gain valuable insights into their applicability and performance across various scenarios.

Gaussian Naïve Bayes

Gaussian Naive Bayes assumes that the features follow a Gaussian (normal) distribution, making it suitable for continuous data where the values of features are real numbers. In this variant, the likelihood of each feature belonging to a particular class is modeled using a Gaussian distribution, characterized by its mean and variance. Gaussian Naive Bayes is particularly effective when dealing with numerical features that exhibit a bell-shaped distribution around their mean, such as height, weight, or temperature. However, it may not perform well with features that have skewed distributions or outliers, as it assumes that the features are normally distributed.

Multinomial Naïve Bayes

Multinomial Naive Bayes, on the other hand, is designed for data with discrete features, typically represented as counts or frequencies. It assumes that the features follow a multinomial distribution, which is suitable for categorical or count-based data. In the car booking example discussed in the preceding section, the hand-worked calculation falls under the Multinomial Naive Bayes classification. Multinomial Naive Bayes is commonly used in text classification tasks, where each feature represents the frequency of a word or term in a document. It works well with data that can be represented as bag-of-words or Term Frequency-Inverse Document Frequency (TF-IDF) vectors. However, it may not be suitable for data with continuous or real-valued features, as it assumes that the features are categorical.

Bernoulli Naive Bayes

Bernoulli Naive Bayes is a variant of Naive Bayes specifically designed for binary or Boolean features, where each feature represents the presence or absence of a particular attribute. It assumes that the features follow a Bernoulli distribution, which is suitable for binary data. Bernoulli Naive Bayes is commonly used in text classification tasks, such as spam detection or sentiment analysis, where each feature represents the presence or absence of a word or term in a document. It is robust to irrelevant features and works well with sparse data. However, it may not capture the frequency of occurrence of features, as it only considers their presence or absence.

When dealing with a dataset that contains both numeric and categorical features, the preferred method depends on the nature of the data and the specific problem at hand. If the categorical features dominate the dataset and the numerical features exhibit a near-normal distribution, Multinomial Naive Bayes can be a suitable choice. This method treats each feature as a separate categorical variable and models the likelihood of each category given the class label. It works well when the categorical features are the primary drivers of the classification decision.

However, if the dataset contains mostly numerical features with a linear relationship with the dependent variable, Gaussian Naive Bayes may be more appropriate. This method assumes that the numerical features follow a Gaussian (normal) distribution and calculates the probability of each class label given the observed numerical values using the Gaussian probability density function.

In cases where the dataset has binary features (only two possible values for each feature), Bernoulli Naive Bayes could be considered. This method is suitable when dealing with binary or Boolean features and calculates the probability of each class label given the presence or absence of each binary feature.

Ultimately, the choice of method depends on the characteristics of the dataset and the specific requirements of the classification task. It may be necessary to experiment with different methods and evaluate their performance using appropriate metrics to determine the most suitable approach for the given dataset.

Applications of Naïve Bayes in Classification Task

Naive Bayes classifiers find significant utility in various classification tasks, particularly those involving data with linear relationships and numerical variables that exhibit near-normal distributions. In scenarios where the relationship between independent and dependent variables follows a linear pattern, Naive Bayes classifiers can effectively model and predict outcomes based on conditional probabilities. This characteristic makes Naive Bayes particularly suitable for tasks where the decision boundaries are linear or can be approximated linearly, such as sentiment analysis in natural language processing or predicting customer churn in marketing.

Moreover, Naive Bayes classifiers perform well when dealing with numerical variables that adhere to a near-normal distribution. By assuming independence between features and applying Bayes' theorem, Naive Bayes classifiers can effectively handle numerical data, provided that the underlying distribution aligns closely with a normal distribution. This assumption enables the classifier to estimate the probabilities of different classes given the observed values of numerical features. Consequently, Naive Bayes classifiers are commonly employed in tasks involving continuous variables, such as predicting the likelihood of default in credit scoring or diagnosing medical conditions based on patient symptoms.

Additionally, Naive Bayes classifiers are known for their simplicity, computational efficiency, and ability to handle large datasets with high-dimensional feature spaces. This makes them particularly suitable for applications where real-time predictions or scalability are essential, such as email spam detection or text categorization. Despite their "naive" assumption of feature independence, Naive Bayes classifiers often perform surprisingly well in practice, especially in situations where the assumptions hold approximately or when sufficient training data is available to compensate for any deviations from these assumptions.

A few popular domains and applications where Gaussian, Multinomial, and Bernoulli Naive Bayes classifiers are prevalent in the modern data-driven industry are as follows:

- **Natural Language Processing (NLP):** Multinomial and Bernoulli Naive Bayes are popular choices for text classification tasks such as sentiment analysis, spam detection, and document categorization.

- **Healthcare**: Gaussian Naive Bayes models can be utilized in medical diagnosis systems where numerical features such as patient vitals are analyzed to predict disease outcomes. Multinomial Naive Bayes models could be applied in healthcare analytics for classifying patient records and medical reports into various categories.

- **Finance**: Gaussian Naive Bayes model can be used in fraud detection systems to analyze transaction data and identify potentially fraudulent activities. The Multinomial Naive Bayes type model could be employed in financial text analytics for sentiment analysis of news articles and social media posts affecting stock prices.

- **E-Commerce**: Multinomial Naive Bayes type model can be employed for product categorization, customer segmentation, and recommendation systems based on user behavior and product attributes. Bernoulli Naive Bayes type of model can be useful for customer churn prediction where binary features represent customer actions or preferences.

- **Social Media Analysis**: The Multinomial Naive Bayes type model can be applied for sentiment analysis of social media posts, comments, and reviews to gauge public opinion on various topics. Bernoulli Naive Bayes is used for user profiling and classification tasks based on binary features such as user interactions.

- **Image Processing**: Gaussian Naive Bayes is utilized for image classification tasks where numerical features represent pixel values or image descriptors.

- **Telecommunications:** Multinomial Naive Bayes type model can be applied in network intrusion detection systems to classify network traffic data into normal and malicious activities.

Overall, the versatility and effectiveness of Naive Bayes classifiers make them valuable tools for a wide range of classification tasks, particularly those involving linear relationships between features and near-normal distributions of numerical variables. By leveraging the simplicity and efficiency of the Naive Bayes approach, practitioners can develop accurate and scalable solutions to various classification problems in diverse domains.

Python Implementation and Use Case

In the first use case, a synthetically generated contrived dataset is considered for this demonstration. The synthetic data represents individuals' ages and Body Mass Index (BMI) measurements, along with corresponding health status labels. The dataset consists of 100 samples, with 40 samples labeled as "Healthy," 30 samples labeled as "Pre-Diabetic," and another 30 samples labeled as "Diabetic." The age values range from 25 to 70 years, while the BMI values vary within the ranges associated with different health categories: 18 to 25 for "Healthy," 25.1 to 29 for "Pre-Diabetic," and above 29 for "Diabetic."

This dataset serves as a simplified representation of individuals' health conditions based on age and BMI. We will apply the Gaussian Naive Bayes algorithm to this dataset without leveraging pre-built libraries such as Scikit-learn, by calculating conditional probability scores and utilizing the Naive Bayes classifier formula to demonstrate the algorithm's functionality with numerical data.

Let us read the data and calculate the class-wise statistics of age and bmi.

```
file_path = 'path_to_your_data/data1_Ch5_Diabetes_Contrived_Data.csv'
df = pd.read_csv(file_path)
# Calculate mean and standard deviation for each class
class_stats = df.groupby('Class').agg({'Age': ['mean', 'std'], 'BMI': ['mean', 'std']})
print(class_stats)
```

The following table lists the class-wise statistics of age and BMI features:

Class	Age mean	Age std	BMI mean	BMI std
Diabetic	56.69	11.34	32.8	3.31
Healthy	33.42	6.49	21.73	2.06
Pre-Diabetic	51.43	9.6	26.57	1.52

Figure 5.1: Class-Wise Statistics of Age and BMI Features

In *Figure* 5.1, the class-wise mean and standard deviation of the Age and BMI features are depicted, illustrating the mean values of the features in relation to each class. The

Naive Bayes as a Linear Classifier

Gaussian Naïve Bayes classification model relies on linearity assumptions and expects numerical features to exhibit a near-normal distribution.

Scaling the data is an essential preprocessing step in many machine learning algorithms, including Naive Bayes. By scaling the data, we ensure that all features have the same scale, which prevents certain features from dominating the learning process due to their larger magnitude. In the context of Gaussian Naive Bayes, scaling the data is particularly important because the algorithm assumes that the features follow a Gaussian (normal) distribution with a mean of 0 and a standard deviation of 1. Standardizing the features to have a mean of 0 and a standard deviation of 1 ensures that they meet this assumption, allowing us to accurately calculate conditional probabilities.

```
from sklearn.preprocessing import StandardScaler
# Initialize the StandardScaler
scaler = StandardScaler()
# Fit and transform the Age and BMI columns
df[['Age', 'BMI']] = scaler.fit_transform(df[['Age', 'BMI']])
# Display the first few rows of the updated DataFrame
print(df.head())
```

Towards the next step, we shall scale the data and display the first five records as shown in *Figure* 5.2.

No	Age	BMI	Class
1	-1.64	-1.28	Healthy
2	-1.27	-0.98	Healthy
3	-0.9	-0.49	Healthy
4	-0.53	-0.19	Pre-Diabetic
5	-0.16	-0.29	Pre-Diabetic

***Figure* 5.2:** *Head of Updated Data Frame Succeeding Scaling*

```
# Calculate mean and standard deviation for each class after scaling
class_stats_scaled = df.groupby('Class').agg({'Age': ['mean', 'std'], 'BMI': ['mean', 'std']})
```

Also, the class-wise statistics got updated as shown in *Figure* 5.3 subsequent to scaling the data.

	Age	Age	BMI	BMI
	mean	std	mean	std
Class				
Diabetic	0.7	0.84	1.15	0.66
Healthy	-1.02	0.48	-1.04	0.41
Pre-Diabetic	0.32	0.71	-0.08	0.3

Figure 5.3: *Class Wise Statistics Succeeding Scaling the Data*

The next step is to define a Gaussian probability density function, also known as the normal distribution, is a fundamental concept in statistics and probability theory. It describes the probability distribution of a continuous random variable that is symmetric and bell-shaped. The formula for the Gaussian probability density function involves two parameters: the mean (μ) and the standard deviation (σ).

$$f(x|\mu,\sigma) = \frac{1}{\sigma\sqrt{2\pi}} e^{\frac{-((x-\mu)^2)}{2\sigma^2}}$$

```
def my_gpdf(x,mean,sd):
    exponent=np.exp(-((x-mean)**2/(2*sd**2)))
    return (1/(np.sqrt(2*np.pi)*sd))*exponent
```

The preceding function computes the probability density of the value 'x' occurring in a normal distribution with the specified mean and standard deviation. It follows the formula of the Gaussian PDF and returns the result. We can use this function to compute the likelihood of observing a specific value under a normal distribution, which is crucial in Gaussian Naive Bayes classification.

Here we are showcasing a step-by-step approach to computing the Gaussian Naïve Bayes classification model formula without relying on the Scikit Learn Library. To achieve this, we have developed a custom Gaussian PDF function for probability calculations. This approach allows us to delve into the underlying mechanics of the model and gain a deeper understanding of its inner workings.

Let us consider a test, using data with [Age=30 years, BMI=20.0], we shall compute class-wise conditional probability using the aforementioned function. Towards the first step, we will convert the test data into a standardized scale.

```
test_age=(30-df['Age'].mean())/df['Age'].std()
test_bmi=(20-df['BMI').mean())/df['BMI'].std()
[test_age,test_bmi]=[-1.2650, -1.3716]
P_healthy=my_gpdf(test_age,class_stats[('Age','mean')]['Healthy'],class_
stats[('Age','std')]['Healthy'])*my_gpdf(test_bmi,class_
stats[('BMI','mean')]['Healthy'],class_stats[('BMI','std')]
```

```
['Healthy'])*(33/100)
P_healthy = 0.1657
P_pre_diab=my_gpdf(test_age,class_stats[('Age','mean')]['Pre-Diabetic'],
class_stats[('Age','std')]['Pre-Diabetic']) *my_gpdf(test_bmi,class_
stats[('BMI','mean')]['Pre-Diabetic'],
class_stats[('BMI','std')]['Pre-Diabetic'])*(35/100)
P_pre_diab= 0.000001801053
P_diab=my_gpdf(test_age,class_stats[('Age','mean')]['Diabetic'],-
class_stats[('Age','std')]['Diabetic'])*my_gpdf(test_bmi,class_
stats[('BMI','mean')]['Diabetic'],class_stats[('BMI','std')]
['Diabetic'])*(32/100)
P_diab=0.00000335517
```

Observing that the probability of being in the healthy class is higher than that of the pre-diabetic and diabetic classes, we conclude that the test record is likely to belong to the healthy class.

Let us consider another test data with [Age=60 years, BMI=31.5], and compute similar calculations and compare the probability scores.

```
[Test_age,test_bmi] = [0.9452,0.89310]
P_healthy = 0.00000000078756
P_pre_diabetic = 0.000893809
P_diabetic = 0.0829
```

Observing that the probability of being in the diabetic class is higher than that of the pre-diabetic and healthy classes, we conclude that the test record is likely to belong to the diabetic class.

A Use Case with GaussianNB Scikit Learn Library

In this section, we delve into a practical application of the Gaussian Naïve Bayes classifier using the Scikit Learn library. Gaussian Naïve Bayes is a powerful tool for classification tasks, particularly when dealing with continuous features that follow a Gaussian distribution. By leveraging the Scikit Learn library, we can efficiently implement the Gaussian Naïve Bayes algorithm and apply it to real-world datasets. This use case will provide valuable insights into how Gaussian Naïve Bayes can be employed in various domains, demonstrating its effectiveness in classification tasks.

This dataset considered for this use case is downloaded from the UCI Machine Learning repository. It is composed of 14 attributes which are age, sex, chest pain type, resting blood pressure, serum cholesterol, fasting blood sugar, resting electrocardiographic results, maximum heart rate achieved, exercise-induced angina, oldpeak ST depression induced by exercise relative to rest, the slope of the peak exercise ST segment, number of major vessels and Thalassemia. This database includes 76 attributes, but all published studies relate to the use of a subset of 14 of them.

Let us load the data and explore its variables.

```
file_path = 'path_to_your_data/data2_Ch5_heart_disease_uci.csv'
df = pd.read_csv(file_path)
```

Let us drop the patient ID and 'dataset' column which indicates the origin city of the patient, as they do not contribute to the model's features.

```
df = df.drop(['id','dataset'], axis = 1)
```

The target variable is '**num**' which is the heart disease category. The dataset does not have enough records for category '**4**', so we shall drop those records and proceed with our analysis with three classes of abnormality, '**1**' being mild, '**2**' being moderate, and '**3**' being severe. Based on domain knowledge, Label-1 (mild) and Label-2 (moderate) features overlap nearly 90%, moreover, we are building a linear model, which does not have the capability to form a non-linear boundary for mild and moderate class. Hence, we combine both Label-1(mild) and Label-2(moderate) categories into a common class. Now, effectively we have Label-0 being normal (no heart disease category), Label-1 being moderate heart disorder, and Label-1 being severe disorder.

```
# Remove records where 'num' column value is 4
df = df[df['num'] != 4]
# Size of the dataframe after removal
df.shape
(891, 14))

# Combine the labels as specified
df['num'] = df['num'].replace({2: 1, 3: 2})
```

In preparation for our analysis, we will delve into Exploratory Data Analysis (EDA) to scrutinize each variable's significance within the dataset and its influence on the dependent variable. Through this process, we aim to uncover patterns, trends, and relationships that can provide valuable insights into the underlying structure of the data. By exploring various aspects such as distributions, correlations, and outliers, we will gain a comprehensive understanding of the dataset's characteristics, enabling us to make informed decisions throughout our analysis.

Exploratory Data Analysis with Heart Disease Dataset

The column names in the dataset are listed as follows with its brief description:

```
column_names = df.columns.tolist()
```

- '**age**': age of the patient

- **'sex'**: gender
- **'cp'**: chest pain type (4 values)
- **'trestbps'**: resting blood pressure
- **'chol'**: serum cholesterol in mg/dl
- **'fbs'**: fasting blood sugar ('1' if > 120 mg/dl or '0' otherwise)
- **'restecg'**: resting electrocardiographic results (values 0,1,2)
- **'thalch'**: maximum heart rate achieved
- **'exang'**: exercise-induced angina
- **'oldpeak'**: ST depression induced by exercise relative to rest
- **'slope'**: the slope of the peak exercise ST segment
- **'ca'**: number of major vessels (0-3) colored by fluoroscopy
- **'thal'**: 0 = normal; 1 = fixed defect; 2 = reversible defect
- **'num'**: Dependent variable, **0** indicates no heart disease, **1** being moderate, and **2** being severe heart disease

We shall begin with the age column and visualize its distribution.

```
sns.histplot(df['age'], kde=True)
```

Figure 5.4 shows a near-normal distribution of age feature which is mandatory for a Naïve Bayes model.

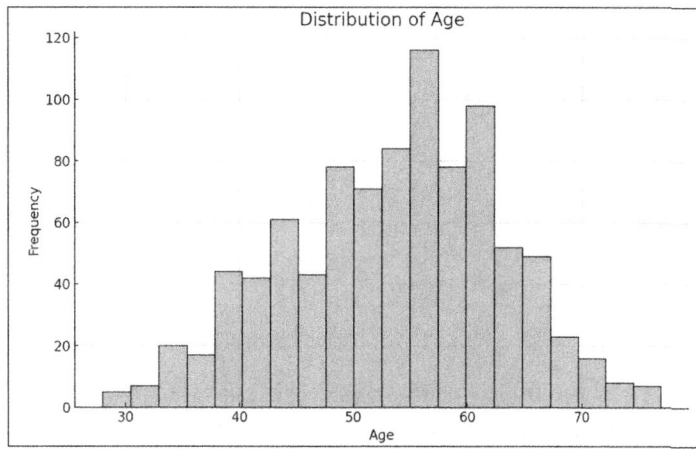

Figure 5.4: *Histogram of Age Feature*

Let us cross-tabulate the gender (**sex**) variable with respect to the dependent variable (num).

```
# Create a cross tabulation of 'sex' and 'num'
cross_tab = pd.crosstab(df['sex'], df['num'], margins=True)
```

Here is a cross tabulation of gender and heart disease categories:

sex	0	1	2
Female	144	40	8
Male	267	334	98

Figure 5.5: Cross Tabulation of Gender and Heart Disease Categories

The *Figure* 5.5 shows the distribution of heart disease categories across males and females. We could notice females have relatively lower counts in higher heart disease categories, with the highest being in category 1 (40). Males have a higher overall prevalence of heart disease compared to females.

We shall explore the next variable, the chest pain type (cp) variable with respect to the categories of heart disease.

```
# Create a cross tabulation of 'cp' (chest pain type) and 'num' (heart disease category)
cp_num_crosstab = pd.crosstab(df['cp'], df['num'], margins=True)
```

Here is a cross tabulation of chest pain type and heart disease category:

cp	0	1	2
asymptomatic	104	286	83
atypical angina	150	21	3
non-anginal	131	51	17
typical angina	26	16	3

Figure 5.6: Cross Tabulation of Chest Pain Type and Heart Disease Category

Figure 5.6 reflects the type of chest pain is a significant indicator of the presence and severity of heart disease. Patients with asymptomatic chest pain are more likely to fall into categories indicating heart disease. Patients with atypical angina and non-anginal chest pain are more likely to be in the `'Label-0'` category, indicating no heart disease. Typical angina, although fewer in number, also shows a higher proportion in the 'Label-0' category, but with notable presence in `'Label-1.'`

The next variable in the data is resting blood pressure, which is a numeric variable. Let us plot the distribution of the values.

```
# Display histogram of the 'trestbps' (resting blood pressure) column
sns.histplot(df[' trestbps '], kde=True)
```

Here is a histogram depicting the resting blood pressure feature:

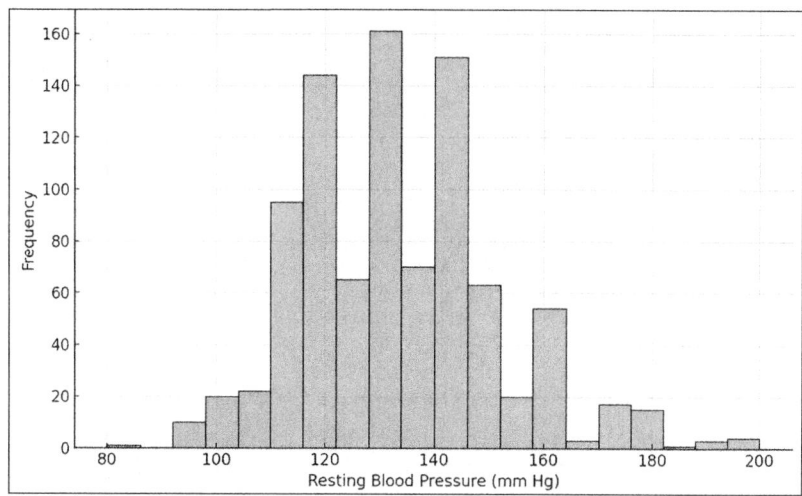

Figure 5.7: Histogram of Resting Blood Pressure Feature

The histogram shown in *Figure* 5.7 indicates the distribution of resting blood pressure (**trestbps**) in the dataset. The majority of individuals have a resting blood pressure in the range of 110 to 140 mm Hg, with a noticeable peak around 120-130 mm Hg, with moderately skewed to the right.

The next variable serum cholesterol (**chol**), there are 165 zero entries in the dataset. Practically cholesterol levels cannot be zero, let us impute the zero entries with the median of the remaining non-zero entries.

```
# Calculate the median of the non-zero entries in 'chol'
chol_median = df[df['chol'] != 0]['chol'].median()

# Impute the zero entries with the calculated median
df['chol'] = df['chol'].replace(0, chol_median)
```

We shall plot the histogram of the imputed cholesterol variable,

```
sns.histplot(df['chol'], kde=True)
```

The distribution shown in *Figure* 5.8 now reflects more realistic values for serum cholesterol.

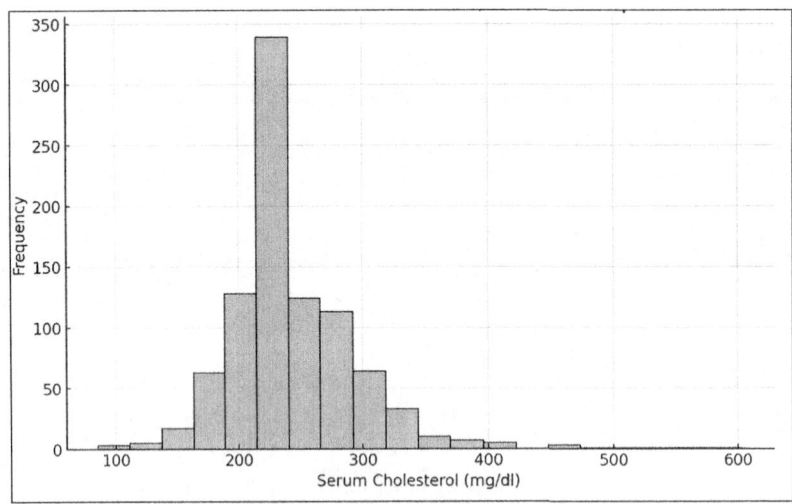

Figure 5.8: *Histogram of the Imputed Cholesterol Feature*

However, the skewness value is approximately 1.547, which indicates that the distribution is skewed to the right, which is not a desirable factor for a linear model such as the Naïve Bayes classifier. Let us impute the outlier values that are above 3 standard deviations (3 sigma) in the standardized scale and we shall plot the updated histogram.

```
# Standardize the 'chol' (serum cholesterol) column
chol_mean = df['chol'].mean()
chol_std = df['chol'].std()
df['chol_standardized'] = (df['chol'] - chol_mean) / chol_std
upper_bound_3sigma=3
# Calculate the median of the non-outlier entries in 'chol'
non_outliers_chol_median = df[df['chol_standardized'] <= upper_
bound_3sigma]['chol'].median()

# Impute the 3-sigma outlier entries with the calculated median
df.loc[df['chol_standardized'] > upper_bound_3sigma, 'chol'] = non_out-
liers_chol_median

#Values got updated in the 'chol' variable, hence chol_standardized can
be dropped
df = df.drop(columns=['chol_standardized'])
sns.histplot(df['chol'], kde=True)
```

The updated histogram in *Figure* 5.9 shows the distribution of serum cholesterol (**chol**) succeeding outlier treatment. The distribution now reflects a more realistic range of serum cholesterol values.

Naive Bayes as a Linear Classifier

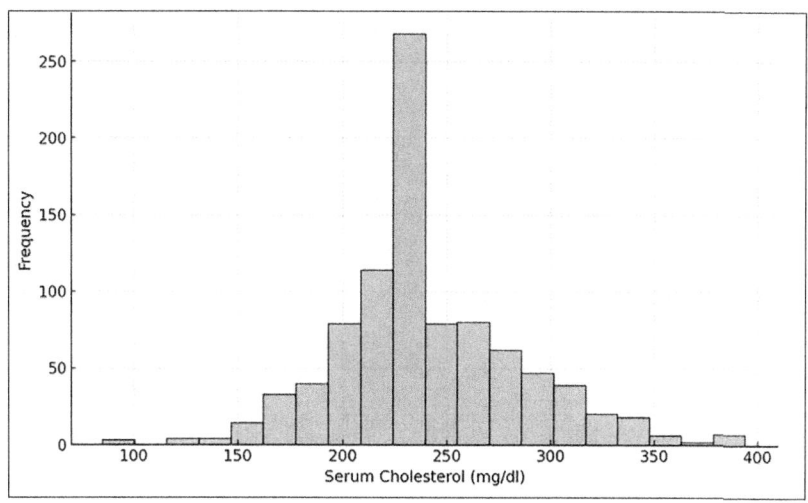

Figure 5.9: *Histogram of the Cholesterol Feature Succeeding Outlier Treatment*

Let us explore the next variable, fasting blood sugar which is a boolean type with '**1**' being above 120 mg/dl and '0' otherwise. The cross-tabulation of fasting blood sugar (fbs) with respect to the heart disease category is shown in *Figure 5.10*, which indicates that elevated fasting blood sugar levels are associated with a higher prevalence of heart disease.

```
# Create a cross tabulation of 'fbs' (fasting blood sugar) and 'num'
(heart disease category)
fbs_num_crosstab = pd.crosstab(df['fbs'], df['num'], margins=True)
```

Here is a cross tabulation of fasting blood sugar and heart disease category:

fbs	0	1	2
False	367	312	79
True	44	62	27

Figure 5.10: *Cross Tabulation of Fasting Blood Sugar and Heart Disease Category*

The next variable is resting electrocardiographic results (**restecg**), let us do the cross tabulation with respect to the heart disease category.

```
# Create a cross tabulation of 'restecg' (resting electrocardiographic
results) and 'num' (heart disease category)
restecg_num_crosstab = pd.crosstab(df['restecg'], df['num'],
margins=True)
```

The *Figure 5.11* suggests that individuals with abnormal resting electrocardiographic results (lv hypertrophy or st-t abnormality) are more likely to have heart disease compared to those with normal results.

restecg	0	1	2
lv hypertrophy	82	68	26
normal	268	226	49
st-t abnormality	61	80	31

Figure 5.11: Cross Tabulation of Resting ECG and Heart Disease Category

The next variable involved in the dataset is maximum heart rate (**thalch**). Let us visualize the histogram of this variable.

```
sns.histplot(df['thalch'], kde=True)
```

The histogram shown in *Figure 5.12* illustrate the distribution of maximum heart rate.

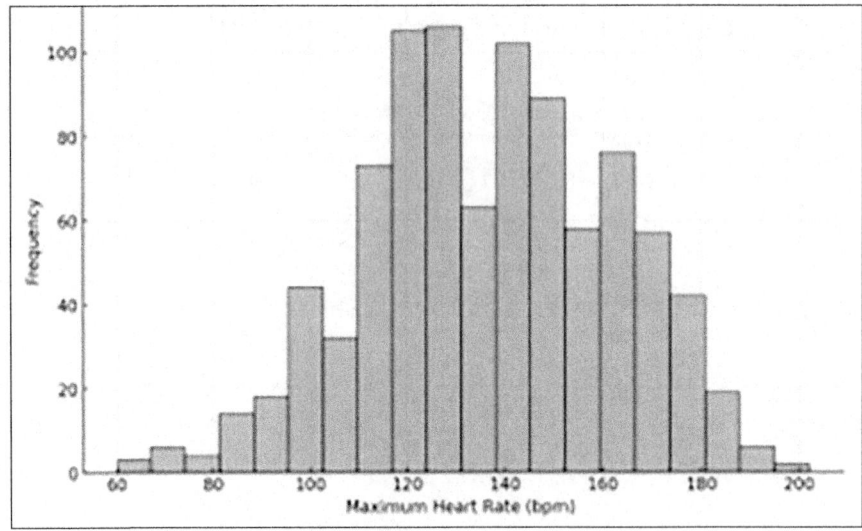

Figure 5.12: Histogram of Maximum Heart Rate

The majority of individuals have a maximum heart rate between 100 and 200 beats per minute, with a peak of around 150 beats per minute. The plot shows a near-normal distribution, which is very favorable for linear models such as the Naïve Bayes classifier.

The next variable is exercise-induced angina (**exang**), meaning pain in the chest due to exercise, which is a categorical feature with majority of individuals who do not experience exercise-induced angina (represented by 0), while a smaller number do

Naive Bayes as a Linear Classifier

(represented by 1). Let us view the cross tabulation of this variable with heart disease category.

```
# Create a cross tabulation of 'exang' (exercise induced angina) and
'num' (heart disease category)
exang_num_crosstab = pd.crosstab(df['exang'], df['num'], margins=True)
```

The *Figure* 5.13 suggests that Patients with exercise-induced angina are more likely to fall into the **'Label-1'** and **'Label-2'** categories, indicating a higher risk of heart disease.

exang	0	1	2
False	347	153	31
True	64	221	75

Figure 5.13*: Cross Tabulation of Exercise-Induced Angina and Heart Disease Category*

The next variable involved in the dataset is ST depression induced by exercise relative to rest (**oldpeak**) which is a numerical variable. Let us visualize the histogram of this variable.

```
sns.histplot(df['oldpeak'], kde=True)
```

The histogram shown in *Figure* 5.14 indicates the distribution of ST depression induced by exercise relative to rest (**oldpeak**). The majority of individuals have an ST depression value close to 0, with the frequency decreasing as the ST depression value increases.

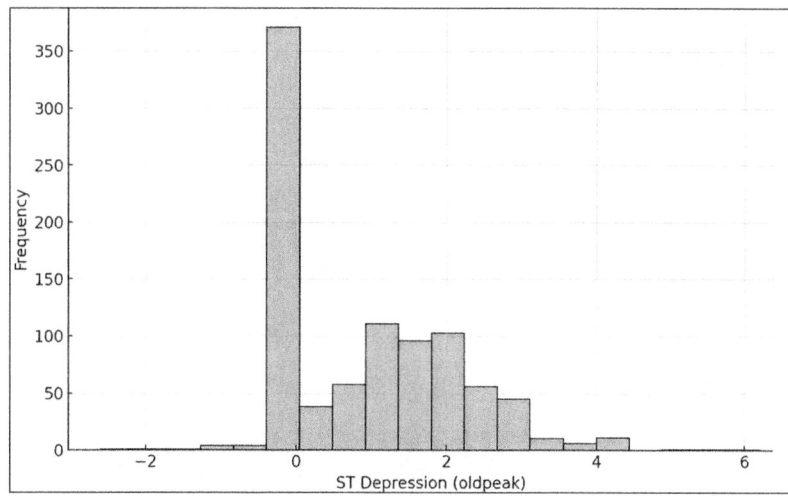

Figure 5.14*: Histogram of Oldpeak Variable*

The next variable is the slope of the peak exercise ST segment which is a categorical feature. Let us view the cross tabulation of this variable with the heart disease category.

```
# Create a cross tabulation of 'slope' and 'num' (heart disease category)
slope_num_crosstab = pd.crosstab(df['slope'], df['num'], margins=True)
```

Figure 5.15 suggests that the type of slope is associated with the presence and severity of heart disease, with flat and down-sloping slopes indicating a higher likelihood of heart disease compared to an up-sloping slope.

slope	0	1	2
downsloping	14	32	18
flat	190	280	71
upsloping	207	62	17

***Figure* 5.15**: *Cross Tabulation of Peak Exercise Segment (ST) and Heart Disease Category*

The next variable is the number of major vessels (0-3) colored by fluoroscopy, which is again a categorical feature. Let us view the cross tabulation of this variable with heart disease category.

```
# Create a cross tabulation of 'ca' and 'num' (heart disease category)
slope_num_crosstab = pd.crosstab(df['ca'], df['num'], margins=True)
```

These observations shown in *Figure* 5.16 suggest a correlation between the number of major vessels colored by fluoroscopy and the severity of heart disease. More vessels colored by fluoroscopy typically indicate a higher severity of heart disease.

ca	0	1	2
0.0	379	200	22
1.0	21	123	31
2.0	8	44	48
3.0	3	7	5

***Figure* 5.16**: *Cross Tabulation of Major Vessels (ca) and Heart Disease Category*

Finally, the last independent variable is '**thal**', which represents a thallium stress test. This test studies how well blood flows through the heart muscle while exercising. The feature with '**0**' indicates normal, '**1**' indicates a fixed defect, and '**2**' indicates a reversible defect. We shall visualize the cross tabulation of this feature with heart disease category.

```
# Create a cross tabulation of 'thal' and 'num' (heart disease category)
slope_num_crosstab = pd.crosstab(df['thal'], df['num'], margins=True)
```

Figure 5.17 reveals, the patients with a normal thallium stress test result are most likely to have no heart disease. Patients with a reversible defect are more likely to have some form of heart disease, with a significant number having moderate to severe heart disease. Fixed defect results show a more even distribution across the heart disease categories but with generally lower counts.

thal	0	1	2
fixed defect	16	39	7
normal	260	62	12
reversable defect	135	273	87

Figure 5.17: *Cross Tabulation of Thallium Stress Test and Heart Disease Category*

Subsequent to completing the exploratory analysis of the heart disease dataset, we have gained valuable insights into the relationships between various attributes and the presence and severity of heart disease. By examining the distributions, identifying outliers, and understanding the correlations between features, we have prepared the data for the next phase. We have handled missing values, standardized the necessary columns, and observed significant patterns through cross tabulations. With this comprehensive understanding of the dataset, we are now well-equipped to proceed with model building. The next step will involve using the Gaussian Naive Bayes classifier to develop a predictive model that can accurately classify and predict heart disease based on the features in our dataset.

Model Building and Evaluation

Previous to feeding the data to the model, it is mandatory to encode all categorical columns to nominal values and the data type needs to be maintained as an object data type.

```
from sklearn.preprocessing import LabelEncoder

# Encode categorical columns
label_encoders = {}
categorical_columns = df.select_dtypes(include=['object', 'bool']).columns
```

```python
for column in categorical_columns:
    label_encoders[column] = LabelEncoder()
    df[column] = label_encoders[column].fit_transform(df[column])

# Convert encoded columns back to object data type
for column in categorical_columns:
    df[column] = df[column].astype('object')

# Type cast 'ca' column as object
df['ca'] = df['ca'].astype(object)
```

Let us define all the updated feature variables in '**X**' and the target variable in '**Y**.'

```python
# Define X and Y variables
X = df.drop('num', axis=1)
Y = df['num']
```

Prior to splitting the records into training and validation sets, all numerical columns are standardized which is very favorable for Gaussian Naïve Bayes Model.

```python
from sklearn.preprocessing import StandardScaler

# Identify numerical columns (excluding object data types)
numerical_cols = X.select_dtypes(include=['int64', 'float64']).columns

# Initialize the standard scaler
scaler = StandardScaler()

# Standardize the numerical columns
X[numerical_cols] = scaler.fit_transform(X[numerical_cols])
```

The dataset is divided into training and validation sets with 70% for training and 30% for validation.

```python
from sklearn.model_selection import train_test_split
# Split the dataset into training and validation sets
xtrain, xtest, ytrain, ytest = train_test_split(X, Y, test_size=0.3, random_state=42)
# Verify the size of each set
xtrain.shape, xtest.shape, ytrain.shape, ytest.shape
((623, 13), (268, 13), (623,), (268,))
```

The Gaussian Naive Bayes model is fitted to the training data, and predictions have been made on the validation set, as follows:

```python
from sklearn.naive_bayes import GaussianNB
# Initialize the Gaussian Naive Bayes classifier
gnb = GaussianNB()
# Fit the model on the training data
gnb.fit(xtrain, ytrain)
```

Naive Bayes as a Linear Classifier

```
# Predict on the validation set
y_pred = gnb.predict(xtest)

#Performance Analysis
from sklearn.metrics import confusion_matrix, classification_report

# Calculate the confusion matrix
conf_matrix = confusion_matrix(ytest, y_pred)

# Calculate the classification report
class_report = classification_report(ytest, y_pred)
```

The confusion matrix has been tabulated and displayed in *Figure* 5.18. Overall, the model has a decent accuracy of **71%** (sum of the diagonals scaled with total validation records), but improvements are needed, especially for better distinguishing between `Class 1` and `Class 2.`

	Predicted 0	Predicted 1	Predicted 2
Actual 0	113	20	0
Actual 1	25	65	19
Actual 2	0	13	13

***Figure* 5.18**: *Confusion Matrix for the Predictions*

The classification report shown in *Figure* 5.19 shows the model performs well for classifying `Class 0` with high precision and recall. The performance drops for `Class 1,` with moderate precision and recall. The model struggles with `Class 2,` showing lower precision and recall.

	precision	recall	f1-score	support
0	0.82	0.85	0.83	133.0
1	0.66	0.6	0.63	109.0
2	0.41	0.5	0.45	26.0
accuracy			0.71	0.71
macro avg	0.63	0.65	0.64	268.0
weighted avg	0.72	0.71	0.71	268.0

***Figure* 5.19**: *Classification Report for the Predictions*

Model Performance Summary

The Gaussian Naive Bayes model was applied to a dataset to classify instances into three different categories of heart disease severity. Here is a summary of the model's performance:

Features Overlap: The features in the dataset show moderate overlap between the three classes. This overlapping nature presents a significant challenge for a linear model such as Gaussian Naive Bayes.

Overall Accuracy: Despite the challenges posed by feature overlap, the model achieved a respectable overall accuracy of 71%. This indicates that the model performs reasonably well in distinguishing between the classes based on the given features.

Given the nature of the dataset, non-linear models could provide significant improvements. Non-linear models can better capture the complexities and interactions between features, leading to improved recall scores for the moderate and severe classes. In subsequent chapters, we will explore various non-linear models, such as decision trees, random forests, support vector machines, and neural networks. These models have the potential to handle the overlapping features more effectively and improve the classification performance for the more challenging classes.

Challenges and Constraints in the Naïve Bayes Model

The Naive Bayes model, while renowned for its simplicity and efficiency, encounters significant limitations when applied to data with complex, non-linear relationships among variables. One primary challenge stems from the model's fundamental assumption of feature independence given the class label. In reality, features often exhibit interdependencies, and the presumption of their independence can lead to suboptimal performance, particularly in cases where the correlation between features significantly influences the output.

Another constraint of the Naive Bayes model is its tendency to perform poorly on imbalanced datasets where some classes are underrepresented. In such scenarios, the model's probability estimates may be biased towards the more frequent classes. This skew can severely affect the model's accuracy, making it less reliable for real-world applications where class distribution is not uniform.

The model also struggles with data that features non-linear relationships between attributes and class labels. Naive Bayes inherently models linear boundaries due to its probabilistic approach, which can be inadequate for capturing complex patterns. This is especially evident in scenarios where the decision boundary between classes is curved or irregular, leading to significant misclassification of instances that lie near these boundaries.

Furthermore, the performance of Naive Bayes is heavily dependent on the accurate estimation of probability distributions for each feature. If the actual distribution of the data deviates from the assumptions made by the model (such as normality in Gaussian Naive Bayes), the reliability of the resulting predictions can be compromised. This model's sensitivity to the distribution of input data underscores its unsuitability for datasets where the underlying distributions are unknown or difficult to estimate accurately.

In summary, while Naive Bayes can provide a robust baseline model due to its simplicity and computational efficiency, its application is best suited for datasets that closely adhere to its underlying assumptions. For data characterized by complex, non-linear relationships and dependencies among features, alternative models that can accommodate such complexities might be more appropriate.

Conclusion

In this chapter, we thoroughly explored the Naive Bayes algorithm, starting with a comprehensive overview, followed by detailed mathematical definitions accompanied by illustrative examples on a contrived dataset. The practical application of the Naive Bayes model in various classification tasks underscores its utility and adaptability across diverse scenarios. Our discussion extended into a Python implementation, where we applied the Naive Bayes model to a real-world dataset, demonstrating its capability to provide reasonably accurate predictions with straightforward implementation.

Despite its evident utility, the Naive Bayes model is not without limitations, particularly when dealing with data characterized by non-linear relationships and interdependent features. As we have seen, while the model excels in scenarios with linear decision boundaries and independent features, its performance can degrade significantly under the complexity of real-world data structures, which often do not conform neatly to these assumptions.

As we transition to the next chapter, we will delve into Decision Trees and Random Forest models well-suited for handling the complexities of non-linear data relationships that pose challenges for models such as Naive Bayes. These methods offer powerful alternatives by constructing decision boundaries that can aptly navigate the intricate patterns found in more complex datasets.

Practice Exercises

1. Consider a dataset with two features, X_1 and X_2, and a binary class label Y. The dataset has the following counts. Calculate P(Y=1|X1=1, X2=1) using the Naive Bayes formula.

   ```
   P(Y=1) =0.4
   P(Y=0) =0.6
   P(X1=1|Y=1) =0.5
   P(X1=1|Y=0) =0.2
   P(X2=1|Y=1) =0.3
   P(X2=1|Y=0) =0.4
   ```

2. A Naive Bayes classifier is used to classify emails as spam or not spam based on the presence of certain words. If the probability of an email being spam is 0.2 and the probability of an email containing the word "free" given that it is spam, is 0.7, while the probability of containing "free" given that it is not spam is 0.1, calculate the probability of an email being spam given that it contains the word "free."

3. For a Naive Bayes classifier used to predict whether a loan will be approved or not, the following probabilities are given. Calculate the probability that a loan will be approved given that the income is high and the credit score is good.

   ```
   P (Approved) =0.6
   P (Declined) =0.4
   P (Income=High|Approved) =0.7
   P (Income=High|Declined) =0.2
   P (CreditScore=Good|Approved) =0.8
   P (CreditScore=Good|Declined) =0.3
   ```

4. Given the contrived data in *Figure 5.17*, identify the challenge faced by the Naive Bayes model when dealing with feature X.

X	Class Y
0	1
0	0
0	1
1	1
1	1

   Figure 5.20: *Contrived Data*

5. In a medical diagnosis scenario, a Naive Bayes classifier is used to predict the presence of a disease. The following probabilities are given. Calculate the probability that a person has the disease given that their test result is positive.

P(Disease)=0.01
P(NoDisease)=0.99
P(TestPositive|Disease)=0.95
P(Test Positive|No Disease) = 0.02

Answers

1. $\dfrac{0.5 \times 0.3 \times 0.4}{0.32 \times 0.36} = 0.52$

2. $P(Spam|Free) = \dfrac{P(Free|Spam) \cdot P(Spam)}{P(Free)} = \dfrac{0.7 \times 0.2}{0.22} = 0.636$

3. $P(Approved|Income=High, CreditScore=Good) = \dfrac{0.7 \times 0.8 \times 0.6}{0.5 \times 0.6} = 1$

4. The challenge here is the zero-frequency problem. For X=1 and Y=0, there are no instances in the training dataset. This means P(X=1|Y=0) =0, which can lead to issues in calculating probabilities. A common way to handle this is by using smoothing.

5. $P(Disease|TestPositive) = \dfrac{0.95 \times 0.01}{0.0293} = 0.324$

Multiple Choice Questions

1. What does the Naive Bayes classifier primarily use to make predictions?

    a. Decision Trees

    b. Neural Networks

    c. Bayes' Theorem

    d. Regression Analysis

2. Which assumption is central to the Naive Bayes classifier?

    a. All variables are equally important

    b. Features depend on each other

    c. There is always a class imbalance

    d. Features are independent given the class

3. Which variant of Naive Bayes is best used for data with a Gaussian distribution?

    a. Multinomial Naive Bayes

    b. Gaussian Naive Bayes

    c. Bernoulli Naive Bayes

    d. Bimodal Naive Bayes

4. What is a major challenge when using Naive Bayes in real-world datasets?

    a. Computing power

    b. Data storage

    c. Feature dependence

    d. Overfitting the model

5. Which of the following is a measure of a classifier's accuracy?

    a. Leverage

    b. F1 Score

    c. Kurtosis

    d. Variance

6. In the context of Naive Bayes, what does the prior probability represent?

    a. The likelihood of the predictors

    b. The initial probability of a class preceding the data is observed

    c. The probability of the predictors given the class

    d. The predictive power of the model

7. What is calculated by dividing the number of true positives by the sum of true positives and false positives?

    a. Recall

    b. Precision

    c. Accuracy

    d. Support

8. When a Naive Bayes classifier makes a prediction, it computes:

    a. The least squares

    b. The mode of the classes

    c. The median of the probabilities

    d. The highest posterior probability

9. What impact does class imbalance have on Naive Bayes classification?

    a. It has no impact on classification accuracy

    b. It can bias the probability estimates towards the majority class

c. It increases computational complexity

d. It simplifies the model's parameters

10. What is used to evaluate the likelihood in Naive Bayes?

a. The class probability of not occurring

b. The joint probability of the predictors

c. The probability of the predictors given the class

d. The ratio of class probabilities

Answers

1. c
2. d
3. b
4. c
5. b
6. b
7. b
8. d
9. b
10. c

Keywords

- Naive Bayes Classifier
- Bayes' Theorem
- Conditional Probability
- Feature Independence
- Class Prior Probability
- Likelihood
- Posterior Probability
- Gaussian Naive Bayes
- Multinomial Naive Bayes

- Bernoulli Naive Bayes
- Class Imbalance
- Feature Extraction
- Model Evaluation
- Confusion Matrix
- Classification Report
- Accuracy
- Precision
- Recall
- F1 Score

References

1. https://archive.ics.uci.edu/dataset/45/heart+disease
2. https://www.kaggle.com/datasets

CHAPTER 6
Tree-Based Machine Learning Models

Introduction

In the previous chapters, we focused extensively on linear models, which are foundational to understanding the principles of Machine Learning. These models, while powerful in their simplicity and ability to provide clear interpretations, often fall short when dealing with complex, non-linear data patterns. Thus, as we turn the page to *Chapter 6, Tree-Based Machine Learning Models*, we begin our exploration into the dynamic realm of non-linear models, starting with Tree-based Machine Learning models. These models are not only pivotal in handling non-linear data efficiently but also offer robustness and high accuracy in diverse scenarios.

This chapter delves with Decision Tree Models, the fundamental building blocks for many advanced non-linear machine learning methods. This chapter aims to equip readers with both a theoretical understanding and practical skills to implement and optimize these models, ensuring a thorough grasp of their applications and nuances. We begin our exploration with Decision Tree Models, the fundamental building blocks of more complex tree-based techniques. Decision trees are simple yet powerful models that partition the data space into subsets based on feature-based questions. This method allows for intuitive decision-making that mimics human decision logic, making them not only effective but also easy to visualize and understand.

Advancing from single trees to the forest, we discuss Random Forest as an ensemble learning technique. By integrating multiple decision trees to make more accurate and stable predictions, Random Forest addresses some of the key limitations of individual decision trees, such as overfitting. Following this, we delve into other ensemble strategies that enhance model performance: Bagging and Boosting. Each technique has its own unique approach, from Bootstrap Aggregating (Bagging), which reduces variance and helps avoid overfitting, to Adaptive Boosting (AdaBoost) and Gradient Boosting Machines (GBM), which sequentially build models to correct the errors of their predecessors.

The chapter culminates in a detailed examination of the differences between Bagging and Boosting, highlighting their strengths and weaknesses. We will also provide a practical guide to implementing these techniques using Python, complete with code snippets and explanations to ensure that readers can not only understand but also apply what they learn directly to real-world datasets.

Structure

In this chapter, we are going to cover the following main topics:

- Overview of Decision Tree Model
- Mathematical Foundation with Hand-Worked Calculation with Contrived Dataset
- Python Implementation and Use Case with Decision Tree
- Limitations and Drawbacks in Decision Tree Models
- Random Forest Model as Ensemble Learning
- Python Implementation and Use Case with Random Forest
- Ensemble Learning: Bagging and Boosting
- Adaptive Boosting Technique
- Gradient Boosting Technique
- Xtreme Gradient Boosting Technique
- Stacking and Voting Ensemble Models

Overview of Decision Tree Model

Decision Tree Models are among the most intuitive and accessible types of machine learning algorithms. Rooted in classical decision-making theory, these models mimic human reasoning by making sequential, hierarchical decisions about the data, leading to a prediction. Decision trees split the data into subsets based on feature-based questions, creating a model that mimics human decision-making logic.

A decision tree is built from a root node to various leaf nodes, each representing classifications or decision outcomes. The nodes represent the decision points where questions about the data are asked, and branches represent the outcome of those questions, leading to further nodes or leaves. The process starts at the root node and splits the data on features that result in the highest information gain or the greatest reduction in impurity. At their core, decision trees use a tree-like graph of decisions and their possible consequences, including chance event outcomes, resource costs, and utility. A typical decision tree is shown in *Figure 6.1*, which demonstrates the concept at two levels, referred to as depth, with branches based on categorical questions. This hierarchical structure, where each decision point (node) leads to further sub-categories (branches), illustrates the decision-making process in a tree-like manner. Each question at a node is categorical, distinguishing between types such as vegetarian versus non-vegetarian or protein versus carbohydrates.

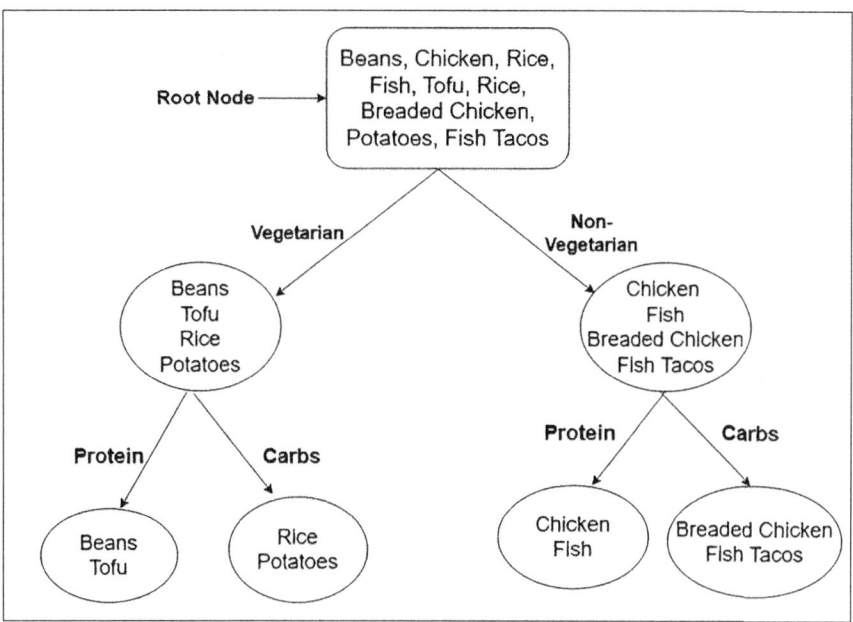

Figure 6.1: Illustrative Example of a Decision Tree

In addition to categorical splits, decision trees can also utilize numerical questions to make decisions. For example, instead of categorizing food items based on type, we could split them based on their caloric value. A numerical split might involve a question such as, "Is the caloric value greater than 100 calories?" This would result in branches for items with calories above or below this threshold, enabling the tree to handle continuous data effectively and make decisions based on numerical values. This flexibility allows decision trees to manage a wide variety of data types, making them versatile tools in machine learning.

Decision trees can handle both categorical and continuous data, making them versatile for classification and regression tasks. In classification, a decision tree makes splits that best separate the classes in the target variable. Each node in the tree acts as a point of decision, branching off into possible outcomes until reaching the leaf nodes, which represent the classification predictions.

In regression tasks, decision trees predict continuous values similar to how they handle classifications. Instead of ending in categories, the leaf nodes represent the average target value of the data points that end up in the leaf. This method can effectively capture the non-linear relationships between features and the target variable.

Mathematical Foundation

The selection of features and the criteria for splitting at each node depend primarily on mathematical measures such as Gini Impurity, Entropy in the case of classification problems, and variance reduction in regression. For classification, Entropy measures the randomness in the information being processed, while the Gini Impurity is a metric to minimize the probability of misclassification. In regression, variance is used as a measure to make decisions at each node, aiming to reduce the variance of the predictions in the subsets formed by the split.

Entropy is calculated using the formula:

$$\text{Entropy}(S) = -\sum_{i=1}^{n} p_i * log_2 p_i$$

Where p_i is the proportion of the number of elements in class i to the number of elements in set S.

Gini impurity can be defined as:

$$\text{Gini}(S) = 1 - \sum_{i=1}^{n} p_i^2$$

Where p_i again represents the proportion of class i elements in the dataset S.

Variance Reduction is commonly used in regression trees, where the aim is to reduce the variance around the mean of the target variable at a specific node. Variance measures how much the data points deviate from the mean of the target variable at that node. The formula for variance at a specific node N is:

$$\text{Variance}(N) = \frac{1}{|N|} \sum_{i \in N} (y_i - \bar{y}N)^2$$

Where y_i is the target value for the ith data point in node N, $\bar{y}N$ is the mean of the target values in node N, and |N| is the number of data points in node N.

Decision Tree as a Classifier: An Illustrative Example with Contrived Dataset

To demonstrate the Decision Tree as a classifier, a contrived dataset comprising 20 records of loan applicants is considered, as shown in *Figure 6.2*. Let us construct a simple decision tree based on the dataset. We will manually calculate the splits based on one or two attributes for illustration.

We will start with the attribute that provides the best split, measured by criteria such as Information Gain or Gini Index.

Tree-Based Machine Learning Models

Let us begin our calculation of the root node entropy with all 20 records. Before the split at the root node, we have 10 (Yes) and 10 (No) records with equal probabilities.

$$\text{Entropy at root node: } -(\tfrac{10}{20} \log_2 \left(\tfrac{10}{20}\right) + \tfrac{10}{20} \log_2 \left(\tfrac{10}{20}\right)) = 1$$

Entropy level "1" indicates 100% randomness with a 50/50 equal chance for a record being considered as Yes or No.

Record Number	Income	Credit Score	Debt-to-Income Ratio	Loan Approved (Yes/No)
1	60000	720	0.3	Yes
2	45000	680	0.4	No
3	75000	740	0.2	Yes
4	50000	700	0.5	No
5	80000	760	0.3	Yes
6	55000	710	0.4	Yes
7	65000	730	0.3	No
8	48000	690	0.5	No
9	85000	770	0.2	Yes
10	52000	705	0.4	Yes
11	70000	725	0.3	No
12	47000	680	0.5	No
13	78000	750	0.2	Yes
14	53000	695	0.4	No
15	72000	735	0.3	Yes
16	46000	675	0.5	No
17	77000	745	0.2	Yes
18	54000	700	0.4	No
19	69000	715	0.3	Yes
20	49000	685	0.5	No

Figure 6.2: *Contrived Data*

Root Node Split

For simplicity, let us consider the Credit Score and a split point of 710, with the split records shown in *Figure 6.3*.

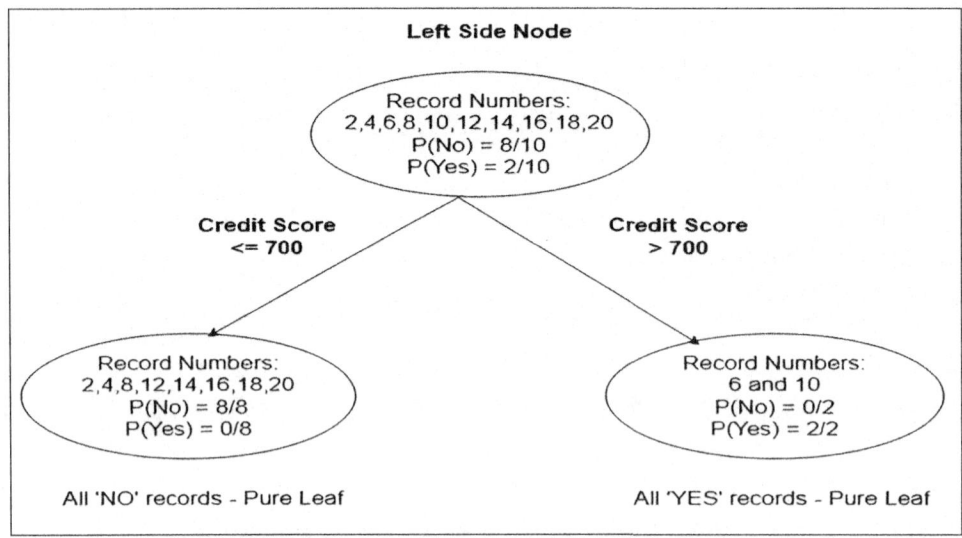

Figure 6.3: *Records after the Root Node Split*

In the left branch (Credit Score ≤ 710), there are 10 records in total. Among these, only 2 applicants were approved for the loan, resulting in a loan approval probability of 20%. The remaining 8 applicants were not approved (No), giving a loan denial probability of 80%. This indicates that applicants with a credit score of 710 or lower have a significantly higher chance of having their loan application denied.

The entropy for the left branch is: $-(0.2 log_2 0.2 + 0.8 log_2 0.8) = 0.722$

In the right branch (Credit Score > 710), there are also 10 records. Here, 8 applicants were approved (Yes) for the loan, leading to a high loan approval probability of 80%. Only 2 applicants were not approved, resulting in a loan denial probability of 20%. This demonstrates that applicants with a credit score above 710 have a much higher likelihood of loan approval.

The entropy for the right branch is: $-(0.8 log_2 0.8 + 0.2 log_2 0.2) = 0.722$

Weighted entropy at depth-1 is calculated by combining the entropy of both sides as follows:

Weighted entropy at depth-1 = $\frac{10}{20} * 0.722 + \frac{10}{20} * 0.722 = 0.361 + 0.361 = 0.722$

The weighted entropy of 0.722 indicates that we have reduced the uncertainty from 100% at the root node to 72.2%. This reduction in uncertainty is referred to as information gain, calculated as 1 - 0.722 = 0.278.

Split of the Right Node at Depth-1

The right node contains all odd-numbered records with a credit score greater than or equal to 710. Using the Debt-to-Income Ratio feature, we found the optimal threshold to further split the records in the right node, as shown in *Figure 6.4*. The chosen threshold is 0.2, which provides the best split with the lowest weighted entropy of approximately 0.551.

The split left branch has 4 records, all with 'Yes' outcomes, while the right branch has 6 records, with 4 'Yes' and 2 'No' outcomes. Let us calculate entropy at this level (depth-2).

$$\text{Entropy (left)} = -(0 log_2 0 + 1 log_2 1) = 0$$
$$\text{Entropy (right)} = -\left(\frac{4}{6} log_2 \frac{4}{6} + \frac{2}{6} log_2 \frac{2}{6}\right) = 0.918$$

The entropy for the left side branch (Debt-to-Income Ratio <= 0.2) is 0.0, indicating a pure node with no uncertainty, called a pure leaf node. The entropy for the right side branch (Debt-to-Income Ratio > 0.2) is approximately 0.918, indicating some level of uncertainty in the classification of records.

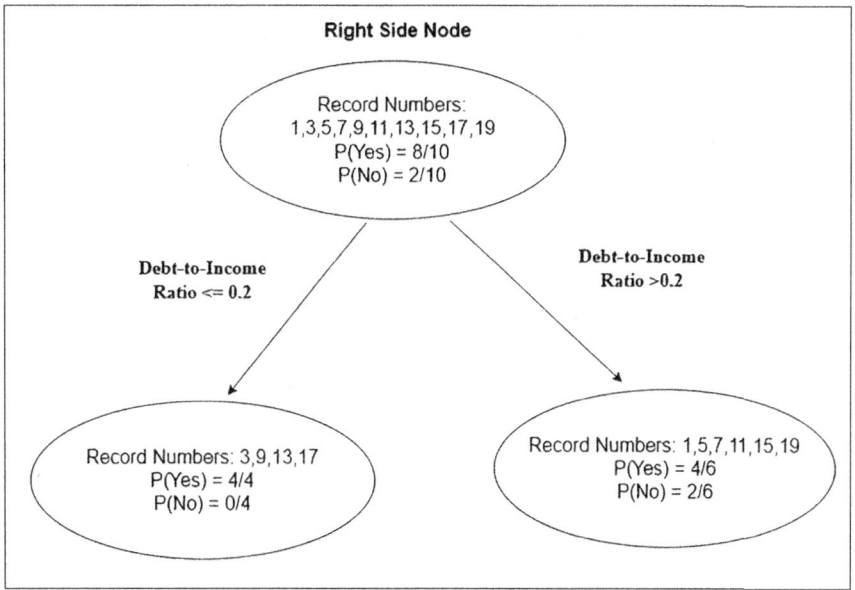

Figure 6.4: *Records after the Right Node Split*

We need to find the weighted entropy at depth-2 at the right branch as follows:

$$\text{Weighted entropy} = \frac{4}{10} * 0 + \frac{6}{10} * 0.918 = 0.5508$$

In the same manner, we need to compute the weighted entropy for the left node splits.

Split of the Left Node at Depth-1

We know the left node contains all even-numbered records with credit scores less than or equal to 710. We further split this node based on the optimal threshold to minimize the entropy. The chosen threshold is 700, which provides the best split with the lowest entropy of zero, indicating a pure leaf, as shown in *Figure* 6.5.

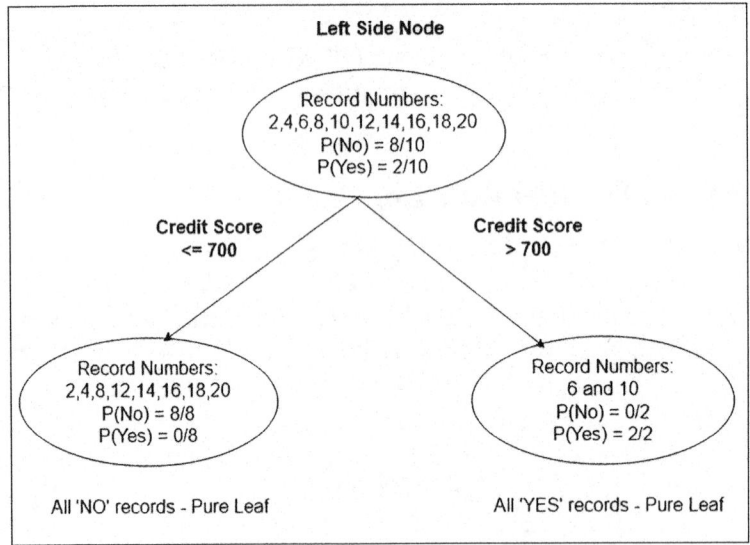

Figure 6.5: *Records after the Left Node Split*

Since we have obtained nodes with zero entropy, we call that node a pure leaf. There is no uncertainty in classifying the records. However, we have uncertainty at the right node split. We proceed with calculating the total entropy at depth-2.

Total entropy at depth-2 = left branch weighted entropy + right branch weighted entropy.

$$= 0 \text{ (completely pure nodes)} + 0.5508 = 0.5508$$

The value 0.5508 indicates that the decision tree has further reduced the entropy from 0.722 at depth-1 to 0.5508 at depth-2, demonstrating an additional information gain of 0.722 - 0.5508 = 0.1712.

Since the left branch at depth-2 has reached pure nodes, no further splitting is possible. However, the right branch at depth-2 still has the potential for additional splits. If we continue in the same manner for two more levels, we will achieve pure nodes. Generally, a decision tree can be trained until it reaches pure nodes, resulting in zero training error. This structure is known as a fully-grown decision tree. However, it is not desirable for practical use because it tends to overfit the training data, capturing noise and details that do not generalize well to new, unseen data. Consequently, this overfitting reduces the model's predictive performance on real-world tasks.

Growing the decision tree fully for the next two steps would lead to a model that overfits the training data, capturing noise and irrelevant patterns. Instead, we should stop this hand-worked illustration of the decision tree classifier at a depth of 2. This results in a pruned tree with better generalization capabilities. Hope this hand-worked illustrative example has provided insight into how a decision tree functions as a classifier.

Python Implementation of Decision Tree Classifier

To demonstrate the Decision Tree as a classifier model, a telecom customer churn dataset is taken from Kaggle. This dataset is commonly used to analyze customer churn in a telecom company. It contains various attributes of the customers along with a target variable that indicates whether a customer has churned.

The attributes are listed as follows:

- `customerID`: Unique identifier for each customer.
- `gender`: Gender of the customer (Male/Female).
- `SeniorCitizen`: Whether the customer is a senior citizen (1, 0).
- `Partner`: Whether the customer has a partner (Yes, No).
- `Dependents`: Whether the customer has dependents (Yes, No).
- `tenure`: Number of months the customer has stayed with the company.
- `PhoneService`: Whether the customer has a phone service (Yes, No).
- `MultipleLines`: Whether the customer has multiple lines (Yes, No, No phone service).
- `InternetService`: Customer's internet service provider (DSL, Fiber optic, No).
- `OnlineSecurity`: Whether the customer has online security (Yes, No, No Internet Service).
- `OnlineBackup`: Whether the customer has online backup (Yes, No, No Internet Service).
- `DeviceProtection`: Whether the customer has device protection (Yes, No, No Internet Service).
- `TechSupport`: Whether the customer has tech support (Yes, No, No Internet Service).
- `StreamingTV`: Whether the customer has streaming TV (Yes, No, No Internet Service).
- `StreamingMovies`: Whether the customer has streaming movies (Yes, No, No Internet Service).

- **Contract**: The contract term of the customer (Month-to-month, One year, Two years).
- **PaperlessBilling**: Whether the customer has paperless billing (Yes, No).
- **PaymentMethod**: The customer's payment method (Electronic check, Mailed check, Bank transfer, Credit card).
- **MonthlyCharges**: The amount charged to the customer monthly.
- **TotalCharges**: The total amount charged to the customer.
- **Churn**: Whether the customer churned (Yes, No).

Let us load the dataset and check the size of the data.

```
import pandas as pd
file_path = 'path_to_your_data/data1_Ch6_Telecom_Customer_Churn.csv'
df = pd.read_csv(file_path)
df.shape
(7043, 21)
```

After a quick visual inspection of the data, the proportion of churn rate is the same for gender and phone service columns. We remove those columns along with **CustomerID**.

```
# Drop the specified columns
df.drop(columns=['customerID', 'gender', 'PhoneService'], inplace=True)
df.shape
(7043, 18)
```

The next step is to use a label encoder to encode the categorical columns with object data types. Additionally, the column **TotalCharges** has been incorrectly typecast as an object and needs to be converted to a numeric datatype.

```
from sklearn.preprocessing import LabelEncoder
# Apply Label Encoding to object columns
label_encoders = {}
for column in df.select_dtypes(include=['object']).columns:
    le = LabelEncoder()
    df[column] = le.fit_transform(df[column])
    label_encoders[column] = le

# Convert TotalCharges to numeric, forcing errors to NaN and then fill
NaN with 0
df['TotalCharges'] = pd.to_numeric(df['TotalCharges'], errors='coerce').fillna(0)
```

Define the target and independent variables to build a decision tree model.

```
# Define the target variable and features
Y = df['Churn']
X = df.drop(columns=['Churn'])
```

Tree-Based Machine Learning Models

Let us split the record into training and validation records.

```
from sklearn.model_selection import train_test_split
xtrain, xtest, ytrain, ytest = train_test_split(X, Y, test_size=0.3, random_state=0)
xtrain.shape, xtest.shape, ytrain.shape, ytest.shape
((4930, 17), (2113, 17), (4930,), (2113,))
```

Let us define and build the decision tree model.

```
# Define and train the decision tree model
from sklearn.tree import DecisionTreeClassifier
from sklearn.metrics import confusion_matrix, classification_report

dt_model = DecisionTreeClassifier(max_depth=5, random_state=0)
dt_model.fit(xtrain, ytrain)

# Predict on the test set
y_pred = dt_model.predict(xtest)

# Compute confusion matrix and classification report
conf_matrix = confusion_matrix(ytest, y_pred)
class_report = classification_report(ytest, y_pred)
# Plot the confusion matrix
plt.figure(figsize=(8, 6))
sns.heatmap(conf_matrix, annot=True, fmt='d', cmap='Blues', xticklabels=['No Churn', 'Churn'], yticklabels=['No Churn', 'Churn'])
plt.title('Confusion Matrix')
plt.xlabel('Predicted')
plt.ylabel('Actual')
plt.show()
```

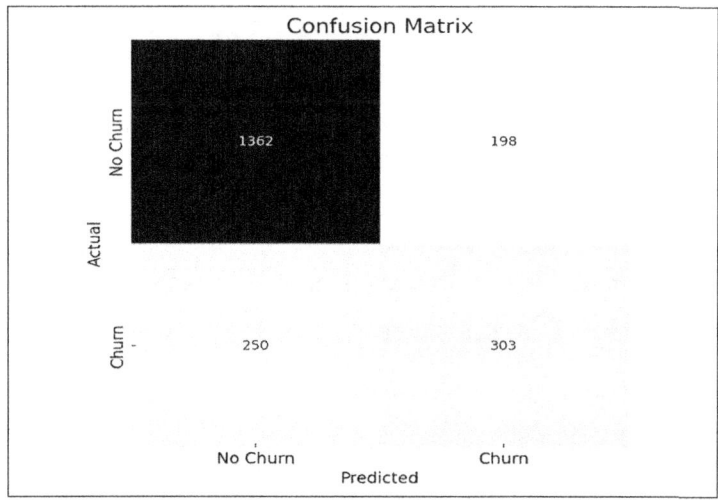

Figure 6.6: *Confusion Matrix of Decision Tree Predictions*

	precision	recall	f1-score	support
No	0.84	0.87	0.86	1560
Yes	0.60	0.55	0.57	553
accuracy			0.79	2113
macro avg	0.72	0.71	0.72	2113
weighted avg	0.78	0.79	0.78	2113

Figure 6.7: Classification Report of Decision Tree Predictions

The confusion matrix shown in Figure 6.6 illustrates the performance of a classification model aimed at predicting customer churn. The model has successfully identified a substantial number of true negatives (1362), indicating strong accuracy in predicting customers who will not churn. Conversely, it also correctly predicted 303 instances of churn (true positives), showing its effectiveness in recognizing potential churn cases. However, the model experienced some shortcomings, misclassifying 198 instances where it predicted churn incorrectly (false positives) and failing to detect churn in 250 cases (false negatives). Overall, the model demonstrates a balanced ability to identify both churn and non-churn cases, although there is room for improvement in reducing both types of errors to enhance its predictive accuracy and reliability.

The classification report shown in Figure 6.7 demonstrates a commendable precision (0.84) and recall (0.87) for predicting the "No" class, which indicates a robust ability to correctly identify customers who will not churn and do so with high reliability. For the "Yes" class, indicating actual churn, the model's performance is notably weaker, with a precision of 0.60 and a recall of 0.55, reflecting a moderate capability in accurately identifying customers likely to churn. This disparity results in an F1-score of 0.57 for the "Yes" class versus 0.86 for the "No" class, suggesting that while the model is reliable in predicting customer retention, it struggles with effectively detecting true churn cases. Overall, the model achieves an accuracy of 0.79. The weighted averages for precision, recall, and F1-score closely mirror this figure, indicating that while the model performs adequately overall, improvements are particularly needed to predict churn more accurately.

Decision Tree as a Regressor: An Illustrative Example with Contrived Dataset

Let us consider a dataset shown in Figure 6.8 with 15 records related to housing prices, featuring two independent variables: 'Size' (measured in square feet) and 'Neighborhood' (with three categories: A, B, and C). The dependent variable is 'Price,' expressed in lacs of INR, ranging from 19 to 40 lacs. This dataset is contrived to facilitate the demonstration of a decision tree Regressor, a machine learning model used to

Tree-Based Machine Learning Models

predict numerical outcomes based on input features. By analyzing how the decision tree splits the data at various points, we can understand the relationship between house size, neighborhood, and pricing, making it an effective tool for illustrating the principles of decision tree regression.

Record	Size (sq ft)	Neighborhood	Price (lacs)
1	1200	A	30
2	1500	B	35
3	900	C	20
4	1800	A	40
5	1600	B	38
6	1000	C	22
7	1300	A	32
8	1400	B	34
9	800	C	19
10	1700	A	39
11	1550	B	36
12	950	C	21
13	1250	A	31
14	1450	B	34.5
15	850	C	19.5

Figure 6.8: *Contrived Dataset*

To demonstrate a decision tree Regressor, we need to calculate the Mean Squared Error (MSE) at the root node and choose an appropriate feature to split the records in a way that reduces the MSE. The average house price across the 15 records is 30.07 lacs, with a corresponding Mean Squared Error (MSE) of 54.67.

Let us split the root node of the 15 records into two nodes, as shown in *Figure* 6.6, based on the threshold of 1100 square feet. We will place records with a size greater than 1100 square feet in the right node and those with a size less than or equal to 1100 square feet in the left node.

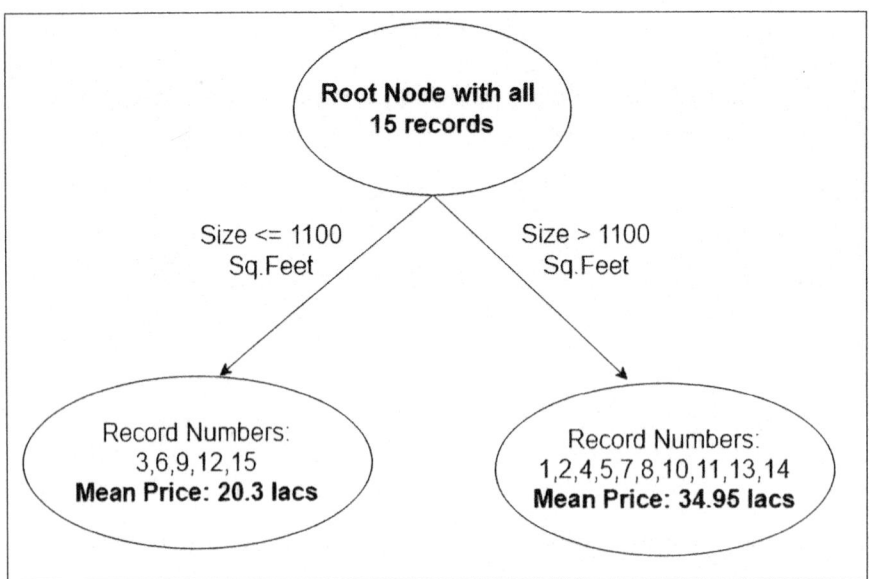

Figure 6.9: Records after the Root Node Split

After splitting the records, the MSE for the left node is calculated to be 1.16, while the MSE for the right node is found to be 10.2625. Hence, the total Mean Squared Error (MSE) at depth-1, after splitting the records, is the sum of the MSE values for the left and right nodes. This results in a total MSE of 1.16 (left node) + 10.2625 (right node) = 11.4225.

The Mean Squared Error (MSE) at the root node, initially calculated as 54.67, has been significantly reduced to 11.4225 after the split. This substantial decrease in MSE demonstrates the effectiveness of the split in improving the prediction accuracy of the decision tree Regressor.

Next, let us further split each side of the branch based on the size of the property feature, growing the tree to a depth of 2.

Split of the Left Node at Depth-1

The left node at depth-1, with an MSE of 1.16, exhibits very minimal error, indicating that the property prices within this node are closely clustered around 20 lacs. This low MSE suggests that the properties in this node are relatively homogeneous in terms of price and thus represent a low-budget segment of the market. Given the minimal variation and the tightly grouped nature of the prices, further splitting of this node is unnecessary. Continuing to split would likely not provide significant additional insights or improvements in prediction accuracy, as the current grouping already effectively captures the characteristics of these low-budget properties.

Split of the Right Node at Depth-1

Let us split the right node of depth-1 based on the size of the property again, using a threshold of 1500 square feet. Properties with a size greater than 1500 square feet will go to the right node, and those with a size less than or equal to 1500 square feet will go to the left node. Then, we will calculate the mean price at each node.

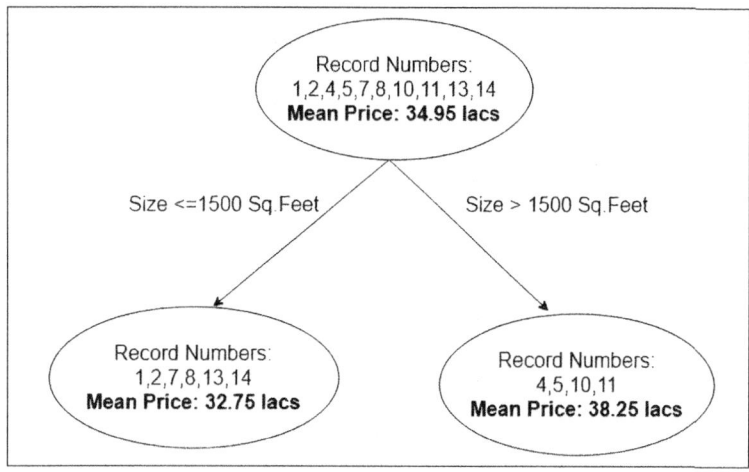

Figure 6.10: Records after the Right Node Split

Figure 6.10 illustrates the mean price for the left node (Size <= 1500 sq. ft) is approximately 32.75 lacs, and the mean price for the right node (Size > 1500 sq. ft) is 38.25 lacs. These nodes represent different segments of the housing market. The node with a mean price of 32.75 lacs captures the moderately priced properties, which tend to have a slightly higher variation but still fall within a mid-range budget. On the other hand, the node with a mean price of 38.25 lacs represents higher-priced properties, indicating a more premium segment of the market. This split effectively distinguishes between moderately priced and high-priced properties, providing clearer insights into the distribution of housing prices within these categories.

The Mean Squared Error (MSE) for the left node (Size <= 1500 sq. ft) is approximately 3.4792, and the MSE for the right node (Size > 1500 sq. ft) is 2.1875. The total MSE after this split is approximately 5.6667. When we add this to the MSE of the left node at depth-1, which was 1.16, the effective training error becomes **5.6667 + 1.16 = 6.8267**. This demonstrates a substantial reduction from the initial MSE of 54.67 at the root node. The reduction in MSE highlights the effectiveness of the decision tree in segmenting the data into more homogenous groups, thereby improving the overall prediction accuracy. The left node at depth-1, with an MSE of 1.16, captures low-budget properties with prices around 20 lacs, while the right node's split identifies moderately priced properties (mean price 32.75 lacs) and high-priced properties (mean price 38.25 lacs). This nuanced segmentation showcases the model's capability to adapt to varying price ranges within the dataset.

Python Implementation of Decision Tree Regressor

To demonstrate the Decision Tree as a Regressor model, a concrete compressive strength dataset is taken from Kaggle. The dataset consists of 1030 entries with 9 columns, capturing various attributes related to concrete production and its compressive strength. The concrete compressive strength is a highly nonlinear function of age and ingredients; employing a non-linear model such as the Decision Tree Regressor is particularly appropriate for this dataset. We will demonstrate how the Decision Tree Regressor learns from the various attributes of the concrete mixtures, including the quantities of different components and the age of the concrete, to make closer predictions.

Let us load the dataset and check the size of the data.

```
import pandas as pd
file_path = 'path_to_your_data/ data2_Ch6_Concrete_Compressive_Strength.csv'
df = pd.read_csv(file_path)
df.shape
(1030, 9)
```

cement	slag	ash	water	superplastic	coarseagg	fineagg	age	strength
141.3	212.0	0.0	203.5	0.0	971.8	748.5	28	29.89
168.9	42.2	124.3	158.3	10.8	1080.8	796.2	14	23.51
250.0	0.0	95.7	187.4	5.5	956.9	861.2	28	29.22
266.0	114.0	0.0	228.0	0.0	932.0	670.0	28	45.85
154.8	183.4	0.0	193.3	9.1	1047.4	696.7	28	18.29

Figure 6.11: Head of the Concrete Dataset

The data is loaded and the first five records are tabulated, as shown in *Figure 6.11*. Each row represents a different concrete mixture, including the quantities of various components (cement, slag, ash, water, superplastic, coarse aggregate, and fine aggregate) in kilograms per cubic meter, the age of the concrete in days, and the resulting compressive strength in megapascals (MPa). To understand the non-linear nature of features with the dependent variable, which is the strength of the concrete, let us plot the correlation matrix in the form of a heatmap and interpret the result.

```
import seaborn as sns
import matplotlib.pyplot as plt
# Calculate the correlation matrix
correlation_matrix = df.corr()
# Plot the heat map
```

```
plt.figure(figsize=(10, 8))
sns.heatmap(correlation_matrix, annot=True, cmap='coolwarm',
linewidths=0.5)
plt.title('Correlation Heatmap of Concrete Compressive Strength
Dataset')
plt.show()
```

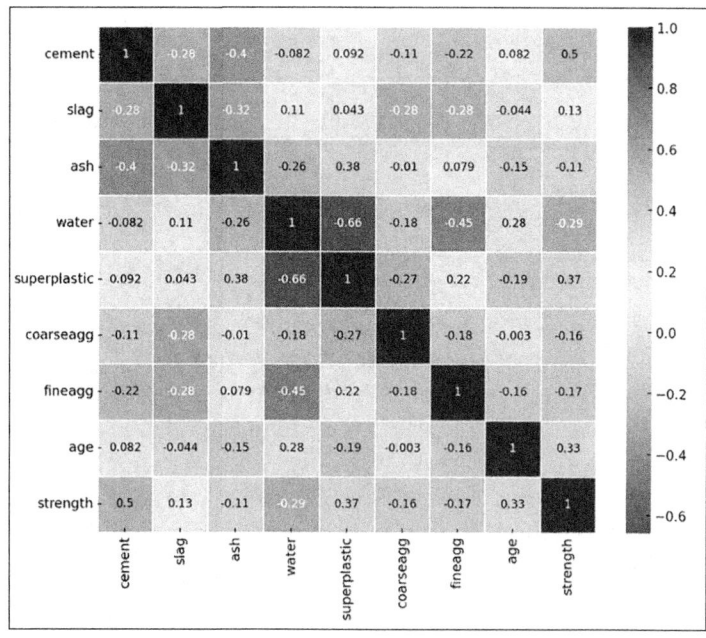

Figure 6.12: *Correlation Heatmap of Concrete Compressive Strength Dataset*

Figure 6.12 shows that the correlation scores are moderate to low, indicating a lack of strong linear relationships between the features and the dependent variable, strength. Therefore, we have chosen to use a non-linear model, such as the decision tree regressor, to address this problem.

In the next step, let us define the independent variables (X) by excluding the 'strength' column from the dataset and designating the **'strength'** column as the dependent variable (Y).

```
# Define independent variables (X) and dependent variable (Y)
X = df.drop('strength', axis=1)
Y = df['strength']
```

Let us perform hyperparameter tuning using **GridSearchCV** for the decision tree Regressor for optimal performance.

```
from sklearn.tree import DecisionTreeRegressor
kf=KFold(n_splits=5,shuffle=True,random_state=0)
from sklearn.model_selection import GridSearchCV,cross_val_score,KFold
dt=DecisionTreeRegressor(random_state=0)
```

```
dt_params= {'max_depth': np.arange(3,10),'min_samples_split':
np.arange(2,10),
'min_samples_leaf': np.arange(2,5)}
GS=GridSearchCV(dt,dt_params,cv=kf,scoring='neg_root_mean_squared_
error')
GS.fit(X,Y)
GS.best_params_
dt_tuned=DecisionTreeRegressor(max_depth=9,min_samples_leaf=2,min_
samples_split=6,random_state=0)
```

Let us conduct k-fold cross-validation using the Root Mean Squared Error (RMSE) metric to assess the model's performance.

```
rmse=cross_val_score(dt_tuned,X,Y,cv=kf,scoring='neg_root_mean_squared_
error')
print([np.mean(np.abs(rmse)),np.std(np.abs(rmse),ddof=1)])
[6.75,0.57]
```

The performance evaluation of the decision tree Regressor model for predicting the compressive strength of concrete, measured in Mega Pascals (MPa), was conducted using 5-fold cross-validation. The mean Root Mean Squared Error (RMSE) across the folds was approximately 6.75 MPa, with a standard deviation of around 0.57 MPa. The individual RMSE values for each fold were 6.76 MPa, 7.21 MPa, 5.85 MPa, 6.68 MPa, and 7.26 MPa, indicating some variability. This suggests that while the model is fairly reliable, there is still room for improvement in reducing the prediction error to achieve more precise and consistent predictions of concrete compressive strength.

Limitations and Drawbacks in Decision Tree Models

One significant limitation of the Decision Tree model is its tendency to overfit the training data. Overfitting occurs when the model becomes too complex, capturing noise and fluctuations in the training dataset rather than general patterns. This overfit nature causes the model to perform exceptionally well on training data but poorly on unseen data, leading to high variability in its performance across different datasets. Consequently, this high variance error makes the model less reliable and robust when applied to new data.

Another drawback of the Decision Tree model is its relatively high average performance error, such as the mean Root Mean Squared Error (RMSE) in regression tasks. The mean RMSE provides a measure of the average prediction error made by the model. In the case of our evaluation, a mean RMSE of approximately 6.75 MPa indicates that, on average, the model's predictions deviate from the actual values by this amount. This level of error suggests that while the model can capture some patterns in the data, it still exhibits considerable inaccuracies.

In classification tasks, the Decision Tree model also shows limitations with its mean accuracy. In the telecom customer churn use case discussed under the Decision Tree as a classifier subsection, the average accuracy is 79%, indicating relatively moderate performance. The mean accuracy, which reflects the proportion of correct predictions, is often moderate for Decision Tree classifiers. This moderate bias error suggests that the model does not fully capture the underlying structure of the data. One reason for this is the model's greedy algorithm, which makes locally optimal choices at each decision node. While this approach can efficiently create a model, it often results in suboptimal overall performance due to its dependency on very few attributes.

Moreover, the Decision Tree model's performance is heavily influenced by the selection of features and the splitting criteria. Because the model tends to focus on specific attributes that may not be the most relevant, it might miss more general patterns that a holistic approach could capture. This greedy dependency on a few attributes can lead to bias errors, as the model may overlook broader relationships within the data. As a result, the model's ability to generalize to new, unseen data is compromised, limiting its practical applicability.

In the next section, we will explore the use of a Random Forest model, which is an ensemble learning method that combines multiple decision trees to improve predictive performance.

Random Forest Model as Ensemble Learning

Random Forest is a versatile machine learning algorithm that operates by constructing a multitude of decision trees at training time. This ensemble technique, which involves building multiple models to solve the same problem, is fundamentally designed to improve predictive accuracy and control overfitting, which is a common issue with single decision trees. The method combines the simplicity of decision trees with flexibility, resulting in a robust algorithm for both classification and regression tasks.

The strength of the Random Forest model lies in its ability to operate numerous uncorrelated decision trees to produce the final output. The algorithm introduces randomness into the model construction process by creating different trees based on different subsets of the data and features. This randomness helps in achieving lower correlation among trees and more robust overall predictions, distinguishing Random Forest from other traditional single models.

The core idea behind Random Forest is to build a forest of trees where each tree is slightly different from the others. When it comes to making predictions, the Random Forest algorithm takes the average of predictions from all the trees (in the case of regression) or the majority vote (in classification), leading to more accurate and stable predictions than any individual tree could provide. Moreover, Random Forest effectively handles both non-linear data and large datasets, making it incredibly efficient for practical applications.

Bagged Decision Trees and Bootstrap Sampling

Random Forest utilizes the bagging (bootstrap aggregation) technique, where multiple decision trees are built on different bootstrap samples of the dataset. A bootstrap sample is a randomly chosen subset of the data, selected with replacement, meaning the same data point can appear multiple times in the sample. This method ensures that each decision tree is trained on a slightly different set of data.

Mathematically, if we have a dataset D with n instances, a bootstrap sample is a subset D_i where 'i' indicates sample index with n instances selected randomly with replacement from D. The process of bootstrapping introduces variability among the decision trees, which enhances the generalization ability of the ensemble.

Each tree in a Random Forest learns from a distinct bootstrap sample and makes its own predictions. This approach helps in reducing the variance component of the prediction error, which is a significant problem in standalone decision trees.

The bagging aspect ensures that the trees in the forest are de-correlated, making the forest more robust to noise and capable of better generalization. It diversifies the models within the ensemble and is particularly effective in scenarios where there are many correlated features in the data.

Figure 6.13 illustrates random forest architecture with individual decision trees that are independently constructed from their respective bootstrapped samples. Each tree is a regressor or classifier depending on the task (predicting a continuous outcome or classifying, respectively). In Random Forest, typically, hundreds of such trees are created; however, we can use **GridSearchCV** to tune and optimize the number of trees.

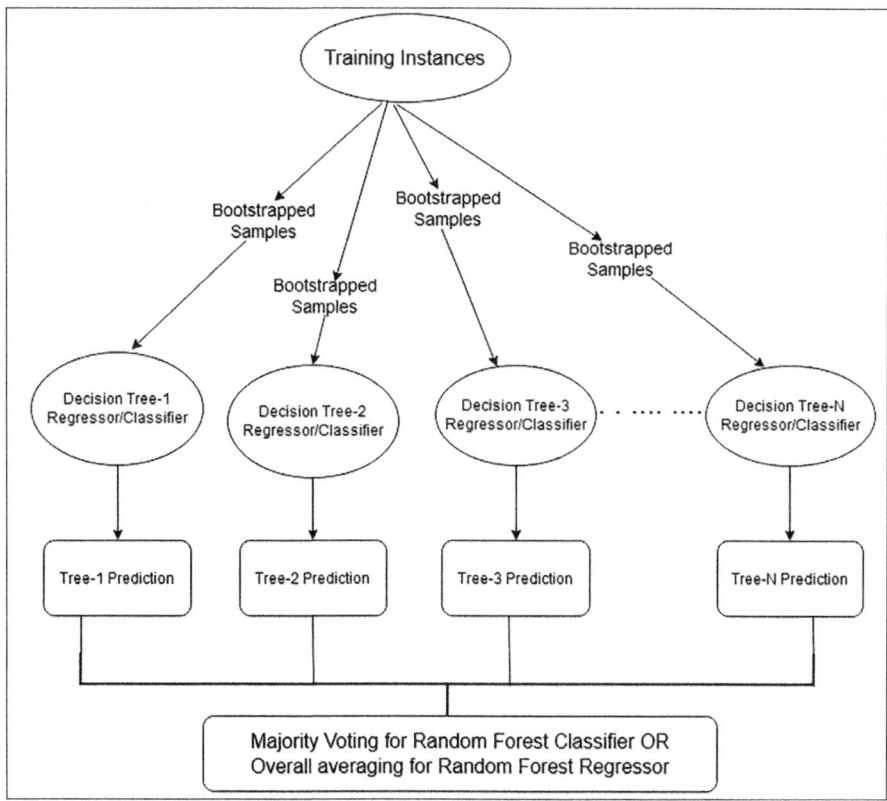

Figure 6.13: *Illustration of Random Forest as Ensemble Learning*

In general, Random Forests significantly improve upon the limitations of individual decision trees by reducing overfitting through averaging and boosting predictive performance with feature and data sample randomness. This robust ensemble method outperforms standalone decision trees in various tasks, offering more reliable and consistent performance across both regression and classification problems. Its ability to deal with a wide range of data types and large feature sets makes Random Forest an essential tool for any data scientist's arsenal.

Python Implementation of Random Forest Models

We will delve into the Python implementation of Random Forest models, extending our analysis from the previous use cases involving decision trees for customer churn prediction in the telecom sector and concrete strength prediction. This segment aims to demonstrate the enhanced performance capabilities of Random Forest models compared to the standalone decision tree models previously discussed.

We will revisit the telecom customer churn prediction and concrete strength prediction scenarios, applying Random Forest to the same datasets used in the decision tree models. By comparing the improved accuracy and reduced error metrics, such as Root Mean Squared Error (RMSE) in the regression task and increased accuracy in the classification task. We will illustrate the practical advantages of using Random Forest in these applications. Through detailed performance analysis, readers will gain insights into how and why Random Forest models outperform their decision tree counterparts, highlighting the significance of ensemble learning in machine learning practice.

Random Forest as a Classifier

Let us load the telecom churn dataset, build a random forest classifier, and compare the performance score with the decision tree classifier. We have already undertaken the necessary data preparation steps, such as handling missing values, encoding categorical variables, and normalizing data in our Decision Tree section. We can proceed directly with defining our feature set X and target variable Y for the Random Forest classifier.

```
# Define the target variable and features from the processed dataframe
Y = df['Churn']
X = df.drop(columns=['Churn'])
```

Let us proceed to define and construct our Random Forest classifier model. However, before we initiate model training, it is essential to fine-tune the hyperparameters of the Random Forest model to ensure optimal performance. We will employ **GridSearchCV** to systematically explore a range of parameter combinations, identifying the most effective settings for our model. This method provides a rigorous approach to hyperparameter optimization, ensuring that we achieve the best possible combination to enhance the predictive accuracy of our Random Forest classifier. Since our goal is to compare the performance of the Random Forest model with that of the decision tree classifier, employing k-fold cross-validation using the recall score will be an appropriate strategy for an effective comparison. This approach will ensure that we have a robust assessment of both models under the same conditions.

Let us go ahead and calculate this to see how the Random Forest model stands up against the decision tree in terms of handling false negatives.

```
from sklearn.model_selection import GridSearchCV,cross_val_score,Kfold
kf=KFold(n_splits=5,shuffle=True,random_state=0)
from sklearn.ensemble import RandomForestClassifier
Rf_params= {'n_estimators': np.arange(3,150),'criterion':
['entropy','gini'],'max_features': ['sqrt','log2']}
GS=GridSearchCV(RF,Rf_params,cv=kf,scoring='recall')
GS.fit(X,Y)
```

```
RF_tuned=RandomForestClassifier(n_estimators=90,criterion='entropy',max_
features='sqrt')
#Define the Decision Tree model used in telecom churn prediction exer-
cise
DT_tuned = DecisionTreeClassifier(max_depth=5, random_state=0)
DT_scores=cross_val_score(DT_tuned,X,Y,cv=kf,scoring='recall')
print([np.mean(np.abs(DT_scores)),np.std(np.abs(DT_scores),ddof=1)])
[0.7869, 0.0137]
RF_scores=cross_val_score(RF_tuned,X,Y,cv=kf,scoring='recall')
print([np.mean(np.abs(scores)),np.std(np.abs(scores),ddof=1)])
 [0.7933,0.0087]
```

Inference

For the Decision Tree model, the mean recall score is 0.7869 with a standard deviation of 0.0137. This suggests that while the decision tree has a decent average performance in terms of recall, its performance consistency across different folds of the data can vary. The relatively higher standard deviation indicates a susceptibility to variability in the dataset, which is a typical sign of overfitting. Decision trees, being greedy learners, often adapt too closely to the training data, capturing noise and detailed fluctuations that do not generalize well to unseen data.

On the other hand, the Random Forest model shows an improved mean recall score of 0.7933 and a notably lower standard deviation of 0.0087. The improvement in the mean recall score, though marginal, indicates a slight enhancement in the model's ability to correctly identify the positive class, which is crucial in scenarios where missing a positive instance (such as churn) can be costly.

More significantly, the reduction in the standard deviation with the Random Forest model points to its greater stability and robustness across different subsets of the dataset. Unlike standalone decision trees, Random Forest mitigates overfitting by averaging the results of multiple decision trees trained on different parts of the data with different subsets of features. This ensemble approach not only stabilizes the model's performance, reducing the impact of outliers and noise, but also improves the generalizability of the model to new, unseen datasets.

Therefore, these scores clearly demonstrate that the Random Forest model provides a more reliable and consistent performance compared to the standalone Decision Tree model. The ensemble technique of Random Forest effectively addresses both the high variance issue common in decision trees and slightly improves the bias, making it a superior choice for both maintaining accuracy and ensuring model reliability across diverse scenarios.

Random Forest as a Regressor

Let us load the concrete compression strength dataset, build a random forest regressor, and compare the performance score with the decision tree regressor. We have already undertaken the necessary data preparation steps for our Decision Tree as a regressor in the preceding subsection, so we can proceed directly with defining our feature set X and target variable Y for the Random Forest Regressor.

```
# Define independent variables (X) and dependent variable (Y)
X = df.drop('strength', axis=1)
Y = df['strength']
```

Let us perform hyperparameter tuning using GridSearchCV for the Random Forest Regressor for optimal performance.

```
from sklearn.model_selection import GridSearchCV,cross_val_score,Kfold
kf=KFold(n_splits=5,shuffle=True,random_state=0)
from sklearn.ensemble import RandomForestRegressor
RF=RandomForestRegressor(random_state=0)
Rf_params= {'n_estimators': np.arange(1,100)}
GS=GridSearchCV(RF,Rf_params,cv=kf,scoring='neg_root_mean_squared_error')
GS.fit(X,Y)
RF_tuned=RandomForestRegressor(n_estimators=93,random_state=0)
rmse=cross_val_score(RF_tuned,X,Y,cv=kf,scoring='neg_root_mean_squared_error')
print([np.mean(np.abs(rmse)),np.std(np.abs(rmse),ddof=1)])
[4.959, 0.30]
```

Inference

The mean Root Mean Squared Error (RMSE) for the Random Forest regressor is 4.959 MPa with a standard deviation of 0.30. This is a substantial improvement over the Decision Tree regressor, which had a mean RMSE of 6.75 MPa and a standard deviation of 0.57.

The lower mean RMSE of the Random Forest indicates a lower bias error, suggesting that the model, on average, makes smaller errors in its predictions. This improvement in bias error means that the Random Forest model is better at capturing the true underlying patterns in the data without being swayed by the noise.

Furthermore, the reduction in standard deviation from 0.57 in the Decision Tree to 0.30 in the Random Forest model underscores a significant decrease in variance error. This lower variance indicates that the Random Forest model is more consistent in its performance across different subsets of the data. It is less likely to be influenced by fluctuations in the training set, thus enhancing its reliability and predictability. This stability is a direct result of the ensemble nature of the Random Forest, where the averaging of predictions from multiple decision trees helps to cancel out individual errors and anomalies.

In summary, the tuned Random Forest regressor not only achieves a more accurate prediction with lower RMSE, indicating reduced bias, but it also demonstrates more consistent results across different data splits, indicating reduced variance. These advantages make the Random Forest regressor a more robust and reliable tool for predicting concrete compressive strength compared to the more simplistic Decision Tree model. This case strongly supports the use of Random Forest in applications where the cost of prediction errors could be high and where model reliability is paramount.

Ensemble Learning: Bagging and Boosting

Ensemble learning is a robust machine learning paradigm where multiple models, often referred to as "weak learners," are strategically combined to form a "strong learner" that ensures better performance than any of the individual models could achieve on their own. This approach leverages the diversity of multiple learning algorithms to reduce bias (the error due to erroneous assumptions in the learning algorithm) and variance (error from sensitivity to small fluctuations in the training set) and improve predictions. The scope of ensemble learning is vast and versatile, encompassing various techniques such as bagging, boosting, and stacking, each suited to different kinds of data and prediction problems.

Bootstrap Aggregation or Bagging

Bagging, or Bootstrap Aggregating, is a powerful ensemble technique that aims to improve the stability and accuracy of machine learning algorithms. It reduces variance and helps to avoid overfitting. Essentially, bagging involves building multiple models (usually of the same type) from different bootstrap samples of the training dataset. The primary goal of bagging is to create several subsets of data from the original dataset, allowing models to train independently on these subsets and then aggregate their individual predictions to form a final consensus, which is typically more robust than a single model. This method leverages the strength of multiple learners to achieve better generalization performance, particularly in complex datasets prone to overfitting.

Bagging is most beneficial when dealing with high-variance algorithms such as decision trees. By training multiple trees on different pieces of the same dataset, bagging takes a more holistic view of the data, thus capturing more diversity in its interpretations. Each individual model learns from a slightly different set of data and makes its predictions, which are then averaged (in regression) or voted on (in classification) to produce the final output. In the preceding section, Random Forest models have an inherent bagging architecture, which is a bag of decision trees. However, in Random Forest, each estimator would randomly select the subset of features to reflect the nature of decision trees. When we construct a bag of other ML models, we do not have these limitations (every estimator utilizes all features).

In practical applications, bagging involves several key strategies. First, the selection of the base estimator: although decision trees are common, any algorithm that is sensitive to the variance in the data can be used. Second, each model in the ensemble is built independently, which allows the training process to be parallelized, resulting in significant efficiency gains. Finally, diversity in the training sets is ensured via the bootstrap process, where each new dataset is generated by random sampling with replacement from the original dataset.

We can import the bagging models from the Scikit-learn library like this:

```
from sklearn.ensemble import BaggingClassifier, BaggingRegressor
```

If we want to construct a bagged Logistic Regression model, which has some variability issues with cross-validation scores, we can construct bagged logistic regression in this manner.

```
base_estimator=LogisticRegression()
LR_bagged=BaggingClassifier(base_estimator, n_estimator = 'n')
```

Using **GridSearchCV**, we can tune the optimal number of estimator values ('n') to the model.

Likewise, we can bag any regression model using **BaggingRegressor**.

Overall, bagging is highly effective in reducing the risk of overfitting while maintaining the ability to capture complex patterns in the data. It tends to perform well on a variety of tasks, including those where the prediction models exhibit significant variance. The aggregated model's performance is often much more reliable and accurate than that of any single constituent model.

Boosting Techniques

Boosting is another form of ensemble technique that aims to create a strong classifier from a number of weak classifiers. This method works in a sequential manner, where each subsequent model attempts to correct the errors of the previous models. Unlike bagging, which aims to reduce variance, boosting focuses on reducing bias and building strong predictive models.

The main objective of boosting is to sequentially improve the prediction accuracy of a model. It starts with a weak model and increases its accuracy iteratively. By focusing on the instances that were previously modeled incorrectly, boosting methods adjust the weight of an instance based on the last classification result, thereby concentrating more on difficult cases that previous models have failed to correctly predict.

Boosting is particularly useful when the base learner is weak and has high bias error. It is most effectively used when you need to minimize bias error. However, unlike bagging, boosting cannot be parallelized, since each classifier needs to be built after evaluating the performance of the previous one, making it a sequential process. Adaptive Boosting (AdaBoost) and Gradient Boosting are two prominent types of boosting techniques used to improve the accuracy of machine learning models. Both methods build a strong classifier by sequentially adding weak classifiers and focusing on instances that previous classifiers misclassified. AdaBoost adjusts the weights of incorrectly classified instances such that subsequent classifiers focus more on difficult cases, while Gradient Boosting optimizes a loss function by adding models that reduce the error gradient.

Adaptive Boosting (AdaBoost) Learning

AdaBoost starts with a base classifier that is trained on the entire dataset and then iteratively adds additional models that correct the errors of the prior models. Initially, all instances in the dataset are given equal weights. After the first classifier is trained, AdaBoost increases the weights of misclassified instances, making them more likely to be correctly predicted in the next round of training. This process is repeated for a specified number of iterations, or until perfect accuracy is achieved on the training set.

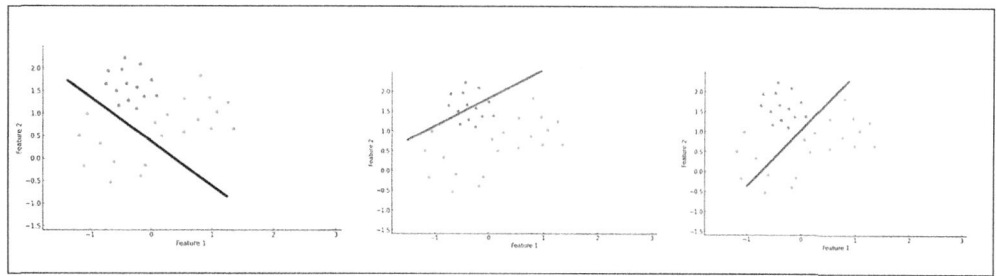

Figure 6.14: *Illustration of AdaBoost Learning*

In *Figure* 6.14, we see a step-by-step visualization of how AdaBoost works to iteratively improve the classification of data points using multiple weak learners (estimators). Each subfigure represents one iteration of the AdaBoost algorithm, with three weak learners shown sequentially.

First Estimator (Leftmost): The first weak learner is a decision boundary (a line in this case) that attempts to separate the two classes of data points (green and purple). This initial model makes several errors, as indicated by the points on the incorrect side of the line.

Second Estimator (Middle): In the second iteration, the AdaBoost algorithm adjusts the weights of the data points, giving higher weights to the points that were misclassified by the first model. The new weak learner is trained on this re-weighted dataset, focusing more on the previously misclassified points. As a result, the decision boundary changes to better classify these challenging points, although it may still make some errors.

Third Estimator (Rightmost): The process repeats for the third weak learner. The data points misclassified by the second learner now have even higher weights, pushing the third learner to correct these mistakes. The final decision boundary again adjusts to further improve classification accuracy, particularly for the difficult points.

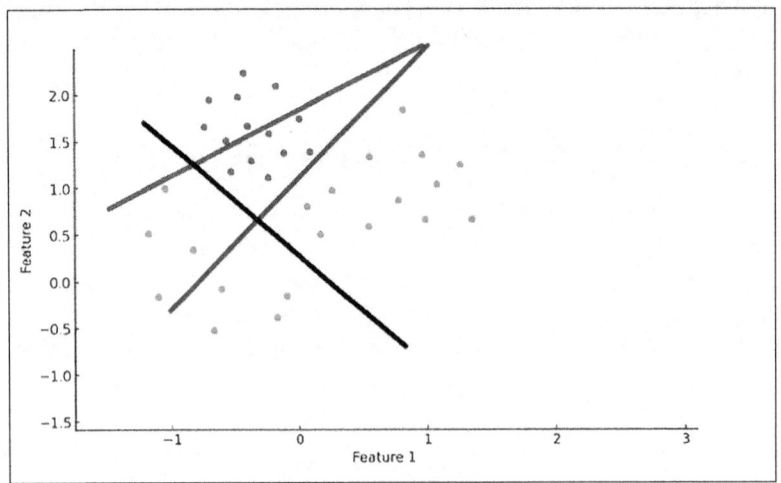

Figure 6.15: Weighted Voter Non-Linear AdaBoost Classifier

Figure 6.15 illustrates the combined effect of the three weak learners. In AdaBoost, the final model aggregates the predictions from all weak learners, typically through a weighted voting mechanism (for classification) or a weighted average (for regression). The figure shows how the individual decision boundaries (represented by different colored lines) contribute to a more complex and accurate decision boundary when combined. This sequential and adaptive nature of AdaBoost enables it to progressively correct errors, making it highly effective in improving prediction accuracy.

We can import the AdaBoost models from the Scikit learn library like this:

from sklearn.ensemble import AdaBoostClassifier, AdaBoostRegressor

If we want to construct a boosted Logistic Regression model, which has a low bias error issue with cross-validation scores, we can construct adaboosted logistic regression in this manner:

base_estimator=LogisticRegression()
LR_boosted=AdaBoostClassifier(base_estimator, n_estimator = 'n')

Using **GridSearchCV**, we can tune the optimal number of estimator values ('n') to the model.

Likewise, we can bag any regression model using **AdaBoostRegressor**. If **base_estimator** is not defined, the decision tree model is considered as the default estimator.

GradientBoost Learning

Gradient Boosting is an advanced machine learning technique used for both classification and regression tasks. It builds an ensemble of weak learners, typically

Tree-Based Machine Learning Models 191

decision trees, in a sequential manner, where each new model aims to correct the errors made by the previous models. Unlike AdaBoost, which adjusts the weights of misclassified instances, Gradient Boosting optimizes a loss function by adding new models that reduce the overall prediction error.

The primary objective of Gradient Boosting is to create a strong predictive model by combining the strengths of several weaker models. Each weak learner is trained to predict the residual errors of the combined ensemble of previous learners. This approach allows Gradient Boosting to reduce both bias and variance, resulting in a highly accurate and robust model.

PersonID	Age	LikesMusic	ReadsBooks	OwnsPet
1	13	False	True	False
2	14	True	False	True
3	15	True	True	False
4	25	False	True	True
5	35	False	False	True
6	49	True	False	False
7	68	True	True	False
8	71	False	True	True
9	73	True	False	True

Figure 6.16: *Contrived Dataset*

Figure 6.16 represents a contrived dataset. We are going to understand gradient boosting for a regression problem, aiming to predict the age of the records as accurately as possible with the least mean squared error (MSE). In gradient boosting, multiple weak learners are combined to form a strong predictor. The process begins with the first estimator, which splits the data based on a feature that best reduces the MSE. For our demonstration, we start by splitting the records using the "`LikesMusic`" variable. This initial split creates two subsets of the data: one for individuals who like music and another for those who do not. By examining how this split impacts the MSE, the algorithm identifies the most effective way to partition the data, setting the foundation for subsequent iterations that iteratively refine the predictions and minimize the overall error.

Here is the decision tree split based on the "`LikesMusic`" attribute. The root contains all records, and the tree splits into two children, as shown in *Figure* 6.17.

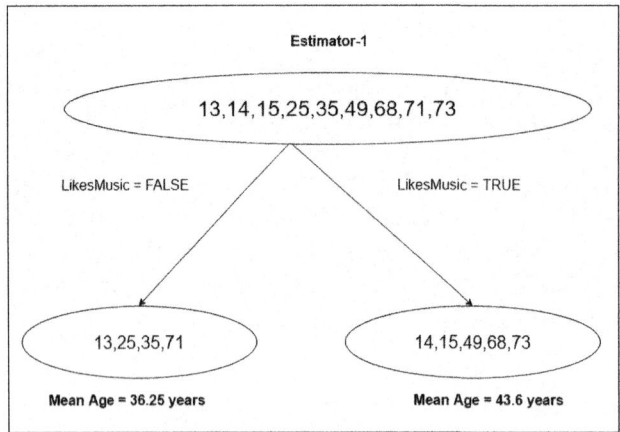

Figure 6.17: Estimator-1 split

After the split, the estimator-1 prediction and its residue are shown in *Figure* 6.18. A decision tree with depth-1 is commonly known as a decision stump, being used in Gradient Boost learning for better control over variance error.

PersonID	Age	LikesMusic	Predicted Age	Residue
1	13	False	36.25	-23.25
2	14	True	43.6	-29.6
3	15	True	43.6	-28.6
4	25	False	36.25	-11.25
5	35	False	36.25	-1.25
6	49	True	43.6	5.4
7	68	True	43.6	24.4
8	71	False	36.25	34.75
9	73	True	43.6	29.4

Figure 6.18: Tree-1 (estimator-1) Prediction

The root mean squared error (RMSE) before the split is 24.02 years. After splitting based on the "`LikesMusic`" variable, the RMSE is found to be 23.71 years. This slight reduction in RMSE still indicates an improvement in prediction accuracy due to the split.

The next step is crucial in the gradient-boosting process. Here, the second estimator will utilize the residuals from the first estimator to make further improvements. By focusing on these residuals, the goal is to identify how we can split the data based on a feature that will further reduce the root mean squared error (RMSE). For this step, we will consider the "`ReadsBooks`" feature to split the residuals, as shown in *Figure* 6.19. This feature is chosen with the intention of finding the most effective way to decrease the error in our predictions, thereby enhancing the overall performance of the model. By carefully analyzing how the residuals split based on whether individuals read books or not, we can refine our predictions and achieve greater accuracy.

Tree-Based Machine Learning Models

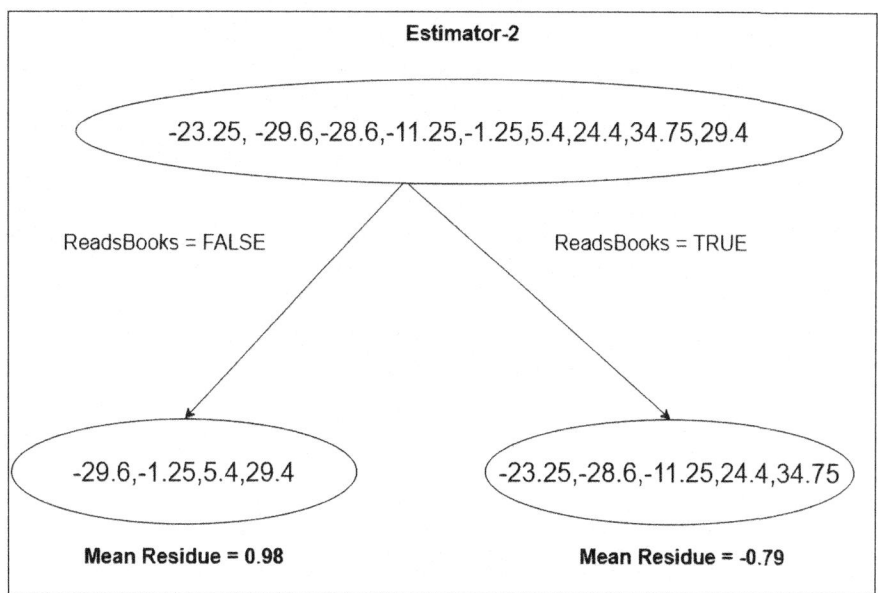

Figure 6.19: Estimator-2 split

PersonID	Age	LikesMusic	ReadsBooks	Tree-1 Prediction	Residue	Tree-2 Prediction	Combined Prediction	Overall Residue
1	13	False	True	36.25	-23.25	-0.79	35.46	-22.46
2	14	True	False	43.6	-29.6	0.98	44.58	-30.58
3	15	True	True	43.6	-28.6	-0.79	42.81	-27.81
4	25	False	False	36.25	-11.25	0.98	37.23	-12.23
5	35	False	False	36.25	-1.25	0.98	37.23	-2.23
6	49	True	False	43.6	5.39	0.98	44.58	4.42
7	68	True	True	43.6	24.4	-0.79	42.81	25.19
8	71	False	True	36.25	34.75	-0.79	35.46	35.54
9	73	True	False	43.6	29.4	0.98	44.58	28.42

Figure 6.20: Gradient Boosted Combined Prediction

By extending this step to multiple levels, we can observe a significant reduction in the RMSE score. This implies that the training error decreases, which in turn helps to better control the bias error. Consequently, the Gradient Boosting technique becomes more effective in capturing the underlying patterns in the data. By refining the model through additional iterations, each subsequent estimator focuses on the residuals left by the previous ones, thereby improving overall predictive accuracy. This iterative process ensures that the model incrementally improves, leading to a more accurate and robust prediction model with lower bias and training errors.

XGBoost Learning

XGBoost, which stands for eXtreme Gradient Boosting, is an advanced implementation of the gradient boosting algorithm designed to enhance performance and speed. It builds on the principles of gradient boosting, where models are sequentially trained to correct the errors of their predecessors by optimizing a loss function. However, XGBoost introduces several innovative features and optimizations that make it more efficient and scalable compared to traditional gradient boosting methods.

Key Features of XGBoost

XGBoost comes with a plethora of additional features that set it apart from standard gradient-boosting algorithms. Some of the key enhancements include:

- **Regularization**: XGBoost incorporates L1 (Lasso) and L2 (Ridge) regularization terms in the objective function, helping to prevent overfitting by penalizing complex estimators.
- **Tree Pruning**: The algorithm uses a depth-first approach for tree construction with a sophisticated pruning mechanism based on the loss function, ensuring that only relevant splits are considered.
- **Handling Missing Values**: XGBoost has a built-in capability to handle missing values, learning the best direction to take when a value is missing, which enhances its robustness.
- **Parallel Processing**: It supports parallel tree construction, making it significantly faster by utilizing multiple CPU cores.
- **Early Stopping**: XGBoost provides an early stopping mechanism that halts training when the performance on a validation set stops improving, saving computational resources.
- **Weighted Quantile Sketch**: This method is used for approximate tree learning, allowing the algorithm to handle large datasets more efficiently.

Limitations of XGBoost

Despite its many advantages, XGBoost is not without limitations. Some of the key challenges include:

- **Complexity**: The added complexity of the algorithm can make it harder to tune compared to simpler methods.
- **Resource Intensive**: Although faster than traditional gradient boosting, XGBoost can still be resource-intensive, requiring significant memory and

Tree-Based Machine Learning Models

computational power, especially for very large datasets.
- **Overfitting**: While regularization helps, there is still a risk of underfitting if the hyperparameters are not tuned carefully.
- **Sensitivity to Parameter Tuning**: XGBoost's performance is highly dependent on the correct tuning of its many hyperparameters, which can be time-consuming and require expertise.

XGBoost represents a significant advancement over traditional gradient boosting methods, offering enhanced performance, speed, and flexibility. Its additional features, such as regularization, parallel processing, and efficient handling of missing values, make it a robust tool for a wide range of machine learning tasks. However, its complexity and sensitivity to parameter tuning require careful handling and expertise. When used effectively, XGBoost can outperform traditional gradient boosting, providing more accurate and reliable models, especially in large-scale and complex data environments.

We can import the Gradient Boost and XGBoost models from the Scikit learn library in the following manner:

```
from sklearn.ensemble import GradientBoostingClassifier, GradientBoostingRegressor
```

Unlike the AdaBoost model, we cannot set a base estimator, the default base estimator is the decision stump in Gradient Boost architecture and the pruned decision tree in XGBoost architecture.

```
GB_Classifier=GradientBoostingClassifier(n_estimator = 'n')
GB_Regressor=GradientBoostingRegressor(n_estimator = 'n')
```

Using **GridSearchCV**, we can tune the optimal number of estimator values ('n') to the models.

```
from xgboost import XGBClassifier,XGBRegressor
XGB_Classifier=XGBClassifier(n_estimator = 'n', alpha=0 to 1, lambda=0 to 1)
XGB_Regressor=XGBRegressor(n_estimator = 'n',alpha=0 to1,lambda=0 to 1)
```

Apart from **n_estimators**, we can tune the regularization parameters such as alpha, lambda, and a few other parameters such as **max_depth**, built-in encoding options for categorical features such as **use_label_encoder** with True or False options. Fine-tuning these parameters based on the specific dataset and problem at hand can significantly improve model performance.

Stacked Ensemble Models

Stacked ensemble models, or stacking, are a sophisticated machine learning technique that combines multiple models (often called base learners or level-0 models) to form a more powerful predictive model. The fundamental concept of stacking involves training several different models on the same dataset and then using another model (referred to as a meta-learner or level-1 model) to combine the predictions from these base learners. This meta-learner learns how to best integrate the outputs of the base models to improve overall prediction accuracy.

- **Base Layer (Level-0 Models)**: Multiple base learners are trained independently on the training dataset. These base learners can be of the same type (for example, all decision trees) or a mix of different algorithms (for example, a combination of decision trees, logistic regression, and Naïve Bayes). Each base learner produces its predictions.

- **Meta Layer (Level-1 Model)**: The predictions from the base learners are then used as input features for the meta-learner. The meta-learner is trained on these predictions to learn how to best combine them to produce a final prediction. Essentially, it learns to correct the weaknesses of the base learners by leveraging their strengths.

The key advantage of stacking is that it allows for the integration of diverse model types, which can capture different aspects of the data patterns, leading to a more robust and accurate final model. This approach can significantly improve predictive performance, especially in complex datasets where no single model performs optimally on its own.

In summary, stacking enhances model performance by intelligently combining different types of models and learning the optimal way to integrate their predictions. This makes it particularly powerful for capturing diverse data patterns and improving prediction accuracy, distinguishing it from bagging and boosting, which rely more on homogeneous model ensembles and sequential error correction, respectively.

We can define the stacking ensemble architecture in a Python environment as follows:

```
base_learners = [('lr', LogisticRegression()),('dt', DecisionTree
Classifier()),
    ('gnb', GaussianNB())]
# Define meta-learner
meta_learner = LogisticRegression()
# Create the StackingClassifier
stacking_model = StackingClassifier(estimators=base_learners, final_
estimator=meta_learner, cv=5)
```

The '**cv**' parameter specifies the cross-validation to use for stacking the predictions. Stacking can be further customized and tuned by experimenting with different base learners, meta-learners, and hyperparameters to achieve optimal performance for your specific dataset and problem.

Voting Ensemble Models

The **VotingClassifier** and **VotingRegressor** are ensemble learning techniques that combine the predictions of multiple base models to improve overall performance. In a **VotingClassifier**, the final prediction is determined by majority voting (hard voting) or averaging the predicted probabilities (soft voting) from each base classifier. This approach leverages the collective wisdom of multiple classifiers, enhancing accuracy and robustness by balancing out individual model errors. Similarly, the **VotingRegressor** combines the predictions of several regression models by averaging their outputs, which tends to produce more stable and reliable predictions. These methods are particularly effective when the base models are diverse and make different types of errors, as the ensemble can smooth out inconsistencies and capitalize on the strengths of each individual model.

However, the voting method treats each model equally and does not learn from their individual strengths and weaknesses. In contrast, stacking involves training a meta-learner on the outputs of the base models to optimize the combination of their predictions. The meta-learner effectively learns how to weigh the contributions of each base model, potentially leading to superior performance. In Python, it can be implemented as follows:

The base learners used for the stacking ensemble model are considered here.

```
from sklearn.ensemble import VotingClassifier
#Create the VotingClassifier
voting_model = VotingClassifier(estimators=base_learners, voting='hard')
```

In the same manner, we can combine multiple regressor models to create a **VotingRegressor** ensemble architecture.

In summary, while both stacking and voting enhance model performance by combining multiple learners, stacking offers a more sophisticated approach that can lead to superior results, albeit at the cost of increased complexity and computational demand. Voting methods, on the other hand, provide a simpler and faster alternative that still benefits from ensemble diversity.

Conclusion

This chapter explored tree-based models and ensemble learning, covering their principles, mathematical foundations, and practical applications. We focused on Decision Trees, explained their structure, mathematical basis, and implementation in Python. While intuitive and interpretable, we noted their limitations, such as overfitting. To overcome these, we introduced Random Forest, demonstrating its effectiveness through Python implementation. We then explored Ensemble Learning techniques, including Bagging and Boosting (AdaBoost, Gradient Boosting, and XGBoost), emphasizing their iterative improvements. Finally, we covered Stacking and Voting ensembles, showcasing how combining multiple models enhances predictive accuracy and robustness.

As we conclude this chapter, we have laid a strong foundation in tree-based and ensemble learning models. In the next chapter, we will explore the Distance-Based Model: K-Nearest Neighbor (KNN), which is another powerful technique capable of learning non-linear and complex data patterns. This model utilizes the proximity of data points to make predictions, providing an intuitive yet effective approach to classification and regression tasks.

Practice Exercises

1. Calculate the information gain for a dataset with the following class distribution before and after a split on attribute X.

   Before split: 10 positives, 10 negatives

   After split:

   X=0: 5 positives, 15 negatives

   X=1: 5 positives, 5 negatives

2. Following is a confusion matrix for a decision tree classifier:

	Predicted Positive	Predicted Negative
Actual Positive	35	15
Actual Negative	10	40

   Figure 6.21: Confusion Matrix

   Calculate the accuracy, precision, recall, and F1-score.

3. Consider a random forest with 100 trees. Each tree is trained on a bootstrap sample of the dataset containing 1000 instances. If each bootstrap sample contains approximately 63.2% of the original instances (due to sampling with replacement), calculate the expected number of unique instances in each bootstrap sample.

4. In an AdaBoost ensemble, the initial weight for each instance is 1n. If a classifier in the first round misclassifies 30 out of 100 instances, calculate the updated weights for the misclassified instances.

5. Calculate the final prediction of an AdaBoost ensemble with three classifiers where each classifier has the following weights and predictions:

Classifier 1: weight = 0.4, prediction = +1

Classifier 2: weight = 0.3, prediction = -1

Classifier 3: weight = 0.5, prediction = +1

6. In a gradient boosting model, the loss function used is the mean squared error (MSE). Given the residuals r=[2,-3,4,-1] from the current iteration, calculate the new predictions if the learning rate (η) is 0.2.

7. Explain how bagging helps to address the bias-variance tradeoff. Provide an example to illustrate your explanation.

8. Describe how boosting affects the bias-variance tradeoff and compare it to bagging. Include the impact of boosting on both bias and variance.

Answers

1. Entropy before split: $H(S) = 1$

   Entropy after split: $H(S \mid X=0) = 0.811$

   Entropy after split: $H(S \mid X=1) = 1$

   Weighted Entropy after the split: $H(S|X) = 2030. 0.811 + 1030. 1 = 0.874$

   Information Gain = 1 − 0.874 = 0.126

2. Accuracy: 75100 = 0.75; Precision: 3545 = 0.778; Recall: 3550 = 0.7; F1-Score: 0.737

3. Expected number of unique instances in each bootstrap sample: 1000×0.632=632

4. Initial weight for each instance: 1100 = 0.01; Error of the classifier: e = 30100 = 0.3; Weight update factor: e1−e = 0.30.7 = 0.429; New weight = 0.01 X 10.429 = 0.0233

5. Final prediction is based on the weighted majority vote:

   Weighted sum=0.4·(+1)+0.3·(−1)+0.5·(+1)=0.4−0.3+0.5=0.6

   Since the weighted sum is positive, the final prediction is +1+1+1.

6. Residuals: r =[2,−3,4,−1]; Update using the learning rate: η·r=0.2·[2,−3,4,−1]=[0.4,−0.6,0.8,−0.2]

7. Bagging (Bootstrap Aggregating) primarily helps to reduce variance without significantly affecting the bias of the model. It does this by training multiple versions of the same model on different bootstrap samples of the training dataset and then averaging their predictions (for regression) or taking a

majority vote (for classification).

8. Boosting is an ensemble technique that sequentially builds a series of models, where each subsequent model attempts to correct the errors made by the previous ones. Unlike bagging, which focuses on reducing variance, boosting aims to reduce both bias and variance, though its primary effect is often on bias.

Multiple Choice Questions

1. What is the primary goal of a Decision Tree model?

    a. To perform linear regression

    b. To minimize overfitting

    c. To make decisions by splitting data into subsets based on feature values

    d. To perform clustering

2. Which of the following is a key disadvantage of Decision Trees?

    a. High bias

    b. Complexity

    c. Overfitting

    d. Underfitting

3. In a Random Forest model, what is the purpose of bootstrap aggregating (bagging)?

    a. To reduce bias

    b. To reduce variance

    c. To increase model complexity

    d. To ensure feature selection

4. Which method is used to prevent overfitting in Decision Trees by removing non-contributory parts of the tree?

    a. Bootstrapping

    b. Bagging

    c. Pruning

    d. Gradient Descent

5. What does AdaBoost focus on when building sequential models?

    a. Increasing model complexity

    b. Correcting misclassified instances

    c. Reducing data size

    d. Combining predictions using averaging

6. Which hyperparameter in Random Forest specifies the number of trees in the forest?

    a. `max_depth`

    b. `min_samples_split`

    c. `n_estimators`

    d. `criterion`

7. What type of ensemble technique is stacking?

    a. Combining multiple models using a meta-learner

    b. Averaging predictions of base models

    c. Using a single model multiple times

    d. Sequentially correcting model errors

8. What does the `'learning_rate'` parameter control in Gradient Boosting?

    a. The contribution of each tree to the final prediction

    b. The number of trees in the model

    c. The depth of each tree

    d. The minimum samples required to split a node

9. Which of the following best describes XGBoost?

    a. A variant of the k-means algorithm

    b. A neural network model

    c. An efficient implementation of Gradient Boosting with additional features

    d. A method for linear regression

10. In a **VotingClassifier**, what does 'soft voting' refer to?

    a. Majority vote of class labels

b. Averaging predicted probabilities
   c. Weighted majority voting
   d. Combining regression outputs

Answers

1. c
2. c
3. b
4. c
5. b
6. c
7. a
8. a
9. c
10. b

Keywords

- Decision Tree
- Root Node
- Leaf Node
- Entropy
- Gini
- Split Criterion
- Pruning
- Overfitting
- Random Forest
- Bootstrap Aggregating (Bagging)
- Ensemble Learning
- Adaptive Boosting (AdaBoost)
- Gradient Boosting

- Extreme Gradient Boosting (XGBoost)
- Stacking
- Voting Classifier
- Voting Regressor
- Meta-Learner
- Base Learner
- Hyperparameters
- Cross-Validation
- Model Tuning

References

1. https://www.kaggle.com/datasets/blastchar/telco-customer-churn
2. https://archive.ics.uci.edu/dataset/165/concrete+compressive+strength

CHAPTER 7
Distance-Based Machine Learning Models

Introduction

This chapter explores Distance-Based Machine Learning Models with a focus on the K-Nearest Neighbor (KNN) algorithm. This chapter aims to provide both theoretical insights and practical skills for implementing and optimizing KNN models. The chapter begins with an introduction to the K-Nearest Neighbor (KNN) model, emphasizing its foundational role in distance-based learning methods. It delves into the mathematical foundation of KNN, using hand-worked calculations on a contrived dataset to explain how distances are computed and predictions are made based on the nearest neighbors. This section aims to clarify the algorithm's mechanics through a step-by-step walkthrough. In the practical sections, the chapter demonstrates the use of KNN as a classifier on a real-world dataset and then explores its application as a regressor, showcasing its versatility in different prediction tasks. The chapter concludes with a discussion on the challenges of KNN models, such as sensitivity to the choice of 'k' and computational inefficiency with large datasets. Understanding these limitations is essential for effectively deploying KNN in practice and recognizing when alternative methods may be more suitable.

Structure

In this chapter, we are going to cover the following main topics:
- Introduction to K-Nearest Neighbor (KNN) Model
- Mathematical Foundation with Hand-Worked Calculation with Contrived Dataset
- Exploring Different Distance Metrics in KNN

- Python Implementation and Use Case with KNN as a Classifier
- Python Implementation and Use Case with KNN as a Regressor
- Limitations in Distance-Based Models

Introduction to K-Nearest Neighbor (KNN) Model

The K-Nearest Neighbor (KNN) model is one of the most fundamental and intuitive machine learning algorithms. At its core, KNN operates on a simple premise: data points that are close to each other in the feature space are likely to share similar characteristics. This concept mirrors human decision-making processes, where we often judge by analogy, comparing new experiences with previous ones to make decisions. In the realm of machine learning, KNN leverages this intuition to perform both classification and regression tasks effectively.

KNN is a type of instance-based learning, also known as lazy learning. Unlike eager learning algorithms, which build a general model during the training phase, KNN defers the generalization process until a query is made to the system. This means that KNN does not make any assumptions about the underlying data distribution and instead relies on the entire training dataset to make predictions. When a new data point needs to be classified or predicted, KNN calculates the distance between this point and all points in the training set, selecting the 'k' closest neighbors based on a chosen distance metric.

Imagine a doctor diagnosing a patient with certain symptoms. The doctor compares the patient's symptoms with past cases in their experience or medical records to make a decision. If the patient has a fever, cough, and sore throat, the doctor might recall similar cases that were diagnosed as the flu. By comparing the new patient's symptoms with those of past patients who had the flu, the doctor can make an informed diagnosis. Similarly, KNN operates by comparing a new data point (the patient's symptoms) with the 'k' nearest data points in the training set (past patient records) to classify the new data point as a particular condition (for example, flu).

Imagine a homeowner wants to estimate the cost of renovating their kitchen. They might ask friends or neighbors who have recently renovated their kitchens for cost estimates. If three neighbors had similar renovations done for ₹36,000, ₹40,000, and ₹38,000, respectively, the homeowner might average these costs to estimate that their own renovation will cost around ₹38,000. This is similar to how KNN regression works: by comparing the new renovation project with similar past projects and averaging their costs to predict the new one. In a KNN regression model, if the homeowner's renovation project is represented as a point in feature space (for example, size of kitchen, quality of materials), the algorithm would find the *k* nearest neighbors (past similar renovation projects) and average their costs to predict the cost of the new renovation.

In both examples, KNN leverages the intuition of comparing new instances with known ones to make effective predictions. This analogy-based decision-making process is what makes KNN both intuitive and powerful for classification and regression tasks. One of the key strengths of KNN is its simplicity and ease of implementation. The algorithm is straightforward: store all the training data, measure distances, and find the majority vote or average of the nearest neighbors. This simplicity, however, does not come at the cost of performance. KNN can be remarkably effective, especially when the structure of the data is not well understood or is highly complex. It is particularly useful in scenarios where decision boundaries are irregular or where the data is too complex for more parametric approaches to handle effectively.

Mathematical Foundation with Hand-Worked Calculation with Contrived Dataset

The KNN algorithm is grounded in a simple but powerful mathematical framework that leverages distance metrics to make predictions. Understanding the mathematical foundation of KNN is crucial for appreciating its strengths and limitations, as well as for effectively tuning the model for optimal performance.

At the core of KNN is the concept of distance, which measures the similarity between data points. The most used distance metric is the Euclidean distance, which calculates the straight-line distance between two points in a multi-dimensional space. Mathematically, the Euclidean distance between two points X_1 and X_2 in n-dimensional feature space is given by:

$$d(X_1, X_2) = \sqrt{\sum_{i=1}^{n}(X_{1i} - X_{2i})^2}$$

This distance metric is intuitive and works well in many scenarios, but other metrics such as Manhattan distance and Minkowski distance can be used depending on the problem characteristics. The Manhattan distance (also known as L1 norm) is defined as:

$$d(X_1, X_2) = \sum_{i=1}^{n}|X_{1i} - X_{2i}|$$

Minkowski distance generalizes both Euclidean and Manhattan distances, with its formula as follows:

$$d(X_1, X_2) = \left(\sum_{i=1}^{n} |X_{1i} - X_{2i}|^p\right)^{1/p}$$

Where p is a parameter that determines the type of distance: p = 2 for Euclidean and p − 1 for Manhattan.

The KNN algorithm involves finding the k closest data points (neighbors) to a given query point X_q. Once the distance between X_q and all points in the training set are computed, the algorithm sorts these distances and selects the k nearest neighbors. For classification tasks, the predicted class of X_q is determined by a majority vote among its k nearest neighbors. If there are ties, they can be resolved by considering the distance-weighted voting, where closer neighbors have a higher influence on the prediction.

In the context of regression, KNN predicts the output value for X_q by averaging the values of its k nearest neighbors. Mathematically, the predicted value is:

$$\hat{y} = \frac{1}{k}\sum_{i=1}^{k} y_i$$

Where y_i are the target values of the k nearest neighbors.

An important aspect of KNN is the choice of k, the number of neighbors to consider. The value of k greatly affects the algorithm's performance. A small k makes the model sensitive to noise and outliers, leading to high variance and potential overfitting. On the other hand, a large k smoothens the predictions and may overlook subtle patterns, causing high bias and underfitting. The optimal k can be determined through cross-validation, where different values of k are tested to find the one that minimizes prediction error.

Another critical factor is the scaling of features. Since KNN relies on distance calculations, features with larger scales can disproportionately influence the results. Therefore, it is essential to standardize or normalize the features so that each one contributes equally to the distance computation. Standardization transforms the features to have zero mean and unit variance, while normalization scales the features to a range of [0, 1].

The mathematical foundation of the KNN model is both elegant and intuitive, rooted in the fundamental concept of distance metrics to gauge similarity between data points. By leveraging various distance measures such as Euclidean, Manhattan, and Minkowski distances, KNN effectively identifies the nearest neighbors to a query point. The algorithm's simplicity lies in its instance-based learning approach, deferring the generalization process until a prediction is needed. This methodology allows KNN to adapt flexibly to different types of data without making strong assumptions about their underlying distributions. Understanding these mathematical principles provides a solid foundation for implementing and fine-tuning KNN models, enabling their effective application in a variety of classification and regression tasks.

Exploring Different Distance Metrics in KNN

In the previous subsection, we delved into the mathematical foundations of various distance metrics used in the KNN algorithm. With a solid understanding of these mathematical principles, we can now explore the nuances of choosing the appropriate distance metric for different scenarios. This subsection will focus on how the choice of distance metric can impact model performance, provide comparisons between different metrics, and discuss how to select the most suitable one for your specific context. By examining these aspects, we aim to equip you with the knowledge to make informed decisions that enhance the effectiveness of your KNN models.

In the KNN algorithm, the choice of distance metric is crucial as it directly influences the model's ability to accurately identify and classify neighbors. Different distance metrics can yield varying results depending on the nature and structure of the data. Understanding the nuances of each metric and knowing when to apply them is key to optimizing the performance of a KNN model.

Euclidean Distance

Euclidean distance is the most widely used and intuitive distance metric, representing the straight-line distance between two points in a multi-dimensional space. It is particularly effective when the data features are continuous and uniformly scaled. However, Euclidean distance can be sensitive to differences in scale across features, meaning it works best when the data is normalized or standardized. For example, in a dataset where features have vastly different ranges, unnormalized Euclidean distance could disproportionately weigh certain features, skewing the results.

Manhattan Distance

Manhattan distance, also known as L1 norm or city block distance, calculates the distance between two points by summing the absolute differences of their coordinates. This metric is often more appropriate in grid-like or high-dimensional spaces where the path taken matters. Manhattan distance can be more robust to outliers compared to Euclidean distance, as it does not square the differences. It is particularly useful in scenarios where movement is constrained along grid paths, such as in certain urban planning or robotics applications.

Minkowski Distance

As discussed in the earlier section, Minkowski distance is a generalization of both

Euclidean and Manhattan distances, parameterized by p. When p-2, it becomes the Euclidean distance, and when p-1, it becomes the Manhattan distance. The flexibility of Minkowski distance allows it to adapt to different data characteristics by adjusting the parameter p. For $p>2$, the metric becomes more sensitive to larger differences in individual feature dimensions, which can be useful in specific contexts but may also exacerbate the influence of outliers.

Cosine Similarity

Cosine similarity measures the cosine of the angle between two vectors, making it particularly useful for text data and high-dimensional datasets. Unlike Euclidean or Manhattan distances, cosine similarity focuses on the orientation rather than the magnitude of the vectors. This makes it ideal for applications such as document similarity or user-item recommendation systems, where the relative distribution of features is more important than their absolute values. Cosine similarity is invariant to vector magnitudes, which helps in scenarios where data vectors have varying lengths.

Hamming Distance

Hamming distance is applicable for categorical variables and binary data, counting the number of positions at which the corresponding elements differ. This metric is useful in fields such as genetics, information theory, and computer science, where data can be represented in binary or categorical forms. Hamming distance is not influenced by the magnitude of differences, making it suitable for comparing sequences of categorical attributes.

Impact on Model Performance

The choice of distance metric can significantly impact the performance of a KNN model. For instance, using Euclidean distance on unnormalized data with varying feature scales can lead to suboptimal results, as certain features may dominate the distance calculations. Conversely, Manhattan distance might perform better in high-dimensional spaces where the relationship between features aligns more with grid-like structures. Cosine similarity, being insensitive to vector magnitudes, is advantageous in text mining applications where document lengths vary widely.

When selecting a distance metric, it is essential to consider the data's characteristics and the specific problem context. Experimenting with different metrics and evaluating their performance through cross-validation can help identify the most suitable metric for a given task. In practice, normalizing or standardizing data before applying distance metrics such as Euclidean or Manhattan can further enhance model performance by ensuring that all features contribute equally to the distance calculations.

In summary, the choice of distance metric in KNN is not merely a technical detail but a critical factor that can shape the algorithm's effectiveness. By understanding and appropriately selecting distance metrics based on the data and problem context, practitioners can significantly improve the performance and reliability of their KNN models.

KNN as a Classifier: An Illustrative Example with Contrived Dataset

To demonstrate KNN as a classifier, a contrived dataset comprises 20 records featuring two numerical columns, Age and Blood Pressure, with a categorical target variable, Health Status, indicating whether an individual is Healthy or Unhealthy, as shown in *Figure 7.1*.

	Age	Blood Pressure	Health Status
1	55	142	Healthy
2	49	117	Healthy
3	56	121	Healthy
4	65	99	Healthy
5	48	112	Healthy
6	59	122	Healthy
7	50	103	Healthy
8	62	126	Healthy
9	48	111	Healthy
10	58	116	Healthy
11	66	111	Unhealthy
12	50	148	Unhealthy
13	52	120	Unhealthy
14	55	104	Unhealthy
15	52	132	Unhealthy
16	47	102	Unhealthy
17	40	123	Unhealthy
18	53	91	Unhealthy
19	41	100	Unhealthy
20	36	123	Unhealthy

Figure 7.1: *Contrived Dataset*

The scatter plot shown in *Figure* 7.2 visualizes the healthcare dataset, with Age on the X-axis and Blood Pressure on the Y-axis. The records are color-coded based on their Health Status: green dots represent Healthy individuals, and red dots represent Unhealthy individuals.

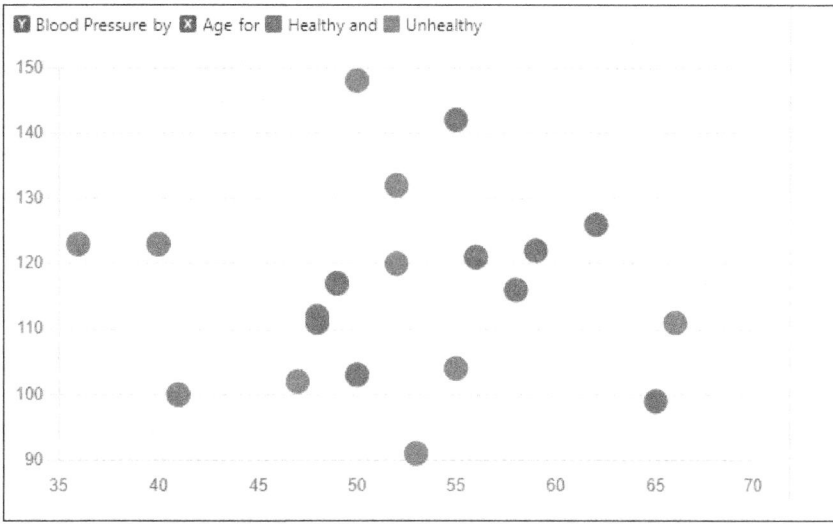

Figure 7.2: *Age versus Blood Pressure Scatter Plot*

From the plot, we can observe some overlap between the two classes, with both Healthy and Unhealthy individuals having similar ranges of Age and Blood Pressure. This overlap highlights the non-linearity in the data; the linear models, such as logistic regression and Naïve Bayes, find it difficult to solve such datasets. However, the KNN model could effectively handle such non-linearity in the data.

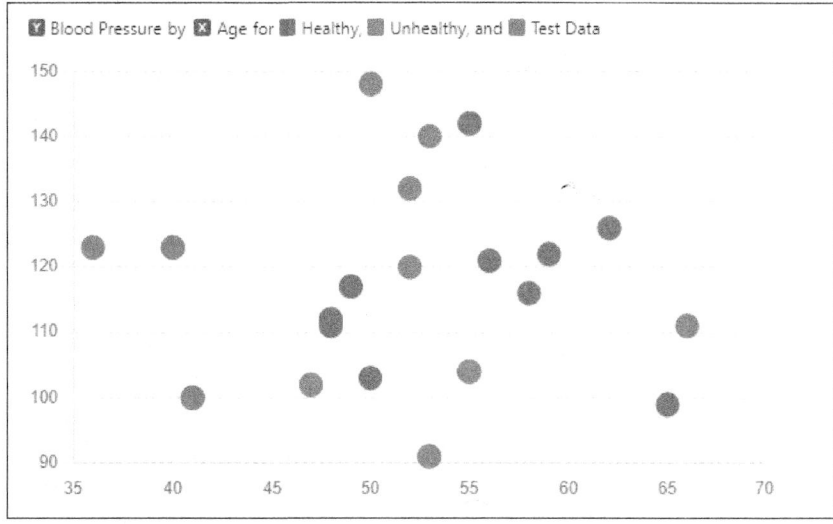

Figure 7.3: *Scatter Plot with Test Data*

In the preceding figure, a single test data point represents an individual aged 53 years with a blood pressure of 140 mmHg. As discussed earlier, KNN is a lazy and instance-based prediction algorithm, meaning it does not calculate any model parameters during the training phase. Instead, it defers computation until a test record is presented. When the test data point (here, the gray data point) is introduced, KNN computes the Euclidean distance (ED) to all other data points in the dataset. Assuming $k=3$, the algorithm sorts the distances from closest to farthest and selects the three closest records. These nearest neighbors are then used to predict the class of the test point, typically by majority voting among the neighbors' classes.

The three closest records are shown in *Figure* 7.4. This illustration demonstrates how the KNN classifier uses the distances to the nearest points to make predictions, showing the importance of the local neighborhood in classification decisions.

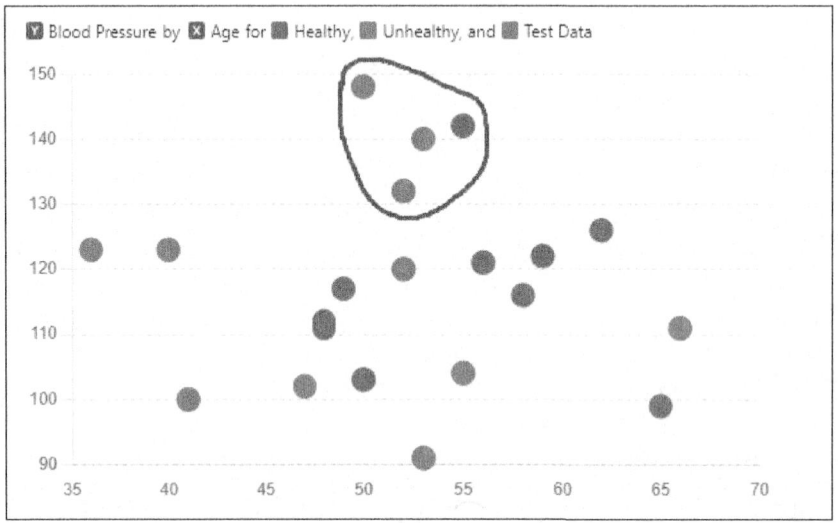

Figure 7.4: *Age versus Blood Pressure with KNN (k=3)*

The closest three datapoints with their Euclidean distance scores are tabulated in *Figure* 7.5.

Age	Blood Pressure	Health Status	Euclidean Distance
55	142	Healthy	2.83
52	132	Unhealthy	8.06
50	148	Unhealthy	8.54

Figure 7.5: *Three Closest Records with Euclidean Distance Score*

In KNN classification, there are two types of voting methods to determine the class of a test record:

Unweighted Voting: Each of the k nearest neighbors contributes equally to the prediction. In this scenario, the class of the test record is determined by the majority class among the nearest neighbors. For the given test data point:

- There are two Unhealthy records and one Healthy record among the three nearest neighbors.
- Therefore, using unweighted voting, the test record is predicted as **Unhealthy**.

Weighted Voting: Each of the k nearest neighbors contributes to the prediction based on their distance to the test point, with closer neighbors having a higher influence. The weight for each neighbor is typically calculated as the inverse of the squared distance. For the given test data point:

Weight of healthy = 1/[2.83]^2 = 0.125

Weight of unhealthy (here, we have 2 records) = 1/[8.06]^2 + 1/[8.54]^2 = 0.0291

Since the weight for the Healthy class (0.125) is greater than the weight for the Unhealthy class (0.0291), the test record is predicted as **Healthy** based on weighted voting.

Choosing between unweighted (uniform) voting and weighted voting depends on the specific requirements and characteristics of the dataset. Generally, unweighted voting is simpler and less prone to overfitting, as it considers the majority class among the nearest neighbors without giving disproportionate influence to any single point. On the other hand, weighted voting assigns more importance to closer neighbors, which can lead to better performance in some cases but also increases the risk of overfitting, particularly if the test data lies near an outlier. This can result in the model losing its generalization capability. Therefore, the choice between 'uniform' or 'weights' as the distance metric can be optimized using grid search hyperparameter tuning when implementing the model in Python, allowing for the best balance between bias and variance for the given data.

KNN as a Regressor: An Illustrative Example with Contrived Dataset

To demonstrate KNN as a regressor, a contrived dataset comprising 15 records, as shown in *Figure 7.6*, each representing a unique car model with three key attributes: engine size (in liters), horsepower, and fuel efficiency (in km per Litre, KMPL). The dataset is designed to explore how engine size and horsepower impact fuel efficiency, making it suitable for demonstrating KNN regression. The dataset includes a slight nonlinearity and randomness to better simulate real-world scenarios. A scatter plot in

Figure 7.4 showing the relationship between engine size and horsepower, with the fuel efficiency values displayed at each point. This visualization helps to understand how fuel efficiency varies with changes in engine size and horsepower.

	Engine_Size	Horsepower	Fuel_Efficiency
1	2.67	120	25.2
2	3.88	138	26.85
3	1.0	285	24.14
4	2.21	311	21.79
5	1.59	156	29.5
6	1.37	211	26.94
7	1.75	77	24.98
8	2.38	389	20.27
9	2.59	387	19.48
10	3.16	92	25.71
11	2.68	383	20.15
12	3.74	71	29.47
13	1.82	366	21.57
14	4.51	279	21.42
15	1.11	334	20.22

Figure 7.6: *Contrived Dataset*

To demonstrate how KNN works as a regressor using the car performance dataset, we will use the *k* parameter set to 3. However, it is important to note that choosing the optimal value for neighbors typically involves performing a grid search and experimenting with validation metrics.

Distance-Based Machine Learning Models

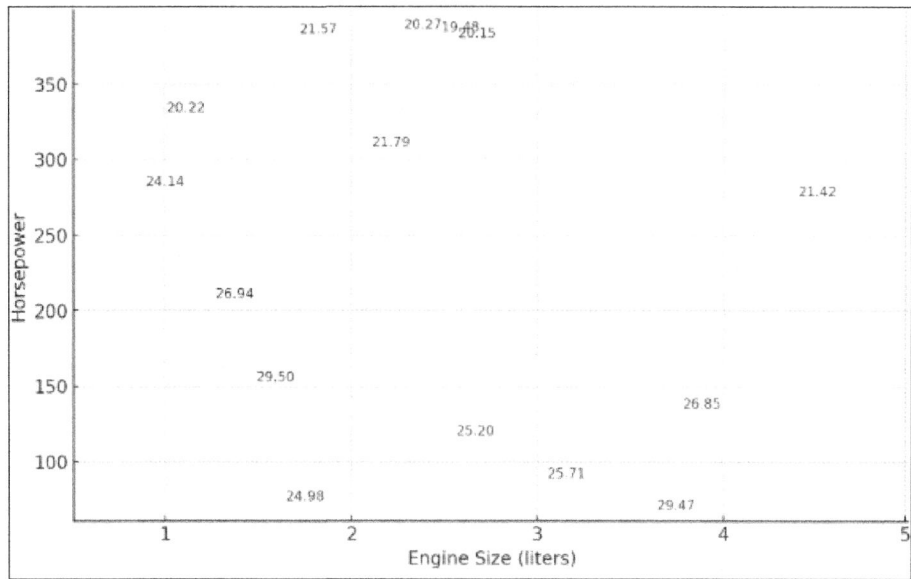

Figure 7.7: Engine Size versus Horsepower Scatter Plot

A test data point marked with a red circular marker is shown in *Figure 7.8*. The test data point has an Engine Size of 1.3 and Horsepower of 155. Using KNN as a regressor, we will compute the fuel efficiency manually using the closest three neighbors.

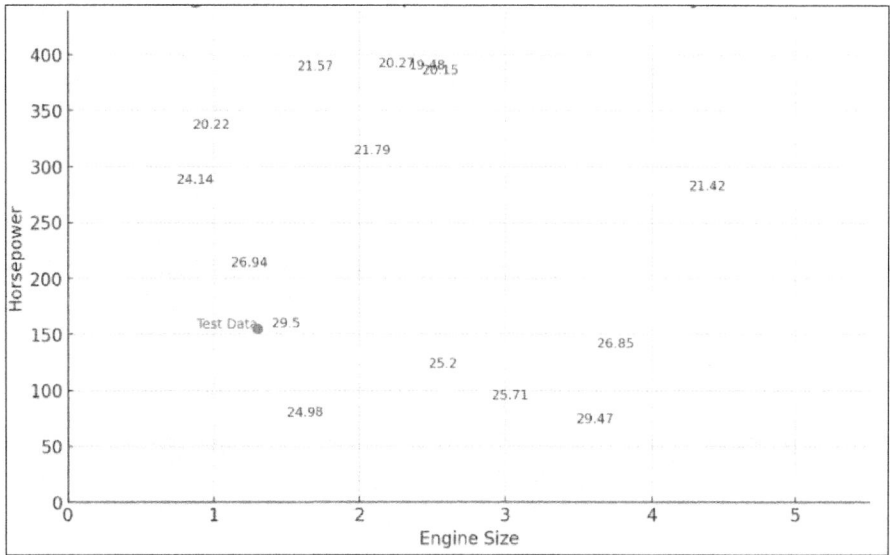

Figure 7.8: Scatter Plot with Test Data

We will compute the Euclidean distances between the test data point and all other records after scaling the independent features to avoid bias. The following figure displays the closest three records along with their distances:

Engine_Size	Horsepower	Fuel_Efficiency	Euclidean_distance
1.59	156	29.5	0.29
1.37	211	26.94	0.48
1.75	77	24.98	0.79

Figure 7.9: Three Closest Records with Euclidean Distance Score

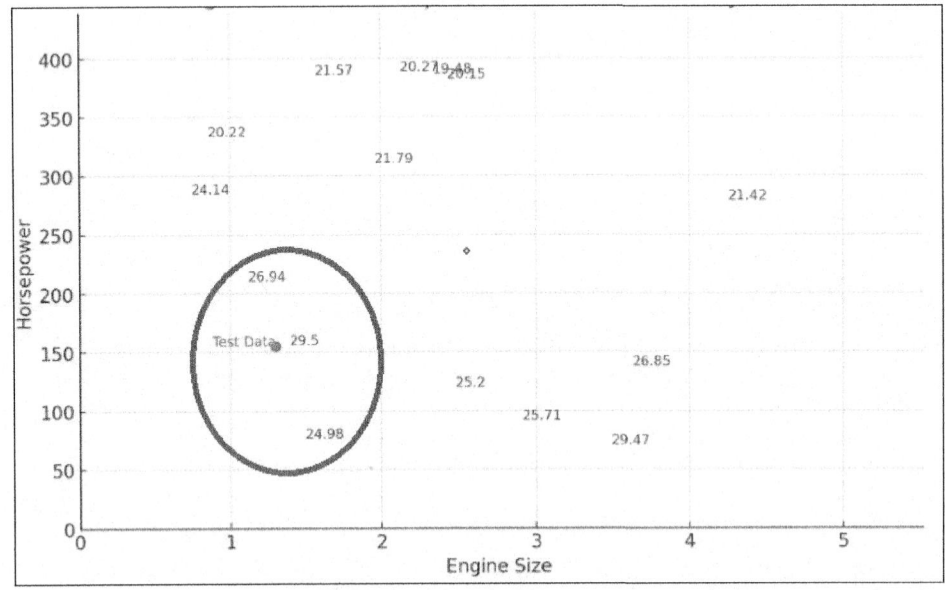

Figure 7.10: Engine Size versus Horsepower with KNN (k=3)

The three closest records are shown in *Figure* 7.10. This illustration demonstrates how the KNN regressor uses the distances to the nearest points to make predictions, showing the importance of the local neighborhood in regression decisions.

In KNN regressor, two types of prediction methods are possible.

Unweighted Average: Each of the k nearest neighbors contributes equally to the prediction. The unweighted average fuel efficiency of the closest three records is 27.14 KMPL. This would be the estimated fuel efficiency for the test data based on the nearest neighbors.

Weighted Average: To predict the fuel efficiency using the KNN regressor based on a weighted average, we can incorporate the Euclidean distance scores into the formula. The weights are typically the inverse of the distance, so closer neighbors will have more influence on the prediction.

We calculate the weights as follows:

$$\text{Weight}_i = \frac{1}{\text{Distance}_i}$$

Next, we compute the weighted average of the fuel efficiencies.

Let us do these calculations in detail:

$$\text{Weight}_1 = \frac{1}{\text{Distance}_1} = \frac{1}{0.29}$$
$$\text{Weight}_2 = \frac{1}{\text{Distance}_2} = \frac{1}{0.48}$$
$$\text{Weight}_3 = \frac{1}{\text{Distance}_3} = \frac{1}{0.79}$$

The weighted average fuel efficiency $FE_{weighted}$ is given by:

$$FE_{weighted} = \frac{FE_1 * Weight_1 * FE_2 * Weight_2 * FE_3 * Weight_3}{Weight_1 * Weight_2 * Weight_3}$$

$$FE_{weighted} = \frac{190.35}{6.80} = 27.99 \text{ KMPL}.$$

Thus, the KNN regressor would predict the fuel efficiency of the test record to be approximately 27.99 KMPL using the weighted average based on the distance scores.

In KNN regression, the choice between using a weighted average versus an unweighted average depends on the desired influence of closer neighbors on the prediction. A weighted average, where weights are typically the inverse or the inverse square of the distances, gives more importance to closer neighbors, leading to a prediction that is more representative of the immediate vicinity of the test point. This method is particularly useful when data points closer to the query point are more relevant. On the other hand, an unweighted average treats all neighbors equally, which can be beneficial when outliers or noise are evenly distributed, or when the relevance of each neighbor is considered equal regardless of distance. The decision should be guided by the specific characteristics of the dataset and the problem context. For most practical purposes, weighted averaging is preferred as it tends to provide more accurate and sensitive predictions.

Python Implementation of KNN Classifier

The Seeds dataset is a well-known dataset in the field of machine learning and agriculture, containing measurements of various geometrical properties of wheat kernels. This dataset includes three varieties of wheat: Kama, Rosa, and Canadian. Each entry in the dataset consists of seven features: area, perimeter, compactness, length of kernel, width of kernel, asymmetry coefficient, and length of kernel groove. The goal is to classify these wheat varieties based on their physical characteristics using a KNN classifier, given its clear, multi-class structure and real-world agricultural context.

Let us load the dataset and display the first five records, as shown in *Figure 7.11*, to understand the feature name and class label. The dataset consists of 210 records with seven independent features. The dependent variable is class name.

```
import pandas as pd
file_path = 'path_to_your_data/ data1_Ch7_seed_dataset.csv'
df = pd.read_csv(file_path)
df.head()
```

area A	perimeter P	compactness	length of kernel	width of kernel	asymmetry coefficient	length of kernel groove	class
15.26	14.84	0.8710	5.763	3.312	2.221	5.220	1
14.88	14.57	0.8811	5.554	3.333	1.018	4.956	1
14.29	14.09	0.9050	5.291	3.337	2.699	4.825	1
13.84	13.94	0.8955	5.324	3.379	2.259	4.805	1
16.14	14.99	0.9034	5.658	3.562	1.355	5.175	1

Figure 7.11: *Head of the Data*

KNN, being a non-parametric model, does not require statistical assumptions about the dataset to be checked, unlike linear models such as logistic regression and Naïve Bayes models. We shall proceed with model building directly.

Being a distance-based model, scaling is mandatory. We standardize the dataset before splitting the records into training and validation data.

```
from sklearn.preprocessing import StandardScaler
# Define X with all features except the last column (class)
X = df.iloc[:, :-1]
# Define Y as the last column (class)
Y = df.iloc[:, -1]
# Initialize the StandardScaler
scaler = StandardScaler()
# Scale X and keep it in X_std
X_std = scaler.fit_transform(X)
```

The next step involves fitting the **GridSearchCV** object to the scaled features (**X_std**) and the target variable (Y). **GridSearchCV** performs an exhaustive search over the specified parameter grid by training and evaluating the model for each combination of parameters using cross-validation.

```
from sklearn.neighbors import KNeighborsClassifier
from sklearn.model_selection import GridSearchCV, cross_val_score, KFold
# Define the KFold cross-validation strategy
kf = KFold(n_splits=3, shuffle=True, random_state=0)
```

Distance-Based Machine Learning Models

```
# Define the KNeighborsClassifier
KNN = KNeighborsClassifier()
params={'n_neighbors':np.arange(3,70),'weights':['uniform','distance']}
```

Here, a parameter grid is defined for the hyperparameter tuning process. The grid includes:

n_neighbors: A range of values from 3 to 69, indicating the number of neighbors to consider in the KNN algorithm.

weights: Two options, '**uniform**' (all points in each neighborhood are weighted equally) and 'distance' (points are weighted by the inverse of their distance).

After fitting, **GridSearchCV** identifies the combination of hyperparameters that yields the best performance based on the specified scoring metric (in this case, the weighted F1 score). We have obtained **n_neighbor** and weights as 12 and 'uniform' respectively.

Now, a KNN classifier model is built with the help of the optimal parameters obtained using GridSearchCV.

```
from sklearn.model_selection import train_test_split
from sklearn.metrics import confusion_matrix,classification_report
X_train, X_test, y_train, y_test = train_test_split(X_std, Y, test_size=0.3, random_state=0)
KNN_tuned = KNeighborsClassifier(n_neighbors=12, weights='uniform')
KNN_tuned.fit(X_train, y_train)
y_pred = KNN_tuned.predict(X_test)
cm=confusion_matrix(ytest,y_pred)
cr=classification_report(ytest,y_pred)
print(cm)
print(cr)
```

Inference

The KNN model performs exceptionally well in classifying the different types of wheat. There are minor misclassifications between Kama Wheat and Rosa Wheat, but Canadian Wheat is perfectly identified. The high precision and recall values indicate the model's reliability and effectiveness in distinguishing between the classes. The confusion matrix for the KNN classifier is shown *Figure* 7.12.

	Predicted Kama Wheat	Predicted Rosa Wheat	Predicted Canadian Wheat
Actual Kama Wheat	17	2	0
Actual Rosa Wheat	3	24	0
Actual Canadian Wheat	0	0	17

Figure 7.12: *Confusion Matrix*

The classification report shown in *Figure 7.13* for the KNN classifier reveals strong performance across all three classes of wheat: Kama Wheat, Rosa Wheat, and Canadian Wheat. The model achieves high precision, recall, and f1-scores, with overall accuracy at 92%. Kama Wheat has a precision of 0.85 and a recall of 0.89, indicating that while most instances are correctly classified, a few are misidentified as Rosa Wheat. Rosa Wheat shows a precision of 0.92 and recall of 0.89, with minimal misclassifications as Kama Wheat. Canadian Wheat is perfectly classified with precision, recall, and f1-score all at 1.00.

	precision	recall	f1-score	support
Kama Wheat	0.85	0.89	0.87	19.0
Rosa Wheat	0.92	0.89	0.91	27.0
Canadian Wheat	1.0	1.0	1.0	17.0
accuracy	0.92	0.92	0.92	0.92
macro avg	0.92	0.93	0.93	63.0
weighted avg	0.92	0.92	0.92	63.0

Figure 7.13: *Classification Report*

These results highlight the model's robustness, particularly its excellent performance in identifying Canadian Wheat, while also indicating that minor improvements could be made to reduce misclassifications between Kama Wheat and Rosa Wheat.

We know KNN is a non-parametric model; hence, there is no scope for boosting the average performance score. However, KNN can be effectively bagged to enhance its stable performance. Bagging involves training multiple KNN models on different random subsets of the data and aggregating their predictions to reduce variance and improve stability.

Python Implementation of KNN Regressor

The dataset used to demonstrate the KNN regressor was created by Angeliki Xifara, a Civil/Structural Engineer, and was processed by Athanasios Tsanas from the Oxford Centre for Industrial and Applied Mathematics, University of Oxford, UK. The dataset, now available on Kaggle, consists of 768 samples and 8 features, designed to predict either heating load or cooling load. In this demonstration, we will focus on using cooling load as the dependent variable, typically (KW/m^2). The unit indicates the amount of cooling energy required per unit area of the building. However, readers are encouraged to apply the same model to predict heating load and compare the performance of both predictions.

Distance-Based Machine Learning Models

Let us load the data and visualize the head of the data, as shown in *Figure 7.14*, to understand its variables.

```
import pandas as pd
file_path = 'path_to_your_data/ data2_Ch7_energy_dataset.csv'
df = pd.read_csv(file_path)
df.head()
```

X1	X2	X3	X4	X5	X6	X7	X8	Y2
0.98	514.5	294.0	110.25	7	2	0.0	0	21.33
0.98	514.5	294.0	110.25	7	3	0.0	0	21.33
0.98	514.5	294.0	110.25	7	4	0.0	0	21.33
0.98	514.5	294.0	110.25	7	5	0.0	0	21.33
0.90	563.5	318.5	122.50	7	2	0.0	0	28.28

Figure 7.14: Head of the Energy Data

This dataset includes the following features:

    X1: Relative Compactness (ratio)

    X2: Surface Area (square meters)

    X3: Wall Area (square meters)

    X4: Roof Area (square meters)

    X5: Overall Height (meters)

    X6: Orientation (Categorical (integer values representing different orientations)

    X7: Glazing Area (percentage %)

    X8: Glazing Area Distribution (Categorical integer values representing different glazing area distributions)

    Y1: Heating Load (target variable: KW/m^2)

    Y2: Cooling Load (target variable: KW/m^2)

Since we are going to predict the cooling load using the KNN regressor model, let us drop the variable **Y1**.

```
df = df.drop(columns=['Y1'])
```

Being a distance-based model, scaling is mandatory. We standardize the dataset before splitting the records into training and validation data. Moreover, there are two categorical variables, X6 and X8. Categorical variables are very sensitive to scaling; we shall explore these columns and choose an appropriate scaling mechanism.

The box plot of cooling load (Y2) with respect to the glazing area distribution (X8) is shown in *Figure 7.15*.

```python
import matplotlib.pyplot as plt
import seaborn as sns
# Create a box plot for cooling load (Y2) with respect to categories in X8
plt.figure(figsize=(10, 6))
sns.boxplot(x='X8', y='Y2', data=df)
plt.xlabel('Glazing Area Distribution (X8)')
plt.ylabel('Cooling Load (Y2) (kW/m²)')
plt.show()
```

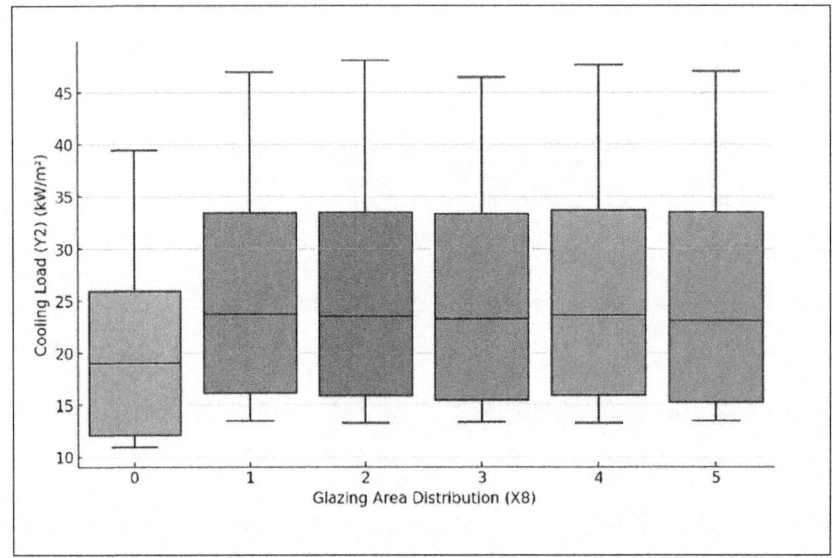

Figure 7.15: *Box Plot of Cooling Load (Y2) with Respect to Glazing Area Distribution (X8)*

The category 1 to 5 has similar distribution with almost same median values; let us bucketize these five categories into single category.

```python
# Bucketize the categories
df['X8'] = df['X8'].apply(lambda x: 1 if x in [1, 2, 3, 4, 5] else 0)
```

Similarly, the box plot of cooling load (Y2) with respect to the orientation (X6) is shown in *Figure 7.16*.

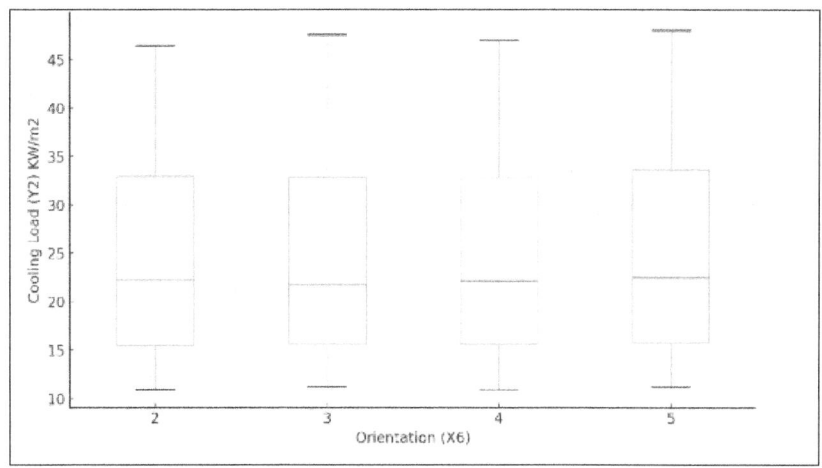

Figure 7.16: *Box Plot of Cooling Load (Y2) with Respect to Orientation (X6)*

The distributions and medians for each category of X6 (orientation) shown in *Figure 7.16* are almost identical, indicating that this feature has minimal variance. As a result, X6 does not significantly contribute to the model and can be dropped to improve model performance and reduce complexity.

```
# Drop the column 'X6'
df = df.drop(columns=['X6'])
```

We can proceed with scaling and model building.

```
from sklearn.preprocessing import StandardScaler
# Define X with all features except the last column (class)
X = df.iloc[:, :-1]
# Define Y as the last column (class)
Y = df.iloc[:, -1]
# Initialize the StandardScaler
scaler = StandardScaler()
# Scale X and keep it in X_std
X_std = scaler.fit_transform(X)
```

The next step involves fitting the **GridSearchCV** object to the scaled features (**X_std**) and the target variable (Y). **GridSearchCV** performs an exhaustive search over the specified parameter grid by training and evaluating the model for each combination of parameters using cross-validation.

```
from sklearn.neighbors import KNeighborsRegressor
from sklearn.model_selection import GridSearchCV, cross_val_score, KFold
# Define the KFold cross-validation strategy
kf = KFold(n_splits=5, shuffle=True, random_state=0)
# Define the KNeighborsRegressor
KNN = KNeighborsRegressor()
params={'n_neighbors':np.arange(3,100),'weights':['uniform','distance']}
```

Here, a parameter grid is defined for the hyperparameter tuning process. The grid includes:

n_neighbors: A range of values from 3 to 99, indicating the number of neighbors to consider in the KNN algorithm.

weights: Two options, 'uniform' (all points in each neighborhood are weighted equally) and 'distance' (points are weighted by the inverse of their distance).

After fitting, **GridSearchCV** identifies the combination of hyperparameters that yields the best performance based on the specified scoring metric (in this case, the root mean squared error). We have obtained **n_neighbor** and weights as 14 and 'distance,' respectively.

Now, a KNN regressor model is built with the help of the optimal parameters obtained using **GridSearchCV**.

```
from sklearn.model_selection import train_test_split
from sklearn.metrics import r2_score
X_train, X_test, y_train, y_test = train_test_split(X_std, Y, test_size=0.3, random_state=0)
KNN_tuned = KNeighborsRegressor(n_neighbors=14, weights='distance')
KNN_tuned.fit(X_train, y_train)
y_pred = KNN_tuned.predict(X_test)
rmse = np.sqrt(np.mean((y_test-y_pred)**2))
r2 = r2_score(y_test, y_pred)
print([rmse,r2])
[1.749,0.9661]
#perform cross-validation
rmse = cross_val_score(KNN_tuned, X_std, Y, cv=kf, scoring='neg_root_mean_squared_error')
# Calculate the mean and standard deviation of the RMSE scores
mean_rmse = np.mean(np.abs(rmse_scores))
std_rmse = np.std(np.abs(rmse_scores),ddof=1)
print([mean_rmse,std_rmse])
[1.686,0.102]
```

Inference

The validation results from the simple train-test split reveal a Root Mean Squared Error (RMSE) of approximately 1.749 KW/m² and an R-squared (R²) score of 0.966. The RMSE indicates that, on average, the model's predictions deviate from the actual cooling load values by 1.749 KW/m². The high R-squared value of 0.966 suggests that the model explains 96.6% of the variance in the cooling load, indicating a strong fit to the data. Cross-validation provides a more thorough and reliable assessment of a model's performance by reducing the dependency on a single split and ensuring that all data points contribute to both training and testing phases. This leads to a more accurate and generalizable evaluation of the model. The cross-validation results for the K-Nearest Neighbors regressor show a mean Root Mean Squared Error (RMSE) of approximately 1.686 KW/m², with a standard deviation of 0.102 KW/m². This indicates that, on average, the model's predictions deviate from the actual cooling load values by about 1.686 KW/m². The relatively low standard deviation suggests that the model's performance is consistent across different folds of the dataset. These results demonstrate that the model is reasonably accurate and reliable in predicting the cooling load (KW/m²), making it a useful tool for estimating energy requirements in building design and energy efficiency applications.

Limitations in Distance-Based ML Models

Distance-based models, particularly the K-Nearest Neighbors (KNN) algorithm, have garnered significant attention for their simplicity and effectiveness in various classification and regression tasks. However, while KNN is a powerful tool, it is not without its limitations. In this subsection, we will explore some of the critical drawbacks inherent to KNN and similar distance-based models.

One of the primary limitations of KNN is its computational inefficiency, especially as the size of the dataset increases. During the prediction phase, KNN must calculate the distance between the query point and every other point in the dataset. This process can be prohibitively time-consuming when dealing with large datasets or high-dimensional data. The computational complexity of KNN is $O(n)$, where n represents the number of training samples, making it less suitable for real-time applications or scenarios where quick predictions are necessary.

Another significant challenge with KNN is its sensitivity to the choice of distance metric. The most used distance metric is the Euclidean distance, which can be effective in certain situations but may not always capture the true relationship between data points in high-dimensional spaces. Different metrics, such as Manhattan or Minkowski distances, might yield better results depending on the nature of the data. However, selecting the appropriate distance metric is often not straightforward and can require extensive experimentation and domain knowledge.

KNN also struggles with the "curse of dimensionality," a phenomenon where the performance of distance-based algorithms degrades as the number of dimensions increases. In high-dimensional spaces, the concept of distance becomes less meaningful because the relative differences between distances diminish. This issue can lead to poor performance, as KNN may not be able to effectively distinguish between the nearest neighbors and other points. Dimensionality reduction techniques, such as Principal Component Analysis (PCA) or t-Distributed Stochastic Neighbor Embedding (t-SNE), are often employed to mitigate this problem, but they add complexity to the model-building process.

One significant drawback of the K-Nearest Neighbors (KNN) algorithm is that it is sensitive to noisy data and outliers. Noisy data refers to data points that are erroneous or irrelevant, often caused by measurement errors, data entry mistakes, or random fluctuations. These inaccuracies can disrupt the algorithm's ability to correctly classify or predict because KNN relies heavily on the local neighborhood of a query point; the presence of noisy data points or outliers can significantly affect the accuracy of the predictions. These aberrant points can distort the true structure of the data, leading to incorrect classifications or regression outputs. Preprocessing steps such as data cleaning, outlier detection, and feature scaling are crucial to minimize the impact of noise and outliers, but they require additional effort and expertise.

Finally, KNN requires careful tuning of hyperparameters, particularly the value of k, the number of nearest neighbors to consider. Selecting an inappropriate value for k can lead to overfitting or underfitting. A small k value can make the model overly sensitive to noise, while a large k value can smooth out important distinctions in the data. Cross-validation techniques are typically used to find the optimal k value, but this process can be time-consuming and computationally expensive.

In conclusion, while KNN is a versatile and intuitive algorithm, it is essential to be aware of its limitations. Its computational inefficiency, sensitivity to distance metrics, challenges with high-dimensional data, vulnerability to noise and outliers, and the need for careful hyperparameter tuning are all factors that must be considered when choosing to use KNN in practical applications. Understanding these limitations allows practitioners to make informed decisions and apply appropriate techniques to mitigate the downsides, thereby harnessing the strengths of KNN more effectively.

Conclusion

In this chapter, we explored the intricacies of distance-based machine learning models, focusing on the K-Nearest Neighbors (KNN) algorithm. We began by introducing the KNN model, discussing its foundational principles and intuitive approach to classification and regression tasks. The algorithm's reliance on the proximity of data points for decision-making highlighted its simplicity and effectiveness in various applications. We examined different distance metrics such as Euclidean, Manhattan, and Minkowski distances, emphasizing how the choice of metric can significantly impact the model's performance. Understanding these metrics is crucial for selecting the appropriate one based on data characteristics and the specific problem at hand. We delved into the mathematical foundation of KNN, using hand-worked calculations on contrived datasets to demonstrate how KNN functions as both a regressor and a classifier. These exercises illustrated the mechanics of KNN and the influence of distance metrics on outcomes. Transitioning from theory to practice, we implemented KNN in Python for classification and regression tasks, showcasing real-world applications and reinforcing theoretical concepts. We addressed the limitations of KNN, including computational inefficiency with large datasets, sensitivity to

Distance-Based Machine Learning Models

distance metrics, and susceptibility to the curse of dimensionality and noisy data. This comprehensive overview of KNN equips readers with a thorough understanding of the algorithm, setting the stage for the next chapter on Support Vector Machines (SVM), a more powerful algorithm capable of handling non-linearity in datasets.

Practice Exercises

1. Given the dataset shown in *Figure 7.17* and using k=3, classify the new point (3,3) using the Euclidean distance metric.

Point	Feature 1	Feature 2	Class
A	1	2	0
B	2	3	0
C	3	3	1
D	6	5	1

***Figure 7.17**: Contrived Dataset*

2. Calculate the Manhattan distance between the new point (3,3) and the points in the dataset shown in the preceding figure.

3. Using the KNN regression algorithm with k=3 and the Euclidean distance metric, predict the value of the new point (3,3) from the data points shown in the following figure:

Point	Feature 1	Feature 2	Value
A	1	2	10
B	2	3	15
C	3	3	20
D	6	5	25
E	5	6	30

***Figure 7.18**: Contrived Dataset*

4. Using the KNN classification algorithm with k=3, classify the new point (4,5) using the dataset shown in *Figure 7.19*. Apply a weighted voting scheme where the weight is the inverse of the distance. Use the Euclidean distance metric.

Point	Feature 1	Feature 2	Class
A	3	4	0
B	5	6	1
C	4	4	1
D	6	7	0

***Figure 7.19**: Contrived Dataset*

5. Using the KNN regression algorithm with k=3, predict the value of the new point (3,3) using the dataset shown in *Figure 7.20*. Apply a weighted average scheme where the weight is the inverse of the distance. Use the Euclidean distance metric.

Point	Feature 1	Feature 2	Value
A	2	2	10
B	4	4	20
C	3	2	15
D	5	5	25

Figure 7.20: Contrived Dataset

Answers

1. D(A, (3,3)) = 2.24 ; d(B,(3,3)) = 1 ; D(C, (3,3)) = 0 ; d(D,(3,3)) = 3.61

   Nearest neighbors: B, C, A (distances 1, 0, and 2.24, respectively)

   Classes of nearest neighbors: 0, 1, 0

   Majority class: 0

2. D(A, (3,3)) = 3 ; d(B,(3,3)) = 1 ; D(C, (3,3)) = 0 ; d(D,(3,3)) = 5

3. D(A, (3,3)) = 2.24 ; d(B,(3,3)) = 1 ; D(C, (3,3)) = 0 ; d(D,(3,3)) = 3.61; d(E,(3,3)) = 3.61; Nearest neighbors: B, C, A (distances 1, 0, and 2.24, respectively); Values of nearest neighbors: 15, 20, 10; Predicted value:15 (average of 3).

4. D(A, (4,5)) = 1.41 ; d(B,(4,5)) = 1.41 ; D(C, (4,5)) = 1 ; d(D,(4,5)) = 2.83 ; Nearest neighbors: C, A, B (distances 1, 1.41, and 1.41, respectively); Weight of C = 11 = 1; Weight of A = 11.41 = 0.71 ; Weight of B = 11.41 = 0.71; Weighted votes of Class-1 : 1.71; Weighted votes of Class-0 : 0.71; New point is classified as class-1.

5. D(A, (3,3)) = 1.41 ; d(B,(3,3)) = 1.41 ; D(C, (3,3)) = 1 ; d(D,(3,3)) = 2.83 ; Nearest neighbors: C, A, B (distances 1, 1.41, and 1.41, respectively); Weight of C = 11 = 1; Weight of A = 11.41 = 0.71 ; Weight of B = 11.41 = 0.71; Weighted value of C = 1 X 15; Weighted value of A = 0.71 X 10 = 7.1 ; Weighted value of B =0.71 X 20 = 14.2;

   Predicted weighted average score = 15+7.1+14.22.42 = 15.

Multiple Choice Questions

1. What is the primary function of the K-Nearest Neighbors (KNN) algorithm?

    a. Data Clustering

    b. Classification and Regression

c. Dimensionality Reduction

d. Data Generation

2. What is a significant drawback of using KNN with high-dimensional data?

    a. Overfitting

    b. Underfitting

    c. Curse of Dimensionality

    d. Lack of Interpretability

3. KNN is particularly sensitive to:

    a. Number of clusters

    b. Activation functions

    c. Noisy data and outliers

    d. Learning rate

4. In the context of KNN, what is the purpose of cross-validation?

    a. To generate new features

    b. To find the optimal value of k

    c. To reduce the dimensionality of data

    d. To normalize the data

5. How does KNN handle a query point during prediction?

    a. By creating decision trees

    b. By calculating distances to all training points

    c. By gradient descent optimization

    d. By splitting the data into clusters

6. Which preprocessing step is crucial for KNN to handle different scales of data features effectively?

    a. Dimensionality reduction

    b. Feature selection

    c. Feature scaling

    d. Data augmentation

7. What challenge does the "curse of dimensionality" present for KNN?

    a. Less data points

    b. Distance metrics become less meaningful

    c. Increased interpretability

    d. Simplified computation

8. In which scenario is KNN likely to perform poorly?

    a. Low-dimensional data with few samples

    b. When data points are linearly separable

    c. Large datasets with high dimensionality

    d. When the value of k is optimally tuned

9. Why is feature scaling important for KNN?

    a. To increase the number of features

    b. To ensure all features contribute equally to distance calculations

    c. To reduce the computational complexity

    d. To eliminate irrelevant features

10. When using KNN for regression, the prediction is typically based on:

    a. The mode of the nearest neighbors' labels

    b. The median of the nearest neighbors' labels

    c. The average of the nearest neighbors' values

    d. The sum of the nearest neighbors' values

Answers

1. b
2. c
3. c
4. b
5. b
6. c

7. b

8. c

9. b

10. c

Keywords

- K-Nearest Neighbors (KNN)
- Distance-Based Models
- Euclidean Distance
- Manhattan Distance
- Minkowski Distance
- Hyperparameters
- Weighted Voting
- Weighted Average
- Non-Parametric Model
- Computational Complexity
- Noisy Data
- Principal Component Analysis (PCA)
- t-Distributed Stochastic Neighbor Embedding (t-SNE)

References

1. https://www.kaggle.com/datasets

2. https://archive.ics.uci.edu/dataset/236/seeds

3. Tsanas, Athanasios; Xifara, Angeliki (2012). "Accurate quantitative estimation of energy performance of residential buildings using statistical machine learning tools". *Energy and Buildings*. 49: 560–567

CHAPTER 8
Support Vector Machines

Introduction

This chapter delves into the powerful and versatile world of Support Vector Machines (SVM), a staple in the toolbox of supervised learning algorithms for both classification and regression tasks. The chapter starts with an in-depth examination of the mathematical underpinnings of SVMs, particularly how they formulate and optimize the hyperplane that serves as the decision boundary between different classes. Following this, the discussion expands to include various kernel functions, which enhance SVMs' capability to handle non-linear data distributions by projecting them into higher-dimensional spaces. The chapter includes a hands-on section on implementing SVMs in Python using the scikit-learn library.

This part of the chapter guides readers through preprocessing data, selecting appropriate kernel functions, and evaluating the performance of the SVM models. By the end of this chapter, readers will not only have a deep understanding of Support Vector Machines but also practical skills and insights to apply these models effectively across various machine learning scenarios.

Structure

In this chapter, we are going to cover the following topics:

- Understanding the Principles of Support Vector Machines
- Mathematical Foundation of Kernel Functions and Their Role in SVMs
- Python Implementation and Use Case with SVM as a Regressor
- Python Implementation and Use Case with SVM as a Classifier
- Pros and Cons of Support Vector Machines

Understanding the Principles of Support Vector Machines

SVMs are renowned for their versatility in machine learning, serving effectively in both classification and regression tasks. This dual capability makes them an indispensable tool for a wide range of applications. At the core of SVMs lies the concept of finding an optimal decision boundary, which is fundamental to their functionality as classifiers. When functioning as a classifier, an SVM aims to identify a hyperplane that distinctly separates different classes within the feature space, ensuring that the margin between these classes is maximized. This approach is crucial for achieving high accuracy and robustness in classification tasks.

The process of finding this optimal hyperplane involves solving a quadratic optimization problem, where the goal is to maximize the margin–the distance between the hyperplane and the nearest data points from each class, known as support vectors. These support vectors are critical as they define the position and orientation of the hyperplane. By maximizing the margin, SVMs strive to reduce the likelihood of misclassifying new data points, thereby enhancing the model's generalization ability. This property is particularly advantageous in high-dimensional spaces, where SVMs excel at distinguishing between classes even when the data is not linearly separable.

In scenarios where the data cannot be separated by a linear hyperplane, SVMs employ a technique known as the kernel trick. This method involves mapping the input features into a higher-dimensional space using a kernel function, where a linear separation becomes feasible, as shown in *Figure* 8.1. Various kernel functions, such as polynomial, radial basis function (RBF), and sigmoid, can be used depending on the nature of the data. The choice of kernel significantly impacts the performance of the SVM, and understanding how to select and apply the appropriate kernel is essential for leveraging the full potential of SVMs.

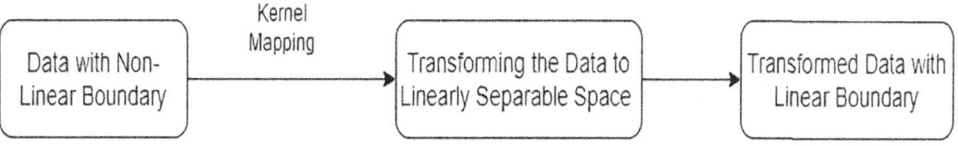

Figure 8.1: *Core Idea of SVM Classifier*

Beyond classification, SVMs also shine in regression tasks, where they are referred to as Support Vector Regression (SVR). In SVR, the objective is to find a function that approximates the target values with a deviation less than a specified threshold, known as the epsilon parameter. The model depicted in *Figure* 8.2 aims to ensure that most of the training data points fall within this epsilon-insensitive tube, minimizing the prediction error while maintaining a balance between complexity and accuracy.

This capability makes SVR highly effective in situations where precise and reliable predictions are necessary, such as in financial forecasting and time-series analysis.

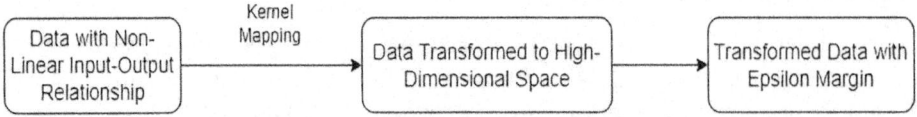

Figure 8.2: Core Idea of SVM Regressor

The flexibility of SVMs in handling both classification and regression tasks is further enhanced by their robustness against overfitting. Overfitting occurs when a model learns the noise in the training data rather than the underlying patterns, leading to poor performance on unseen data. SVMs mitigate this risk by focusing on the support vectors and maximizing the margin, which helps in maintaining a simpler and more generalizable model. Additionally, the regularization parameter (C) in SVMs allows for controlling the trade-off between maximizing the margin and minimizing classification errors, providing a mechanism to fine-tune the model's complexity.

Another notable advantage of SVMs is their effectiveness in high-dimensional spaces. In many practical applications, data can have many features, making traditional classification and regression algorithms prone to performance degradation. SVMs, however, are well-suited for such environments due to their reliance on support vectors and the kernel trick, which enables them to handle complex and high-dimensional data without significant loss of accuracy. This property has made SVMs a popular choice in fields such as bioinformatics, text classification, and image recognition.

Despite their many strengths, SVMs consist of challenges. One of the primary difficulties lies in the selection of the appropriate kernel and its parameters. An incorrect choice can lead to suboptimal performance, and finding the right combination often requires experimentation and cross-validation. Additionally, SVMs can be computationally intensive, especially with large datasets, as the optimization problem scales with the number of data points. Efficient implementations and techniques such as Sequential Minimal Optimization (SMO) have been developed to address these issues, making SVMs more scalable and practical for large-scale applications.

In practical terms, the implementation of SVMs involves several steps, including data preprocessing, selecting the kernel function, tuning hyperparameters, and evaluating the model's performance. Data preprocessing may involve normalizing the features to ensure that they have similar scales, which can improve the convergence of the optimization algorithm. Selecting the kernel function requires understanding the nature of the data and the relationships between features. Hyperparameter tuning, particularly the regularization parameter (C) and the kernel parameters, is crucial for achieving optimal performance, often requiring techniques such as grid search and cross-validation.

To illustrate the application of SVMs, consider a binary classification problem in the field of medical diagnosis. Suppose we have a dataset containing various health metrics of patients, and the goal is to classify whether a patient has a particular disease. By using an SVM classifier, we can identify the decision boundary that best separates the healthy and diseased patients based on their health metrics. The SVM will maximize the margin between the two classes, ensuring that the model generalizes well to new patients. If the relationship between health metrics and the disease is non-linear, a kernel function can be used to map the data into a higher-dimensional space where a linear separation is possible.

Mathematical Foundation of Kernel Functions and Their Role in SVMs

Kernel functions play a pivotal role in Support Vector Machines (SVMs) by enabling them to perform efficiently in high-dimensional spaces. At a high level, kernel functions are mathematical tools that transform the original input data into a higher-dimensional space, where it becomes easier to separate data points using a linear boundary. This transformation helps SVMs to create more complex decision boundaries, thereby improving their performance on non-linear classification tasks. The concept of kernel functions allows SVMs to leverage powerful feature spaces without explicitly computing the coordinates in that space, which is known as the "kernel trick." This approach not only enhances computational efficiency but also expands the applicability of SVMs to a wider range of problems.

Types of Kernel Functions

There are several types of kernel functions, each suited for different kinds of data and tasks. Here are the most commonly used kernel functions, along with their mathematical representations and examples:

- **Linear Kernel**: The linear kernel is the simplest form of kernel function. It is used when the data is linearly separable in the original feature space. The linear kernel function is defined as:

$$K(x_i, x_j) = x_i \cdot x_j$$

  Where x_i and x_j are input vectors. This kernel does not perform any transformation and is equivalent to the standard dot product.

- **Polynomial Kernel:** The polynomial kernel represents the similarity of vectors in a polynomial feature space. It is defined as:

$$K(x_i, x_j) = (x_i \cdot x_j + c)^d$$

Where c is a constant term (trading off the influence of higher-order versus lower-order terms), and d is the degree of the polynomial.

- **Radial Basis Function (RBF) Kernel**: The RBF kernel, also known as the Gaussian kernel, is popular for its ability to handle non-linear data. It is defined as:

$$K(x_i, x_j) = e^{-\frac{\|x_i - x_j\|^2}{2\sigma^2}}$$

Where σ is a parameter that determines the width of the Gaussian function.

- **Sigmoid Kernel**: The sigmoid kernel, also known as the hyperbolic tangent kernel, is related to neural networks. It is defined as:

$$K(x_i, x_j) = \tanh(\propto (x_i, x_j) + c)$$

- **Custom Kernels**: In some cases, it might be beneficial to design a custom kernel that is specifically tailored to the problem at hand. Custom kernels can be constructed by combining standard kernels or by designing new ones that capture the desired features of the data. A custom kernel could be a combination of a polynomial and RBF kernel:

$$K(x_i, x_j) = (x_i, x_j + 1)^2 + e^{-\frac{\|x_i - x_j\|^2}{2\sigma^2}}$$

By understanding and utilizing these various types of kernel functions, SVMs can be adapted to a wide range of problems, making them a versatile tool in the field of machine learning.

Kernel Trick

In *Figure* 8.3, we see a two-dimensional scatter plot depicting two classes of data points. The blue points form a circular pattern surrounding a cluster of green points in the center. This kind of arrangement presents a classic example of non-linearly separable data, where no straight line can effectively divide the two classes. Traditional linear models, such as Logistic Regression or Naïve Bayes, fail to find an appropriate boundary that separates these classes because they only consider linear relationships. The challenge with non-linear boundaries is that the decision surface needed to separate the classes is not a straight line but rather a more complex shape, such as a circle or an ellipse in this case.

Support Vector Machines   237

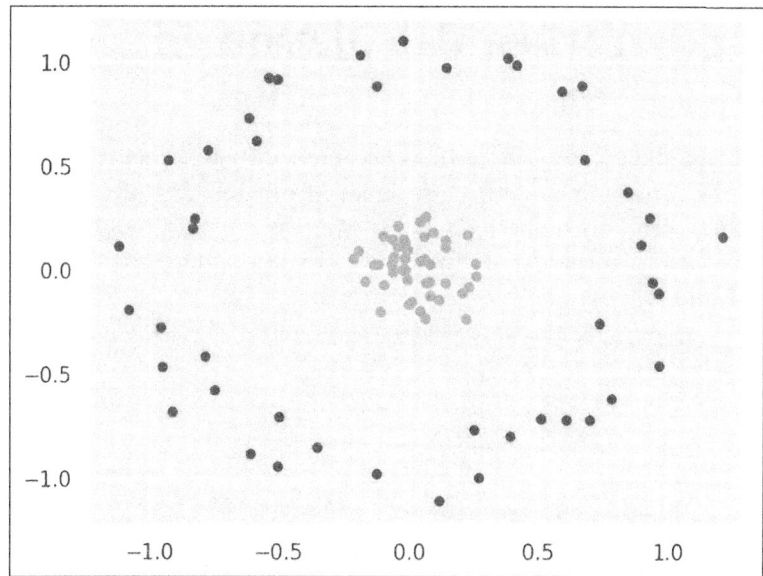

Figure 8.3: *2D Scatter Plot with Non-Linear Boundary*

Figure 8.4 demonstrates how a kernel function, specifically the Radial Basis Function (RBF) kernel, can address this issue by transforming the original features into a higher-dimensional space. In this elevated space, the data points are mapped in such a way that the non-linear relationships in the original 2D space become linear. The figure shows that the green and blue points, initially entangled in a circular pattern, are now separated along a new dimension (the vertical axis), making them linearly separable.

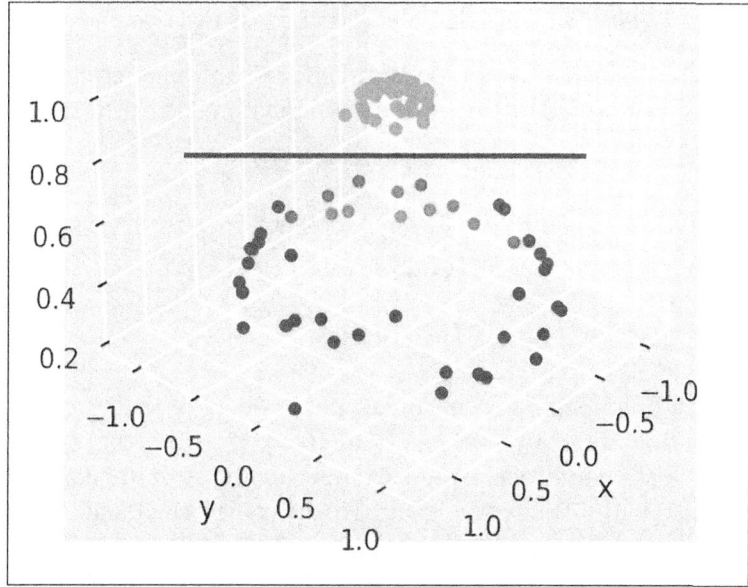

Figure 8.4: *3D Scatter Plot after RBF Transformation*

SVM Hand-Worked Calculation with Contrived Dataset

Consider a contrived dataset with two classes, each with four records, and each record has two features. The points with class label -1 are located away from the origin, forming a square with coordinates [(4,4), (4, −4), (−4, −4), and (−4,4)]. The points with class label 1 are closer to the origin, forming a smaller square with coordinates [(2,2), (2, −2), (−2, −2), and (−2,2)].

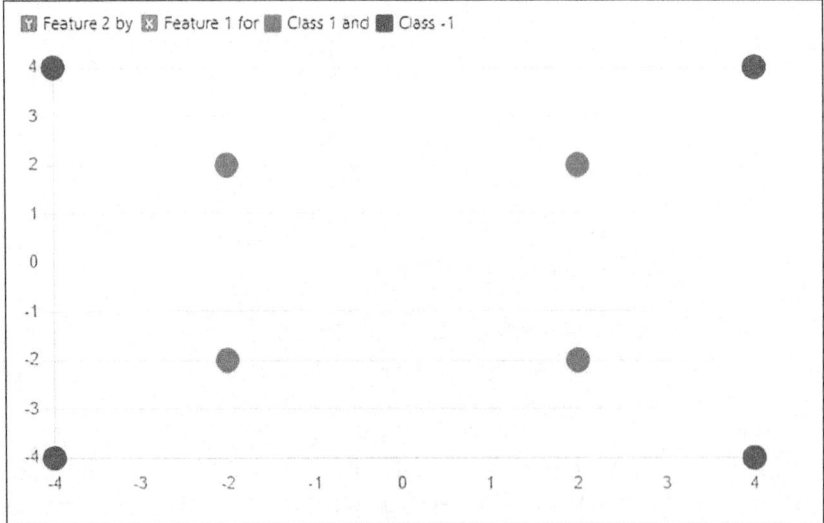

Figure 8.5: *Linearly Non-Separable Contrived Data*

Let us apply polynomial kernel function to the aforementioned contrived data points and visualize the transformed feature space. The polynomial kernel function is defined as follows:

$$\emptyset(x_1, x_2) = \begin{cases} x_1 = 8 - x_2 + |x_1 - x_2|, if \sqrt{x_1^2 + x_2^2} > 4 \\ x_2 = 8 - x_1 + |x_1 - x_2|, \\ \quad otherwise \\ x_1 = x_1 \ and \ x_2 = x_2 \end{cases}$$

After applying the polynomial kernel function, we observe that the red data points remain unchanged at their original positions [(2,2), (2, −2), (−2, −2), and (−2, 2)]. In contrast, the blue data points are mapped to new locations in the feature space [(4,4), (20,12), (12,12), and (12,20)]. The scatter plot of these transformed data points, as shown in *Figure* 8.6, illustrates how the polynomial kernel mapping renders the data points linearly separable in the new feature space, highlighting the effectiveness of this kernel function in solving a linearly non-separable data point.

Support Vector Machines

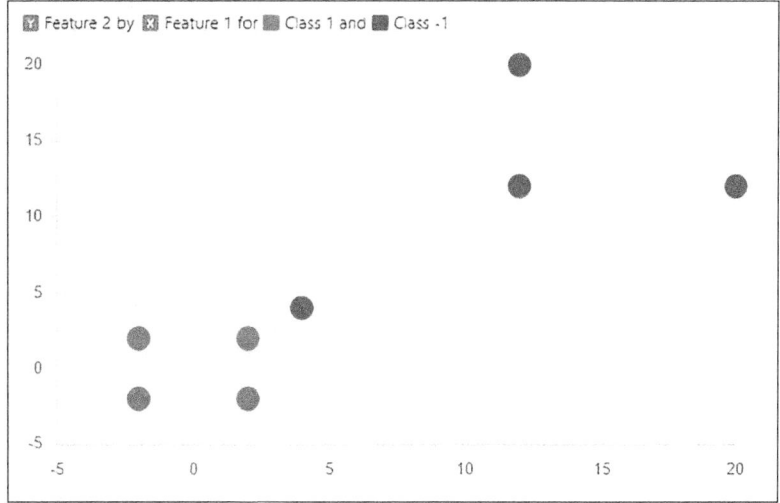

Figure 8.6: *Data Points after Kernel Mapping*

The next step is to calculate the decision boundary with maximum margins between the two classes, we need to identify the support vectors. In this case, the support vectors are [2,2] (red) from class -1 and [4,4] (blue) from class 1.

The support vectors, including the bias term '1,' are represented as follows:

$$\tilde{S_1} = \begin{pmatrix} 2 \\ 2 \\ 1 \end{pmatrix} \text{ belongs to label 1}$$

$$\tilde{S_2} = \begin{pmatrix} 4 \\ 4 \\ 1 \end{pmatrix} \text{ belongs to label -1}$$

Let us define X and Y as the coefficients that, when applied to the support vectors, satisfy the SVM conditions for maximal margin. The values X and Y can be used to construct the optimal hyperplane and determine the decision boundary.

We can frame the equations using $\tilde{S_1}$ and $\tilde{S_2}$ with two unknown variables, X and Y, as follows:

$$\tilde{S_1} \cdot \tilde{S_1} X + \tilde{S_1} \cdot \tilde{S_2} Y = -1$$
$$\tilde{S_2} \cdot \tilde{S_1} X + \tilde{S_2} \cdot \tilde{S_2} Y = 1$$

$$\begin{pmatrix} 2 \\ 2 \\ 1 \end{pmatrix} \cdot \begin{pmatrix} 2 \\ 2 \\ 1 \end{pmatrix} X + \begin{pmatrix} 2 \\ 2 \\ 1 \end{pmatrix} \cdot \begin{pmatrix} 4 \\ 4 \\ 1 \end{pmatrix} Y = 1$$

$$\begin{pmatrix} 4 \\ 4 \\ 1 \end{pmatrix} \cdot \begin{pmatrix} 2 \\ 2 \\ 1 \end{pmatrix} X + \begin{pmatrix} 4 \\ 4 \\ 1 \end{pmatrix} \cdot \begin{pmatrix} 4 \\ 4 \\ 1 \end{pmatrix} Y = -1$$

$$9X + 17Y = 1$$
$$17X + 33Y = -1$$

By solving the preceding equations, we obtained the value of X and Y as follows:

X = 6.25 and Y = -3.25

Substitute these values into the final expression to define the SVM maximum margin decision boundary as $X.\tilde{S_1} + Y.\tilde{S_2}$.

$$6.25\,\tilde{S_1} - 3.25\,\tilde{S_2} = 6.25 \begin{pmatrix} 2 \\ 2 \\ 1 \end{pmatrix} - 3.25 \begin{pmatrix} 4 \\ 4 \\ 1 \end{pmatrix} = \begin{pmatrix} -0.5 \\ -0.5 \\ 3 \end{pmatrix}$$

The final vector represents the model parameters of the SVM with $W_1 = -0.5$, $W_2 = -0.5$ and bias of 3. The decision boundary of SVM in the X_1 and X_2 feature space is given by the equation: $-0.5\,X_1 - 0.5\,X_2 + 3 = 0$. This can be expressed as Y = mX + c form as follows:

$-0.5\,X_2 = 0.5\,X_1 - 3$

$X_2 = -X_1 + 6$

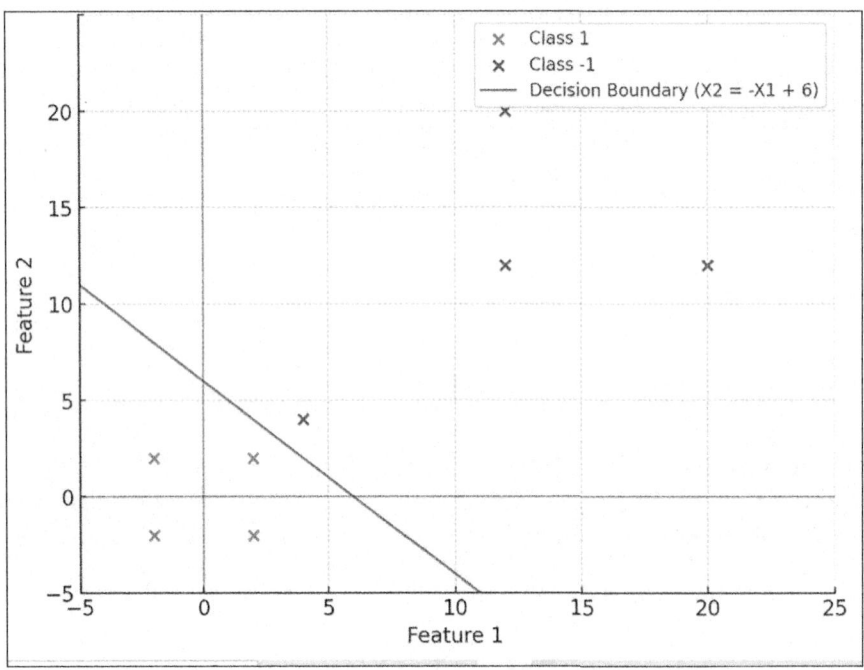

Figure 8.7: *Linear Decision Boundary in Transformed Feature Space*

The final scatter plot shown in Figure 8.7 visually represents how a polynomial kernel can transform data points to aid in classification, with a clear decision boundary separating different classes in the transformed feature space. This hand-worked calculation and visualization provide a concrete example of how kernel functions, such as the polynomial kernel, transform data points into a higher-dimensional feature space where they become linearly separable.

Properties of Kernel Functions

Kernel functions possess several key properties that make them powerful tools for transforming data into higher-dimensional spaces, where it becomes easier to classify using linear boundaries. One fundamental property is **symmetry**. A kernel function K(is symmetric if K(= K(for all vectors . This symmetry ensures that the relationship between any pair of data points is consistent regardless of the order in which they are considered, which is crucial for maintaining the integrity of the distance or similarity measure in the transformed space.

Additionally, kernel functions exhibit the property of **invariance to input transformations**. This means that certain transformations applied to the input data do not affect the kernel function's output. For example, in the case of the Radial Basis Function (RBF) kernel, the output remains invariant to translations and rotations of the input data. This invariance allows the SVM to handle various data transformations without the need for explicit preprocessing steps, making it more robust to changes in the data distribution.

Lastly, **scalability** is a practical property of kernel functions that determines their applicability to large datasets. Efficient computation of the kernel function, particularly in the case of non-linear kernels such as RBF, is crucial for scalability. This includes the ability to compute the kernel function quickly and to handle large kernel matrices in memory. Techniques such as kernel approximation methods (for example, Random Fourier Features) can help scale kernel methods to larger datasets by approximating the kernel function with a lower-dimensional feature map, thereby reducing computational complexity and memory requirements.

These properties collectively enable kernel functions to transform complex, non-linear relationships in the data into a space where linear classification methods can be effectively applied. This makes kernel functions a cornerstone of Support Vector Machines and other kernel-based learning algorithms, enhancing their versatility and performance across various machine learning tasks.

Python Implementation and Use Case with SVM as a Regressor

Let us consider the Boston Housing Dataset, which is widely used in regression analysis and machine learning, as it has non-linear characteristics and is very suitable for demonstrating the SVM Regressor.

This dataset contains information collected by the U.S. Census Service concerning housing in the area of Boston, Massachusetts. It has 506 rows and 14 columns, where each row represents a different town or suburb in Boston, and each column represents a different attribute or feature of the housing market in those areas. The columns in the dataset are as follows:

- **crim**: Per capita crime rate by town.
- **zn**: Proportion of residential land zoned for lots over 25,000 sq. ft.
- **indus**: Proportion of non-retail business acres per town.
- **chas**: Charles River dummy variable (1 if tract bounds river; 0 otherwise).
- **nox**: Nitrogen oxides concentration (parts per 10 million).
- **rm**: Average number of rooms per dwelling.
- **age**: Proportion of owner-occupied units built prior to 1940.
- **dis**: Weighted distances to five Boston employment centers.
- **rad**: Index of accessibility to radial highways.
- **tax**: Full-value property tax rate per $10,000.
- **ptratio**: Pupil-teacher ratio by town.
- **black**: 1000(Bk-0.63)21000(Bk - 0.63)^21000(Bk-0.63)2, where BkBkBk is the proportion of Black residents by town.
- **lstat**: Percentage of lower status of the population.
- **medv**: Median value of owner-occupied homes in $1000s.

Let us load the data, display the head of the data, and understand its shape.

```
import pandas as pd
file_path = 'path_to_your_data/ data1_Ch8_Boston_Housing_Price_dataset.csv'
df = pd.read_csv(file_path)
df.shape
(506, 14)
```

	CRIM	ZN	INDUS	CHAS	NOX	RM	AGE	DIS	RAD	TAX	PTRATIO	BLACK	LSTAT	MEDV
1	0.00632	18.0	2.31	0.0	0.538	6.575	65.2	4.09	1.0	296.0	15.3	396.9	4.98	24.0
2	0.02731	0.0	7.07	0.0	0.469	6.421	78.9	4.9671	2.0	242.0	17.8	396.9	9.14	21.6
3	0.02729	0.0	7.07	0.0	0.469	7.185	61.1	4.9671	2.0	242.0	17.8	392.83	4.03	34.7
4	0.03237	0.0	2.18	0.0	0.458	6.998	45.8	6.0622	3.0	222.0	18.7	394.63	2.94	33.4
5	0.06905	0.0	2.18	0.0	0.458	7.147	54.2	6.0622	3.0	222.0	18.7	396.9	5.33	36.2

Figure 8.8: Boston Housing Price Dataset

Figure 8.8 represents the first five records with 14 columns. The last column (**'medv'**) is the variable we need to predict, which is the price of the property given in U.S dollars (**$1000**).

Support Vector Machines

```
# Define independent variables (X) and dependent variable (Y)
X = df.drop('medv', axis=1)
Y = df['medv']
```

Let us perform hyper parameter tuning using **GridSearchCV** for the SVM Regressor for optimal performance.

```
from sklearn.preprocessing import StandardScaler
# Initialize the StandardScaler
scaler = StandardScaler()
# Scale X and keep it in X_std
X_std = scaler.fit_transform(X)
```

The next step involves fitting the **GridSearchCV** object to the scaled features (**X_std**) and the target variable (**Y**). **GridSearchCV** performs an exhaustive search over the specified parameter grid by training and evaluating the model for each combination of parameters using cross-validation.

```
from sklearn.svm import SVR
from sklearn.model_selection import GridSearchCV, cross_val_score, KFold
# Define the KFold cross-validation strategy
kf = KFold(n_splits=3, shuffle=True, random_state=0)
# Define the SVM Regressor
SVM = SVR()
params={'kernel':['poly','rbf','sigmoid'], 'C':np.arange(1,30,0.1), 'degree':np.arange(2,10)}
```

Here, a parameter grid is defined for the hyperparameter tuning process. The grid includes:

kernel: Specifies the kernel type to be used in the algorithm.

C: Regularization parameter. It controls the trade-off between achieving a low training error and a low testing error (generalization). Higher values of C aim to fit the training data better, potentially at the cost of generalization.

degree: Degree of the Polynomial kernel function (ignored for other kernels)

Now a SVM regressor model is built using the optimal parameters obtained using **GridSearchCV**. The optimal values are found to be the **'rbf'** kernel with C=25.

Let us define a tuned SVM regressor as follows:

```
GS=GridSearchCV(SVM,params,cv=kf,scoring= 'neg_root_mean_squared_error')
GS.fit(X_std,Y)
GS.best_params_
SVM_tuned = SVR (kernel = 'rbf', C=25)
kf=KFold(n_splits=5,shuffle=True,random_state=0)
scores=cross_val_score(SVM_tuned,X_std,Y,cv=kf,scoring='neg_root_mean_squared_error')
```

```
print('Mean RMSE',np.mean(np.abs(scores)))
print('STD RMSE',np.std(np.abs(scores),ddof=1))
[3.432, 0.817]
```

To compare the performance of SVM regressor, we define and fit a Linear Regression model to this dataset and interpret the results

```
from sklearn.linear_model import LinearRegression
LR=LinearRegression()
kf=KFold(n_splits=5,shuffle=True,random_state=0)
scores=cross_val_score(LR,X_std,Y,cv=kf,scoring='neg_root_mean_squared_error')
print('Mean RMSE',np.mean(np.abs(scores)))
print('STD RMSE',np.std(np.abs(scores),ddof=1))
[4.837, 0.729]
```

Inference

The SVM regressor model performs exceptionally well in The Mean RMSE for the SVM regressor is 3432 USD. This means that on average, the predicted house prices differ from the actual prices by 3432 USD. The standard deviation of RMSE for the SVM regressor is ± 817 USD. This indicates that the errors in prediction vary by 817 USD around the mean error.

On the other hand, the Linear Regression model has a higher average prediction error of 4837 USD ± 729 USD, indicating a higher bias in its predictions. Therefore, the SVM regressor is more effective for this dataset in predicting house prices with lower bias and better overall accuracy. Despite the slight overfitting indicated by the increased variance error, the SVM regressor significantly reduces the bias error compared to the Linear Regression model, making it a more accurate predictor overall. However, this increase in variance error can be controlled by performing **bagging** on the SVM model. This would result in a more accurate and stable model for predicting house prices.

Python Implementation and Use Case with SVM as a Classifier

Let us consider the dataset pertains to a study of diabetes in Pima Indian women from UCI machine learning repository. Each row represents an individual's medical record, consisting of various health-related metrics, with the aim of predicting whether the individual has diabetes (class variable: 0 or 1). The dataset includes nine attributes: pregnancy week, plasma glucose concentration measured two hours into an oral glucose tolerance test, diastolic blood pressure, triceps skin fold thickness, 2-hour serum insulin level, body mass index (BMI), diabetes pedigree function (a measure of diabetes likelihood based on family history), age, and a class variable indicating the presence of diabetes.

Support Vector Machines

Let us read the dataset and display the head of the data to understand its structure and shape.

```
import pandas as pd
file_path = 'path_to_your_data/data2_Ch8_Pima-indians-diabetes_dataset.csv'
df = pd.read_csv(file_path)
df.shape
(768, 9)
```

preg	plas	pres	skin	test	mass	pedi	age	class
6	148	72	35	0	33.6	0.627	50	1
1	85	66	29	0	26.6	0.351	31	0
8	183	64	0	0	23.3	0.672	32	1
1	89	66	23	94	28.1	0.167	21	0
0	137	40	35	168	43.1	2.288	33	1

Figure 8.9: *Head of the Diabetes Dataset*

The first five records are shown in *Figure* 8.9, indicates the instances of '0' entries in several columns of our dataset, which indicate the non-availability of data rather than actual zero values. To address this issue and ensure the integrity of our analysis, we are going to perform imputation by replacing these '0' entries with the median of the non-zero entries in the respective columns. This approach helps in maintaining the dataset's consistency and provides more accurate insights by using a central tendency measure for imputation.

```
# Calculate the median of non-zero entries in the 'preg' pregnancy week column
median_non_zero_preg = df[df['preg'] != 0]['preg'].median()
# Replace '0' entries with the median
df['preg'] = df['preg'].replace(0, median_non_zero_preg)
# Calculate the median of non-zero entries in the 'plas' glucose concentration column
median_non_zero_plas = df[df['plas'] != 0]['plas'].median()
# Replace '0' entries with the median
df['plas'] = df['plas'].replace(0, median_non_zero_plas)
# Calculate the median of non-zero entries in the 'pres' blood pressure column
median_non_zero_pres = df[df['pres'] != 0]['pres'].median()
# Replace '0' entries with the median
```

```
df['pres'] = df['pres'].replace(0, median_non_zero_pres)
# Calculate the median of non-zero entries in the 'skin' skin fold 
thickness column
median_non_zero_skin = df[df['skin'] != 0]['skin'].median()
# Replace '0' entries with the median
df['skin'] = df['skin'].replace(0, median_non_zero_skin)
# Calculate the median of non-zero entries in the 'test' serum insulin 
column
median_non_zero_test = df[df['test'] != 0]['test'].median()
# Replace '0' entries with the median
df['test'] = df['test'].replace(0, median_non_zero_test)
 # Calculate the median of non-zero entries in the 'mass' body mass 
index column
median_non_zero_mass = df[df['mass'] != 0]['mass'].median()
# Replace '0' entries with the median
df['mass'] = df['mass'].replace(0, median_non_zero_mass)
# Calculate the median of non-zero entries in the 'pedi' pedigree 
function column
median_non_zero_pedi = df[df['pedi'] != 0]['pedi'].median()
# Replace '0' entries with the median
df['pedi'] = df['pedi'].replace(0, median_non_zero_pedi)
# Calculate the median of non-zero entries in the 'age' column
median_non_zero_age = df[df['age'] != 0]['age'].median()
# Replace '0' entries with the median
df['age'] = df['age'].replace(0, median_non_zero_age)
```

	preg	plas	pres	skin	test	mass	pedi	age
count	768.0	768.0	768.0	768.0	768.0	768.0	768.0	768.0
mean	4.42	121.66	72.39	29.11	140.67	32.46	0.47	33.24
std	2.98	30.44	12.1	8.79	86.38	6.88	0.33	11.76
min	1.0	44.0	24.0	7.0	14.0	18.2	0.08	21.0
25%	2.0	99.75	64.0	25.0	121.5	27.5	0.24	24.0
50%	4.0	117.0	72.0	29.0	125.0	32.3	0.37	29.0
75%	6.0	140.25	80.0	32.0	127.25	36.6	0.63	41.0
max	17.0	199.0	122.0	99.0	846.0	67.1	2.42	81.0

***Figure 8.10**: Summary Statistics of Imputed Data*

We have successfully imputed the '0' entries in all independent variable columns with the median of the non-zero entries. The summary statistics of the dataset, after performing the imputation, are shown in *Figure* 8.10. These statistics provide an

Support Vector Machines

overview of the central tendency, dispersion, and range of the dataset, ensuring the integrity and consistency of the data for further analysis.

```
# Define independent variables (X) and dependent variable (Y)
X = df.drop('class', axis=1)
Y = df['class']
```

Let us perform hyperparameter tuning using **GridSearchCV** for the SVM classifier for optimal performance.

```
from sklearn.preprocessing import StandardScaler
# Initialize the StandardScaler
scaler = StandardScaler()
# Scale X and keep it in X_std
X_std = scaler.fit_transform(X)
```

The next step involves fitting the **GridSearchCV** object to the scaled features (**X_std**) and the target variable (**Y**). **GridSearchCV** performs an exhaustive search over the specified parameter grid by training and evaluating the model for each combination of parameters using cross-validation.

```
from sklearn.svm import SVC
from sklearn.model_selection import GridSearchCV, cross_val_score, KFold
# Define the KFold cross-validation strategy
kf = KFold(n_splits=3, shuffle=True, random_state=0)
# Define the SVM Classifier
SVM = SVC()
params={'kernel':['poly','rbf','sigmoid'], 'C':np.arange(1,30,0.1), 'degree':np.arange(2,10)}
GS=GridSearchCV(SVM,params,cv=kf,scoring= 'roc_auc')
GS.fit(X_std,Y)
GS.best_params_
```

Now, a SVM classifier model is built using the optimal parameters obtained using **GridSearchCV**. The optimal values are found to be the **'rbf'** kernel with C=0.5.

Let us define a tuned SVM classifier as follows:

```
SVM_tuned = SVR (kernel = 'rbf', C=0.5)

from sklearn.model_selection import cross_val_score
    scores=cross_val_score(SVM_tuned,X_std,Y,cv=3,scoring='roc_auc')
print(scores)
[0.822,0.801,0.879]
print('Mean', np.mean(scores))
Mean [0.834]
print('STD', np.std(scores,ddof=1))
STD [0.04]
```

Inference

The implementation of the SVM classifier on the Pima Indians dataset has yielded promising results, as indicated by the cross-validation scores, with a Receiver Operating Characteristic - Area Under Curve (ROC-AUC) of [0.822, 0.801, 0.879]. The mean ROC-AUC score of 0.834 suggests that the SVM model has a good ability to distinguish between the positive and negative classes, which is a strong indicator of its classification performance. The standard deviation of 0.04 indicates that the model's performance is relatively stable across different folds of the dataset. These results reflect that the SVM classifier is a reliable and robust model for predicting outcomes on this particular dataset, showing consistent performance with a reasonable margin of variability.

Pros and Cons of Support Vector Machines

SVMs are highly regarded in the realm of machine learning for their robust performance and versatility. They excel in high-dimensional spaces, providing effective classification and regression solutions even when the number of features is large. SVMs are particularly known for their ability to minimize overfitting through margin maximization and their adaptability via the kernel trick, which allows them to handle both linear and non-linear data efficiently. These strengths make SVMs a powerful tool for a variety of applications, from text classification to bioinformatics. A few of the pros of SVMs are listed as follows:

Effective in High-Dimensional Spaces: One of the key strengths of SVMs is their effectiveness in high-dimensional spaces. SVMs perform well when the number of dimensions (features) exceeds the number of samples, making them suitable for text classification problems where the feature space is often very large. This capability is due to the fact that SVMs rely on support vectors, which are the data points that lie closest to the decision boundary, thereby defining the optimal hyperplane irrespective of the dimensionality.

Robust to Overfitting: SVMs are designed to find the hyperplane that maximizes the margin between classes, which inherently reduces the risk of overfitting. This robustness is particularly evident in high-dimensional spaces, where the risk of overfitting is higher. By focusing on the support vectors and maximizing the margin, SVMs often generalize well to unseen data, especially in cases where the dataset has a clear margin of separation.

Versatile Kernel Trick: The flexibility of SVMs is significantly enhanced by the use of the kernel trick, which allows the algorithm to fit the maximum-margin hyperplane in a transformed feature space. This transformation can handle non-linear relationships between features, making SVMs highly versatile. Common kernels such as polynomial, radial basis function (RBF), and sigmoid can be applied to transform the input space, enabling SVMs to solve complex classification and regression problems that are not linearly separable.

Effective for Various Data Types: SVMs can handle both continuous and categorical data efficiently. They are also well-suited for problems where the data points are not linearly separable. With the appropriate kernel function, SVMs can classify data points that lie in non-linear decision boundaries, providing a robust solution for a wide range of classification problems, including image recognition, bioinformatics, and text categorization.

While SVMs offer powerful and versatile solutions for many classification and regression tasks, they come with certain limitations. SVMs can be computationally intensive, especially with large datasets, and are sensitive to the choice of kernel and hyperparameters, which can complicate their implementation. Additionally, they may struggle with noisy data and overlapping classes. They lack straightforward probabilistic interpretation, making them less ideal for some applications where these factors are critical. A few of the cons of SVMs are listed as follows:

Computationally Intensive: One of the significant drawbacks of SVMs is their computational complexity, particularly in training. The quadratic programming problem that SVMs need to solve can be computationally expensive, especially for large datasets. The time complexity grows quadratically with the number of samples, making it less practical for very large datasets. This can result in long training times and high memory usage, which might be prohibitive for certain applications.

Sensitive to Kernel Parameters: The performance of SVMs is highly dependent on the choice of kernel and the parameters associated with it. Selecting the right kernel and tuning hyperparameters (such as the regularization parameter (C) and the kernel parameters) can be challenging and often require extensive experimentation and cross-validation. Poor parameter tuning can lead to suboptimal performance, making SVMs less straightforward to implement compared to other machine learning algorithms that might be more forgiving in this aspect.

Less Effective on Noisy Data: SVMs can be sensitive to noisy data and overlapping classes. In cases where the data is not clearly separable or contains a significant amount of noise, SVMs might struggle to find a suitable hyperplane, resulting in lower classification accuracy. The presence of outliers can also skew the decision boundary, as SVMs attempt to maximize the margin, potentially leading to poor generalization on new data.

Limited Probabilistic Interpretation: Unlike some other classification algorithms, SVMs do not provide direct probabilistic interpretations of the classification outcomes. While methods such as Platt scaling can be used to convert SVM outputs into probabilities, these approaches are approximate and add another layer of complexity to the model. This limitation can be a disadvantage in applications where understanding the probability of predictions is crucial for decision-making.

Difficulty in Choosing the Right Kernel: Choosing the appropriate kernel for a specific problem can be a non-trivial task. The selection depends on the underlying data distribution and the specific problem at hand. There is no one-size-fits-all kernel, and the trial-and-error process of kernel selection can be time-consuming. Additionally, some kernels may lead to overfitting if not chosen carefully, adding to the complexity of using SVMs effectively.

While SVMs present some challenges, such as computational demands and sensitivity to parameter selection, their strengths in handling high-dimensional data, reducing overfitting, and adapting to various types of data with kernel functions make them a valuable tool in the machine learning toolkit. With careful application and tuning, SVMs can deliver robust and reliable performance across a wide array of tasks, demonstrating their enduring relevance and utility in the ever-evolving field of data science and AI.

Conclusion

In this chapter, we learned the multifaceted nature of SVM, a cornerstone technique in the machine learning domain. We began with a thorough understanding of the principles of SVMs, exploring how they function as powerful classifiers and regressors by identifying the optimal hyperplane that separates different classes with the maximum margin.

We then ventured into the mathematical foundation of kernel functions, which play a crucial role in extending the capabilities of SVMs to handle non-linear data. Understanding these mathematical underpinnings is essential for leveraging SVMs effectively, especially when dealing with complex datasets. The chapter also included practical aspects with Python implementations of SVMs. These sections not only demonstrated the practical utility of SVMs in real-world scenarios but also equipped readers with the necessary skills to implement SVMs using Python, fostering a hands-on learning experience. Finally, we analyzed the pros and cons of SVM, providing a balanced view of their strengths and limitations.

In the next chapter, we will embark on a journey into the world of Artificial Neural Networks (ANNs), exploring their foundational concepts and structures. This chapter will provide an introduction to how ANNs mimic the human brain to perform complex tasks, setting the stage for understanding deep learning models.

Practice Exercises

1. Given the data points shown in *Figure 8.11* with the following points and their respective classes, use the SVM algorithm to find the optimal hyperplane that separates the classes. Assume a linear kernel. Find the equation of the separating hyperplane.

Support Vector Machines

Point	Feature 1	Feature 2	Class
A	1	2	+1
B	2	3	+1
C	3	3	-1
D	4	4	-1

Figure 8.11: *Contrived Dataset*

2. Calculate the value of the polynomial kernel function K(x,y)=(x.y+1)^2 for the vectors x=[1,2] and y=[3,4].

3. Given the RBF (Gaussian) kernel function $K(x, y) = \exp(-\gamma\|x - y\|^2)$ with γ = 0.5, calculate the kernel value for the vector x=[1,2] and y=[2,3].

4. Explain the role of the kernel trick in Support Vector Machines (SVM). Why is it particularly useful for non-linear data? Provide an example to illustrate your explanation.

5. Discuss the trade-offs between using a linear SVM and a non-linear SVM with an RBF kernel. Under what circumstances might you prefer one over the other?

6. You have trained an SVM classifier on a binary classification problem. The confusion matrix shown in *Figure 8.12* summarizes the results of the classifier on the test dataset.

	Predicted Positive	Predicted Negative
Actual Positive	40	10
Actual Negative	5	45

Figure 8.12: *Confusion Matrix*

Using this confusion matrix, calculate the following performance metrics for the SVM classifier:

a. Accuracy

b. Precision

c. Recall (Sensitivity)

d. F1-Score

Answers

1. Let us assume w1=1w_1 = 1w1=1 and w2=−1w_2 = -1w2=−1. The support vectors are typically the closest points to the hyperplane:

   For point A: 1·1+(−1)·2+b=1

   For point D: 1·4+(−1)·4+b=−1

   Solving these equations:

   1−2+b=1⇒b=2

   4−4+b=−1⇒b=−1

   The separating hyperplane is x1−x2+b=0 with b=1.5. Therefore, the equation is x1−x2+1.5=0.

2. x.y=1.3+2.4=3+8=11

   $K(x,y)=(11+1)^2 = 144$

3. $\|x - y\|^2 (1-2)^2 + (2-3)^2 = 2; \exp(-0.5 \cdot 2) = \exp(-1) = 0.3679$

4. The kernel trick in Support Vector Machines (SVMs) allows the algorithm to operate in a high-dimensional, implicit feature space without ever computing the coordinates of the data in that space. Instead, it computes the inner products between the images of all pairs of data in the feature space. This is particularly useful for non-linear data because it enables SVM to find a linear separating hyperplane in a higher-dimensional space, where the data becomes linearly separable.

5. When deciding between using a linear SVM and a non-linear SVM with an RBF kernel, several trade-offs need to be considered, including model complexity, computational efficiency, and the nature of the data.

6. Accuracy: 85/100 = 0.85; Precision: 40/45 = 0.8889 or 88.89% ; Recall (Sensitivity): 40/50 = 0.80 or 80%; F1-Score = 0.8413 = 84.13%

Multiple Choice Questions

1. What is the primary goal of a Support Vector Machine (SVM)?
   a. Minimizing error rate
   b. Finding the optimal hyperplane
   c. Reducing dimensionality
   d. Increasing computational speed

2. What does the kernel trick in SVM enable?
   a. Simplification of linear data
   b. Reduction of data size
   c. Transformation of input features into higher-dimensional spaces
   d. Acceleration of the training process
3. Which function is crucial for SVM to handle non-linear data?
   a. Activation function
   b. Kernel function
   c. Loss function
   d. Regularization function
4. In the context of SVM, what does the hyperplane do?
   a. Reduces error rate
   b. Increases computational efficiency
   c. Separates different classes with maximum margin
   d. Maps data to lower dimensions
5. Which of the following is a strength of SVMs?
   a. Fast training on large datasets
   b. Robust performance in high-dimensional spaces
   c. Easy parameter tuning
   d. Low sensitivity to noise
6. What is one of the challenges associated with using SVMs?
   a. Poor performance in high-dimensional spaces
   b. Computational intensity
   c. Lack of flexibility with non-linear data
   d. Insufficient support for classification tasks
7. In Python implementations of SVMs, which library is commonly used?
   a. TensorFlow
   b. Keras

c. Scikit-learn

  d. PyTorch

8. Which aspect of SVM helps in deciding the margin between classes?

   a. Loss function

   b. Support vectors

   c. Activation function

   d. Bias term

9. What kind of data transformation does the kernel trick apply in SVM?

   a. Linear to non-linear

   b. Non-linear to linear

   c. Two-dimensional to three-dimensional

   d. Sparse to dense

10. When applying SVM, what is an important consideration for achieving good performance?

    a. Increasing the number of features

    b. Parameter tuning

    c. Reducing the number of data points

    d. Using a simple linear kernel

Answers

1. b
2. c
3. b
4. c
5. b
6. b
7. c
8. b

9. b

10. b

Keywords

- Support Vector Machines (SVM)
- Hyperplane
- Maximum Margin
- Kernel Functions
- Kernel Trick
- Non-linear Data
- Higher-Dimensional Spaces
- Computational Intensity
- Parameter Tuning
- Kernel Mapping
- Radial Basis Function (RBF)
- Polynomial Kernel
- Sigmoid Kernel
- Linear Kernel
- SVM Regressor
- SVM Classifier

References

1. https://www.kaggle.com/datasets/uciml/pima-indians-diabetes-database
2. https://www.kaggle.com/datasets/schirmerchad/bostonhoustingmlnd

CHAPTER 9
Introduction to Artificial Neural Networks

Introduction

In this chapter, we are going to learn about the fascinating world of Artificial Neural Networks (ANNs), which form the backbone of many modern machine learning and deep learning applications. ANNs are inspired by the structure and functioning of the human brain, aiming to replicate its ability to learn from data and make intelligent decisions. This chapter will provide a comprehensive introduction to the fundamental concepts and principles that underpin neural networks, setting a solid foundation for more advanced topics in subsequent chapters.

We will start with the fundamentals of artificial neural networks, exploring how these models are designed to process complex patterns and relationships within data. By understanding the basic building blocks of ANNs, including neurons and connections, we will gain insight into how these models are capable of performing tasks such as classification, regression, and even more intricate operations like image and speech recognition.

Moreover, we will explore the significance of activation functions, which are crucial components that enable neural networks to capture non-linear patterns in the data. Finally, we will break down the layers in neural networks, examining the roles of input, hidden, and output layers, and how they work together to transform inputs into meaningful outputs. This holistic overview will equip you with the knowledge and skills to start building and experimenting with your own neural network models.

Structure

In this chapter, we are going to cover the following main topics:

- Fundamentals of Artificial Neural Networks
- Structure and Architecture of Artificial Neural Networks
- Activation Functions and their Significance
- Layers in Neural Networks: Input, Hidden, and Output layers

Fundamentals of Artificial Neural Networks

ANNs are inspired by the remarkable capabilities of the human brain, particularly how biological neurons process and transmit information. In the human brain, billions of neurons communicate with each other through complex networks. The structure of a biological neuron is shown in *Figure 9.1*, which depicts that each neuron receives signals through its dendrites, processes these signals in the cell body or soma, and transmits the output through its axon to other neurons. This process of signal transmission and processing forms the basis of learning and decision-making in biological systems.

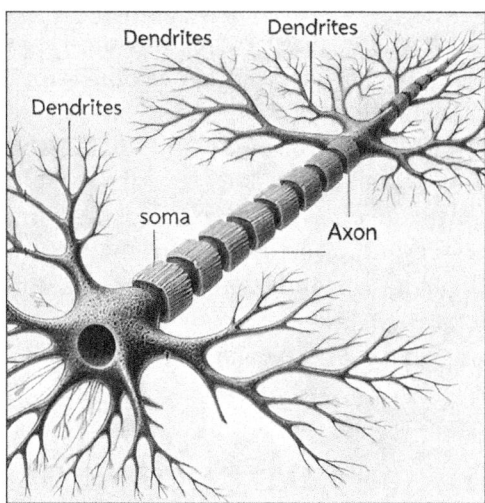

Figure 9.1: Biological Neuron

The concept of ANNs mimics this biological process. In an ANN, the fundamental unit is an artificial neuron, which is designed to simulate the behavior of a biological neuron. Just as a biological neuron receives input signals, an artificial neuron receives input data. These inputs are then weighted and summed, and the result is passed through an activation function to produce an output. This output can be transmitted to other artificial neurons, forming a network that can learn from data and make predictions.

The idea of using artificial neurons to replicate brain function was first proposed by Warren McCulloch and Walter Pitts in 1943. They created a mathematical model of a neuron that could perform simple logical functions, laying the groundwork for neural networks. This model, known as the McCulloch-Pitts neuron, was a significant step toward developing more complex neural networks. Their pioneering work demonstrated that networks of artificial neurons could, in theory, perform any computation that a digital computer could.

Frank Rosenblatt further advanced the field in 1958 with the development of the perceptron, an early type of neural network capable of learning from data. Rosenblatt's perceptron could classify input data into two categories by adjusting the weights of the inputs based on the errors it made during training. This learning process, known as supervised learning, was a critical advancement that allowed neural networks to improve their performance over time through exposure to data.

The analogy between biological neurons and artificial neurons is more than just a superficial comparison. Just as the brain learns and adapts through experience, ANNs learn from data by adjusting the weights of their connections. This learning process is driven by algorithms that optimize these weights to minimize errors, much like how the brain strengthens or weakens synapses based on the frequency and intensity of signals.

One of the most influential figures in the development of ANNs is Geoffrey Hinton, often referred to as the "godfather of deep learning." Hinton's work on backpropagation, a method for training neural networks, has been pivotal in making ANNs practical and efficient. Backpropagation involves computing the gradient of the loss function with respect to each weight by the chain rule, allowing the network to adjust the weights in a way that reduces the overall error. This technique has enabled the training of deep neural networks, which consist of many layers of interconnected neurons. This fundamental understanding of artificial neurons and their learning processes is essential for anyone looking to explore the capabilities and applications of neural networks. As we move forward in this chapter, we will delve deeper into the structure and architecture of these networks, exploring how they can be configured to tackle a wide range of problems.

Structure and Architecture of Artificial Neural Networks

The journey into the structure and architecture of Artificial Neural Networks (ANNs) begins with the seminal work of Warren McCulloch and Walter Pitts in the 1940s. They introduced the McCulloch-Pitts model, as shown in *Figure* 9.2, a mathematical model of a neuron that laid the groundwork for modern neural networks. This model treated the neuron as a binary threshold unit, where inputs are either excitatory or inhibitory.

When the weighted sum of the inputs exceeded a certain threshold, the neuron would "fire," producing an output of 1; otherwise, the output would be 0. This simplistic model demonstrated that networks of such neurons could perform logical operations and provided a theoretical foundation for more complex neural architectures.

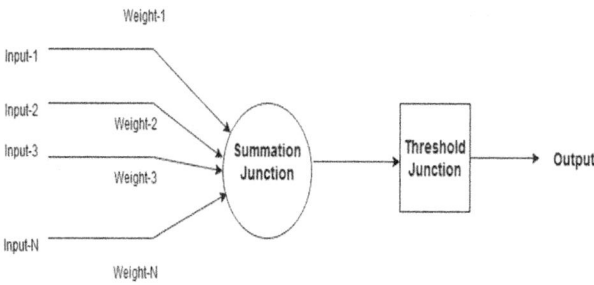

Figure 9.2: McCulloch-Pitts Model

Building on the McCulloch-Pitts model, Frank Rosenblatt developed the perceptron in 1958. The perceptron is a single-layer neural network consisting of input nodes, weights, a bias, and an output node. Each input node receives a signal, which is multiplied by a corresponding weight. These weighted inputs are then summed, and a bias term is added to the sum. This value is passed through an activation function (often a step function in the case of the basic perceptron) to produce the output. If the result is above a certain threshold, the perceptron outputs one class; otherwise, it outputs another. The perceptron was one of the first algorithms capable of learning weights from data, using a simple learning rule to minimize classification errors.

Despite its simplicity, the single-layer perceptron has limitations. It can only solve linearly separable problems, where a single straight line (or hyperplane in higher dimensions) can separate the data into different classes. This limitation was highlighted by Marvin Minsky and Seymour Papert in their 1969 book "Perceptrons," which showed that the perceptron could not solve the XOR problem, a simple problem where the classes are not linearly separable. This revelation led to a temporary decline in interest in neural networks, but it also paved the way for the development of more advanced models.

To overcome the limitations of the single-layer perceptron, researchers introduced the concept of Multi-Layer Perceptrons (MLPs). An MLP consists of an input layer, one or more hidden layers, and an output layer. Each layer is composed of multiple neurons, with each neuron in one layer connected to every neuron in the subsequent layer, as shown in *Figure 9.3*. This fully connected structure allows MLPs to learn complex, non-linear relationships between inputs and outputs. The key innovation in MLPs is the addition of hidden layers, which enable the network to capture intricate patterns and dependencies in the data that single-layer perceptrons cannot.

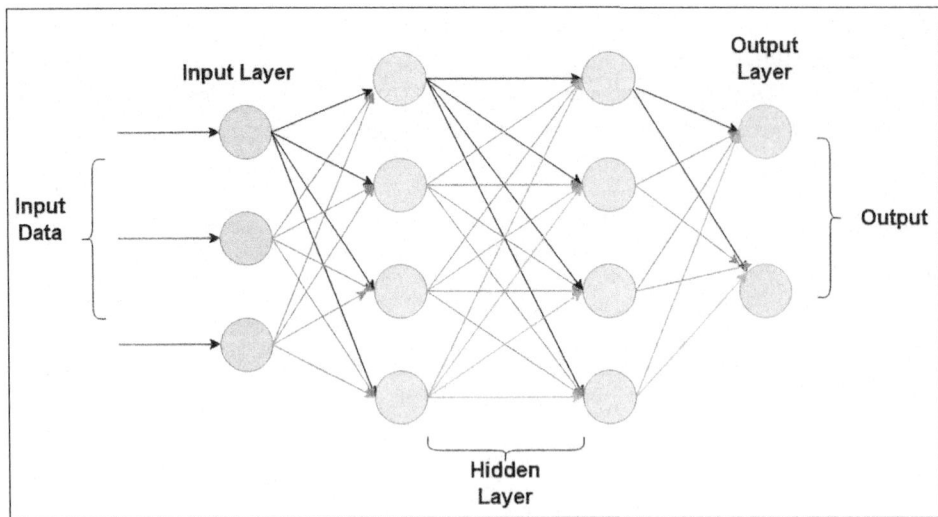

Figure 9.3: *Multi-Layer Perceptron Architecture*

Training an MLP involves adjusting the weights of the connections to minimize the error between the predicted and actual outputs. This is achieved through a process called *backpropagation*, introduced by Geoffrey Hinton and others in the 1980s. Backpropagation works by computing the gradient of the loss function (which measures the difference between predicted and actual outputs) with respect to each weight by the chain rule. These gradients are then used to update the weights, iteratively reducing the error. We will delve into these techniques in detail in the next chapter, where we explore the mathematical foundations and practical implementations of backpropagation and gradient descent.

The architecture of an MLP can be varied by changing the number of layers and the number of neurons in each layer. Deeper networks with more hidden layers can model more complex functions, but they also require more data and computational power to train effectively. The choice of architecture depends on the specific problem at hand and the characteristics of the data. Despite the increased complexity, MLPs have proven to be powerful tools in a wide range of applications, from image recognition to natural language processing.

In summary, the evolution from the McCulloch-Pitts model to multi-layer perceptrons represents a significant advancement in the field of neural networks. While the single-layer perceptron introduced the basic concepts of weighted inputs and activation functions, it was the development of multi-layer architectures and the backpropagation algorithm that truly unlocked the potential of neural networks to solve complex, real-world problems. As we continue to explore ANNs, understanding these foundational structures and architectures will be crucial for leveraging their full capabilities.

Activation Functions and Their Significance

Activation functions play a crucial role in ANNs, determining the output of each neuron in the network. They introduce non-linearity into the model, enabling it to learn and represent complex patterns in the data. Without activation functions, neural networks would be limited to linear mappings, severely restricting their ability to solve complex tasks. In this section, we will explore the most commonly used activation functions, their mathematical formulations, and their significance in the context of neural networks.

- **Sigmoid Function:** The sigmoid function is one of the earliest activation functions used in neural networks, as shown in *Figure* 9.4, which typically looks like an "S" shape, asymptotically approaching 0 for large negative inputs and 1 for large positive inputs.

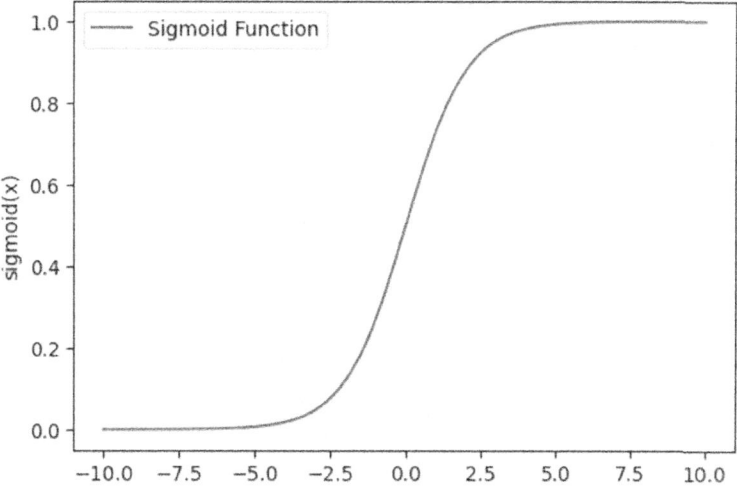

Figure **9.4**: *Sigmoid Activation Function*

It maps input values to a range between 0 and 1, making it useful for binary classification tasks. The sigmoid function is defined as:

$$\sigma(x) = \frac{1}{1 + e^{-x}}$$

The sigmoid function squashes large positive values to near 1 and large negative values to near 0, providing a smooth gradient. However, one of the main drawbacks of the sigmoid function is the vanishing gradient problem, where gradients become very small for large positive or negative inputs, making it difficult for the network to learn effectively during backpropagation.

○ **Hyperbolic Tangent (tanh) Function:** The hyperbolic tangent (tanh) function is similar to the sigmoid function but maps input values to a range between -1 and 1, as shown in *Figure 9.5*. This allows the outputs to be zero-centered, which can help with the convergence of the training process.

The tanh function is defined as:

$$tanh(x) = \frac{e^x - e^{-x}}{e^x + e^{-x}}$$

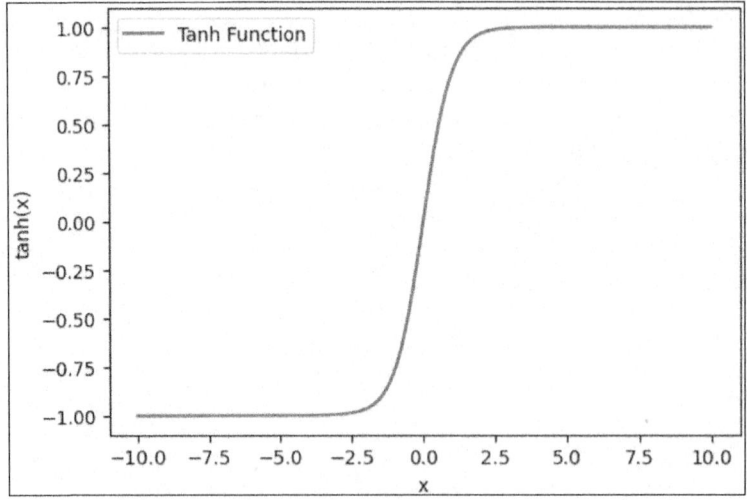

Figure 9.5: *Hyperbolic Tangent Activation Function*

Like the sigmoid function, tanh also suffers from the vanishing gradient problem, but it generally performs better in practice because its outputs are centered around zero, making it easier for the optimization algorithm to adjust weights.

- **Softmax Activation Function**

    The softmax activation function is primarily used in the output layer of neural networks for multi-class classification problems. It converts the raw output scores (logits) from the network into probabilities, which are easier to interpret and compare. Each probability represents the likelihood of the input belonging to a particular class.

Given an input vector $z=[z_1, z_2,.....z_k]$, where 'k' is the number of classes, the softmax function is:

$$\sigma(z_i) = \frac{e^{z_i}}{\sum_{j=1}^{k} e^{z_i}}, \text{ for i = 1, 2, 3, k}$$

The outputs of the softmax function form a probability distribution over the classes. Each output value can be interpreted as the probability of the input belonging to the corresponding class. The softmax function is differentiable, which makes it suitable for use in neural networks. The exponential function magnifies the differences between input scores, which can help in distinguishing between classes with varying levels of confidence.

- **Rectified Linear Unit (ReLU) Function**

    The Rectified Linear Unit (ReLU) function has become one of the most popular activation functions in deep learning due to its simplicity and effectiveness. It addresses the vanishing gradient problem by allowing gradients to flow more freely. The ReLU function is defined as:

    ReLU(x)=max(0,x)

ReLU outputs the input directly if it is positive; otherwise, it outputs zero, as shown in *Figure 9.6*.

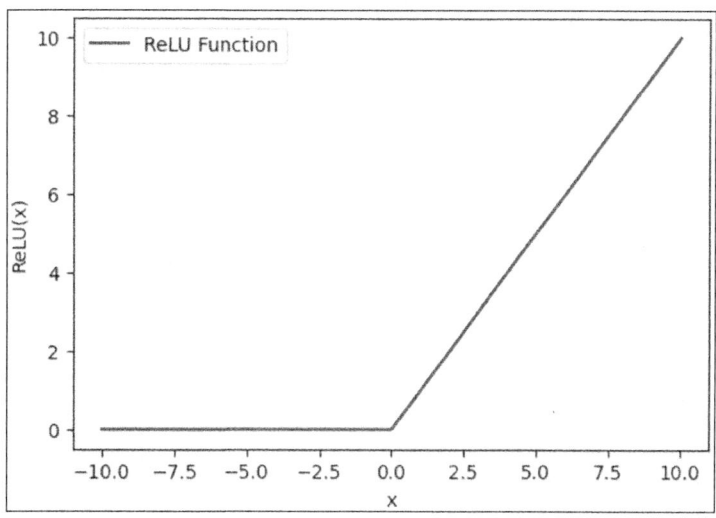

Figure 9.6: *ReLU Activation Function*

This non-linear activation function is computationally efficient and helps networks converge faster. However, ReLU can suffer from the *"dying ReLU"* problem, where neurons can become inactive and only output zero, which can be mitigated by variants such as Leaky ReLU.

- **Leaky ReLU Function:**

    The Leaky Rectified Linear Unit (Leaky ReLU) activation function is a variant of the ReLU activation function commonly used in neural networks. While the ReLU function outputs zero for all negative input values, the Leaky ReLU introduces a small slope to allow a small, non-zero gradient when the unit is not active. This helps to address the problem of "dying ReLUs," where neurons can become inactive and only output zero for any input, effectively ceasing to learn. By allowing a small gradient when the input is negative, Leaky ReLU ensures that neurons do not become inactive during training. The small slope for negative values helps maintain a gradient flow through the network, which can lead to better convergence during training.

Leaky ReLU(x)=max(σx,x)

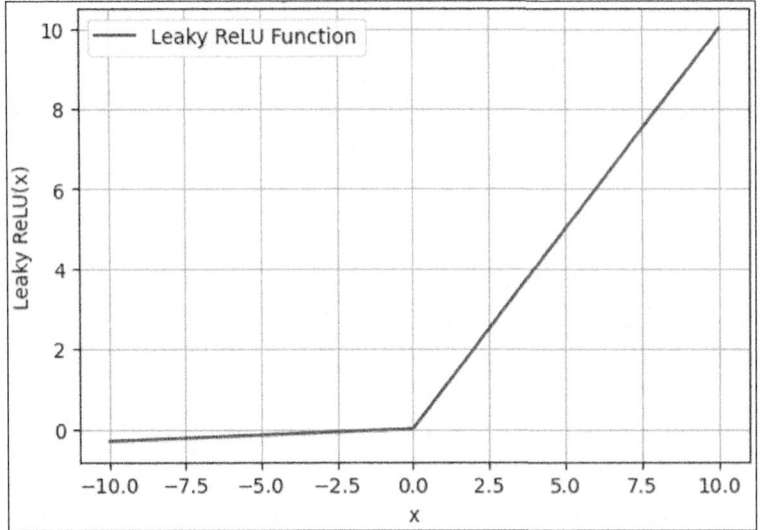

Figure 9.7: *Leaky ReLU Activation Function*

In the *Figure* 9.7, the Leaky ReLU function outputs the input directly if it is positive, and for negative inputs, it outputs a small, non-zero value determined by the slope α, which is typically set to a small constant such as 0.03.

Layers in Neural Networks

Neural networks are structured in layers, each serving a distinct purpose in the process of learning and making predictions. Understanding the roles and functionalities of the different layers—input, hidden, and output—is essential for designing and working with neural networks effectively.

Input Layer

The input layer is the first layer in a neural network. It serves as the gateway for the data to enter the network. Each neuron in this layer represents a feature or attribute of the input data. For instance, in an image recognition task, the input layer's neurons might correspond to pixel values. The number of neurons in the input layer equals the number of features in a tabular dataset. The primary role of the input layer is to accept the input data and pass it to the subsequent layers for further processing. The input layer does not perform any computations or transformations. It simply feeds the input values into the network. Each neuron in the input layer receives a single value from the input data. This value is typically pre-processed and normalized to ensure that all input values are within a similar range, which helps in the efficient training of the network. These input values are then passed on to the neurons in the next layer, known as the hidden layer.

Pre-Processing and Normalization

Data pre-processing is an essential step before feeding the input layer. This includes various techniques, such as:

- **Normalization**: Scaling the input data to a standard range, typically between 0 and 1 or -1 and 1. This helps in accelerating the convergence during training and improves the numerical stability of the model.
- **Standardization**: Transforming the input data to have a mean of 0 and a standard deviation of 1. This is particularly useful when the input features have different units or scales.
- **Encoding**: Converting categorical data into numerical format using techniques such as one-hot encoding or label encoding. This ensures that the network can process non-numeric data.
- **Dimensionality Reduction**: Techniques such as Principal Component Analysis (PCA) can be used to reduce the number of input features, thereby simplifying the model and reducing computational load.

Importance of the Input Layer

The design and configuration of the input layer are critical for the following reasons:

- **Representation of Data**: The input layer must accurately represent the input data to ensure that the subsequent layers receive meaningful information for processing. Any loss or distortion of information at this stage can negatively impact the network's performance.
- **Influence on Network Architecture**: The number of neurons in the input layer determines the initial shape and complexity of the network. An incorrect number of neurons can lead to underfitting (too few neurons) or overfitting (too many neurons).
- **Compatibility with Data**: The input layer must be designed to handle the specific type of input data, whether it is images, text, or numerical data. This ensures that the network can effectively learn and generalize from the input data.

Hidden Layers

Hidden layers are the intermediate layers between the input and output layers. They are where the actual learning and processing take place. Each hidden layer consists of neurons that apply activation functions to their inputs, enabling the network to learn complex patterns and representations. Unlike the input and output layers, hidden layers do not directly interact with the external environment but play a pivotal role in transforming input data into a form that the network can use to make accurate predictions.

Hidden layers perform a series of transformations on the input data, extracting features and learning representations that are necessary for making accurate predictions. The depth (number of hidden layers) and width (number of neurons per hidden layer) of the network influence its capacity to learn and generalize. Neurons in hidden layers typically use non-linear activation functions, as discussed in the preceding section. These functions introduce non-linearity into the network, allowing it to model complex relationships in the data. As data passes through each hidden layer, the network captures higher-level features. In a deep network for an image dataset, early layers might learn coarse features such as shape and structure, while deeper layers learn finer features such as edges.

Number of Hidden Layers and Neurons

The architecture of an ANN, including the number of hidden layers and the number of neurons in each layer, is a critical factor in its performance. This is often determined through experimentation and validation, as there are no definitive rules.

- **Shallow Networks**: Networks with one or two hidden layers are known as shallow networks. They are suitable for simpler problems where the relationship between input and output is relatively straightforward.
- **Deep Networks**: Networks with multiple hidden layers are known as deep networks. They are capable of modeling complex, hierarchical relationships in the data. Each successive hidden layer captures increasingly abstract features.

Role in Learning

Hidden layers play several key roles in the learning process of an ANN:

- **Feature Extraction**: The initial hidden layers often act as feature extractors, identifying important patterns and representations in the input data. For example, in image recognition, early layers may detect edges and textures. Let us consider a classifier designed to recognize three animal species: dog, cat, and rabbit. In the input layer, raw features such as the animal's height, weight, skin tone, and ear shape are fed into the network. The hidden layers transform these raw features into higher-level representations. For example, the first hidden layer might group features to represent general shapes (for example, tall animals with long legs for dogs, and small and compact shapes for rabbits). Deeper layers may combine these patterns into more specific traits, such as recognizing a bushy tail as a defining feature of dogs or floppy ears for rabbits. This transformation allows the network to focus on meaningful patterns while ignoring irrelevant noise.

- **Feature Transformation**: Subsequent hidden layers transform these features into more abstract representations. For example, higher layers in an image recognition network might identify shapes and objects.
- **Hierarchy of Concepts**: Deep networks create a hierarchy of concepts, with each layer building upon the previous layer's output. This hierarchical learning enables the network to understand complex data structures.

Challenges and Considerations

While hidden layers are fundamental to the success of artificial neural networks, their design and implementation come with a set of challenges and considerations. Properly addressing these challenges is crucial for building effective and efficient neural networks. Some of the primary challenges include the risk of overfitting, computational complexity, and issues related to gradient stability during training. Understanding and mitigating these challenges is essential for ensuring that the network generalizes well to new data, trains efficiently, and achieves optimal performance.

- **Overfitting**: Deep networks with many hidden layers can overfit the training data, especially if there is insufficient training data. Regularization techniques such as dropout, L2 regularization, and early stopping can help mitigate over fitting. For example, consider a classifier designed to recognize three animal species: dog, cat, and rabbit. The network might learn that a specific pattern of fur color is unique to a training example of a dog, leading to incorrect classifications when encountering new dog images with slightly different fur patterns. Over fitting results in a model that performs well on training data but poorly on unseen data.
- **Underfitting**: If the network architecture is too simple (for example, only one hidden layer with a small number of neurons), it might fail to capture the complexity of the data. For instance, the model may incorrectly classify rabbits and cats together because it has not learned to differentiate based on their ear shape or tail length. Underfitting occurs when the model lacks the capacity to learn the underlying patterns and generalizes poorly, resulting in low accuracy on both training and test data.
- **Computational Complexity**: More hidden layers and neurons increase the computational complexity of the network, requiring more processing power

and memory. This can be a challenge when working with large datasets or limited computational resources.

- **Vanishing and Exploding Gradients**: In very deep networks, gradients can become extremely small (vanishing gradient problem) or very large (exploding gradient problem) during backpropagation. This can impede the training process. Techniques such as gradient clipping, batch normalization, and using appropriate activation functions (for example, ReLU) can help address these issues.

Output Layers

The output layer is the final layer in the neural network, responsible for producing the final prediction or classification. The number of neurons in the output layer depends on the type of task the network is designed for. The output layer aggregates the features learned by the hidden layers and maps them to the desired output format. For a regression task, the output layer typically has one neuron that outputs a continuous value. For a classification task, the output layer has as many neurons (one-hot encoded) as there are classes, and it outputs probabilities or class labels. The activation function used in the output layer depends on the nature of the task. For binary classification, a sigmoid activation function is commonly used, outputting values between 0 and 1. For multi-class classification, a softmax activation function is used, producing a probability distribution over the classes. The output layer's predictions are compared with the true labels using a loss function, such as mean squared error for regression or cross-entropy for classification. The loss function quantifies the prediction error, guiding the network's learning process during training.

Interactions Between Layers

The layers in a neural network are interconnected through weights and biases. During the forward pass, data flows from the input layer, through the hidden layers, to the output layer, undergoing transformations at each step. During the backward pass (backpropagation), the network adjusts its weights and biases based on the loss function's gradient, minimizing the prediction error.

- **Feedforward**: In the feedforward process, each neuron in a layer receives input from neurons in the previous layer, applies an activation function, and passes the result to neurons in the next layer.
- **Backpropagation**: Backpropagation is the learning algorithm used to train the network. It involves computing the gradient of the loss function with respect to each weight by the chain rule and updating the weights to minimize the loss. For example, if the network misclassifies a cat as a rabbit, the error is calculated using a loss function. This error is then propagated backward

through the network, adjusting weights in each layer to improve the model's ability to differentiate cats from rabbits in the next iteration.

A detailed discussion on backpropagation learning, including the mathematical foundations and step-by-step computations, will be covered in the next chapter. This will provide an in-depth understanding of how neural networks learn and optimize their parameters.

Conclusion

In this chapter, we delved into the foundational aspects of Artificial Neural Networks (ANNs), exploring their fundamental principles, structure, and architecture. We began by understanding the basic concepts and history of ANNs, highlighting their ability to mimic the human brain's neural networks and their application in solving complex problems.

We then examined the intricate structure and architecture of ANNs, emphasizing the importance of various components such as neurons, connections, and layers. We discussed how these elements come together to form networks capable of learning and adapting to data. The significance of activation functions was also explored in depth, showcasing their critical role in introducing non-linearity into the network, enabling ANNs to model complex relationships.

The discussion on layers in neural networks provided a comprehensive view of the input, hidden, and output layers. We examined the purpose and functionality of each layer, noting how they contribute to the network's ability to process and transform data from raw input to meaningful predictions.

Throughout this chapter, we have laid a solid foundation for understanding ANNs, setting the stage for more advanced topics. In the next chapter, we will delve into the details of training neural networks, with a particular focus on the backpropagation algorithm and the mathematics behind it. This will further enhance our understanding of how ANNs learn and improve their performance over time.

Practice Exercises

1. Consider a neural network with three output classes. Suppose the raw output scores (logits) from the network are z= [1.0, 2.0, 3.0]. Calculate the Softmax scores.

2. Consider a neuron with an input vector x=[0.5,−1.5,2.0] and weight vector w=[0.4,−0.9,0.1], with a bias term b=0.2. Calculate the output of this neuron using the sigmoid activation function.

3. Calculate the output of a ReLU activation function for the input vector x=[-2,3,-1,5].

4. Given the actual values y=[1,0,1] and predicted probabilities from a neural network =[0.8,0.3,0.9], calculate the mean squared error.

5. Assume a neural network with one hidden layer of two neurons. The input to the hidden layer is x=[0.5,-1], weights are w1=[0.5,-0.5] and w2=[-1.5,1], and biases are b1=0.2 and b2=-0.3. Calculate the output using the sigmoid activation function.

Answers

1. [0.09, 0.245, 0.665]

2. 0.876

3. The output vector is [0,3,0,5].

4. MSE = 0.0467

5. The outputs of the hidden layer neurons are approximately [0.679,0.113].

Multiple Choice Questions

1. What is the primary role of the input layer in a neural network?

    a. To classify the input data into categories

    b. To transform input data using non-linear activation functions

    c. To receive input data and pass it to subsequent layers

    d. To prevent overfitting during model training

2. Which activation function is typically used in the output layer of a neural network for multi-class classification?

    a. ReLU

    b. Tanh

    c. Sigmoid

    d. Softmax

3. What does the term 'neuron' in a neural network refer to?

    a. A type of deep learning model

    b. A processing unit that receives, processes, and transmits information

c. The connection between layers in a network

   d. The loss function used in network training

4. Which of the following is a characteristic of the ReLU activation function?

   a. Outputs a 0 for positive inputs

   b. Outputs the input itself if it is negative

   c. Outputs the input itself if it is positive and 0 if it is negative

   d. Outputs 1 for any positive input

5. What is a common issue associated with the sigmoid activation function?

   a. It cannot output negative values

   b. It is computationally expensive

   c. It may lead to vanishing gradients

   d. It only works with binary classification

6. Which technique is used to prevent neurons from dying in a network that uses ReLU activation functions?

   a. Normalization

   b. Dropout

   c. Using Leaky ReLU instead of ReLU

   d. Applying softmax

7. What does overfitting in a neural network mean?

   a. The model performs poorly on the training data

   b. The model performs well on the training data but poorly on unseen data

   c. The model requires more hidden layer

   d. The model does not use enough epochs during training

8. Which of the following is a benefit of using deep neural networks?

   a. They require fewer computational resources

   b. They can model complex hierarchical relationships in the data

   c. They are less prone to overfitting

   d. They do not require activation functions

9. What is the purpose of the backpropagation process in neural networks?
    a. To increase the number of layers dynamically during training
    b. Non-linear to linear
    c. To adjust weights and biases to minimize the loss function
    d. To increase the speed of the forward pass in the network
10. What role does the softmax function play in a neural network?
    a. It is used as a loss function
    b. It enhances the non-linearity of the mode
    c. It prevents the model from overfitting
    d. It converts logits to probabilities that sum to one

Answers

1. c
2. d
3. b
4. c
5. c
6. c
7. b
8. b
9. c
10. d

Keywords

- Artificial Neural Networks (ANNs)
- Neurons
- Connections
- Layers
- Input Layer

- Hidden Layers
- Output Layer
- Activation Functions
- Sigmoid Function
- Tanh Function
- Rectified Linear Unit (ReLU)
- Leaky ReLU
- Softmax Function
- Weighted Sum
- Bias Term
- Non-linearity
- Feature Extraction
- Feature Transformation
- Overfitting
- Computational Complexity
- Vanishing Gradient Problem
- Exploding Gradient Problem
- Regularization
- Backpropagation
- Gradient Descent
- Loss Function

References

1. https://shorturl.at/UdMIJ

CHAPTER 10
Training Neural Networks

Introduction

This chapter delves into the intricate world of training neural networks, providing both foundational knowledge and practical techniques essential for mastering this area of machine learning. The chapter begins with a thorough exploration of gradient descent and optimization techniques, detailing the methods that underpin the learning mechanisms of neural networks.

Following this, we move to backpropagation learning, a key concept that underlies multi-layer neural network training. This discussion includes a thorough examination of the backpropagation algorithm's mechanics, showcasing its role in the efficient adjustment of weights in the network, based on the gradients of the loss function.

It then transitions into fine-tuning model parameters, offering insights into how subtle adjustments can significantly enhance model performance. The practical application of these concepts is demonstrated through coding examples using ScikitLearn, providing a hands-on approach to implementing and training neural networks. Additionally, the chapter addresses the challenges commonly encountered in traditional neural networks dealing with unstructured data such as image, video, speech, and text datasets. The chapter concludes with a brief introduction to Convolutional Neural Networks (CNNs), which have the ability to handle data such as images and speech.

Structure

In this chapter, we are going to cover the following main topics:

- Gradient Descent and Backpropagation Algorithm
- Fine-Tuning Model Parameters
- Coding Neural Networks in Python Using Scikit Learn
- Challenges in Traditional Neural Networks and the Birth of Deep Learning Models with CNN capability

Gradient Descent and Backpropagation Algorithm

In the broader context of neural networks, understanding the fundamentals of gradient descent and gradient calculations, as elaborated in *Chapter 4, Regression versus Classification Models*, is crucial. This knowledge serves as the backbone for appreciating how these concepts apply specifically to neural network architectures. Neural networks without hidden layers function similarly to linear regression models; they are essentially linear classifiers. In such configurations, the neural network uses input features directly, applies a set of weights, and produces output predictions through a linear combination of those inputs. While this can be effective for linearly separable data, it significantly limits the network's ability to handle complex patterns or non-linear relationships. The output in these scenarios is merely a direct projection of input data into the output space, governed by linear transformations.

The introduction of hidden layers is a game-changer for neural network capabilities. As discussed in the previous chapter, hidden layers allow the network to transform input data into more abstract and composite representations. Each neuron in a hidden layer transforms its input through a non-linear activation function before passing it on. This non-linearity is crucial; it allows the network to learn and model non-linear relationships, making it possible to tackle problems that are not linearly separable by creating complex boundaries based on the learned features.

This capability is amplified through the use of backpropagation, a method essential for learning in multilayer networks. Backpropagation uses the chain rule of calculus to iteratively calculate gradients for each weight in the network by moving backward from the output layer to the input layer. It adjusts each weight in the network by taking into account the error made by the network (the difference between the predicted output and the actual output) and how much each weight contributed to that error. This method not only helps in fine-tuning the weights in the output and hidden layers but also refines the feature extraction processes performed by the hidden layers.

The process of backpropagation in a multi-layered setup involves several critical steps:

- **Forward Pass**: During the forward pass, input data is passed through the network, layer by layer, until it reaches the output layer where the final prediction is made.
- **Loss Calculation**: The loss (or error) is calculated at the output, usually by a loss function suited to the task (for example, mean squared error for regression or cross-entropy for classification).
- **Reverse Pass**: The gradient of the loss function with respect to each weight is calculated, starting from the output back to the inputs. This calculation

considers the non-linear activations applied at each hidden layer, allowing the error to propagate back through the network.

Through this mechanism, neural networks can adjust their internal parameters (weights) to minimize errors, making them incredibly effective at handling complex, non-linear problems across a myriad of applications in various fields. By learning to manipulate these weights effectively through backpropagation and gradient descent, neural networks develop a robust capability to solve non-linear problems in regression and classification task.

We are going to extend the mathematics of gradient descent discussed in Linear Regression and Logistic Regression in the context of neural network learning.

ANN as a Classifier

The backpropagation algorithm, central to training neural networks, relies heavily on the chain rule of calculus to compute the gradients of the loss function with respect to each weight in the network. This process involves breaking down the gradient into a product of three components, each corresponding to different parts of the neural network's structure and function. We will go through how these components are calculated and how they contribute to the overall gradient computation.

Initially, we shall consider ANN as a classifier to work out these components. Let us consider the net value at the summing point of a neural network node as:

net = $w_b + w_1 * x_1 + w_2 * x_2 + \cdots w_p * w_p$, where w_b is the bias weight and w_1 to w_p represent the weights of input features x_1 to x_p.

When a non-linear sigmoidal activation function is applied over the net, the output is represented as $\hat{y} = f(net) = \frac{1}{1+e^{-(net)}}$

The objective of a gradient descent is to train the values of and that minimize the cost function, which we will define as the Sum Squared Error (SSE) across all output nodes of a neural network architecture with a scaling factor 1/2 for mathematical convenience:

$$\text{Loss} = SSE = \frac{1}{2}\sum_{i=1}^{n}(y_i - \hat{y}_i)^2$$

The chain rule in the calculus allows us to combine three gradient components to calculate the gradient of the loss (cost) function with respect to the weights in the network:

$$\frac{\partial Loss}{\partial w} = \frac{\partial Loss}{\partial \hat{y}} \frac{\partial \hat{y}}{\partial net} \frac{\partial net}{\partial w}$$

Training Neural Networks 277

The first component of the gradient calculation is the derivative of the loss function with respect to the output of the network. This component measures how the error (or loss) changes with respect to changes in the network's output. This component, often referred to as the error signal, indicates the magnitude and direction in which the network's output should be adjusted to minimize the loss.

The second component is the derivative of the activation function with respect to the weighted sum of inputs (net) for each neuron. This component captures how the activation function modifies the input received from the previous layer. This derivative tells us how sensitive the activation of a neuron is to changes in its input and is crucial for understanding how changes in the input propagate through the activation function.

The third and last component is the derivative of the weighted sum of inputs (net) with respect to the individual weights. This component quantifies how the input to the neuron changes with respect to each weight associated with the inputs.

Hence, the overall gradient of the loss function can be interpreted as:

- **Error Signal**: How much the error changes with respect to the network's output.
- **Activation Gradient**: How much the neuron's activation changes with respect to its net.
- **Input Contribution**: How much the input to the neuron depends on the specific weight being adjusted.

The following figure depicts a simple neural network architecture with one hidden layer. In this network, we have two input features (x_1 and x_2) connected to the hidden layer neurons. The connections between the inputs and the hidden layer neurons are weighted by w_1, w_2, w_3, and w_4, with additional biases (w_{bias1} and w_{bias2}) applied to each hidden neuron. The net outputs of the hidden layer neurons are then passed through a sigmoid activation function to produce these hidden layer activations called h_1 and h_2. The hidden layer outputs are subsequently connected to the output layer, where they are weighted by v_1 and v_2, with an additional bias v_{bias}. The net value at the output neuron is then passed through a sigmoid activation function, resulting in the final output, denoted as ŷ or 'out.'

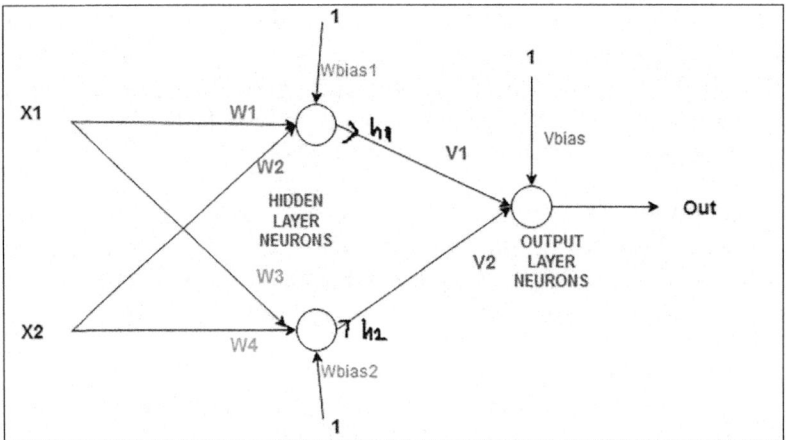

Figure 10.1: *Single Hidden Layer Architecture*

We will use this specific architecture as a reference to apply the three components of the gradient calculation. We will explore how to calculate the gradient of the loss (or cost) function with respect to the weights in the network, focusing on each layer's contribution to the overall gradient. This will include exploring backpropagation learning by applying the chain rule, a fundamental concept for training neural networks effectively.

A feedforward flow is the process by which input data is propagated through the network layers to produce an output. This process involves passing the input data through the network's connections, applying the respective weights and biases, and using activation functions to transform the signals before they reach the output layer.

- **Input Layer**: The process begins with the input features (x_1 and x_2) being fed into the network. These inputs represent the raw data that the network will process to generate a prediction.

$$net_1 = w_1 * x_1 + w_2 * x_2 + w_{bias1}$$

$$net_2 = w_3 * x_1 + w_4 * x_2 + w_{bias2}$$

- **Hidden Layer (Weighted Sum and Activation)**: The inputs are first multiplied by their corresponding weights and summed up along with the biases to compute the net input for each neuron in the hidden layer. The net inputs for the hidden layer neurons are calculated as follows:

$$h_1 = \text{Activation}(net_1)$$

$$h_2 = \text{Activation}(net_2)$$

These net inputs (net_1 and net_2) are then passed through an activation function,

Training Neural Networks

typically a non-linear function such as the sigmoid, ReLU, or tanh. The outputs of these activations are the hidden layer outputs, h_1 and h_2,

$$net_{out} = v_1 * h_1 + v_2 * h_2 + v_{bias}$$

- **Output Layer (Weighted Sum and Activation)**: The hidden layer outputs h_1 and h_2 are then fed into the output layer. Similar to the hidden layer, these outputs are multiplied by their corresponding weights and summed up along with the bias to compute the net input to the output neuron:

$$Out = \hat{y} = \frac{1}{1+e^{-net_{out}}}$$

This net value (net_{out}) is passed through an activation function (commonly the sigmoid function for binary classification tasks and the softmax function for multiclass classification) to produce the final output of the network.

- **Error Gradient Calculation:** To understand how the error gradient is calculated in a neural network using the chain rule, let us focus on two specific weights: v_1 in the output layer and w_1 in the hidden layer. These examples will illustrate how the gradients are computed and how they contribute to the overall learning process. The same principles can be extended to other weights and bias terms in the network.

To begin with, we will calculate the error gradient to adjust the v_1 weight in the output layer. As previously discussed, the total gradient is represented as a product of three components:

$$\frac{\partial Loss}{\partial v_1} = \frac{\partial Loss}{\partial \hat{y}} \frac{\partial \hat{y}}{\partial net_{out}} \frac{\partial net_{out}}{\partial v_1}$$

Component-1: $\frac{\partial Loss}{\partial \hat{y}} = \frac{\partial(\frac{1}{2}((y-\hat{y})^2))}{\partial \hat{y}}$

$$\frac{\partial Loss}{\partial \hat{y}} = -(y - \hat{y})$$

Component-2: $\frac{\partial \hat{y}}{\partial net_{out}} = \frac{\partial(\frac{1}{1+e^{-net_{out}}})}{\partial net_{out}}$

$$\frac{\partial \hat{y}}{\partial net_{out}} = \frac{e^{-net_{out}}}{(1 + e^{-net_{out}})^2}$$

$$\frac{\partial \hat{y}}{\partial net_{out}} = \hat{y} * (1 - \hat{y})$$

Component-3: $\frac{\partial net_{out}}{\partial v_1} = \frac{\partial(h_1 * v_1 + h_2 * v_2 + v_{bias})}{\partial v_1}$

$$\frac{\partial net_{out}}{\partial v_1} = h_1$$

Now, let us combine all three components to calculate the error gradient for adjusting the v_1 weight in the output layer as follows:

$$\frac{\partial Loss}{\partial v_1} = -(y - \hat{y}) * \hat{y} * (1 - \hat{y}) * h_1$$

In a similar manner, we proceed with the calculation of the error gradient for the w_1 weight in the hidden layer. The total gradient is represented as a product of three components as follows:

$$\frac{\partial Loss}{\partial w_1} = \frac{\partial Loss}{\partial h_1} \frac{\partial h_1}{\partial net_{h_1}} \frac{\partial net_{h_1}}{\partial w_1}$$

Since the loss function is not directly represented as a function of h_1, we will expand the first component into three components for easier computation. Upon doing so, we realize that these components are essentially the output layer's error gradient scaled by the output layer weight (in this case, v_1). This is why the process is referred to as backpropagation.

$$\frac{\partial Loss}{\partial h_1} = \frac{\partial Loss}{\partial \hat{y}} \frac{\partial \hat{y}}{\partial net_{out}} \frac{\partial net_{out}}{\partial h_1}$$

$$\frac{\partial Loss}{\partial h_1} = -(y - \hat{y}) * \hat{y} * (1 - \hat{y}) * \frac{\partial net_{out}}{\partial h_1}$$

We know that, $\frac{\partial net_{out}}{\partial h_1} = \frac{\partial (h_1 * v_1 + h_2 * v_2 + v_{bias})}{\partial h_1} = v_1$

We can notice that the first two components are the same as we have computed at the output layer and the last component is v_1, which is a weight. Hence, we can say the output layer error gradient is propagated back for the hidden layer weight calculation.

$$\frac{\partial Loss}{\partial h_1} = -(y - \hat{y}) * \hat{y} * (1 - \hat{y}) * v_1$$

We can logically re-write the expression $\frac{\partial Loss}{\partial w_1} = \frac{\partial Loss}{\partial h_1} \frac{\partial h_1}{\partial net_{h_1}} \frac{\partial net_{h_1}}{\partial w_1}$ as follows:

$$\frac{\partial Loss}{\partial w_1} = (\text{Output Layer Error Gradient} * v_1) * \left(\frac{\partial h_1}{\partial net_{h_1}} \frac{\partial net_{h_1}}{\partial w_1}\right)$$

$$\frac{\partial Loss}{\partial w_1} = (\text{Output Layer Error Gradient} * v_1) * [h_1 * (1 - h_1) * x_1]$$

$$\frac{\partial Loss}{\partial w_1} = (\text{Back propagated } v_1 \text{ scaled Output Gradient}) * (\text{Derivative of hidden activation}) * (\text{input})$$

Training Neural Networks

Since the loss is not directly related to the hidden layer, we decomposed the error into components that include the output error, scaled by the output weight v_1, and the derivative of the hidden layer activation function. This process, known as backpropagation, efficiently propagates errors backward through the network, enabling the adjustment of all weights in the network, layer by layer. The gradients calculated for each weight contribute to refining the model's ability to classify data accurately, driving the learning process in multi-layer neural networks.

ANN as a Regressor

In this section, we extend the principles of neural network training to regression tasks, where the goal is to predict continuous values rather than discrete classes. Similar to the classifier, an Artificial Neural Network (ANN) as a regressor follows the same fundamental structure, involving input, hidden, and output layers. However, the primary difference lies in the nature of the output and the loss function. The process of calculating error gradients to adjust the network's weights remains largely the same as in classification, relying on the backpropagation algorithm.

Refer to *Figure 10.1*, using the architecture as described earlier, with the only difference being that in this regression scenario, the output node does not have an activation function. Instead, the final output is simply the net input to the output neuron, that is, Output = Net. This simplifies the error gradient calculation since there is no activation function applied at the output layer, making the gradient directly proportional to the error in the predicted value.

$$\frac{\partial Loss}{\partial v_1} = \frac{\partial Loss}{\partial \hat{y}} \frac{\partial \hat{y}}{\partial net_{out}} \frac{\partial net_{out}}{\partial v_1}$$

Component-1: $\dfrac{\partial Loss}{\partial \hat{y}} = \dfrac{\partial (\frac{1}{2}((y-\hat{y})^2))}{\partial \hat{y}}$

$$\frac{\partial Loss}{\partial \hat{y}} = -(y - \hat{y})$$

Component-2: $\dfrac{\partial \hat{y}}{\partial net_{out}} = \dfrac{\partial (net)}{\partial net_{out}}$

$$\frac{\partial \hat{y}}{\partial net_{out}} = 1$$

Component-3: $\dfrac{\partial net_{out}}{\partial v_1} = \dfrac{\partial (h_1 * v_1 + h_2 * v_2 + v_{bias})}{\partial v_1}$

$$\frac{\partial net_{out}}{\partial v_1} = h_1$$

To begin with, we will calculate the error gradient to adjust the v_1 weight in the output layer. As previously discussed, the total gradient is represented as a product of three components:

$$\frac{\partial Loss}{\partial v_1} = -(y - \hat{y}) * 1 * h_1$$

Now, let us combine all three components to calculate the error gradient for adjusting the v_1 weight in the output layer as follows:

$$\frac{\partial Loss}{\partial w_1} = \frac{\partial Loss}{\partial h_1} \frac{\partial h_1}{\partial net_{h_1}} \frac{\partial net_{h_1}}{\partial w_1}$$

In a similar manner, we proceed with the calculation of the error gradient for the w_1 weight in the hidden layer. The total gradient is represented as a product of three components as follows:

Since the loss function is not directly represented as a function of h_1, we will expand the first component into three components for easier computation. Upon doing so, we realize that these components are essentially the output layer's error gradient scaled by the output layer weight (in this case, v_1). This is why the process is referred to as backpropagation.

$$\frac{\partial Loss}{\partial h_1} = \frac{\partial Loss}{\partial \hat{y}} \frac{\partial \hat{y}}{\partial net_{out}} \frac{\partial net_{out}}{\partial h_1}$$

$$\frac{\partial Loss}{\partial h_1} = -(y - \hat{y}) * 1 * \frac{\partial net_{out}}{\partial h_1}$$

We know that, $\frac{\partial net_{out}}{\partial h_1} = \frac{\partial (h_1 * v_1 + h_2 * v_2 + v_{bias})}{\partial h_1} = v_1$

We can notice that the first two components are the same as we have computed at the output layer, and the last component is v_1, which is weight. Hence, we can say the output layer error gradient is propagated back for the hidden layer weight calculation.

$$\frac{\partial Loss}{\partial h_1} = -(y - \hat{y}) * 1 * v_1$$

$$\frac{\partial Loss}{\partial w_1} = -(y - \hat{y}) * 1 * v_1 * [h_1 * (1 - h_1) * x_1]$$

We can observe that the only difference compared to the classifier is that the term $\hat{y} * (1 - \hat{y})$, which represents the derivative of the sigmoid activation function in the classification scenario, is replaced by **1** in this case. This happens because, in the regressor, there is no activation function in the output layer, meaning that f'(net) = 1, simplifying the gradient calculation for the output layer.

Fine-Tuning Model Parameters

Fine-tuning model parameters is an essential aspect of optimizing the performance of ANNs. It involves carefully adjusting key hyperparameters that govern the learning process of the network. While training a neural network, these hyperparameters influence how well the model learns, its convergence speed, and its ability to generalize to unseen data. Fine-tuning these parameters is critical for ensuring that the network performs efficiently and effectively in both classification and regression tasks.

The weight update rule in neural network learning is given as:

$$weight_{new} = weight_{old} - learning\ rate * \frac{\partial Loss}{\partial weight}$$

- **Learning Rate:** The learning rate controls how much the weights are updated during each iteration of the training process. A higher learning rate causes the model to update the weights more significantly with each step, potentially speeding up convergence. However, if the learning rate is too high, the network may overshoot the optimal weights and fail to converge properly. On the other hand, a very low learning rate will make the training process slow, requiring many more iterations to reach an optimal solution. Thus, selecting the right learning rate is crucial for achieving an efficient balance between speed and accuracy.
- **Batch Size:** Batch size refers to the number of training examples processed in one forward and backward pass. A larger batch size provides a more accurate estimate of the gradients but requires more memory, while a smaller batch size introduces more noise into the gradient calculation but consumes less computational resources. Fine-tuning the batch size helps in determining the balance between computational efficiency and the quality of gradient estimates, directly influencing the network's performance during training.
- **Number of Epochs:** The number of epochs defines how many times the network will process the entire training dataset. More epochs allow the model to learn from the data multiple times, leading to improved performance. However, too many epochs may lead to overfitting, where the model becomes overly specialized to the training data and performs poorly on unseen data. Fine-tuning the number of epochs involves finding the optimal point where the model learns sufficiently without overfitting.
- **Momentum:** Momentum is an optimization technique that helps accelerate gradient descent by incorporating the previous gradient update. It works by adding a fraction of the previous gradient to the current update, allowing the model to build velocity in directions where the gradient consistently points. This not only prevents the model from getting stuck in local minima but also helps reduce oscillations, especially when navigating complex

and noisy loss landscapes. By introducing momentum, the optimizer gains the ability to smooth out the gradient updates, leading to faster and more stable convergence. Fine-tuning the momentum parameter can significantly improve both the stability and the speed of the convergence during the training process, especially for deep neural networks where loss landscapes can be highly irregular.

- **Adagrad**: Adagrad, short for Adaptive Gradient Algorithm, is an optimization technique that adjusts the learning rate dynamically based on the historical gradients for each parameter. Unlike standard gradient descent, where a fixed learning rate is used, Adagrad assigns smaller learning rates to parameters that have been updated frequently, while parameters that are updated less frequently retain larger learning rates. This allows Adagrad to handle sparse data effectively and ensures that learning slows down for features that have already been sufficiently learned. However, one limitation of Adagrad is that the learning rate tends to decrease significantly over time, which can cause the model to stop learning prematurely in the later stages of training.

- **RMSprop**: RMSprop, or Root Mean Square Propagation, was developed to counteract the decaying learning rate issue in Adagrad. It works by maintaining a moving average of the squared gradients for each parameter, and this average is then used to scale the learning rate. The key idea is to keep the learning rate large enough even after many iterations, allowing the model to continue learning. RMSprop divides the learning rate by the square root of the average of recent squared gradients, effectively preventing the learning rate from shrinking too much. This makes it particularly well-suited for training deep neural networks, where the loss surface can be complex and gradients vary across different dimensions.

- **Adam**: Adaptive Moment Estimation (Adam) is one of the most widely used optimization algorithms in deep learning. It combines the benefits of both momentum and RMSprop by maintaining two moving averages: one for the gradients (such as momentum) and one for the squared gradients (such as RMSprop). The first moment (mean of the gradients) helps guide the search in the right direction, while the second moment (mean of the squared gradients) ensures that the learning rate adapts based on the gradient's magnitude. Adam also includes bias correction terms, which adjust the estimates of the moments to ensure they are unbiased, especially at the beginning of training when the moments can be close to zero. Adam is known for its robust performance, making it well-suited for a wide range of deep learning tasks, including training large-scale models. It is efficient, has a low memory requirement, and works well with sparse gradients.

- **Regularization Techniques:** Regularization is important to prevent overfitting, especially in deep networks. Techniques such as L2 regularization, dropout, and early stopping are commonly used. L2 regularization adds a penalty term to the loss function to discourage large weights, while dropout randomly deactivates a fraction of neurons during training to prevent co-adaptation. Fine-tuning the regularization parameters ensures that the model generalizes well to new data without overfitting.

- **Weight Initialization:** Proper weight initialization is essential to ensure that the network starts training from a balanced point. Poor initialization can lead to slow convergence or prevent the model from learning altogether. Techniques such as Xavier initialization or 'He' initialization are commonly used for deeper networks to ensure that the gradients neither vanish nor explode during training.

Fine-tuning the hyperparameters of a neural network is crucial for optimizing its performance. There are several strategies to achieve this, each designed to systematically adjust key parameters. Common strategies include grid search, which exhaustively explores all possible combinations of hyperparameters; random search, which randomly samples parameter values within predefined ranges; and manual tuning, which leverages the practitioner's insights to iteratively adjust parameters based on performance metrics. Additionally, modern approaches such as Bayesian optimization and Hyperband use intelligent algorithms to automate the fine-tuning process, offering a more efficient and data-driven approach to finding optimal configurations. These strategies ensure that the neural network achieves the best possible balance between learning speed, accuracy, and generalization.

While fine-tuning, it is crucial to monitor the network's performance using metrics such as training and validation loss, accuracy, and convergence speed. Early stopping is a useful strategy to halt the training process if the validation performance starts degrading, thus preventing overfitting. By carefully adjusting hyperparameters, the network can be guided to learn efficiently, converge quickly, and generalize well to new data.

Coding Neural Networks in Python

In this section, we will dive into the practical implementation of ANNs using Python, focusing specifically on the powerful scikit-learn library. We will explore how to use MLPClassifier for classification tasks and MLP Regressor for regression tasks, providing hands-on examples to solidify your understanding of how ANNs function in real-world scenarios.

Moving forward, in the next chapters, we will transition to more advanced frameworks such as TensorFlow and Keras, which are widely used for building state-of-the-art deep learning models. These frameworks will allow us to develop more complex neural networks and explore deep learning architectures such as Convolutional Neural Networks (CNNs) and Recurrent Neural Networks (RNNs).

To begin, we will demonstrate how to solve the classic X-OR problem, which is a linearly non-separable dataset, using a step-by-step mathematical breakdown of the neural network's calculations. This will provide an intuitive understanding of how ANNs work to solve non-linear problems. Following this, we will apply ANNs to a real-world use case with tabular data, showcasing their capability as both a classifier and a regressor. These examples will serve as a foundation for understanding how neural networks are implemented and fine-tuned using scikit-learn, setting the stage for more advanced deep learning topics in the following chapters.

Solving X-OR Problem Using ANN

The X-OR problem is a classic example in the field of machine learning and ANNs, highlighting the ability of neural networks to solve problems that are not linearly separable. Traditional linear models, such as logistic regression or single-layer perceptrons, fail to solve the X-OR problem because the classes cannot be separated with a straight line. However, an ANN with a hidden layer can successfully solve this problem by transforming the input space into one where the classes become linearly separable. We will solve the X-OR problem using an ANN with a single hidden layer containing three neurons. We will break down the steps mathematically, showing how the hidden layer and non-linear activation functions enable the network to classify X-OR inputs correctly.

The X-OR problem has two inputs, x_1 and x_2 with the following truth table.

x_1	x_2	XOR Output
0	0	0
0	1	1
1	0	1
1	1	0

Figure 10.2: X-OR Truth Table

```
from random import choice
from numpy import array,dot,random
import numpy as np
import matplotlib.pyplot as plt
%matplotlib inline
#X-OR (linearly non-separable problem)
train_data=[(array([0,0,1]),0),(array([0,1,1]),1),(ar-
ray([1,0,1]),1),(array([1,1,1]),0)]
v=random.rand(3,3) #weights connecting input to hidden layer
w=random.rand(4,1)#weights connecting hidden to output layer
eta=0.45
n=15000
#Training
```

```
for i in range(n):
  x,expected=choice(train_data)
  net1=dot(x,v)
  y=sig_act(net1) #hidden layer output
  bias=np.array([1]) #input to bias at output layer
  y_in=np.concatenate((y,bias),axis=0)
  net2=dot(y_in,w)
  y_pred=sig_act(net2) #output layer response
  #output layer error gradient
  delta_out=(expected-y_pred)*y_pred*(1-y_pred)
  #updating the Hidden-Output weight
  w=w+(eta*delta_out*y_in.reshape(-1,1)) matrix
  #Output error propagates to hidden layer
  bp=delta_out*w[:3]
  y_dash=y*(1-y)
  y_dash.reshape(-1,1)
  delta_hid=np.multiply(y_dash.reshape(-1,1),bp)
  v[:,0]=v[:,0]+(eta*delta_hid[0]*x)
  v[:,1]=v[:,1]+(eta*delta_hid[1]*x)
  v[:,2]=v[:,2]+(eta*delta_hid[2]*x)
```

By repeatedly performing feedforward and backpropagation over multiple training epochs, the network gradually learns to classify the X-OR inputs correctly. The hidden layer neurons enable the network to map the X-OR inputs to a space where they can be separated linearly, which allows the output neuron to make the correct classification.

```
#Testing (feedforward flow only)
for x,_ in train_data:
      net1=dot(x,v)
      y=sig_act(net1) #(3x1)
      bias=np.array([1]) #input to bias at output layer
      y_in=np.concatenate((y,bias),axis=0)
      net2=dot(y_in,w)
      y_pred=sig_act(net2)
   print("{} :-> {}".format(x[:3],y_pred))
```

Output:

[0 0 1]: [0.03965356]

[0 1 1]: [0.96708234]

[1 0 1]: [0.96532844]

[1 1 1]: [0.03809788]

The outputs show that the neural network is performing well in classifying the input data into two classes. For inputs where the output should be close to 1, the network gives high values (for example, 0.967, 0.965), indicating strong confidence in the positive class. For inputs where the output should be close to 0, the network produces low values (for example, 0.039, 0.038), indicating strong confidence in the negative class.

After the network has been trained, the hidden layer maps the input features into a higher-dimensional space where the previously inseparable points can now be separated more easily. This is one of the key strengths of neural networks, particularly with non-linear activation functions in the hidden layers.

We will visualize this transformation by plotting the input features in a 3D space, showing how the neural network's hidden layer effectively maps the data points to a higher-dimensional space. The points that were originally non-separable will now appear separable after being passed through the hidden layer. The convincing probability scores generated by the neural network will help illustrate how the network assigns class labels based on this transformation.

```
hidden_neurons=np.array([[0.5, 0.5, 0.5],[0.39,0.12,0.97],[0.45,0.11,
0.97],[0.67, 0.85, 0.99]])
import pandas as pd
HN=pd.DataFrame(hidden_neurons,columns=['H1','H2','H3']) HN
['label']=['0','1','1','0']
#3D scatter plot
import plotly.express as px
fig = px.scatter_3d(HN, x='H1', y='H2', z='H3',color=HN.label)
fig.show()
```

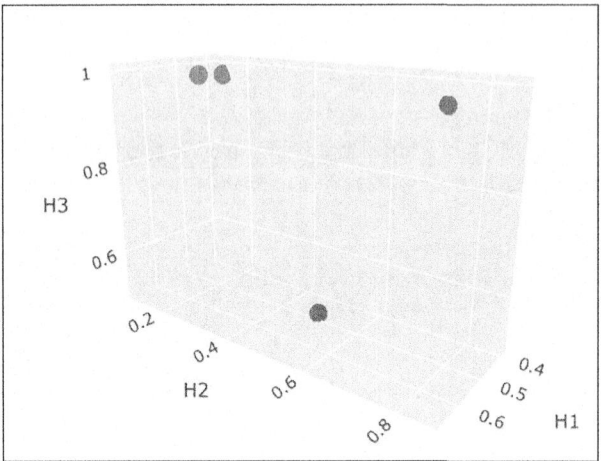

Figure 10.3: 3D Plot of Hidden Layer Output

By visualizing the data in the preceding figure after it has been processed by the hidden layer, we can observe how the network learns to distinguish between different classes. This graphical representation will provide an intuitive understanding of how neural networks handle non-linear problems by transforming the input space into one where a clear decision boundary can be drawn, allowing for accurate classification.

ANN as a Classifier Use Case

To demonstrate ANN as a classifier, a popular wine dataset is often used in machine learning to classify wine cultivators based on a set of chemical properties. It contains 13 chemical attributes measured for 178 samples of wine, each corresponding to one of three different cultivators. The dataset is useful for demonstrating how a neural network (ANN) can be applied to solve classification problems, where the goal is to predict the wine cultivator based on the chemical composition of the wine.

Features in the wine dataset are:

- **Cultivator**: The class label representing one of the three wine cultivators (target variable).
- **Alcohol**: Alcohol content in the wine.
- **Malic_Acid**: The amount of malic acid in the wine.
- **Ash**: The ash content of the wine.
- **Alcalinity_of_Ash**: The alkalinity of the ash in the wine.
- **Magnesium**: The magnesium content of the wine.
- **Total_phenols**: Total phenols in the wine.
- **Flavanoids**: Flavonoid content in the wine.
- **Nonflavanoid_phenols**: Non-flavonoid phenols in the wine.
- **Proanthocyanins**: Proanthocyanins content in the wine.
- **Color_intensity**: Intensity of the color in the wine.
- **Hue**: The hue of the wine.
- **OD280**: Optical density ratio measured at 280 nm, related to the concentration of phenolic compounds.
- **Proline**: The amount of proline, an amino acid found in the wine.

The goal of the classification problem is to build a neural network that can classify the wine into one of the three cultivators based on the 13 chemical properties. The Cultivator column is the target variable, and the remaining columns are the features used to make the classification.

Let us load the data and check the head of the data.

```
import numpy as np
import pandas as pd
import matplotlib.pyplot as plt
%matplotlib inline
import seaborn as sns
from sklearn.neural_network import MLPClassifier
```

```
from sklearn.preprocessing import StandardScaler
from sklearn.model_selection import KFold,cross_val_score
A=pd.read_csv('/content/drive/My Drive/Case Studies Mahesh Anand/wine.
xls',names =
["Cultivator", "Alchol", "Malic_Acid", "Ash", "Alcalinity_of_Ash",
"Magnesium", "Total_phenols", "Flavanoids", "Nonflavanoid_phenols",
"Proanthocyanins", "Color_intensity", "Hue", "OD280", "Proline"])
# plot the scatterplot to visualize the clusters
plt.rcParams['figure.figsize'] = [15,8]
sns.scatterplot(x = 'Flavanoids', y = 'OD280', data = A, hue =
'Cultivator',palette=['red','green','blue'])
# set the axes and plot labels
# set the font size using 'fontsize'
plt.title('scatter plot', fontsize = 15)
plt.xlabel('Flavanoids', fontsize = 15)
plt.ylabel('OD280', fontsize = 15)
# display the plot
plt.show()
```

To better understand the complexity and distribution of the data, a scatter plot of two prominent features, Flavanoids and OD280, is shown in *Figure* 10.4. These two chemical properties are important features for distinguishing between different cultivators of wine. However, as seen in the scatter plot, the data points from the different cultivators tend to overlap, highlighting the complexity of the dataset and the challenge of classifying the wines based on these features alone.

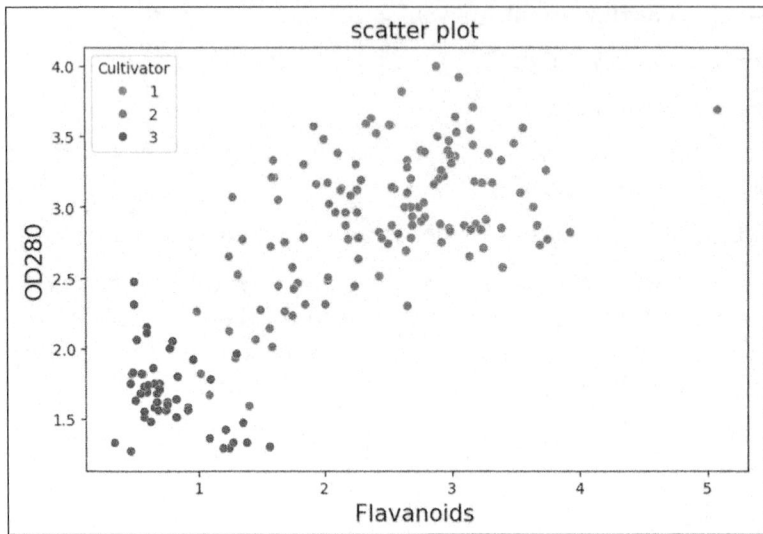

***Figure* 10.4**: *Scatter Plot Showing Linearly Non-Separable Data Points*

Let us prepare the dataset for building the ANN by separating the features (input

Training Neural Networks

variables) from the target variable (output). The X and Y variables represent the input features and the target variable, respectively.

```
X=A.drop('Cultivator',axis=1)
Y=A['Cultivator']
```

Towards the next step, let us standardize the input features to ensure each feature has a mean of 0 and a standard deviation of 1, which is important for many machine learning algorithms, including ANNs, as it helps the model converge faster and perform better.

```
from sklearn.model_selection import train_test_split
xtrain,xtest,ytrain,ytest=train_test_split(X_std,Y,test_size=0.2,random_state=0)
ANN_model=MLPClassifier(hidden_layer_sizes=(20))
```

Towards the next step, we are dividing the dataset into training and testing sets using the **train_test_split** function from the scikit-learn library. This is a crucial step in model development as it allows us to evaluate how well the model performs on unseen data after being trained.

In this step, we experimented with a neural network architecture featuring one hidden layer with 20 neurons. The architecture has proven effective in classifying the overlapping records in the wine dataset, successfully handling the complexity of the data that a simpler model might struggle with. The neural network was built using the MLPClassifier from the scikit-learn library.

```
ANN_model.fit(xtrain,ytrain)
y_pred=ANN_model.predict(xtest)
from sklearn import metrics
cm=metrics.confusion_matrix(ytest,y_pred)
print(cm)
[14  0  0]
[ 0 16  0]
[ 0  0  6]
cr=metrics.classification_report(ytest,y_pred)
print(cr)
```

	precision	recall	f1-score	support
1	1.00	1.00	1.00	14
2	1.00	1.00	1.00	16
3	1.00	1.00	1.00	6
accuracy			1.00	36
macro avg	1.00	1.00	1.00	36
weighted avg	1.00	1.00	1.00	36

Figure 10.5: *Classification Report of Wine Data Classification*

The results shown in *Figure 10.5* show perfect precision, recall, and F1-scores for all classes. The model uses one hidden layer with 20 neurons, which was manually fine-tuned to achieve the best classification accuracy for this dataset. When experimenting with fewer neurons (such as 15 or less), the model began to misclassify some overlapping data points, especially in the more complex regions of the dataset where the features of different classes overlap. The diagonal entries shown in the confusion matrix (14, 16, and 6) represent the correctly classified instances for each class. The process of manually fine-tuning the number of neurons helped identify the optimal configuration. While fewer neurons resulted in misclassification, increasing the hidden layer size to 20 neurons provided the network with enough capacity to correctly classify all instances, including those in the overlapping regions.

ANN as a Regressor Use Case

In this section, we will explore the use of ANN as a Regressor, focusing on predicting continuous values. We will use the same dataset that was demonstrated for K-Nearest Neighbors (KNN) regression in *Chapter 7, Distance-Based Machine Learning Models*. The dataset was originally created by Angeliki Xifara, a Civil/Structural Engineer, and processed by Athanasios Tsanas from the Oxford Centre for Industrial and Applied Mathematics, University of Oxford. It is now publicly available on Kaggle. The dataset consists of 768 samples and 8 features that represent various building characteristics, such as surface area, wall area, and roof area. The goal is to predict either the heating load or the cooling load required for the building. In this demonstration, we will focus on using cooling load as the dependent variable, which is measured in KW/m^2. This unit reflects the amount of energy required per unit area to cool the building.

The step-by-step approach for implementing ANN as a Regressor is explored in the following section. Let us load the dataset and perform similar pre-processing steps as we did for the KNN Regressor in *Chapter 7, Distance-Based Machine Learning Models*.

```
import pandas as pd
import matplotlib.pyplot as plt
import seaborn as sns
from sklearn.preprocessing import StandardScaler
from sklearn.neighbors import MLPRegressor
from sklearn.model_selection import KFold, train_test_split
from sklearn.metrics import r2_score
import numpy as np
# Load the dataset
df = pd.read_csv('file_path/data2_Ch7_energy_dataset.csv')
df.head()
```

	X1	X2	X3	X4	X5	X6	X7	X8	Y1	Y2
0	0.98	514.5	294.0	110.25	7.0	2	0.0	0	15.55	21.33
1	0.98	514.5	294.0	110.25	7.0	3	0.0	0	15.55	21.33
2	0.98	514.5	294.0	110.25	7.0	4	0.0	0	15.55	21.33
3	0.98	514.5	294.0	110.25	7.0	5	0.0	0	15.55	21.33
4	0.90	563.5	318.5	122.50	7.0	2	0.0	0	20.84	28.28

Figure 10.6: *Head of the Data*

```
# Drop the column 'Y1'
df = df.drop(columns=['Y1'])
# Bucketize the categories in 'X8'
df['X8'] = df['X8'].apply(lambda x: 1 if x in [1, 2, 3, 4, 5] else 0)
# Drop the column 'X6'
df = df.drop(columns=['X6'])
# Define X with all features except the last column (class)
X = df.iloc[:, :-1]
# Define Y as the last column (class)
Y = df.iloc[:, -1]
# Initialize the StandardScaler
scaler = StandardScaler()
# Scale X and keep it in X_std
X_std = scaler.fit_transform(X)
xtrain,xtest,ytrain,ytest=train_test_split(X_std,Y,test_size=0.3,random_state=0)
```

The hidden layer neurons were manually tuned to achieve optimal performance for the regression task. After experimenting with various configurations, the following architecture provided the best results.

```
ANN=MLPRegressor(hidden_layer_sizes=(50,50,50,50,50,60),activation='relu',batch_size=20,random_state=1)
ANN.fit(xtrain,ytrain)
y_pred = ANN.predict(xtest)
# Calculate RMSE and R^2 score
rmse = np.sqrt(np.mean((ytest - y_pred) ** 2))
r2 = r2_score(ytest, y_pred)
print([rmse, r2])
[1.694,0.9681]
```

When we applied KNN as a Regressor to this dataset, it produced a Root Mean Squared Error (RMSE) of 1.749 KW/m², indicating that, on average, the model's predictions deviate from the actual cooling load values by 1.749 KW/m². The R-squared (R^2) score was 0.966, suggesting that the KNN model explains 96.6% of the variance in the cooling load, indicating a strong fit to the data. However, when we implemented the same task using a multi-layer Artificial Neural Network (ANN) model, the performance improved slightly. The ANN model achieved an RMSE of 1.694 KW/m² and an R-squared (R^2) score of 0.9681, showing a marginal improvement over KNN. This improvement highlights the ability of ANN to capture non-linear relationships more effectively, even though the performance gain is subtle.

Challenges in Traditional Neural Networks

While we have explored multi-layer feedforward ANN models for solving both classification and regression problems on tabular data, it is important to acknowledge that traditional ANN models often struggle to outperform other machine learning models such as K-Nearest Neighbors (KNN), Decision Trees, Random Forests, and Support Vector Machines (SVMs). These models possess similar capabilities when it comes to handling non-linear problems and, in some cases, can perform more efficiently on tabular data, especially when the dataset is not too large or complex. Despite the flexibility of ANNs in learning from data, traditional ANNs have not stood out as a clear superior option in the landscape of machine learning for many of these tasks, particularly when simpler and more interpretable models can achieve similar results.

One of the key limitations of traditional ANNs, specifically Multi-Layer Perceptrons (MLPs), is their performance on structured tabular data, where they may not provide significant improvements over the aforementioned algorithms. In this context, models such as Random Forest and SVM can often perform better due to their ease of interpretability, lower computational costs, and ability to handle non-linearities efficiently. This is one reason why traditional ANN models, while powerful in theory, did not make significant advancements in practical applications in the early stages of AI development.

The landscape of artificial intelligence began to shift in the early 2000s when the focus of research and industry moved toward unstructured data, such as images, videos, and text, rather than structured tabular data. Traditional ANN models such as MLPs were not well-suited to handle this new demand due to their limitations in effectively capturing spatial or sequential information, which is often present in unstructured data. However, the introduction of Convolutional Neural Networks (CNNs) fundamentally changed the perception of neural networks. CNNs, with their ability to capture local patterns and hierarchical structures in data such as images and videos, revolutionized the AI field. CNNs demonstrated that neural networks could excel in domains where traditional machine learning models struggled, paving the way for the deep learning era.

At the same time, the industry saw significant advancements in Graphics Processing Unit (GPU) technology. GPUs, with their parallel processing capabilities, were far better suited for the heavy computational demands of training deep neural networks, particularly CNNs. Before the widespread adoption of GPUs, training deep neural networks was prohibitively slow, limiting their practical use. The confluence of improved hardware (GPUs) and the development of CNNs created the perfect storm for deep learning to take off. This evolution allowed neural networks to handle increasingly complex tasks involving vast amounts of data and deeper network architectures.

Prior to these advancements, the classical MLP models of ANN struggled to gain significant traction. Despite their theoretical promise, MLPs were limited by their inability to efficiently process high-dimensional unstructured data, such as images or videos, and were outperformed by models better suited for structured data. The turning point came when the industry recognized the potential of deep networks, such as CNNs, which were capable of processing unstructured data in a way that traditional models could not. CNNs' ability to extract hierarchical features from images and videos made them indispensable for applications such as image recognition, video analysis, and even natural language processing when combined with other architectures.

Furthermore, deep learning became a dominant force as the AI community shifted focus from shallow networks such as MLPs to deeper architectures that could learn increasingly abstract representations from data. The limitations of traditional neural networks in handling complex tasks were gradually overcome as CNNs and other deep learning models continued to evolve.

Despite the rise of advanced neural network architectures such as CNNs, the feedforward layer, specifically the classical Multi-Layer Perceptron (MLP), continues to play a crucial role in decision-making within deep learning models. In many state-of-the-art models, particularly those used for image recognition or object detection, CNN layers are primarily responsible for feature extraction. These convolutional layers act as automatic feature engineers, progressively learning hierarchical features from raw data, such as edges, textures, and complex shapes in images.

However, after these features are extracted and processed through multiple convolutional layers, they are typically flattened into a vector form and passed through one or more fully connected (feedforward) layers. In this stage, the feedforward network functions as the decision-making component of the model, transforming the learned features into meaningful outputs. For tasks such as image classification, the feedforward layer outputs probability scores for each class, helping the model determine the most likely category for a given input. Similarly, in more complex tasks such as object detection and localization, the feedforward network outputs logit scores or net values, which are used to predict bounding boxes for objects in images. This shows that, while convolutional layers handle the bulk of feature extraction, the feedforward MLP remains essential in translating those features into actionable decisions, and its role will be further explored in the upcoming chapters.

Evolution of Technology Stack and Structured Data

Traditional neural networks were developed in an era where computational power, data storage, and processing capabilities were significantly limited, restricting their ability to handle complex patterns or large-scale unstructured data. By examining the evolution of technology stacks and data processing methodologies, we can better appreciate the obstacles faced by early neural networks and how these challenges paved the way for the development of modern architectures and frameworks. Understanding this progression helps contextualize why traditional neural networks struggled with scalability, adaptability, and performance in real-world scenarios and highlights the advancements that have enabled their resurgence in contemporary AI applications. The following figure reflects the transition from traditional technology stacks and data handling approaches to contemporary practices, highlighting the advancements.

Era	Technology Stack	Data Characteristics	Challenges	Modern Advancements
1970s - 1980s	Mainframe Systems, Rule-Based Systems	Small, Structured Tabular Data	Limited processing power, reliance on human-crafted rules.	Introduction of relational databases and SQL for structured data management.
1990s - Early 2000s	Client-Server Architecture, Statistical Models	Structured Data with Simple Features	Difficulty scaling and capturing complex relationships in data.	Rise of machine learning algorithms (e.g., Decision Trees, SVMs) for improved predictions on structured data.
2010s	Big Data Tools (Hadoop, Spark), GPUs	Large, Semi-Structured, and Unstructured Data	Inability of traditional statistical models to handle high-dimensional data.	Emergence of Neural Networks and deep learning frameworks (e.g., TensorFlow, PyTorch) to process complex data.
2020s and Beyond	Cloud Computing, Pre-trained Models, MLOps	Heterogeneous, Multi-Modal Data	Managing real-time insights and end-to-end AI/ML pipelines.	Use of pre-trained CNNs, RNNs, and transformers to solve image, speech, and text processing challenges.

Figure 10.7: Evolution of Technology Stack and Data Processing

This transition has not only overcome the limitations of traditional approaches but also paved the way for more sophisticated architectures capable of handling real-world problems across diverse domains. Through this transition, we will explore how CNNs have become the cornerstone of modern AI applications in the following chapter.

Conclusion

In this chapter, we explored the foundational principles of training neural networks, focusing on the critical role played by gradient descent and the backpropagation algorithm in optimizing model weights. These algorithms enable neural networks to learn from data by minimizing the loss function and improving performance iteratively.

We also discussed the importance of fine-tuning model parameters to achieve optimal results and demonstrated how to code neural networks in Python using scikit-learn, providing a practical understanding of the implementation process. The challenges faced by traditional neural networks, particularly in handling unstructured data, were highlighted, paving the way for more advanced architectures.

With the rise of deep learning models and the introduction of CNNs, the limitations of classical ANNs were overcome, revolutionizing AI's ability to process complex data. In the next chapter, we will delve into the world of deep learning models, exploring their capabilities and applications in detail.

Practice Exercise

1. Consider a neural network with one output neuron and two hidden neurons in the hidden layer. The weights from the input to the hidden layer are $w_1=0.4$ and $w_2=-0.2$, and the weights from the hidden layer to the output are $v_1=0.3$ and $v_2=-0.5$. If the target output is 1 and the v_1 and predicted output from the network is 0.6, calculate the gradient of the loss with respect to v_1 and v_2 using backpropagation. Assume the hidden activations are $h_1=0.7$ and $h_2=0.3$.

2. Suppose a neuron in a hidden layer has an incoming weight of $w=0.5$, and after calculating the gradient of the loss with respect to the weight, you obtain $\frac{\partial L}{\partial w} = -0.3$. If the learning rate is $\eta=0.01$, what will the updated weight be after one iteration of gradient descent?

3. A neural network is trained on a dataset containing 10,000 samples. If the batch size is set to 50, how many iterations (or updates) will the model perform in one epoch of training?

4. A neuron in a network uses the sigmoid activation function $\sigma(z) = \frac{1}{1+e^{-z}}$. Given an input value of $z=0.8$, calculate the derivative of the sigmoid function at this point $\sigma'(z)$.

5. Consider a binary classification problem where the target output is $y=1$ and the predicted probability from the model is $\hat{y} = 0.7$. Using the binary cross-entropy loss function $L= -[y.\log(\hat{y})+(1-y).\log(1-\hat{y})]$. Calculate the value of the loss.

Answers

1. −(1−0.6) x 0.7=−0.4 x 0.7=−0.28; −(1−0.6)x0.3=−0.4x0.3=−0.12
2. 0.5−0.01x(−0.3)=0.503
3. (Total Samples)/(Batch Size)= 10000/50 =200
4. $\sigma(0.8) = \frac{1}{1+e^{-0.8}} = 0.68997$; $\sigma'(0.8) = 0.68997 \times (1-0.68997) = 0.21398$
5. 0.3567

Multiple Choice Questions

1. What is the key function of the backpropagation algorithm in training neural networks?

    a. To initialize the weights of the network

    b. To update weights by minimizing the loss function

    c. To classify input data into categories

    d. To prevent overfitting by regularizing the model

2. Which of the following is crucial in controlling how much a model's weights are updated during training?

    a. Batch size

    b. Epochs

    c. Learning rate

    d. Activation function

3. What is the primary reason for fine-tuning hyperparameters in a neural network?

    a. To increase the number of hidden layers

    b. To adjust learning rates and prevent overfitting

    c. To decrease the training time

    d. To remove irrelevant features from the input data

4. In neural networks, which component helps determine how frequently the model's weights are updated?

    a. Number of neurons

    b. Batch size

c. Number of layers

   d. Loss function

5. Which of the following challenges is most common in traditional neural networks when handling unstructured data?

   a. High computation cost

   b. Inability to solve regression problems

   c. Difficulty in capturing spatial patterns

   d. Overfitting in all situations

6. What is the main purpose of weight initialization in training neural networks?

   a. To ensure the model converges faster

   b. To avoid using activation functions

   c. To increase the complexity of the model

   d. To improve the visualization of data

7. Which of the following optimizers is most commonly associated with improving gradient descent performance?

   a. Adam

   b. RMSprop

   c. Adagrad

   d. All of the above

8. In scikit-learn, which model is used for creating feedforward neural networks for regression tasks?

   a. MLP Classifier

   b. Decision Tree Regressor

   c. MLP Regressor

   d. Random Forest Classifier

9. Which activation function is often used in the hidden layers of a neural network to introduce non-linearity?

   a. Softmax

   b. ReLU

c. Sigmoid

d. Linear

10. Why do we use batch size during training?

    a. To increase model complexity

    b. To process a subset of the data in each iteration, improving efficiency

    c. To prevent the model from using activation functions

    d. To initialize weights in the network

Answers

1. b
2. c
3. b
4. b
5. c
6. a
7. d
8. c
9. b
10. b

Keywords

- Artificial Neural Networks (ANNs)
- Gradient Descent Learning
- Cost Function/Loss Function
- Cross Entropy
- Learning Rate
- Backpropagation
- Chain Rule
- Weight Update
- Optimization

- Scikit-Learn
- ANN as a Classifier
- ANN as a Regressor
- Multi-Layer Perceptron (MLP)
- Training
- Model Evaluation
- Regularization
- Validation/Testing
- Root Mean Squared Error
- R-Squared Value
- Cross Validation
- Convolutional Neural Networks (CNN)
- Feature Extraction
- Deep Learning
- Object Detection
- Bounding Box Regressor

References

1. https://cs.stanford.edu/people/karpathy/convnetjs/demo/classify2d.html
2. https://playground.tensorflow.org/
3. http://karpathy.github.io/neuralnets/

CHAPTER 11
Introduction to Convolutional Neural Networks

Introduction

This chapter takes readers into the transformative world of Convolutional Neural Networks (CNNs), a key architecture in deep learning designed specifically to handle unstructured data, such as images, videos, text, and speech. The chapter begins by discussing the evolution of neural networks from handling structured tabular data to the development of advanced techniques that allow for effective processing of unstructured data types.

We then transitioned to the Introduction of CNNs, which revolutionized the way neural networks process visual and sequential data. Readers will learn about the unique architecture of CNNs, how they differ from traditional feed forward neural networks, and why they are so effective in recognizing patterns within images and other forms of unstructured data.

The chapter also explores the role of filters in CNNs, where small learnable kernels slide over the input data to capture essential features, such as edges, textures, and shapes. Additionally, the chapter covers essential operations such as max pooling, which helps reduce the dimensionality of feature maps, and the ReLU activation function, which introduces non-linearity to the network and improves its ability to learn complex patterns. By the end of this chapter, readers will gain a solid foundational understanding of CNNs, including the fundamental operations and structures that make them indispensable in modern-machine learning applications.

Structure

In this chapter, we are going to cover the following main topics:

- Evolution of Neural Networks for Unstructured Data, such as Image, Video, Text, and Speech
- Introduction of Convolutional Neural Networks (CNN)
- Role of Filters in CNN
- Role of ReLU Activation Function

Evolution of Neural Networks for Unstructured Data

The evolution of neural networks for unstructured data, such as images, video, text, and speech, represents a pivotal shift in the field of machine learning. Traditional feed forward neural networks and earlier models such as multilayer perceptrons (MLPs) were initially limited in their ability to handle structured data such as tabular data with fixed input dimensions. However, as the need to process more complex and unstructured data types such as images, audio, and text grew, the limitations of traditional models became apparent. The introduction of Convolutional Neural Networks (CNNs) marked a major breakthrough in neural network development, enabling models to effectively process unstructured data and opening up new possibilities for artificial intelligence applications.

The early work on neural networks for image data can be traced back to the late 1980s when Yann LeCun and his colleagues at AT&T Bell Labs introduced the LeNet-5 architecture. This model was designed for handwritten digit recognition and played a significant role in the development of CNNs for image data. LeNet-5 introduced key concepts, such as convolutional layers and pooling layers, which became fundamental components of CNNs. The architecture demonstrated the power of CNNs to automatically learn hierarchical features from pixel data, significantly outperforming traditional methods in image recognition tasks. The success of LeNet-5 provided the foundation for further advancements in deep learning for unstructured data.

The research in CNNs for image data surged as computational power increased and large datasets became more accessible. One of the most significant milestones came in 2012 when Alex Krizhevsky, Ilya Sutskever, and Geoffrey Hinton from the University of Toronto introduced the AlexNet model. AlexNet won the ImageNet Large Scale Visual Recognition Challenge (ILSVRC) by a large margin, reducing the error rate to nearly half of the previous best-performing model. The success of AlexNet demonstrated the effectiveness of deeper and more complex CNN architectures for image classification, driven by the availability of large labeled datasets (such as ImageNet) and the use of

Graphics Processing Units (GPUs) for training. AlexNet's success is widely recognized as the moment that sparked the deep learning revolution in computer vision.

While 2D CNNs proved highly successful in image classification, the need to handle video data where both spatial and temporal information is important led to further adaptations of CNN architectures. The extension of CNNs to video data was addressed through the development of 3D Convolutional Neural Networks (3D CNNs), which apply convolutional operations across both spatial and temporal dimensions. This allowed models to capture motion and changes over time, making 3D CNNs particularly effective in tasks such as action recognition and video classification. Significant contributions to this area were made by Karen Simonyan and Andrew Zisserman from the Visual Geometry Group (VGG) at the University of Oxford, whose work on Two-Stream CNNs in 2014 further advanced video classification by combining spatial and temporal streams to handle motion information.

In parallel, CNNs also evolved to handle time series data, such as speech, audio, and music. These types of data are often represented as sequences, making 1D CNNs particularly suitable for processing them. One of the earliest applications of CNNs in speech recognition was pioneered by George Dahl and his colleagues at the University of Toronto in 2011, where they demonstrated how CNNs could be applied to acoustic modeling in speech recognition systems. Unlike 2D CNNs, which work on grid-like structures such as images, 1D CNNs operate on one-dimensional sequential data, making them ideal for tasks involving audio signals, music analysis, and other time-dependent data. These networks are capable of capturing temporal dependencies and identifying patterns over time, allowing them to excel in tasks such as speech recognition and music genre classification.

The adaptation of CNNs for speech recognition, along with advancements in deep learning frameworks such as TensorFlow and PyTorch, accelerated the development of robust models for handling audio and speech data. Research labs such as Google Brain and academic institutions such as Carnegie Mellon University (CMU) made significant contributions to the development of deep learning models for natural language processing (NLP) and speech recognition. For instance, Google's WaveNet model, introduced in 2016, utilized CNNs for high-quality audio generation, revolutionizing speech synthesis and pushing the boundaries of audio-based neural network applications.

As CNNs matured, their ability to process unstructured data expanded beyond vision and audio into the realm of text and natural language. The architecture of CNNs was adapted for tasks such as text classification, sentiment analysis, and document classification, where CNNs helped capture local dependencies and extract important features from sequential data. Pioneering work by researchers such as Yoon Kim from Harvard University in 2014 showcased how CNNs could outperform traditional NLP methods such as recurrent neural networks (RNNs) in certain tasks, especially those involving text classification. Kim's work demonstrated that CNNs could efficiently model the local features of text, such as n-grams, and provided a computationally efficient alternative to RNNs in many NLP applications. The significant milestones in CNN development are illustrated in *Figure 11.1*.

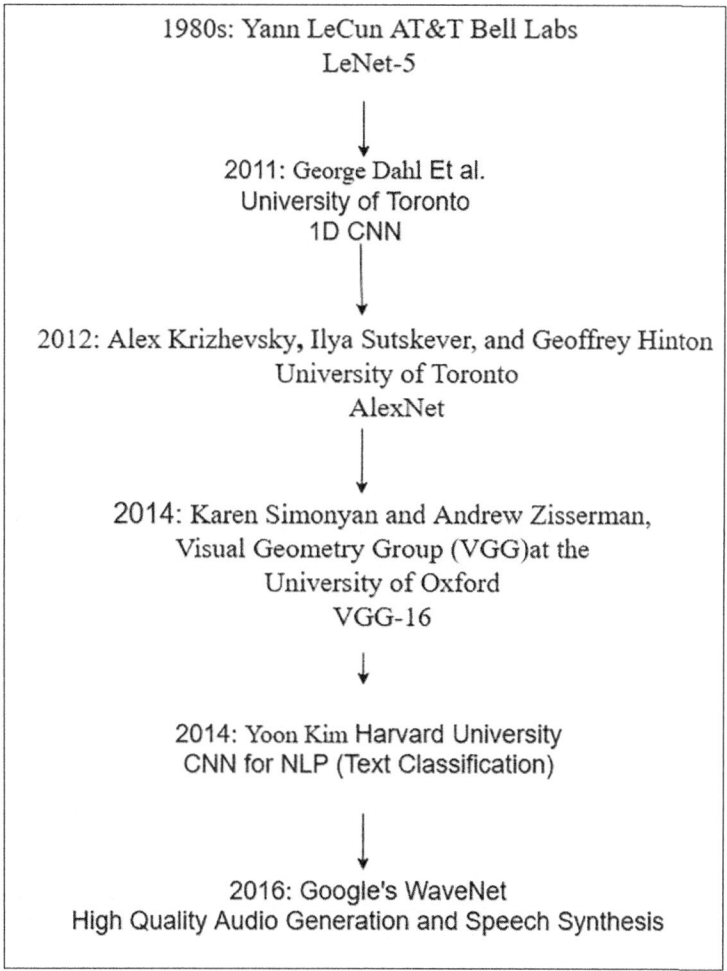

Figure 11.1: *Significant Milestones in CNN Development*

Introduction of Convolutional Neural Networks (CNNs)

Convolutional Neural Networks (CNNs) have revolutionized deep learning by enabling models to excel at processing unstructured data, such as images, video, and audio. Unlike traditional feedforward neural networks, CNNs are designed to automatically detect spatial hierarchies in data through specialized operations such as convolution and pooling. In this section, we will explore the core components of CNNs, including the mathematical operations behind convolution, the role of filters and padding, max pooling, ReLU activation, and the flattening step in CNN architecture.

Convolution Operations in CNN

At the heart of a CNN is the convolution operation, which helps extract features, such as edges, textures, and patterns from input data. Mathematically, the convolution operation involves sliding a small matrix (filter) over the input image or data to compute a weighted sum of the input values. This operation can be represented as:

$$z(i,j) = \sum_m \cdot \sum_n I(i+m, j+n) * K(m,n)$$

Where:

I(i,j) is the input image matrix

K(m,n) is the filter (or kernel) matrix

z(i,j) is the resulting convolved feature map

The filter size in CNNs, typically ranging from 3×3 to 5×5, plays a crucial role in determining how much local information the network considers at each step of the convolution process. A smaller filter, such as 3×3, captures fine-grained details, such as edges or small textures, making it suitable for identifying intricate patterns in the input data. On the other hand, a larger filter, such as 5×5, captures broader features, such as larger shapes or textures, enabling the network to understand more extensive structures. The size of the filter directly influences how much of the input is "seen" at once by the convolutional layer.

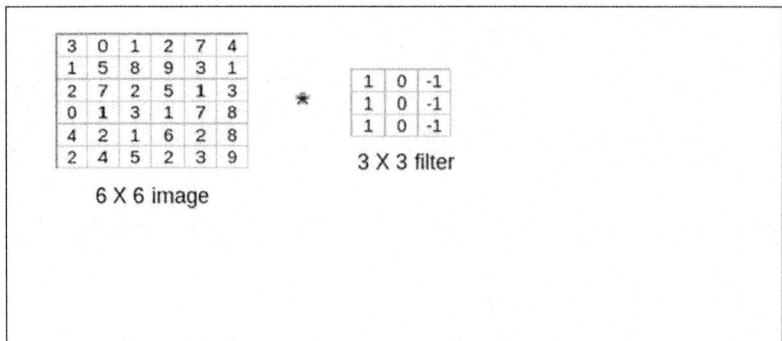

Figure 11.2: *Image and filter representation*

Consider a representative 6×6 image and a 3×3 filter, as shown in *Figure* 11.2. The convolution operation involves sliding a 3×3 filter over the 6×6 image, performing element-wise multiplication, and summing the results at each step. To demonstrate

Introduction to Convolutional Neural Networks

the calculation for the top-left corner of the image as shown in *Figure* 11.3, place the 3×3 filter on the top-left corner of the 6×6 image and perform element-wise multiplication between the overlapping elements of the filter and the image, then sum the result as follows:

$$(3\times1) + (1\times1) + (2\times1) + (0\times0) + (5\times0) + (7\times0) + (1\times-1) + (8\times-1) + (2\times-1) = -5.$$

```
Image Block:          Filter:
3  0  1               1  0  -1
1  5  8               1  0  -1
2  7  2               1  0  -1
```

Figure 11.3: *Top-left corner representation*

The result of each operation forms an element in the convolved output matrix, as shown in *Figure 11.4*.

-5	-4	0	8
-10	-2	2	3
0	-2	-4	-7
-3	-2	-3	-16

Figure 11.4: *Convolved output matrix*

One of the key strengths of CNNs is their ability to apply multiple filters at each convolutional layer. Each filter detects a different set of features, such as edges, gradients, corners, or textures, allowing the network to learn a wide variety of representations from the input. These filters act like feature detectors, automatically learning the most relevant characteristics from the data without manual feature engineering. By stacking multiple layers of filters, CNNs progressively build hierarchical representations of the data. In early layers, the filters capture low-level features (for example, edges), while in deeper layers, the filters capture more complex structures, such as shapes or objects. This ability to learn hierarchical features is one of the reasons CNNs perform so well in tasks such as image recognition and object detection.

However, as the convolution operation progresses through the layers, the spatial dimensions of the feature map tend to decrease. This shrinking of dimensions can lead to a loss of crucial spatial information, especially in deeper layers where the network is expected to capture high-level features. To address this, padding is applied to the input data as shown in *Figure 11.5*. The padding adds extra rows and columns of zeros around the border of the input matrix, allowing the network to maintain the original spatial dimensions of the data. By preserving the spatial size, padding ensures that the network can apply multiple convolutions without reducing the size of the feature maps too quickly, which could otherwise lead to the loss of important edge or boundary information.

```
0  0  0  0  0  0  0  0
0  3  0  1  2  7  4  0
0  1  5  8  9  3  1  0
0  2  7  2  5  1  3  0
0  0  1  3  1  7  8  0
0  4  2  1  6  2  8  0
0  2  4  5  2  3  9  0
0  0  0  0  0  0  0  0
```

Figure 11.5: Input image after zero padding

We will slide the 3×3 filter used earlier over the 8×8 padded image and compute the element-wise product and sum, just like we did earlier. Let us go through the first couple of steps as an example. Starting with the top-left corner of the padded matrix (first 3×3 block) as shown in *Figure 11.6*:

```
Image Block:        Filter:
0  0  0             1  0  -1
0  3  0             1  0  -1
0  1  5             1  0  -1
```

Figure 11.6: Top-left corner representation after padding

Element-wise multiplication and sum: (0×1)+(0×0)+(0×−1)+(0×1)+(3×0)+(0×−1)+(0×1)+(1×0)+(5×−1) = −5

Move the filter one step to the right:

(0×1)+(0×0)+(0×−1)+(3×1)+(0×0)+(1×−1)+(1×1)+(5×0)+(8×−1) = −5

In a similar way, we can slide over the entire image to get the convolved response equal to the size of input image 8×8.

Understanding Strides in Convolution Operation

The stride in a convolution operation refers to the number of steps the filter moves across the input data during the convolution process. A stride of 1 means the filter moves one pixel at a time, while a stride of 2 moves the filter two pixels at a time, and so on. The stride has a direct impact on the size of the output feature map, as it controls how much the input data is "sampled" during the convolution. In this convolution operation, we used a stride of 1. This means that for each step, the filter moves one position to the right across the image matrix, and once it reaches the end of the row, it moves one step down to the next row.

Mathematically, the relationship between the stride and the output dimensions is given by:

$$O = \frac{(I - F + 2P)}{S} + 1$$

Where S is the stride. A smaller stride results in more overlap between the filter positions, producing a larger output feature map that retains more spatial details from the input. Conversely, a larger stride skips more positions, resulting in a smaller feature map that captures less detailed but more abstract information.

Impact of Small Versus Large Strides

A small stride ensures that the filter examines every possible position in the input, leading to a dense feature map with high spatial resolution. This is particularly useful when working with data that contains fine-grained details, such as medical images or satellite images, where preserving local features is critical. However, smaller strides increase computational complexity since the network has to process more overlapping regions.

A larger stride reduces the overlap between filter positions, resulting in a more compact feature map. This can be advantageous when working with high-resolution inputs or when a reduction in spatial dimensions is desirable to manage computational costs. For instance, in real-time applications such as video analysis or edge devices with limited processing power, larger strides can help reduce latency by simplifying the network's computations. However, this comes at the cost of losing some fine-grained spatial details.

The choice of stride depends on the task and the nature of the input data. Smaller strides are typically used in the early layers of a CNN to capture intricate patterns and preserve spatial information. Larger strides are more commonly used in deeper layers or in architectures designed for tasks, such as object detection, where reducing the feature map size helps focus on higher-level abstractions. Strides, along with filter size and padding, must be carefully tuned during experimentation to balance computational efficiency and model performance effectively.

Max Pooling Layer in CNN

After the convolution operation, the next key step in a CNN is often a max pooling layer. The purpose of max pooling is to reduce the spatial dimensions of the feature maps (height and width) while retaining the most important features. This process helps reduce the computational load, prevents overfitting, and makes the network more robust to small distortions and translations in the input. In a max pooling operation, a small window (usually 2×2 or 3×3) slides over the feature map, similar to the way a filter does in convolution. However, instead of performing a weighted sum, the max pooling operation selects the maximum value from the window. For example, in a 2×2 max pooling window, the highest value within each 2×2 region of the feature map is retained, and the other values are discarded.

Consider the feature map we have obtained in the earlier section, shown in *Figure 11.4*. If we apply a 2×2 max pooling window, we retain the following values as shown in *Table 11.1*:

-2	8
0	-3

Table 11.1: *Feature Map after Max pooling*

Thus, after max pooling, the spatial dimensions of the feature map are reduced, but the most dominant features in each region are retained.

Importance of Max pooling

Max pooling is an essential layer in CNNs because it reduces the spatial size of feature maps while retaining important information.

- **Dimensionality Reduction**: Max pooling reduces the size of the feature maps, which lowers the computational cost for the network. Smaller feature maps mean fewer parameters in the subsequent layers, making the model more efficient and faster to train.

- **Feature Preservation**: By taking the maximum value in each window, max pooling retains the most prominent or important features while discarding less important information. This allows the network to focus on key aspects of the data, such as edges or patterns in images.

- **Translation Invariance**: Max pooling makes CNNs more robust to small shifts or distortions in the input. For example, if an object in an image is slightly shifted or rotated, max pooling ensure that the key features (such as edges or shapes) are still detected, even if they appear in slightly different positions.

- **Overfitting Prevention**: By reducing the number of parameters in the network, max pooling helps prevent overfitting, especially in cases where the network might otherwise memorize noise or irrelevant details in the training data.

The next step after max pooling is to transition from the spatial representation of features to a format suitable for decision-making. This requires flattening the 2D feature maps into a single one-dimensional vector that can serve as input to the fully connected layers. In the flatten layer, we reorganize the extracted features into a vector format without losing any valuable information. Let us take a detailed look into the functionality and importance of the flatten layer in the next section.

Flatten Layer

The flatten layer in a CNN acts as a bridge between the convolutional and pooling layers, which extract features from the input data, and the fully connected layers, which perform the final classification or regression tasks. After a series of convolution and pooling operations, the data is represented as a multi-dimensional array of features (feature maps). To feed these features into a fully connected layer, the flatten operation converts the multi-dimensional feature maps into a single-dimensional vector.

Importance of Flattening

Flattening ensures that all of the learned features from the convolutional and pooling layers are preserved and passed on to the fully connected layers for final decision-making.

- **Dimensional Transition**: It transitions data from the structured, multi-dimensional format used in convolutional layers to the one-dimensional format required for the fully connected layers.
- **Feature Representation**: The flattened vector retains all the learned features from the previous layers, making them accessible for higher-level processing and decision-making.
- **Input to Fully Connected Layers**: Without flattening, the fully connected layers cannot process the extracted features, making this step essential for model architecture.

For example, if the output of a pooling layer is a feature map of size 4×4×8 (height, width, and depth), flattening this feature map produces a vector of size 4×4×8=128, which becomes the input for the next layer.

After flattening, the extracted 1D features are ready to be processed for decision-making. The next step involves connecting these features to a classical feedforward neural network, where the network determines the appropriate decision based on the learned patterns. This fully connected layer enables the model to classify the image or make predictions depending on the task at hand. Let us explore the functionality and significance of this layer in detail in the next subsection.

Fully Connected FeedForward Layer

The fully connected layer is the final component of a CNN, where the network consolidates the features learned from earlier layers to make predictions. This layer is equivalent to the layers in traditional feedforward neural networks, where each neuron is connected to every neuron in the previous layer. It takes the flattened vector from the preceding layer as input and outputs either probability scores for classification tasks or continuous values for regression tasks.

Steps in Fully Connected Layers

1. **Feature Consolidation:** The input from the flatten layer is multiplied with weights and added to biases, followed by the application of activation functions. This operation aggregates the features learned by the network.

2. **Prediction:** For classification, the final output layer often uses a softmax activation function to convert raw scores into probabilities for each class. For regression tasks, no activation or linear activation is used to produce continuous outputs.

Example:

In an image classification task with three categories (for example, Cat, Dog, and Rabbit), the fully connected layer will output three values corresponding to the probability of the input belonging to each category. The class with the highest probability is selected as the model's prediction.

Importance of Fully Connected Layers

The main function of the fully connected layers is to make decisions based on the features learned by the convolutional layers.

- **Decision Making**: These layers transform learned features into actionable outcomes, such as class probabilities or regression outputs.
- **Generalization**: Fully connected layers enable the network to generalize learned patterns to unseen data, making the model robust.
- **Integration**: They consolidate the hierarchical features learned from convolutional layers into a meaningful prediction.

Together, the flatten and fully connected layers mark the transition from feature extraction to decision-making in CNNs. While convolutional and pooling layers focus on detecting patterns and reducing spatial dimensions, these layers ensure that the learned features are transformed into accurate predictions or classifications, completing the CNN pipeline.

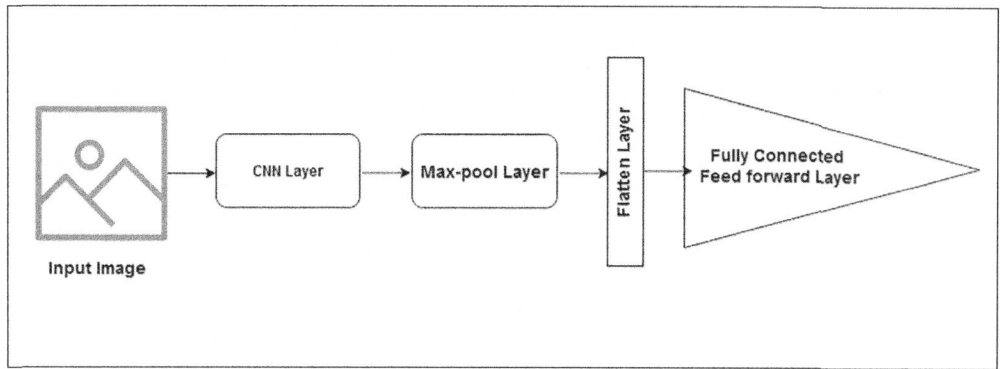

Figure 11.7: *End-to-End Architecture of CNN*

Figure 11.7 depicts the complete workflow of the CNN steps we have discussed, illustrating how the input image progresses through convolution, pooling, flattening, and fully connected layers to generate the final output. The flow diagram indicates a single convolutional layer followed by max pooling. However, in real-world problems, different configurations are often used, such as a series of convolutional layers followed by max pooling or multiple convolutional layers before applying one max pool operation. The choice of configuration depends on how well the layers represent the features of the input image. During the training process, experimentation with various configurations allows us to determine the optimal setup that best captures the essential patterns and delivers the highest performance for the given task.

Role of Filters in CNN

Although we have already discussed convolutional operations using 2D filters or kernel functions, it is essential to delve deeper into the scope and role of filters in CNNs. Filters, essentially 2D representations of traditional neural network weights, play a critical role in feature extraction. Before the advent of CNNs, researchers relied heavily on hand-curated feature engineering for image processing tasks, which required significant domain expertise in computer vision. CNNs revolutionized this approach by enabling automatic feature extraction. Through gradient descent learning, CNNs update these filters (2D weights) dynamically, allowing them to adapt to the patterns in the data without manual intervention.

Filters in CNNs are designed to capture specific patterns or features within the input image. For instance, a filter might detect vertical edges, horizontal edges, or textures such as corners and curves. During the convolution operation, the filter slides over the input image, computing dot products between the filter values and the overlapping input pixels. The resulting feature map highlights regions of the image where the filter detects its specific pattern. Multiple filters are applied in each convolutional layer, enabling the network to capture a wide variety of low-level and high-level features, such as edges in the initial layers and complex shapes in deeper layers.

One of the most significant advantages of filters in CNNs is their ability to maintain spatial relationships within an image. Unlike fully connected layers, which treat inputs as flat vectors, convolutional layers use filters to preserve the spatial structure of the data. This enables CNNs to effectively analyze visual patterns such as the arrangement of pixels in an image, making them particularly suited for tasks such as image recognition and object detection. Filters also enable parameter sharing, where the same filter is used across different parts of the input, reducing the number of trainable parameters and improving computational efficiency.

The size of the filter significantly impacts the features it captures. Smaller filters such as 3×3, focus on fine details and local patterns while larger filters such as 5×5 or 7×7 capture broader and more global patterns. The choice of filter size depends on the nature of the input data and the desired features. For instance, smaller filters are commonly used in deeper networks to progressively refine features, while larger filters may be suitable for capturing global context in earlier layers. Experimentation during training helps identify the most effective filter sizes for a specific problem.

Filters in CNNs are initialized with random weights and are refined during the training process through backpropagation and gradient descent. During training, the network adjusts the filter weights to minimize the loss function, optimizing its ability to detect meaningful features in the input data. This automatic learning of filter weights is a significant departure from traditional image processing methods, where filters were manually designed and fixed. By learning from data, CNN filters adapt to diverse datasets and tasks without requiring domain-specific feature engineering.

The depth of a convolutional layer determines the number of filters applied, with each filter producing a separate feature map. For example, a convolutional layer with 64 filters will generate 64 feature maps, each highlighting a different aspect of the input data. These feature maps are then passed to subsequent layers, where additional filters refine and combine the extracted features to build hierarchical representations. This process enables CNNs to transition from detecting simple edges to recognizing complex objects or patterns.

Role of ReLU Activation Function in CNNs

The Rectified Linear Unit (ReLU) activation function is a pivotal component in CNNs, enabling the network to model complex, non-linear relationships within data. By introducing non-linearity, ReLU transforms the linear operations performed during convolution into a form capable of capturing intricate patterns and dependencies. Without activation functions such as ReLU, CNNs would be equivalent to linear models, significantly limiting their ability to handle real-world tasks such as image recognition or object detection.

Mathematically, the ReLU activation function is expressed as:

$$f(x) = max\,(0, x)$$

This means that any negative value in the feature map is replaced with zero, while positive values remain unchanged. This simple yet powerful operation ensures that the network remains computationally efficient while discarding irrelevant or less important features represented by negative values.

One of the key benefits of ReLU is its ability to mitigate the vanishing gradient problem, a common issue in deep networks where gradients become too small during backpropagation, hindering effective weight updates. Unlike sigmoid or tanh activations, which compress values into a bounded range and cause gradients to diminish, ReLU preserves a strong gradient for positive inputs. This characteristic allows CNNs to learn faster and converge more effectively during training, particularly in deeper architectures with multiple layers.

ReLU also introduces sparsity into the network. By setting negative values to zero, it effectively reduces the number of active neurons, resulting in a sparse representation of the data. This sparsity enhances the network's computational efficiency by reducing the number of calculations required and helps mitigate overfitting by preventing the network from relying too heavily on any specific feature. Sparse activations force the network to generalize better, improving its ability to handle unseen data.

In CNN layers, ReLU is typically applied after the convolution operation to introduce non-linearity and enable the network to capture complex features. For example, after a convolutional layer extracts features, such as edges or corners, applying ReLU ensures that only the most relevant features are passed to the next layer. This activation step helps highlight the features that contribute positively to the task at hand, such as identifying objects in an image.

ReLU's simplicity also makes it computationally efficient compared to other activation functions. It involves a straightforward thresholding operation, requiring minimal computational overhead, which is particularly important in large-scale networks or when processing high-dimensional data such as images or videos. This efficiency contributes to the widespread adoption of ReLU in modern deep-learning architectures.

Although ReLU is highly effective, it is not without limitations. One notable issue is the dying ReLU problem, where neurons can become inactive if their weights cause all outputs to be negative during training. In such cases, the gradient becomes zero, preventing the neuron from updating its weights and contributing to the learning process. Variants such as Leaky ReLU and Parametric ReLU (PReLU) address this issue by allowing a small gradient for negative inputs, ensuring that all neurons remain active to some extent.

Conclusion

In this chapter, we explored the fundamental concepts of Convolutional Neural Networks (CNNs), highlighting their pivotal role in processing unstructured data, such as images and videos. Beginning with the evolution of neural networks, we discussed how CNNs addressed the limitations of manual feature engineering through using filters, enabling automated and efficient feature extraction.

The key components of CNNs, including convolutional layers, max pooling, flattening, and fully connected layers, were examined in detail. These elements work together to detect hierarchical features and translate them into actionable predictions. The importance of operations such as ReLU activation and the configuration of filters was emphasized, demonstrating their contribution to the network's ability to learn complex patterns.

CNNs have transformed the field of computer vision and beyond, laying the foundation for advanced AI applications. In the next chapter, we will explore specific CNN architectures and their real-world applications, delving deeper into their design and implementation.

Practice Exercises

1. Consider a 32x32 input image passed through a convolutional layer with the following parameters:
    - Filter size: 3x3
    - Stride: 1
    - Padding: 1 (same padding)
    - Number of filters: 16

    Calculate the dimensions of the output feature map.

2. An input feature map of size 28×28×32 is passed through a max pooling layer with the following parameters:
    - Pool size: 2×2
    - Stride: 2
    - No padding is applied

    Calculate the dimensions of the output feature map.

3. A convolutional layer has the following configuration:
   - Input depth: 32
   - Filter size: 3×33 \times 33×3
   - Number of filters: 64
   - Bias is added for each filter

   Calculate the total number of trainable parameters in this convolutional layer.

4. A fully connected layer has the following configuration:
   - Input features: 128
   - Output neurons: 64

   Each neuron in the output layer has a bias term. Calculate the total number of trainable parameters in this fully connected layer.

Answers

1. Output = $\frac{(32-3+2 \times 1)}{1} + 1 = 32$, Dimension = 32 x 32 x 16
2. Output = $\frac{(28-2)}{2} + 1$; Dimension = 14 x 14 x 32
3. Total parameters = (3 x 3 x 32 +1) x 64 = 18,496
4. Total parameters = (128 x 64) + 64 = 8,256

Multiple Choice Questions

1. What is the primary role of filters in a CNN?
   a. To reduce the dimensionality of the input data
   b. To capture specific features such as edges and textures
   c. To add non-linearity to the network
   d. To connect neurons across layers

2. Which activation function is most commonly used in CNNs to introduce non-linearity?
   a. Sigmoid
   b. Tanh
   c. ReLU
   d. Softmax

3. What does max pooling do in a CNN?
   a. It normalizes the feature maps
   b. It selects the maximum value in a local region
   c. It adds non-linearity to the data
   d. It converts the 2D feature maps into 1D vectors
4. What is the purpose of padding in CNNs?
   a. To add noise to the data for better generalization
   b. To reduce the size of feature maps
   c. To preserve spatial dimensions during convolution
   d. To increase the number of filters
5. What is the function of the flatten layer in a CNN?
   a. To reduce the spatial dimensions of feature maps
   b. To convert 2D feature maps into a 1D vector
   c. To apply non-linear activation to the data
   d. To select important features from the data
6. What is the main benefit of ReLU activation in CNNs?
   a. Avoids the exploding gradient problem
   b. Prevents overfitting
   c. Mitigates the vanishing gradient problem
   d. Reduces the size of the feature maps
7. Which operation is used to reduce the computational complexity in a CNN?
   a. Convolution
   b. Pooling
   c. Fully Connected Layers
   d. Padding
8. What does a stride of 1 in convolution indicate?
   a. The filter moves one step horizontally or vertically
   b. The filter size is 1x1

Introduction to Convolutional Neural Networks

      c. The filter skips every other input

      d. The convolution operates only on the center of the input

9. Why are hierarchical features important in CNNs?

      a. They ensure the model converges faster

      b. They allow the network to detect patterns ranging from simple to complex

      c. They increase the dimensionality of the data

      d. They eliminate the need for activation functions

10. What issue can occur with ReLU that is addressed by variants such as Leaky ReLU?

      a. Overfitting due to excessive neuron activations

      b. Neurons becoming inactive due to negative inputs

      c. Lack of feature detection in deep layers

      d. Insufficient gradient during training

Answers

1. b
2. c
3. b
4. c
5. b
6. c
7. b
8. a
9. b
10. b

Keywords

- Convolutional Neural Networks (CNNs)
- Filters
- Kernel Functions
- Feature Maps
- Padding
- Stride
- Max Pooling
- ReLU Activation Function
- Flatten Layer
- Fully Connected Layer
- Feature Extraction
- Leaky ReLU
- Parametric ReLU (PReLU)
- Sparsity
- Softmax
- tanh
- Dimensionality Reduction
- ImageNet

References

1. http://deeplearning.stanford.edu/tutorial/supervised/ConvolutionalNeuralNetwork/
2. https://cs231n.github.io/convolutional-networks/

CHAPTER 12
Classification Using CNN

Introduction

In this chapter, we delve into the practical application of Convolutional Neural Networks (CNNs) for classification tasks, focusing on both image and time-series data.

The chapter begins with dataset preparation for image classification tasks, a critical step that ensures the input data is well-structured and preprocessed for training. We then explore training and fine-tuning the model for optimal performance using Conv2D layers, examining the importance of hyperparameter tuning and strategies for achieving robust results.

To measure the effectiveness of a CNN model, we introduce evaluation metrics for assessing image classification results, such as accuracy, precision, recall, F1-score, and confusion matrices. These metrics provide insights into the model's performance and its ability to generalize to unseen data.

Beyond images, CNNs are also highly effective for time-series classification tasks, where the sequential nature of data requires specific preprocessing and handling. This section discusses how to prepare datasets for such tasks and outlines how Conv1D layers can be leveraged for extracting temporal features. We also address the importance of fine-tuning for optimal results in these scenarios.

The chapter concludes with a comprehensive implementation in Python using the TensorFlow-Keras framework, demonstrating step-by-step workflows for both image and time-series classification tasks. By the end of this chapter, readers will have gained the knowledge and skills to apply CNNs to real-world classification problems across diverse data types.

Structure

In this chapter, we will cover the following main topics:

- Dataset Preparation for Image Classification Tasks
- Training and Fine-Tuning the Model for Optimal Performance Using Conv2D layers
- Evaluation Metrics for Image Classification
- Dataset preparation for Time-Series Classification Tasks
- Training and Fine-Tuning the Model for Optimal Performance Using Conv1D layers
- Implementation in Python Using Tensorflow-Keras Framework

Dataset Preparation for Image Classification Tasks

Preparing a dataset is the foundational step in building any image classification model. The quality of the dataset directly impacts the model performance, making it essential to ensure the data is well-structured, diverse, and representative of the problem being addressed. This subsection outlines key considerations and steps involved in preparing datasets for image classification tasks.

- **Data Collection:** The first step is collecting a dataset that represents the categories to be classified. Publicly available datasets, such as CIFAR-10, MNIST, or ImageNet, provide a good starting point for common image classification tasks. For custom applications, data can be collected using sensors, cameras, or web scraping. Ensuring a balanced representation of all categories is crucial to prevent biases during model training.
- **Data Annotation and Labeling:** Once the images are collected, they are labeled with the corresponding class. For example, in a dataset for classifying animals, each image should be tagged with its respective label, such as "cat," "dog," or "rabbit." Proper labeling ensures the model learns accurate relationships between image features and their corresponding classes.
- **Data Cleaning:** Raw datasets often contain noisy, irrelevant, or corrupted images that can adversely affect model training. Cleaning the dataset involves removing duplicate, blurry, or incorrectly labeled images. This step ensures the training process focuses on relevant and high-quality data, improving the model's ability to generalize.
- **Data Augmentation:** Data augmentation techniques are employed to artificially expand the dataset by applying transformations, such as rotation, flipping, zooming, cropping, and brightness adjustments. This enhances the model's

robustness by teaching it to recognize patterns regardless of variations in image orientation or lighting conditions. Augmentation also helps mitigate overfitting, especially when the dataset size is limited.

- **Data Preprocessing:** Preprocessing involves resizing images to a uniform dimension, normalizing pixel values to fall within a specific range (such as 0 to 1), and encoding labels into a numerical format. Additionally, images are often converted to grayscale or RGB channels based on the model requirements. Preprocessing ensures the data is compatible with the input layer of the CNN model and accelerates convergence during training.
- **Splitting the Dataset:** To evaluate the model's performance, the dataset is typically divided into training, validation, and test sets. A common split is 70-20-10, where 70% of the data is used for training, 20% for validation, and 10% for testing. The training set is used to optimize model weights, the validation set helps tune hyperparameters, and the test set assesses the model's generalization ability.
- **Balancing the Dataset:** Imbalanced datasets, where certain categories have significantly more samples than others, can lead to biased predictions. Techniques such as over-sampling, under-sampling, or class weighting can address this issue, ensuring that the model gives equal importance to all categories during training.
- **Preparing Data Pipelines:** Efficient data pipelines streamline the process of loading and preprocessing images during training. Libraries such as TensorFlow and PyTorch provide utilities to create input pipelines that load batches of images, apply augmentations, and preprocess data on the fly, enabling faster and more efficient training.

Training and Fine-Tuning the Model for Optimal Performance Using Conv2D Layers

Training and fine-tuning a CNN is a critical process that determines its effectiveness in performing image classification tasks. It involves carefully designing the network's architecture and optimizing hyperparameters, such as the number of filters, filter size, activation functions, learning rate, and number of epochs to achieve high accuracy and generalization.

At the heart of CNNs are Conv2D layers, which are specifically designed to process 2D spatial data such as images. These layers apply convolutional operations to extract meaningful patterns from the input data. Unlike traditional fully connected layers that lose spatial relationships, Conv2D layers preserve the spatial structure of the input, allowing the model to identify critical patterns, such as edges, corners, textures, and other features. This ability makes Conv2D layers particularly powerful for image-related tasks.

As data progresses through multiple Conv2D layers, the network builds a hierarchical understanding of the input. Early layers in the CNN typically learn simple, low-level features, such as horizontal or vertical edges.

These features are crucial for detecting boundaries and basic shapes within the image. As the data flows deeper into the network, subsequent Conv2D layers capture increasingly complex and abstract patterns, such as textures, object parts, or even entire objects. This progressive learning enables CNNs to handle intricate classification tasks, making them indispensable for computer vision applications ranging from handwritten digit recognition to medical imaging and autonomous vehicles.

A popular problem for demonstrating the power of Conv2D-based CNNs is the MNIST dataset, which consists of 70,000 grayscale images of handwritten digits (0 to 9). The dataset includes 60,000 training images and 10,000 test images, with each image having a resolution of 28×28 pixels. The goal is to classify each image into one of the ten digit classes. Using a Conv2D-based CNN, the task of recognizing handwritten digits can be solved with high accuracy, showcasing the model's ability to learn patterns inherent in the data.

Implementing a CNN for MNIST Classification

The implementation of a CNN for image classification can be efficiently carried out using TensorFlow and Keras, two widely used frameworks in the deep learning community. TensorFlow provides a robust backend for building, training, and deploying machine learning models, while Keras offers a high-level API that simplifies the process of creating neural networks. Using these frameworks, we can design a CNN model tailored to the dataset at hand, incorporating layers, such as Conv2D, MaxPooling2D, and Dense for feature extraction and decision-making. The process includes loading and preprocessing the dataset, constructing the CNN architecture, compiling the model with appropriate loss functions and optimizers, and training it over multiple epochs to achieve optimal performance. The combination of TensorFlow's computational efficiency and Keras's user-friendly interface makes it an ideal choice for implementing CNNs for image classification tasks, such as MNIST.

The following code demonstrates a Python implementation utilizing TensorFlow and Keras:

```
# Let us begin by importing all the necessary libraries required for
building and evaluating our CNN model.
import tensorflow as tf
from tensorflow.keras.models import Sequential
from tensorflow.keras.layers import Conv2D, MaxPooling2D, Flatten, Dense
from tensorflow.keras.utils import to_categorical
from sklearn.metrics import classification_report
```

Classification using CNN

```python
from keras.datasets import mnist
(xtrain,ytrain),(xtest,ytest)=mnist.load_data()
#Represent Training & Testing samples suitable for TensorFlow backend
x_train=xtrain.reshape(xtrain.shape[0],28,28,1).astype('float32')
x_test=xtest.reshape(xtest.shape[0],28,28,1).astype('float32')
#Encoding the output class label (One-Hot Encoding)
y_train=to_categorical(ytrain,10)
y_test=to_categorical(ytest,10)
#Model Building
model=Sequential()
model.add(Conv2D(8,kernel_size=(5,5),input_shape=(28,28,1),activation='relu'))
model.add(MaxPooling2D(pool_size=(2,2)))
model.add(Conv2D(4,(3,3),activation='relu'))
model.add(MaxPooling2D((2,2)))
model.add(Flatten())
model.add(Dense(32,activation='relu'))
model.add(Dense(10,activation='softmax'))
#Compile and Train the model
model.compile(loss='categorical_crossentropy',optimizer='adam',metrics=['accuracy'])
model.fit(x_train,y_train,batch_size=500,epochs=100,verbose=1,validation_data=(x_test,y_test))
#Predictions and classification report
y_pred = model.predict(x_test)
y_pred_classes = y_pred.argmax(axis=1)
print(classification_report(y_test, y_pred_classes))
```

The results in this classification report shown in *Figure* 12.1 summarize the performance of the CNN model on the MNIST dataset for handwritten digit recognition.

	precision	recall	f1-score	support
0	0.98	0.99	0.99	980
1	0.98	0.99	0.99	1135
2	0.98	0.97	0.97	1032
3	0.96	0.99	0.98	1010
4	0.99	0.97	0.98	982
5	0.98	0.98	0.98	892
6	0.98	0.98	0.98	958
7	0.98	0.96	0.97	1028
8	0.98	0.98	0.98	974
9	0.96	0.97	0.97	1009
accuracy			0.98	10000
macro avg	0.98	0.98	0.98	10000
weighted avg	0.98	0.98	0.98	10000

Figure 12.1: *Classification Report for MNIST Dataset*

The CNN model demonstrates excellent classification performance on the MNIST dataset, achieving high precision, recall, and F1-scores across all digit classes. The high accuracy of 98% confirms the effectiveness of Conv2D layers in extracting relevant features and the robustness of the model in handling handwritten digit recognition tasks. These results validate the suitability of the CNN for image classification problems.

Evaluation Metrics for Image Classification

Evaluating the performance of an image classification model is a critical step in the machine learning pipeline. It helps ensure that the model generalizes well to unseen data and provides actionable insights into its strengths and limitations. In this section, we will explore key evaluation metrics used in image classification tasks, highlighting their significance and practical applications.

The results in our classification report summarize the performance of the CNN model on the MNIST dataset for handwritten digit recognition. Let us analyze the key metrics provided:

- **Precision:** Precision represents the proportion of correctly classified instances among all instances predicted to belong to a class. In this report, precision values are consistently high (around 0.96–0.99) across all digit classes, indicating that the model rarely misclassifies one digit as another.
- **Recall:** Recall measures the proportion of correctly identified instances out of the total actual instances of a class. The recall values also range from 0.96 to 0.99, showing that the model effectively identifies instances of each digit with minimal omissions.
- **F1-Score:** The F1-score is the harmonic mean of precision and recall, providing a balanced measure of the model's performance. All classes show F1-scores between 0.97 and 0.99, reflecting a strong balance between precision and recall across the dataset.
- **Support:** Support indicates the number of actual instances of each class in the dataset. Each digit class has a sufficient number of samples (ranging from 892 to 1135), ensuring the model's evaluation is reliable.
- **Accuracy**: The model achieves an overall accuracy of 0.98, meaning it correctly classifies 98% of the test samples.
- **Macro Average**: The macro average calculates the unweighted mean of the metrics across all classes, giving equal importance to each class. It shows 0.98 for precision, recall, and F1-score, indicating consistent performance across all digits.
- **Weighted Average**: The weighted average accounts for the support of each

class when calculating the mean. It also yields 0.98, showing the model performs well even with varying class sizes.
- **Confusion Matrix:** The confusion matrix provides a detailed breakdown of model predictions across all classes. It is a table that shows the number of true positives, true negatives, false positives, and false negatives for each class. This matrix is invaluable for identifying specific classes where the model may be underperforming or prone to errors.
- **ROC-AUC Score:** The Receiver Operating Characteristic (ROC) curve plots the true positive rate against the false positive rate at various thresholds. The Area Under the Curve (AUC) quantifies the overall performance of the model, with values closer to 1 indicating better performance. Although commonly used in binary classification, this metric can be extended to multi-class problems.
- **Top-k Accuracy:** Top-k accuracy measures whether the correct class is within the top k predictions of the model. This metric is particularly relevant in problems with a large number of classes, such as object recognition in images. For instance, in ImageNet, top-5 accuracy is often reported.

Choosing the right evaluation metrics depends on the specific requirements of the classification task. For balanced datasets, accuracy may suffice as a measure of performance. However, for imbalanced datasets or high-stakes applications, metrics, such as precision, recall, F1-score, and ROC-AUC provide deeper insights. Employing a combination of these metrics ensures a comprehensive evaluation, allowing practitioners to fine-tune the model for both effectiveness and reliability.

In the following subsection, we will explore how CNNs can be adapted for 1-dimensional datasets, such as time-series data, for classification tasks. Unlike 2D image data, time-series data has a sequential structure where the order of observations is critical. Examples include stock prices, sensor readings, and speech signals. By leveraging Conv1D layers, CNNs can effectively extract temporal patterns and features from time-series data, enabling accurate classification.

Dataset Preparation for Time-Series Classification

In the following subsection, we will explore how CNNs can be adapted for 1-dimensional datasets, such as time-series data, for classification tasks. Unlike 2D image data, time-series data has a sequential structure where the order of observations is critical. For example, stock prices, sensor readings, and speech signals. By leveraging Conv1D layers, CNNs can effectively extract temporal patterns and features from time-series data, enabling accurate classification. To begin, we will discuss the critical steps involved in preparing datasets for time-series classification, ensuring they are formatted and preprocessed for optimal performance in CNN-based models.

To understand the process of preparing time-series data for classification tasks, we will consider a use case involving an Electroencephalogram (EEG) dataset. This dataset provides a rich example of sequential data, where temporal dependencies play a crucial role in analysis and classification. The dataset used in this study consists of EEG recordings aimed at examining the neural correlates of genetic predisposition to alcoholism. EEG data were collected from 64 electrodes strategically placed on the scalps of subjects, with signals sampled at 256 Hz, resulting in a temporal resolution of 3.9 milliseconds per epoch for a duration of one second. This setup provides a rich time-series dataset for analyzing brain activity patterns.

Subjects in the study were categorized into two groups: alcoholic and control. They were exposed to visual stimuli designed to evoke distinct brain responses. The stimuli included a single image (S1) or two sequential images (S1 and S2). When two stimuli were shown, they were either in a matched condition (where S1 was identical to S2) or a non-matched condition (where S1 and S2 differed). The images were selected from the 1980 Snodgrass and Vanderwart picture set, which is known for its standardized characteristics, making it ideal for controlled experiments.

This dataset is particularly valuable for time-series classification tasks as it not only contains rich temporal patterns but also represents a clear binary classification problem distinguishing between alcoholic and control subjects based on EEG responses. The inherent structure of the data provides an excellent opportunity to demonstrate the power of 1D CNNs in extracting meaningful features from sequential data for classification. In the following subsections, we will prepare this dataset for training and explore how Conv1D layers can be utilized to achieve accurate classification results.

Let us build a 1D CNN architecture to classify the alcoholic and control subjects in the EEG dataset. The following Python code demonstrates the step-by-step process of data preparation and model development. To begin, we will import all the necessary libraries and load the EEG dataset, ensuring the data is ready for preprocessing and analysis.

```
#Step-1
import os,sys
from keras.models import Sequential
from keras.layers import Dense,BatchNormalization
from keras.utils import to_categorical
import numpy as np
import pandas as pd
import matplotlib.pyplot as plt
from keras import backend as K
from keras.layers import Dropout, Flatten, Dense, Conv1D,MaxPooling1D
from keras.layers import Dropout
from keras.layers import Flatten
from IPython.display import display
from PIL import Image
```

Classification using CNN

```
from sklearn.utils import shuffle
from sklearn.model_selection import train_test_split
from sklearn import metrics
%matplotlib inline
#Loading the dataset
path1 = "/DL/alcoholic"
path2 = "/DL/control"
files1 = os.listdir(path1)
num_samples1 = len(files1)
#Let us read a sample file and check the shape of the data
e = pd.read_csv(path1+'/'+files1[0])
e.shape
(16384, 10)
```

After loading the EEG dataset, we observed that each sample has a length of 16,384, which represents the time-series data collected over a specific period. The dataset contains 10 columns, each representing different attributes. To proceed with the analysis, we need to extract the specific column containing sensor data for all files corresponding to both the alcoholic and control categories.

Step 2 ensures that only the relevant time-series data is used for training the 1D CNN model, enabling accurate classification of the two groups. Let us demonstrate this data extraction process in Python.

```
#Step-2
#Extracting the sensor value
dat_alcoholic=np.zeros((num_samples1,16384))
for i,file in enumerate(files1):
  eeg = pd.read_csv(path1+'/'+file)
  dat_alcoholic[i,:]=eeg['sensor value']
#Similarly extracting the sensor value from control folder
files2 = os.listdir(path2) # stores the file name alone
num_samples2=len(files2)
dat_control=np.zeros((num_samples2,16384))
for i,file in enumerate(files2):
  eeg = pd.read_csv(path2+'/'+file)
  dat_control[i,:]=eeg['sensor value']
dat_alcoholic.shape
(50, 16384)
dat_control.shape
(237, 16384)
```

To facilitate training the 1D CNN model, we need to combine these two datasets into a single 2D array of shape (287, 16384). This consolidated dataset allows each row to represent one EEG sample, making it convenient to feed into the 1D CNN architecture, where each row corresponds to one training instance. The labels for each sample can then be assigned as 0 for control and 1 for alcoholic, enabling the model to learn the classification task effectively. Towards step 3, we proceed with concatenating the data and preparing it for the CNN model.

```
#Step-3
dat_complete=np.concatenate((dat_alcoholic,dat_control),axis=0)
dat_complete.shape
(287, 16384)
```

Step 4 is to initialize the labels for the two classes, alcoholic and control, which will be used to train the 1D CNN model.

```
#Step-4
#initialize the labels
label = np.zeros((num_samples,),dtype=int)
label[:num_samples1]=1 # Alcoholic
label[num_samples1:]=0 # Controls
```

Step 5 is to shuffle the dataset and split it into training and testing sets. This ensures that the model is trained on a diverse subset of the data and tested on unseen samples to evaluate its performance.

```
#Step-5
data,Label = shuffle(dat_complete,label,random_state=2)
xtrain,xtest,ytrain,ytest = train_test_split(data,Label,test_size=.3,random_state=4)
xtrain.shape,xtest.shape
(200, 16384), (87, 16384))
```

To ensure compatibility with the TensorFlow-Keras framework, it is necessary to convert the data type of the input features to float32. This data type is the standard for numerical computations in TensorFlow and is optimized for faster processing and efficient memory usage during training.

```
#Step-6
#convert to float
x_train = xtrain.astype('float32')
x_test = xtest.astype('float32')
```

Step 7 involves reshaping the input data to ensure it meets the TensorFlow-Keras framework's requirement for 1D CNN models. TensorFlow expects the input data to be in a specific shape that corresponds to the number of samples, the time-series length, and the number of channels (features) per time step (1 in this case, as we are using a single sensor's data).

```
#Step-7
x_train=x_train.reshape(x_train.shape[0],x_train.shape[1],1) x_test=x_test.reshape(x_test.shape[0],x_test.shape[1],1) x_train.shape,x_test.shape
((200, 16384, 1), (87, 16384, 1))
```

Step 8 involves converting the integer labels into a binary format using one-hot encoding. One-hot encoding transforms categorical integer labels into a binary matrix, where each class is represented as a unique binary vector. This is required for classification tasks when using categorical cross-entropy as the loss function in TensorFlow-Keras, which expects labels in a one-hot encoded format.

```
#Step-8
y_train = to_categorical(ytrain)
y_test = to_categorical(ytest)
```

Training and Fine-Tuning the Model

The next step involves building the 1D CNN model, which extracts temporal features using Conv1D, processes them through pooling and dense layers, and outputs class probabilities. This model is designed using the sequential API, which is intuitive for building layer-by-layer architectures; however, in the next chapter on transfer learning, we will explore the functional API, which is particularly suited for working with pre-trained models and more complex designs.

```
#Step-9
model = Sequential()
model.add(Conv1D(12,kernel_size=3,input_shape=(x_train.shape[1],1),
activation='relu'))
model.add(BatchNormalization())
model.add(MaxPooling1D(pool_size=4))
model.add(Flatten()) # acts as the i/p layer to dense which is 1st
hidden layer
model.add(Dense(256,activation='sigmoid'))
model.add(Dropout(0.1))
model.add(Dense(128,activation='relu'))
model.add(Dense(num_classes, activation='sigmoid'))
```

This architecture is lightweight yet powerful, capable of learning temporal dependencies in the EEG dataset. The model is now ready for compilation and training, which we will proceed with in the next step.

The model was compiled using the binary cross-entropy loss function, which is suitable for binary classification tasks, along with the Stochastic Gradient Descent (SGD) optimizer to update weights during training. The training process was carried out over 20 epochs with a batch size of 10, and the verbose=2 setting provided detailed updates for each epoch in the console.

During training, the model demonstrated convergence within the 20-epoch range, showing a steady decrease in the loss function initially, followed by a saturation zone where the loss values stabilized. This indicates that the model effectively minimized the error and reached an optimal point, balancing training and validation performance.

The saturation zone for the loss function reflects that further training would yield diminishing returns, suggesting the model has adequately learned from the data.

The final step (step 10) in evaluating the model's performance involves generating predictions on the test set and analyzing the results using a classification report and a confusion matrix.

```
#Step-10
y_predict = model.predict(x_test)
y_pred = [ ]
for val in y_predict:
  y_pred.append(np.argmax(val))
print(y_pred)
cr = metrics.classification_report(ytest,y_pred)
print(cr)
cm = metrics.confusion_matrix(ytest,y_pred)
print(cm)
```

	Predicted Control (0)	Predicted Alcoholic (1)
Actual Control (0)	71	0
Actual Alcoholic (1)	3	13

Figure 12.2: Confusion Matrix of EEG classification

The confusion matrix presented in Figure 12.2 highlights that while the model performs well, it is not flawless in identifying alcoholic cases, with a sensitivity score of 81.25% due to a few missed detections. In contrast, the model is exceptionally accurate in classifying control cases, achieving a specificity score of 100% with no false positives.

```
              precision    recall  f1-score   support

           0       0.96      1.00      0.98        71
           1       1.00      0.81      0.90        16

    accuracy                           0.97        87
   macro avg       0.98      0.91      0.94        87
weighted avg       0.97      0.97      0.96        87
```

Figure 12.3: Classification Report of EEG classification

The classification report shown in Figure 12.3, the model correctly classified 97% of all test samples, showcasing its strong overall performance. It excels in recognizing "Control" samples with perfect recall and precision. However, for the "Alcoholic" class, although precision is perfect, the recall is slightly lower at 81%, indicating some alcoholic cases were not identified.

We have demonstrated the implementation of TensorFlow-Keras using Python for two distinct use cases, showcasing the versatility of convolutional neural networks. For image classification, we utilized Conv2D layers to process spatial features in 2D data, achieving high accuracy in tasks such as handwritten digit recognition using the MNIST dataset. Additionally, we applied Conv1D layers to analyze sequential data from the EEG dataset, effectively extracting temporal patterns to classify alcoholic and control subjects. These examples highlight the adaptability of CNNs to handle both spatial and temporal data, demonstrating their power in solving diverse real-world classification problems.

The two use cases achieved promising results, but there remains significant scope for improvement through hyperparameter tuning. By systematically experimenting with parameters such as the number of filters, kernel size, activation functions, learning rate, batch size, and the number of layers, practitioners can significantly enhance the model's ability to learn and generalize. Effective tuning ensures that the network captures meaningful patterns while avoiding overfitting or underfitting. The scope of hyperparameter tuning extends beyond performance optimization; it also influences training stability, computational efficiency, and model robustness, making it an indispensable part of designing and training CNNs for complex classification tasks.

Conclusion

In this chapter, we explored the practical applications of convolutional neural networks for classification tasks, focusing on both image and time-series data. We began by discussing dataset preparation techniques, emphasizing the importance of pre-processing and structuring data for optimal performance. Using Conv2D layers, we demonstrated the successful classification of handwritten digits from the MNIST dataset, showcasing the power of CNNs in extracting spatial features for image-based tasks.

We extended the capabilities of CNNs to sequential data by implementing Conv1D layers for the classification of EEG signals, effectively capturing temporal patterns in the dataset. The models were evaluated using comprehensive performance metrics, including precision, recall, and F1 scores, highlighting their strengths and areas for improvement. Additionally, we underscored the importance of hyperparameter tuning in enhancing model performance and adapting CNN architectures to diverse datasets.

Through these use cases, we illustrated the versatility and adaptability of CNNs in handling a variety of classification problems. In the next chapter, we will explore the concept of transfer learning using pre-trained models, examining how CNNs can be leveraged for advanced applications, thereby extending their utility to diverse real-world challenges.

Practice Exercises

1. Consider a 1D CNN model applied to a sequential dataset with the following details:

    a. The input sequence has a length of 1000 time steps

    b. The model applies a Conv1D layer with 32 filters and a kernel size of 5

    c. The stride is set to 1, and no padding is used

    d. Number of filters: 16

    Calculate the length of the output sequence after the convolution operation. If the next layer applies MaxPooling1D with a pool size of 2, calculate the length of the output sequence after pooling.

2. You are designing a Conv2D-based CNN for image classification with the following details:

    a. The input image size is 64×64 pixels (height x width)

    b. The first Conv2D layer has 16 filters with a kernel size of 3×3, a stride of 1, and padding set to "same"

    c. The output of the Conv2D layer is passed through a MaxPooling2D layer with a pool size of 2×2 and a stride of 2

    Calculate the dimensions of the feature map after the Conv2D layer. Calculate the dimensions of the feature map after the MaxPooling2D layer.

3. You are analyzing the performance of a CNN model on a binary classification problem with the following details:

    Confusion matrix for the test dataset:

    [[90, 10]

    [15, 85]]

    Total test samples: 200

    a. Calculate the accuracy of the model

    b. Compute the precision and recall for the positive class

    c. What does the F1-score indicate for this model?

Answers

1. Output length = $\frac{(1000-5)}{1} + 1 = 996$;

   Output length after maxpooling = $\frac{996}{2} = 498$

2. Dimensions after Conv2D: 64 × 64 × 16
   Dimensions after MaxPooling2D: 32 × 32 × 16

3. Accuracy = $\frac{(85+90)}{200} = 87.5\%$; Precision = $\frac{(85)}{85+10} = 89.47\%$;
   Recall = $\frac{85}{85+15} = 85\%$; F1 – score = $2 \times \frac{(.89 \times .85)}{(.89 + .85)} = 87.4\%$

Multiple Choice Questions

1. What is the primary role of Conv2D layers in CNNs?

   a. Extract temporal patterns from sequential data

   b. Extract spatial features from 2D data such as images

   c. Normalize data during training

   d. Reduce the dimensions of input data

2. Which of the following datasets is commonly used for benchmarking image classification models?

   a. CIFAR-10

   b. EEG dataset

   c. Kaggle Titanic dataset

   d. UCI Diabetes dataset

3. Why do we use one-hot encoding for labels in classification tasks?

   a. To improve model accuracy

   b. To normalize the input data

   c. To convert categorical labels into a binary format compatible with the loss function

   d. To simplify the training process

4. What is the primary function of the MaxPooling layer in a CNN?

a. Normalize feature maps

b. Reduce the spatial dimensions of feature maps while retaining critical information

c. Flatten the feature maps for dense layers

d. Add non-linearity to the model

5. What is the function of the flatten layer in a CNN?

   a. To reduce the spatial dimensions of feature maps

   b. To convert 2D feature maps into a 1D vector

   c. To apply non-linear activation to the data

   d. To select important features from the data

6. Which metric is most useful for evaluating the ability of a model to identify all positive instances in a dataset?

   a. Precision

   b. Accuracy

   c. Recall

   d. F1-Score

7. What is the primary difference between Conv2D and Conv1D layers in CNNs?

   a. Conv2D processes spatial data, while Conv1D processes sequential data

   b. Conv2D is used for classification, while Conv1D is used for regression

   c. Conv1D is faster than Conv2D for all datasets

   d. Conv2D requires one-hot encoded data, while Conv1D does not

8. What is the purpose of Batch Normalization in a CNN model?

   a. To reduce the spatial dimensions of feature maps

   b. To improve convergence speed and stability during training

   c. To prevent overfitting by randomly dropping neurons

   d. To flatten the feature maps for dense layers

9. Which preprocessing step is essential for Conv1D layers to process sequential

data?

   a. One-hot encoding

   b. Normalizing pixel values

   c. Reshaping data to include the channel dimension

   d. Applying MaxPooling

10. Why is hyperparameter tuning important in CNN models?

   a. Helps generate new training data

   b. Optimizes the model's architecture and improves performance

   c. Ensures data preprocessing is accurate

   d. Reduces the dataset size

Answers

1. b
2. a
3. c
4. b
5. b
6. c
7. a
8. b
9. b
10. b

Keywords

- Conv2D Layers
- Conv1D Layers
- MNIST Dataset
- Sequential Data
- Image Classification

- Time-Series Classification
- Feature Extraction
- Pre-Trained Models
- Transfer Learning
- Confusion Matrix
- Classification Report
- Precision
- Recall
- F1-score
- Accuracy
- Sensitivity
- Specificity
- Hyperparameter Tuning

References

1. https://archive.ics.uci.edu/dataset/121/eeg+database

Chapter 13
Pre-Trained CNN Architectures

Introduction

In this chapter, we explore the fascinating world of pre-trained convolutional neural network (CNN) architectures, which have become a cornerstone of modern deep learning applications. Pre-trained models leverage extensive training on large datasets, such as ImageNet, to provide powerful feature extraction capabilities, drastically reducing the computational and time requirements for training new models from scratch.

We begin by introducing some of the most popular pre-trained CNN architectures, including VGGNet, ResNet, and MobileNet, each of which has revolutionized the field with unique innovations and breakthroughs. This will be followed by a discussion on transfer learning, a technique that utilizes pre-trained models to adapt their knowledge to new tasks, highlighting its significance in accelerating training and improving performance, especially when data availability is limited.

The chapter also covers practical implementation aspects, showcasing how transfer learning can be applied using pre-trained CNN models to solve various tasks. We delved into using pre-trained models as feature extractors, demonstrating their ability to extract meaningful representations from input data. Finally, we present case studies across diverse domains, such as healthcare, agriculture, and industry automation, illustrating the effectiveness of pre-trained architectures in solving real-world problems.

Structure

In this chapter, we will cover the following main topics:

- Introduction to Popular Pre-Trained CNN Architectures
- Transfer Learning and its Significance in Deep Learning
- Implementing Transfer Learning with Pre-Trained CNN Models

- Pre-Trained CNN Model as a Feature Extractor
- Case Studies Showcasing the Effectiveness of Pre-Trained Architectures in Various Domains

Introduction to Popular Pre-Trained CNN Architectures

The field of CNN has witnessed significant advancements over the years, driven by the development of innovative architectures that pushed the boundaries of computer vision tasks. This section introduces some of the most influential pre-trained CNN architectures, highlighting their origins, training datasets, contributions, and real-world applications. The models we will explore include AlexNet (2012), VGGNet (2014), GoogleNet/Inception (2014), ResNet (2015), DenseNet (2017), and EfficientNet (2019). Each of these architectures has played a pivotal role in shaping modern deep learning, demonstrating their utility across a variety of applications, such as image recognition, object detection, and medical diagnostics.

Let us begin with AlexNet, the first architecture that marked a significant leap in deep learning performance.

AlexNet

AlexNet, developed by Alex Krizhevsky, Geoffrey Hinton, and Ilya Sutskever at the University of Toronto, revolutionized the field of computer vision by winning the ImageNet Large Scale Visual Recognition Challenge (ILSVRC) in 2012. This architecture introduced a breakthrough in deep learning by significantly improving performance on image classification tasks. Trained on the massive ImageNet dataset, containing over 1.2 million labeled images across 1000 categories, AlexNet achieved top-5 error rates of 16.4%, nearly halving the error of its competitors.

The architecture features eight layers, including five convolutional layers followed by three fully connected layers. Notable innovations in AlexNet include using ReLU activation for faster training, dropout for regularization to prevent overfitting, and GPU acceleration to handle the computational complexity of deep networks. These features set the stage for a new era of deep learning.

AlexNet's success demonstrated the power of deep CNNs in handling large-scale datasets, inspiring the development of subsequent architectures. Its applications extend beyond image classification, influencing advancements in areas such as medical imaging, video analysis, and autonomous driving systems.

VGGNet

VGGNet, developed by Karen Simonyan and Andrew Zisserman at the University of Oxford's Visual Geometry Group (VGG), made significant strides in computer vision by introducing a deeper network architecture. It was presented in 2014 as part of the ILSVRC competition, where it secured second place in the classification task with a top-5 error rate of 7.3% on the ImageNet dataset. VGGNet stood out for its simplicity and elegance, setting a benchmark for designing deep convolutional networks.

The key innovation of VGGNet lies in its use of small 3×3 convolutional filters stacked together to increase the depth of the network. This approach allowed the network to capture complex hierarchical features while keeping the number of parameters manageable. VGGNet was released in multiple configurations, with VGG16 (16 weight layers) and VGG19 (19 weight layers) being the most popular.

Although computationally intensive due to its large parameter size, VGGNet's straightforward design made it a foundational model for transfer learning. Its pre-trained weights have been extensively used in applications such as facial recognition, medical imaging, and style transfer, proving the versatility of this architecture. VGGNet's influence is evident in the design principles of modern deep learning models, emphasizing the importance of depth in neural networks.

GoogleNet/Inception

GoogleNet, also known as Inception, was introduced by a team of researchers at Google led by Christian Szegedy in 2014 as part of their submission to the ILSVRC competition. This architecture marked a major leap in efficiency and performance, winning the competition with a top-5 error rate of just 6.7% on the ImageNet dataset. The name "Inception" was inspired by the movie *Inception*, with the phrase "we need to go deeper" symbolizing the architectural depth.

The Inception architecture introduced the revolutionary concept of Inception modules, which use parallel convolutional layers with different filter sizes (for example, 1×1, 3×3, 5×5) and pooling layers. This design allows the network to capture multi-scale features while reducing computational costs.

GoogleNet is 22 layers deep and uses global average pooling instead of fully connected layers, which decreases its parameter count. This design made it possible to build deep yet efficient networks, paving the way for modern architecture.

GoogleNet's applications extend to areas, such as object detection (for example, R-CNN variants), video analysis, and medical diagnostics. It is particularly known for its balance between depth, efficiency, and accuracy, which set a new standard for designing scalable deep learning architectures.

ResNet

ResNet, short for Residual Networks, was introduced by Kaiming He, Xiangyu Zhang, Shaoqing Ren, and Jian Sun from Microsoft Research in 2015. This ground-breaking architecture won the ILSVRC competition with a remarkable top-5 error rate of just 3.57%, surpassing human-level performance on the ImageNet dataset. ResNet addressed a critical challenge in deep learning: the vanishing gradient problem, which often limits the depth of neural networks.

The key innovation of ResNet lies in its use of residual connections or skip connections. These connections bypass one or more layers, allowing the network to learn residual functions instead of direct mappings. This approach enabled the construction of extremely deep networks, such as ResNet-50 and ResNet-101, with up to 152 layers. By alleviating issues related to gradient flow, ResNet made it feasible to train very deep models without performance degradation.

ResNet's success demonstrated that depth alone does not guarantee better performance; instead, effective learning depends on efficient gradient flow and proper architectural design. Its residual connections have become a standard component in modern deep-learning architectures.

Applications of ResNet are vast, ranging from image classification and object detection to segmentation and feature extraction for medical imaging, autonomous driving, and video analytics. Its introduction marked a significant milestone in deep learning, solidifying the importance of depth and optimization in CNN design.

DenseNet

DenseNet, short for Dense Convolutional Network, was introduced by Gao Huang, Zhuang Liu, Laurens van der Maaten, and Kilian Q. Weinberger in 2017. This architecture, developed at Cornell University and Tsinghua University, brought a novel approach to designing deep networks by introducing dense connectivity between layers. DenseNet achieved competitive performance on datasets such as ImageNet and CIFAR-10 while significantly reducing the number of parameters compared to previous models such as ResNet.

The key innovation in DenseNet is its dense connections, where each layer is directly connected to every subsequent layer in a feedforward manner. Unlike traditional architectures, where layers pass information sequentially, DenseNet ensures that each layer receives input from all previous layers and passes its own feature maps to all subsequent layers. This design encourages feature reuse, leading to more efficient learning and reducing redundancy in feature extraction.

DenseNet also addresses the vanishing gradient problem by providing short paths for gradient flow, making it easier to train very deep networks. DenseNet-121,

DenseNet-169, and DenseNet-201 are among the popular configurations, each named after the number of layers.

DenseNet has been widely adopted in applications requiring efficient architectures, such as image classification, biomedical image segmentation, and object recognition. Its dense connectivity pattern has inspired subsequent advancements in neural network design, highlighting the importance of feature reuse and efficient parameter utilization.

MobileNet

MobileNet, introduced by Andrew G. Howard and his team at Google in 2017, revolutionized CNN design for mobile and embedded devices by offering a lightweight and efficient architecture. Designed specifically for resource-constrained environments, MobileNet achieved a significant reduction in computational cost without compromising much on accuracy, making it ideal for applications in mobile and edge computing.

The key innovation of MobileNet lies in its use of depthwise separable convolutions, a two-step process that splits standard convolutions into depthwise and pointwise convolutions. Depthwise convolutions apply a single filter per input channel, while pointwise convolutions use 1×1 filter to combine the outputs from the depthwise step. This approach drastically reduces the number of parameters and computations compared to traditional convolution operations.

MobileNet was trained on the ImageNet dataset and demonstrated competitive performance while being much smaller and faster than architectures such as VGGNet or ResNet. It also introduced a width multiplier and resolution multiplier, allowing developers to tradeoff between accuracy and efficiency based on specific hardware constraints.

Applications of MobileNet include real-time image recognition, object detection (for example, MobileNet-SSD), and tasks in augmented reality and IoT devices. Its versatility and efficiency have made it a popular choice for on-device AI applications, inspiring the development of subsequent versions, such as MobileNetV2 and MobileNetV3, which further improve performance and scalability.

EfficientNet

EfficientNet, introduced by Mingxing Tan and Quoc V. Le from Google Research in 2019, represents a major advancement in the design of scalable and efficient convolutional neural networks. This architecture was developed with the goal of achieving state-of-the-art performance on tasks like image classification while significantly reducing computational complexity and model size. EfficientNet achieved a top-1 accuracy of

84.4% on the ImageNet dataset, outperforming previous architectures with fewer parameters.

The key innovation of EfficientNet lies in its compound scaling method, which uniformly scales the depth, width, and resolution of the network. Traditional approaches often scale one dimension at a time, leading to suboptimal results. In contrast, EfficientNet uses a systematic scaling formula to balance all three dimensions, optimizing performance while minimizing computational overhead.

EfficientNet models, such as EfficientNet-B0 to EfficientNet-B7, are built using Mobile Inverted Bottleneck Convolution (MBConv) layers, which enhance efficiency and accuracy. The lightweight design of these models makes them ideal for deployment in resource-constrained environments, such as mobile devices and edge computing.

Applications of EfficientNet span a wide range of domains, including medical imaging, autonomous vehicles, and real-time video analytics. Its combination of accuracy and efficiency has made it a popular choice for modern deep-learning tasks, setting a new benchmark for scalable CNN architectures.

Transfer Learning and its Significance in Deep Learning

Transfer learning has become a cornerstone of modern deep learning, enabling practitioners to solve complex problems with limited data and computational resources. It is leveraging a model trained on a large dataset to adapt to a new task, often in a different domain or with a smaller dataset. This approach has proven highly effective, significantly improving the efficiency and performance of deep learning models across various applications. Here, we explore transfer learning in detail, breaking it into key concepts, methodologies, benefits, and applications.

Traditional machine learning models are typically trained from scratch for a specific task, requiring substantial labeled data and computational power. Transfer learning shifts this paradigm by reusing pre-trained models as a foundation for new tasks. This is based on the idea that the features learned by a model on one task, especially on large-scale datasets such as ImageNet, can be applied to other related tasks. For instance, features such as edges, corners, and textures learned by a CNN trained on ImageNet can be highly valuable for other vision tasks, even with significantly smaller datasets.

Types of Transfer Learning

There are primarily two approaches to applying transfer learning:

- **Feature Extraction:** In this method, the pre-trained model is used as a fixed

feature extractor. The learned weights of the convolutional layers are frozen, and the output feature maps are passed to a new classifier tailored for the specific task. This approach is effective when the new task is similar to the original training task, and the dataset is small.
- **Fine-Tuning:** Fine-tuning involves unfreezing some or all layers of the pre-trained model and retraining it on the new dataset. This allows the model to adjust its weights to better suit the new task while retaining the general knowledge it has already learned. Fine-tuning is particularly useful when the target dataset differs significantly from the dataset used to train the pre-trained model.

Benefits of Transfer Learning

Some of the key benefits of transfer learning are listed as follows:
- **Efficiency in Training:** Training a deep neural network from scratch can be computationally expensive, often requiring days or weeks on high-performance hardware. Transfer learning significantly reduces this burden by starting with a pre-trained model that already encapsulates general knowledge, requiring fewer epochs and less data for convergence.
- **Handling Limited Data:** One of the biggest challenges in deep learning is the availability of labelled data. Transfer learning enables effective model training even with small datasets by leveraging features learned from larger datasets. This is particularly impactful in domains such as healthcare, where obtaining labeled data is costly and time-consuming.
- **Improved Generalization:** Models trained using transfer learning tend to generalize better to unseen data. The use of pre-trained features provides a robust starting point, minimizing overfitting and improving performance on test datasets.
- **Cost-Effectiveness:** By reusing pre-trained models, transfer learning reduces the need for expensive computational infrastructure and extensive labeling efforts, making deep learning more accessible to small organizations and researchers.

Implementing Transfer Learning with Pre-Trained CNN Models

Transfer learning is typically implemented using deep learning frameworks, such as TensorFlow, PyTorch, and Keras. The steps involve:
1. Loading a pre-trained model such as ResNet or VGGNet

2. Freezing the initial layers to retain their learned weights
3. Adding new layers tailored to the target task, such as fully connected layers for classification
4. Fine-tuning the model on the target dataset with appropriate hyperparameter tuning

In this section, we will explore the step-by-step implementation of transfer learning for a practical weed recognition task using the popular Plant Seedlings Dataset. Transfer learning allows us to leverage the power of pre-trained CNN architectures to classify plant species with minimal data and training time, making it an ideal approach for this problem. By utilizing pre-trained models such as Vgg16, we will demonstrate how to adapt these architectures to recognize and classify plants at various growth stages effectively. This hands-on Python exercise not only highlights the efficiency of transfer learning but also provides a solid foundation for applying these techniques to similar tasks in agriculture and beyond.

Introduction to the Problem Statement

The Plant Seedlings Dataset is a publicly available resource designed to facilitate research in plant species recognition. It contains approximately 960 images of unique plants across 11 different species; these classes include Charlock, Cleavers, Loose Silky-bent, Common Wheat, Maize, Fat Hen, Shepherd's Purse, Scentless Mayweed, Common Chickweed, Small-flowered Cranesbill, and Sugar Beet. Each class reflects unique characteristics and growth patterns, making this dataset a robust resource for training and evaluating weed recognition algorithms. The diversity of plant types also poses a practical challenge, as it requires models to generalize across varying shapes, textures, and growth stages. This dataset was recorded at Aarhus University Flakkebjerg Research Station in collaboration with the University of Southern Denmark and Aarhus University.

The dataset serves as a robust foundation for developing and evaluating algorithms aimed at weed recognition and plant classification. This problem statement not only highlights the utility of transfer learning for agricultural research but also underscores its potential in creating scalable solutions for real-world challenges such as automated weed control and precision farming.

The following code demonstrates a Python implementation utilizing TensorFlow and Keras:

Toward step 1, let us import all the necessary libraries and load the image data for training by iterating through directories containing class-specific images.

Pre-trained CNN Architectures

```
# Step-1: Let us import all the necessary libraries and load the image
data
from tensorflow.keras import applications
from keras.models import Sequential, Model
from keras.layers import Dropout, Flatten, Dense
from keras import backend as K
from keras.callbacks import ModelCheckpoint, EarlyStopping
from tensorflow.keras.optimizers import SGD
from sklearn import metrics

x_train=[ ]
y_train= [ ]
import cv2
for j in os.listdir(i):
    try:
        dummy = cv2.imread('/content/drive/My Drive/DL/train/' + i +
"/" + j)
        dummy = cv2.resize(dummy, (128, 128))
        x_train.append(dummy)
        y_train.append(i)
    except Exception as e:
        print(e)
```

OpenCV (cv2) library is used to read images from a specified path, resize them to 128×128 pixels for consistency, and append them to the **x_train** list. Corresponding class labels (folder names) are stored in the **y_train** list. Only valid directories are processed, and a try-except block ensures that errors during image loading or resizing do not interrupt the workflow. This step ensures the dataset is structured with resized image arrays and corresponding labels, ready for further preprocessing or model training.

The following step 2 converts the list of images (**x_train**) into a NumPy array, which is the standard format for efficient numerical computations in Python.

```
#Step-2
x_train=np.array(x_train)
x_train.shape
(3571, 128, 128, 3)
```

The resulting shape indicates that the dataset contains 3571 images, each resized to 128×128 pixels, with three color channels (RGB).

```
cv2_imshow(x_train[2000,:,:,:])
```

The command serves as a sanity check by visualizing an image from the dataset as shown in *Figure 13.1* to ensure the preprocessing steps were executed correctly. Here, **x_train** [2000,:,:,:] selects the image at index 2000 from the NumPy array **x_train**. This command displays the selected image, allowing us to verify that the images were loaded, resized, and stored properly. Such checks are critical in identifying issues such as incorrect data formatting or unexpected transformations before proceeding with model training.

```
y_train[2000]
'Scentless Mayweed'
#Step-3
import pandas as pd
import numpy as np
dum = pd.get_dummies(y_train)
encoded_labels = dum
y_train = dum
y_train = np.array(y_train)
y_train.shape
(3571, 11)
```

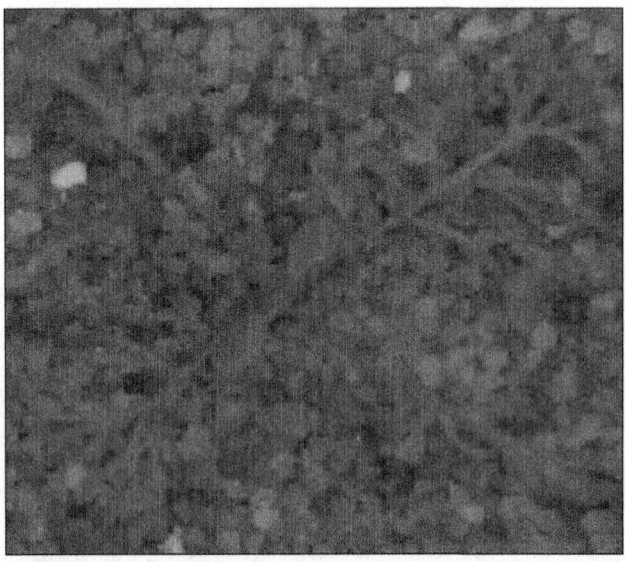

Figure 13.1: Sample Image of Scentless Mayweed from the Preprocessed Dataset (Index 2000)

In step 3, the string labels in **y_train** are converted into a one-hot encoded format using the **pd.get_dummies()** function from the pandas library. Each unique class label is represented as a binary column, where the presence of a specific class is denoted by '1', and all other classes are marked as '0'. This process transforms the labels into a binary matrix suitable for multi-class classification tasks. The encoded labels are then stored back into **y_train**, ensuring compatibility with machine learning frameworks such as TensorFlow/Keras. Finally, the labels can be converted into a NumPy array for efficient computation during model training.

```
#Step-4
from sklearn.model_selection import train_test_split
x_train2, x_val, y_train2, y_val = train_test_split(x_train, y_train, test_size=0.2, random_state=2)
```

Pre-trained CNN Architectures

The step 4 splits the dataset into training and validation sets using the **train_test_split** function from **sklearn.model_selection**. Here, 80% of the data is allocated to **x_train2** and **y_train2** for training, while the remaining 20% is set aside as **x_val** and **y_val** for validation.

```
x_train2.shape
(2856, 128, 128, 3)
x_val.shape
(715, 128, 128, 3)
#Step-5
x_train2 = x_train2/255.0
x_val = x_val/255.0
```

In step 5, the pixel values in the training and validation datasets (**x_train2** and **x_val**) are normalized by dividing each value by 255.0. Since the original pixel values range from 0 to 255 (for 8-bit images), this operation scales the values to a range between 0 and 1. Normalization helps improve the training process by ensuring the model converges faster and achieves better performance. It also prevents issues related to large input values, such as exploding gradients, making the training process more stable and efficient.

```
#Step-6
model = applications.VGG16(weights = "imagenet",include_top=False,
input_shape = (128, 128, 3))
```

The step-6 initializes the pre-trained VGG16 model as a feature extractor by loading its convolutional layers with weights trained on the ImageNet dataset. By setting **include_top=False**, the fully connected layers are removed, allowing us to customize the model for our specific task. The input shape is defined as 128×128×3, matching the resized RGB images. The pre-trained convolutional layers will extract hierarchical features, such as edges, textures, and patterns, which can then be passed to new classification layers added on top. This approach forms the basis of transfer learning, enabling efficient model adaptation to the plant species classification task.

```
#Step-7: Freeze the layers which we don't want to train. In this we are
freezing the first 10 layers.
for layer in model.layers[:11]:
layer.trainable = False
#Adding custom Layers (Fully Connected Layer Design)
cnn_out = model.output
ip_feat = Flatten()(cnn_out)
HL1 = Dense(1024, activation="relu")(ip_feat)
DO1 = Dropout(0.3)(HL1)
HL2 = Dense(1024, activation="relu")(DO1)
HL3 = Dense(64, activation="relu")(HL2)
predictions = Dense(11, activation="softmax")(HL3)
```

```
# creating the final model
model_final = Model(model.input,predictions)
# compile the model
model_final.compile(loss = "categorical_crossentropy", optimizer ='sgd',
metrics=["accuracy"])
```

The step-7 customizes the pre-trained VGG16 model for the plant species classification task by freezing the first 10 layers to retain their pre-trained weights and prevent updates during training. New fully connected layers are added to the model to adapt it for the specific task. The output of the VGG16 convolutional layers is flattened, followed by two dense layers with 1024 neurons each and ReLU activation, a dropout layer for regularization, and additional dense layers, including the final layer with 11 neurons (matching the number of classes) and a softmax activation for multi-class classification. The final model is compiled with the categorical cross-entropy loss function, the SGD optimizer, and accuracy as the evaluation metric. This architecture combines the pre-trained feature extraction capability of VGG16 with task-specific classification layers.

```
#Step-8
checkpoint = ModelCheckpoint("/content/drive/My Drive/DL/plant_vgg16_
best.h5", monitor='val_accuracy', verbose=1, save_best_only=True,
mode='auto')
early = EarlyStopping(monitor='val_accuracy', min_delta=0, patience=20,
verbose=1, mode='auto')
#an absolute change of less than min_delta , will count as no improve-
ment (threshold value) epochs=50
# Train the model model_final.fit(x_train2, y_train2, epochs = epochs,
validation_data=(x_val, y_val), callbacks = [checkpoint, early])
```

In step-8, the **ModelCheckpoint** callback is used to save the model with the highest validation accuracy to the specified file path, **plant_vgg16_best.h5**. The EarlyStopping callback monitors validation accuracy and stops training if there is no significant improvement (as defined by **min_delta=0**) for 20 consecutive epochs. The model is then trained for up to 50 epochs on the training set **(x_train2, y_train2)**, with validation performed on the validation set **(x_val, y_val)**. The specified callbacks ensure efficient training by retaining the best model and avoiding unnecessary overtraining.

```
#Step-9
y_pred=trained_model.predict(x_val)
```

In step-9, we generate predictions for the validation dataset **x_val** using the trained model. The **predict()** function outputs the probabilities for each class, as the final layer of the model uses a softmax activation. Each row in **y_pred** corresponds to a sample in the validation set and contains a vector of probabilities for all classes. The class with the highest probability can be considered the model's predicted class for that sample.

Pre-trained CNN Architectures

The step-10 is essential for evaluating the model's performance using metrics, such as accuracy, confusion matrix, or classification report. Let us convert the predicted probabilities (**y_pred**) and true one-hot encoded labels (**y_val**) into class labels. Using **np.argmax()**, the index of the maximum value is extracted for each sample, representing the predicted or actual class. The resulting lists, **y_label** (predicted classes) and **y_actual** (true classes), contain integer class labels for all validation samples. These labels are then used to calculate performance metrics, such as accuracy, confusion matrix, or classification report, for evaluating the model.

```
#Step-10
y_label=[]
for i in np.arange(y_pred.shape[0]):
    y_label.append(np.argmax(y_pred[i]))
y_actual=[]
for i in np.arange(y_val.shape[0]):
    y_actual.append(np.argmax(y_val[i]))
cr=metrics.classification_report(y_actual,y_label)
print(cr)
cm=metrics.confusion_matrix(y_actual,y_label)
print(cm)
```

The classification report shown in *Figure* 13.2 summarizes the model's performance on the validation dataset across 11 classes.

	precision	recall	f1-score	support
0	0.92	0.97	0.94	70
1	0.89	0.89	0.89	38
2	0.99	0.96	0.98	110
3	0.78	0.86	0.82	29
4	0.91	0.94	0.92	77
5	0.96	0.95	0.95	113
6	0.95	0.80	0.87	25
7	0.91	0.97	0.94	76
8	0.88	0.81	0.84	26
9	0.97	0.96	0.96	92
10	0.91	0.86	0.89	59
accuracy			0.93	715
macro avg	0.92	0.91	0.91	715
weighted avg	0.93	0.93	0.93	715

Figure 13.2: *Classification Report of Plant Species Dataset*

Despite freezing the first 10 layers of the pre-trained VGG16 model, the results are highly promising, achieving an overall accuracy of 93%. The model demonstrates strong precision, recall, and F1-scores across most classes. However, there is room for further improvement, particularly in under-represented or challenging classes, such as 3 and 6. By unfreezing a few additional convolutional layers and allowing them to fine-tune the target dataset, the model can better adapt to task-specific features, potentially improving the performance beyond **95%**. This highlights the flexibility and power of transfer learning when combined with strategic layer tuning.

Pre-Trained CNN Model as a Feature Extractor

Feature extraction is a powerful technique in deep learning where pre-trained convolutional neural network (CNN) models extract meaningful features from input data, which can then be used for specific tasks, such as classification, object detection, or clustering. Rather than training a CNN model from scratch, which is computationally expensive and time-consuming, feature extraction leverages the pre-trained convolutional layers of popular architectures, such as VGG, ResNet, or Inception. These models, having been trained on massive datasets such as ImageNet, learn to capture hierarchical features, starting from low-level edges and textures to high-level shapes and object components.

In traditional machine learning, feature engineering was a labor-intensive process requiring domain expertise to extract features manually. CNN-based feature extraction eliminates this manual process by learning generalizable representations directly from the data. Pre-trained models act as efficient feature extractors because their convolutional layers have already learned robust filters for detecting edges, curves, textures, and patterns that are universal across a wide variety of images. These features, extracted as outputs from convolutional and pooling layers, serve as inputs to new task-specific classifiers, such as fully connected layers or traditional machine learning models including Support Vector Machines (SVM).

Feature extraction works particularly well when the new dataset is small or similar to the dataset on which the CNN was originally trained. For example, if a pre-trained model such as VGG16 has learned features on the ImageNet dataset, which consists of millions of natural images, its convolutional base can be reused to extract features from a smaller dataset like the Plant Seedlings Dataset. The extracted features contain rich spatial and structural information that can significantly improve the performance of a new model while reducing training time.

The key steps in feature extraction involve loading a pre-trained model, removing or freezing the top layers (fully connected layers), and using the convolutional base to generate feature maps for input images. These feature maps are then flattened or pooled to form a compact representation that can be passed to a new custom classifier. This method is especially effective in transfer learning scenarios where models trained on large-scale data are adapted for tasks with limited training data.

By using pre-trained CNN models for feature extraction, deep learning practitioners can build highly accurate models with fewer resources, making it an efficient and scalable approach for solving real-world problems across diverse domains, such as medical imaging, agricultural analysis, and autonomous systems.

Exploring Different Configurations of Pre-Trained CNNs

Pre-trained models offer flexibility and can be configured or used in different ways depending on the requirements of a specific task. These models, trained on large-scale datasets such as ImageNet, serve as a strong foundation for a wide range of applications. They can be utilized for direct inference, feature extraction, or fine-tuning, allowing users to adapt them effectively to their datasets. The choice of configuration depends on factors, such as the size of the target dataset, computational resources, and the level of similarity between the source and target tasks. In this section, we will explore various ways to configure and use pre-trained models to achieve optimal results for different tasks.

Pre-Trained Models as Direct Inference

A pre-trained model for direct inference is a machine learning model that has already been trained on a large dataset to learn patterns and features relevant to a specific task, allowing it to be used immediately to make predictions or analyze new data without requiring further training. These models are built and fine-tuned by experts on extensive datasets, enabling them to generalize well to new, similar tasks in the same domain. Direct inference involves using the model as-is, leveraging its pre-learned knowledge to efficiently solve problems, such as classifying images, recognizing speech, or processing text, without additional computational resources or retraining.

Pre-trained models, such as VGG16 or ResNet, can be utilized directly for inference without additional training or fine-tuning. These models are already trained on large-scale datasets such as ImageNet, which contains over a million images across 1000 classes, enabling them to generalize well for tasks involving natural images. The model can be loaded this way:

```
model = VGG16 ( weights = 'imagenet', input_shape=(256,256,3))
```

In this case, the VGG16 model is loaded with weights='imagenet' and configured to accept input images of size (256, 256, 3). This means the input images need to be resized to match the model's expected dimensions, where 256x256 represents the spatial resolution, and 3 indicates the RGB color channels. Once the model is loaded, it can be used for direct inference on new images.

```
model.predict (test_image_with_size_256×256×3)
```

The `model.predict` method takes an input image (reshaped to the required size) and outputs the predicted probabilities for each class. This approach is particularly useful for quick testing and evaluation when the target task aligns closely with the ImageNet dataset. It eliminates the need for retraining, allowing practitioners to obtain predictions rapidly and use them in downstream applications, such as classification, anomaly detection, or initial benchmarking.

Full Model Training Configuration with Pre-Trained CNNs

In this configuration, the entire pre-trained CNN architecture is used for training on a customized dataset. Unlike configurations where certain layers are frozen to retain pre-trained weights, here all layers are made trainable using the command:

```
for layer in model.layers:
    layer.trainable = True
```

By setting trainable = True, the model's weights in all layers (including convolutional and fully connected layers) are updated during back propagation. This approach is particularly useful when the target dataset differs significantly from the original dataset (for example, ImageNet) that the model was trained on. For instance, datasets involving medical images, satellite imagery, or domain-specific tasks often have unique patterns and features that require retraining the full model by configuring the output layer according to number of classes.

Customizing Only the Dense Layer (Fully Connected Layer)

In this configuration, only the fully connected dense layers (FCL) are customized while retaining the pre-trained weights of the convolutional layers in a CNN architecture. This approach allows us to leverage the powerful feature extraction capabilities of the convolutional base without altering its pre-trained weights. The VGG16 model is loaded with weights trained on the ImageNet dataset, and the argument `include_top=False` ensures that the original fully connected layers (top classification layers) are excluded.

```
from keras.models import Model
model = VGG16 ( weights = 'imagenet', include_top=False, input_shape=(256,256,3))
X=model.output
X=Flatten()(X)
```

Pre-trained CNN Architectures

```
X=Dense(128,activation= 'Relu')(X)
Out = Dense (3, activation = 'softmax')(X)
Final_model = Model (model.input, out)
```

The last CNN layer output, which contains the extracted feature maps, is accessed using **model.output**. To feed these feature maps into a new classifier, a Flatten layer is added to transform the multi-dimensional output into a 1D vector. Custom dense layers are then added on top of the pre-trained base:

- A dense layer with 128 neurons and ReLU activation for learning task-specific features.
- A final dense layer with 3 neurons and softmax activation to classify the input into 3 target classes.

Customizing only the dense layers while freezing the convolutional layers significantly reduces training time and computational cost because the pre-trained convolutional filters are not updated. This approach is ideal for smaller datasets or tasks where the features learned from large-scale datasets such as ImageNet (for example, edges, shapes, and textures) are sufficient to solve the problem.

For example, in a plant species classification task, the convolutional layers extract hierarchical features such as leaf texture and structure, while the newly added dense layers focus on task-specific classification. This configuration strikes a balance between leveraging pre-trained knowledge and introducing new layers for fine-tuned decision-making.

Transforming Images into Feature Vectors Using Pre-Trained CNNs

In this configuration, a pre-trained CNN model is used solely for feature extraction without altering its weights. The fully connected output layer which performs classification is discarded to access the penultimate hidden layer's output. This hidden layer produces a high-dimensional feature vector that captures meaningful patterns from the input image.

To implement this, the pre-trained model is loaded, and the final dense classification layer is removed. Specifically, using **model.layers[-2].output**, we access the second-to-last hidden layer, which in this case consists of 4096 neurons (for VGG16). This allows us to extract a 4096-dimensional feature vector from input images:

final_model = Model(model.inputs, model.layers[-2].output)

By running final_model.predict(test_img), the extracted feature vector is returned. This vector represents a rich set of learned features, such as edges, shapes, and textures, which can be used as input to traditional machine learning models (for example, SVM, Logistic Regression) or for clustering tasks.

The extracted feature vectors can be applied to tasks such as image classification, anomaly detection, or image retrieval, where a new lightweight classifier or model is trained on top of these features. This method significantly reduces computational cost and training time while leveraging the robust feature extraction capabilities of pre-trained CNN architectures.

Case Studies Showcasing the Effectiveness of Pre-Trained Architectures in Various Domains

Pre-trained CNN architectures have revolutionized the field of computer vision by enabling rapid and efficient solutions across a variety of domains. Their ability to learn rich, hierarchical features from large-scale datasets like ImageNet makes them highly adaptable for solving complex real-world problems. By leveraging transfer learning, pre-trained models can be fine-tuned or used as feature extractors to achieve remarkable performance, even with limited domain-specific data. In this section, we will explore several case studies that demonstrate the effectiveness of pre-trained CNN models across diverse applications, including medical imaging, agriculture, autonomous systems, and retail e-commerce. These case studies showcase the flexibility of pre-trained architectures and their role in addressing domain-specific challenges while significantly reducing computational effort and training time.

MedNet: Pre-Trained Model for Medical Imaging Tasks

The MedNet architecture is a custom-designed deep convolutional neural network (DCNN) specifically tailored for medical imaging tasks. Unlike many transfer learning approaches that adapt popular pre-trained models such as VGG16 or ResNet50 trained on datasets such as ImageNet, MedNet was developed by a team of researchers from the Department of Computer Science, University of Missouri, Columbia, MO, USA. This model serves as a baseline for future research in medical image classification and analysis. MedNet distinguishes itself by being tailored to capture subtle and complex patterns in medical scans, which are often not present in general-purpose datasets. Its design enables it to act as a strong baseline model for future research, offering a foundation for advancing medical imaging applications, such as disease diagnosis, anomaly detection, and segmentation. By addressing domain-specific challenges in medical data, MedNet sets a benchmark for developing highly accurate and reliable solutions in healthcare imaging.

SatlasPretrain: Satellite Imagery Analysis

SatlasPretrain: A Large-Scale Dataset for Remote Sensing Image Understanding was developed by researchers at Allen Institute for AI (AI2), including Mohammadreza Mostajabi and colleagues. These models incorporate backbones such as ResNet, which have been pre-trained on large-scale datasets such as ImageNet. By fine-tuning these architectures on the SatlasPretrain dataset, the models achieve improved performance on a wide range of geospatial tasks, including planetary and environmental monitoring. The integration of these pre-trained backbones allows the SatlasPretrain models to effectively process diverse satellite and aerial imagery, facilitating applications, such as detecting solar farms, wind turbines, offshore platforms, and tree cover. This approach leverages the strengths of established CNN architectures to address the unique challenges present in remote sensing data.

A Mobile-Based DL Model for Cassava Disease Diagnosis

Researchers from the Department of Entomology, College of Agricultural Sciences, Penn State University, State College, PA, United States, and the International Institute of Tropical Agriculture (IITA), Dar es Salaam, Tanzania, developed a fine-tuned deep learning model deployed as a mobile application. This app is designed to identify foliar symptoms of three cassava diseases, two types of pest damage, and nutrient deficiencies. Serving as a practical tool for farmers and agricultural workers, it enables real-time, in-field diagnosis of cassava health issues, facilitating timely and well-informed decisions for effective crop management. The researchers utilized the MobileNet architecture, pre-trained on the COCO dataset (Common Objects in Context), which comprised 1.5 million images across 80 object categories. They employed transfer learning to fine-tune the model parameters to their specific dataset of cassava leaf images. This integration of deep learning models into mobile technology exemplifies the potential for AI-driven solutions to address agricultural challenges, particularly in resource-limited settings.

Fashion and Apparel Classification Using CNNs

Researchers from the Austrian Institute of Technology and Zalando SE conducted a study titled "Fashion and Apparel Classification using Convolutional Neural Networks". The study evaluated five different CNN architectures, including clean and pre-trained models. Among the pre-trained models, architectures such as VGG16, VGG19, and InceptionV3 were analyzed. These models were pre-trained on large-scale datasets such as ImageNet and then fine-tuned for specific tasks in fashion image classification. The research aimed to enhance meta-data enrichment for e-commerce applications by improving the accuracy of fashion and apparel image classification. The models were evaluated on tasks including person detection, product classification, and gender classification across both small and large-scale datasets. The findings indicated that fine-tuning pre-trained models yielded higher accuracy compared to training models from scratch, demonstrating the effectiveness of transfer learning in this domain. This study underscores the potential of leveraging pre-trained CNN architectures in developing efficient and accurate fashion image classification systems for e-commerce platforms.

Industrial Automation and Machine Vision

Researchers Ioannis D. Apostolopoulos and Mpesiana Tzani from the Department of Informatics and Telecommunications, University of Athens, Greece, conducted an in-depth study titled "Industrial Object, Machine Part, and Defect Recognition Towards Fully Automated Industrial Monitoring Employing Deep Learning: The Case of Multilevel VGG19." The study introduced a modified version of the well-known VGG19 architecture, referred to as Multipath VGG19 (MVGG19), to address challenges in industrial automation and machine vision. Unlike traditional approaches, MVGG19 was fine-tuned specifically for recognizing machine parts and detecting manufacturing defects in industrial settings, making it highly specialized for automated monitoring systems.

The model was tested on various industrial datasets and demonstrated a significant improvement in classification accuracy compared to traditional methods. Specifically, MVGG19 achieved an average classification improvement of 6.95%, highlighting its robustness and adaptability to complex industrial patterns. By enabling precise defect detection and object recognition, this solution advances the automation of quality control processes in manufacturing plants. The study illustrates the potential of deep learning models such as VGG19 to revolutionize industrial monitoring, reducing downtime, and improving production efficiency through real-time automated inspection systems.

Defense Sector: Automatic Target Recognition

Researchers Antoine d'Acremont, Ronan Fablet, Alexandre Baussard, and Guillaume Quin from Lab-STICC, ENSTA Bretagne, Brest, France, conducted a study titled "CNN-Based Target Recognition and Identification for Infrared Imaging in Defense Systems." The research aimed to address critical challenges in Automatic Target Recognition (ATR) for defense applications using infrared imaging. Leveraging the power of Convolutional Neural Networks (CNNs), the study focused on improving the identification and classification of military targets under low-visibility conditions where traditional vision systems struggle.

The CNN-based approach demonstrated significant improvements in recognition accuracy, particularly for detecting and classifying targets from infrared imagery.

Pre-trained CNN Architectures

The deep learning model effectively handled variations in target size, orientation, and environmental noise, which are common in defense operations. By integrating CNNs into defense systems, the study showcased the potential for enhanced surveillance, real-time decision-making, and increased situational awareness. This work highlights the growing role of deep learning in modern defense technologies, offering robust and reliable solutions for automated target recognition and strengthening national security efforts.

The case studies presented in this section demonstrate the versatility and effectiveness of pre-trained CNN architectures across diverse domains, including agriculture, defense, industrial automation, and beyond. These real-world applications highlight how leveraging pre-trained models significantly accelerates development, reduces computational costs, and enhances performance in complex tasks. From improving industrial defect detection to advancing target recognition in defense systems, these models have proven to be indispensable tools in solving domain-specific challenges. As the adoption of pre-trained architectures continues to grow, their ability to integrate seamlessly into various industries underscores their transformative potential. These success stories not only validate the robustness of pre-trained CNNs but also pave the way for further innovation, inspiring future advancements in deep learning-driven solutions across emerging domains.

Conclusion

In this chapter, we explored the remarkable advancements brought by pre-trained CNN architectures and their widespread applications across various domains. Beginning with an introduction to popular models, such as AlexNet, VGG, ResNet, Inception, Xception, DenseNet, MobileNet, and EfficientNet, we discussed their evolution, design principles, and contributions to the field of computer vision. These models, trained on massive datasets such as ImageNet, provide a robust foundation for tackling real-world problems with minimal retraining.

We delved into transfer learning, emphasizing its significance in leveraging pre-trained models for new tasks, reducing both the time and computational resources required for training. Through detailed implementation examples, we showcased how transfer learning can be applied for tasks like image classification using frameworks such as TensorFlow and Keras. Furthermore, we discussed different configurations of pre-trained models, full model training, fine-tuning, and feature extraction—demonstrating their adaptability to varied use cases.

The chapter concluded with compelling case studies highlighting the effectiveness of pre-trained CNN architectures across diverse domains, including industrial automation, defense systems, agriculture, and medicine. These examples underscored the transformative impact of these models in solving complex, real-world challenges, reaffirming their versatility and reliability. In the next chapter, we will explore the most fascinating world of sequence data modeling using Recurrent Neural Networks (RNNs).

Practice Exercises

1. A pre-trained CNN model uses an input image of size 224 × 224 × 3. The first convolutional layer has 32 filters of size 3 × 3, with a stride of 1 and padding of 1. Calculate the output dimensions (height, width, and depth) of the feature map after the first convolutional layer.

2. After the convolution layer in Exercise 1, a 2 × 2 max pooling layer with a stride of 2 is applied. Calculate the output dimensions after the pooling layer.

3. You have a fully connected (Dense) layer with 512 input neurons and 256 output neurons. The activation function is ReLU. Calculate the total number of trainable parameters in this layer, including biases.

4. A pre-trained VGG16 model processes an input image of size 256 × 256 × 3. After passing through the convolution and pooling layers, the feature map size is reduced to 8 × 8 × 512. Calculate the total number of features that will be fed into the first dense layer if we apply Flattening.

5. You are working on a transfer learning problem using the ResNet50 architecture pre-trained on the ImageNet dataset. The task is to classify 10 categories of traffic signs. The images in your dataset are of size 100 × 100 × 3. Configure the following hyperparameters for optimal performance:

    a. Should `include_top` be set to True or False? Explain why.

    b. What input size should be specified in the pre-trained model?

    c. Suggest a suitable optimizer and loss function for this classification problem.

Answers

1. $Output\ Size = \frac{(224-3+2(1))}{1} + 1 = 224;$

   $Final\ Output\ Dimensions = 224 \times 224 \times 32$

2. $Output\ height/width: \frac{(224-2+2(0))}{2} + 1 = 112$

   $Final\ Output\ Dimensions = 112 \times 112 \times 32$

3. Parameters= 512 × 256 +256 = 131328
4. Total Features= 8 × 8 × 512 = 32768
5. Setting `include_top = False` excludes the fully connected (Dense) layers specific to the ImageNet classification task (1,000 categories). Since the traffic signs dataset has only 10 categories, a new classifier needs to be added to the model to match this task.
6. ResNet50 was trained on ImageNet, where the standard input size is 224 × 224 × 3. Therefore, the traffic sign images (100 × 100 × 3) should be resized to this standard size during preprocessing to ensure compatibility.
7. Adam is effective for deep learning tasks as it adapts the learning rate dynamically, ensuring faster convergence. Categorical cross entropy is suitable for multi-class classification tasks, such as the 10-class traffic sign recognition problem.

Multiple Choice Questions

1. Which of the following was the first popular pre-trained CNN model that demonstrated groundbreaking success on ImageNet?

    a. ResNet

    b. AlexNet

    c. VGG16

    d. MobileNet

2. What is the primary purpose of transfer learning in deep learning?

    a. To train a model from scratch on a new dataset

    b. To reuse a pre-trained model for solving a related task

    c. To reduce the size of the model

    d. To perform gradient descent optimization

3. Which pre-trained model introduced residual connections to solve the vanishing gradient problem?

    a. VGG16

    b. InceptionNet

    c. ResNet

    d. DenseNet

4. The term "feature extraction" in pre-trained models refers to:
   a. Using a CNN to generate features without retraining its weights
   b. Training the entire model for a specific task
   c. Adding new layers to extract low-level features
   d. Reducing the number of filters in convolutional layers

5. Which of the following challenges was MobileNet primarily designed to address?
   a. High computational costs in large CNNs
   b. Vanishing gradient problem
   c. Feature map redundancy in convolution layers
   d. Overfitting on small datasets

6. What is a key advantage of using pre-trained CNN architectures such as VGG, ResNet, or DenseNet?
   a. Require no data preprocessing
   b. Provide state-of-the-art performance with minimal retraining
   c. Eliminate the need for labeled data
   d. Do not require GPUs for training

7. Which pre-trained model family is well-known for its lightweight architecture suitable for mobile and embedded devices?
   a. ResNet
   b. DenseNet
   c. MobileNet
   d. XceptionNet

8. What is the primary purpose of freezing layers in a pre-trained CNN during transfer learning?
   a. To train the entire model faster
   b. To prevent the pre-trained weights from being updated
   c. To eliminate redundant layers
   d. To increase the number of parameters for learning

9. What is a significant advantage of using pre-trained models for tasks such as image classification and object detection?

   a. Eliminate the need for labeled datasets

   b. Improve accuracy while reducing training time and computation

   c. Automatically solve data imbalance issues

   d. Do not require any fine-tuning

10. What is the main benefit of using pre-trained CNNs on datasets with limited labeled data?

    a. Reduces the need for GPUs

    b. Prevents overfitting without additional preprocessing

    c. Leverages learned features from large datasets to achieve good performance

    d. Eliminates the need for data augmentation

Answers

1. b
2. b
3. c
4. a
5. a
6. b
7. c
8. b
9. b
10. c

Keywords

- Pre-Trained CNN Models
- Transfer Learning
- AlexNet

- VGG16/VGG19
- ResNet (Residual Networks)
- InceptionNet
- XceptionNet
- Pre-Trained Models
- DenseNet
- MobileNet
- EfficientNet
- Fine-Tuning
- Feature Extraction
- Fully Connected Layers
- Convolutional Layers
- Automatic Target Recognition (ATR)
- Specificity
- Industrial Defect Detection
- Plant Disease Classification
- ImageNet Dataset

References

1. https://vision.eng.au.dk/plant-seedlings-dataset/
2. https://arxiv.org/abs/2110.06512
3. https://www.computer.org/csdl/proceedings-article/iccv/2023/071800q6726/1TJfWdaSyha
4. https://ceur-ws.org/Vol-2009/fmt-proceedings-2017-paper2.pdf
5. https://paperswithcode.com/paper/industrial-object-machine-part-and-defect
6. https://pubmed.ncbi.nlm.nih.gov/31052320/

CHAPTER 14
Introduction to Recurrent Neural Networks

Introduction

In this chapter, we delve into the fascinating domain of Recurrent Neural Networks (RNNs), a pivotal advancement in deep learning tailored to handle sequential data. Unlike feed-forward neural networks, RNNs are designed to capture temporal dependencies, making them ideal for tasks involving sequences, such as time-series forecasting, speech recognition, and text analysis.

We begin by exploring the basics of sequential data and time-series analysis, providing insights into the unique characteristics of data that depend on temporal order. This foundational understanding highlights why traditional neural network architectures struggle to process such data effectively.

Next, we introduce the concept of recurrent connections in neural networks, elucidating how these connections enable RNNs to retain information across time steps. By revisiting the architecture and working principle of a basic RNN, we will uncover how these networks process sequences and propagate information through recurrent loops.

However, no discussion about RNNs would be complete without addressing their challenges. This chapter also examines the limitations of RNNs, including issues such as vanishing gradients and difficulties in capturing long-term dependencies. These limitations set the stage for understanding more advanced architectures such as LSTMs and GRUs, which we will explore in subsequent chapters.

Structure

In this chapter, we will cover the following main topics:

- Basics of Sequential Data and Time-Series Analysis
- Understanding the Need for Recurrent Connections in Neural Networks
- Architecture and Working Principle of a Basic RNN
- Limitations of RNN

Basics of Sequential Data and Time-Series Analysis

Sequential data is a unique form of data where the arrangement or order of the observations is as significant as the data itself. This characteristic distinguishes it from traditional datasets, which are often analyzed under the assumption that each data point is independent of others. In sequential data, the sequence carries meaningful information, such as trends or patterns that unfold over time. For instance, the sequence of daily temperatures provides insight into weather patterns that individual temperature readings cannot reveal. *Figure 14.1* illustrates the time series of daily female births in Melbourne, Australia, spanning the years 1981 to 1990.

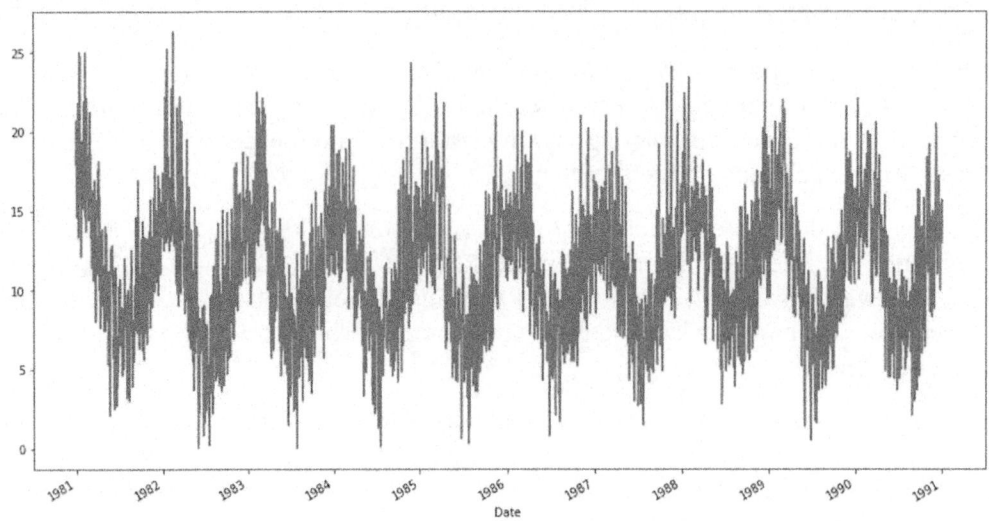

Figure 14.1: *Daily Total Female Birth in Melbourne, Australia During 1981-1990*

Unlike independent data points, sequential data inherently captures relationships across time or positions within the sequence. This means that each data point's value is influenced not just by its intrinsic properties but also by its relation to the preceding and succeeding data points. For example, the value of a stock price at a given time is influenced by prior movements in the market, reflecting a dependency that must be considered for accurate analysis. Ignoring these dependencies can result in incomplete or misleading insights.

The analysis of sequential data is critical in many domains where temporal or sequential order provides essential context. For example, in finance, the trends in stock market prices over time are studied to predict future movements or identify risk patterns. Similarly, weather data, collected as a sequence over time, is analyzed to understand climate patterns or forecast upcoming conditions. Speech signals and natural language sequences, such as sentences, also fall under this category, where the sequence of sounds or words determines meaning.

Time-Series Analysis

Time-series data is often decomposed into several underlying components that explain its structure and patterns. These components include Level, Trend, Seasonality, and Noise, which can combine either additively or multiplicatively. Understanding these components is fundamental for analyzing, modeling, and forecasting time-series data. The Level represents the baseline value of the time series, which is the average or constant part of the data when all other components (trend, seasonality, noise) are removed. It reflects the overall magnitude or central tendency of the female birth rate data as shown in *Figure 14.2*.

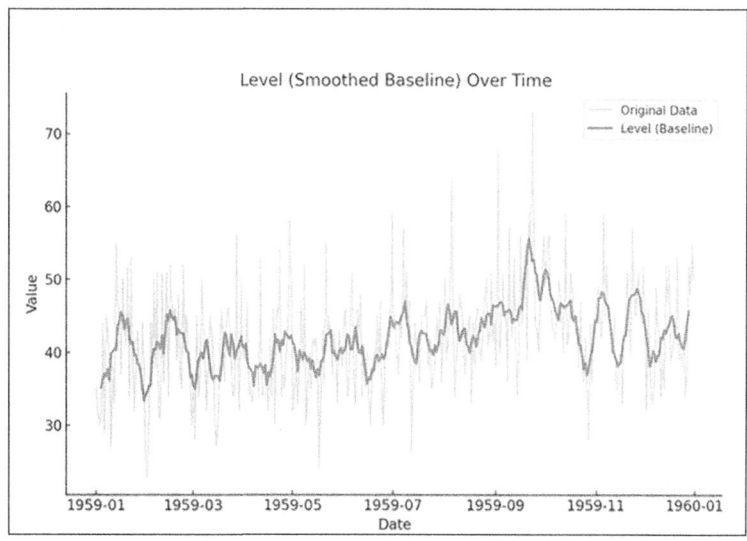

Figure 14.2: *Smoothed Baseline (Level) of Daily Female Births Over Time*

The seasonality component captures periodic fluctuations that occur at regular intervals, such as daily, monthly, or yearly cycles. These patterns are often driven by external factors, such as weather, holidays, or business cycles. For example, retail sales may peak during the holiday season. The seasonality in female birth rate data is observed and represented as the monthly average number of female births for 1959, as shown in *Figure* 14.3, which reflects the seasonal variations in births across the year.

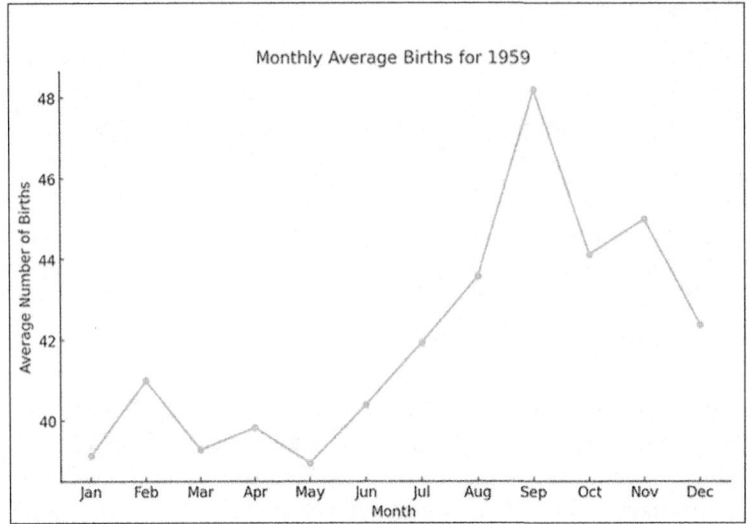

Figure 14.3: *Monthly Average Births for 1959 Showing Seasonality*

Consider another time series data shown in *Figure* 14.4, an air passenger's dataset (1949–1960), a classic time series dataset often used for analyzing and modeling temporal patterns in passenger traffic. The dataset records monthly totals of international airline passengers, measured in thousands, over 12 years. It is widely cited and originates from Box and Jenkins' work on time series analysis.

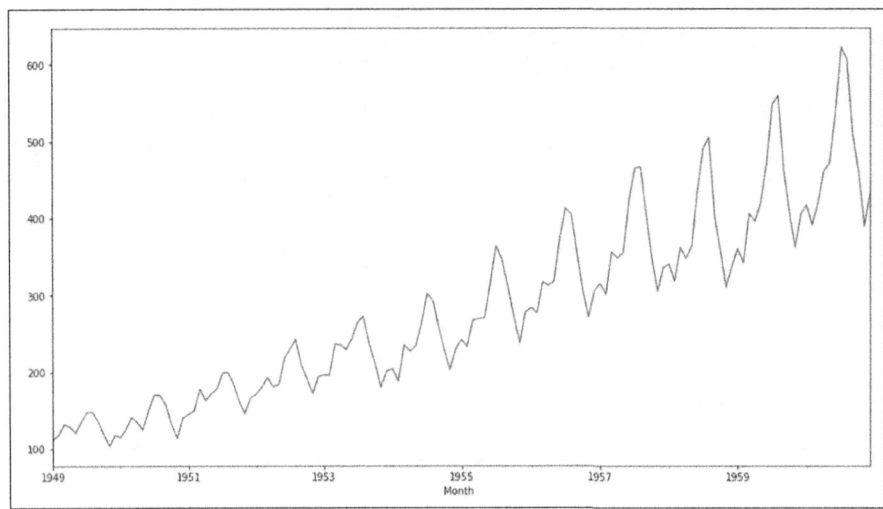

Figure 14.4: *Monthly Airline Passengers (1949–1960): Data from Box and Jenkins' Time Series Analysis*

The Trend in a time series data represents the long-term movement or direction in the data over time. A time series may exhibit an upward or downward trend due to factors, such as economic growth, population increase, or other underlying changes. The trend in airline passenger data is shown in *Figure* 14.5, highlighting the long-term direction or pattern in the data while filtering out seasonal and random variations.

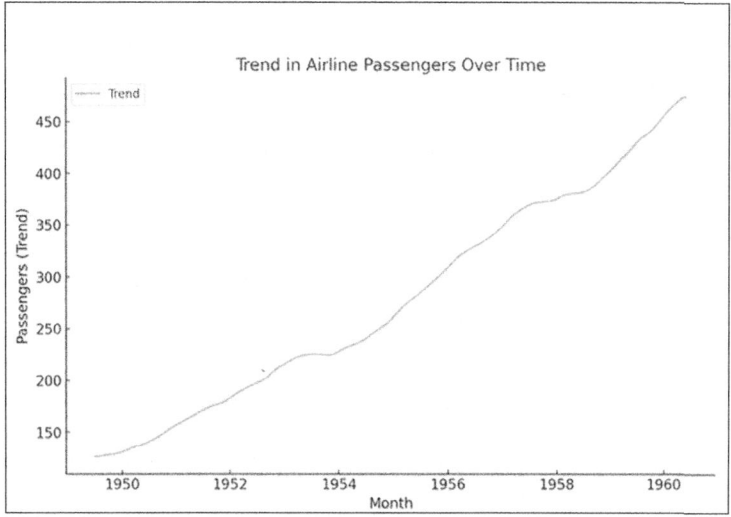

Figure 14.5: *Trend in Airline Passengers Over Time*

The noise component in a time series represents random variations or anomalies in the data that cannot be attributed to trend, seasonality, or level. It captures unpredictable and irregular fluctuations.

The decomposition of time-series data into Level, Trend, Seasonality, and Noise is essential for understanding its structure and preparing it for forecasting. This framework enables a systematic approach to analyzing and forecasting time-series data across various domains.

Classical modeling approaches such as Moving Average (MA), Autoregressive (AR), Autoregressive Moving Average (ARMA), and Autoregressive Integrated Moving Average (ARIMA) have been foundational in time-series analysis. These models are particularly effective in capturing linear dependencies and trends in sequential data. The AR model focuses on past values to predict future ones, while MA captures the influence of past errors. ARMA combines these two methods, and ARIMA extends ARMA by incorporating differencing to handle non-stationary data. However, these models have limitations when dealing with complex, non-linear patterns, or high-dimensional data often found in real-world scenarios. Additionally, classical methods struggle with multivariate time-series, or scenarios where relationships span long-term dependencies. In modern contexts, these challenges have spurred a transition to neural network-based models, which excel at capturing both linear and non-linear dependencies in sequential data, enabling robust and scalable solutions.

Challenges in Analyzing Sequential Data

Analyzing sequential data poses significant challenges due to its inherently dynamic and interconnected nature. Unlike traditional datasets where observations can be treated as independent, sequential data requires models that can account for dependencies across time or sequence positions. This interconnectedness adds complexity to the analysis, as each data point carries not only its intrinsic information but also the contextual information from its relationship with surrounding data points. For example, in a weather dataset, the temperature at a given hour depends on preceding temperatures, which must be factored into any meaningful analysis.

Traditional machine learning models often fall short of capturing these temporal dependencies. Models such as linear regression, decision trees, or even classical neural networks treat each observation as independent, ignoring the sequential context critical to understanding the underlying patterns. This limitation becomes evident in tasks such as time-series forecasting, where the inability to model temporal relationships can lead to inaccurate predictions and suboptimal insights.

Moreover, real-world sequential data introduces additional complexities. It is often noisy, containing outlier values or sudden shifts that do not follow established patterns. Irregular sampling rates, such as missing data points in a time-series dataset, add another layer of difficulty, as the sequence's continuity is disrupted. Sequential data can also be multidimensional, with multiple variables evolving simultaneously over time. For instance, in financial datasets, stock prices, trading volumes, and economic indicators may interact dynamically, further complicating the modeling process.

A deep understanding of sequential data is crucial for designing models that not only predict future trends but also uncover the underlying relationships within the data. Proper preprocessing, feature engineering, and selection of the right architecture are vital steps in ensuring successful outcomes in sequential data analysis. In a feedforward neural network, data flows in a single direction from input to output without loops, treating each input independently, while a recurrent neural network uses loops to feed information from previous time steps back into the network, allowing it to "remember" past inputs and process sequential data such as text or time series, making the computation process fundamentally different between the two architectures as shown in *Figure 14.6*.

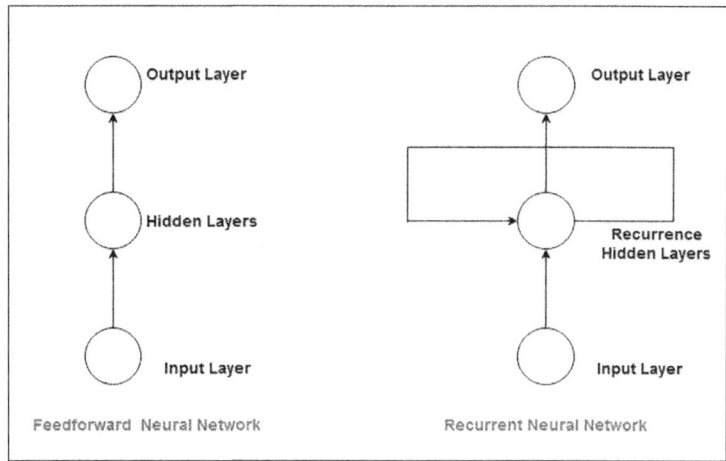

Figure 14.6: *Feedforward and Recurrent Neural Network Comparison*

RNNs are specifically designed to process sequential data by introducing recurrent connections, allowing the model to retain information from previous steps in the sequence. This capability enables RNNs to capture temporal dependencies effectively and learn patterns that unfold over time. By maintaining a "memory" of prior observations, RNNs can model complex relationships in sequential data, making them particularly well-suited for tasks, such as time-series forecasting, speech recognition, and text generation.

This section sets the stage for understanding the inherent challenges of sequential data and the need for neural networks capable of leveraging temporal dependencies, paving the way for exploring Recurrent Neural Networks in subsequent sections.

Understanding the Need for Recurrent Connections in Neural Networks

Sequential data such as time series, speech, and text inherently contains temporal dependencies where the meaning or value of a current data point often depends on previous data points. Traditional neural network architectures such as feedforward neural networks treat input data as independent, ignoring the sequential relationships that are vital for tasks involving context or time-dependent patterns. This limitation creates a need for a specialized approach that can capture these dependencies effectively.

For example, in natural language processing, the meaning of a word in a sentence depends on the preceding words. Similarly, in financial time-series data, the value of a stock today may depend on its historical values over the past days or weeks. A model that processes each input independently cannot effectively account for these contextual relationships, leading to suboptimal performance in such tasks.

Challenges of FeedForward Models for Sequential Data

Let us consider the sentence: "The cat sat on the mat." This is a simple, sequential sentence where understanding depends on the order and relationships between the words. A feedforward neural network processes input data independently, treating each word as a distinct entity without accounting for its position or relation to other words. This creates significant challenges for tasks such as next-word prediction or sequence classification.

Next Word Prediction Challenge

Suppose we want the model to predict the next word after "on the." If the input to a feedforward network consists of the independent words:

- Input: ["The", "cat", "sat", "on", "the"]
- Output: Prediction

A feedforward network lacks memory and does not retain the sequence context (for example, "sat on the" suggests "mat"). Instead, it treats these inputs as unrelated features, making it difficult to infer the correct next word, "mat." For example, it might incorrectly predict "dog" or "chair," as it cannot associate prior words to form a meaningful context.

Sequence Classification Challenge

If we want to classify the entire sentence as a specific label, say "Action at a Location," the feedforward model struggles to associate individual words to generate a meaningful sequence representation. The sentence requires context to connect "cat" with "sat" and "mat" with "location." A feedforward network processes each word separately, failing to link them as a coherent sequence. This can result in incorrect classification due to missing relationships, such as identifying the subject ("cat") and its action ("sat") together with the location ("mat").

The primary limitation is that feedforward networks treat all inputs as independent and lack mechanisms to retain or process prior information. Sequential data, however, inherently depends on:

1. **Temporal Order**: The sequence in which events or words occur is crucial
2. **Context**: Words or events gain meaning only in relation to their preceding or succeeding elements

Without mechanisms such as recurrent connections or memory, feed-forward networks fail to:

- Retain information about previous words (for example, "sat on the")
- Capture dependencies between distant words (for example,"cat" and "mat")

Recurrent connections in neural networks address this gap by enabling the network to "remember" information from previous time steps. This memory allows the network to dynamically update its understanding of the data as new inputs arrive. By introducing a feedback loop within the network, recurrent architectures effectively process sequential data while maintaining contextual awareness. This makes them particularly suited for applications such as time-series forecasting, machine translation, and speech recognition, where temporal dependencies are crucial.

Recurrent Connections in Neural Networks

Recurrent connections in neural networks address the fundamental limitation of traditional feed-forward architectures by introducing the concept of "memory." This enables the network to retain information from previous time steps and use it to inform decisions about the current input. Unlike feedforward models, which process data independently, recurrent neural networks (RNNs) create a feedback loop that allows information to flow from one time step to the next. This dynamic updating mechanism enables the network to build a contextual understanding of sequential data, making it particularly well-suited for tasks where the order and relationship between inputs matter.

For instance, in time-series forecasting, recurrent connections allow the model to capture patterns over time, such as seasonal trends or recurring behaviors, which are critical for accurate predictions. In applications such as machine translation, RNNs can maintain the context of a sentence as they process words sequentially, ensuring the translation preserves the intended meaning. Similarly, in speech recognition, recurrent architectures help decode audio signals by analyzing the flow of phonemes over time, enabling the recognition of entire words and sentences rather than isolated sounds.

The feedback loop in RNNs not only allows them to maintain contextual awareness but also dynamically adapts their understanding of the data as new inputs arrive. For example, in stock market analysis, the model can use recent price movements to predict future trends while continuously updating its predictions as new data points are added. This ability to adapt makes RNNs highly effective for scenarios where real-time data processing is required, such as live weather forecasting or sentiment analysis on streaming social media data.

Moreover, recurrent connections enable RNNs to handle sequences of varying lengths, a crucial feature for tasks such as natural language processing (NLP). For instance, RNNs can process short phrases such as "Hello world" as effectively as they can process longer texts such as "Once upon a time, in a land far away." This flexibility ensures that the network does not impose rigid constraints on the input data, making it versatile across a wide range of sequential applications.

In the following section, we will delve deeper into the detailed architecture and the underlying mathematical principles of RNNs, exploring how they function and are trained to handle such complex tasks.

Architecture and Working Principle of a Basic RNN

In this section, we will delve into the fundamental architecture and working principles of a basic RNN. RNNs are designed to handle sequential data by "remembering" information from previously processed inputs. This capability makes them well-suited for tasks, such as language modeling, time series forecasting, and speech recognition. Here, we will build our understanding step-by-step, starting with the structural aspects of a simple RNN cell and then examining how the network evolves its hidden state over time.

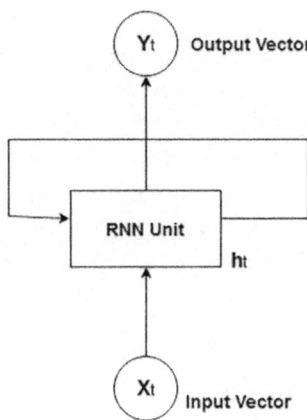

Figure 14.7: *Structure of RNN Architecture*

Let us start by visualizing a basic RNN architecture shown in *Figure* 14.7. At its heart, an RNN unit is a small computational unit that takes an input vector and a hidden state vector from the previous time step and then produces a new hidden state.

Introduction to Recurrent Neural Networks

Conceptually, you can imagine the RNN unit as a function that reads the current input x_t at time t and the previous hidden state h_{t-1} and outputs a new hidden state h_t. This hidden state is essentially a summary of all the relevant information that the network has encountered in the sequence so far. Internally, the RNN cell contains parameters such as weight matrices and bias vectors that transform and combine x_t and h_{t-1}. The first step during the forward pass involves computing a weighted combination of the current input and the previous hidden state. We typically define:

$$h_t = \tanh(W_{hh}.h_{t-1} + W_{xh}.x_t + b_h)$$

where W_{xh} is the weight matrix connecting the input to the hidden layer, W_{hh} is the recurrent weight matrix connecting the hidden state at t-1 to the hidden state at t, and b_h is a bias vector.

The function f(.) is often a nonlinear activation function, such as hyperbolic tangent (tanh). This ensures that the hidden state can capture non-linear relationships across time.

Once we have computed the hidden state h_t, we may also produce an output at each time step, which is typically defined as:

$$\hat{y}_t = W_{hy}.h_t + b_y$$

Where W_{hy} is the weight matrix mapping the hidden state to the output, and b_y is a corresponding bias. Depending on the task, the output could represent a probability distribution over vocabulary words (in the case of language modeling) or a predicted numerical value (in the case of time series forecasting). By applying the same computations at each time step, we effectively "unfold" the RNN in time, creating a computational graph that shows how hidden states and outputs evolve as we move forward in a sequence as depicted in *Figure* 14.8 for three time steps.

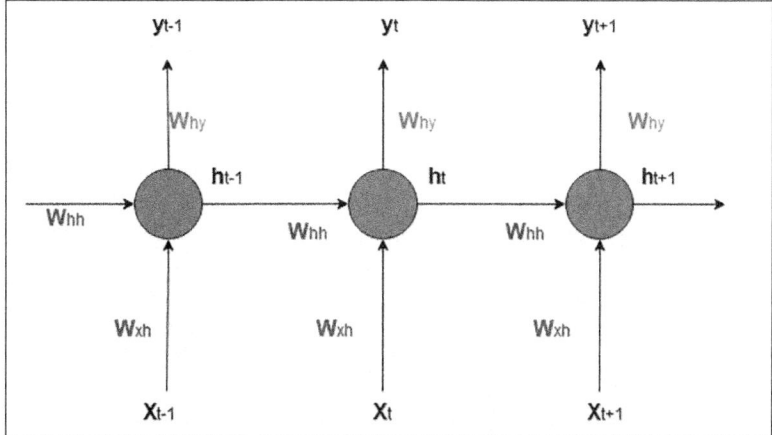

Figure 14.8: *Unfolding RNN Over Time*

By repeatedly applying the same cell parameters across all time steps, the network "unrolls" across a sequence, allowing it to learn temporal patterns and long-term dependencies.

Training the RNN Architecture

From a training perspective, the RNN's objective is to adjust the parameters such that the network can accurately predict desired outputs given the sequence of inputs. This is typically done using an adaptation of the standard gradient-based optimization methods called Backpropagation Through Time (BPTT). BPTT involves unrolling the RNN for a fixed number of time steps and then computing gradients of a loss function with respect to each parameter by back-propagating through the unfolded network. While this process is computationally more expensive than standard backpropagation in feedforward networks, it allows the RNN to learn from sequences of arbitrary length.

Let us consider a basic RNN that processes a sequence of two inputs $\{x_1, x_2\}$. We assume an initial hidden state h_0, which can be a vector of zeros.

At the first time step (t=1) during the forward pass, the hidden state and output state response are given as:

$$h_1 = \tanh(W_{xh} \cdot x_1 + W_{hh} \cdot h_0 + b_h)$$
$$y_1 = W_{hy} \cdot h_1 + b_y$$

In the second time step (t=2), the network again uses the same parameters but now takes x_2 and h_1 as inputs:

$$h_2 = \tanh(W_{xh} \cdot x_2 + W_{hh} \cdot h_1 + b_h)$$
$$y_2 = W_{hy} \cdot h_2 + b_y$$

If we denote the loss at each time step as L_1 and L_2 (for example, cross-entropy loss in language modeling or mean squared error in time series prediction), then the total loss across these two steps is often a simple sum:

$$L = L_1 + L_2$$

Backpropagation Through Time

To train the RNN, we need to compute gradients of L with respect to all parameters $W_{xh}, W_{hh}, W_{hy}, b_h$, and b_y. BPTT conceptually "unrolls" the RNN into two feedforward-like layers corresponding to the two time steps. We then back-propagate the error signals from each time step through this unrolled structure.

Introduction to Recurrent Neural Networks

Output Gradients

For each time step t ∈ {1, 2}, we first compute $\frac{\partial L}{\partial y_t}$

The loss function can be defined as $L = \frac{1}{2}[y - \tanh(W_{hy}.h_2 + b_y)]$

Since, $y_t = W_{hy}.h_t + b_y$, we apply the chain rule:

$$\frac{\partial L}{\partial W_{hy}} = \frac{\partial L}{\partial y_t} \cdot \frac{\partial y_t}{\partial net} \cdot \frac{\partial net}{\partial W_{hy}}$$

$$\frac{\partial L}{\partial W_{hy}} = \sum_{t=1}^{2} \left(\frac{\partial L}{\partial y_t} \cdot h_t\right)$$

$$\frac{\partial L}{\partial b_y} = \sum_{t=1}^{2} \left(\frac{\partial L}{\partial y_t}\right)$$

Hidden State Gradients

The gradient flows back from y_t into h_t. For each time step:

$$\frac{\partial L}{\partial h_t} = \frac{\partial L}{\partial y_t}.W_{hy} + \text{(gradient coming from future time steps)}$$

At $t = 2$, there is no future time step (since we have considered 2 step unroll)

$$\frac{\partial L}{\partial h_2} = \frac{\partial L}{\partial y_2}.W_{hy}$$

At $t = 1$, the gradient coming from the future (time step 2) also matters:

$$\frac{\partial L}{\partial h_1} = \frac{\partial L}{\partial y_1}.W_{hy} + \left[\frac{\partial L}{\partial h_2}.f'(z_2)\right].W_{hh}$$

Where $z_2 = W_{xh}.x_2 + W_{hh}.h_1 + b_h$ is the pre-activation at time step-2, and $f'(z_2)$ represents the element-wise multiplication by the derivative of the activation function at z_2. This term captures how changes in h_1 propagate to the loss at time step-2.

Parameter Gradients

Each hidden state h_t depends on both x_t and h_{t-1} for $t = 2$:

$$\frac{\partial L}{\partial W_{xh}} = \left[\frac{\partial L}{\partial h_2}.f'(z_2)\right].x_2$$

$$\frac{\partial L}{\partial W_{hh}} = \left[\frac{\partial L}{\partial h_2}.f'(z_2)\right].h_1$$

$$\frac{\partial L}{\partial b_h} = \left[\frac{\partial L}{\partial h_2}.f'(z_2)\right]$$

Similarly, at $t = 1$:

$$\frac{\partial L}{\partial W_{xh}} = \left[\frac{\partial L}{\partial h_1}.f'(z_1)\right].x_1$$

$$\frac{\partial L}{\partial W_{hh}} = \left[\frac{\partial L}{\partial h_1}.f'(z_1)\right].h_0$$

$$\frac{\partial L}{\partial b_h} = \left[\frac{\partial L}{\partial h_1}.f'(z_1)\right]$$

We sum the contributions from both time steps to get the total gradient with respect to each parameter. Finally, an optimization algorithm (for example, stochastic gradient descent or Adam) uses these gradients to update the model parameters.

By unrolling for two time steps, we have seen how the hidden state influences both h_t and h_{t+1}. In practice, this unrolling can continue for many time steps (or even the full length of the input sequence). Though more computationally demanding than standard backpropagation in feed-forward networks, BPTT captures dependencies across time, enabling the RNN to learn how earlier inputs affect later outputs.

Limitations of RNN

In this section, we will examine some of the key limitations of basic RNNs. While RNNs excel at capturing sequential dependencies, especially for short sequences, several challenges arise when dealing with longer contexts or complex patterns. The vanishing and exploding gradient problems, difficulties with long-range dependencies, and issues around computational efficiency are a few of the most notable hurdles. By understanding these limitations, we can better appreciate why more advanced architectures, such as Long Short-Term Memory (LSTM) networks and Gated Recurrent Units (GRUs), have been developed, as they offer explicit mechanisms to mitigate the effects of vanishing and exploding gradients. In the next chapter, we will explore these models in greater depth, examining how they address the shortcomings of basic RNNs and enable more robust learning over longer sequences. In the following section, let us see how these limitations manifest in practice and what potential workarounds or solutions researchers have adopted over time.

- **Vanishing Gradient Problem:** One of the most prominent issues with basic RNNs is the vanishing gradient problem. During the BPTT process, gradients flow backward from the final time step to earlier ones. For very long sequences, this backward flow often becomes negligible by the time it reaches the initial steps, causing the network to "forget" critical information that appeared far in the past. As the gradients exponentially shrink, the parameters in earlier time steps barely get updated, resulting in poor performance on tasks that require long-term memory, such as long-text comprehension or complex time-series forecasting. This phenomenon limits an RNN's ability to learn dependencies beyond a certain temporal window, making it difficult to capture important contextual clues when sequences span hundreds or thousands of steps.

- **Difficulty in Capturing Long-Range Dependencies:** Even if we address vanishing and exploding gradients through techniques, such as careful initialization, gradient clipping, or certain activation functions, basic RNNs still struggle to capture dependencies that stretch far across time. Consider a language modeling task where the meaning of a word at the beginning of a paragraph influences how we interpret a subsequent phrase at the end of the paragraph. A standard RNN might not maintain a coherent representation of that early information by the time it needs to predict the final words. This deficiency becomes critical in applications, such as machine translation, sentiment analysis of extended texts, and scientific document classification. Consequently, while basic RNNs are still useful for relatively short sequences, they are often outperformed by architectures specifically designed to handle longer contexts.

- **Computational Bottlenecks:** From a computational perspective, RNNs can be quite resource-intensive to train, especially when unrolled over many time steps. Each step in the sequence depends on the previous hidden state, making it challenging to parallelize computations across different parts of the sequence. This sequential nature contrasts with feedforward or convolutional architectures that can often process large batches in parallel. Training time increases substantially as the sequence length grows, and GPU utilization may not be as efficient because the core operation recurrent updates must be performed step-by-step. As a result, practitioners frequently truncate the backpropagation window to a fixed size to balance memory constraints and training speed, but this truncation can further degrade the network's ability to learn long-range dependencies.

- **Memory Constraints in Long Sequences:** Memory constraints also pose a problem in both practical and theoretical senses. As we unroll an RNN over many time steps, the computational graph grows, leading to increased memory usage. For tasks that process very long sequences, such as natural language documents, video frames, or sensor data streams, this can quickly become impractical. Additionally, storing intermediate activations is crucial for BPTT, which multiplies the memory cost. Many real-world problems demand real-time processing, compounding the difficulty when deploying RNNs on devices with limited memory and computational power. Though partial unrolling and gradient truncation methods exist to address these constraints, they inherently limit the model's capacity to truly learn long-term dependencies.

All these limitations, including vanishing and exploding gradients, difficulties in capturing long-range dependencies, computational bottlenecks, and high sensitivity to hyperparameters, underscore the need to advance the basic RNN framework. Researchers have put forward a variety of solutions, including specialized gating mechanisms (as in LSTMs and GRUs) and other memory-augmented models capable of maintaining richer histories. In many fields, attention methods and Transformer architectures have gone a step further, drawing focus away from strictly recurrent cells. Despite these developments, the classic RNN still serves as a crucial cornerstone in sequence modeling. By recognizing its limitations, we can better appreciate why modern approaches have evolved in the manner they have. In the next chapter, we will discuss these advanced architectures in detail, highlighting how they address the core challenges outlined here.

Conclusion

In this chapter, we explored the foundational concepts of sequential data and time-series analysis, emphasizing the unique challenges and complexities associated with processing such data. Traditional machine learning models often fall short when capturing temporal dependencies, highlighting the need for specialized architectures such as RNNs.

We then delved into the significance of recurrent connections in neural networks, which enable models to "remember" past information and dynamically update their understanding of data sequences. This capability has made RNNs indispensable for applications, such as natural language processing, time-series forecasting, and speech recognition. The architecture and working principle of a basic RNN were thoroughly examined, along with the underlying mathematical foundations, including gradient calculations and the concept of BPTT, which enables the training of RNNs by updating weights based on sequential dependencies.

Despite their groundbreaking contributions, RNNs face notable limitations, such as vanishing and exploding gradients, which hinder their ability to process long sequences effectively. These limitations pave the way for advancements such as Long Short-Term Memory (LSTM) networks and Gated Recurrent Units (GRUs), which address these challenges. In the next chapter, we will explore these advanced recurrent architectures, diving deeper into their designs and capabilities, which have further revolutionized the handling of sequential data.

Practice Exercises

1. Consider an RNN with the following parameters:

    - Input size: 3
    - Hidden layer size: 4
    - Output size: 2

    If the weight matrices are initialized as follows:

    - W_x: 4×3
    - W_h: 4×4
    - W_y: 2×4

2. How many total trainable parameters does the RNN have, including biases?

3. Given an input x_t=[1,2,−1], previous hidden state h_{t-1} = [0.5,−0.5,0.3,−0.2], weight matrices W_x =[[0.2,0.1,−0.1],[0.3,−0.2,0.2],[−0.3,0.4,−0.2],[0.1,−0.1,0.5]], and W_h =[0.2,−0.1,0.1,0.4],[−0.2,0.3,−0.3,0.1],[0.3,−0.4,0.2,−0.2],[0.1,0.2,−0.1,0.3]],and bias b = [0.1,−0.1,0.2,0.1], calculate the net input for h_t.

4. If an RNN processes a sequence of length 10, and each time step takes 0.5 seconds to compute, how long will a full forward pass for one sequence take?

5. A basic RNN is unrolled for 5 time steps during training. If the loss gradient at the final time step is 0.8, and the gradient diminishes by half at each preceding step, what is the gradient value at the first time step?

6. Consider a sequence-to-sequence RNN model where the input sequence is of length 4 and the output sequence is of length 3. If the hidden state dimension is 5 and the input vector size is 3, how many times does the model update its hidden states during a forward pass?

Answers

1. $W_x = 4 \times 3 = 12$, $W_h = 4 \times 4 = 16$, $W_y = 2 \times 4 = 8$

   Biases = Hidden layer Bias (4) + Output layer Bias (2) = 6

   Total = 12 + 16 + 8 + 6 = 42

2. Each time step computes one hidden state, since there are five time steps, the RNN will perform 5 hidden state calculations.

3. $h_t = \tanh(W_x \cdot x_t + W_h \cdot h_{t-1} + bias)$

   Net input matrix before applying: [1.02, -0.56, 0.31, 0.14]

4. Time per sequence = Number of time steps × Time per step = 10 × 0.5 = 5 seconds

5. Gradient diminishes by half, so:

   Gradient at step 5: 0.8

   Step 4: 0.8×0.5=0.4, Step 3: 0.4×0.5=0.2, Step 2: 0.2×0.5=0.1, Step 1: 0.1×0.5=0.05

6. The hidden state is updated for each input time step during encoding, so it is updated 4 times for the input sequence. During decoding, the hidden state is updated for each output time step, so it is updated 3 times for the output sequence. Hence, the total hidden state updates are 7.

Multiple Choice Questions

1. What is the primary feature of sequential data?

    a. Independent data points

    b. High dimensionality

c. Temporal dependencies

   d. Sparse representation

2. Why do traditional feed-forward networks fail in processing sequential data?

   a. They do not use activation functions

   b. They lack memory of past inputs

   c. They only work with linear data

   d. They require labeled data for training

3. What is the role of recurrent connections in RNNs?

   a. To reduce computation time

   b. To enable the network to process independent inputs

   c. To remember information from previous time steps

   d. To increase the size of the network

4. Which of the following is a key component of RNN architecture?

   a. Dropout layer

   b. Feedback loop

   c. Convolutional layer

   d. Pooling layer

5. What problem does Back Propagation Through Time (BPTT) solve in RNNs?

   a. Reduces the model size

   b. Enables sequential gradient updates

   c. Removes temporal dependencies

   d. Simplifies network training

6. What is the purpose of unrolling an RNN during training?

   a. To process inputs in parallel

   b. To visualize temporal dependencies

   c. To compute gradients for each time step

   d. To reduce overfitting

7. Which activation function is commonly used in the hidden layers of basic RNNs?

   a. ReLU

   b. Sigmoid

   c. Tanh

   d. Softmax

8. In time-series analysis, what does temporal dependency refer to?

   a. Data points that are randomly sampled

   b. Data points that are unrelated to each other

   c. Data points that are influenced by preceding values

   d. Data points that have no missing values

9. Which field is NOT a common application of RNNs?

   a. Image classification

   b. Time-series forecasting

   c. Speech recognition

   d. Natural language processing

10. Which of the following is a direct consequence of the vanishing gradient problem in RNNs?

    a. Reduced model size

    b. Inability to learn long-term dependencies

    c. Increased model complexity

    d. Faster convergence during training

Answers

1. c
2. b
3. c
4. b
5. b

6. c
7. c
8. c
9. a
10. b

Keywords

- Sequential Data
- Temporal Dependencies
- Time-Series Analysis
- Recurrent Neural Network (RNN)
- Recurrent Connections
- Feedback Loop
- Back Propagation Through Time (BPTT)
- Unrolled RNN
- Context Awareness
- Memory in Neural Networks
- Training Sequential Data
- Limitations of RNNs
- Natural Language Processing (NLP)
- Time-Series Forecasting
- Speech Recognition
- Long-Term Dependencies
- Short-Term Dependencies
- Sequential Processing
- Gradient Descent in RNNs
- Sequence-to-Sequence Modeling

References

1. https://www.cs.cmu.edu/~bhiksha/courses/deeplearning/Fall.2016/pdfs/Werbos.backprop.pdf
2. https://www.sciencedirect.com/science/article/pii/S0950705124004593?via%3Dihub

CHAPTER 15
Introduction to Long Short-Term Memory (LSTM)

Introduction

This chapter explores the transformative advancements in sequential data processing introduced by Long Short-Term Memory (LSTM) networks. Traditional Recurrent Neural Networks (RNNs), despite their effectiveness in modeling short-term dependencies, face significant challenges when tasked with capturing long-term relationships in data. LSTMs were developed to overcome these limitations, offering a robust solution to the vanishing gradient problem and enabling the efficient handling of long-term dependencies.

This chapter begins by addressing the core issues of traditional RNNs, particularly their inability to retain information over extended sequences. We then highlight the advantages of LSTMs, showcasing their unique ability to learn and retain long-term dependencies. Following this, the architecture and working principles of LSTMs will be explored in detail, including their memory cell, gating mechanisms, and how they facilitate selective information flow. Finally, we will introduce the Gated Recurrent Unit (GRU), a simplified version of the LSTM, comparing its design and functionality to help readers grasp the nuances of gated architectures.

Structure

In this chapter, we are going to cover the following main topics:

- Overcoming the Long-Term Dependency Problem in RNN
- Advantages of LSTMs over Traditional RNNs
- Architecture and Working Principle of LSTM
- Simplified Representation of LSTM as Gated Recurrent Unit (GRU)

Overcoming the Long-Term Dependency Problem in RNN

In this section, we will take a closer look at the long-term dependency challenge inherent in basic Recurrent Neural Networks (RNNs). Recall that the foundation of an RNN lies in passing information from one time step to the next through its hidden state. While this architecture works well for sequences of moderate length, it struggles as the time span grows larger. Information from early inputs can fade away, leaving the network with insufficient context to make accurate predictions at later steps. This phenomenon is sometimes referred to as the vanishing gradient problem, where gradient signals become extremely small when they are backpropagated over many time steps. Conversely, when gradients become excessively large, we encounter the exploding gradient problem. Both scenarios inhibit effective learning of long-range dependencies. As a result, text generation, language translation, and other tasks requiring significant contextual awareness often surpass the capabilities of basic RNNs. Let us discuss some of the strategies that have been developed to address these limitations.

- **Gradient Clipping:** One of the more straightforward solutions to mitigate exploding gradients is gradient clipping. The idea is simple yet effective: during backpropagation, we compute the norm of the gradient vector, and if it exceeds a predefined threshold, we scale it down to match that threshold. This will prevent excessively large updates to the RNN's parameters, avoiding numerical instabilities or abrupt changes in the loss function. Gradient clipping helps stabilize training, particularly in the early stages when weight updates can be chaotic. Although it does not directly resolve the vanishing gradient problem, this technique serves as a useful safeguard against gradient explosions in the unrolled computation graph of an RNN. Many modern deep learning frameworks offer built-in routines for gradient clipping, reinforcing its importance as a standard practice in sequential model training.

- **Careful Initialization and Activation Functions:** Another approach to partially alleviating long-term dependency issues revolves around careful initialization of RNN parameters and the choice of activation functions. If the recurrent weight matrix is initialized improperly, say, with values too large, then repeated multiplications over time steps can quickly inflate gradient magnitudes, leading to exploding gradients. Conversely, if weights are too small, the gradients can diminish prematurely. Orthogonal initialization and controlled variance scaling are popular strategies to ensure stable gradients. Furthermore, the selection of activation functions, such as tanh or sigmoid, can have a considerable impact. Tanh, for example, naturally keeps values within a -1 to 1 range, thereby reducing the likelihood of extreme activations but still risking saturation for large inputs. ReLU functions avoid saturation for positive inputs, although they can suffer from "dead" neurons if hidden states remain in the negative regime. By adjusting these factors, we can mitigate, though not entirely resolve, the challenges of modeling long-term dependencies.

- **Skip Connections and Residual Networks:** Besides addressing gradients directly, some architectural modifications can help RNNs capture more extended contexts. One notable idea involves incorporating skip connections or residual pathways into the recurrent computation. These connections effectively allow information to bypass certain layers or time steps, offering a more direct route for gradients to flow backward through the network. While skip connections are more commonly associated with feedforward and convolutional neural networks (for instance, in ResNet architectures), they can be adapted for use in RNNs. By creating shortcuts that circumvent intermediate transformations, the network can retain earlier signals and thus mitigate the depth-related degradation of information. Although not as widely used as in CNN-based models, skip connections in recurrent architectures remain an active area of research and can offer promising results in tasks requiring extended memory.

- **Dilated Recurrent Networks:** Another intriguing approach is the use of dilated recurrent networks, which introduce a notion of skipping specific time steps in the recurrent connection. Rather than updating the hidden state at every consecutive time step, the RNN updates at intervals or "dilations," for instance, every second or third time step. By spacing out the updates, the network can effectively observe patterns over broader temporal spans without drastically increasing the depth of the computation graph. This method can be particularly useful in time series analysis, where sampling rates and repetitive patterns can be accounted for through controlled dilations. Though not a universal fix for all long-range dependency issues, dilated recurrence can broaden an RNN's receptive field, enabling it to focus on strategically chosen time steps for both forward and backward passes.

- **External Memory Augmentation:** Beyond purely architectural changes within the RNN cell, researchers have explored the idea of augmenting RNNs with external memory modules. These modules act like differentiable memory banks that store and retrieve information over a longer span than the basic hidden state can manage. By employing specialized read and write operations, the RNN can selectively interact with the memory, retaining relevant details from distant time steps. These approaches, sometimes classified under the banner of memory-augmented neural networks, can better handle tasks such as question answering or summarization, where it is crucial to recall information from far back in the input sequence. However, these methods can introduce additional complexity, both in terms of architectural design and training procedures, and often require meticulous tuning to realize their full potential in real-world applications.

While the strategies described in this section can address certain facets of the long-term dependency problem, a truly robust solution lies in specialized gating mechanisms. This leads us to the development of LSTM networks and GRUs, both of which offer more systematic ways to regulate the flow of information through time. By explicitly controlling what to remember and what to forget, these models significantly reduce the problems of vanishing and exploding gradients. In the following section, we will explore how LSTMs implement gating and memory cells and why they are particularly effective for tasks requiring long-range context retention.

Advantages of LSTMs over Traditional RNNs

The real breakthrough in sequence data modeling came with the development of LSTM networks by Hochreiter and Schmidhuber in 1997. LSTMs introduced a novel memory cell structure and gating mechanisms that allow the network to retain, forget, or update information dynamically, effectively solving the long-term dependency problem. By enabling selective memory retention and addressing the vanishing gradient issue, LSTMs provide a powerful solution for processing sequential data. They ensure that essential context is preserved across long sequences, allowing models to understand intricate temporal relationships. This breakthrough has made LSTMs indispensable in fields, such as natural language processing, speech synthesis, and time-series forecasting. Let us explore the key advantages that set LSTMs apart from traditional RNNs.

- **Addressing the Vanishing Gradient Problem:** One of the most significant advantages of LSTM networks over traditional RNNs is their ability to mitigate the vanishing gradient problem. In traditional RNNs, the gradients during backpropagation through time (BPTT) tend to diminish exponentially as they propagate backward through longer sequences. This makes it difficult for the model to update weights effectively for earlier time steps, causing the network to "forget" long-term dependencies. LSTMs address this issue by incorporating a unique memory cell structure and gating mechanisms that allow gradients to flow unimpeded over time. This innovation ensures that important information can be retained and updated dynamically, enabling LSTMs to learn dependencies over much longer sequences.

- **Selective Memory Retention:** LSTMs introduce three specialized gates, such as input gate, forget gate, and output gate, that work together to control the flow of information. The forget gate enables the network to discard irrelevant information, while the input gate decides what new information to store. The output gate determines what part of the memory to expose as output. This selective retention mechanism is what allows LSTMs to process both short-term and long-term dependencies effectively, giving them a significant edge in tasks that require a nuanced understanding of sequential data, particularly for language modeling.

- **Handling Long-Term Dependencies:** Traditional RNNs struggle with long-term dependencies, especially in applications where the context from earlier time steps is crucial for predictions. LSTMs excel in these scenarios due to their ability to retain essential information over extended sequences. For instance, in natural language processing tasks such as text generation or translation, the ability of LSTMs to remember context from earlier sentences ensures coherence and semantic accuracy in generated text.

- **Enhanced Learning Capacity for Complex Patterns:** The advanced memory mechanisms in LSTMs enable them to learn complex temporal patterns that traditional RNNs cannot handle effectively. This makes them particularly useful for applications such as speech recognition, where nuanced patterns in audio signals need to be identified over time. Similarly, in time-series forecasting, LSTMs can model intricate trends and seasonality better than RNNs, leading to more accurate predictions.

- **Robustness to Noise in Sequential Data:** Sequential data, such as sensor readings or stock market trends, often contains noise that can interfere with learning. Traditional RNNs lack the ability to filter out irrelevant information effectively. LSTMs, on the other hand, leverage their gating mechanisms to discard noisy or redundant information during training. This selective filtering improves the robustness of LSTMs and enhances their performance in real-world scenarios.

- **Improved Training Stability:** Traditional RNNs often suffer from unstable training dynamics due to their difficulty in maintaining meaningful gradients over long sequences. LSTMs overcome this instability through their memory cell structure, which ensures smooth gradient flow and reduces the likelihood of exploding gradients. This stability enables LSTMs to converge faster and achieve better generalization.

- **Versatility in Applications:** LSTMs have demonstrated remarkable versatility across a wide range of applications, including natural language processing, speech synthesis, and biomedical time-series analysis. Their ability to adapt to diverse data types and capture both short-term and long-term dependencies makes them indispensable in modern AI applications.

- **Compatibility with Modern Deep Learning Frameworks:** The widespread support for LSTMs in modern deep learning frameworks, such as TensorFlow and PyTorch, has made them accessible to researchers and practitioners. These frameworks provide pre-built implementations of LSTMs, making it easier to design, train, and deploy models for sequential data processing tasks.

- **Foundation for Advanced Variants:** LSTMs serve as the foundation for many advanced architectures, including Bidirectional LSTMs and GRUs. These variants build upon the principles of LSTMs, offering improved efficiency and performance for specific tasks. Understanding the advantages of LSTMs is thus essential for appreciating the broader ecosystem of sequence modeling architectures.

However, to truly appreciate how LSTMs manage information flow, we must explore their internal design more closely. In the following section, we will delve into the structural components of an LSTM cell and learn how each gate operates behind the scenes. By examining these details, we can see precisely how LSTMs outperform traditional RNNs and why they continue to play a pivotal role in many state-of-the-art sequence-based models.

Architecture and Working Principles of LSTM

In this section, we will dive into the internal design of LSTM networks. Building on the motivations outlined in the previous sections, an LSTM cell addresses the limitations of traditional RNNs by incorporating a more sophisticated mechanism to control how information flows through time. Rather than relying on a single hidden state that repeatedly transforms with each time step, an LSTM maintains two primary components: a cell state and a hidden state. The cell state acts as a long-term memory, while the hidden state plays a more immediate, short-term role. Together, these components enable the network to decide what information to keep, what to discard, and how to update its internal representation of the sequence. Because the LSTM cell is specifically designed to combat vanishing and exploding gradients, it can more effectively capture long-range dependencies across many time steps.

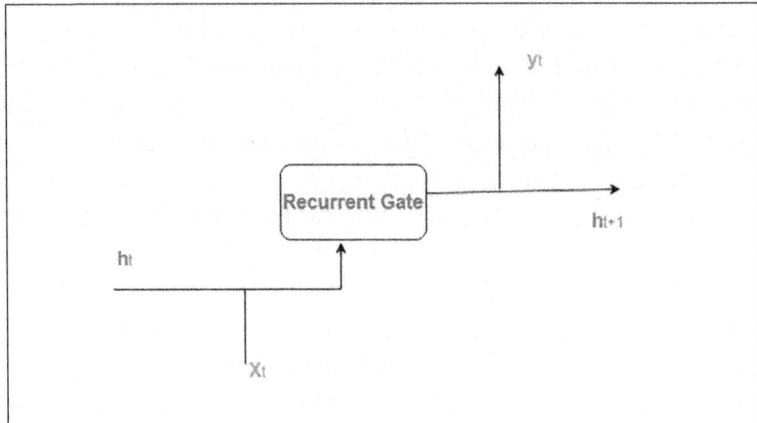

Figure 15.1: Basic RNN Unit

Let us start by visualizing a basic RNN unit; there is effectively a single "gate" or transformation as shown in *Figure 15.1*. Since there is only one hidden state, the

Introduction to Long Short-Term Memory (LSTM)

network can struggle with long-term dependencies; it has no explicit mechanism to decide which information to keep or forget over many time steps. Despite these limitations, basic RNN units can still be effective for short-sequence applications where the dependencies between time steps are limited. For instance, they are well-suited for tasks such as next-word prediction in a short sentence or sentiment analysis of brief texts, where the context required for accurate predictions does not span over a long sequence. Additionally, basic RNNs can be employed in time-series forecasting for small datasets, such as predicting stock prices or weather conditions for a short horizon, where the model can efficiently capture dependencies within a limited time frame.

Another example of their utility is in speech recognition for isolated words, where the sequence of phonemes or sound frames is relatively short, and the context is localized. While these applications showcase the potential of basic RNNs, they also highlight their constraints. As the length of the sequence increases, the network struggles to retain relevant information, often leading to the vanishing gradient problem during training.

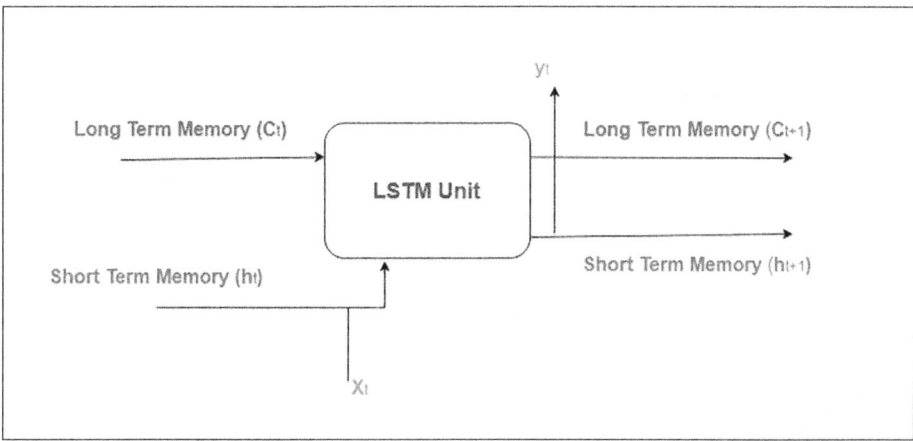

Figure 15.2: LSTM Unit with Short-Term and Long-Term Memory

Whereas in the LSTM unit, there are two distinct forms of memory known as short-term memory (the hidden state, h_t); this is analogous to the hidden state in RNN and is used for immediate computations at each time step and a long-term memory (the cell state, c_t) as shown in *Figure 15.2*. This acts as a "protected" conveyor belt of information that can carry important data across many time steps without being overwritten at every step. This design explicitly manages what is kept or forgotten over time, mitigating the vanishing and exploding gradient issues common in basic RNNs. The output y_t typically depends on the updated hidden state h_{t+1}, which is itself influenced by the long-term memory c_{t+1}.

The Core Gates of LSTM

At the heart of every LSTM cell are three gates, as shown in *Figure 15.3*: forget, input or update, and output. These gates serve as checkpoints for the flow of information, enabling the network to selectively modify its cell state. The forget gate determines which parts of the previous cell state should be retained, the input or update gate regulates what new information should be added, and the output gate controls how much of the updated cell state is shared with the rest of the network as the hidden state.

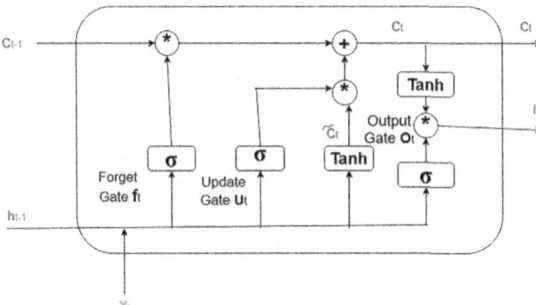

Figure 15.3: LSTM Architecture with Memory Gates

This gating system offers a level of explicit control absent in standard RNNs, which rely on a single hidden state transformation. Internally, each gate is typically implemented using a sigmoid activation function σ(·), producing outputs between 0 and 1 that act like "switches" or "weights." By carefully adjusting these values, the LSTM can learn to remember context over long spans or quickly forget irrelevant details while mitigating issues of gradient decay or explosion.

Forward Pass

At each time step t, the LSTM cell receives three inputs:

- The current input
- The previous short-term memory (hidden state) h_{t-1}
- The previous long-term memory (cell state) C_{t-1}

Forget Gate

The forget gate decides which parts of the previous cell state should be retained:

$$f_t = \sigma\left(w_f[h_{t-1}, x_t] + b_f\right)$$

Where, $[h_{t-1}, x_t]$ is the concatenation of the hidden state and input vector. A value of $f_t \approx 1$ means "keep most of what's in C_{t-1}" while $f_t \approx 0$ means "forget it". For example, imagine you are reading a long story and have a mental checklist of details to keep track of.

Introduction to Long Short-Term Memory (LSTM)

At some point, you realize that certain information, such as the color of a minor character's shirt, is irrelevant to the plot moving forward. The forget gate in an LSTM serves this purpose: it decides what to let go of from past information. If a detail no longer contributes to the ongoing narrative, the forget gate "zeros it out" so the model does not waste its finite memory capacity holding onto unimportant things. This frees up space to remember only what truly matters for making predictions in later steps.

Update Gate

The update gate decides how much new information to add to the cell state:

$$u_t = \sigma(w_u[h_{t-1}, x_t] + b_u)$$

This gate "opens" or "closes" the cell to fresh inputs. With the story analogy, after deciding what is no longer needed, you come across a new piece of critical information, perhaps a twist in the plot or a fresh clue that could be important later. The update gate's role is to decide how much of this new detail should be added to your ongoing mental record. If it is highly relevant, then you incorporate it into your memory; if it is only marginally important, then you add it more sparingly. In this way, the update gate ensures that your knowledge stays relevant and grows in response to genuinely noteworthy events in the sequence.

Candidate Cell State

In parallel, the candidate cell state $\tilde{C}_t$ is computed:

$$\tilde{C}_t = \tanh(w_c[h_{t-1}, x_t] + b_c)$$

This represents the new information proposed for inclusion in long-term memory. Continuing with our story analogy, the candidate cell state can be thought of as the new proposed storyline you come up with after reading the latest chapter. It is the initial draft of what might become part of your "master record" (your long-term memory). Before you add any fresh details to your ongoing mental narrative, you first consider them in a rough form: "Should I incorporate this plot twist or character clue?" That consideration forms your candidate cell state. Some of these details may be highly relevant and deserving of full attention, whereas others are less critical. The update gate then decides just how much of these proposed elements make it into your long-term memory.

Cell State Update

Once you have your candidate additions to the storyline, you must merge them with the details you are already carrying in your memory. This merging step is the cell state update. It integrates what remains useful from the old memory (after the forget gate has discarded unimportant parts) with the new insights you have just encountered (the candidate state). The result is your updated mental record, a blend of what was already there and the new, carefully filtered information. By revising this record at every step, the LSTM ensures it continuously balances the significance of past knowledge with fresh data from the evolving sequence. After deciding what to forget and what to add, the new long-term memory C_t is updated as:

$$C_t = f_t \odot \overline{C_{t-1}} + u_t \odot \tilde{C}_t$$

Where $\odot$ denotes element-wise multiplication. This is the crux of LSTM's ability to control long-term information flow:

- Forget Gate f_t zeros out unneeded parts of the old state.
- Update Gate u_t integrates relevant new candidate values $\tilde{C}_t$.

C_t carries information across time steps without being fully overwritten at every update and provides resilience against vanishing and exploding gradients by limiting how quickly information fades or amplifies.

Output Gate and Final Hidden State

Finally, the output gate determines how much of the updated cell state contributes to the new hidden state h_t:

$$o_t = \sigma(w_o[h_{t-1}, x_t] + b_o)$$
$$h_t = o_t \odot \tanh(C_t)$$

Here, $\tanh(C_t)$ is a "filtered" view of the long-term memory, scaled by o_t. Continuing the storyline analogy, once you have updated your long-term memory with fresh information, you still need to decide how much of that comprehensive knowledge to bring forward into your current focus. The output gate makes that choice. If you imagine you are about to share a quick recap of the story so far, you would not list every single detail; you would emphasize the most critical or relevant parts. The output gate, similarly, regulates which portion of the updated memory is "exposed" as your working summary at this moment, ensuring that only the information most pertinent to the current step is placed front and center.

The updated hidden state h_t can be used to generate an output y_t (for example, through a linear or softmax layer), and it also serves as a bridge to the next time step. Also, h_t interacts with the current input x_t to propose new content for long-term storage. $\tilde{C}_t$. This short-term memory is crucial for interfacing with the world (or the rest of the network), reflecting the LSTM's best guess at what matters most in the current moment. Think of this as the succinct highlight reel of the ongoing story. It is not the entire novel (which would be too large and unwieldy) but rather the most actionable elements you need right now, either for predicting the next part of the plot or for generating a response in a conversation.

In summary, at each temporal step, the LSTM cell effectively balances what to remember and what to forget, so it can manage both immediate and extended context. It does this by maintaining two forms of memory: a short-term memory (h_t) for immediate processing and a long-term memory (C_t) for carrying important information over many time steps. First, it decides which parts of its existing long-term memory are no longer relevant and should be discarded. Next, it determines what new insights from the current input and recent short-term memory need to be added to the long-term store. Finally, the cell determines how much of this updated long-term memory to share back out as a fresh short-term memory for downstream tasks. This interplay of "forgetting," "updating," and "outputting" ensures the LSTM can hold onto crucial details while discarding obsolete ones, all without overwhelming the network's capacity to learn from longer sequences.

Training the LSTM Model

Training LSTMs follows the same principle as Backpropagation Through Time (BPTT) used in basic RNNs: unroll the network over a certain number of time steps as discussed in the preceding chapter, which computes the loss at each step and then backpropagate gradients through the unrolled graph. The only major difference is that the gradient now also flows through the gating mechanisms and the cell state. Concretely:

- Each gate has associated parameters: (w_f, b_f, w_u, b_u, w_o, b_o, w_c, b_c) that govern how h_{t-1} and x_t affect the forget, update, and output signals.
- During backpropagation, gradients with respect to these parameters are computed based on partial derivatives that pass through $\sigma(.)$ and tanh.
- The cell state gradient must be tracked carefully over many steps to handle long-range dependencies; this is precisely what LSTM was designed to do more effectively than a vanilla RNN.

In essence, the mathematics of BPTT remains the same conceptually, but LSTMs add additional computational paths for the gradients via the forget, update, and output gates, as well as the cell state itself. This helps maintain stable gradients over longer sequences, addressing the vanishing/exploding gradient problem more effectively. Despite its robust handling of long-range dependencies and its mitigation of vanishing and exploding gradients, LSTM architecture does come with drawbacks that can affect both its training efficiency and model simplicity. The multiple gating mechanisms, dual memory states, and additional parameter sets add layers of complexity, making LSTMs computationally heavier to train. Furthermore, while the network can process inputs in batches, the sequential nature of its hidden-state updates often leads to slower convergence compared to purely feedforward models. Recognizing these challenges, practitioners sought a simpler yet effective approach for retaining context across time steps without fully replicating LSTM's complexity. This exploration led to the Gated

Recurrent Unit (GRU), a more streamlined architecture that approximates many of the benefits of LSTMs through fewer gates and reduced parameter overhead. In the next section, we will dive into GRU in detail, unpacking its internal components and contrasting its design with the more elaborate structure of LSTMs.

Applications and Use-Case of LSTM Models

Let us navigate a few popular applications where LSTM networks have proven particularly influential, along with key publications or research references.

- LSTMs have been widely used to model the probability distribution over sequences of words, enabling tasks such as text generation, next-word prediction, and language understanding. Originally introduced by Hochreiter and Schmidhuber (1997) in their seminal paper *Long Short-Term Memory* (Neural Computation, 9(8), 1735–1780), this architecture has demonstrated a remarkable ability to capture long-range dependencies in textual data.

- LSTM-based encoders and decoders have shown remarkable success in translating sentences between languages by effectively capturing long-range context in both source and target sequences. Sutskever, Vinyals, and Le (2014), in their groundbreaking NeurIPS paper *Sequence to Sequence Learning with Neural Networks*, demonstrated how an LSTM encoder-decoder framework can learn a continuous representation of an input sentence, enabling the decoder to produce a coherent translation. Further advancements came from Bahdanau, Cho, and Bengio (2015) in their paper *Neural Machine Translation by Jointly Learning to Align and Translate*, where they introduced an attention mechanism that allows the model to focus on specific parts of the input sentence at each step of decoding. Together, these studies laid the groundwork for modern neural machine translation systems, establishing LSTMs as a cornerstone in sequence-to-sequence modeling.

- Graves, Mohamed, and Hinton (2013), in their paper *Speech Recognition with Deep Recurrent Neural Networks* presented at the IEEE International Conference on Acoustics, Speech and Signal Processing (ICASSP), leveraged LSTMs to develop end-to-end speech recognition systems. By harnessing the model's capacity to preserve information over extended time intervals, they demonstrated notable improvements in accuracy and more robust handling of variable-length inputs, illustrating the practical benefits of using LSTMs for real-world speech applications.

- Gers, Schmidhuber, and Cummins (2000), in their work *Learning to Forget: Continual Prediction with LSTM* published in Neural Computation, demonstrated how LSTMs excel at capturing temporal patterns and seasonality in complex time series data such as stock prices, weather forecasting, and sensor readings by effectively handling nonlinear dynamics and extended dependencies that often overwhelm traditional models.

- Vinyals, Toshev, Bengio, and Erhan (2015), in their CVPR paper *Show and Tell: A Neural Image Caption Generator*, combined convolutional neural networks (CNNs) for visual feature extraction with LSTMs functioning as decoders, thereby producing descriptive sentences for images and effectively bridging the gap between vision and natural language processing.

Simplified Representation of LSTM as Gated Recurrent Unit (GRU)

In this section, we will explore the GRU, often hailed as a streamlined alternative to the LSTM network. While LSTMs have gates for forgetting, updating, and producing outputs, plus a separate cell state and hidden state, GRUs merge some of these concepts into a simpler architecture. The motivation behind the GRU was to preserve LSTM's ability to manage long-range dependencies while reducing the complexity that can hinder training speed and interpretability. By combining the forget and input gates into a single "update gate" and removing a separate cell state, GRUs achieve competitive performance on many tasks with fewer parameters. This simpler design not only lowers computational overhead but also makes it easier to implement, tune, and interpret certain types of sequential problems.

A key difference between LSTMs and GRUs lies in how many states each retains at any given time step. In an LSTM, we maintain two distinct forms of memory: a cell state for long-term information and a hidden state for short-term or immediate outputs. In contrast, the GRU stores all necessary information in a single hidden state. There is no dedicated cell state; instead, the GRU carefully decides which parts of the previous hidden state to keep or discard via its gating mechanism. This consolidation effectively "approximates" the role of the LSTM cell state within the hidden state itself. While it may not always capture as nuanced a division between long-term and short-term memory, in practice, GRUs often match or even surpass LSTMs on tasks, such as language modeling, speech recognition, and other sequential problems, especially when data or resources are limited.

Update Gate: Merging Forget and Input Gates

The GRU's update gate, denoted, merges the responsibilities of the LSTM's forget gate and input gate into one, as shown in *Figure 15.4*.

Instead of separately deciding what to forget and what to add, the GRU uses a single update decision.

$$u_t = \sigma(w_u[C_{t-1}, x_t] + b_u)$$

$$\tilde{C}_t = \tanh(w_c[C_{t-1}, x_t] + b_c)$$
$$C_t = u_t \odot \tilde{C}_t + (1 - u_t) \odot \overline{C_{t-1}}$$

Here, $\sigma(\cdot)$ is the sigmoid function, mapping values to the range [0,1]. Conceptually, u_t tells the GRU how much of the past information to carry forward versus how much of the new information to incorporate into the next state. If u_t is close to 0, then the unit leans towards preserving most of C_{t-1}; if it is near 1, then the unit is more inclined to replace it with a fresh update.

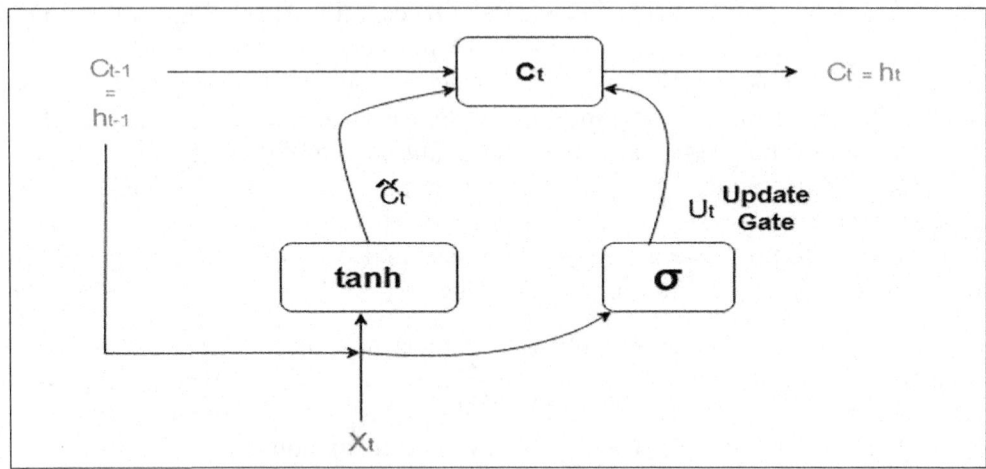

Figure 15.4: *GRU Architecture with Combined Gates*

Hence, GRU combines what would be the forget and input gates into a single update gate u_t. Instead of independently learning two gating values, u_t and its complement $(1-u_t)$ jointly decide the ratio of "old content" versus "new content". Thus, the update gate simplifies the logic used by LSTM's forget and input gates, making the gating mechanism more compact. In contrast, LSTMs rely on two independent gates (forget and input) to achieve a similar effect, resulting in a more complex design. By unifying these gates, GRUs maintain competitive performance, often with fewer parameters and faster convergence, making them a popular alternative to LSTMs in tasks that demand efficient handling of long-range dependencies.

From a high-level perspective, a GRU "approximates" LSTM behavior. In that it aims to learn long-term dependencies by deciding what to keep from the past and what to update at each step. However, GRUs do it more compactly. They do not have an explicit cell state separate from the hidden state; instead, the hidden state itself carries both short-term and long-term information as needed. Although this can lead to slightly less flexibility in theory, LSTM has more nuanced control via three gates plus a distinct cell state. Empirical evidence suggests that GRUs can perform just as well in many scenarios. Their simpler structure can also be easier to interpret and tune, which is particularly beneficial when working with limited data or constrained computing resources. The GRU often strikes an attractive balance between performance and efficiency for real-world tasks that require iterative refinement of hidden states but do not necessarily demand the full complexity of LSTM gating.

Pros and Cons of GRU Compared to LSTM

Though both GRUs and LSTM networks tackle the problem of learning long-range dependencies in sequential data, they do so with slightly different designs. LSTMs use separate gates for forgetting, inputting, and outputting information and distinguish between a cell state and a hidden state. GRUs consolidate some of these functions to form a simpler gating mechanism, often leading to fewer parameters and potentially faster training. However, this streamlined approach also removes certain degrees of control that LSTMs provide. In the following section, we explore the key advantages and limitations of GRUs in comparison to LSTMs.

Pros of GRU Compared to LSTM

Let us outline the key benefits that GRUs offer compared to LSTMs.

- **Simpler Architecture**: GRUs use only two gates (update and reset) instead of LSTM's three (forget, input, output), and they omit a separate cell state. This reduced complexity can mean fewer parameters to train, leading to faster convergence and lower memory usage.
- **Comparable Performance**: In many real-world tasks such as language modeling, speech recognition, or time series forecasting, GRUs are able to match or exceed LSTMs' performance, especially when data size or complexity is moderate.
- **Faster Convergence**: Thanks to the simplified gating structure, GRUs often converge more quickly in practice, making them attractive for rapid experimentation or when computational resources are limited.

Cons of GRU Compared to LSTM

While GRUs offer a more streamlined architecture and can perform on par with or even surpass LSTMs in many settings, these simplifications do come with certain drawbacks. Here, we discuss some of the key limitations of GRUs in comparison to LSTMs.

- **Less Granular Control**: By merging the forget and input gates, GRUs sacrifice some of the fine-grained regulation that LSTMs provide when discarding old information and incorporating new data.

- **No Separate Cell State**: By merging the forget and input gates, GRUs sacrifice some of the fine-grained regulation that LSTMs provide when discarding old information and incorporating new data.
- **Task-Dependent Efficacy**: While GRUs generally perform well, certain tasks with extremely long sequences or more intricate dependencies may still benefit more from the more nuanced gating structure of an LSTM.

Applications and Use-Case of GRU Models

Let us walk through a few popular applications where GRU networks have proven particularly compact and scalable, along with key publications or research references.

- Cho, van Merriënboer, Gulcehre, Bahdanau, Bougares, Schwenk, and Bengio (2014), in their paper *Learning Phrase Representations using RNN Encoder–Decoder for Statistical Machine Translation* (EMNLP), were among the first to showcase how GRUs can be leveraged in sequence-to-sequence models. By employing a GRU-based encoder to digest input text and a GRU-based decoder to generate translations, their system captured the essence of a sentence in a compact hidden representation. This simpler, yet efficient, architecture demonstrated competitive performance with LSTMs, highlighting the practicality of GRUs for transforming one language into another.
- Li, Zheng, and Li (2018) proposed GRU-based networks in *Enhancing Stock Price Movement Prediction with GRU-based Neural Networks* to forecast stock prices and detect temporal patterns more effectively. They found that GRUs outperformed traditional methods and sometimes even surpassed LSTMs, thanks to fewer parameters and more straightforward gating mechanisms. This success illustrated how GRUs can handle real-world time series that exhibit seasonal fluctuations, trends, and abrupt market shifts.
- Zhou, Shi, Tian, Qi, Li, and Hao (2016), in their paper *Text Classification Improved by Integrating Bidirectional GRU with Two-dimensional Max Pooling* (Neurocomputing), demonstrated how GRUs could be adapted for document classification tasks. By encoding sentences in both forward and backward directions with a bidirectional GRU, the network captured contextual nuances often missed by more rigid architectures. Their results showed that GRUs could be a strong backbone for analyzing text data across domains, such as sentiment analysis, topic modeling, and more.
- Zhang, Wu, Zhu, and Du (2019), in *Attention-based Fully Convolutional Network for Speech Emotion Recognition* (IEEE Access), integrated GRUs to refine temporal dependencies in speech signals. Although the core framework was convolutional, they employed a GRU layer to distill sequential patterns essential for detecting emotions in audio data. The combination enhanced robustness to variations in speech cadence and intonation, thereby improving recognition accuracy across multiple emotion categories.

- Venugopalan, Rohrbach, Donahue, Mooney, Darrell, and Saenko (2015), in their work *Sequence to Sequence – Video to Text* (ICCV), illustrated how a GRU could serve as a decoder for generating descriptive sentences from video frames. The model produced coherent sentences that captured key events in a video by blending convolutional features for visual context with a GRU's gating to preserve long-range temporal structure. This demonstrated GRUs' strength in multimodal tasks where temporal cues and visual inputs must be combined effectively.

In the next chapter, we will build upon these real-world applications by demonstrating a series of LSTM and GRU-based use cases in Python. From language modeling and time series forecasting to more specialized tasks, we will walk through hands-on examples, highlighting the practical advantages and key implementation details of LSTM and GRU networks.

Conclusion

In this chapter, we explored the transformative impact of LSTM networks in addressing the limitations of traditional RNNs. We began by understanding the challenges of learning long-term dependencies in RNNs, particularly the vanishing gradient problem, and how LSTMs were designed to overcome these issues through their innovative architecture. By introducing memory cells and gating mechanisms, LSTMs enable efficient handling of sequential data, making them indispensable in modern AI applications.

We further examined the advantages of LSTMs over traditional RNNs, highlighting their ability to retain long-term information, manage complex patterns, and improve training stability. These qualities have made LSTMs a preferred choice in fields ranging from natural language processing to time-series analysis. The chapter also detailed the architecture and working principles of LSTMs, explaining the roles of input, forget, and output gates, as well as the underlying mathematics that power their operations. Additionally, we introduced the Gated Recurrent Unit (GRU) as a simplified variation of LSTMs, providing a comparative understanding of these powerful sequential models.

With a solid understanding of LSTM and GRU architectures, the next chapter will delve into real-world use cases of these models. We will explore their transformative role in solving practical challenges, including text generation, machine translation, and forecasting, further illustrating their versatility and impact across domains.

Practice Exercises

1. Consider an LSTM model with an input sequence length of 10, an input feature size of 8, and a hidden state dimension of 16. If the model uses a single LSTM

layer, how many weights (parameters) are there in total for this LSTM layer? Assume the LSTM has the standard gates: input, forget, output, and cell state.

2. Consider an LSTM model where the hidden state dimension is 20, and the input feature size is 15. For the output gate equation $o_t = \sigma(w_o[h_{t-1},x_t]+b_o)$ determine:
   The size of the concatenated vector $[h_{t-1},x_t]$
   The size of the weight matrix w_o
   The size of the bias vector b_o

3. In an LSTM, the hidden state dimension is 16, and the input feature size is 12. The cell state C_t is
   updated using the equation: $C_t = f_t \odot \overline{C_{t-1}} + u_t \odot \tilde{C}_t$
   Where, $f_t, u_t,$ and $\tilde{C}_t$ are vectors with dimensions equal to the hidden state. Determine:
   - The size of $f_t, u_t,$ and $\tilde{C}_t$
   - The size of the weight matrix w_f associated with the <u>forget gate</u>
   - The number of learnable parameters for the forget gate, considering biases

4. Consider a GRU model where the hidden state dimension is 10, and the input feature size is 8. For the update gate equation: $u_t = \sigma(w_u[h_{t-1},x_t]+b_u)$, Determine:
   - The size of the concatenated vector $[h_{t-1},x_t]$
   - The size of the weight matrix w_u
   - The size of the bias vector b_u

Answers

1. Input-to-hidden weights: Input size ×Hidden size × 4 = 8×16×4=512

   Hidden-to-hidden weights: Hidden size × Hidden size ×4 = 16×16×4=1024

   Bias terms: Hidden size×4 = 16×4=64. The total number of parameters is 1600.

2. Size of the concatenated vector: 35, size of the weight matrix: 35 × 20, size of the bias is 20

3. All these vectors are related to the hidden state and have the same size as the hidden state dimension: Size = 16, Size of the Weight Matrix = 28 × 16, Number of Learnable Parameters for the Forget Gate = 464

4. Size of the concatenated vector: 18, size of the weight matrix: 18 × 10, size of the bias : 10

Multiple Choice Questions

1. What is the primary function of the forget gate in an LSTM?
   a. To add new information to the cell state
   b. To remove irrelevant information from the cell state
   c. To decide the final output of the LSTM
   d. To initialize the hidden state

2. Which of the following is a key difference between an LSTM and a GRU?
   a. GRUs have separate cell states, while LSTMs do not
   b. LSTMs use three gates, while GRUs use two gates
   c. LSTMs are faster to train than GRUs
   d. GRUs are not suitable for sequential data

3. The vanishing gradient problem is effectively addressed in LSTMs through:
   a. Batch normalization
   b. Memory cells and gating mechanisms
   c. Weight regularization techniques
   d. Increasing the number of layers

4. What role does the output gate play in an LSTM?
   a. It determines which information is discarded
   b. It updates the hidden state with new input
   c. It decides which part of the cell state is passed to the hidden state
   d. It resets the cell state after each time step

5. What is the purpose of the input gate in an LSTM?
   a. To decide what part of the hidden state should be output
   b. To decide what new information to store in the cell state
   c. To remove irrelevant information from the cell state
   d. To pass the hidden state directly to the output layer

6. How does a GRU simplify the LSTM architecture?
   a. By combining the forget and input gates into a single update gate
   b. By removing the hidden state entirely

c. By using a linear activation function instead of tanh
d. By eliminating the need for backpropagation

7. What is the function of the cell state in an LSTM?
    a. To store the output of the previous layer
    b. To provide a path for gradients to flow during training
    c. To act as the activation function for the hidden state
    d. To regulate the learning rate of the model

8. Which of the following best describes a common application of LSTMs?
    a. Image classification tasks
    b. Temporal data processing and sequence modeling
    c. Dimensionality reduction of static datasets
    d. Feature extraction from structured tabular data

9. Why are GRUs often preferred over LSTMs in certain applications?
    a. GRUs require fewer parameters and are computationally faster
    b. GRUs have a more complex architecture for better accuracy
    c. GRUs are specifically designed for image data
    d. GRUs do not require training like LSTMs

10. What is the role of the reset gate in a GRU?
    a. To determine how much past information should be forgotten
    b. To decide what information to store in the hidden state
    c. To regulate the flow of gradients during backpropagation
    d. To initialize the cell state

Answers

1. b
2. b
3. c
4. b
5. b
6. a

7. b
8. b
9. a
10. a

Keywords

- Long-Term Dependency
- Vanishing Gradient Problem
- Backpropagation Through Time (BPTT)
- Memory Cell
- Input Gate
- Forget Gate
- Output Gate
- Gated Recurrent Unit (GRU)
- Temporal Dependencies
- Sequential Data
- Selective Memory Retention
- Exploding Gradient Problem
- Encoder-Decoder Architecture
- Machine Translation
- Speech Recognition
- Temporal Data Processing

References

1. https://web.stanford.edu/class/cs379c/archive/2018/class_messages_listing/content/Artificial_Neural_Network_Technology_Tutorials/OlahLSTM-NEURAL-NETWORK-TUTORIAL-15.pdf

2. https://cs224d.stanford.edu/lectures/CS224d-Lecture10.pdf

CHAPTER 16
Application of LSTM in NLP and TS Forecasting

Introduction

The advent of Long Short-Term Memory (LSTM) and Gated Recurrent Unit (GRU) architectures has revolutionized the way sequential data is processed and analyzed. In this chapter, we will delve into the practical applications of these advanced recurrent neural networks across diverse domains such as time-series forecasting and natural language processing. We will begin with an exploration of different design strategies of LSTMs, highlighting their configurations as encoder-only, encoder-decoder, and decoder-only models, each tailored to specific tasks and challenges.

The chapter progresses into the realm of time-series forecasting and language modeling, showcasing the role of LSTMs in understanding the numerical sequence and textual data and generating meaningful outputs. Furthermore, we explore their application in language translation and chatbot modeling, demonstrating how these architectures enable seamless communication in multiple languages and real-time conversational agents. This chapter bridges the gap between theoretical understanding and practical application through Python implementations using the TensorFlow-Keras framework, equipping readers with the tools to harness the full potential of LSTM and GRU networks in sequential data tasks.

All the use cases designed in this chapter in each section are for educational purposes with smaller prototypes; the LSTM model effectively handles the training sample size. However, in real-world scenarios where applications demand large volumes of training data and scalability, GRU models are often preferred. Also, in the preceding chapter, we extensively discussed the pros and cons of LSTM and GRU models. Readers are advised to select the model that best suits their requirements and aligns with the specific needs of the problem statement. While all the use cases are equally applicable for GRU models, we will refer to LSTM throughout this chapter. Readers are encouraged to replace the LSTM function with GRU and explore the exercises for deeper insights.

Structure

In this chapter, we will cover the following main topics:

- Time-Series Forecasting using LSTM Architecture and its Implementation in Python
- Different Design Strategies of LSTM as Encoder only, Encoder-Decoder and Decoder only Model
- Language Modelling and Sentiment Analysis using LSTMs and its Implementation in Python
- Language Translation and Chatbot Modeling using LSTMs and its Implementation in Python

TS Forecasting Using LSTM and its Implementation

In *Chapter 14, Introduction to Recurrent Neural Networks*, we extensively covered the fundamentals of sequential data and the approaches required for time-series forecasting, laying a strong foundation for understanding temporal dependencies. With this knowledge, we now focus on applying these concepts to a practical problem statement. For this section, we have chosen the popular Google stock price time-series dataset, which provides daily stock data spanning from January 3, 2012 to December 30, 2016.

The dataset includes five key variables, which include 'open', 'high', 'low', 'close', and 'volume'. Among these, we will focus on the 'open' price variable to design and implement a LSTM model for forecasting purposes.

Time-series (TS) forecasting for stock prices is inherently challenging due to the volatile and unpredictable nature of financial markets. Factors such as market trends, economic indicators, and external shocks can cause significant fluctuations in stock prices. The 'open' price is particularly significant as it serves as the initial value for daily trading and reflects the market's sentiment at the start of each trading session. Our objective is to forecast the 'open' price for future days based on historical trends, leveraging the sequential processing capabilities of LSTMs to capture temporal dependencies in the data. However, readers are encouraged to experiment with this use case using any other variable from the dataset, such as 'high', 'low', or 'volume', to explore different forecasting scenarios.

The Google stock price dataset offers an ideal scenario for demonstrating the power of LSTM models.

With over five years of data, it provides sufficient historical context to train a robust model capable of identifying complex patterns. By focusing on a single variable, the 'open' price, we simplify the analysis, making it accessible for educational purposes while highlighting the core aspects of LSTM – based forecasting. This approach allows us to demonstrate how to preprocess data, design an LSTM architecture, and evaluate the model's performance step by step. The goal of this exercise is not only to forecast the stock price but also to showcase the practical implementation of LSTMs in Python using

the TensorFlow-Keras framework. Readers will gain hands-on experience in data preparation, model design, and performance evaluation.

Although this example uses a relatively small dataset, the principles and techniques discussed can be scaled to more complex, real-world applications involving larger datasets and additional variables. This ensures that the knowledge gained here remains applicable to diverse time-series forecasting tasks.

As the first step, we will import all the necessary libraries required to implement this forecasting problem.

```
import numpy as np
import pandas as pd
import matplotlib.pyplot as plt
%matplotlib inline
from sklearn.preprocessing import MinMaxScaler
from keras.models import Sequential
from keras.layers import Dense,LSTM
```

Next, we will load the training dataset, `Google_Stock_Price_Train.csv`, and display the first few records to examine the data structure as shown in *Figure 16.1*.

```
dat_train=pd.read_csv('/filepath/Google_Stock_Price_Train.csv')
dat_train.shape
(1258,6)
dat_train.head()
```

	Date	Open	High	Low	Close	Volume
0	1/3/2012	325.25	332.83	324.97	663.59	7,380,500
1	1/4/2012	331.27	333.87	329.08	666.45	5,749,400
2	1/5/2012	329.83	330.75	326.89	657.21	6,590,300
3	1/6/2012	328.34	328.77	323.68	648.24	5,405,900
4	1/9/2012	322.04	322.29	309.46	620.76	11,688,800

Figure 16.1: *Head of the Google Stock Price Train data*

After loading the data, we will visualize the time-series column for the 'open' variable using a line plot as shown in *Figure 16.2*.

```
plt.plot(dat_train['Open'])
```

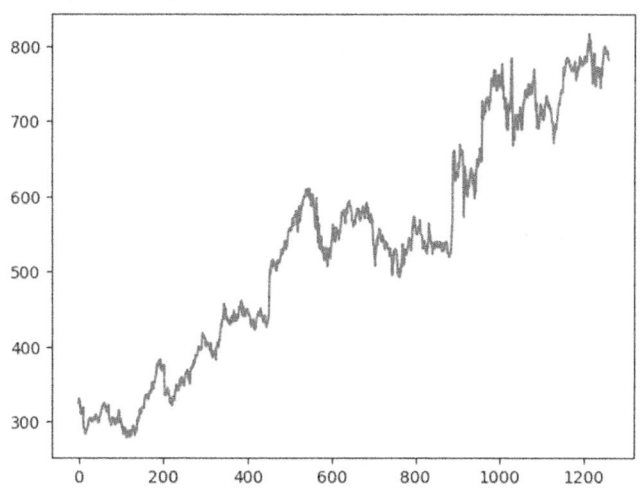

Figure 16.2: *Time-Series Visualization of Google Stock 'Open' Prices*

In the next step, we will extract the 'open' column and scale the data using a Min-Max Scaler as follows.

```
training_set=dat_train.iloc[:,1:2].values
sc=MinMaxScaler(feature_range=(0,1))
training_set_sc=sc.fit_transform(training_set)
```

Next, we will prepare the time-series data by creating sequences with 60 time steps as input and one output. This means that for every sequence of 60 consecutive days (representing the lag), the model will forecast the 'open' price for the next day. In this case, a 60-day lag corresponds to approximately two months of trading data, which we have chosen for demonstration purposes.

However, the selection of an appropriate lag period is highly dependent on domain knowledge, particularly in stock market trading. Factors such as market trends, volatility, and seasonal patterns can influence the optimal lag period. A well-informed lag period can significantly enhance the model's ability to capture relevant dependencies in the data and improve forecasting accuracy.

Readers are encouraged to experiment with different lag periods to better understand their impact on the model's performance. By trying various configurations, such as shorter or longer lags, readers can gain valuable insights into the fine-tuning process and the role of temporal dependencies in time-series forecasting. This hands-on approach will also help in developing a deeper appreciation of the complexities involved in stock price prediction.

```
X_train=[]
y_train=[]
for i in range(60,1258):
    X_train.append(training_set_sc[i-60:i,0])
    y_train.append(training_set_sc[i,0])
    X_train,y_train=np.array(X_train),np.array(y_train)
X_train.shape,y_train.shape
((1198,60), (1198,))
```

Now, we reshape the **X_train** dataset to make it compatible with the TensorFlow workflow, which expects the input data for LSTM models to be in a specific three-dimensional format:

(Number of Samples, Time Steps, Features).

```
X_train=np.reshape(X_train,(X_train.shape[0],X_train.shape[1],1))
X_train.shape,y_train.shape
((1198,60,1), (1198,))
```

We now proceed to design the LSTM model, starting with the initialization of a Sequential model. The first layer added is an LSTM layer:

```
model=Sequential()
model.add(LSTM(units=100,input_shape=(X_train.shape[1],1)))
```

The number of units (or neurons) in the LSTM layer is set to 100. These units represent the dimensionality of the output space for this layer. The choice of 100 units is a starting point and can be fine-tuned based on the complexity of the data and the length of the time steps (lags).

Here, **X_train.shape[1]** corresponds to the time steps (60 in this example). The number of LSTM units directly impacts the model's capacity to learn and represent temporal patterns. Readers are encouraged to experiment with this hyperparameter, adjusting it based on the size of the dataset, the length of the time steps, and the complexity of the forecasting problem. Fine-tuning this value is a crucial step in optimizing the model's performance.

Application of LSTM in NLP and TS Forecasting

Next, we configure the output layer and proceed to compile and train the model:

`model.add(Dense(1))`

Since this is an autoregressive task where we predict a single numeric value (the 'open' price), the output layer consists of a single node.

`model.compile(optimizer='adam', loss='mean_squared_error')`

We use the Adam optimizer for efficient training and mean squared error (MSE) as the loss function to minimize the prediction error for the numeric target. The model is trained for 100 epochs with a batch size of 32. A batch size of 32 is a common choice balancing training speed and memory usage.

`model.fit(X_train, y_train, epochs=100, batch_size=32)`

Readers are encouraged to experiment with the number of epochs and batch size to observe their impact on training dynamics and forecasting accuracy.

To prepare the validation data for the LSTM model, we begin by loading the Google Stock Price Test dataset containing 20 records from January 3, 2017, onwards. To account for the 60-day lag, we concatenate the **'open'** price column from the training and test datasets, extracting the last 60 days from the training data and all 20 test records.

```
dat_test=pd.read_csv('/filepath/Google_Stock_Price_Test.csv')
real_stock_price=dat_test.iloc[:,1:2].values
dat_total = pd.concat((dat_train['Open'], dat_test['Open']), axis=0)
dat_total=pd.concat((dat_train['Open'],dat_test['Open']),axis=0)
inputs=dat_total[len(dat_total)-len(dat_test)-60:].values
inputs=inputs.reshape(-1,1)
inputs_sc=sc.transform(inputs)
X_test=[]
for i in range(60,inputs.shape[0]):
  X_test.append(inputs_sc[i-60:i,0])
X_test=np.array(X_test)
X_test=np.reshape(X_test,(X_test.shape[0],X_test.shape[1],1))
X_test.shape
(20, 60, 1)
```

The extracted data is reshaped and scaled using the same Min-Max Scaler applied during training. Sequential time-series inputs are then generated, where each sequence consists of 60 time steps, creating the necessary lagged data for prediction. Finally, the validation data is reshaped into a 3D format of (20, 60, 1), ensuring compatibility with the LSTM model's input requirements. This preparation allows the trained model to make accurate predictions and evaluate its performance on the unseen validation dataset.

In the final step, we use the trained LSTM model to predict the 'open' stock price for the prepared validation data. The predictions are generated using the following command:

```
predicted_stock_price = model.predict(X_test)
```

Since the model outputs scaled values, we apply the inverse transformation to return the predictions to their original scale, matching the actual stock prices:

```
predicted_stock_price = sc.inverse_transform(predicted_stock_price)
```

To evaluate the model's performance, we compare the predicted stock prices with the actual values from the test dataset. The performance is quantified using the Root Mean Squared Error (RMSE), which provides a measure of the average deviation between the predicted and actual values.

```
mse=np.mean((real_stock_price-predicted_stock_price)**2)
rmse=np.sqrt(mse)
print(rmse)
```

13.17056

On average, the model's predictions differ from the actual values by approximately 13.17 USD.

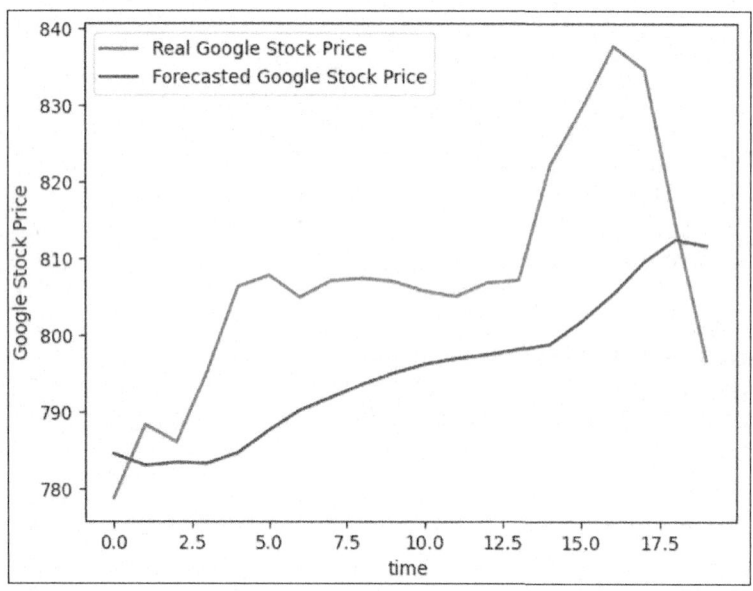

Figure 16.3: *Google Stock 'Open' Prices Forecasting using LSTM Model*

Additionally, we generated a time-series visual comparison plot as shown in *Figure 16.3* to observe how closely the predicted values align with the actual stock prices, highlighting the model's forecasting accuracy. This combined numerical and visual evaluation offers a comprehensive understanding of the model's effectiveness in time-series forecasting.

```
#Visualizing the results
plt.plot(real_stock_price,color='red',label='Real Google Stock Price')
plt.plot(predicted_stock_price,color='blue',label='Forecasted Google
Stock Price')
plt.title('Google Stock Price Forecasting Model using RNN')
plt.xlabel('time')
plt.ylabel('Google Stock Price')
plt.legend()
plt.show()
```

A few key observations from the plot indicate that the general trend of the forecasted prices closely follows the actual stock price, indicating that the model captures the overall pattern and temporal dependencies effectively. Unlike traditional RNNs, which often suffer from vanishing gradient issues leading to degraded performance over extended sequences, the LSTM model efficiently retains information across time steps using its gating mechanism. The RMSE score of 13.17056 USD indicates a relatively low prediction error, highlighting the model's precision. In contrast, an RNN-based model would likely yield higher RMSE scores due to its limited memory and inability to maintain context over longer sequences. The improved accuracy and reduced bias in predictions underscore the LSTM's superiority in handling complex sequential data such as stock prices. While the predicted values align well with the actual prices during gradual changes, there are noticeable discrepancies during sudden spikes or dips, such as towards the 15th time step. This discrepancy highlights the model's limitation in fully capturing abrupt fluctuations, which is common in stock market prediction due to its highly dynamic nature.

Overall, the graph reflects that the LSTM model performs well for smooth trends, but further tuning or incorporating additional features may help improve its responsiveness to sudden market shifts.

Different Design Strategies of LSTM Architecture

The versatility of LSTM networks lies in their ability to adapt to various sequential modeling tasks through different architectural configurations. Depending on the nature of the problem, LSTMs can be designed as Encoder-only, Encoder-Decoder, or Decoder-only models, each tailored to address specific requirements of sequence processing. These design strategies enable LSTMs to handle a wide array of applications, from sequence classification and forecasting to translation and sequence generation. We will examine each of these configurations in greater detail in this section, beginning with the LSTM as an encoder, which works especially well for tasks requiring a fixed-length representation of sequential data.

LSTM as Encoder

The LSTM encoder-only architecture serves as a fundamental building block for applications requiring an understanding of input sequences. The encoder-only configuration is especially beneficial for tasks that aim to learn a fixed-length representation or embedding from a variable-length input sequence. This embedding serves as a compressed summary that captures both short-term and long-term dependencies in the sequence. Unlike feedforward networks, the encoder leverages the sequential nature of LSTMs to effectively "encode" the temporal relationships present in the input data.

A practical example of an encoder-only LSTM is found in time-series classification tasks, such as identifying anomalies in sensor data or predicting a class label for a sequence. For instance, in detecting equipment failures in an industrial setting, an encoder LSTM can process historical sensor readings and output a single label indicating normal or abnormal operation. The LSTM encoder converts the entire input sequence into a fixed-dimensional representation, which is then fed to a dense layer for classification. This approach ensures that the temporal patterns within the input sequence are effectively captured and utilized for accurate predictions.

The architecture typically consists of an input layer, a stacked LSTM layer or layers, and a fully connected dense layer that maps the encoded sequence representation to the output space as shown in *Figure 16.4*. The LSTM layers process the input sequence step by step, maintaining a hidden state and cell state that encapsulate the learned information from the previous steps. At the final time step, the hidden state of the LSTM acts as the encoded representation of the input sequence, summarizing all the temporal dependencies observed.

One of the advantages of the encoder-only architecture is its simplicity and efficiency, making it well-suited for applications where a single label or decision is required from a sequence. For instance, in sentiment analysis of text data, the encoder can process the entire sentence or paragraph and output a sentiment score or class label. Similarly, in biomedical signal processing, an encoder-only LSTM can classify ECG data into categories such as normal or arrhythmic, leveraging its ability to capture intricate temporal patterns.

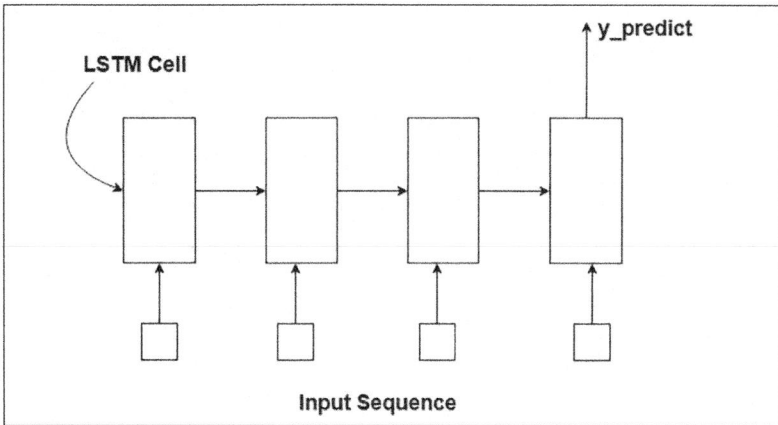

Figure 16.4: Encoder-Only LSTM Configuration

While the encoder-only architecture is effective for tasks requiring a single output, it has its limitations in applications like sequence-to-sequence mapping, where the output sequence may differ in length or structure from the input sequence. To address these scenarios, advanced designs such as encoder-decoder architectures are employed, which will be discussed in the next section. Nonetheless, the encoder-only LSTM remains a cornerstone of sequential data modeling, particularly for classification and regression tasks where sequence embeddings are critical for downstream predictions.

LSTM as Encoder-Decoder

The Encoder-Decoder architecture with LSTMs is a transformative design that extends the capability of sequential models to handle complex tasks, such as machine translation, text summarization, and sequence-to-sequence (Seq2Seq) prediction. Unlike the Encoder-only configuration, which focuses on extracting a fixed-length representation of sequential data, the Encoder-Decoder design processes input sequences into meaningful representations and subsequently generates output sequences.

In this configuration, the Encoder LSTM processes the input sequence and condenses it into a fixed-length context vector. This vector serves as a compressed representation of the input, encapsulating its temporal dependencies and semantic meaning. The Decoder LSTM then takes this context vector and generates the output sequence step-by-step as shown in *Figure* 16.5, starting with the Start of Sequence (SOS). Each step of the Decoder depends on both the context vector and the previously generated output, creating a dynamic, context-aware sequence generation process till it generates an End of Sequence (EOS) token.

For example, in machine translation, the Encoder processes the source sentence (for example, in English) into a context vector, which the Decoder uses to generate the target sentence (for example, in French) one word at a time. This allows the system to translate sequences of varying lengths while preserving the contextual integrity of the input.

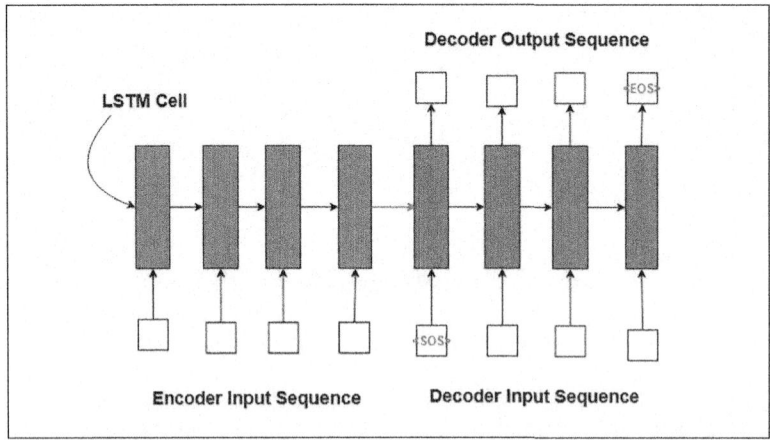

Figure 16.5: Encoder-Decoder LSTM Configuration

Apart from machine translation, the Encoder-Decoder LSTM configuration is widely used in diverse applications, such as text summarization, question-answering systems, and speech-to-text processing. In text summarization, the Encoder converts lengthy documents into a condensed semantic representation, which the Decoder then reconstructs into a concise summary. Similarly, in question-answering tasks, the Encoder processes the context or passage, while the Decoder generates relevant answers based on the encoded information. In speech-to-text systems, audio signals are encoded into feature-rich vectors by the Encoder and subsequently decoded into textual sequences. This architecture is also integral to video captioning, where visual frames are encoded, and the Decoder generates descriptive sentences. The versatility of the Encoder-Decoder framework makes it indispensable in applications requiring seamless handling of variable-length input and output sequences.

LSTM as Decoder

The Decoder-only LSTM configuration represents a simplified yet powerful model tailored for sequence generation tasks. Unlike the Encoder-Decoder configuration, where both components collaborate to handle input-output relationships, the Decoder-only architecture focuses solely on generating sequences based on contextual cues or prompts. This makes it particularly effective in tasks requiring autonomous sequence generation, such as text prediction, creative writing, and real-time speech synthesis. In this configuration, the model takes an initial input (for example, a seed or trigger word appended with context vector) as shown in *Figure 16.6* and generates the subsequent sequence iteratively. Each generated token is appended to the input sequence and fed back into the model as the next input.

This recurrent feedback mechanism enables the model to capture the evolving context, allowing for coherent and contextually relevant outputs. For instance, in language modeling, the Decoder-only LSTM predicts the next word in a sentence based on the previously generated words, ensuring grammatical and semantic consistency.

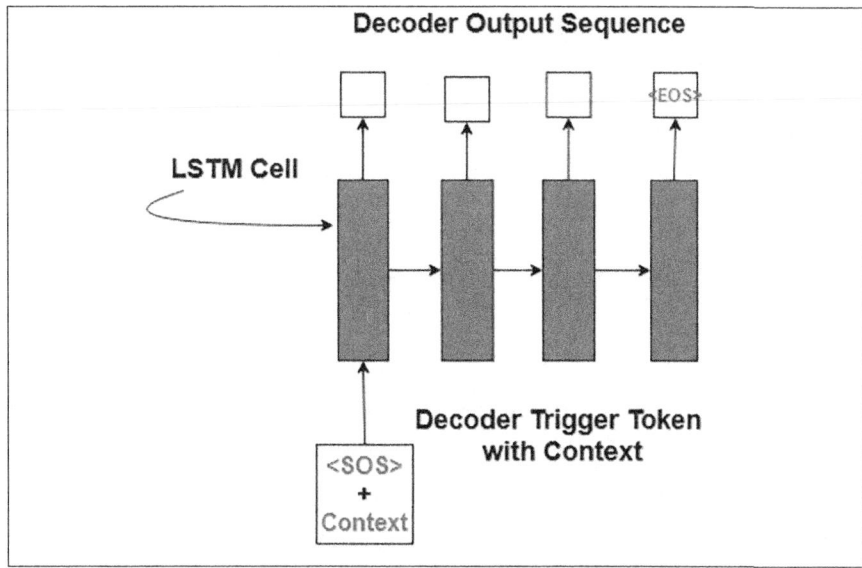

Figure 16.6: *Decoder-Only LSTM Configuration*

A notable strength of the Decoder-only LSTM lies in its ability to operate without explicit reliance on an Encoder. This eliminates the need for a separate encoding process, reducing computational complexity and training time. However, this simplicity comes with a trade-off; the model relies heavily on the initial input and its capacity to maintain long-term dependencies. Properly initializing the model with meaningful context is critical to its performance, particularly in complex applications such as story generation or speech synthesis.

One of the most prominent use cases of Decoder-only LSTMs is in text auto-completion systems, such as predictive keyboards and conversational agents. In these scenarios, the model dynamically generates text based on user input, enhancing communication efficiency. Similarly, in creative fields, Decoder-only LSTMs are employed to generate poetry, music compositions, and even artwork descriptions, demonstrating their versatility in handling structured yet open-ended tasks.

In addition to text-based applications, Decoder-only LSTMs are employed in audio synthesis, particularly in text-to-speech (TTS) systems. Here, the model takes textual input and generates corresponding audio sequences, producing natural-sounding speech. This application highlights the model's ability to handle sequential data across modalities, further underscoring its flexibility and adaptability. Overall, the Decoder-only LSTM configuration is a cornerstone in sequence generation tasks, offering a streamlined yet highly capable approach to producing coherent and contextually aligned outputs. Its application spans a wide range of domains, from enhancing user experiences in real-time systems to driving creativity in content generation.

Each configuration caters to specific applications, from compressing and representing complex input sequences to generating coherent outputs autonomously. These designs form the backbone of various breakthroughs in machine translation, text generation, and sequence modeling. As we transition to the next section, we will explore the practical implementation of these concepts through language modeling and sentiment analysis using Python, providing readers with hands-on experience in applying LSTMs to real-world scenarios.

Language Modelling and Sentiment Analysis

This section delves into the practical application of LSTMs for two essential tasks in natural language processing: language modeling and sentiment analysis. Language modeling involves predicting the next word in a word sequence, enabling tasks such as text generation, auto-completion, and more. On the other hand, sentiment analysis focuses on understanding the emotional tone of a given text, classifying it as positive, negative, or neutral, among other sentiments. By leveraging the sequential processing capability of LSTMs, we will implement these use cases step by step in Python. The next word prediction task will highlight how LSTMs can capture context and dependencies in a word sequence, while the sentiment analysis use case will demonstrate how LSTMs excel in understanding nuanced patterns in text data for classification. Through these implementations, readers will gain a deeper understanding of LSTM's versatility in tackling real-world language-based challenges.

Language Modelling using LSTM

In this use case, we will explore how an LSTM model can be used for language modeling to predict the next word in a sequence. Language modeling is a fundamental task in natural language processing, enabling applications, such as text generation, autocomplete, and machine translation. To demonstrate this concept, we will use the popular nursery rhyme "Mary had a little lamb" as our training data. This poem, with its simple structure and repetitive patterns, serves as an excellent example to illustrate how an LSTM model can learn the sequential order of words and predict the next word based on context. By training the LSTM model on this dataset, we aim to showcase its ability to grasp patterns, dependencies, and word relationships, ultimately generating the correct word predictions that align with the flow of the poem. Through this exercise, readers will gain practical insights into implementing and training an LSTM model for next-word prediction in Python.

Application of LSTM in NLP and TS Forecasting

To get started with this exercise, we first need to load all the necessary libraries required for essential functionalities for text preprocessing, model building, and training the LSTM model.

```
import numpy as np
from keras.preprocessing.text import Tokenizer
from keras.utils import np_utils
from keras.models import Sequential
from keras.layers import Dense
from keras.layers import LSTM
from keras.layers import Embedding
from keras.utils import pad_sequences
```

We can load the text of the poem either by reading it from an external file or, given its small size, by directly assigning it to a variable in our script. This approach ensures flexibility in handling input data while keeping the implementation simple for this use case.

```
data = """Mary had a little lamb, little lamb, little lamb. Mary had
a little lamb\n its fleece was white as snow. And everywhere that Mary
went, Mary went, Mary went\n everywhere that Mary went, the lamb was
sure to go. It followed her to school one\n day, school one day, school
one day. It followed her to school one day, which was\n against the
rule. It made the children laugh and play, laugh and play, laugh and\n
play. It made the children laugh and play to see a lamb at school. So
the teacher\n turned him out, turned him out, turned him out. So the
teacher turned him out and\n sent him straight away"""
```

The next step involves converting the words in the poem into numerical representations, which are required for training the LSTM model.

```
tokenizer = Tokenizer()
tokenizer.fit_on_texts([data])
encoded = tokenizer.texts_to_sequences([data])[0]
```

A **Tokenizer** object is first created and trained on the text using **fit_on_texts**, which maps each unique word in the data to a unique integer. The **texts_to_sequences** function then encodes the poem into a sequence of integers, where each word is replaced by its corresponding integer, enabling the model to process the text numerically.

Knowing the vocabulary size is essential for defining the size of the embedding layer and ensuring the model can correctly map each unique word to its corresponding numerical representation during training. This ensures that the model's input and embedding layers are properly configured to handle all words in the dataset. The vocabulary size shows the total number of unique words in the text plus one (to account for the reserved padding or unknown token, if needed).

```
vocab_size = len(tokenizer.word_index) + 1
print('Vocabulary Size: %d' % vocab_size)
Vocabulary Size: 45
```

Next, we generate line-by-line sequence encodings to prepare the dataset for training the LSTM model. For each tokenized line, shorter sub-sequences are iteratively created.

For instance: "fleece" → "fleece, was" → "fleece, was, white" → "fleece, was, white, as" → "fleece, was, white, as, snow".

```
sequences = list()
for line in data.split('\n'):
  encoded = tokenizer.texts_to_sequences([line])[0]
  for i in range(1, len(encoded)):
    sequence = encoded[:i+1]
    sequences.append(sequence)
print('Total Sequences: %d' % len(sequences))
```

Each sub-sequence is appended to the **sequences** list, creating a dataset of sequences where each sequence's last token serves as the target for prediction during training. By the end of the process, all lines are transformed into sequential datasets of varying lengths, and the total number of sequences is printed, which indicates the size of the dataset prepared for the LSTM model. This method allows the model to learn word relationships incrementally within the context of the poem.

There are various approaches to preparing input sequences for an LSTM model. In this example, we have generated variable-length sequences, which can be padded with zeros to ensure uniformity. Alternatively, readers can explore fixed-length input sequences, such as using two words as input to predict the next word, or three words as input for one-word output. These variations allow flexibility in designing the training data and offer opportunities to experiment with how sequence length impacts the model's learning and predictive performance.

```
max_length = max([len(seq) for seq in sequences])
sequences = pad_sequences(sequences, maxlen=max_length, padding='pre')
print('Max Sequence Length: %d' % max_length)
Max Sequence Length: 7
```

The maximum sequence length (**max_length**) is calculated by finding the longest sequence in the dataset. Then, all sequences are padded to this maximum length using **pad_sequences**, ensuring they are of uniform size. The padding='pre' option adds zeros at the beginning of shorter sequences to align them with the longer ones. This uniformity is essential for training the LSTM model, as it requires inputs of consistent dimensions. The output, "**Max Sequence Length: 7**," indicates that all sequences are now of length 7, facilitating efficient model training.

```
sequences = np.array(sequences)
X, y = sequences[:,:-1],sequences[:,-1]
y = np_utils.to_categorical(y, num_classes=vocab_size)
```

We prepare the data for training by splitting the sequences into inputs () and outputs (). The sequences are first converted to a NumPy array for efficient manipulation.

The input features () are extracted as all elements except the last word in each sequence, while the target output () is the last word in each sequence. To enable the model to predict word probabilities, the target output is one-hot encoded, ensuring that each target is represented as a vector of size equal to the vocabulary size. This encoding helps the LSTM model learn to predict the next word as a probability distribution over the vocabulary.

Following data preparation, we proceed to construct the model outlined as follows:

```
model = Sequential()
model.add(Embedding(vocab_size, 10, input_length=max_length-1))
x & y model.add(LSTM(50))
model.add(Dense(vocab_size, activation='softmax'))
print(model.summary())
# compile network
model.compile(loss='categorical_crossentropy', optimizer='adam',
metrics=['accuracy'])
# fit network
model.fit(X, y, epochs=500, verbose=2)
```

A sequential model is built to train on the prepared sequences with an embedding layer, which transforms each unique word into a dense vector of fixed dimensions, capturing its semantic meaning in a continuous vector space. This representation helps the model learn relationships between words, such as similarities and contextual associations, making it more effective for sequential tasks. Here, the embedding layer initializes the vocabulary with 10-dimensional dense word vectors and takes input sequences of length max_length-1 (excluding the target word). The LSTM layer with 50 units processes the embedded sequences, capturing temporal dependencies and relationships between words. A dense layer with a softmax activation outputs probabilities over the vocabulary, enabling the model to predict the next word. The model is compiled with the categorical cross-entropy loss function, suitable for multi-class classification, and the Adam optimizer, known for efficient convergence. Finally, the model is trained over 500 epochs, iteratively learning the sequence patterns to predict the next word in the input context.

To test the model, let us create a user-defined function to iteratively generate a sequence of words using the trained language model. Starting with an initial seed word or phrase, the function predicts the next word based on the current context and appends it to the input text. This updated input is then used for subsequent predictions, allowing the model to dynamically extend the sequence one word at a time. The function creates coherent sequences that reflect the patterns learned during training by repeatedly encoding the input, padding it to the required length, and mapping the predicted word index back to its corresponding word. This iterative process is useful for tasks, such as text generation and auto-completion, demonstrating the model's ability to understand and generate meaningful language.

```
# generate a sequence from a language model
def generate_seq(model, tokenizer, max_length, seed_text, n_words):
  in_text = seed_text
  # generate a fixed number of words
  for _ in range(n_words):
    # encode the text as integer
    encoded = tokenizer.texts_to_sequences([in_text])[0]
    # pre-pad sequences to a fixed length
    encoded = pad_sequences([encoded], maxlen=max_length, padding='pre')
    # predict probabilities for each word
    yhat = np.argmax(model.predict(encoded), axis=-1)
    # map predicted word index to word
    out_word = ''
    for word, index in tokenizer.word_index.items():
      if index == yhat:
        out_word = word
   break
    # append to input in_text += ' ' + out_word
return in_text
```

Let us evaluate the model using the function we have created. Starting with the seed phrase "**fleece was**," the model generates a sequence of five additional words by predicting the next word iteratively and appending it to the input.

```
# evaluate model
print(generate_seq(model, tokenizer, max_length-1, 'fleece was', 5))
fleece was white as snow and every
```

The generated output highlights the model's ability to learn and reproduce the contextual flow of the poem. While this example demonstrates the application of LSTMs in language modeling, the next use case will explore how LSTMs can be employed in sentiment analysis to classify the emotional tone of a given text, further showcasing the versatility of these models in natural language processing tasks.

Sentiment Analysis using LSTM

In this use case, we will explore the application of LSTM models for sentiment analysis using a dataset of airline passenger tweets, featuring feedback on Virgin America and a few other airlines. The dataset captures passengers' sentiments as positive, negative, or neutral, along with associated metadata such as tweet ID, creation time, and location.

Application of LSTM in NLP and TS Forecasting

For this exercise, we filter out neutral sentiments, focusing solely on positive and negative sentiments to train the LSTM model. Unnecessary columns, including tweet ID, creation time, location, and other metadata, are removed to streamline the dataset for analysis. The cleaned dataset uses the tweet text as input and the corresponding sentiment labels, positive or negative, as the output. This task highlights how LSTMs can effectively process textual data to classify emotional tones, offering practical insights into sentiment-based categorization.

To get started with this exercise, we first need to load all the necessary libraries required for essential functionalities for text preprocessing, model building, and training the LSTM model.

```
import numpy as np
import pandas as pd
from tensorflow.keras.preprocessing.text import Tokenizerfrom tensorflow.keras.utils import to_categorical
from tensorflow.keras.preprocessing.sequence import pad_sequences
from keras.models import Sequential
from keras.layers import LSTM,Dense,Dropout,Embedding
from sklearn.model_selection import train_test_split
```

Let us load the dataset, extract the relevant columns containing the tweet text and sentiment labels, and display the shape of the resulting data to understand its structure and size.

```
df=pd.read_csv('/filepath/Tweets.csv', sep=',')
tweet_df = df[['text','airline_sentiment']]
tweet_df.shape
(14640, 2)
```

We shall classify tweets as either negative or positive, so we will filter out rows with neutral sentiment. The filtered head of the dataset is shown in *Figure* 16.7.

```
tweet_df = tweet_df[tweet_df['airline_sentiment'] != 'neutral']
tweet_df.head()
```

	text	airline_sentiment
1	@VirginAmerica plus you've added commercials t...	positive
3	@VirginAmerica it's really aggressive to blast...	negative
4	@VirginAmerica and it's a really big bad thing...	negative
5	@VirginAmerica seriously would pay $30 a fligh...	negative
6	@VirginAmerica yes, nearly every time I fly VX...	positive

Figure 16.7: *Head of the Tweet Dataset*

```
tweet_df.shape
(11541, 2)

# Reset the index and drop the old index
tweet_df = tweet_df.reset_index(drop=True)
```

The filtered dataset size indicates 11541 tweets with two columns, indicates tweet and sentiment column. Also, the dataset's index is reset, and the old index is dropped to ensure a clean, sequential indexing of rows, which is useful for maintaining consistency during data preprocessing and analysis.

```
# convert airline_sentiment to numeric
sentiment_label = tweet_df.airline_sentiment.factorize()
Y_encoded = to_categorical(sentiment_label[0])
```

The sentiment labels are converted to numeric values using factorization, which assigns a unique integer to each sentiment category, followed by one-hot encoding to the sentiment labels, transforming the numeric values into binary vectors. Each sentiment is represented as a vector with a single "1" indicating the class and "0s" elsewhere, making the labels compatible with the categorical output expected by the LSTM.

```
tweet = tweet_df.text.values
tokenizer = Tokenizer()
tokenizer.fit_on_texts(tweet)
encoded_docs = tokenizer.texts_to_sequences(tweet)
```

The tweet text data is tokenized and converted into a numerical format suitable for model training. Subsequently, the tweets are transformed into sequences of integers where each word in a tweet is replaced by its corresponding numeric representation. This encoding process enables the LSTM model to process textual data as numerical input while preserving the semantic structure of the original tweets.

The encoded sequences are standardized to a uniform length of 30 tokens by applying padding. Shorter sequences are padded with zeros at the beginning, ensuring consistent input dimensions for the LSTM model.

```
padded_sequence = pad_sequences(encoded_docs, maxlen=30)
vocab_size = len(tokenizer.word_index) + 1
#plus 1 added to accomodate the index '0' for padding tokens
```

This standardization is crucial for efficient processing, as LSTM models require fixed-length input sequences for training and prediction. After completing the encoding and padding of the sequences, we perform a sanity check by randomly inspecting a specific tweet, such as at index 100. This step helps verify that the text data has been correctly transformed into its corresponding padded numerical representation, ensuring the preprocessing pipeline is functioning as expected.

```
print(tweet[100])
print(encoded_docs[100])
```
@VirginAmerica I don't understand why you need a DM to give me an answer on if you have a damaged luggage policy.
[103, 3, 89, 344, 64, 6, 94, 4, 250, 1, 234, 19, 40, 310, 10, 82, 6, 25, 4, 1230, 146, 554]

Let us split the dataset into training and testing subsets to evaluate the model's performance.

```
x_train,x_test,y_train,y_test=train_test_split(padded_sequence,Y_encoded,test_size=0.3, random_state=0)
 x_train.shape,x_test.shape,y_train.shape,y_test.shape
((8078, 30), (3463, 30), (8078, 2), (3463, 2))
```

Seventy percent of the data is used for training (**x_train** and **y_train**), while the remaining thirty percent is reserved for testing (**x_test** and **y_test**). This ensures a balanced evaluation by training the model on one subset and validating its accuracy on unseen data.

```
# Build the model
embedding_vector_length = 128 #128 features
model = Sequential()
model.add(Embedding(vocab_size, embedding_vector_length,input_length=30))
model.add(LSTM(256))
model.add(Dense(2, activation='sigmoid'))
model.compile(loss='binary_crossentropy',optimizer='adam',metrics=['accuracy'])
model.fit(x_train,y_train,validation_data=(x_test,y_test), epochs=20, batch_size=32)
```

The LSTM model is constructed with an embedding layer that maps words to 128-dimensional vectors, followed by an LSTM layer with 256 units to capture temporal dependencies in the text data. The final fully connected layer consists of two output nodes with a sigmoid activation function, designed to classify the sentiments as positive or negative. The model is compiled using binary cross-entropy loss and the Adam optimizer, ensuring efficient training and performance tracking through the accuracy metric. The model is trained on the training data for 20 epochs with a batch size of 32 while validating its performance on the test data after each epoch. For demonstration purposes, training is limited to 20 epochs to achieve satisfactory performance. However, readers are encouraged to experiment with different batch sizes and tune the number of epochs to optimize results further. After training, the model's performance is tested with a few random tweets as follows:

```
test_tweet1 ="On time arrival, and great baggage handling"
tw = tokenizer.texts_to_sequences([test_tweet1])
tw = pad_sequences(tw,maxlen=30)
```

```
prediction = np.argmax(model.predict(tw))
sentiment_label[1][prediction]
'positive'
test_tweet2 ="Delayed on-boarding, need to wait for 30 min to receive the baggage"
tw = tokenizer.texts_to_sequences([test_tweet2])
tw = pad_sequences(tw,maxlen=30)
prediction = np.argmax(model.predict(tw))
sentiment_label[1][prediction]
'negative'
```

This use case demonstrates the effectiveness of LSTM models in sentiment analysis by correctly classifying airline passenger tweets as positive or negative. While the model achieves reasonable performance in this demonstration, further fine-tuning hyperparameters, additional training epochs, or expanding the dataset could enhance its accuracy.

Language Translation and Chatbot Modeling

In this section, we explore the implementation of encoder-decoder-based LSTM architecture for two practical applications: language translation and chatbot modeling. Building on the encoder-decoder design discussed in the preceding section, we will first implement a language translation task where English sentences are used as input and French sentences as output, demonstrating the ability of LSTMs to learn complex sequence-to-sequence mappings. Extending the same architecture, by replacing the training dataset with pairs of questions and answers on a specific topic, we can train the encoder-decoder LSTM to develop a chatbot application. These examples illustrate the versatility of LSTM models in handling diverse sequence-based tasks.

To get started with this exercise, we first need to load all the necessary libraries required for essential functionalities for text preprocessing, model building, and training the LSTM based encoder-decoder architecture.

```
import os, sys
from keras.models import Model
from keras.layers import Input, LSTM, Dense, Embedding
from keras.preprocessing.text import Tokenizer
from keras.utils import pad_sequences
from keras.utils import to_categorical
import numpy as np
import matplotlib.pyplot as plt
```

The configuration for the language translation task is designed to balance model complexity and computational efficiency. To accommodate hardware limitations, the dataset can be reduced to 5000 sentences, or up to 20,000 for larger capacity systems. Each sentence is truncated or padded to a maximum length of 50 tokens, ensuring uniform input dimensions. The vocabulary size is limited to the top 20,000 words based on frequency, and word embeddings are set to a dimension of 100 to provide rich semantic representations. These configurations collectively optimize the model for effective learning while managing resource constraints. It reads the data line by line, extracting English sentences as inputs and French sentences as outputs. For French sentences, it creates two separate versions: one for decoder input with a special <sos> token indicating the start of a sequence and another for decoder output with a <eos> token marking the end of the sequence.

```
BATCH_SIZE = 64
EPOCHS = 30
LSTM_NODES =256
#reduce the sentences to 5000 if you have limitation in RAM
NUM_SENTENCES = 20000
MAX_SENTENCE_LENGTH = 50
MAX_NUM_WORDS = 20000
EMBEDDING_SIZE = 100
```

We proceed with the data preparation by loading the training dataset outlined as follows:

```
input_sentences = []
output_sentences = []
output_sentences_inputs = []
count = 0
for line in open(r'/filepath/fra.txt', encoding="utf-8"):
    count += 1
    if count > NUM_SENTENCES:
    break
    if '\t' not in line:
    continue
    input_sentence, output,*rest = line.rstrip().split('\t')
    output_sentence = output + ' <eos>'   #decoder output
    output_sentence_input = '<sos> ' + output #decoder input input_
    sentences.append(input_sentence)
    output_sentences.append(output_sentence) output_sentences_inputs.
    append(output_sentence_input)
print("num samples input:", len(input_sentences))
print("num samples output:", len(output_sentences))
print("num samples output input:", len(output_sentences_inputs))
```

These steps ensure the model learns to translate English to French while correctly handling the sequence structure. The process is limited to a specified number of sentences to manage computational requirements, and the code verifies the number of processed samples for input and output consistency.

After completing the data preparation, a quick sanity check is performed on index 200 to verify the processed data.

```
print(input_sentences[200])
print(output_sentences[200])
print(output_sentences_inputs[200])
Drop it!
Laisse tomber ! <eos>
<sos> Laisse tomber !
```

The English input sentence is "Drop it!" with the corresponding French output sentence "**Laisse tomber ! <eos>**" for the decoder output and "**<sos> Laisse tomber !**" for the decoder input. This ensures input and output sequences have been correctly formatted for the language translation task. Later, tokenization and padding are applied to the input sentences to prepare them for model training.

```
input_tokenizer = Tokenizer(num_words=MAX_NUM_WORDS) input_tokenizer.fit_on_texts(input_sentences)
input_integer_seq = input_tokenizer.texts_to_sequences(input_sentences)
word2idx_inputs = input_tokenizer.word_index
print('Total unique words in the input: %s' % len(word2idx_inputs))
max_input_len = max(len(sen) for sen in input_integer_seq)
print("Length of longest sentence in input: %g" % max_input_len)
Total unique words in the input: 3452
Length of longest sentence in input: 5
```

The tokenizer processes the input English sentences, converting each word into a corresponding integer based on its frequency, creating sequences of integers. A word-to-index dictionary is generated to map each word to its assigned integer, and the total number of unique words in the input is calculated. Additionally, the length of the longest sentence is determined to ensure that all input sequences are standardized for the model. These steps are essential for transforming raw text data into a structured numerical format suitable for processing by the LSTM model. Similarly output French sentences are tokenized and prepared as follows:

```
output_tokenizer = Tokenizer(num_words=MAX_NUM_WORDS, filters='')
output_tokenizer.fit_on_texts(output_sentences + output_sentences_inputs)
output_integer_seq = output_tokenizer.texts_to_sequences(output_sentences)
output_input_integer_seq = output_tokenizer.texts_to_sequences(output_sentences_inputs)
word2idx_outputs = output_tokenizer.word_index
print('Total unique words in the output: %s' % len(word2idx_outputs))
num_words_output = len(word2idx_outputs) + 1
max_out_len = max(len(sen) for sen in output_integer_seq)
print("Length of longest sentence in the output: %g" % max_out_len)
Total unique words in the output: 9431
Length of longest sentence in the output: 12
```

From the comparison of the number of unique words in the input and the output, it can be concluded that English sentences are normally shorter and contain a smaller number of words on average, compared to the translated French sentences. Next, we need to pad the input. The reason behind padding the input and the output is that text sentences can be of varying length, however LSTM expects input instances with the same length. Therefore, we need to convert our sentences into fixed-length vectors.

```
encoder_input_sequences = pad_sequences(input_integer_seq, maxlen=max_input_len)
print("encoder_input_sequences.shape:", encoder_input_sequences.shape)
print("encoder_input_sequences[200]:", encoder_input_sequences[200])
encoder_input_sequences.shape: (20000, 5)
encoder_input_sequences[200]: [  0   0   0 303   4]
```

In the encoder, zeros were padded at the beginning. The reason behind this approach is that encoder output is based on the words occurring at the end of the sentence; therefore, the original words were kept at the end of the sentence, and zeros were padded at the beginning. On the other hand, in the case of the decoder, the processing starts from the beginning of a sentence, and therefore post-padding is performed on the decoder inputs and outputs. A sanity check is performed on index 200 to verify the processed data.

```
decoder_input_sequences = pad_sequences(output_input_integer_seq, maxlen=max_out_len, padding='post')
print("decoder_input_sequences.shape:", decoder_input_sequences.shape)
print("decoder_input_sequences[200]:", decoder_input_sequences[200])
decoder_input_sequences.shape: (20000, 12)
decoder_input_sequences[200]: [  2 195 491   4   0   0   0   0   0   0   0   0]
print(word2idx_outputs["<sos>"])
print(word2idx_outputs["laisse"])
print(word2idx_outputs["tomber"])
print(word2idx_outputs["!"])
2
195
491
4
```

Towards the next step, external GloVe embeddings are loaded for the English sentences to provide pre-trained word vectors that capture semantic relationships between words. A dictionary is created to map each word in the GloVe file to its corresponding embedding vector. For the input sentences, a matrix is initialized to store the embedding vectors for the most frequent words, as determined by the tokenizer. Each word in the vocabulary is then matched with its pre-trained GloVe embedding vector, and these vectors are populated into the embedding matrix. If a word does not have a pre-trained embedding, it remains as a zero vector. For the decoder side (French sentences), the default Keras embedding layer is used, highlighting the flexibility of choosing between pre-trained embeddings and trainable embeddings. Readers are encouraged to experiment with different combinations, such as using GloVe for both sides and Keras embedding for both, to observe their impact on model performance.

```
#word embeddings
from numpy import array
from numpy import asarray
from numpy import zeros
embeddings_dictionary = dict()
glove_file = open(r'/filepath/glove.6B.100d.txt', encoding="utf8")
for line in glove_file:
records = line.split()
word = records[0]
vector_dimensions = asarray(records[1:], dtype='float32')
embeddings_dictionary[word] = vector_dimensions
glove_file.close()
num_words = min(MAX_NUM_WORDS, len(word2idx_inputs) + 1)
embedding_matrix = zeros((num_words, EMBEDDING_SIZE))
for word, index in word2idx_inputs.items():
embedding_vector = embeddings_dictionary.get(word)
if embedding_vector is not None:
embedding_matrix[index] = embedding_vector
#embedding layer for encoder (encoder_embedding) #num_words=3453
(english)
embedding_layer = Embedding(num_words, EMBEDDING_SIZE, weights=
[embedding_matrix], input_length=max_input_len)
```

To make predictions, the final layer of the model will be a dense layer; therefore, we need the outputs in the form of one-hot encoded vectors since we will be using softmax activation function at the dense layer. To create such a one-hot encoded output, the next step is to assign 1 to the column number that corresponds to the integer representation of the word. For instance, the integer representation for laisse tomber! is [2 195 491 4 0 0 0 0 0 0 0]. In the **decoder_targets_one_hot** output array, in the second column of the first row, '1' will be inserted. Similarly, at the 195 index of the second row, another '**1**' will be inserted, and so on.

```
decoder_targets_one_hot = np.zeros((len(input_sentences),max_out_len,
num_words_output),dtype='float32')
decoder_targets_one_hot.shape
(20000, 12, 9432)
decoder_output_sequences = pad_sequences(output_integer_seq,
maxlen=max_out_len, padding='post')
for i, d in enumerate(decoder_output_sequences):
for t, word in enumerate(d):
decoder_targets_one_hot[i, t, word] = 1
```

The core encoder-decoder design begins with defining the encoder, which processes the input English sentence. The encoder starts with an input placeholder for sequences of the maximum input length, followed by a custom embedding layer utilizing GloVe embeddings to transform words into dense vector representations. The LSTM layer in the encoder processes these embeddings and outputs its final hidden and cell states, which encapsulate the context of the input sequence. These states are passed to the decoder as the initial state to maintain continuity between the input and output sequences.

```
#Define the encoder
encoder_inputs_placeholder = Input(shape=(max_input_len,))
#custom made embedding_layer using Glove for english words
x = embedding_layer(encoder_inputs_placeholder)
encoder = LSTM(LSTM_NODES, return_state=True)
encoder_outputs, h, c = encoder(x)
encoder_states = [h, c]
```

The decoder, designed to generate French translations, begins with an input placeholder for the output sequence. It uses a Keras embedding layer to create trainable embeddings for the French words. The decoder LSTM processes these embeddings while initializing its state with the encoder's final states, ensuring that the output generation is contextually aligned with the input sequence. The decoder produces outputs for each time step, forming the basis for generating the translated sentence. This design effectively links the input and output sequences through shared states, enabling sequence-to-sequence translation.

```
#Define the decoder
decoder_inputs_placeholder = Input(shape=(max_out_len,))
#Keras Embedding Layer
decoder_embedding = Embedding(num_words_output, EMBEDDING_SIZE)
decoder_inputs_x = decoder_embedding(decoder_inputs_placeholder)
decoder_lstm = LSTM(LSTM_NODES, return_sequences=True,return_state=True)
decoder_outputs,_,_= decoder_lstm(decoder_inputs_x, initial_state=
encoder_states)
```

Finally, the output from the decoder LSTM is passed through a dense layer to predict decoder outputs, as shown here:

```
decoder_dense = Dense(num_words_output, activation='softmax') decoder_
outputs = decoder_dense(decoder_outputs)
model = Model([encoder_inputs_placeholder,decoder_inputs_placeholder],
decoder_outputs) model.compile(optimizer='rmsprop',loss='categorical_
crossentropy',metrics=['accuracy']) r = model.fit( [encoder_input_se-
quences, decoder_input_sequences], decoder_targets_one_hot, batch_
size=BATCH_SIZE, epochs=EPOCHS, validation_split=0.1, )
```

The model is compiled using the RMSprop optimizer and categorical cross-entropy loss, suitable for multi-class prediction tasks, with accuracy as the performance metric. During training, the model learns to map input sequences to target sequences by minimizing the loss function, leveraging one-hot encoded target sequences for comparison. The training process is carried out in batches, over multiple epochs, with a validation split to monitor performance on unseen data and ensure the model generalizes well.

To prepare the trained model for deployment in a production environment, it is modified to handle real-time input for inference. The encoder is restructured to return its final hidden and cell states as outputs, representing the context of the input sequence. These states are then passed to the decoder, which is adapted to process one word at a time, enabling step-by-step sequence generation. The decoder is redesigned to accept the current decoder hidden and cell states as additional inputs, ensuring continuity between time steps. The decoder's embedding layer is adjusted to accommodate single-word inputs, and the LSTM outputs both the next word prediction and updated hidden and cell states.

```
encoder_model = Model(encoder_inputs_placeholder, encoder_states)
decoder_state_input_h = Input(shape=(LSTM_NODES,))
decoder_state_input_c = Input(shape=(LSTM_NODES,))
decoder_states_inputs = [decoder_state_input_h, decoder_state_input_c]
decoder_inputs_single = Input(shape=(1,))
decoder_inputs_single_x = decoder_embedding(decoder_inputs_single)
decoder_outputs, h, c = decoder_lstm(decoder_inputs_single_x, initial_state=decoder_states_inputs)
decoder_states = [h, c]
decoder_outputs = decoder_dense(decoder_outputs)
decoder_model = Model( [decoder_inputs_single] + decoder_states_inputs, [decoder_outputs] + decoder_states )
idx2word_input = {v:k for k, v in word2idx_inputs.items()}
idx2word_target = {v:k for k, v in word2idx_outputs.items()}
```

These modifications are essential for real-time decoding during inference, where the model generates one word at a time based on the previous word and context. Additionally, dictionaries mapping indices to words for both input and output vocabularies are prepared, facilitating the conversion of predictions into human-readable text. This setup ensures the trained model is production-ready for dynamic sequence-to-sequence tasks, such as language translation or chatbot responses.

The final step involves creating a user-defined function to interact with the trained model for translating input sentences. At each step, the decoder model outputs a probability distribution over the target vocabulary, along with updated hidden and cell states, which are fed back into the decoder for the next prediction. The predicted word is added to the output sentence unless the <eos> token is encountered, signaling the end of the sequence. This iterative process continues until the maximum sequence length is reached or the <eos> token is predicted.

```
def translate_sentence(input_seq):
    states_value = encoder_model.predict(input_seq)
    target_seq = np.zeros((1, 1))
```

```
        target_seq[0, 0] = word2idx_outputs['<sos>']
        eos = word2idx_outputs['<eos>']
        output_sentence = []
        for _ in range(max_out_len):
            output_tokens, h, c = decoder_model.predict([target_seq] +
            states_value)
            idx = np.argmax(output_tokens[0, 0, :])
            if eos == idx:
                break
            word = ''
            if idx > 0:
                word = idx2word_target[idx]
                output_sentence.append(word)
            target_seq[0, 0] = idx
            states_value = [h, c]
    return ' '.join(output_sentence)
```

This function finally returns the generated sentence, providing a seamless way to test and use the model for language translation tasks. When testing the translation function with a randomly picked sentence (for example, index 17820), the function demonstrates remarkable accuracy, returning a translation that is almost at a commercial-grade level of quality. The selected input sequence is passed through the encoder to generate context states, and the decoder iteratively predicts the target words, forming the complete translated sentence.

```
i=17820
input_seq = encoder_input_sequences[i:i+1]
translation = translate_sentence(input_seq)
print('-')
print('Input:', input_sentences[i])
print('Response:', translation)
Input: I need more time.
Response: j'ai besoin de temps.
```

This result showcases the effectiveness of the encoder-decoder LSTM architecture, even in its prototype form with limited training data. However, it is important to emphasize that this implementation is primarily designed for academic demonstration purposes. Real-life language translation systems require significantly larger and more diverse training datasets, along with more complex architectures and optimizations, to handle the nuances and scalability challenges of production-grade applications. Such enhancements ensure robust performance across varied linguistic contexts and large-scale deployments.

Readers are encouraged to experiment with this implementation by using a dataset like **chatbot_QandA.txt**, which contains pairs of questions and answers. By fine-tuning the initial configurations, such as adjusting the maximum input length for questions and the maximum output length for answers, the same encoder-decoder architecture can be adapted to train a chatbot. This exercise will help readers understand how sequence-to-sequence models can be leveraged for applications beyond language translation. Exploring this architecture with different datasets and configurations enables readers to grasp its flexibility and practical utility, laying the groundwork for deploying advanced conversational AI systems or domain-specific chatbots.

Conclusion

In this chapter, we explored the transformative capabilities of LSTM architectures in handling sequential data for a wide range of applications. Beginning with time-series forecasting, we demonstrated how LSTMs can effectively model and predict temporal patterns, showcasing their relevance in financial and stock market analysis. We then delved into different design strategies, including encoder-only, encoder-decoder, and decoder-only configurations, highlighting their strengths in tasks such as machine translation and chatbot modeling.

The chapter also featured practical implementations of language modeling for next-word prediction and sentiment analysis for airline passenger feedback, providing readers with hands-on experience in applying LSTMs to real-world scenarios. Each use case emphasized the adaptability of LSTM architectures and their ability to generalize across diverse datasets. Finally, we introduced an encoder-decoder architecture for language translation, illustrating how such models can be extended for chatbot applications with appropriate dataset modifications.

As we wrap up this chapter, we move toward the final chapter of this book, titled *Emerging Trends and Ethical Considerations in AI*. In the next chapter, we will delve into cutting-edge advancements in AI, focusing on its applications in computer vision and natural language processing, while also addressing the critical ethical considerations shaping the future of AI technologies.

Practice Exercises

1. Consider a language translation model using an encoder-decoder LSTM architecture. The input vocabulary size is 10,000, and the output vocabulary size is 8,000. Each word in the input and output is represented by a 100-dimensional embedding. The maximum input sequence length is 30 words, and the maximum output sequence length is 40 words. Calculate the total number of parameters for the embedding layers in the model.

2. An LSTM model is designed for a time-series forecasting task with the following configuration:
Number of units in the LSTM layer: 128
Input sequence length: 60
Number of features per time step: 1

Calculate the total number of trainable parameters in the LSTM layer. Assume the LSTM uses forget gates, input gates, and output gates.

3. In a language translation task using an encoder-decoder LSTM architecture, the input sequence is represented as ["cat", "is", "on", "the", "mat"]. After tokenization, the integer sequence is [12, 5, 16, 7, 22]. The maximum sequence length is set to 8, and padding is applied to ensure uniform input length.
   - Show the padded sequence after applying pre-padding
   - Explain why padding is necessary in LSTM models and how it helps during training

4. In a sentiment analysis use case, the LSTM model is trained on 10,000 tweets with a vocabulary size of 5,000 unique words. Each tweet is padded to a length of 50 words. The embedding layer is initialized with pre-trained embeddings of dimension 100.
   - Calculate the size of the embedding matrix used in the model
   - Explain why the embedding dimension does not depend on the length of the padded sequences

5. During the training of an encoder-decoder LSTM for language translation, the training data contains 15,000 input sentences with a maximum length of 20 words, and the vocabulary size is 10,000 for both input and output. If the encoder LSTM has 128 units and the decoder LSTM has 256 units:
   - Calculate the total number of weights in the encoder LSTM
   - Explain how the hidden states from the encoder are passed to the decoder

Answers

1. Input Embedding Layer Parameters: Vocabulary size × Embedding dimension = 10,000 × 100
   Output Embedding Layer Parameters: 8000 × 100
   Total Embedding Layer Parameters: 10, 00,000 + 8, 00,000 = 18, 00,000

2. Parameters = 4 × (128 × (128 + 1 + 1)) = 66,560

3. Padded Sequence: [0, 0, 0, 12, 5, 16, 7, 22]. Padding is necessary for maintaining uniform input dimensions, facilitating batch processing, and ensuring computational efficiency in LSTM models.

4. Size of embedding matrix = 5000 × 100 = 5, 00,000. The embedding dimension reflects the representation of individual words, independent of the sequence length, which is only a structural requirement for LSTM models.

5. Weights = 4 × (10,000 + 128) = 51, 80,672 weights. The encoder's hidden and cell states are passed to the decoder to maintain contextual information for sequence generation.

Multiple Choice Questions

1. In an encoder-decoder LSTM model for language translation, the encoder's main role is to:
   a. Generate the final output sentence
   b. Capture the context of the input sequence
   c. Tokenize the input sentence
   d. Translate words individually

2. What is the purpose of adding the <sos> and <eos> tokens in language translation tasks?
   a. To increase the vocabulary size
   b. To handle unknown words during translation
   c. To define the start and end of the sentence
   d. To improve model accuracy

3. Which of the following tasks is NOT a typical application of LSTMs?
   a. Image recognition
   b. Sentiment analysis
   c. Language modeling
   d. Time-series prediction

4. In sentiment analysis, one-hot encoding is used to:
   a. Tokenize the text data
   b. Represent sentiment labels as binary vectors
   c. Reduce the dimensionality of the dataset
   d. Pad the input sequences

5. What is the significance of using word embeddings in NLP tasks?
   a. To convert words into one-hot vectors
   b. To handle missing words in the dataset
   c. To represent words as dense vectors capturing semantic meaning
   d. To improve the accuracy of numerical computations

6. In a language modeling task, padding sequences is necessary to:
   a. Reduce the size of the dataset

b. Ensure all input sequences are of the same length

c. Increase the vocabulary size

d. Handle unknown words

7. What metric is typically used to evaluate a time-series forecasting model?

   a. F1 Score

   b. Root Mean Squared Error (RMSE)

   c. BLEU Score

   d. Precision

8. In a sequence-to-sequence architecture, the hidden states from the encoder are:

   a. Discarded after training

   b. Directly passed to the softmax layer

   c. Used to initialize the decoder's hidden states

   d. Replaced with embedding vectors

9. What is the primary reason to use an encoder-decoder LSTM for chatbot modeling?

   a. To handle variable-length input and output sequences

   b. To improve computational efficiency

   c. To generate one-hot encoded outputs

   d. To increase the training speed

10. What is the primary role of the decoder in an encoder-decoder LSTM architecture?

    a. To preprocess the input data

    b. To predict the next word or token in the sequence

    c. To generate embeddings for input sentences

    d. To initialize the hidden state of the encoder

Answers

1. c

2. c

3. a

4. b
5. c
6. b
7. b
8. c
9. a
10. b

Keywords

- Sequential Data
- Time-Series Forecasting
- LSTM Encoder-Decoder Model
- Word Embeddings
- Tokenization
- Language Modeling
- Sentiment Analysis
- Neural Machine Translation (NMT)
- Chatbot Architecture
- Sequence-to-Sequence Learning
- Padding and Truncation
- Vocabulary Size
- Encoder-Decoder Architecture
- Encoder Hidden States
- Decoder Outputs
- Pre-trained Word Embeddings

References

1. https://ojs.bbwpublisher.com/index.php/PBES/article/view/4361https://cs224d.stanford.edu/lectures/CS224d-Lecture10.pdf
2. https://repository.rit.edu/cgi/viewcontent.cgi?article=12309&context=theses

Chapter 17
Emerging Trends and Ethical Considerations in AI

Introduction

As we conclude this foundational journey through the principles and applications of AI, we step into the rapidly evolving landscape of advanced AI technologies and their broader implications.

The chapter begins with advanced applications of CNNs in critical domains, such as object detection and face recognition, showcasing their transformative impact on industries ranging from security to healthcare. It then transitions to discussing how LSTMs have evolved into more sophisticated architectures such as transformer models, which power today's modern Generative AI (GenAI) systems. These transformer models are at the core of large language models (LLMs) such as ChatGPT, driving innovations in natural language understanding and generation. The chapter delves into the challenge of ethical considerations in AI and its far-reaching economic, cultural, and social impacts.

This chapter is designed to provide an overarching view rather than exhaustive detail. This chapter aims to inspire readers to investigate these cutting-edge topics further, offering an overview to spark curiosity among readers and encourage further exploration.

Structure

In this chapter, we will cover the following main topics:

- Advanced Applications of CNN in Object Detection and Face Recognition
- Advanced Applications of LSTM in the Form of Transformer Models

- Scope of GenAI in Modern Day ChatGPT
- Ethical Challenges and Societal Responsibilities in AI
- Balancing Risks and Benefits in the AI landscape
- Economic, Cultural, and Social Impacts of AI

Advanced Applications of CNN in Object Detection and Face Recognition

Object detection has been one of the cornerstone applications of CNNs, marking a shift from identifying "what" is in an image to pinpointing "where" objects reside. The journey began with simpler models using sliding window techniques and bounding box regressors that scanned an image patch by patch, classifying each region for potential objects. While effective for basic tasks, this approach suffered from computational inefficiency and limited scalability to complex scenes with multiple objects.

- **RCNN:** The introduction of Region-based Convolutional Neural Networks (RCNN) by researchers at UC Berkeley marked a groundbreaking advancement in the field of object detection. At its core, RCNN divided the task of object detection into manageable steps, beginning with the generation of region proposals—areas within an image that were likely to contain objects. These proposals were then cropped and resized to a uniform size, enabling efficient feature extraction using a CNN. The extracted features were subsequently fed into a classifier to determine the class of the object within each region. This structured approach allowed RCNN to achieve significantly higher accuracy than earlier methods, making it a milestone in computer vision research.

  Despite its success in boosting detection performance, RCNN faced significant limitations in terms of computational efficiency. The process of generating region proposals relied on external algorithms such as Selective Search, which were slow and resource-intensive. Furthermore, each region proposal had to be individually processed by the CNN, resulting in redundant computations when overlapping regions shared similar features. This inefficiency limited RCNN's applicability in real-time scenarios, such as autonomous driving or live surveillance, where speed is critical. However, RCNN laid the foundational framework for subsequent advancements like Fast RCNN and Faster RCNN, which refined and streamlined these steps, transforming object detection into a more practical and scalable solution.

- **Fast RCNN and Faster RCNN:** Fast RCNN, developed as an enhancement to the original RCNN, addressed many of its computational inefficiencies while maintaining high accuracy in object detection tasks. Unlike RCNN, which independently processed each region proposal through a CNN, Fast RCNN introduced a single feature map approach. By passing the entire image through the CNN once, it generated a shared feature map, which was then divided into region-specific segments using region proposals. This shared feature map eliminated the need for redundant computations, dramatically improving the processing speed. Additionally, Fast RCNN incorporated the concept of Region of Interest (RoI) pooling, which standardized the size of region proposals to a fixed resolution, making them compatible with fully connected layers. The network could now perform classification and bounding box regression in a single forward pass, reducing the multi-step complexity seen in RCNN.

Faster RCNN represented a significant leap forward by introducing Region Proposal Networks (RPNs), which generated region proposals directly from the shared feature map created by CNN. The RPN was a lightweight, fully connected network that identified potential object locations by predicting objectness scores and refined bounding box coordinates. This integration eliminated the dependency on external proposal generation algorithms, significantly accelerating the object detection pipeline. Faster RCNN maintained high accuracy while achieving substantial speed improvements, making it more suitable for real-time applications.

- **The Emergence of YOLO:** The introduction of the "You Only Look Once" (YOLO) framework marked a transformative moment in object detection. Unlike earlier RCNN-based models, which relied on a multi-step process involving region proposals, feature extraction, and classification, YOLO approached object detection as a unified regression task. This innovative method processed the entire image in a single pass through the neural network, predicting bounding boxes and class probabilities simultaneously as shown in *Figure 17.1*. By treating object detection as a global optimization problem, YOLO achieved remarkable speed without compromising accuracy. This efficiency made YOLO ideal for real-time applications, such as surveillance systems, robotics, and autonomous vehicles, where rapid decision-making is critical.

At the core of YOLO's architecture is the division of the input image into an grid, where each grid cell is responsible for detecting objects whose center lies within it. Each grid cell predicts bounding box coordinates, objectness scores, and class probabilities, all in one go. This direct prediction approach eliminated the need for separate region proposal networks and intermediate processing steps. The end-to-end architecture allowed YOLO to balance global context with local features, improving its ability to detect multiple objects in diverse and cluttered environments. YOLO's use of a single convolutional neural network for both localization and classification tasks significantly reduced computational overhead, enabling it to process dozens of frames per second. Its design also minimized false positives by considering the spatial relationships within the image, making it robust for complex scenes. YOLO's real-time detection capabilities revolutionized fields, such as autonomous driving, where detecting pedestrians, vehicles, and traffic signs quickly and accurately is vital for safety.

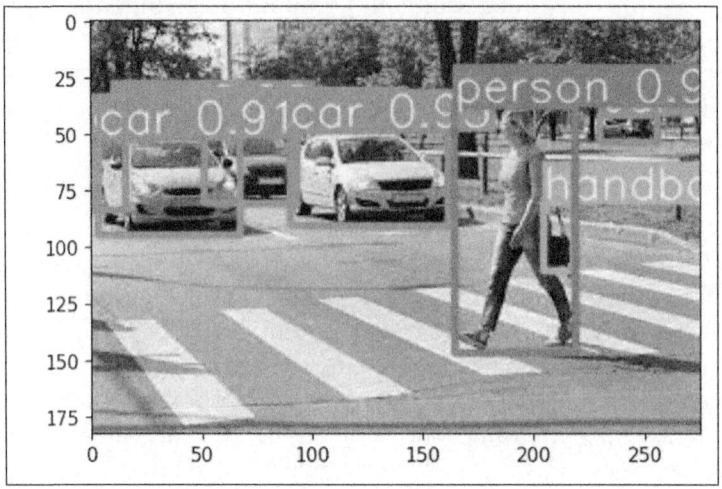

Figure 17.1: YOLO Multi-Object Detection

YOLO's influence extended beyond traditional object detection applications. Its combination of speed and accuracy inspired new research directions and adaptations for tasks such as instance segmentation and real-time video analysis. As one of the most cited and widely implemented frameworks, YOLO remains a cornerstone in the evolution of computer vision technologies.

- **Semantic Segmentation with Unet:** Semantic segmentation represents a significant leap in computer vision by assigning a meaningful label to every pixel in an image, enabling a fine-grained understanding of scenes. Unlike object detection, which identifies discrete objects within bounding boxes, semantic segmentation delineates the exact shape and location of objects as shown in *Figure 17.2*. The Unet architecture, introduced by researchers at the University of Freiburg for biomedical image segmentation, became a landmark model in this domain. Designed to handle challenges such as limited data and complex shapes, Unet employs an encoder-decoder structure. The encoder extracts hierarchical features through convolutional and pooling layers, compressing the spatial dimensions while retaining semantic information. The decoder then up-samples these features, restoring the spatial dimensions while preserving critical details.

  The versatility of Unet extends far beyond its original biomedical applications. In autonomous navigation, Unet-based models segment roadways, obstacles, and traffic signs, enabling self-driving cars to interpret their surroundings with remarkable accuracy. Similarly, in agriculture, Unet aids in segmenting crops and weeds from aerial imagery, streamlining precision farming efforts. The model's adaptability also makes it invaluable in remote sensing, where it processes satellite imagery for tasks such as land cover classification and disaster assessment.

Furthermore, the principles behind Unet have influenced generative models, such as GANs (Generative Adversarial Networks), forming the backbone of tasks such as image synthesis and style transfer. This transition to generative applications culminates in cutting-edge models such as stable diffusion architectures, where Unet-inspired designs contribute to photorealistic image generation. By bridging pixel-level precision with contextual understanding, Unet continues to shape the landscape of computer vision.

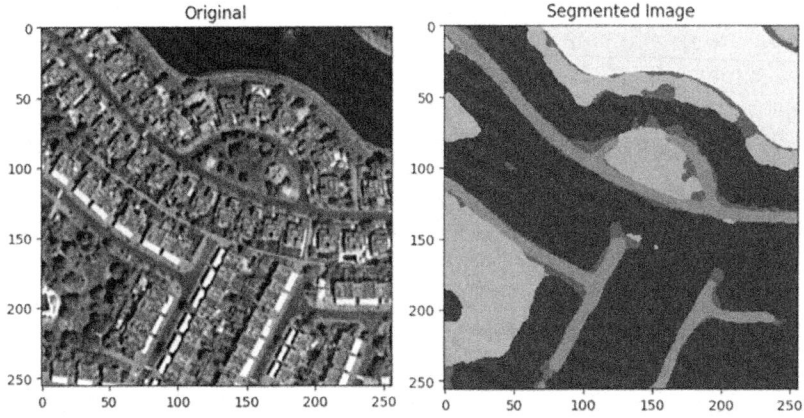

Figure 17.2: *U-Net Based Semantic Segmentation*

The principles behind Unet have laid the foundation for advanced generative models, particularly in the realm of image generation. When combined with Generative Adversarial Networks (GANs), Unet-style architectures enable tasks such as image inpainting, style transfer, and even creating photorealistic images. GAN-based models, leveraging segmentation as a pre-processing step, have been instrumental in modern-day applications, such as Stable Diffusion and DALL-E.

Face Recognition: Face recognition has emerged as a transformative application of CNNs, particularly in biometric security systems, where accuracy and reliability are paramount. CNNs excel in face recognition by learning high-dimensional feature representations that encode unique characteristics of a face, such as shape, texture, and subtle variations. Unlike traditional methods relying on handcrafted features, CNN-based models autonomously learn discriminative features from raw pixel data, making them robust to variations in lighting, pose, and expression. Pioneering architectures such as DeepFace, developed by Facebook's AI Research team, marked a significant milestone by achieving near-human accuracy in face verification tasks. DeepFace employs a deep neural network to extract face embeddings, mapping each face into a latent space where distances between embeddings correspond to similarity.

Building upon these foundations, FaceNet, introduced by Google researchers, further refined the approach to face recognition. FaceNet leverages a triplet loss function to directly optimize the embeddings, ensuring that faces of the same individual cluster closely together in the latent space, while faces of different individuals are spaced apart. This approach allows for efficient face verification, clustering, and even one-shot learning, where the system can recognize individuals with minimal training data. Beyond theoretical advancements, CNN-based face recognition models have been integrated into real-world systems, from unlocking smartphones and enhancing airport security to monitoring attendance in workplaces and improving personalized user experiences. As face recognition technology continues to evolve, challenges such as privacy concerns and ethical implications remain at the forefront, requiring balanced innovation to ensure both utility and user trust.

The advancements in object detection, face recognition, and image segmentation exemplify the transformative impact of CNNs across domains. As these architectures evolve, their influence extends beyond traditional applications, paving the way for creative innovations in AI-driven imaging solutions. In the following sections, we will explore how similar advancements in sequential modeling, such as LSTMs, have inspired modern transformer models, reshaping NLP and other sequential tasks.

Advanced Applications of LSTM in the Form of Transformer Models

The evolution of deep learning architectures has seen significant milestones, one of which is the transformation of LSTM-based models into the more advanced Transformer models. LSTM networks have been widely celebrated for their ability to address long-term dependencies in sequential data. However, their sequential processing nature posed challenges, especially with large datasets, as it limited parallelization and increased computational time. Transformer models, introduced in the groundbreaking paper "Attention is All You Need" by Vaswani et al., redefined the landscape by overcoming these limitations. Transformers abandoned the recurrent structure of LSTMs and relied solely on the self-attention mechanism, enabling parallel processing of input sequences while maintaining contextual awareness. This innovation significantly improved efficiency and scalability, making transformers the go-to architecture for tasks that involve long sequences.

Despite their differences, Transformer models are conceptually rooted in the principles established by LSTMs. The gating mechanisms in LSTMs responsible for selectively updating and forgetting information share a philosophical similarity with the attention mechanism in transformers.

Emerging Trends and Ethical Considerations in AI 445

While LSTMs use gates to manage information flow across time steps, transformers pay attention to weighing the importance of different parts of the input sequence. This transition highlights how the limitations of LSTMs inspired the design choices in transformers, such as positional encoding as shown in *Figure* 17.3 to retain sequence order. As a result, tasks that were once dominated by LSTM-based models, such as machine translation, text summarization, and speech recognition, have witnessed dramatic performance improvements with the adoption of transformers.

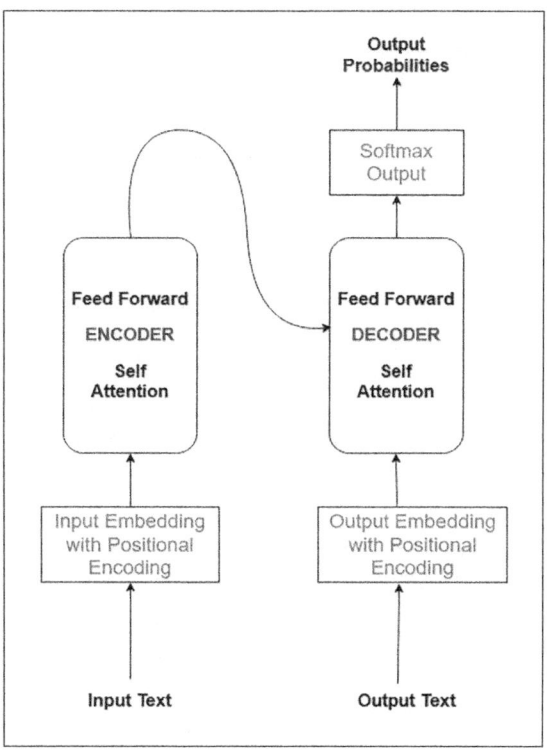

Figure 17.3: *Encoder-Decoder Transformer Architecture*

This section delves into how transformers have taken center stage in modern AI applications across diverse domains.

- **Machine Translation:** In NLP, machine translation stands as one of the most impactful applications of transformer models. Tools such as Google Translate have moved beyond LSTM-based architectures to adopt transformer models such as the Transformer and its successors. The ability of transformers to process entire input sequences simultaneously, coupled with their contextual awareness through self-attention, has resulted in significant improvements in translation accuracy and fluency. Beyond single-language translation, transformer models have become the foundation for multilingual systems capable of real-time processing. Architectures such as FLAN-T5 and Generative Pre-trained Transformer (GPT) can handle multiple languages within a single model, reducing the need for separate systems for each language pair. This capability is especially critical for global applications requiring dynamic translation in real-world settings, such as international meetings, travel assistance, and cross-border commerce. Additionally, the ability to incorporate transfer learning has enabled transformer models to be fine-tuned on specific languages or domains, further enhancing their adaptability and performance. These innovations have positioned transformers as indispensable tools for breaking language barriers, fostering global collaboration, and bridging cultural divides in an increasingly interconnected world.

- **Text Generation and Summarization:** Text generation has undergone a paradigm shift with the introduction of transformer architectures, such as GPT. Historically reliant on LSTMs, text generation often faced challenges in maintaining coherence over long passages and in effectively capturing nuanced contexts. GPT and its successors have overcome these limitations by leveraging self-attention mechanisms and vast training datasets. These models excel at generating text that is not only syntactically correct but also contextually rich, demonstrating an understanding of the nuances of human language. Applications such as content creation for articles, automated storytelling, and conversational chatbots have greatly benefited from this advancement. For instance, GPT-based systems can create compelling narratives, compose creative content, or generate realistic responses in dialogues, rivaling human-like linguistic capabilities. This innovation has transformed industries ranging from digital marketing to entertainment, where the demand for scalable and personalized content generation continues to grow.

- **Sentiment Analysis and Opinion Mining:** Sentiment analysis, which historically relied heavily on LSTM networks for sequence processing, has reached new heights with the advent of transformer models such as Bidirectional Encoder Representations from Transformers (BERT). LSTMs, while effective, often struggled with fully understanding the context due to their sequential processing nature, which limited their ability to account for complex interdependencies between words. Transformers, on the other hand, leverage bidirectional processing through self-attention mechanisms, enabling them to consider both preceding and succeeding words simultaneously. This holistic understanding allows transformers to better capture the nuances of sentiment embedded in the text, including subtle contextual cues that can alter the sentiment of a phrase. For instance, understanding the sentiment in a sentence like "The movie was surprisingly not bad" requires recognizing that "not bad" conveys a positive sentiment despite the presence of a negative word.

  This enhanced capability has made transformer-based models indispensable for various applications. In social media monitoring, for example, organizations can analyze public sentiment about brands, products, or events in real-time, gaining valuable insights to shape marketing strategies or address public concerns. Customer feedback analysis is another area where transformers shine, helping companies decode complex customer sentiments from reviews and surveys, thus improving product development and customer service. Similarly, in financial markets, sentiment analysis powered by transformers can be used to gauge public and investor sentiment, providing actionable insights for market trend prediction. By surpassing the limitations of traditional LSTM-based models, transformer architectures have redefined the accuracy and scope of sentiment analysis, making them critical tools in today's data-driven decision-making landscape.

- **Speech-to-Text and Voice Synthesis:** Transformers have profoundly impacted speech-processing tasks, setting new benchmarks in both accuracy and efficiency. One of the most notable advancements is speech-to-text transcription, where models such as Wav2Vec and Whisper leverage transformer architectures to achieve exceptional performance. Unlike traditional LSTM-based systems that process audio sequences sequentially, transformers use self-attention mechanisms to capture long-term dependencies across entire audio inputs simultaneously. This approach not only enhances accuracy but also ensures resilience to noise, a common challenge in real-world applications. For instance, Whisper, a cutting-edge transformer model by OpenAI, excels at transcribing speech even in noisy environments, such as crowded streets or poor audio recordings. This capability has unlocked new possibilities for automated transcription services, enabling their use in scenarios where traditional models struggled to deliver consistent results.

    In parallel, transformers have significantly advanced voice synthesis technologies, including text-to-speech (TTS) generation. By leveraging their capacity to model intricate temporal dependencies in audio sequences, transformer-based systems produce speech that sounds remarkably natural and expressive. These models are particularly adept at capturing subtle variations in pitch, tone, and rhythm, which are crucial for replicating human-like speech. Unlike earlier LSTM-based approaches, which often suffered from monotonic or robotic-sounding outputs due to limited context modeling, transformer-based TTS models ensure fluid and engaging voice generation. Applications of this technology span a wide range of domains, from virtual assistants and audiobooks to accessibility tools for visually impaired users. By bridging the gap between textual inputs and dynamic audio outputs, transformers have redefined the boundaries of what is achievable in speech processing, making them indispensable tools in the field.

- **Image Captioning in Computer Vision:** Transformers have made a significant impact in the field of computer vision, particularly in image captioning, where their sequence modeling capabilities shine. Image captioning involves generating descriptive textual captions that accurately reflect the content of an image, requiring the ability to connect visual features with linguistic constructs. Transformers excel in this task by analyzing visual data through advanced attention mechanisms and mapping it to corresponding textual representations. Unlike traditional methods that rely on separate feature extraction and language generation stages, transformer-based architectures seamlessly integrate these processes, enabling a more cohesive and accurate understanding of images.

One of the critical advantages of using transformers for image captioning is their ability to model complex relationships across both spatial and sequential dimensions. By employing vision-language models such as the Vision Transformer (ViT) as shown in *Figure* 17.4, these systems can analyze intricate patterns in visual inputs and generate contextually rich and grammatically correct descriptions or object detection in an image.

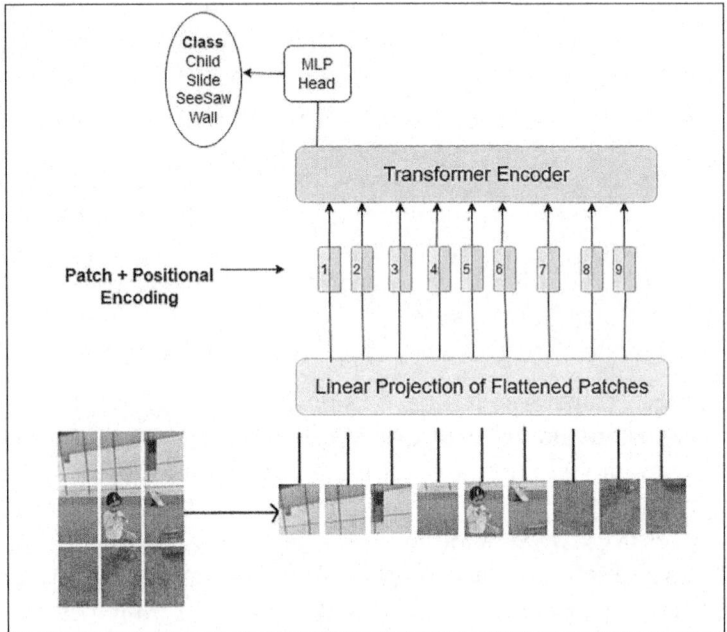

Figure 17.4: *Vision Transformer (ViT) Architecture*

Beyond accessibility, transformer-driven image captioning also plays a pivotal role in content indexing and retrieval systems. For instance, e-commerce platforms benefit from automatic captioning of product images to enhance search engine optimization (SEO) and improve user experiences. Similarly, digital asset management systems leverage this capability for organizing and retrieving visual content based on textual queries and streamlining workflows in creative industries and media archives. The synergy of transformers in processing both images and text has not only redefined the capabilities of image captioning but also expanded its applicability across diverse domains.

- **Video Analysis and Understanding:** Video analysis, a challenging domain requiring the modeling of temporal dependencies, has also benefited from transformer architectures. Transformers process sequences of frames in a video, identifying patterns and relationships across time to enable applications, such as action recognition, video summarization, and anomaly detection. Their parallel processing capabilities make them particularly suited for handling the vast amount of data inherent in video tasks. One of the unique strengths of transformers lies in their ability to handle multimodal data. Applications such as visual question answering (VQA) and audio-visual speech recognition rely on transformers to integrate information from multiple modalities. This cross-modal understanding has opened new avenues for research and applications, ranging from interactive AI assistants to advanced surveillance systems.

Scope of GenAI in Modern Day ChatGPT

Transformer models have become the cornerstone of modern natural NLP, revolutionizing how machines understand and generate human language. ChatGPT, one of the most prominent examples, is built on the GPT architecture. This architecture, developed by OpenAI, leverages the transformer's self-attention mechanism to understand context in a text sequence effectively. During pre-training, the model learns language patterns and relationships by predicting the next word in massive datasets comprising books, articles, and online content. This self-supervised learning phase equips the model with a broad understanding of language. In the fine-tuning phase, the model is refined on domain-specific or task-specific datasets using supervised learning, aligning it more closely with practical applications such as conversational AI or customer support systems. Transformer models such as GPT-3 and ChatGPT represent some of the largest neural networks ever trained, with billions of parameters. This scale enables them to capture subtle nuances in language and deliver human-like responses. The scalability of transformers is further enhanced by innovations such as parallelization and model compression techniques. These advancements make it feasible to deploy large-scale models in real-world applications, from virtual assistants to content generation.

Generative AI, as exemplified by ChatGPT, marks a paradigm shift in artificial intelligence by enabling machines to create rather than merely analyze or classify. ChatGPT, based on the GPT architecture, leverages generative AI to produce coherent, contextually relevant, and human-like text. Unlike traditional AI models focused on predefined tasks, ChatGPT represents a dynamic framework capable of generating content, answering questions, summarizing text, translating languages, and much more. This versatility positions ChatGPT as a transformative tool across industries. We shall navigate the diverse scope of GenAI in modern tools such as ChatGPT, exploring its multimodal capabilities and transformative potential across various applications.

- **Enhanced Conversational AI:** The most prominent application of ChatGPT lies in conversational AI. It acts as a sophisticated virtual assistant capable of engaging in multi-turn conversations with users. By understanding context through advanced transformer architectures, ChatGPT excels in maintaining conversational flow, adapting tone, and generating empathetic responses. This capability finds applications in customer service, technical support, and personal assistance, where real-time, human-like interaction is critical.

- **Generative Capabilities in Content Creation:** ChatGPT's ability to generate text spans creative and practical domains. From drafting articles, blogs, and social media posts to generating code snippets and creative stories, the model has proven to be a powerful content generation tool. These capabilities are revolutionizing industries, such as journalism, marketing, and software development by streamlining processes, reducing turnaround times, and augmenting human creativity.

- **Education and Learning Assistance:** In education, ChatGPT is emerging as a personalized tutor capable of addressing diverse learning needs. The model can explain complex concepts, generate practice questions, and even simulate real-world problem-solving scenarios. Its ability to adapt responses based on user queries enhances personalized learning experiences, making education more accessible and engaging.

- **Applications in Healthcare:** Generative AI-powered models such as ChatGPT have shown promise in healthcare applications, including patient interaction, medical literature summarization, and assisting healthcare professionals in decision-making. While heavily regulated to ensure ethical and accurate outputs, these systems offer the potential to triage symptoms, explain medical procedures, and provide mental health support through empathetic conversation.

- **Driving Innovation in Multimodal AI:** ChatGPT's potential is not limited to text; it is evolving into a multimodal AI capable of integrating text with other data forms such as images and audio. For instance, ChatGPT could analyze an image alongside textual input to provide detailed responses or recommendations. This multimodal integration broadens its scope to applications, such as video content generation, interactive storytelling, and enhanced customer engagement tools.

The scope of ChatGPT is continually expanding with advancements in generative AI. Models such as GPT-4 and beyond promise greater contextual awareness, improved accuracy, and integration with real-time data sources. As generative AI evolves, ChatGPT will likely transition from a conversational tool to a comprehensive AI assistant capable of seamlessly interacting across domains, making it an indispensable component of the digital future.

Ethical Challenges and Societal Responsibilities in AI

AI technologies have revolutionized industries, but their rapid development comes with ethical challenges. While AI enhances efficiency, automates complex tasks, and improves decision-making, its misuse or unintended consequences raise concerns. Ethical dilemmas emerge when AI systems operate without transparency, accountability, or fairness. For instance, facial recognition systems, while beneficial in security, have been criticized for racial and gender biases, potentially leading to wrongful identifications and unjust consequences. We will explore critical issues such as bias, transparency, and accountability in AI systems, while also addressing the broader implications of AI on privacy, decision-making, and social equity.

- **Transparency and Explainability in AI Models:** One of the foremost ethical concerns in AI is the lack of transparency, often referred to as the "black box" problem. Complex models, particularly deep learning architectures, make predictions without providing interpretable reasoning. This opaqueness creates challenges in sectors like healthcare or legal systems, where explainability is critical for trust and accountability. To address these challenges, researchers are actively developing interpretable AI frameworks and tools. Techniques such as Local Interpretable Model-Agnostic Explanations (LIME), Shapley Additive Explanations (SHAP), and counterfactual reasoning aim to shed light on the inner workings of AI systems. These methods provide stakeholders with a better understanding of how input features influence outcomes, thereby fostering trust. Moreover, regulatory frameworks like the European Union's General Data Protection Regulation (GDPR) are pushing for "right to explanation," demanding that organizations deploying AI systems ensure a level of interpretability. This regulatory pressure has further amplified the need for explainable AI systems, making transparency not just an ethical priority but also a legal requirement in many regions.

- **Bias in AI Algorithms and Its Impact:** Bias in AI models arises when training data reflects societal prejudices, leading to discriminatory outcomes. This issue is particularly troubling in sensitive applications, such as hiring, credit scoring, and law enforcement. AI systems trained on biased datasets may perpetuate or even amplify inequalities. Tackling bias requires diverse datasets, rigorous testing, and the inclusion of ethical considerations during the design phase.

- **Data Privacy Concerns:** AI systems rely heavily on vast amounts of data, often including sensitive personal information. This dependency raises concerns about data privacy and security. Unauthorized access, data breaches, or misuse of personal information can erode trust and violate individuals' rights. The use of AI in surveillance systems has sparked debates over privacy infringement and potential misuse by authoritarian regimes. While AI-driven surveillance can enhance security, its misuse for mass monitoring or suppression of dissent raises societal concerns. Striking a balance between security and individual rights is essential to maintaining public trust. Addressing these challenges requires a proactive and multi-layered approach. Robust data protection measures, such as encryption, anonymization, and secure storage protocols, are essential for safeguarding sensitive information. Ethical AI development must prioritize transparency, informing users about how their data will be used and obtaining explicit consent for data collection. Regulations such as the GDPR in the European Union serve as benchmarks for ensuring privacy compliance, mandating strict data protection standards, and empowering individuals with control over their personal information.

- **Societal Responsibilities in AI:** AI systems can inadvertently exclude vulnerable groups if they are not designed inclusively. For instance, voice recognition systems often fail to recognize accents or dialects which put non-native speakers at a disadvantage. Ensuring inclusivity in AI design is not only a technical challenge but also a moral imperative. To address these issues, developers must prioritize diversity in training data and rigorously evaluate models for fairness across demographic groups. Collaboration with sociologists, ethicists, and community representatives can offer valuable insights into the societal impacts of AI systems. Additionally, employing techniques such as fairness-aware machine learning and bias mitigation algorithms can help create more equitable outcomes. By embedding inclusivity into every stage of AI development, we can work towards technology that bridges societal divides rather than exacerbates them, fostering equitable access and empowering all users to benefit from AI-driven advancements.

Creating ethical AI is not solely the responsibility of developers. Policymakers, industry leaders, and society at large must collaborate to establish guidelines and standards. Initiatives such as the EU's Ethics Guidelines for Trustworthy AI emphasize the need for fairness, transparency, and accountability in AI systems, setting a global benchmark for ethical practices. To address these challenges, ethics must be integrated into every stage of AI development. From data collection and model training to deployment and monitoring, ethical considerations should guide decision-making. Education and awareness among AI practitioners, coupled with robust ethical frameworks, are essential for aligning technological advancements with societal values and responsibilities.

Balancing Risks and Benefits in the AI Landscape

The rapid advancement of artificial intelligence has ushered in transformative changes across industries, presenting a unique blend of opportunities and challenges. As AI continues to evolve, striking the right balance between its potential benefits and associated risks becomes crucial. This equilibrium is not merely a technical challenge but a societal responsibility, requiring collaboration among technologists, policymakers, and stakeholders.

AI systems have demonstrated unparalleled efficiency in automating repetitive tasks, streamlining workflows, and driving innovation. For instance, in healthcare, AI assists in diagnosing diseases through image analysis, reducing diagnostic time while enhancing accuracy. In logistics, predictive algorithms optimize supply chains, minimizing delays and cutting costs. These advancements, while beneficial, demand careful consideration of the underlying systems to ensure they are accessible, ethical, and reliable.

Over-reliance on AI systems poses a significant risk. Automated decision-making systems, if left unchecked, could lead to critical failures in sectors, such as finance or healthcare. For example, a flawed credit scoring model might deny loans to deserving candidates, while an error in medical diagnosis algorithms could jeopardize patient outcomes. To mitigate such risks, there is a need for robust validation, regular audits, and mechanisms to intervene when systems fail.

One of the most debated risks of AI adoption is the displacement of jobs. Automation is reshaping industries by replacing routine manual tasks with machines. While this creates opportunities for new, AI-driven roles, it also necessitates upskilling workers to remain relevant. Governments and corporations must invest in education and reskilling programs to bridge this transition, ensuring workers are equipped to thrive in an AI-powered economy.

A significant risk lies in the perpetuation of biases within AI models. While previous discussions have addressed bias at a design level, balancing risks and benefits also involves ensuring fairness in deployment. Companies deploying AI solutions must conduct real-world assessments to identify unintended consequences and recalibrate models accordingly. This effort goes beyond development, extending into implementation and monitoring.

High-stakes applications, such as autonomous vehicles or facial recognition, bring unique challenges. These systems must navigate complex ethical landscapes, including safety concerns and potential misuse. For instance, autonomous vehicles face the moral dilemma of prioritizing passengers versus pedestrians in unavoidable accidents. Stakeholders must collaboratively define ethical frameworks and legal standards to govern such scenarios.

Another critical element in balancing AI risks and benefits is maintaining accountability. Decision-making systems must remain transparent, with humans retaining oversight in critical processes. AI systems should assist rather than replace human judgment in sensitive areas, such as judicial verdicts or medical prescriptions. Establishing clear lines of accountability ensures that when errors occur, responsibility can be traced and addressed.

The energy consumption associated with training and deploying large AI models is another pressing concern. While AI delivers immense value, its environmental footprint cannot be ignored. Balancing risks and benefits requires exploring energy-efficient AI techniques and renewable energy sources to power computational infrastructures.

Ultimately, achieving balance in the AI landscape depends on public trust. Transparency, ethical practices, and user education are pivotal in fostering trust. Companies must openly communicate the limitations of their systems, empowering users to make informed decisions. Public trust also hinges on clear regulations and the ethical alignment of AI solutions with societal values.

By carefully weighing the risks and benefits, stakeholders can harness AI's transformative potential while minimizing its adverse effects. Achieving this balance will require proactive measures, robust governance, and an unwavering commitment to ethical principles, ensuring that AI serves humanity in a sustainable and equitable manner.

Economic, Cultural, and Social Impacts of AI

In the final section of this chapter, we will navigate the multifaceted economic, cultural, and social impacts of AI. This exploration will highlight how AI is transforming industries, influencing cultural norms, and reshaping societal structures while addressing the opportunities and challenges that come with these advancements.

- **Economic Transformation:** Artificial intelligence is reshaping economies by automating repetitive tasks and enhancing productivity. While this leads to significant cost savings and efficiency for businesses, it also raises concerns about job displacement. Sectors such as manufacturing, logistics, and customer service have witnessed automation replacing human roles in mundane tasks. However, AI is also creating new job opportunities in fields such as data science, AI ethics, and machine learning engineering. Policymakers and organizations must focus on reskilling and upskilling the workforce to bridge the gap between displacement and the emergence of new roles.
- **Cultural and Social Influence:** AI is revolutionizing the media and entertainment industries by enabling the creation of immersive experiences. Content platforms such as Netflix and Spotify use AI to curate personalized recommendations, enhancing user engagement. Moreover, AI-generated art and music are challenging traditional notions of creativity, sparking debates about authorship and authenticity. While these innovations enrich cultural experiences, they also raise ethical concerns regarding intellectual property

and the potential for homogenization of content. Social media platforms leverage AI for content moderation, targeted advertising, and user engagement. While this improves platform efficiency, it also amplifies ethical issues, such as echo chambers, misinformation, and surveillance. The cultural impact of AI in social media is profound, influencing public opinion and shaping societal norms. Addressing these challenges requires transparency, accountability, and stringent regulatory frameworks. AI is empowering individuals and organizations to advocate for social change. Sentiment analysis tools gauge public opinion on pressing issues, while AI-powered simulations model the impact of policies before implementation. These applications enhance decision-making in governance and activism, enabling informed advocacy and fostering societal progress.

In conclusion, the economic, cultural, and social impacts of AI are multifaceted, offering immense potential to transform society while presenting significant challenges. Striking a balance between innovation and ethical responsibility is critical to ensuring that AI benefits all segments of society equitably.

Conclusion

In this chapter, we explored the transformative advancements and ethical challenges in artificial intelligence, highlighting applications such as CNNs for object detection and face recognition, and the role of transformer models in large language systems. We examined the expanding potential of generative AI, exemplified by ChatGPT, in multimodal interactions, content creation, and personalized learning. Ethical considerations, including transparency, fairness, and inclusivity, were emphasized alongside the need to balance AI's immense potential with its risks. Additionally, we reflected on AI's economic, cultural, and social impacts, showcasing its influence on industries, cultural norms, and societal structures.

It is our hope that this book has provided you with a strong foundational knowledge in AI, empowering you to seamlessly transition into more advanced developments in this rapidly evolving field.

Multiple Choice Questions

1. Which of the following is a primary concern regarding data privacy in AI systems?

    a. Lack of training data

    b. Unauthorized access and data breaches

    c. High computational cost

    d. Limited scalability

2. What is one key benefit of AI in logistics?

    a. Creating autonomous vehicles

    b. Optimizing supply chains and reducing delays

    c. Developing more durable packaging materials

    d. Enhancing employee productivity through manual interventions

3. What is the "black box" problem in AI?

    a. An issue with hardware compatibility

    b. Lack of transparency in AI decision-making processes

    c. A technical error during neural network training

    d. A bias in the input training dataset

4. Which term refers to AI's role in automating repetitive tasks to improve efficiency?

    a. Neural processing

    b. Predictive modeling

    c. Task automation

    d. Autonomous learning

5. How can inclusivity in AI systems be ensured?

    a. By increasing the number of layers in neural networks

    b. By using a single type of dataset for training

    c. By designing systems that consider diverse user demographics

    d. By only focusing on technical optimization

6. What is the significant cultural impact of AI adoption?

    a. Replacing traditional forms of employment entirely

    b. Fostering cross-cultural understanding through language translation tools

    c. Eliminating all forms of human intervention in decision-making

    d. Creating uniform cultural practices globally

7. Why is explainability crucial in AI systems used in healthcare?
   a. To improve computational speed
   b. To provide interpretable reasoning for medical decisions
   c. To replace doctors entirely in diagnosis
   d. To minimize the cost of AI deployment
8. What is a potential economic risk associated with widespread AI adoption?
   a. Increased job opportunities in all sectors
   b. Creation of completely bias-free systems
   c. Job displacement due to automation
   d. Reduced reliance on technology
9. What is the primary goal of balancing risks and benefits in AI deployment?
   a. Maximizing AI profits at all costs
   b. Ignoring ethical considerations in AI design
   c. Ensuring accessible, fair, and responsible AI systems
   d. Reducing computational resources without affecting user needs
10. What is one of the main societal risks of AI?
    a. Encouraging inclusivity in decision-making systems
    b. Excluding marginalized groups due to biased designs
    c. Reducing automation in public services
    d. Eliminating privacy concerns completely

Answers

1. b
2. b
3. b
4. c
5. c
6. b

7. b

8. c

9. c

10. b

Keywords

- Object Detection
- Face Recognition
- YOLO Framework
- Unet Architecture
- Semantic Segmentation
- Transformer Models
- ChatGPT
- Generative AI
- Multimodal AI
- Ethical AI
- Bias in AI
- Data Privacy
- Explainability in AI
- Societal Impacts of AI
- AI Regulations
- Pre-trained Word Embeddings
- General Data Protection Regulation (GDPR)
- Local Interpretable Model-Agnostic Explanations (LIME)
- Shapley Additive Explanations (SHAP)

References

1. https://indiaai.gov.in/article/ethics-for-ai-challenges-resolution

2. https://www.coe.int/en/web/human-rights-and-biomedicine/common-ethical-challenges-in-ai

3. https://www.unesco.org/en/artificial-intelligence/recommendation-ethics

Index

A

Activation Functions 261
Activation Functions,
    significance
  Hyperbolic Tangent
    (tanh) 262
  Leaky ReLU 263
  Rectified Linear Unit
    (ReLU) 263
  Sigmoid 261
  Softmax Activation 262
AI, challenges 451, 452
AI, history 2, 3
AI, impacts 454
AI, milestones 3-5
AI Risks, balancing 452, 453
ANN as a Classifier 276
ANN as a Classifier,
    configuring 276-279
ANN as a Classifier,
    use cases 289, 290
ANN as a Regressor 281
ANN as a Regressor,
    preventing 281, 282
ANN as a Regressor,
    use cases 292, 293
ANNs, architecture 258-260
ANNs, concepts 257, 258
Artificial Intelligence
    (AI) 2
Artificial Neural Networks
    (ANNs) 257

B

Backpropagation 275

Backpropagation,
    steps 376-378
  Forward Pass 275
  Loss Calculation 275
  Reverse Pass 275
Bagging 187, 188
Bank Loan Defaulter,
    case study
  Incomplete Data, handling 20
  Rule Brittleness 20
  Scalability 20
Big Data Variables 28, 29
Boosting 188
Boosting, techniques
  AdaBoost 189, 190
  GradientBoost 190-193
  Stacked Ensemble Models 195
  VotingClassifier 196, 197
  XGBoost 194
Bootstrap Aggregating 187

C

CNNs, implementing 324, 325
CNNs, points
  Flatten Layer 311
  Full Connected Layer 312
  Max Pooling 310
CNNs, role 313, 314
CNNs, sections
  ALexNet 340
  DenseNet 342
  EfficientNet 343, 344
  GoogleNet/Inception 341
  MobileNet 343
  ResNet 342
  VGGNet 341

Coding Neural Networks (CNNs) 285
Conventional Programming 30, 31
Convolutional Neural Networks (CNNs) 305
Convolution Operations 306
Convolution Operations, architecture 306-308

D

Data-Driven AI 27
Data-Driven AI, applications
  Image-Based Datasets 39
  Tabular Datasets 38, 39
  Text-Based Datasets 39, 40
  Time Series Dataset 40
Data-Driven AI, challenges
  Bias/Data, representation 42
  Cloud, dominance 42
  Cyber Threats 41
  Data Security, governance 42
  Ethical/Responsible AI, considering 41
  Framework Diversity 41
Data-Driven AI, fundamentals 27, 28
Data-Driven Approach 31, 32
Data Preparation 55
Data Preparation, points
  Feature, scaling 60, 61
  Miss Values, handling 58, 59
  Outlier Treatment 62
Data Preparation With Python, optimizing 56
Data Pre-Processing 265
Data Pre-Processing, techniques
  Dimensionality 265
  Encoding 265
  Normalization 265
  Standardization 265
Dataset Preparation 322

Dataset Preparation, steps
  Data Annotation/Labeling 322
  Data Augmentation 322
  Data Cleaning 322
  Data Collection 322
  Data Pipelines 323
  Data Preprocessing 323
  Dataset, balancing 323
  Data Splitting 323
Decision Tree 164
Decision Tree, architecture 165
Decision Tree, attribute
  Left Node, splitting 170, 171
  Right Node, splitting 169
  Root Node Split 167, 168
Decision Tree Classifier 171
Decision Tree Classifier, attributes 171, 172
Decision Tree, limitations 180, 181
Decision Tree Mathematic, foundation 166
Decision Tree Regressor 174
Decision Tree Regressor, configuring 175, 176
Decision Tree Regressor, features
  Left Node, splitting 176
  Right Node, splitting 177
Decision Tree Regressor, implementing 178-180
Distance Metrics 208
Distance Metrics, impact 209
Distance Metrics, types
  Cosine Similarity 209
  Euclidean Distance 208
  Hamming Distance 209
  Manhattan Distance 208
  Minkowski Distance 208

E

EDA, architecture 65-72

EDA, observations
  EU Sales 72
  JP Sales 72
  NA Sales 72
EDA, points
  Bivariate Analysis 103-105
  K-Fold Cross-Validation 108
  MLR Model, implementing 105-107
Ensemble Learning 187
Expert Systems 12
Expert Systems, configuring 13
Exploratory Data Analysis 144-150
Exploratory Data Analysis (EDA) 64, 101
Exploratory Data Analysis, points
  Model Evaluation, building 153-155
  Model Performance 156

F

Fine-Tuning 323, 324
Fine-Tuning, architecture 331-333
Fine-Tuning Model Parameters 283
Fine-Tuning Model Parameters, rule
  Adagrad 284
  Adam 284
  Batch Size 283
  Epochs Number 283
  Learn Rate 283
  Momentum 283
  Regularization 284
  RMSprop 284
  Weight, initializing 285
Flattening 311
Flattening, layers
  Connected 311
  Dimensional 311
  Feature Representation 311
Flatten Layer 311
Fully Connected Layers 312
Fully Connected Layers, features
  Decision Making 312
  Generalization 312
  Integration 312
Fully Connected Layers, steps
  Feature Consolidation 312
  Prediction 312

G

Gated Recurrent Unit (GRU) 397
GaussianNB 143
GaussianNB, configuring 143, 144
Gen AI, capabilities
  Content Creation 450
  Conversational, enhancing 450
  Education/Learn, assistance 450
  Healthcare 450
  Multimodal AI 450
Gradient Descent 95, 96, 275
Gradient Descent Mathematic, calculations 96, 97
Gradient Descent With Data, demonstrating 97-99
GRU, benefits
  Comparable Performance 399
  Faster Convergence 399
  Simpler Architecture 399
GRU Gates, merging 397, 398
GRU, limitations
  Less Granular Control 399
  Separate Cell State 400
  Task-Dependent, efficacy 400
GRU, use cases 400

H

Hidden Layers 266
Hidden Layers, challenges
  Computational Complexity 267
  Gradients, vanishing 268
  Overfitting 267
  Underfitting 267

Hidden Layers, roles
  Feature Extraction 266
  Feature Transformation 267
  Hierarchy 267
Hidden Layers, rules
  Deep Networks 266
  Shallow Networks 266

I

IDE, architecture 57
IDE, tools
  Google Colab 57
  Jupyter Notebook 56
  Online Editors 57
  PyCharm 56
  Spyder 56
Image Classification 326
Image Classification, metrics
  Accuracy 326
  Confusion Matrix 327
  F1-Score 326
  Macro Average 326
  Precision 326
  Recall 326
  ROC-AUC Score 327
  Support 326
  Top-k Accuracy 327
  Weight Average 326
Inference Engines 11, 12
Input Layers 264
Input Layers, reasons
  Data, compatibility 265
  Data, representating 265
  Network, influence 265
Integrated Development Environment (IDE) 56

K

Kernel Functions 235
Kernel Functions, configuring 236, 237
Kernel Functions, properties 241

Kernel Functions, types
  Custom 236
  Linear 235
  Polynomial 235
  Radial Basis Function (RBF) 236
  Sigmoid 236
K-Fold Cross-Validation 108
K-Fold Cross-Validation, configuring 108, 109
K-Fold Cross-Validation, reasons
  Bias Reduction 108
  Efficient Data 108
  Generalizability 108
K-Nearest Neighbor (KNN) 205, 206
KNN Algorithm 206
KNN Algorithm, configuring 206, 207
KNN as a Classifier 210
KNN as a Classifier, architecture 211-213
KNN as a Regressor 213
KNN as a Regressor, configuring 213-217
KNN Classifier 217-219
KNN Classifier, inference 219, 220
KNN, limitations 225, 226
KNN Regressor 220
KNN Regressor, configuring 221-224
KNN Regressor, features 221
KNN Regressor, inference 224, 225
Knowledge Representation 14
Knowledge Representation, configuring 14-16

L

Language Translation 426
Language Translation, architecture 426-433
Linear Models 118

Linear Models, pattern
  Homoscedasticity 118
  Independence,
    observations 118
  Multicollinearity 118
  Outliers, influence 118
Linear Regression 93
Linear Regression Coefficients,
    interpreting 94, 95
Linear Regression Mathematical,
    operations 93, 94
Logistic Regression 109, 110
Logistic Regression Coefficients,
    interpretation 117
Logistic Regression Data,
    illustrative 111-113
Logistic Regression Model,
    implementing 113-116
Long-Term Dependency 386
Long-Term Dependency,
    limitations
  Gradient Clipping 386
  Initialization/Activation 386
  Memory Augmentation 387
  Recurrent Networks 387
  Residual Networks 387
LSTM, points
  Language Modelling 418-421
  Sentiment Analysis 422-426
LSTMs 388
LSTMs, advantages 388, 389
LSTMs, applications
  Computer Vision 447
  Machine Translation 445
  Sentiment Analysis 446
  Text Generation 446
  Video Analysis 449
  Voice Synthesis 447
LSTMs, gates
  Candidate Cell 393
  Cell State 393
  Forget 393
  Forward Pass 392
  Update 393
LSTMs, implementing 407-412
LSTMs Model, training 395
LSTMs Model, use cases 396

LSTMs, principles 390
LSTMs, strategies
  Decoder 416, 417
  Encoder 414
  Encoder-Decoder 415

M

Machine Learning (ML) 30
Max Pooling 310
Max Pooling, features
  Dimensionality Reduction 310
  Preservation 310
  Prevention, overfitting 311
  Translation Invariance 310
ML, architecture 49
ML, components
  Algorithms 52
  Evaluating 53, 54
  Features 51
  Labels 51, 52
  Training Process 52
  Validation/Testing 53
ML, lifecycle 36-38
ML Model, evaluation 83, 84
ML, models 49, 50
MLOps 54
MLOps, platforms
  AWS SageMaker 54
  Dababricks MLflow 54
  Google Vertex AI 54
  Microsoft Azure ML Studio 54
MLOps, tools
  Airflow 55
  Docker 55
  Kubeflow 55
MLR Dataset, optimizing 99, 100
MLR With Python,
    implementing 100, 101
ML, types
  Reinforcement Learning (RL) 35
  Supervised Learning (SL) 32
  Unsupervised Learning (UL) 33
Model Evaluation 120
Model Evaluation,
    configuring 120-122
Multiple Linear Regression (MLR) 99

N

Naive Bayes Algorithm
     (NBA) 133
Naive Bayes Model (NVM) 156
NBA, calculations 133, 134
NB Classifier, applications 138
NB Classifier, extending 134-136
NB Classifier, industry
  E-Commerce 139
  Finance 139
  Healthcare 139
  Image, processing 139
  Natural Language
       Processing (NLP) 139
  Social Media, analyzing 139
  Telecommunications 139
NB Classifier, types
  Bernoulli Naive
       Bayes 137, 138
  Gaussian Naive Bayes 137
  Multinomial Naive
       Bayes 137
NB With Python,
     implementing 140-142
Neural Networks 264
Neural Networks,
     challenges 294, 295
Neural Networks,
     evolution 296-304
Neural Networks, functions
  Backpropagation 268
  Feedforward 268
Neural Networks, layers
  Hidden Layers 266
  Input Layers 264
  Output Layers 268

O

Object Detection 440
Object Detection, approach
  Faster RCNN 440
  RCNN 440
  Semantic Segmentation 442
  YOLO 441
Outlier Treatment 62, 63
Outlier Treatment, scenarios
  Capping 62
  Imputation 62
  Interquartile Range (IQR) 62
  Transformation 62
  Trimming/Removing 62
  Z-score Method 62
Output Layers 268

P

Pediatric, case study
  Adaptability 20
  Rule Explosion 19
  Uncertainty, handling 20
Pre-Trained CNNs 352
Pre-Trained CNNs, use cases
  Cassava Disease Diagnosis 357
  Defense Sector 358
  Fashion/Apparel
       Classification 357
  Industrial Automation 358
  MedNet 356
  SatlasPretrain 357
Pre-Trained CNNs, ways
  Direct Inference 353
  Feature Vectors,
       extracting 355
  Full Model, training 354
  Fully Connected Layer
       (FSL) 354
Problem Statement 346
Problem Statement,
     configuring 346-350
Production/Manufacturing,
     case study
  Adaptability 20
  Noisy Data, handling 20
  Rule Maintenance 20

R

Random Forest 181
Random Forest, models
  Random Forest as a Classifier 184
  Random Forest as a
       Regressor 185, 186

Index   465

Random Forest, utilizing 182, 183
Recurrent Connections 373
Recurrent Connections,
        configuring 373, 374
Reinforcement Learning
        (RL) 35, 36
ReLU Activation Function 314, 315
RNNs Architecture 374, 375
RNNs Architecture, training 376
RNNs, limitations 378, 379
Rule-Based System 5, 6
Rule-Based System, case studies
    Finance/Banking 17
    HealthCare/Medical
        Diagnosis 16
    Production Industry/
        Manufacturing 18
Rule-Based System,
        components 7-9
Rule-Based System, history 6, 7
Rule-Based System, limitations 19
Rule-Based System, sections
    Bank Loan Defaulter 20
    Pediatric 19
    Production/Manufacturing 20
Rule-Based System, trends 21

S

Sequential Data 366, 367
Sequential Data,
        challenges 370, 371
Sequential Data, tasks
    Next Word Prediction 372
    Sequence Classification 372, 373
SL, purpose
    Classification Models 82, 83
    Regression Models 81, 82
Stacked Ensemble Models 196
Stacked Ensemble Models,
        outputs
    Base Layer 196
    Meta Layer 196
Strides 309
Strides, types
    Larger 309
    Small 309

Supervised Learning
        (SL) 32, 33, 81
Support Vector Machines
        (SVMs) 233
SVM as a Classifier 244
SVM as a Classifier,
        configuring 244-247
SVM as a Classifier, inference 248
SVM as a Regressor 241
SVM as a Regressor, dataset 242
SVM as a Regressor,
        implementing 242-244
SVM as a Regressor,
        inference 244
SVMs, cons
    Computationally
        Intensive 249
    Kernel Parameters 249
    Noisy Data 249
    Probabilistic Interpretation 249
    Right Kernal 250
SVMs Dataset,
        optimizing 238-240
SVMs, pros
    Effective Data 249
    High Dimensional Space 248
    Robust, overfitting 248
    Versatile Kernal Trick 248
SVMs, structures 233-235
Symbolic Reasoning 9
Symbolic Reasoning,
        architecture 9, 10
Symbolic Reasoning, factors
    AI Approaches, integrating 10
    Ethical/Social, implications 10
    Inference Mechanisms 10
    Scalability/Efficiency 10
    Uncertainty, handling 10

T

Time-Series Classification 327
Time-Series Classification,
        configuring 328-330
Time-Series Data 367
Time-Series Data,
        configuring 367-369

Transfer Learning 344
Transfer Learning, approaches
  Feature Extraction 344
  Fine-Tuning 345
Transfer Learning, benefits
  Cost-Effectiveness 345
  Efficiency 345
  Generalization,
      improving 345
  Limited Data, handling 345
Transfer Learning With CNN,
      implementing 345, 346

U

Unsupervised Learning
      (UL) 33-35
Unsupervised Learning
      (USL) 73
USL, points
  Hierarchical Clustering 77-81
  K-Means Clustering 74-77

X

XGBoost 194
XGBoost, challenges
  Complexity 194
  Overfitting 195
  Parameter, tuning 195
  Resource Intensive 194
XGBoost, features
  Early, stopping 194
  Miss Value, handling 194
  Parallel, processing 194
  Regularization 194
  Tree Pruning 194
  Weighted Quantile
      Sketch 194
X-OR Problem 286
X-OR Problem,
      optimizing 286-288

Printed in Great Britain
by Amazon